Perspectives on Argument

Nancy V. Wood

The University of Texas at Arlington

PRENTICE HALL
Upper Saddle River, New Jersey, 07458

Library of Congress Cataloging-in-Publication

Wood, Nancy V.
    Perspectives on argument / Nancy V. Wood. — 2nd ed.
       p.   cm.
    Includes indexes.
    ISBN 0–13–096448–4
    1. English language—Rhetoric.   2. Persuasion (Rhetoric)
  3. College readers.   I. Title.
  PE1431.W66   1998
  808′.0427—dc21   97–12903
                                 CIP

Editorial director: Charlyce Jones Owen
Assistant development editor: Kara Hado
Managing editor: Bonnie Biller
Production liaison: Fran Russello
Project manager: Pine Tree Composition
Manufacturing manager: Nick Sklitsis
Prepress and manufacturing buyer: Mary Ann Gloriande
Cover design: Pat Wosczyk
Marketing manager: Rob Mejia

Credits

Jerry Adler, "Building a Better Dad" from *Newsweek* (June 17, 1996). Copyright © 1996 by Newsweek, Inc.
    Reprinted with the permission of *Newsweek*.
Lois Agnew, "Special Education's Best Intentions." Reprinted with the permission of the author.
Credits continue on page 655, which constitutes an extension of the copyright page.

This book was set in 10/12 Palatino by Pine Tree Composition, Inc.,
and was printed and bound by *Hamilton Printing Company*.
The cover was printed by *Phoenix Color Corp.*

 © 1998, 1995 by Prentice-Hall, Inc.
Simon & Schuster/A Viacom Company
Upper Saddle River, New Jersey 07458

Printed in the United States of America
10 9 8 7 6 5 4 3

ISBN: 0-13-096448-4

Prentice-Hall International (UK) Limited, *London*
Prentice-Hall of Australia Pty. Limited, *Sydney*
Prentice-Hall Canada Inc., *Toronto*
Prentice-Hall Hispanoamericana, S.A., *Mexico*
Prentice-Hall of India Private Limited, *New Delhi*
Prentice-Hall of Japan, Inc., *Tokyo*
Simon & Schuster Asia Pte. Ltd., *Singapore*
Editora Prentice-Hall do Brasil, Ltda., *Rio de Janeiro*

Contents

Alternate Table of Contents

MAJOR WRITING ASSIGNMENTS (Other writing assignments, in addition to those listed here, appear in the Exercises and Activities sections at the ends of the chapters.)

Issue Proposal, 25
  Provides initial information about an issue and shows how to test it to see if it is arguable.

Argument Style Paper, 47
  Describes student's usual style of argument and analyzes the outside influences on this style.

Analyze the Rhetorical Situation, 83
  Analyzes the elements of the rhetorical situation in a written essay.

Summary-Response Paper, 88
  Summarizes an essay and provides the writer's response to its ideas.

Exploratory Paper, 115, 116
  Describes three or more perspectives on an issue and helps writers identify their own perspective.

Toulmin Analysis, 150
  Analyzes the claim, support, and warrants in student-provided essays, cartoons, advertisements, or letters to the editor.

Position Paper Based on "The Reader," 237
  Develops a claim through research in "The Reader" and the employment of the Toulmin model, the claim questions, and the types of proof.

CLASS PROJECTS

Class Literary Debate, 301

Students divide into three groups of prosecution, defense, and jury to conduct a debate about a character in a play.

Class Symposium, 390

Students organize into small symposium groups to read abstracts and answer questions.

EXAMPLES OF ARGUMENT STRATEGIES IN "READER" ARTICLES

1. **Argument Papers.** *Exploratory:* Bates, 547; Mathews, 581. *Rogerian:* Carter, 650; Negroponte, 605. *Position:* Gingrich, 636; Rotundo, 444.
2. **Claims.** *Fact:* Cohen, 517; West, 561; Faludi, 630; H. L. Gates Jr., 576. *Definition:* Dalzell, 554; Rotundo, 444; Newman, 503. *Cause:* Males and Docuyanan, 518; Postman, 593; Vitz, 538. *Value:* Dickerson, 523; Hacker, 565; Authors of "Watching TV," 603. *Policy:* Canada, 527; Romo and Falbo, 482; Pollitt, 464. *Inferred claim (Irony):* Borkat, 478; Swift, 618. *Qualified claim:* Faludi, 630.
3. **Language and Style.** *Language that appeals to logic:* Sizer, 480; Mill, 536; Sollod, 472. *Language that appeals to emotion:* Friedan, 434; Glaser, 459; Califano, 495. *Language that develops ethos:* Darrow, 505; DuBois, 572.
4. **Organizational Patterns.** *Claim plus reasons:* Alter, 457. *Cause-effect:* Friedan, 434; *Chronological/narrative:* Dickerson, 523; *Comparison-contrast:* Hamill, 599; Connors, 431; *Problem-solution:* Califano, 495; Juarez, 486; Lykken, 624; Wagner and Guttman, 490; Newman, 515.
5. **Proofs:Ethos:** *Self as authority:* Adler, 452; DuBois, 572; Gates, 607. *Quoted authorities:* Males and Docuyanan, 518; Kadi, 612; Cowley and Hager, 644.
6. **Proofs:Logos.** *Sign:* Young, 550; *Induction:* Gutmann, 646; Wiesenfeld, 475; *Cause:* Postman, 593. *Deduction:* Sollod, 472; Katz, 470. *Analogy:* Hamill, 599; Bacon, 469; Pollitt, 464; Milton, 535. *Definition:* Bennett, 463; Sullivan, 461; Gabriel, 555. *Statistics:* Kadi, 612; Conniff, 628; Gramm, 498; Newman, 515.
7. **Proofs:Pathos.** *Motives:* Newman, 515; Herd, 633; Cowley and Hager, 644. *Values:* FitzPatrick, 513; Landers, 635; Isasi-Diaz, 587.
8. **Refutation.** Sullivan, 461; Bennett, 463; Wang and Wu, 566
9. **Adaptation to Rhetorical Situation.** Juarez, 486; Orenstein, 545; Swift, 618.
10. **Support.** *Examples:* Hentoff, 541; Theroux, 449; Tannen, 426; Orenstein, 545; Bates, 547. *Facts:* Cohen, 517; Califano, 495; Kadi, 612. *Graphs:* Mathews, 581. *Narration:* Dickerson, 523; Hacker, 565. *Personal examples:* H. L. Gates, 576; Glaser, 459; Herd, 633; B. Gates, 607; Brennan, 501; Wiesenfeld, 475.
11. **Warrants.** Alter, 457; Darrow, 505; Friedan, 434; Gramm, 498; Henry, 441; Katz, 470.

Preface

PURPOSE

The most important purpose of this book is to teach students strategies for critical reading, critical thinking, research, and writing that will help them participate in all types of argument both inside and outside of the classroom. A basic assumption is that argument exists everywhere and that students need to learn to participate productively in all forms of argument including those they encounter in school, at home, on the job, and in the national and international spheres. Such participation is critical not only in a democratic society, but also in a global society in which issues become more and more complex each year. Students who use this book will learn to identify controversial topics that are "at issue," to read and form reactions and opinions of their own, and to write argument papers that express their individual views and perspectives.

A central idea of this book is that modern argument is not always polarized as right or wrong, but that instead it often invites a variety of perspectives on an issue. Another idea, equally important, is that not all argument results in the declaration of winners. The development of common ground and either consensus or compromise are sometimes as acceptable as declaring winners in argument. Students will learn to take a variety of approaches to argument, including taking a position and defending it, seeking common ground at times, withholding opinion at other times, negotiating when necessary, and even changing their original beliefs when they can no longer make a case for them. The perspectives and abilities taught here are those that an educated populace in a world community needs to coexist cooperatively and without constant destructive conflict.

SPECIAL FEATURES

Both instructors and students who pick up this book have the right to ask how it differs from some of the other argument texts that are presently available. They deserve to know why they might want to use this book instead of another. This text, which is targeted for freshmen and sophomores enrolled in argument or argument and literature classes in two-year and four-year colleges, is both a reader and a rhetoric. Within this reader and rhetoric format are a number of special features that when taken together, make the book unique.

- **Reading, critical thinking, and writing** are taught as integrated and interdependent processes. Comprehensive chapters on the reading and writing processes show how they can be adapted to argument. Extensive instruction in critical reading and critical thinking appear throughout. Assignments and questions that invite critical reading, critical thinking, and original argumentative writing appear at the end of every chapter in "The Rhetoric" and at the end of every section of "The Reader."

- **Cross-gender** and **cross-cultural communication styles** are presented in a unique chapter that provides for a classroom in which every student can find a voice. Students learn to identify and develop their own unique styles of argument and to recognize how their styles may have been influenced by family background, gender, ethnic background, or country of origin. Also included are international students' perspectives on the argument styles of their countries. Many readings in the book are by authors of varied cultural and ethnic backgrounds.

- **Explanations of the elements and structure of argument** include the **Toulmin model of argument,** the **classical modes of appeal,** the **traditional categories of claims** derived from classical stasis theory, and the **rhetorical situation.** Theory is integrated and translated into language that students can easily understand and apply. For example, students learn to apply theory to recognize and analyze the parts of an argument while reading and to develop and structure their own ideas while writing.

- **Audience analysis** includes the concepts of the familiar and the unfamiliar audience as well as Chaim Perelman's concept of the universal audience.

- **Productive invention strategies** help students develop ideas for papers.

- **Library and on-line research is presented as a creative activity** that students are invited to enjoy. Workable strategies for research and note taking are provided. Students are taught to document researched argument papers according to both **MLA** and **APA style.**

- **Exercises, class projects, and writing assignments at the ends of the chapters invite individual, small group, and whole class participation.** Collaborative exercises encourage small groups of students to engage in critical thinking, and whole class projects invite students to participate in activities that require an understanding of argument. Classroom-tested **writing assignments** include the **exploratory paper,** which teaches students to explore several different perspectives on an issue, the **critical analysis paper,** which teaches students to analyze and evaluate a written argument, and the **researched position paper,** which teaches students to take a position on an issue and defend it. **Examples of student papers** are provided for each major type of paper. The writing assignments in this book are models for assignments that students are likely to encounter in their other classes.

- **Summary charts at the end of the rhetoric section present the main points of argument** in a handy format. They also integrate the reading and writing processes for argument by placing strategies for both side by side and showing the interconnections.

- **A total of 123 different readings** in the rhetoric section and "The Reader" provide students with multiple perspectives on the many issues presented throughout the book. Fifteen of these readings are argument papers written by students.
- **The readings in "The Reader" are clustered under nineteen subissues** that are related to the seven major general issue areas that organize "The Reader." This helps students focus and narrow broad issues. Furthermore, the readings in each subissue group "talk" to each other, and questions invite students to join the conversation.

NEW TO THIS EDITION

- **Two new chapters** teach special applications of argument theory.
  - **"Rogerian Argument and Common Ground"** teaches an alternate strategy to use when the traditional confrontational style of argument is not working.
  - **"Argument and Literature"** teaches students to recognize argument in literature and to write arguments of their own about literature.
- **Sixty-five percent of the reading selections are new.** A total of 80 of the 123 reading selections in this edition appear for the first time.
- **Two new issue areas** that explore the issues associated with **Modern Electronic Media** and **Social Responsibility** appear in "The Reader."
- **Nine new issue questions,** each accompanied by sets of 3–6 essays to provide different perspectives on the questions, appear in "The Reader." These questions include, "**Do Men and Women Students Learn Differently** in the Classroom?" "**What Is a Family?** Does It Have to Be Traditional?" "**How Much Should Schools Change** to Help Students Succeed?" "What Should Be Done With **Young Offenders?**" "Should the **Internet Be Censored** or Screened to Protect Users?" "What **Effect Do Computers Have** on Their Users?" "Who Should Share **Responsibility for the Children?**" "Who Should Take **Responsibility for the Poor?**" and "Who Should Be **Responsible for** the Life and Death Decisions That Affect the **Terminally Ill?**"
- **Examples of how to locate and cite Internet materials and use on-line databases** appear in the chapter on invention and research.
- **Nine new examples of student writing** provide models for an issue proposal, a Toulmin analysis, Rogerian argument (one is written in letter format), an analysis of an argument made by a literary character, a position paper that demonstrates how to use argument theory for invention, and an annotated bibliography.
- **Nine new whole class projects** include debates, symposia, literary debates, critical reading and analysis sessions, and class reporting sessions. All create opportunities for students to participate in major argument activities.

- **New Questions on the Chapter** and **Questions on the Essays for Analysis** appear at the end of each of the twelve chapters. These can be used as reading quizzes and as questions for discussions.
- **Revised exercises and writing assignments** appear throughout the book. Many small changes have been made in response to advice from instructors who taught with the first edition.
- **Films and literature related to "The Reader" issues** are listed in the introductions to each issue area and invite students to extend their perspectives on the issues through these art forms.
- **An Alternate Table of Contents** provides (1) an alphabetical **listing of all of the issues in the book** to help students discover paper topics and related essays, (2) an annotated list of the **major writing assignments** that include clear instructions and models to help students complete them, (3) an annotated list of the **class projects** along with clear instructions for organizing and executing them, and (4) **examples of some of the argument strategies** that appear in the essays in "The Reader." Students may consult these to increase their understanding of argument theory.

ORGANIZATION

The book is organized into four parts and, as much as possible, chapters have been written so that they stand alone. Instructors may thus assign them either in sequence or in a more preferred order to supplement their own course organization.

Part One: Engaging with Argument for Reading and Writing.   This part introduces students to issues and the characteristics of argument in Chapter 1, helps them begin to develop a personal style of argument in Chapter 2, and provides them with processes for reading and writing argument in Chapters 3 and 4. Writing assignments include the issue proposal, the argument style paper, the analysis of the rhetorical situation paper, the summary-response paper, and the exploratory paper.

Part Two: Understanding the Nature of Argument for Reading and Writing.   This part identifies and explains the parts of an argument according to Stephen Toulmin's model of argument in Chapter 5, explains the types of claims and purposes for argument in Chapter 6, and presents the types of proofs along with clear examples and tests for validity in Chapter 7. Chapter 8 teaches students to use Rogerian argument strategies to achieve common ground when traditional strategies are not working, and Chapter 9 explains how to use argument theory to gain new perspectives in reading imaginative literature. Writing assignments include the Toulmin analysis, the position paper based on "The Reader," the Rogerian argument papers, the argument and literature papers, and the critical analysis paper.

Part Three: Writing a Research Paper That Presents an Argument. This part teaches students to write a claim, clarify purpose, and analyze the audience in Chapter 10, to use various creative strategies for inventing ideas and gathering research materials in Chapter 11, and to organize, write, revise, and prepare the final manuscript for a researched position paper in Chapter 12. Methods for locating and using resource materials in the library and on-line are presented in Chapters 11 and 12.

Part Four: The Reader. This part is organized around the broad issues of men's and women's roles, education, crime and the treatment of criminals, freedom of speech, racism in America, modern electronic media, and social responsibility. Strategies and questions to help students explore issues and move from reading and discussion to writing are also included.

THE INSTRUCTOR'S MANUAL

In preparing the Instructor's Manual, my coauthors and I have included chapter-by-chapter suggestions for using the book in both the traditional and the computer classrooms. We have also included sample syllabi. Two instructors have written day-by-day teaching journals in which they detail how they worked with this book in class and how the students responded. Also included in the manual are strategies for teaching students to use electronic data bases, the Internet, and other resources for conducting on-line and library research. Another chapter suggests how student argument papers can be developed with the help of tutors in a writing center and by on-line moos and chat groups. A set of class handouts ready for photocopying is also provided. Copies of this manual may be obtained from your Prentice Hall representative.

ACKNOWLEDGMENTS

My greatest debt is to my husband, James A. Wood, who has also taught and written about argument. He helped me work out my approach to argument by listening to me, by discussing my ideas, and by contributing ideas of his own. The process renewed my faith in peer groups and writing conferences. Most writers, I am convinced, profit from talking through their ideas with someone else. I was lucky to find someone so knowledgeable and generous with his time and insights.

I also owe a debt to the freshman English program at The University of Texas at Arlington. When I joined the department a few years ago, I found myself caught up in the ideas and controversies of this program. It provided me with much of the interest and motivation to write this book.

For the past several years I have trained the graduate teaching assistants in our department who teach argument. An exceptionally alert group of these students volunteered to meet with me and recommend revisions for this second edition. They include Lynn Atkinson, J. T. Martin, Kimberly Ellison, Corri Wells, Steve Harding, Barbara Chiarello, Collin G. Brooke, Tracy Bessire, Cheryl Brown, Matthew Levy, Alan Taylor, and Deborah Reese. I hope they will be pleased when they see that I have followed many of their suggestions for improvement. Many other graduate teaching assistants in our program have also taught with this book and have made useful recommendations and suggestions. I am grateful to them for their insight and enthusiasm.

I am also indebted to other colleagues and friends who have helped me with this book. James Kinneavy is the originator of the exploratory paper as it is taught in this book. Audrey Wick, Director of Freshman English at our University and a seasoned teacher of argument, read and critiqued every essay in the present Reader. No essay is included that does not bear her stamp of approval. She also provided me with one of her favorite class projects, the literary debate that appears at the end of Chapter 9 on argument and literature. My colleague Tim Morris helped me think through some of the ideas in Chapter 9, and he provided me with many excellent examples of poems and other literary works that make arguments. I owe a special debt of gratitude to Samantha Masterton who provided research assistance and other types of creative help for this edition. She made a thorough critique of all of the chapters, she classroom tested all of the class exercises and writing assignments, and she contributed many excellent suggestions for improving chapters and exercises. I have followed her suggestions throughout. She also contributed materials to some of the chapters and to the Instructor's Manual, and she helped locate and organize articles for "The Reader." Beth Brunk, Corri Wells, Deborah Reese, Cheryl Brown, Samantha Masterton, and Leslie Snow have all either provided chapters or have co-authored chapters in the Instructor's Manual. Beth Brunk formatted and typed it. It has been a constant pleasure to work with these bright, energetic, and creative colleagues, and I am grateful to all of them for the contributions they have made to this second edition.

I wish I had the space to acknowledge by name the many students from argument classes, including my own, who read the first edition and made recommendations for this second edition. Some of them also contributed their own essays to be used as examples, and their names appear on their work. I paid particularly close attention to these student's comments, and I know their suggestions and contributions have made this a better book for other argument students throughout the country.

At Prentice Hall, my greatest debt is to Phil Miller, President, Humanities and Social Sciences, who got me started with this project. I also thank Kara Hado, assistant development editor, and Charlyce Jones Owens, Editorial Director of Humanities and Social Sciences. These individuals provided excellent help with all of the various stages of writing and final editing. Thanks also to Rob Mejia, Marketing Manager, who helped me develop some of the more user-friendly features of the book. Patty Sawyer of Pine Tree Composition, Inc. did a thorough and conscientious job of seeing the book through all phases of production. Fred

Courtright did a superb job of obtaining all of the permissions for this edition. I have felt very fortunate to work with such conscientious, reliable, and capable professionals.

Other colleagues around the country provided additional ideas and recommended changes that have helped improve both the first and second editions of this book. They include Margaret W. Batschelet, University of Texas at San Antonio; Linda D. Bensel-Meyers, University of Tennessee; Gregory Clark, Brigham Young University; Dan Damesville, Tallahassee Community College; Alexander Friedlander, Drexel University; William S. Hockman, University of Southern Colorado; James Kinneavy, University of Texas at Austin; Elizabeth Metzger, University of South Florida; Margaret Dietz Meyer, Ithaca College; Susan Padgett, North Lake College; Randall L. Popken, Tarleton State University; William E. Sheidley, United States Air Force Academy; Diane M. Thiel, Florida International University; and Jennifer Welsh, University of Southern California. I am grateful to them for the time and care they took reviewing the manuscript.

Finally, I thank all of you who use this book. I would like to hear about your experiences with it, and I am especially interested in your ideas for improving the chapters and readings. My e-mail address is woodnv@utarlg.uta.edu.

This book has been a genuinely collaborative effort, and I expect that it will continue to be. I hope students will profit from the example and learn to draw on the expertise of their instructors and classmates to help them write their papers. Most writing is more fun and more successful when it is, at least partly, a social process.

N. V. W.

PART ONE

Engaging with Argument for Reading and Writing

The strategy in these first four chapters is to introduce you to issues and the special characteristics of argument in Chapter 1, to help you begin to develop a personal style of argument in Chapter 2, and to help you develop your processes for reading and writing argument in Chapters 3 and 4. The focus in these chapters is on you and how you will engage with argument both as a reader and as a writer. When you finish reading Part One:

- You will understand what argument is and why it is important in a democratic society.
- You will have found some issues (topics) to read and write about.
- You will have analyzed your present style of argument and considered ways to adapt it for special contexts.
- You will have new strategies and ideas to help you read argument critically.
- You will have adapted your present writing process to help you think critically and write argument papers.
- You will have experience with writing an issue proposal, a summary-response paper, and an exploratory argument paper.

CHAPTER 1

A Perspective on Argument

You engage in argument, whether you realize it or not, nearly every day. Argument deals with *issues,* or the topics that have not yet been settled, topics that invite two or more differing opinions and that are, consequently, subject to question, debate, or negotiation. Pick up today's newspaper and read the headlines to find some current examples. Here are some issues raised by headlines of the past: Should pornography on the Internet be censored? Who should pay for health care? Should same-sex marriages be legal? Are American industrial executives overpaid? What is the best way to slow population growth in Third World countries? Should politicians be more ethical than everyone else? What should be done about the latest crime wave? Or, think of examples of issues that may be closer to your daily experience: Should one "eat, drink, and be merry," or exercise daily and avoid fatty foods? Which is the more important consideration in selecting a major: finding a job or enjoying the subject? How can one minimize the frustrations caused by limited campus parking? Is it good or bad policy to go to school and work at the same time?

All of these issues, whether they seem remote or close to you, are related to the big issues that have engaged human thought for centuries. In fact, all of the really important issues—those dealing with life and death, the quality of life, ways and means, war and peace, the individual and society, the environment— these and others like them are discussed, debated, and negotiated somewhere in the world on a regular basis. There are usually no simple or obvious positions to take on such important issues. Still, the positions we do take on them and, ultimately, the decisions and actions we take in regard to them can affect our lives in significant ways. In democratic societies, individuals are expected to engage in effective argument on issues of broad concern. They are also expected to make moral judgments and to evaluate the decisions and ideas that emerge from argument.

The purpose of this book is to help you participate in two types of activities: evaluating other people's arguments and creating arguments of your own. The book is organized in parts, and each part will help you become a more effective participant in the arguments that affect your life. Part One will help you engage with argument personally as you begin to identify the issues, the argument styles, and the processes for reading and writing that will work best for you; Part

Two will help you understand the nature of argument as you learn more about its essential parts and how they operate in argument to convince an audience; Part Three will provide you with a process for thinking critically and writing an argument paper that requires both critical thought and research; Part Four will provide you with many good examples of effective argument to analyze and draw on as you create original arguments of your own.

WHAT IS YOUR CURRENT PERSPECTIVE ON ARGUMENT?

You may never have been in an argument class before. If that is the case, as it is with most students, you will have a few ideas about argument, but you will not have a totally clear idea about what you will be studying in this class. It is best to begin the study of any new subject by thinking about what you already know. Then you can use what you know to learn more, which is the way all of us acquire new knowledge.

What does the word "argument" make you think about? The following list contains some common student responses to that question. Place a check next to those that match your own. If other ideas come to your mind, add them to the list.

_____ 1. It is important to include both sides in argument.

_____ 2. Argument is "an argument," with people mad and yelling at each other.

_____ 3. Argument is a debate in front of a judge; one side wins.

_____ 4. Argument takes place in courtrooms before judges and juries.

_____ 5. Argument is what I'd like to be able to do better at home, at work, with my friends so that I'd win more, get my way more often.

_____ 6. Argument is standing up for your ideas, defending them, and minimizing the opposition by being persuasive.

_____ 7. Argument requires one to keep an "open mind."

_____ 8. Argument papers are difficult to write because they require more than a collection of personal feelings and opinions about a subject.

_____ 9. Argument, to me, is like beating a dead horse. I have done papers in high school about subjects I'm supposed to care about, like abortion, homosexuality, drugs, capital punishment. They're old news. They no longer spark my imagination.

_____ 10. Argument is something I like to avoid. I see no reason for it. It makes things unpleasant and difficult. And nothing gets settled anyway.

_____ 11. _____

_____ 12. _____

Whether your present views of argument are positive, negative, or just vague, it's best to acknowledge them so that you can now begin expanding on them or even modifying some of them in order to develop a broad perspective on argument.

A definition of argument at this point should help clarify the broad perspective we are seeking for this word. There are many approaches and views of argument, and consequently various definitions have been suggested by argument theorists. Some focus on identifying opposing views, providing evidence, and declaring winners. Others emphasize reasoning, understanding, agreement, and consensus. Both types of definition are useful depending on the context and the purpose of the argument. Chaim Perelman, a respected modern argument theorist, provides the definition that we will use in this book. Perelman suggests that the goal of argument "is to create or increase the adherence of minds to the theses presented for their [the audience's] assent."[1] In other words, the goal of argument is at times to create agreement about controversial issues among participants and at other times merely to increase the possibility of agreement. This definition is broad enough to include both argument that focuses on opposing views and the declaration of winners and argument that emphasizes understanding and results in consensus. This definition further invites argument participants either to agree to the best position on a matter of dispute or to create a new position that all participants can agree on. Using this definition as a starting point, we can now add to it and consider argument in its broadest sense.

DEVELOPING A BROAD PERSPECTIVE ON ARGUMENT

Think about the implications of this idea: *Argument is everywhere.*[2] It is not only found in obvious places such as courts of law, legislative assemblies, or organized debates. Indeed, it is a part of all human enterprise, whether at home, at school, at work, or on the national or international scene. Home argument, for example, might center on spending money, dividing the household work, raising the children, and planning for the future. School argument might include such issues as increasing student fees, finding parking, understanding grades, or selecting classes and professors. Work argument might focus on making hiring decisions, delegating responsibility, or establishing long-term goals. National argument might deal with providing health care, abolishing crime, or electing leaders. International argument might deal with protecting human rights, abolishing hunger, or negotiating international trade agreements. Thus argument appears in virtually any context in which human beings interact and hold divergent views about topics that are at issue. Furthermore, argument is a perspective, a

---

[1]Chaim Perelman and L. Olbrechts-Tyteca, *The New Rhetoric: A Treatise on Argumentation* (Notre Dame, IN: Notre Dame Press, 1969), p. 45.

[2]I am indebted to Wayne Brockriede for this observation and for some of the other ideas in this chapter. See his article "Where Is Argument?" *Journal of the American Forensic Association,* Spring 1975, pp. 179–182.

point of view that people adopt to identify, interpret, analyze, communicate, and try to reach settlements or conclusions about subjects that are at issue.

If we accept the idea that argument can, indeed, be found anywhere, then we discover that it can also appear in several different forms and involve varying numbers of people. Argument can take eight different forms, as in the following list. Some, like organized debate and courts of law, will not surprise you. Others may.

Forms of Argument

1. *Debate, with participants on both sides trying to win.*   In a debate, people take sides on a controversial issue that is usually stated as a proposition. For example, the proposition "Resolved that health care be affordable for all Americans" might be debated by an affirmative debater arguing in favor of this idea and a negative debater arguing against it. A judge, who listens to the debate, usually selects one of the debaters as the winner. The debaters do not try to convince one another, but instead they try to convince the judge who is supposed to be impartial. Debates are useful for exploring and sometimes resolving issues that have distinct pro and con sides. Debates on television often feature people who hold conflicting views. The judge for these programs is the viewing public who may or may not pick a winner. Certainly the participants give the impression that they hope viewers will side with one or the other of them.

2. *Courtroom argument, with lawyers pleading before a judge and jury.*   As in a debate, lawyers take opposing sides and argue to convince a judge and jury of the guilt or innocence of a defendant. Lawyers do not try to convince one another. Also as in debate, someone is designated the winner. Television provides opportunities to witness courtroom argument, particularly on cable channels devoted exclusively to televising real trials. You can also visit court, since trials are open to the public.

3. *Dialectic, with people taking opposing views and finally resolving the conflict.* In dialectic, two or more people argue as equals to try to discover what seems to be the best position. A questioning strategy is often used to test the validity of each of the opposing views. The ancient philosopher Plato used this form of argument in his dialogues to examine such questions as what is truth, what is the ideal type of government, and what is more important: honesty and justice or political power. Dialectic is used by some professors to help students think about and finally arrive at positions that can be generally accepted by most of the class. For example, dialectic might be used to ascertain students' views on academic honesty or political action. Participants explain and justify their own positions and test others' positions. The object is to discover a common bedrock of ideas that everyone can agree on. There are no winners. There is, instead, a consensual discovery of a new position on the issue that is agreeable to everyone.

4. *Single-perspective argument, with one person arguing to convince a mass audience.*   We encounter argument in single-perspective form constantly on television and in newspapers, journals, books, and public speeches. It is usually clear

what the issue is and what position is being taken. Other opposing views, if referred to at all, are usually refuted. Specific examples of such argument range from a politician trying to influence voters to change their ideas about taxes, to an environmentalist trying to influence management to eliminate toxic waste, to an advertiser trying to sell blue jeans. The arguer does not usually know what immediate effect the message has had on the audience unless a poll or vote is taken, unless there is an opportunity for the readers to write letters to the editor, or unless there is a publicized change in policy or behavior. It is not clear, in other words, whether anyone "wins."

5. *One-on-one, everyday argument, with one person trying to convince another.* Convincing another person, one on one, is very different from convincing an impartial outside judge or a large unspecified audience. In the one-on-one situation, one person has to focus on and identify with the other person, think about what he or she wants and values, and be conciliatory if necessary. Each person either wins, loses, or is partially successful in winning. Examples of this form of argument might include convincing a partner to sell the business, convincing an employment officer to hire a favored candidate, or convincing a potential customer to buy a car.

6. *Academic inquiry, with one or more people examining a complicated issue.* The purpose of academic argument is to discover new views, new knowledge, and new truths about a complex issue. For example, physicists engage in academic inquiry about the nature of gravity, historians about the causes of major wars, or political scientists about the benefits of a strong state government. There are no clear-cut pro and con positions, no judges, and no emphasis on winning. Instead, anyone can participate, and there are potentially as many views as there are participants. Inquiry is a common form of argument that you will encounter in many of your college classes, where you will also be assigned to write inquiry papers. Virtually every discipline includes matters that are still open to inquiry, matters that people are still thinking and arguing about. Many professors expect their students to be able to identify the issues for inquiry in an academic discipline and also to participate in the ongoing search for answers. Imagine, for example, people reasoning together in a sociology class about whether war is ever justified, or in a psychology class about whether discrimination can ever be eliminated from society. These are not simple questions with yes or no answers. Inquiry can, however, produce insight into very difficult questions, with each new participant contributing a new reason, a new example, or a new angle that the others may not have considered. As the conversation progresses, participants achieve better understanding through mutual feedback, and some may even change their minds in order to bring their ideas in line with those of other participants. The inquiry form of argument is appropriate for the complex issues that one can find in every area of study and in every field of human endeavor. Like other forms of argument, it focuses on an issue and examines evidence. It is conducted through a cooperative search for knowledge, however, rather than on finding a winning position at the expense of others. Its result, ideally, is a consensus theory of truth, even though it may take some time to reach it.

7. *Negotiation, with two or more people working to reach consensus.* This is an important form of argument that is used to create the plans of action that solve problems. Both the Palestinians and the Israelis, for example, could not claim ownership of the same land, so a joint plan for separate states had to be negotiated. One country could not kill sea life that another country depended on, so rights to the sea had to be negotiated. Closer to home, people negotiate who gets the car, who picks up the check, or who takes out the newspapers. Negotiation most often takes place between two people, one on one, or in group meetings. It involves both competition and cooperation, and, in order for it to be successful, everyone must state his or her favored position and support it. Everyone must also be willing to listen to alternative views and reasons and modify original views in order to reach consensus.

8. *Internal argument, or working to convince yourself.* Internal argument is used by all of us for individual decision making and also to increase our own levels of motivation. New Year's resolutions are one example of internal argument and decision making. As in other forms of argument, different possibilities are identified, reasons both for and against are considered, and conclusions are finally reached.

Now reconsider some of the student perspectives on argument listed at the beginning of this chapter. Most of those ideas fit into one of the eight forms of argument just described. The exception is item 2, argument defined as "an argument," with people mad and yelling at each other. No argument can be effective when people stop listening, stop thinking, and engage in vocal fighting, so "an argument" is not part of the broad perspective on argument defined in this chapter. Look back also at item 8 (argument is difficult to write because it requires more than opinion), item 9 (I'm tired of some of the topics for argument), and item 10 (argument makes me uncomfortable). If you found yourself initially in sympathy with those responses, you may now have discovered forms of argument that could be acceptable vehicles for your ideas. Here is the list again: debate, courtroom argument, dialectic, single-perspective argument, one-on-one argument, academic inquiry, negotiation, and internal argument. Which have been successful forms for you in the past? Which others are you drawn to? Why?

These examples and explanations of forms of argument demonstrate that effective argument does not take place automatically. Special conditions are necessary, in fact, if argument is to be effective. Let's look at some of those conditions to further expand our perspective on argument.

UNDER WHAT CONDITIONS DOES ARGUMENT WORK BEST?

To work best, argument requires (1) an arguable issue, (2) a person who will argue, (3) an audience that will listen, (4) some common ground between the arguer and the audience, (5) a forum in which the argument can take place, and

(6) some changes in the audience. Let's look at some optimal requirements for each of these important elements.

1. **An issue.** An argument needs to have as its central focus an issue that has not yet been settled. Furthermore, there must be the potential for at least two or more views on that issue. For example, some people seem to think that the handgun issue has only two sides—that is, everyone should, by constitutional right, be allowed to own handguns, or no one should be allowed to own them. Between these two extreme views, however, people can and do take a variety of positions, including the view that owning and using handguns may be acceptable under certain conditions but not others.

2. **An arguer.** Every argument requires an arguer who is willing, interested, and motivated to take a position on an issue, get information and think about it, and communicate it to others. This person needs to develop expertise on an issue and be willing to take the risk to express his or her own ideas about it. Furthermore, the arguer should be willing to go beyond the "current wisdom" about an issue and give fresh perspectives and approaches that will suggest original insights to the audience. For example, an individual arguing for tougher handgun laws needs to present fresh reasons and evidence to get people's attention and agreement.

3. **An audience.** Every argument needs an audience that is willing to listen or read and consider new views or perspectives. The audience should also be capable of understanding, thinking, questioning, discussing, and answering. It may be composed of one or more people who are personally known to the arguer, or it may be unknown, in which case the arguer must imagine and invoke its background, motives, and values. The arguer should want to communicate with this audience. It should not be composed of people who are usually ignored or who are not respected by the arguer. It is a compliment to draw someone into discussion on an issue, so the audience should be valued, and, to be effective, the arguer must show that he or she cares about the audience, its interests, and its state of mind. This approach will assure a willing audience that listens and does not shut the arguer out or otherwise try to escape. Receptive audiences are potentially willing to change their minds, a desirable outcome of argument.[3] Consider, for example, an audience member who favors handgun ownership, who is a parent of schoolchildren, and who is willing to listen to an opposing view because a respectful fellow parent has described the number of children who own handguns in their children's school.

4. **Common ground.** Effective argument requires a community of minds that is achieved through common language and the establishment of some common ground that is relevant to the issue. People from different countries obviously need a common language, but they also need an understanding and respect

---

[3]Some of the observations in this chapter about the special conditions for argument, especially for the audience, are derived from Perelman and Olbrechts-Tyteca, *The New Rhetoric,* Part 1.

for one another's cultural differences in order to argue effectively. People from different disciplines must be able to understand and respect one another's technical jargon and other words and concepts central to the understanding of a particular field of study. In addition, they need to share some background, values, and views to make communication possible. Three situations are possible when one works to establish common ground in argument. First, if two parties agree totally, they do not argue. For example, two parents who agree that their child should go to college do not argue about that part of the child's future. Second, if two parties are too far apart, they usually do not understand one another well enough to argue. The United States did not have enough common ground with Iraq in 1991 to work out differences, and the two countries went to war. There were several causes for this war. Iraq had invaded Kuwait, and the United States was committed to help this country maintain its independence. Kuwait's independence was important to the United States because Kuwait was a major source of U.S. oil. Finally, Iraq was developing a powerful military with nuclear potential, so it seemed important to the United States to stop that military growth. Common ground in this situation virtually did not exist, and, as a result, reasoned argument gave way to "an argument," and many people were killed. The third possible situation for establishing common ground creates more effective conditions for argument than do the first two. Common ground may be established through the discovery of common interests—common ideas, motives, or values—or even through recognizing common friends or enemies. As soon as two parties realize they have something in common, they can more easily achieve identification, even if it is minimal, and engage in constructive argument. Imagine, once again, two parties who disagree on handgun ownership. One party believes handgun ownership should be forbidden to stop random killing. The other party believes people should own handguns to protect themselves from random killers. Both agree that random killing is bad and must be stopped, and this basic agreement provides the common ground they need to begin to engage in constructive argument about handgun ownership. Figure 1.1 provides a diagram of these three possible situations for establishing common ground in argument.

5. **A forum.**   People need safe forums for argument where they can feel creative and know they will be heard. Such widely available forums include magazines and journals, newspapers, books, letters and reports, television programs of all sorts, courtrooms, legislative assemblies, motion pictures, art, drama, fiction, poetry, advertisements, and music. College is another safe forum for arguments. Professors and students argue in class, at meals, and in dorms and apartments. Outside speakers present argument. The argument class, with its discussions, papers, and other assignments, can be a safe forum for practicing argument, particularly if both the students and the instructor work to create an environment in which all students participate and are respected.

6. **Audience outcomes.**   Successful arguments should produce changes in the audience. These changes will vary with the audience and situation. At times the audience becomes convinced and decides to change its mind. Or a successful negotiation is achieved, people find themselves in consensus, a deci-

THE ISSUE: WAS HUMAN LIFE CREATED OR DID IT EVOLVE

Possibility 1: Complete agreement and not argument. **Two creationists believe the biblical language about the six days of creation literally, agree totally, and share the same common ground.**

Possibility 2: Total disagreement, no common ground, and no argument. **A creationist literally believes the biblical six days of creation, and an evolutionist believes that human life evolved from a single cell over eons of time. They disagree totally, and there is no common ground.**

Possibility 3: Two parties discover something in common and there is a possibility of argument. **Another creationist allows that biblical language may be metaphorical and therefore that creation may have occurred over eons of time. An evolutionist also believes humans took eons to evolve. They share common ground on that point, but disagree on other points.**

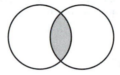

Figure 1.1   Establishing Common Ground.

sion is reached, and a plan of action is proposed. Other arguments may not have such clear-cut results. A hostile audience may be brought to a neutral point of view. A neutral audience may decide to take a stand. Sometimes, it is a significant accomplishment to get the audience's attention and to raise its level of consciousness. This success can lay the groundwork for a possible future change of mind.

At times an event can create a massive change in the way that people view issues. The Million Man March held in Washington, D.C. in the fall of 1995 changed many peoples' perceptions about the size, commitment, and solidarity of the black male community. The Stand for Children demonstration held in Washington, D.C. in the summer of 1996 also changed public perceptions about the issues that are of major concern to women. As a number of private American citizens and public organizations prepared to assemble at the Stand for Children demonstration, Betty Friedan wrote in *The New Yorker* that the probable outcome of the Stand for Children rally would be "to bring out some new thinking that has been quietly bubbling under the surface." The demonstration, she predicted, would help identify the "most urgent concerns of women today." These would not be the "gender issues" (abortion, date rape, sexual harassment, pornography, and the like) that have engaged women in the past, but, instead, there would be a change in focus to the issues associated with "jobs and families." Women will not abandon their concern for gender issues, she says, but the Stand for Children demonstration will largely refocus their attention on a concern for children and their future. In her article, she claimed a major shift in thinking would come about as a result of the demonstration.[4] And, indeed, in the months that followed this gathering of some 200,000 people, in much of the writing and discussion about women's issues that appeared in the public press, there did seem to be a new interest and concern for children, including adequate family and public resources for their care and their future. The event seemed to create the change in focus that Friedan predicted.

How much can you expect to change people's thinking as you discuss and write about the issues that are important to you? Some students in argument class wonder if they must convince their teachers along with their classmates of their point of view in every paper they write if they are to get good grades. This demand may be too great, since audiences and the outcomes of argument vary so much. Convincing the teacher and your fellow students that the argument paper is effective with a particular audience is probably the best possible outcome in argument class. As one professor put it, "My ambition is to return a paper and say that I disagreed with it completely—but the writing was excellent—A!"[5]

UNDER WHAT CONDITIONS
DOES ARGUMENT FAIL?

We have just examined the optimal conditions for argument. Now let's look at the conditions that can cause it to flounder or fail. No argument, we have seen, can take place when there is no real disagreement, no uncertainty, or no possibility for two or more views. Also, neutral people who do not have enough interest in an issue to form an opinion do not argue. For example, some young people do not want to argue about possible retirement plans because they are neutral on this issue. Argument also cannot take place unless people perceive an issue as a subject for argument. An example might be a college orientation session where various department representatives argue in favor of their areas as majors. This is not an issue for students who have already decided, and thus they will not identify issues or perceive this session as a forum for argument.

Big problems or risky problems that may require radical change are difficult for some people to argue about. Finding a new career or dissolving a longtime relationship may fit into this category, and many people, wisely or not, tend to

---

[4]Betty Friedan, "Children's Crusade," *The New Yorker,* June 3, 1996, pp. 5–6.
[5]Hilton Obenzinger, "The Israeli-Palestinian Conflict: Teaching a Theme-Based Course," *Notes in the Margins,* Winter 1994, p. 12.

leave such difficult issues alone rather than argue about them. Religious issues or issues that threaten global disaster are also sometimes too big, too emotional, or too scary for many people to argue about. At the other extreme, some issues may be perceived as low risk, trivial, boring, or even ridiculous. Some family arguments fall into this category, like what to eat for dinner. One person may care, but the rest do not.

Arguments that lack common ground among participants do not work well. It is sometimes difficult to establish common ground and argue constructively with "true believers," for example, who have made up their minds on certain issues and will not listen, budge, or change. Racial bigots fall into this category. It is also difficult to argue with some religious people who take certain issues on faith and do not perceive them as subjects for argument. In fact, argument often fails when one participant perceives a topic as an issue and the other does not. Again, there is no common ground. Finally, argument cannot take place when one party is not motivated to argue. "Don't bring that up again" or "I don't want to discuss that" puts an end to most argument. The "Calvin and Hobbes" cartoon in Figure 1.2 provides a similar example.

We have already described the audience outcomes of effective argument. When argument is not working, as in the situations just described, the outcomes are negative also. Sometimes poor argument results in a standoff: both parties agree to keep their original views and not to cross the line. Or emotions run strong, verbal fighting breaks out, and extreme views are expressed. No one agrees with anyone else. People shake their heads and walk away, or they become hurt and upset. Some individuals may become strident, wanting to debate everyone to demonstrate that they are right. When classroom argument results in such negative outcomes, some students drop the class, others become silent and refuse to participate, and everyone becomes confused.

One important aim of this book is to provide you with the insight and skill to manage these negative situations so that more constructive argument can take place. Students are in an excellent position to overcome some of the fear, resistance, and aversion associated with difficult issues and, by using evidence and

Figure 1.2 When Argument Fails.

good sense, get to work and face some of them. Understanding audience members, especially their attitudes, needs, and values, is an important first step. Another useful idea to keep in mind is that most arguers have more success with some audiences than with others depending upon the amount of common ground. Even in the most difficult situations, some common ground can usually be found among people who seem to disagree on almost everything else. Recent research suggests that one vehicle for establishing common ground is through narratives, with each side relating personal experiences and stories. Even the most hostile adversaries can usually relate to one another's personal experiences and find some unity in the common villains, heroines, or themes in their stories. What sometimes also happens in this process is that the issues themselves change or are transformed in ways that make them easier for both parties to argue.[6]

Arguing effectively in difficult situations requires a conscious effort to avoid both stereotypical reactions and entrenched behavioral patterns. Past habits must be replaced with new strategies that work better. It is sometimes difficult to make such changes because habits can be strong, but it is possible to do so, and the stakes are often high, especially when the choice is constructive argument or verbal fighting and standoffs.

ENGAGING WITH ISSUES

The most easily arguable issues, to summarize, are those that invite two or more views, that are perceived by all parties as issues, that are interesting and motivating to all participants, and that inspire research, information gathering, and original thought. They also promise common ground among participants, and they do not appear too big, too risky, too trivial, too confusing, too scary, or too specialized to discuss profitably. But you may also find yourself drawn to some of the more difficult issues that do not meet all of these criteria, and you should not necessarily shun them just because they are difficult. You will need to work with your audience in creative ways and consider the entire context for argument, regardless of the nature of the issues you select. Most important is that you now identify some issues that are arguable and important to you and to your classroom audience. Identifying issues will help you keep a high level of motivation and receive the maximum instructional benefits from argument class. Finding your own arguable issues is much better than accepting assigned issues as writing topics.

So now the search begins. What will help you find your arguable issues? Issues exist in contexts, and the issues most engaging to you will probably emerge from those parts of your life that demand your greatest attention and energy. For

---

[6]Linda Putnam in the keynote speech at the Texas Speech Communication Association Conference, October 1993, reported these results from her study of negotiations between teachers and labor union leaders.

example, people who are compellingly engaged with their professions think about work issues, new parents think about child-rearing issues, dedicated students think about the issues raised in class, and many teenagers think about peer-group issues. To begin the search for your issues, examine those parts of your life that demand your most concentrated time and attention right now. Also, think about some of the special characteristics of issues in general. Here are a few of them:

Issues Are Compelling.   People get excited about issues, and they usually identify with a few in particular. In fact, most people can quickly name one or more issues that are so important to them that they think about them often. Some people even build careers or change careers because of issues that are vital to them. People who devote large amounts of time and study to particular issues become the "experts" on those issues. Can you think of some of your own issues that are particularly compelling to you?

Issues Often Originate in Dramatic Life Situations.   Things happen—a teenager gets shot at school, several major companies decide to downsize and lay off workers, a doctor helps a terminally ill patient to die, an oil spill pollutes a beach and kills the wildlife. To understand these occurrences better, people react to them intellectually, and then issues emerge. Are companies making too much money and at the expense of employee morale? Should teenagers, or should anyone, be allowed to purchase guns? Should doctors help patients die or should they be required to let nature take its course? Which is more important, economic growth or environmental protection? Because of their dramatic origins, many issues are intensely interesting to many people. Pay attention to the stories that are newsworthy this week and identify the issues that are associated with them. Select the ones that interest you the most.

Current Issues Are Related to Enduring Issues.   Current issues can be linked to enduring issues, those that have engaged people for many ages. For example, the current issues about military spending have their roots in the age-old issues that are associated with war. Is war ever justified? Should a country constantly be prepared for war? The abortion issue has its roots in the enduring issues about life. Should life be protected at all costs? Should the individual or a social agency have the greater control over one's life? Think about the enduring issues that engage you. They may help you find your arguable issues.

Issues Go Underground and Then Resurface.   Public concern with particular issues is not constant. Experts may think about their issues continuously, but the public usually only thinks about an issue when something happens that brings it to public attention. How to deal with increasing population is an example of such an issue. Experts on that issue may think about it daily, but the general public may think about it only when census figures are released or when an international meeting on the subject commands media attention. Such issues are, of course, always lurking in the background, always important. But we do not think about all of them all of the time. Think back. Are there some issues that used to concern you that you have neither thought about nor read about for a long time? What are they?

Issues Sometimes Get Solved, but Then New Ones Emerge.   Some issues command so much public attention that the people who can do something about them finally perceive them as problems and pass laws or take other measures to solve them. As soon as an issue is solved, however, other, related issues spring up in its place. For example, for many years, people argued about what to do about health care. As soon as Health Maintenance Organizations (HMOs) became widely accessible, new issues emerged that focused on the quality of care patients received in these organizations and how physicians could profit economically from these changes in the delivery of health care. Are there any new issues of this type that might interest you? Think of problems that now seem solved but probably aren't fully solved.

Issues Seem to Be Getting More Complex.   The world's issues seem to become more and more complex as the world becomes more complex. In an interview, the actress Susan Sarandon, who has always been engaged with social issues, stated that in the mid- to late-1960s, when she was in college, the issues seemed simpler, more black and white. The issues at that time, for example, centered on civil rights and the Vietnam war. "We were blessed with clear-cut issues," she says. "We were blessed with clear-cut grievances. Things were not as gray as they are now."[7]

Because issues are now more complex, people need to learn to engage with them in more complex ways. The word "perspectives" as used in this book refers not only to a broader perspective on issues and argument itself, but also to the variety of different perspectives that individuals can take on particular issues. Few issues are black and white or can be viewed as pro or con anymore. Most invite several different ways of looking at them

As you develop your own perspectives on the complex issues that engage you, keep in mind that it takes many years to become an expert. You will want to look at what the experts say. But you will not have the background and information to write as comprehensively as they do. When you write your own argument, you will want to write on a limited aspect of your issue, one that you can learn enough about. Limiting your topic will permit you to get the information and gain the perspective to be convincing. Suggestions to help you limit your approach to a complex issue will be made in future chapters.

---

[7]Ovid Demaris, "Most of All, the Children Matter," *Parade,* March 1, 1992, pp. 4, 5.

Some Examples of Arguable Issues

Looking at examples of some of the issues that typically engage people should help you select the ones that will interest you. Date rape, political correctness, hate language, the treatment of criminals, environmental protection, gay rights, men's and women's roles and responsibilities, and censorship are issues that often interest students. In the 1996 presidential campaign, a number of public issues, such as the right to legal abortion, welfare reform, taxation policies, youth violence, and immigration commanded fairly constant attention from the candidates. Campaign issues do not change radically from one election to the next, although certain issues may receive more attention some years than others. In Box 1.1 some contemporary public issues have been linked with enduring issues to demonstrate the timeless quality of most of them. See if you can add additional examples of your own as you read through those in the "current" column.

Box 1.2 illustrates some of the issues you are likely to encounter in your other classes in college. These are examples of issues that your professors argue about, the subjects for academic inquiry. You may be expected to take positions and develop arguments yourself on these or similar issues if you take classes in some of these subjects. As you read, try to add additional examples from your own classes.

HOW SHOULD YOU ENGAGE WITH ISSUES?

Boxes 1.1 and 1.2 represent only a sampling of issues. When you start focusing on issues, you will identify many more. Here are some final suggestions to help you engage with issues:

- Listen for issues in all of your classes and identify them with a circled *I* in the margins of your lecture notes. Ask your professors to identify the major issues in their fields.
- Read a newspaper daily, if possible, or at least three or four times a week. If you do not subscribe to a newspaper, read one or more of them in the library or set up a newspaper recycling system in class. You will find stories about issues throughout the paper. The opinion and editorial pages, however, are the best source.
- Read a news magazine, like *Time* or *Newsweek,* on a regular basis, and look for issues.
- Concentrate your television viewing on programs where issues are discussed: news programs and programs that focus on interviews about issues, like "The Newshour with Jim Lehrer," "To the Contrary," "Crossfire," "Firing Line," "CNN Presents," "Nightline," "This Week with David Brinkley," "Meet the Press," or "60 Minutes." Some of these programs focus mainly on debate and pro and con argument, and others explore an issue from several perspectives.

What Are Some Public Issues?

CURRENT ISSUES	ENDURING ISSUES
Ways and Means Issues	
Should everyone pay taxes and in what proportion to their income? Should free trade be limited? How much business profit can be sacrificed to keep the environment clean and safe? Should scholarships and fellowships be taxed? How should we finance health care?	Where should a government get money, and how should it spend it?
Quality of Life Issues	
Should more resources be directed to protecting the environment? Are inner cities or rural areas better places to live? How can we improve the quality of life for children and senior citizens?	What is a minimum quality of life, and how do we achieve it?
Personal Rights Versus Social Rights Issues	
Should individuals, the government, or private business be responsible for the unemployed? health care? day care? the homeless? senior citizens? drug addicts? AIDS victims? race problems? minority problems? dealing with criminals? worker safety? deciding who should buy guns?	Can individuals be responsible for their own destinies, or should social institutions be responsible? Can individuals be trusted to do what is best for society?

continued

BOX 1.1   Examples of Current and Enduring Public Issues.

War and Peace Issues

How much should the government spend on the military?	Is war justified, and should countries stay prepared for war?
Should the United States remain prepared for a major world war?	
Should you, your friends, or your family be required to register for the draft?	

Self-Development Issues

What opportunities for education and training should be available to everyone?	What opportunities for self-development should societies make available to individuals?
Should the welfare system be revised to include opportunities for self-development?	
Should gays be allowed the same opportunities to participate in society as other people?	

Human Life Issues

Should abortions be permitted?	Should human life be protected under any conditions?
Should capital punishment be permitted?	
Is mercy killing ever justifiable?	

Foreign Affairs Issues

Which is wiser, to support an American economy or a global economy?	In world politics, how do we balance the rights of smaller countries and different ethnic groups against the needs of larger countries and international organizations?
How much foreign aid should we provide, and to which countries?	
Should college graduates be provided with opportunities for foreign service?	
Should the U.S. defend foreign countries from aggressors?	

Law and Order Issues

Is the judicial system effective?	What is an appropriate balance between the welfare and protection of society as a whole and the rights of the individual?
Does the punishment always fit the crime?	
Is police brutality a problem in your community?	

BOX 1.1   Examples of Current and Enduring Public Issues (*continued*)

What Are Some Academic Issues?

In Physics—Is there a unifying force in the universe? Is there enough matter in the universe to cause it eventually to stop expanding and then to collapse? What is the nature of this matter?

In Astronomy—What elements can be found in interstellar gas? What is the nature of the asteroids?

In Biology—What limits, if any, should be placed on genetic engineering?

In Chemistry—How can toxic wastes best be managed?

In Sociology—Is the cause of crime social or individual? Does television have a significant negative effect on society?

In Psychology—Which is the best approach for understanding human behavior, nature or nurture? Can artificial intelligence ever duplicate human thought?

In Anthropology—Which is more reliable in dating evolutionary stages, DNA or fossils?

In Business—Can small privately owned businesses still compete with giant conglomerate companies? Are chief executive officers paid too much?

In Mathematics—Are boys naturally better than girls at math? Should calculators be encouraged? Should calculators be allowed in testing situations?

In Engineering—How important should environmental concerns be in determining engineering processes? To what extent, if any, are engineers responsible for the social use of what they produce? How aggressive should we be in seeking and implementing alternative sources of energy? Should the government fund the development of consumer-oriented technology to the same extent that it funds military-oriented technology?

In History—Have historians been too restrictive in their perspective? Does history need to be retold, and, if so, how? Is the course of history influenced more by unusual individuals or socioeconomic forces?

In Political Science—Where should ultimate authority to govern reside, with the individual, the church, the state, or social institutions? Is power properly divided among the three branches of government in the United States?

In Communication—How can the best balance be struck between the needs of society and freedom of expression in the mass media? How

continued

BOX 1.2   Examples of Academic Issues across the Disciplines.

much impact, if any, do mass media have on the behavior of individuals in society?

In English—Is the concept of traditional literature too narrowly focused in English departments? If yes, what else should be considered literature?

BOX 1.2 Examples of Academic Issues Across the Disciplines. (*continued*)

- Browse at the newsstand or in the current periodicals in the library and look for issues.
- Browse in the new-books section of the library and look for books that address issues.
- Listen for issues in conversations and discussions with other students. If you get confused, ask, "What is at issue here?" to help focus an argumentative discussion.
- Study the table of contents of this book and sample some of the issues in the various readings at the ends of chapters and in "The Reader." Notice that "The Reader" is organized around broad issue areas and specific issues that are related to them. The articles have been selected to provide various perspectives, both historic and modern, on many specific current and enduring issues.
- Begin discussing and writing about some of the ideas you get from reading and listening to other people's arguments.

EXERCISES AND ACTIVITIES

1. CLASS PROJECT: "ARGUMENT IS EVERYWHERE"

Test the idea that argument can be found everywhere. Each member of the class should bring in an example of an argument and explain why it can be defined in this way. Each example should focus on an issue that people are still arguing about and on which there is no general agreement. Look for examples in a variety of contexts: newspapers, magazines, the Internet, television, motion pictures, music, sermons, other college classes, and in conversations and other printed material that you find at work, at school, and at home. Bring in actual examples of articles, letters to the editor, bumper stickers, advertisements, or other easily transportable arguments, or bring in clear and complete descriptions and explanations of arguments you cannot bring to class, like lectures, television shows, or billboards. Students should give two- to three-minute oral reports on the arguments they select that includes a description of the six requirements for an argument described in this chapter: an issue, an arguer, an audience, possible common ground between them, a forum, and some expected changes in the audience (pp. 9–11). The class should decide if all examples described in this activity are, indeed, examples of argument.

2. **GROUP WORK AND CLASS DISCUSSION: WHAT MAKES A GOOD ARGUMENT?**

Both of the following arguments were submitted to and accepted by the *New York Times* for publication. The first was written by a college student and the second by a married couple. Why do you think these arguments were selected for publication? Write the title "Characteristics of Effective Argument" at the top of a sheet of paper and divide the sheet into two columns by drawing a line down the middle. List the subtitles "Argument 1" and "Argument 2" at the top of the two columns. Now list the conditions, special characteristics, and qualities of each of these arguments that contribute to their success as arguments. Note also how they are different from each other. At the bottom of each column you might also list any weaknesses. Use what you have learned from this chapter and your own past experience with argument to do this critique and evaluation. Now discuss the results. Compile a class list of the best argumentative features of each essay, as well as a list of the weaknesses. Keep a copy of this class list. It is a starting point. You will add to it as you learn more about what it takes to make a good argument. Establishing these characteristics will help you recognize good argument when you read and also help you write better argument yourself.

ARGUMENT 1

SOME COLLEGE COSTS SHOULD BE TAX DEDUCTIBLE

Davidson Goldin

Ithaca, N.Y.

As the Government spends increasingly less on student financial aid, many leading colleges and universities are using a greater percentage of tuition revenues for scholarships. Just as income tax breaks are given for charitable contributions, this portion of tuition should be tax deductible.

Statistics compiled by the Consortium on Financing Higher Education, which does research and analysis for 32 member colleges, show the growing importance of tuition for scholarships. In 1980, the consortium schools spent an average 9.8 percent of tuition revenues on financial aid; last year, that figure rose to 15.9 percent. It will continue to rise as Federal and state financing drops further.

The median tuition at the consortium schools in 1991 was approximately $15,000 per year. These schools devoted an average of $2,400 from each student's tuition to discounts for students with financial need.

Of the consortium schools, the University of Chicago spent the largest portion of tuition on aid in 1991: 30.7 percent of its $15,135 tuition. Brown, Cornell,

Columbia, Johns Hopkins, Stanford, Wesleyan and Williams spent 14 percent to 16 percent. Princeton spent the least, 1.4 percent, but it finances an unusually large portion of student aid from its permanent endowment. Other schools include Rochester (28.6 percent), Harvard (8.6 percent) and Pennsylvania (19.5 percent).

After four years, families paying full tuition often provide more than $10,000 for easing the economic burden of others but do not receive any tax relief for this contribution to society. Scholarships based on financial need promote a socioeconomically diverse student body, and they enable economically strapped students to attend top schools.

Many tax-deductible contributions enhance the quality of life in a community or promote social, cultural and educational programs—gifts to orchestras, churches, social welfare agencies and libraries, and so on. All donations to colleges are tax deductible, whether the money is used for scholarships, an endowed professorship or a new building.

Tuition, unlike these voluntary contributions, is obligatory. Yet the portion of tuition that directly finances scholarships is in effect a charitable contribution, so it deserves the same tax treatment. In the tuition bill, schools should disclose the percentage of tuition set aside specifically for financial aid. Unlike the portions of tuition that pay for the educational enterprise—faculty and administration salaries, security and maintenance—the amount allotted for aid does not directly benefit those who provide the money.

Many families considered able to afford exorbitant tuition fees are hard-pressed to pay the bill. Many parents have refinanced their homes, incurred long-term debt and forfeited countless purchases and opportunities to pay for a college education.

All students benefit from the social and economic diversity that would be impossible without scholarships. Our society, which similarly thrives on diversity, should reward those who pay extra to make it possible.[8]

ARGUMENT 2

WE'RE GOOD REPUBLICANS—AND PRO-CHOICE

Beverly G. Hudnut and William H. Hudnut 3d

Indianapolis

An open letter to the Republican National Committee:

Last year, during the 18th week of Beverly's pregnancy, we discovered through testing that our baby suffered from grave defects that would have pre-

---

[8]*New York Times*, April 18, 1992, Sec. A, p. 5.

vented him from becoming a healthy human being. Anencephaly was just one problem. Ultrasound and, later, an autopsy revealed several more.

After talking with our families, physicians and pastors, we decided to terminate the pregnancy. It was a heart-wrenching decision, because we wanted our baby very badly and already loved him dearly. But we felt that our decision was the only good one to make, grounded as it was in sound professional advice, the love of family and friends, and our faith.

At the time, Bill was in his 16th year as Republican Mayor of Indianapolis. So ours was a public decision as well as a private one. We issued a news release, and tried to be upfront with the press. The outpouring of love and support from all over the country—mostly from people who had struggled with the same decision—was heartwarming.

We would have been terribly upset if an outside force, namely government, had prevented us from following the dictates of our conscience in this matter. Granted, our case represents a small fraction of the total number of abortions performed in the U.S., but nonetheless we feel constrained to ask: Why should political parties, our party in particular, stake out a position on abortion? Why borrow trouble on a matter on which people are so seriously divided?

It seems to us that under traditional minimalist Republican policy, government would choose *not* to interfere with a woman's right to make her own decision about whether or not to bear a child. We consider ourselves to be good members of the Republican team. It has been fairly easy to keep quiet about the abortion issue in the past and vote for candidates in spite of their position on abortion. It was perhaps easy because we felt protected by the *Roe* v. *Wade* decision. Following the same logic, it is now easy to speak up publicly because our party leaders are encouraging the Supreme Court to reverse *Roe* v. *Wade*.

If the Court takes steps this year to dilute laws determining whether or not a woman has control over her choice about bearing a child, we fear for our party in this year's election and those in the future. Pro-choice Republicans can no longer afford to keep their opinions to themselves. There are many of us with different political beliefs who find ourselves in the middle. Our voices are not being heard, primarily because we have kept quiet, and no forum of discussion has existed to date to learn from one another. Surely we are mature enough as a country to be able to talk civilly about abortion without yelling or screaming or trying to force our viewpoint on others.

When Beverly applied to testify at Tuesday's party platform meeting in Salt Lake City, she was told that the Republican National Committee had already selected its speakers on "both sides" of the abortion issue. The response perplexed us, because this complex subject has more sides than two. How about a third side? Granted, we are pro-choice, but why not simply leave abortion out of the platform, which has opposed abortion in recent years. As soon as a party or politician or citizen takes a stand on abortion, an "us against them" situation is set in place, leaving little room for dialogue or diversity of opinion.

In his book, *Life Itself,* Roger Rosenblatt wrote that we have to "learn to live on 'uncommon ground' in the matter of abortion; that we must not only accept but embrace a state of tension that requires a tolerance of ambivalent feelings, respect for different values and sensibilities, and no small amount of compassion." We call on our party leadership to take a stand on that "uncommon ground" by not taking a stand on abortion.[9]

3. **READING, DISCUSSION, AND WRITING ASSIGNMENT: COMPELLING ISSUES**
   "We're Good Republicans—and Pro-Choice" in Exercise 2 illustrates a married couple's engagement with an issue. Note how compelling and complex issues can become for individuals.
   1. **Class discussion.** What issue has been compelling to the Hudnuts? What is original about their perspective on this issue? Why did they become interested in it? How have their views changed over time? What caused them to change some of their views on this issue?
   2. **Writing assignment.** Write a two-page paper in which you identify two issues that are of compelling interest to you. In your paper describe your views on the issues and explain why you hold them. Most people hold their particular views for interesting reasons. Where did they come from? Also, describe how they have changed over time, if at all, and what caused them to change.

4. **WRITING ASSIGNMENT: ISSUE PROPOSAL**
   Your instructor may from time to time require you to write a proposal in which you will provide initial information about an issue that is of interest to you and that you will write about at length later in either one paper or in a series of papers. Here are instructions for writing such a proposal.
   a. **Select an issue.** Identify an issue that you care about, that you have not yet made up your mind about, and that you would like to study. To help you find an issue, look through the table of contents for "The Reader" in this book and find the issue question that is most interesting to you. Or, make a class list of all of the issues that are of current concern to the students in your class and select the issue that is of greatest interest to you. Most students have "their issue," one that they really care about. What is yours?
   b. **Test the issue.** When you have selected your issue, apply the "Twelve Tests of an Arguable Issue" to make certain that it is an arguable issue. If all of your answers are "yes," you will be able to work with your issue productively. If any of your answers are "no," you may want to modify your issue or switch to another one.

---

[9]*New York Times,* May 29, 1992, Sec. A, p. 15.

Twelve Tests of an Arguable Issue

Change or modify your issue if you cannot answer "yes" to all of these questions.

Your issue (write as a question): _____

Yes _____ No _____   1. Is this an issue that has not been resolved or settled?

Yes _____ No _____   2. Does this issue potentially inspire two or more views?

Yes _____ No _____   3. Are you interested and engaged with this issue, and do you want to communicate with an audience about it?

Yes _____ No _____   4. Can you inspire your audience to be sufficiently interested to pay attention?

Yes _____ No _____   5. Do other people, besides you, perceive this as an issue?

Yes _____ No _____   6. Is this issue significant enough to be worth your time?

Yes _____ No _____   7. Is this a safe issue for you? Not too risky? Scary? Will you be willing to express your ideas?

Yes _____ No _____   8. Will you be able to establish common ground with your audience on this issue, that is, a common set of terms, some common background and values?

Yes _____ No _____   9. Can you get information and come up with convincing insights on this issue?

Yes _____ No _____ 10. Can you eventually get a clear and limited focus on this issue, even if it is a complicated one?

Yes _____ No _____ 11. Is it an enduring issue, or can you build perspective by linking it to an enduring issue?

Yes _____ No _____ 12. Can you predict some audience outcomes? (Think of your classmates as the audience. Will they be convinced? Hostile? Neutral? Attentive? Remember, any outcomes at all can be regarded as significant in argument.)

---

   c. **Write a one-page issue proposal.** Include the following information.
   - Introduce the issue and then present it in question form.
   - Explain why it is compelling to you.
   - Describe what you already know about it.
   - Explain what more you need to learn

An example of an issue proposal written by a student appears on page 27.

**Student
Paper**

ISSUE PROPOSAL ON AFFIRMATIVE ACTION

Jeanna Fuston

To counter centuries of discrimination, racism, and dispossession, the federal government and many state governments over the years have implemented affirmative action programs to make economic, occupational, and educational opportunities available to minority workers and minority-owned businesses. While many Americans believe that affirmative action represents little more than reverse discrimination, others defend it wholeheartedly, arguing that its benefits to society and to the advancement of traditionally alienated groups far outweigh its costs. Should affirmative action be preserved, perhaps in a modified form, or should it be abolished?

I am interested in this issue because I like to follow politics, and recently affirmative action has come into the forefront of political discussion. Also, I believe that access to education is critical for minorities, and affirmative action still provides opportunities for some groups of students that might not otherwise be available.

I know that some people believe that affirmative action gives an unfair advantage to minority students and workers and that it is no longer necessary. These people either want to modify it or secure its abolition. The opposition is fierce, however. Women, African-Americans, and other minorities who have benefitted from affirmative action in education and employment argue that members of minority populations have not yet gained equal footing and, without affirmative action, racial and gender disparities will surely return to the levels of two decades ago. The most recent and aggressive attack against affirmative action came in California where Governor Pete Wilson used its abolition as a plank in his campaign platform. Moreover, the University of California system voted to suspend affirmative action quotas in school admissions and hiring.

I need more information about the legislative enactments concerning affirmative action programs, particularly those enacted by the federal government. Also I need to find out what the various proposals are for revision. I would like to examine current statistics on minority employment compared to those of twenty years ago.

5. QUESTIONS ON THE CHAPTER
   a. Provide three examples of your own to illustrate the statement, "Argument is everywhere."
   b. What are some of the defining characteristics of debate, courtroom argument, academic inquiry, and negotiation?
   c. What are some of the conditions necessary for argument to work best?
   d. What are some of the conditions that may cause argument to fail?
   e. Describe some of the special characteristics of issues.
   f. What are some examples of enduring issues?
   g. What are some examples of contemporary issues?

h. What are some of the issues you will probably encounter in your other classes this semester?

i. What did you think of when you encountered the word "argument" before you read this chapter? What do you think now?

6. QUESTIONS ON THE ESSAYS FOR ANALYSIS

a. "Some College Costs Should Be Tax Deductible," page 22. What are your opinions on college costs? Why do you hold these opinions? What is your reaction to Goldin's ideas? Do you have any ideas of your own to help make college more affordable for more people?

b. "We're Good Republicans—and Pro-Choice," page 23. What is your reaction to the Hudnut's decision to seek an abortion? Why do you hold your views? What do these authors mean by the concept "uncommon ground"? How could you apply this concept to another difficult issue where an agreement to seek uncommon ground might facilitate constructive argument?

CHAPTER 2

Develop Your Personal Argument Style

Some students resist the idea of finding issues and participating in argument because they think they will be required to take an opposing view, to debate, or to be contentious or aggressive in class, and they feel that they do not do these things well. This chapter will develop the important idea that everyone can and should participate in argument, but that not everyone may participate in the same way. You have already developed your own personal style of argument, and it has probably been developed by several influences in your background. Many of the students who read and commented on this chapter in the first edition of this book identified family and cultural backgrounds as particularly potent forces in forming the ways in which they argue. In addition, some researchers think that men tend to argue differently from women, that some Asians argue differently from Europeans and Americans, and that blacks and Hispanics may have distinctive styles that are influenced by their cultures. We will look at some of these causes for differences in this chapter, and you may want to argue about them. They are controversial. This chapter invites differing views on the issues it raises.

The final purpose of this chapter is to encourage you and your classmates to become aware at the outset of how each of you argues best. Thus you will learn to recognize, rely on, and perhaps even improve your existing style of argument. You will also learn from others how to modify or change to another style in certain situations when your preferred style may not be working well. This process will help you learn flexibility. Finally, you will learn to recognize and adapt to other people's styles, and you will therefore become a more sensitive and persuasive arguer, more likely to establish the common ground essential for the give and take of argument.

Individual tendencies and preferences in argument are present in many but not all argumentative situations. If you discover, for example, that you prefer reaching consensus in most instances over winning the argument, this discovery does not mean that you should always argue for consensus. Furthermore, if you discover that you are reluctant to participate in argument, your reluctance does not mean that you cannot find a way to participate. An awareness of individuals' predominant styles should reduce the dissonance and discomfort experienced by some people in argument classes where a single argument style or perspective may seem to dominate. By acknowledging instead that individualistic and preferred perspectives and styles not only exist but also are valued, everyone in class should feel empowered to join the ongoing conversation about issues with confidence and skill. The goal is to create and maintain an inclusive classroom where everyone has a voice and where every approach and style is tolerated and understood. This is a worthy "real-life" goal as well for a world in which cultural, racial, and gender diversity often influence the nature and special characteristics of the ongoing conversations about issues.

INDIVIDUAL STYLES OF ARGUMENT

Most contemporary argument classes are composed of varied groups of male and female students representing several races and cultural backgrounds from various parts of the world, and it is usually pretty clear from the first week in class that not all students regard argument in the same way nor will they argue in the same way. In fact, when students are asked to describe their styles of argument— that is, what they do when they have to be convincing—individual differences in style and strategy surface right away. Some of these differences seem to be related to home training and role models, others may be related to gender, others to the background and experience provided by different cultures or nationalities. Modern research indicates that men and women describe different approaches to argument often enough to suggest that gender may contribute to differences in argument style. African-American, Asian-American, Hispanic-American, and Native American cultures may also produce recognizably distinct styles and approaches. Finally, international students, particularly those from non-Western cultures, sometimes describe approaches to argument that are distinctive and even unique, especially when compared to others.

These differences among styles are usually neither consistent nor strong enough for typecasting. In fact, in some studies, a sizable minority of men indicate they prefer the styles that some researchers have identified as predominantly female.[1] Also, a particular style may be more convincing in some contexts than in others, so that students who have a preferred style find that they vary it at times to meet the demands of particular argumentative situations. Thus no single style emerges as best for all occasions for anyone. For example, one student in the group that test-read this book reported that when he argues with close friends about baseball players he always wants to be right, he is very contentious and argumentative, and he expects to win. On the job, however, where he has low status in an office of four women, he never argues to win but rather tries to achieve agreement or consensus. Another student said she argues most aggressively

---

[1]Carol S. Pearson, "Women as Learners: Diversity and Educational Quality," *Journal of Developmental Education,* Winter 1992, p. 10.

when she is secure in her knowledge about the subject. She is tentative or even silent when she is not sure of her facts. Students also point out that there is a difference between home or "kitchen" argument and argument that takes place in school or on the job. Home argument may be more emotional and less controlled, especially in some cultures, than the reasoned discourse that one associates with school or work. Now, let us look at some of the factors that may influence the ways in which you prefer to argue.

DO EARLY TRAINING AND ROLE MODELS INFLUENCE ARGUMENT STYLE?

Students often identify their early home training as an influence on their style. Some students from military families, for example, say that argument was not encouraged at home. Instead, orders were given in military fashion, and opposing views were not encouraged. Other students, such as those whose parents are teachers, lawyers, or politicians, have reported that arguing about issues occurred frequently in their households. Also, students tend to identify the well-known arguers who are most like themselves as the role models they like to imitate as they develop their own styles. They watch such individuals on television or in the movies and, when they are in argumentative situations, they find they tend to imitate the styles of the people whom they admire.

DO MEN AND WOMEN ARGUE DIFFERENTLY?

Some, but certainly not all, people think there are differences in the ways that men and women argue, and that the basis for these differences lies in the power relationships that exist between the sexes in certain situations. You can decide what you think. Those who favor this view point out that men may often be better able to dominate an argument, while women may tend to remain silent. Men are thus perceived to have more personal power in these situations. In an essay entitled "The Classroom Climate: Still a Chilly One for Women," Bernice Sander describes the results of some unequal male-female power relationships. Even though most people think that women talk more than men in everyday situations, she says, a number of studies show that in formal situations, such as a class, a meeting, or a formal group discussion where argument is conducted, the stereotype of women talking the most does not hold up. In these situations men often talk more than women. Men, Sander claims, talk for longer periods, take more turns, exert more control over what is said, and interrupt more often. Furthermore, their interruptions of women tend to be trivial or personal, and thus they often get women off the track and cause the focus of the discussion to change.[2]

---

[2]See *Educating Men and Women Together*, ed. Carol Lasser (Urbana and Chicago: University of Illinois Press, 1987), p. 188.

Sociologist Deborah Tannen in her best-selling book *You Just Don't Understand: Women and Men in Conversation* also provides detailed descriptions of some differences between men and women arguing.[3] Tannen asserts that many men make connections with one another primarily through conflict. (She qualifies this assertion because she realizes that she cannot generalize about *all* men.) Men see the world as competitive, and the competition can be either friendly and involved or unfriendly. Men, furthermore, like self-display and achieve it often by reporting what they see and what they know. Typical male behavior is centered on "the idea of contest, including combat, struggle, conflict, competition, and contention." As evidence, Tannen quotes Walter Ong, a scholar of cultural linguistics, who reminds us that many men enjoy ritual combat such as rough play and sports. Friendship among men often takes the form of friendly aggression. Ong also asserts, according to Tannen, that in daily argument men expect the discussion to stick to the rules of logic. They expect argument to be adversarial, to include clash, to take the form of debate, and to rely primarily on logic.

On the other hand, Tannen says most women do not like ritualized combat. They do not like conflict, either, and will often try to avoid it at all costs. Women, according to Tannen, tend to be the peacemakers and to want to work for the general good. They are as interested in making connections with other people as men are in competing. Making connections and keeping the peace are such strong tendencies in women's argument that even when women are being competitive and critical, they often mask their actual intentions with apparent cooperation and affiliation. Women, in fact, are often less direct than men in argumentative situations, and their indirect style sometimes causes men to think that women are trying to be devious and to manipulate them.

To summarize Tannen, men's power comes from acting in opposition to others and to natural forces. Women's power comes from their place in a community. For women, in fact, life is often a struggle to keep from being cut off from the group and to stay connected with the community.

Linguistics professor Susan Herring has conducted research on men's and women's styles in electronic argument on the Internet. She identifies some differences in style that she claims are gender-related. Slightly more than two-thirds of the men she studied are much more aggressive than women in their electronic messages. Men write longer posts, are adversarial, and they do not seem to mind criticism or ridicule since they say they do not take insults and "flaming" personally. Women, on the other hand, say they dislike this type of interaction, are typically either silent "lurkers" or, when they do participate, they typically hedge, apologize, or ask questions rather than making assertions.[4]

---

[3]Deborah Tannen, *You Just Don't Understand: Women and Men in Conversation* (New York: Ballantine Books, 1990). See Chapter 6, "Community and Context."

[4]Susan Herring, "Gender Differences in Computer-Mediated Communication." Speech to the American Library Association, panel entitled "Making the Net*Work*: Is There a Z39.50 in Gender Communication?", Miami, June 27, 1994.

Recent studies of the leadership styles of men and women confirm some of the generalizations about gender differences made by Tannen, Herring, and other researchers. Women leaders, for instance, are usually described as more democratic and affiliative, and men as more authoritarian and hierarchical. One study, for example, surveyed more than 1,000 male and female leaders from a variety of cultures and backgrounds. Women, it was discovered, were most interested in creating a sense of social equality in their groups and in building a consensus of opinion among members of the group. Men, on the other hand, were more interested in competing for rank and status in the groups.[5]

Another effort to study some of the possible differences between men and women identifies additional characteristics that could affect their argument styles. Mary Belenky and her associates conducted in-depth interviews of 135 women who were either students in universities or who were clients in social service agencies.[6] Interviewees were asked about preferred types of classrooms for the exchange of ideas. These researchers discovered that debate—the style of argument that has dominated Western education and that is typically associated with the "masculine adversary style of discourse"—was never selected by women as a classroom forum for exchange and discussion. Instead, women students more typically gravitated toward the class in which there was a sense of community as opposed to a sense of hierarchy. In hierarchical groups some people possess more power and, consequently, more ability to be heard than others. In groups that favor community, equality is favored and power relationships become less important.

Critics of this study point out that Belenky and her associates only asked women about their preferences and did not include any men in this study. Many men, if provided the chance, may have expressed the same preferences as the women, that is, they too would have preferred "connected" classrooms with a sense of community to adversarial, doubting classrooms where debate is favored over collaboration.[7]

The requirements of a particular situation may be more influential than gender in determining the argumentative style that an individual or a group prefers at a particular time. In some cases males find they prefer connection and consensus over contention and winning, and many females like the excitement and energy associated with winning debates. One young male student, for example, when asked to describe his style of argument, said that it was important to him to keep the peace, to negotiate, to work things out, and to gain consensus in argument. When he discovered that some of these qualities may be associated with fe-

---

[5]William F. Allman, "Political Chemistry," *U.S. News & World Report*, November 2, 1992, p. 65.

[6]See Mary Field Belenky, Blythe McVicker Clinchy, Nancy Rule Goldberger, and Jill Mattluck Tarule, *Women's Ways of Knowing: The Development of Self, Voice, and Mind* (New York: Basic Books, 1986), especially Chapter 10, "Connected Teaching."

[7]Richard Fulkerson, "Transcending Our Conception of Argument in Light of Feminist Critiques," paper presented at the Rhetoric Society of America Conference, Tucson, Arizona, May 1996.

male styles of argument, he quickly changed his description of himself, saying, instead, that he liked to win at any cost. Apparently this young man did not want his classmates to question his masculinity, so he switched his description of himself to one less accurate. Actually, however, when questioned, a number of the male students in class admitted they preferred negotiation over winning at any cost. And the women in the class, even those who preferred to think of themselves as winners, still strongly supported the idea of men as negotiators rather than aggressive winners.

The tendency to prefer the consensual style of argument, sometimes associated with females, is often evident among "real-world" groups of men, including those in business and politics. One manager, for example, describes himself in the *Harvard Business Review* as a "soft" manager. He explains that this description does not mean he is a weak manager. As a soft manager, he welcomes argument and criticism from subordinates, is often tentative in making difficult decisions, admits his own human weaknesses, and tries to listen to employees and understand them. In other words, he stresses connection over conflict, and negotiation over winning. He believes that these qualities make him more human, more credible, and more open to change than the classic leaders of business with their "towering self-confidence, their tenacity and resolution, their autocratic decision making, and their invulnerable lonely lives at the top."[8]

Other examples of male and female characteristics in argument can be found in the language of politics. Maureen Dowd, writing in the *New York Times Magazine,* analyzes the language used by politicians in a recent election. "Politicians and their strategists," she claims, "have long been entranced by the image of themselves as warriors. Certainly, it is more romantic for a politician to think of himself as a warrior than as a bureaucrat, hack, pencil-pusher, or blowhard."[9] The very next day after Dowd's article appeared, a male politician was quoted in another newspaper as saying,

> Today it looks as if the Indians are about to overwhelm the wagon train. The wagons are circled and the arrows are flying. . . . We're going to begin a cavalry charge, which is going to bring us into the battle. . . . We've waited to get out on the playing field. The last three weeks has reminded me of a locker room before a big game—everybody nervous, everybody ready—tomorrow, we go charging down the chute.[10]

This quotation, according to Dowd's analysis, would be typical of the language used by many male politicians who gravitate toward male styles of argument. Notice the images associated with battle and sports.

---

[8]William H. Peace, "The Hard Work of Being a Soft Manager," *Harvard Business Review,* November–December 1991, pp. 40–42, 46–47.

[9]Maureen Dowd, "Guns and Poses," *New York Times Magazine,* August 16, 1992, pp. 10, 12.

[10]Karen Potter, "Gramm Gets 'Em Going with a Little Pre-Speechmaking," *Fort Worth Star-Telegram,* August 17, 1992, Sec. A, p. 6.

Dowd, in her article, also contrasts the old "blood-and-guts" politicians with the new "touchy-feely" politicians who exhibit many of the traits some theorists identify as female:

> Bill Clinton and Al Gore, the first baby-boomer ticket, have shared intimacies about their search for the inner man. They have used the sort of feel-better jargon never before heard in the manly arena of politics. They talk about confronting problems, connecting with people, shattering emotional barriers, embracing the pain and working it out with counseling and self-examination.

Personally, Dowd says, she is thrilled with this new approach and sees it as a "welcome respite from the war talk that usually drives politics."[11] She does not see it as a weakness or as a feminization of style, but as a new style that can also be strong and effective.

As you analyze your own argument style and those of your classmates, you may discover that the people who break the hypothetical male-female stereotypes are some of the most effective arguers in class. In a recent discussion about argument, one woman commented that she disagreed so totally with an anti-gay rights group in her part of the country that she absolutely did not want to cooperate with them in any way or try to reach consensus. Instead, she wanted to argue and win. In another discussion, a businessman made the point that if he didn't work for consensus in his business he wouldn't get anywhere with his fellow workers and nothing would ever be accomplished. Deborah Tannen makes a plea for the flexibility that can come from adapting features of both adversarial and consensual styles. Both men and women, she says, could benefit from being flexible enough to borrow one another's best qualities: "Women who avoid conflict at all costs," she suggests, "would be better off if they learned that a little conflict won't kill them. And men who habitually take oppositional stances would be better off if they broke their addiction to conflict." Such flexibility has other advantages as well. It is also useful to realize that what may sometimes seem like an unfair or irrational approach to argument may simply be a manifestation of a particular individual's style. Such a realization makes it less frustrating, usually, to argue with such an individual.[12]

DOES CULTURE INFLUENCE ARGUMENT STYLE?

Now consider the possibility that members of different cultural groups in America may exhibit distinct styles of argument, and that individuals learn these styles through affiliation with their groups. Here are some differences that may be influenced by cultural identity, as well as by experience.

---

[11]Dowd, "Guns and Poses," p. 10.
[12]Tannen, *You Just Don't Understand*, p. 187.

Some people think that many African-Americans tend to focus strongly on issues and that, even though they make effective use of logical and ethical appeal, they sometimes also make superior use of emotional appeal. African-American students report that much of their experience with argument styles comes from family interactions and also from the broad American cultural backdrop for the African-American culture. The many African-American magazines and publications on modern bookstore shelves attest to this group's strong interest in the issues that impact the African-American culture. Two other distinctly black forums for argument are available to many African-Americans: rap music, which is relatively new, and the black church, which is old and traditional. Both provide members of the black race with the opportunity to observe and imitate distinctive black styles of argument.

Contemporary issues, presented forcefully and emotionally, form the main content of much rap music, as Sister Souljah, the New York rapper, recognizes. "I think it would be a good idea," she says, "for members of Congress and the Senate and all people who consider themselves policy makers to listen to the call of help that is generated by rap artists." She sees rap music as a deliberate effort to organize black people to think about issues and to engage in social action. She and other rap artists have, in fact, organized a ten-point program to engage African-Americans in such issues as African life, economics, education, spirituality, defense, and how not to support racism.[13] Reviews of rap music also sometimes stress the argumentative slant of some of this music. Rap has been described as "so topical that it'll probably leave newsprint on your ears" and as a "checklist of intractable Big Issues set to a metal soundtrack."[14]

The black church is also regarded by many as another potent forum for argument. In an article describing a protest against a questionable court decision, the author observes that the African-American church was at the forefront of the protest, "stepping into its time-honored role in politics and advocacy for social change."[15] Some of the most influential African-American leaders who have addressed black issues have also been preachers in black churches. Included in this group are Martin Luther King, Jr., Malcolm X, and Jesse Jackson.

The following description of his argument style was provided by a black student in an argument class. As you can see, he attributes some of his preferences and characteristics as an arguer to the fact that he is young, black, and male.

> What influences my style of argument the most is the fact that I am a young black male. The fact that I am young makes me want to be fair and direct with my opponent. That is, I attempt to be free of vagueness, ambiguity, and fallacies. Also, the

---

[13]Sheila Rule, "Rappers' Words Foretold Depth of Blacks' Anger," *New York Times,* May 26, 1992, Living Arts Section, pp. B1–B2.

[14]John Austin, "Noize from the 'Hood,'" *Forth Worth Star-Telegram,* Arts and Entertainment, March 2, 1993, p. 1.

[15]Gracie Bonds Staples and Anjetta McQueen, "Ministers Lead Prayers in Call for Awakening," *Fort Worth Star-Telegram,* March 27, 1993, p. 1.

fact that I am black affects the way I approach my audience. For instance, I tend to use emotional language, and my language is sometimes racially manipulative. I think that blacks tend to see people's race before they see people's attitudes and feelings. Finally, the fact that I am a male probably influences my argument. I think that males tend to be a bit more harsh in their argument. They tend to want to "rock the boat" and stir some emotions. I think that this is a strong tendency in my argument style. The use of facts, emotions, fairness, and strong language is very typical of black argument.[16]

Some Asian-American students, according to recent researchers, may be more reluctant than other students to participate in argument because of their cultural background. Students who have spent a portion of their school years in Japan, China, or other Far Eastern Asian countries or whose parents or grandparents come from these countries may regard argument class as an odd environment that has little to do with them. This statement may be particularly true if they view these classes as places where pro and con issues are debated and winners are declared. The reason is that argumentation and debate are not traditionally practiced in some of the Asian countries in the Far East. Carl Becker, a professor of Asian curriculum research and development, explains some of the reasons for the lack of argumentation in the Far East. For these Asians, sympathetic understanding and intuition are a more important means of communication than are logic and debate. Furthermore, many Asians do not like to take opposite sides in an argument because they do not like becoming personal rivals of those who represent the other side. They value harmony and peace, and argument, as they perceive it, has the potential to disturb the peace.[17] A friend who taught for a brief period in Japan reported that he could not get his Japanese students to take pro and con sides on an issue and debate it. Instead, they all insisted on taking the same side.[18] A book published a few years ago in Japan teaches Japanese how to say "no" to Americans. Taking an opposing stance and defending it is a skill that must be learned in Japan. It is not part of the traditional culture. Read the short article provided in exercise 5 at the end of this chapter for some examples of what Japanese really mean when they say "yes" to people outside their culture.

Here is the self-reported argument style of a young male Asian-American in an argument class. This account was written at the beginning of the semester.

My style of argument is to avoid argument as much as possible. I think that I argue more with other men than I do with women. I think the reason I don't argue a lot is because I analyze the situation a bit too much, and I can pretty much tell what the outcome is going to be. During argument I usually blank out what the other person is saying and think about when they are going to stop talking.[19]

---

[16]Provided by Kelvin Jenkins, with permission.

[17]Carl B. Becker, "Reasons for the Lack of Argumentation and Debate in the Far East," *International Journal of Intercultural Relations,* vol. 10 (1986), 75–92.

[18]Interview with Clyde Moneyhun.

[19]Jim Lui. Quoted with permission.

He was more comfortable and skilled with argument at semester's end. He credited argument class, finally, with teaching him to listen more, argue more, and be less self-centered.

An Asian international student who petitioned to be excused from argument class said that, for her, the idea of such a class was very confusing because she could not understand why she or any other student should spend time arguing and trying to convince others to agree with their points of view. She associated such activity with advertising and selling and could not envision it as useful in other contexts. Ironically, this student went on to write a convincing argument about why she should not have to take an argument class. This was an important issue for her, and she wrote a good argument in spite of her reluctance to participate in it.

The Asian students who test-read this book warned that not all Asian cultures are the same, and that the reluctance to argue may be stronger in some Asian cultures than others. For example, a Sri Lankan student pointed out that in her country, as well as in India and Bangladesh, argument is encouraged. Students also observed that there is a tradition of lively, contentious, and even combative "kitchen" arguments among close family members in some Asian cultures. This, they say, is typical of the Korean culture. Amy Tan, in her books about her childhood in a Chinese immigrant household, gives examples of the lively home argument in that culture as well. Outside of the home, however, Asians may tend to be reluctant to enter into argument. For students reluctant to speak out, argument class is a safe place for developing and practicing that special ability.

Since the Hispanic culture promotes strong family ties and group values, many Hispanic students seem to favor connection over contention, and negotiation over winning. Here is a female Hispanic student describing her style of argument.

> What I like best about my current style of argument is the fact that I listen and try to understand others' points of view. I also like the fact that I can express my feelings without hurting other people. A negotiated solution eventually comes through. I would like to be more assertive. The ideal arguer, for me, is the one who can accept it if she is wrong.

The three descriptions of argument style that you just read were written by students enrolled in argument classes who responded to an assignment that asked them to describe their current argument styles. These students, along with more than 600 additional students, also completed a questionnaire about their argument styles, and, in addition, they were asked to identify their gender and cultural background. The idea was to see if the links between style and gender and background characteristics already discussed in this chapter seemed to have any validity.

The students were questioned in three areas. First, they were asked how they viewed the outcomes of argument. Then they were asked to report on their personal participation in argument. Finally, they were asked about their present style of argument. Several possible answers were provided for each of the three items, and students were asked to identify one item under each question that best described them, and then to identify two others that also described them, but perhaps not quite so forcefully. The questions appear in Box 2.1. As you read them, answer them yourself. Under each question identify the item you agree with most as number 1. Then number as 2 and 3 the additional items that also describe your opinions and practices.

You may now want to compare your own answers to the questions with those reported by other students. The 647 argument-class students who completed this questionnaire one week after classes started also identified themselves as male or female and as white, black, Asian, or Hispanic. Sixty-nine percent of them were second-semester freshmen, 19 percent were sophomores, and 12 per-

---

How Would You Answer These Questions? Check All Responses That Apply to You

Question 1. How would you describe the usual outcomes of argument?

_____ Argument helps people understand each other's points of view.
_____ Argument separates and alienates people.
_____ Argument causes conflict and hard feelings.
_____ Argument resolves conflict and solves problems.
_____ Argument can change people's minds.
_____ Argument rarely changes other people's minds.

Question 2. How would you describe your personal participation in argument?

_____ Argument makes me feel energized, and I like to participate.
_____ Argument makes me uncomfortable, and I dislike participating.
_____ I participate a lot.
_____ I participate sometimes.
_____ I never participate.
_____ I think it is fun to argue.
_____ I think it is rude to argue.

Question 3. What is your style of argument at present?

_____ I am contentious and enjoy conflict.
_____ I am a peacekeeper, and I value conflict resolution.
_____ I try to win and show people I am right.
_____ I try to listen, understand, make connections, negotiate solutions.
_____ I tend to use reason and facts more than emotion.
_____ I tend to use emotion more than reason and facts.

BOX 2.1 Student Questionnaire on Attitudes and Style in Argument.

cent were juniors and seniors. Also, 53 percent were male and 47 percent were female. Of the males, 69 percent were white, 9 percent were black, 12 percent were Asian, and 10 percent were Hispanic. Of the females, 64 percent were white, 15 percent were black, 13 percent were Asian, and 8 percent were Hispanic. The percentages were weighted to indicate the relative strength of preference for each group in order to make more accurate comparisons.

One of the most interesting results of this study was that no items on the questionnaire were rejected by all students. Every item on the questionnaire was marked by at least a few students as being typical or somewhat typical of themselves. These students' responses suggest the wide diversity of attitudes and preferences among them.

In answer to the first question about argument outcomes, both male and female students overwhelmingly favored the response that the best outcome of argument is to help them "understand others." Scoring highest in this area, however, were Asian men. "Changing minds" and "resolving conflict" were in second and third places among the preferences of the entire group. Clearly more students thought argument resolves conflict than causes it. Only a few students indicated that argument separates and alienates people. There was essentially no difference between male and female responses to this first question.

Male and female students also were very similar in their assessment of their participation in argument. Most students reported that they "participated sometimes" instead of "never" or "a lot." Both women and men reported that they are energized by argument, they like it, and they find it "fun to argue." Asian women were the largest identifiable group among those students who said they found argument "uncomfortable" so that they disliked participating. Certainly not all of them, however, responded in this way. African-American men and women ranked themselves slightly higher than the other groups in perceiving argument as energizing and enjoyable. Only a few students, and about the same number of males as females, thought it was "rude to argue" and said they "never participated."

Male and female students differed more in their responses to question 3, "What is your style of argument at present?" than they did in their responses to the other two questions. "Listening and connecting" was the style favored over the others by both men and women of all groups, but more women than men identified themselves with this style. More females than males also reported that they use emotion in argument more than reason, and more males than females favored reason and facts over emotion. White males said they "try to win" more than the other groups. Asian males and females identified themselves as "peacekeepers" somewhat more than did the other groups, even though a significant number of the students in the other groups saw themselves this way as well. Finally, only a few of the men and even fewer of the women said they were "contentious" and that they "enjoyed conflict."

Although no Native American students participated in this study, research concerning Native American culture and values suggests that Native American students value community and cooperation more than rivalry and competition.

Furthermore, in traditional Native American culture young people are expected to agree with authority figures, especially with those seen as older and wiser. Native American students are often, as a consequence, reluctant to debate, particularly with the teacher.[20]

We concluded that the differences among these groups of students are certainly not great enough to create stereotypes. College students, in fact, often break stereotypes because of their close association with one another, which often results in greater flexibility, adaptability, and increased tolerance, and because of their common goal to become educated. The strongest tendencies among these students that seem to confirm the notion that gender and cultural background may have influence over them as arguers were that Asian students were less enthusiastic about argument than the others, that white males liked to win more than any of the other groups, and that more females than males said they typically try to listen and connect.

Some findings, however, are not typical of some of the tendencies described by recent researchers. For instance, listening, understanding, making connections, and negotiating solutions was a preferred style for nearly as many men as for women, and the contentious, conflictive style was less popular with both groups. Also, it seems clear that these students as a group value knowing the facts, are suspicious of too much emotion particularly if it results in anger and loss of control, and have positive opinions about the outcomes and uses of argument.

The study mainly emphasizes the many differences in argument style that can be found in argument classrooms. The study confirms the importance of the goals for argument class listed at the beginning of this chapter: students need to learn to value one another's styles, to develop flexibility by extending their own styles and learning to borrow from others, and to adapt to styles other than their own.

DO DIFFERENT COUNTRIES HAVE DIFFERENT STYLES OF ARGUMENT?

Argument class can often be thought of as a microcosm of the larger world, particularly when the students in it represent a variety of different countries and cultures. Cultural backgrounds outside of the United States can sometimes exert a powerful influence over the way in which individual people view and practice argument. Studying argument across cultures is a complicated field, and most of its findings are tentative because of the vast individual differences in people from culture to culture. Still, even tentative findings are important for the argument

---

[20]B. C. Howard, *Learning to Persist/Persisting to Learn* (Washington, DC: Mid-Atlantic Center for Race Equity, American University, 1987). Quoted in Pearson, "Women as Learners," p. 6.

classroom. Hypothesizing about how argument differs according to nationality helps students focus on the preferences in argument styles that may be typical of certain groups and cultures. Developing an awareness of these characteristics and preferences and learning to adapt to them not only helps students achieve the goals of the inclusive argument classroom, but also helps prepare students for lifelong communicating and negotiating with people from other countries and cultures.

Here are some examples of some possible differences. Deborah Tannen claims that argument in some societies is a way of coming together, a pleasurable sign of intimacy, a kind of game that people play together. This observation is particularly true of Italy, Greece, and Eastern Europe. To outsiders, the argument in these countries may seem to be contentious, "an argument," rather than reasoned inquiry into issues. Italian *discussione* strikes outsiders as loud, contentious arguing, but to Italians it is a friendly game. Greeks and East Europeans may appear bossy and overbearing. In their view, however, they are showing friendly caring.[21]

In the following essay, Nilesh Bhakta, a student from Zimbabwe, describes a different attitude and style of argument in his country.

ARGUMENT IN ZIMBABWE

Nilesh Bhakta

Zimbabwe is located in central Africa, south of the equator. It is a landlocked country surrounded by South Africa to the south, Mozambique to the east, and Zambia to the north and northwest. The argument styles used in Zimbabwe are somewhat different from those used here in the United States. Very, very rarely are arguments based upon emotional appeals or ethical virtues.

From a very young age, children are taught to respect their elders (mainly grandparents) who are considered to be wise and knowledgeable. As a result, children and everyone else are not allowed to argue with them, since it shows their lack of respect. With parents, however, it is somewhat relaxed. Most children are allowed to question or bring up their own perspectives on an issue. *But* whatever are the parents' views, that is what the whole family adapts to. This view is then readily accepted (with no arguments to preserve respect) among family members, thus creating a sense of unity within the family. This unity symbolizes the "traditional closely knit" meaning of family.

There are three general races widespread in Zimbabwe—the natives (blacks), Europeans (whites), and the Asians. Because of the colonial class system imposed by the colonial power (whites at the top, Asians in the middle, and

---

[21]Tannen, *You Just Don't Understand*, pp. 160–162.

blacks at the bottom), there tends to be very little argument across the different races. The main reason for this avoidance of argument is the fear that it may spark violence. Thirteen years after independence, this situation still exists. Maybe the new generation that has grown up after independence will overcome this barrier.

The logical approach seems to be the dominant style among people of similar age groups and races. They tend to favor direct relationships, like stating a problem and a solution. With this approach it is easier to follow and understand the problem at hand. And since most of the population is uneducated, the logical approach is the widely used style, since it makes the issue easier to grasp.[22]

International students in your class may be able to provide additional examples that represent predominant styles of argument, along with an analysis of what causes them, in their countries and cultures.

Some researchers have speculated about the reasons for the differences in argument styles among different cultures. *Preferred cultural values* and *preferred patterns of thinking* may be the two major factors that differentiate argument styles across cultures.[23] Differences in value systems from culture to culture are often particularly obvious. For example, Americans who relocate to Saudi Arabia are sometimes surprised when they receive copies of newspapers from outside the country. Before the newspapers are delivered, the Saudi censors use wide felt-tipped ink pens to obliterate visual material that is offensive to their cultural values. Pictures of a ballerina's legs and arms may be colored over, as well as other parts of the female anatomy usually kept covered in Arab countries.

You may want to discuss with your classmates, particularly if some of them come from other countries or have lived in another country for awhile, what values and patterns of thinking are preferred in their cultures since these are believed to have an effect on the common ground that is established in cross-cultural argument.[24] For example, according to some researchers, Americans value individual achievement, hard work, and independence, and, in their patterns of thinking, they tend to prefer generalizations backed by examples and experience to pure reasoning unaccompanied by examples. Japanese, like Americans, also value achievement, but, in addition, they also value serenity and self-confidence. Characteristic of their thinking patterns are the preferences to make suggestions, to give hints, and to communicate indirectly. Researchers who have studied Japanese argument claim that the Japanese like ambiguity, or saying

---

[22]Used with permission.

[23]Gregg B. Walker, "Assessing Multicultural Argument in the Law of the Sea Negotiations: A Rationale and Analytical Framework," *Spheres of Argument: Proceedings of the Sixth SCA/AFA Conference on Argumentation,* ed. Bruce E. Gronbeck (Annandale, VA: Speech Communication Association, October 1989), pp. 600–603.

[24]See Walker, "Assessing Multicultural Argument," pp. 600–601. Walker summarizes the results of considerable cross-cultural research into the values and patterns of thought preferred by different cultures. See his article for additional sources and information. Pearson, "Women as Learners," p. 6, also summarizes some of the cultural values included here.

one thing and meaning something else. They often use understatement. Their communication can seem incomplete to outsiders because they often omit logical links, expecting others to infer them. Japanese dislike contention and debate.[25]

You see that understanding the value systems and preferred patterns of reasoning of other cultures can be very important in establishing the common ground necessary for productive argument across cultures. As you read newspaper accounts of intercultural communication and argument, watch for the problems and misunderstandings that can arise from an absence of shared values and shared ways of thinking. Here are two examples:

1. **A Japanese Example.** In an article concerning deliberations in Japan about whether or not that country should have a permanent seat on the United Nations Security Council, David Sanger wrote in the *New York Times:*

> The Tokyo Government has not wanted to appear to be openly seeking the Security Council seat, even though countries with far less economic power sit there today. But there is also an underlying fear that Japan, if given a bully pulpit, may have little to say. "We might be ashamed to raise our hand," Seiki Nishihiro, a former Deputy Defense Minister, said during a recent conference.[26]

Nishihiro's comment is puzzling unless one recalls a possible Japanese reluctance to participate in contentious debate, which is a regular feature of the Security Council.

2. **A Russian Example.** A human interest story about an international student from Russia says she was confident she would do well on her first exam. She studied hard, memorized the material, and wrote it well in the exam booklet. She was surprised, however, when she received a D grade. Her professor had penalized her for writing only what the book said and for not including her own opinions.[27]

This incident can be puzzling unless one realizes that not all countries and cultures encourage critical thinking, evaluative opinion, and argument. Totalitarian governments like the former Soviet Union, in fact, discouraged or even forbade diverse opinion in public forums.

Argument is fundamental to democracy, and it flourishes in democratic societies. In totalitarian societies, however, if it exists at all, it usually must go underground. Thus, the argument in such countries may be found in the secret meetings of opposition political groups or in private meetings of citizens. Written argument may appear in underground newspapers or in material written by dissidents or political exiles. Forums for argument in such societies are severely lim-

---

[25]Michael David Hazen, "The Role of Argument, Reasoning and Logic in Tacit, Incomplete and Indirect Communication: The Case of Japan," in *Spheres of Argument: Proceedings of the Sixth SCA/AFA Conference on Argumentation,* ed. Bruce E. Gronbeck (Annandale, VA: Speech Communication Association, 1989).

[26]*New York Times,* May 5, 1992, Sec. A, p. 1.

[27]David Wallechinsky, "This Land of Ours," *Parade,* July 5, 1992, p. 4.

ited compared to those in democratic societies. Some international students from such countries may, at first, find it difficult to participate in argument.

The following account was written by a Russian student describing Soviet and post-Soviet argument in her country. Notice that the Soviet Communist government was never completely successful in eliminating argument among Russian citizens.

FROM SHOES AND FISTS TO GLASNOST: ARGUMENT IN RUSSIA

Nadejda Michoustina

FIRST DOG: How are things different under Yeltsin?

SECOND DOG: Well, the chain is still too short and the food dish is still too far away to reach, but they let you bark as loud as you want.

A post-Soviet political anecdote

When in the early 1960s Nikita Khruschev shook his fist and threatened the United Nations with a shoe, the former Soviet leader was regarded as comical rather than convincing, ridiculous rather than persuasive. When in the early 1990s the debates in the Russian Parliament moved from words to blows, the diagnosis became obvious: the Parliament lacked argumentation skills, and the causes were many.

Russians historically have been influenced by the habits and traditions of authoritarian rule which provides a belief system to live by, whether it is Communism or Russian Orthodoxy. Five centuries of absolutism from Ivan the Terrible to Leonid Brezhnev have left the Russian people uncomfortable with the Western notion of the democratic process.

Most Russians through habit have looked to the state, the ruler, the parent, or the teacher as the authority figures that provide ideology and purpose, law and order, age and status, and the indisputable truths to live by. To take an opposing side on issues in most cases has meant also to become a personal rival of authorities or even to risk becoming a political prisoner. The Communist Party line kept the Russians numb, choked their public voices, denied them the means of communication and civilized argumentation, drowned them in the foam of the Party press, kept them impotent and powerless politically, and suspicious and frightened socially.

Fear, however, did not make all Russians totally submissive or silent. Even under Communist rule they distrusted the media, questioned the authorities, and were suspicious and skeptical. Cynical jokes, political anecdotes, and personal opinions, however, were voiced in the private spaces of kitchens rather than in public forums. The kitchen became a free-speech arena, a hot line for political debates, and a tribune for personal opinions. Russians by nature love to argue, and they argue in order to grasp a notion of what they consider truth. To most Russians truth is not merely a matter of testing the accuracy of a proposition; instead, it is a human virtue, an indicator of human "goodness."

History has taught Russians to be skeptical and distrustful, but it has not provided them with the tools and techniques of argumentation. Argument in Russia is bare, straightforward, and at times crude. Because for centuries argumentation and rhetoric have neither been taught nor publicly practiced, Russians tend to believe that actions speak louder than words, and that loud words speak for themselves. Russian argument is almost always contentious and presupposes "winners" and "losers." It usually is not settled until one side is willing to yield to the other.

It was not until the late 1980s that the huge army of in-kitchen debaters were given a public microphone. Even though the word *glasnost* does not correspond to the American freedom of speech, it comes from the Russian word *glas*, voice, and literally means voiceness or speaking out. Along with *glasnost*, words like "pluralism" and "compromise" now have entered the pages of Russian newspapers and are also a part of the vocabulary of Russian political leaders. Modern Russians are gradually realizing that the Parliament is not that far removed from the kitchen and that pounding shoes do not speak so eloquently as words.[28]

All participants in argument, whether they come from democratic or totalitarian societies, need to work to establish common ground if argument across cultures and gender boundaries is to be successful. This effort can be difficult and time-consuming. An issue that historically has been argued and debated through the ages is the fishing, navigation, and territorial rights to the oceans of the world. In the 1970s the United Nations Conference on the Law of the Sea was charged with the task of reaching agreement among nations on access to and use of the seas. This group spent nine years engaged in intercultural argument and negotiation, finally reaching agreement on some but not all of the issues raised by this subject.[29]

President Boris Yeltsin of Russia made an effective attempt to achieve common ground on his visit to Japan in late 1993 when there was considerable tension between the two countries. Unlike some of his predecessors, Yeltsin is accomplished in building common ground. Soon after arriving in Japan he apologized for Russia's treatment of thousands of Japanese prisoners of war who were sent to Siberia after World War II. More than 60,000 of them died, and many Japanese believed an apology was long overdue. Later, Yeltsin repeated this apology to the Japanese prime minister and, at the same time, bowed deeply to express his remorse, a gesture that is valued in the Japanese culture.[30] His efforts,

---

[28]Used with permission.

[29]Walker, "Assessing Multicultural Argument," pp. 599–600.

[30]David E. Sanger, "Yeltsin, in Tokyo, Avoids Islands Issue," *New York Times,* October 14, 1993, Sec. A, p. 5.

according to reports, relieved a considerable amount of tension between the two countries because of the common ground he established. When common ground is not established, the consequences can be devastating. Wars are a frequent alternative to productive argument and successful negotiations, especially when the differences among the arguing parties are extreme.

The consequence of all people knowing how to argue effectively to resolve differences in personal, national, and international relationships is potentially a very powerful idea. Think of a country and a world where major problems are resolved through profitable argument instead of through confrontation, shouting orders, having arguments, fighting, or even going to war. You will often fervently disagree with other people. In fact, life would be boring if you never disagreed. Yet, even when you disagree, even when you decide to enter an ongoing argument, you can learn to use a style that is comfortable and natural for you. And that approach is preferable to the alternatives: either remaining silent or becoming involved in destructive arguments that solve nothing and that may even cause harm.

EXERCISES AND ACTIVITIES

1. **SELF EVALUATION: ANALYZE YOUR PREDOMINANT ARGUMENT STYLE**
   Box 2.2 provides a summary of some of the characteristics of consensual and adversarial styles of argument. As you read the lists, check the items that are most typical of you. Does one list describe your style of argument better than the other? Or can your style best be described by items derived from both lists? From this analysis, how would you say you prefer to argue?

2. **WRITING ASSIGNMENT: THE ARGUMENT STYLE PAPER**
   Think about the last time you had to convincingly argue for a certain point of view. Write a 500-word paper in which you describe your predominant argument style. Include the following information:

   a. When you argued, what was the issue that you were arguing about?
   b. What were you trying to achieve?
   c. What did you do to achieve it?
   d. Was that typical of your usual style of argument?
   e. If yes, say why; and if no, say why and describe your usual style.
   f. What has influenced your style of argument? Consider home training, role models, gender, culture, nationality, national heritage, or any other life experiences that have influenced you.
   g. How would you describe your ideal arguer, and how would you like to be more like this person in your own arguing?
   h. What do you like best about your current style of argument? What would you like to change? How can you become more flexible in your style?

Which Describes You Best?

CONSENSUAL STYLE	ADVERSARIAL STYLE
_____ To be indirect	_____ To be direct and open
_____ To give reasons	_____ To reach conclusions
_____ To prefer cooperation	_____ To prefer competition
_____ To favor group consensus	_____ To favor individual opinions
_____ To like affiliation	_____ To like conflict
_____ To hate to fight	_____ To like to fight
_____ To avoid confrontation	_____ To like confrontation
_____ To avoid contentious argument	_____ To like contentious argument
_____ To be nonaggressive	_____ To be aggressive
_____ To solicit many views on an issue	_____ To tend to see issues as two-sided, pro and con, right or wrong
_____ To be both logical and emotional	_____ To be primarily logical
_____ To try to make connections	_____ To be adversarial
_____ To prefer negotiating	_____ To prefer winning
_____ To favor the personal example, story, anecdote	_____ To favor abstract ideas
_____ To want to keep the community strong	_____ To want to keep the individual strong

BOX 2.2   Two Styles of Argument.

3. CLASS PROJECT: ANALYZE ARGUMENT STYLES AND CREATE AN IDEAL CLASSROOM ENVIRONMENT FOR ARGUMENT

Read aloud the argument style papers written by class members. Discuss the different styles described in these papers and some of the influences that have helped create them. Discuss creating a classroom environment that can accommodate all of these styles.

To get you started, Jürgen Habermas, a modern European rhetorician, describes his version of an ideal environment for argument.[31] Read each item, decide whether you agree or disagree, and explain why. What would you eliminate? Why? What would you add? Why?

a. Each person should have the freedom to express ideas and critique other's ideas directly, openly, and honestly.

---

[31]Habermas's ideas are summarized by James L. Golden, Goodwin F. Berquist, and William E. Coleman in *The Rhetoric of Western Thought*, 4th ed. (Dubuque, IA: Kendall Hunt, 1989), p. 438.

b. The use of force and personal power that tend to inhibit some participants are to be eliminated.

c. Arguments based on an appeal to the past and tradition are to be exposed. These arguments superimpose the past on the present, and everyone does not share the same past.

d. The aim of argument is to arrive at truth through consensus and an adherence of minds.

e. _____

f. _____

g. _____

4. GROUP WORK AND CLASS DISCUSSION: ANALYZE STYLES AS INFLUENCED BY GENDER, NATIONALITY, AND CULTURAL BACKGROUND

Read the following four articles and discuss them in small groups of four or five students each. Appoint a scribe to record your findings and report them to the class. The following will help organize your discussion.

a. Identify some of the effective argument strategies in each of the essays.

b. Identify the gender and cultural background of each of the authors. How does each author draw on the experiences associated with gender and/or cultural background to strengthen these arguments?

c. Could each of these articles have been written as convincingly by a member of another culture or gender? Provide specific details to show why or why not.

d. How can you use your culture, gender, or nationality as a resource in writing your own argument? Be creative in your answer to this question.

Essay 1 is by Shirlee Taylor Haizlip who has also written *The Sweeter the Juice: A Family Memoir in Black and White.*

Essay

WE KNEW WHAT GLORY WAS

Shirlee Taylor Haizlip

When I was growing up in the 40's and 50's, my father would pack up the car every August and squeeze in my mother, four children, several dolls and a picnic lunch. It was the time before air-conditioning, and the drive was hot, dusty and, after New York, without bathrooms.

We left long before dawn, because for a dark-skinned man driving a large shiny sedan holding a white-looking wife, the journey from Connecticut to the South was not without peril. It was essential that each leg of the trip be made before nightfall. We knew that safety lay within the homes and the churches of my father's friends and colleagues, the black ministers we would visit. They were our underground railroad.

My father was a Baptist pastor who ministered to a medium-sized black church in a Connecticut mill town. His father was a minister who had founded a major black Baptist church in Washington. At the beginnings of their careers, both had led small country churches in North Carolina, Virginia and West Virginia. Later, as popular officers of the National Baptist Convention and known for their dramatic oratory, the two were frequent guest preachers at rural churches throughout the South.

Traditionally, my father and his father before him preached a week of revival services at these houses of worship. After my grandfather died, my father continued to return to the South each year. For him, the churches were touchstones of faith, of culture, of triumph over slavery. For him, they were living, breathing links to the past and an indestructible foundation for the future.

There was more than a spiritual connection. When they were in college, my four uncles, all of whom played musical instruments and had glorious voices, would sometimes join my father and present musical programs of spirituals and the light joy as he brought the worshipers to their feet with promises of survival now and salvation later. In that place, at that time, we knew what glory was.

After the service, in the pitch blackness of a muggy summer night, we would drive back to our host's house, listening to parish gossip and ghost stories, accept offers of freshly made iced tea and every once in a while homemade ice cream. Sweetly, another church night had ended.

The best was yet to come. At the close of the week, we celebrated the homecoming, the end of the week-long revival, behind the church, where picnic benches were felicitously placed among sweet-smelling pines. We ate miles of delicious food and drank lakes of sweet punch.

Usually there was a modest graveyard somewhere near the picnic grounds. We did not play there. Our parents had taught us better than that. Mold-covered gravestones barely hinted at the life stories they marked. The bones of slaves lay side by side with the bones of their emancipated children. All of their spirits were free to be free, at last.

As I grew older, I would learn about the lives of the church members from the comfort of my mother's side. I would grow to understand that there, in that place, every single church member was *somebody*.

In God's house, if nowhere else, they were C.E.O.'s and presidents, directors and chairmen, counselors and managers. In God's house, if nowhere else, they were women of infinite grace and men of profound dignity. Forever, amen.

With traditions that began in slavery, the parishioners carried forward, bit by precious bit, the dreams of their forebears. In their roles as deacons, trustees, missionaries and choir members, those domestics, handymen, cotton and tobacco farmers and teachers sang and prayed on hard, scrabbly benches, validating and celebrating themselves and one another, warmly and well, week after week, year after year, generation after generation.

Surely their oils and essences seeped into the well-worn pews. Surely the whorls of their fingertips left lovely striations in the wood, at which their grandbabies would stare before they fell off to sleep.

Not only did they tend to the church's business, they looked after classics to appreciative Southern congregations, all too often deprived of other cultural experiences.

At other times, my dad, resplendent in a white suit, would offer solo recitals. When he crooned "Danny Boy" or "When I Grow Too Old to Dream" in his high tenor vibrato and with exquisite diction, the fans moved a little faster, the backs sat up a little straighter and the shouts of "Sing it, Rev!" were as heartfelt as they were for his renditions of "Amazing Grace" or "His Eye Is on the Sparrow."

I cannot hear the Three Tenors sing without thinking of my father standing in the pulpit of a spare little church, singing like a melancholy angel.

To reach many of the churches, we drove up deserted dirt roads covered by gracefully arching kudzu-fringed trees. Just when we thought we would never get there, a clearing materialized. There at its edge stood the church, often the only building for miles around, plain as a line drawing in a children's coloring book, more often than not in need of a fresh coat of paint. Never lonely looking, it seemed instead a natural part of the landscape, splendid in its simplicity.

Before the service, with admonitions of keeping our "best" clothes clean fading in our ears, my siblings and I would play with other children, running and jumping, catching fireflies, hiding and seeking in the darkening silver twilight. Each night, the revival crowd would get bigger and livelier. By the end of the week, the church was full, the room was hot and the penitents were saved.

During every service, I watched as my father, in high Baptist style, "picture painted" the stories of Moses and Job, Ruth and Esther. I listened as he moaned and hummed and sang the tales of W. E. B. Du Bois and Frederick Douglass, the Scottsboro Boys and Emmett Till. I clapped for the elderly and the infirm, encouraged the young to learn, learn, learn and rallied their communities in times of economic stress, natural disaster or social crisis. It did not escape my understanding that the church encompassed all. Seldom were there outcasts.

For me as a child, those beautiful little structures were places beyond enchantment. As an adult, I understood that the churches were indeed the collective soul of black folks.

I never thought that this particular reality could end. Although I have visited the South as an adult and know that some of those churches have been abandoned, enlarged or modernized, in my mind's eye all of them remain storybook sanctuaries, testament to my own faith, the faith of my father, his father and the larger black community.

Heartsick now, my soul's light has been dimmed. Church after church in the South has been destroyed by fire, torched by arsonists. I watch the television images as long as I can. Then I hide my eyes behind my fingers, peeking at the screen as if it were a horror film, while hellish flames consume the heavenly places of my youth.

I ask my father across the void, Who will put out the flames, Dad? Where can we go now to be safe?[32]

Essay 2 is by Chancellor Chang-Lin Tien who has been chancellor of the University of California, Berkeley since July 1990.

Essay

A VIEW FROM BERKELEY

Chancellor Chang-Lin Tien

When the debate over affirmative action in higher education started to simmer, the stance I took as the chancellor of the University of California at Berkeley seemed to surprise many people.

To be sure, my view—that we *should* consider race, ethnicity and gender along with many other factors in admissions—has put me at odds with some constituencies, including the majority of the Regents of the University of California. Last July, these officials voted to end affirmative action admission policies.

And with California voters to decide later this year whether to end all state affirmative action programs, silence might seem a more prudent course for the head of a major public university. We already have enough battles to fight, my staff sometimes reminds me: declining public funding, for example.

A few students and friends have hinted that it might make more sense for me, as an Asian-American, to oppose affirmative action.

Asian-Americans, who are not considered underrepresented minorities under affirmative action, have divergent views. Some are disturbed by the "model minority" stereotype; they say it pits them against other minorities and hides the discrimination they still face. Others—including the two Asian-American Regents who voted to end affirmative action—believe the only fair approach is to base admissions on academic qualifications. That also opens the door to more Asians.

So why do I strongly support affirmative action? My belief has been shaped by my role in higher education. And by my experience as a Chinese immigrant. I know first-hand that America can be a land of opportunity. When I came here, I was a penniless 21-year-old with a limited grasp of the language and culture. Yet I was permitted to accomplish a great deal. My research in heat transfer contributed to better nuclear reactor safety and space shuttle design. My former students are professors and researchers at some of America's best schools and business concerns.

---

[32]*New York Times*, June 23, 1996, Sec. A, p. 13.

But as I struggled to finish my education here, I also encountered the ugly realities of racial discrimination. This, too, is part of America's legacy and it is inextricably connected to the need for affirmative action.

When I first arrived in this country in 1956 as a graduate student, for example, I lived in Louisville, Ky. One day I got on a bus and saw that all the black people were in the back, the white people in the front. I didn't know where I belonged, so for a long time I stood near the driver. Finally, he told me to sit down in the front, and I did. I didn't take another bus ride for a whole year. I would walk an hour to avoid that.

I served as a teaching fellow at Louisville for a professor who refused to pronounce my name. He addressed me as "Chinaman." One day he directed me to adjust some valves in a large laboratory apparatus. Climbing a ladder, I lost my balance and instinctively grabbed a nearby steam pipe. It was scorchingly hot and produced a jolt of pain that nearly caused me to faint. Yet I did not scream. Instead, I stuffed my throbbing hand into my coat pocket and waited until the class ended. Then I ran to the hospital emergency room, where I was treated for a burn that had singed all the skin off my palm.

Outwardly, my response fit the stereotype of the model-minority Asian: I said nothing and went about my business. But my silence had nothing to do with stoicism. I simply did not want to endure the humiliation of having the professor scold me in front of the class.

Of course, four decades later, there have been major civil rights advances in America. But serious racial divisions remain. That's why colleges and universities created affirmative admissions programs. The idea was to open the doors to promising minority students who lacked educational and social opportunities.

As Berkeley's chancellor, I have seen the promise of affirmative action come true. No racial or ethnic group constitutes a majority among our 21,000 undergraduates. And Berkeley students enter with higher grades and test scores than their predecessors. They graduate at the highest rate in our history.

I think that affirmative action should be a temporary measure, but the time has not yet come to eliminate it. Educational opportunities for inner-city minority students, for example, still contrast dramatically with those of affluent students in the suburbs, where many white families live.

And as a public institution, the university needs to look at broader societal needs, including greater leadership training of California's African-American and Hispanic population.

I try to explain this when, as occasionally happens, Asian-American or white friends complain to me that their child, a straight-A student, didn't get into Berkeley because we give spaces to others. I also say that we use admission criteria other than test scores, grades and ethnicity, including a genius for computers, musical talent, geographical diversity.

Besides, a straight-A average wouldn't guarantee admission to Berkeley even if there were no affirmative action. For a freshman class with 3,500 places, we get about 25,000 applicants. This year, 10,784 of them had a 4.0 high school record.

What's more, helping minority students may not be the most compelling reason for preserving affirmative action.

Every time I walk across campus, I am impressed by the vibrant spirit of this diverse community. In teeming Sproul Plaza, the dozens of student groups who set up tables represent every kind of social, political, ethnic and religious interest. In the dorms, students from barrios, suburbs, farm towns and the inner city come together.

When there are diverse students, staff and faculty (among whom there are still too few minorities) everybody stands to gain.

Of course, interactions between students of different backgrounds can bring misunderstanding. Some white students tell me they feel squeezed out by black and Latino students they believe are less deserving, as well as by overachieving Asian-American students. Some African-American and Latino students confide they sometimes feel their professors and white classmates consider them academically inferior, a view that's slow to change even when they excel.

Still, the overall message I get time and again from students and recent graduates is that they have valued the chance to challenge stereotypes.

So I was stunned by the Regents' decision to end affirmative action admissions policies, which goes into effect by 1998. I even debated whether to resign.

In Chinese, however, the character for "crisis" is actually two characters: one stands for danger and the other for opportunity. And I took the Chinese approach. Noting that the Regents had reaffirmed their commitment to diversity when they discarded affirmative action, I decided to stay to try to make a difference.

Recently, I joined the superintendents of the major urban school districts of the San Francisco Bay area to announce a campaign: The Berkeley Pledge.

Under this program, Berkeley is deepening its support for disadvantaged youth trying to qualify for admission. One way will be to provide educational expertise for teachers; another will be to create incentives for pupils at selected school "pipelines" that begin in kindergarten. We also are stepping up our recruitment of exceptional minority students.

America has come a long way since the days of Jim Crow segregation. It would be a tragedy if our nation's colleges and universities slipped backward now, denying access to talented but disadvantaged youth and eroding the diversity that helps to prepare leaders.[33]

Essay 3 is by Ernest Martinez, an instructor in inmate vocational education at Wasco State Prison in Wasco, California.

---

[33]*New York Times*, Education Special Section, March 31, 1996, p. 30.

GIVING PEOPLE A SECOND CHANCE

Ernest Martinez

I am very proud of being Mexican American and am both privileged and honored to have been blessed with a career as an educator. Yet, I sometimes think that when discussing the many Hispanic issues that we often attribute to a fractured American society, I believe we often do to ourselves what we don't want others to do to us: ostracize ourselves. On the one hand, we rally together as Hispanics to seek out equal opportunity and revel in the triumphs of our unity. But on the other hand, when we hear of our many Hispanic brethren who are ex-convicts who need employment avenues for reentry into society, we close our eyes and ears to their cry for assistance. We blame society for their plight and thrust the burden of our people on the very government we condemn for lack of opportunity.

For the past several years, I have been part of the lives of inmates by teaching them vocational studies. These inmates are an example to us all that it is only by the grace of God that we are not in their place. We can all attest to the fact that we have done something for which we have simply not been caught—for example, drinking alcoholic beverages as minors, or driving without a license, or hanging around with the wrong people and being at the wrong place at the wrong time, or telling little "white lies" while filing our taxes. These are all examples of "crimes" that we've gotten away with. And instead of being imprisoned, we are known as law abiding citizens. The inmates of Wasco State Prison have not been so lucky, graced or blessed.

I believe many of the inmates with whom I work are persons like you and me. Unfortunately, they took "the road less traveled," and found themselves in a situation that was beyond their ability to handle or solve. This is not only "man as the problem," but the "problems of man." There are many parallels that we can draw between ourselves—those of us in the professional and business communities in need of not only able but willing people—and the backgrounds, personalities, character traits, abilities, needs, and yes, even aspirations, of the many prison inmates wanting and asking for a "Chapter Two" in their lives.

The business environment today is not solely based on equipment, products, or services. It's dependent on the skills, talents, and savvy of people. We're not only in an information age today; we are in an Age of Man, whereby sales can only be made and increased through the interpersonal relationships that we create between provider and consumer, between our companies and our customers. The world-respected organization, business, and management guru Dr. Peter Drucker has said, "Show me an organization or business that does not believe people are their greatest resource and I'll show you an organization with built-in limits to its success, and perhaps one destined for certain failure." Remember the old saying, "*El ojo del amo engorda el caballo*." Only if we can secure our fiscally solvent present can we launch into a more expansive tomorrow. And, again, we can only do this if we focus on people as our greatest asset today.

I am of the ardent belief that many prison inmates are highly functional, tremendously skilled, fabulously talented, and often technically gifted. Some are inordinately intelligent, while others are blessed simply with the extraordinary ability to work diligently. I've learned over the years working as educator of vocational studies with inmates that their crime was more a matter of poor judgment rather than of faulty character. And while not so naive as to believe that all inmates are worthy of a "Chapter Two," I can empathize with how hard it is to take a breath when one is in a whirlwind. The momentum of the moment is a tremendous force in this "survival of the fittest" society.

This is not to mean that we are to be guilt-driven, but rather people-motivated. This is not to promote philanthropy, but to be responsible in not overlooking a pool of prospective employees that is often not considered in the equation. This is not to say that every prison inmate is right for our companies, but to instead entertain the financial and accessible feasibility of hiring persons (both men and women) who want to work hard and need the opportunity to do so. And, this is not about hiring the "lessor among us," but to seek the "gold hidden behind and beneath a bushel."

Yes, many among the prison population are the very best of people, both in skill and desire, and in character and spirit. These people represent a select group who did the crime and served their time. They possess abilities, skills, and talents that range from refined artistic propensities, technical adeptness, and computer literacy, to management skills, professional polish, and interpersonal qualities. And, while they may need the power of your push or the compassion of your pull, they are people who can and will show a watching world that it is possible to "turn a large ship in a harbor."

If they can turn their lives around from the dungeons of prison to the epic of hope, they can also be a tremendous testimony to what is possible in the world of Hispanic business and to society at large.[34]

Essay 4 is by Judy Brady. This famous essay first appeared in *Ms. Magazine* in 1971.

WHY I WANT A WIFE

Judy Brady

I belong to that classification of people known as wives. I am A Wife. And, not altogether incidentally, I am a mother.

Not too long ago a male friend of mine appeared on the scene fresh from a recent divorce. He had one child, who is, of course, with his ex-wife. He is look-

---

[34]*Hispanic*, June 1996, p. 64.

ing for another wife. As I thought about him while I was ironing one evening, it suddenly occurred to me that I, too, would like to have a wife. Why do I want a wife?

I would like to go back to school so that I can become economically independent, support myself, and, if need be, support those dependent upon me. I want a wife who will work and send me to school. And while I am going to school I want a wife to take care of my children. I want a wife to keep track of the children's doctor and dentist appointments. And to keep track of mine, too. I want a wife to make sure my children eat properly and are kept clean. I want a wife who will wash the children's clothes and keep them mended. I want a wife who is a good nurturant attendant to my children, who arranges for their schooling, makes sure that they have an adequate social life with their peers, takes them to the park, the zoo, etc. I want a wife who takes care of the children when they are sick, a wife who arranges to be around when the children need special care, because, of course, I cannot miss classes at school. My wife must arrange to lose time at work and not lose the job. It may mean a small cut in my wife's income from time to time, but I guess I can tolerate that. Needless to say, my wife will arrange and pay for the care of the children while my wife is working.

I want a wife who will take care of *my* physical needs. I want a wife who will keep my house clean. A wife who will pick up after my children, a wife who will pick up after me. I want a wife who will keep my clothes clean, ironed, mended, replaced when need be, and who will see to it that my personal things are kept in their proper place so that I can find what I need the minute I need it. I want a wife who cooks the meals, a wife who is a *good* cook. I want a wife who will plan the menus, do the necessary grocery shopping, prepare the meals, serve them pleasantly, and then do the cleaning up while I do my studying. I want a wife who will care for me when I am sick and sympathize with my pain and loss of time from school. I want a wife to go along when our family takes a vacation so that someone can continue to care for me and my children when I need a rest and change of scene.

I want a wife who will not bother me with rambling complaints about a wife's duties. But I want a wife who will listen to me when I feel the need to explain a rather difficult point I have come across in my course of studies. And I want a wife who will type my papers for me when I have written them.

I want a wife who will take care of the details of my social life. When my wife and I are invited out by my friends, I want a wife who will take care of the babysitting arrangements. When I meet people at school that I like and want to entertain, I want a wife who will have the house clean, will prepare a special meal, serve it to me and my friends, and not interrupt when I talk about things that interest me and my friends. I want a wife who will have arranged that the children are fed and ready for bed before my guests arrive so that the children do not bother us. I want a wife who takes care of the needs of my guests so that they feel comfortable, who makes sure that they have an ashtray, that they are passed the hors d'oeuvres, that they are offered a second helping of the food, that their wine glasses are replenished when necessary, that their coffee is served to them as they like it. And I want a wife who knows that sometimes I need a night out by myself.

I want a wife who is sensitive to my sexual needs, a wife who makes love passionately and eagerly when I feel like it, a wife who makes sure that I am satisfied. And, of course, I want a wife who will not demand sexual attention when I am not in the mood for it. I want a wife who assumes the complete responsibility for birth control, because I do not want more children. I want a wife who will remain sexually faithful to me so that I do not have to clutter up my intellectual life with jealousies. And I want a wife who understands that *my* sexual needs may entail more than strict adherence to monogamy. I must, after all, be able to relate to people as fully as possible.

If, by chance, I find another person more suitable as a wife than the wife I already have, I want the liberty to replace my present wife with another one. Naturally, I will expect a fresh, new life; my wife will take the children and be solely responsible for them so that I am left free.

When I am through with school and have a job, I want my wife to quit working and remain at home so that my wife can more fully and completely take care of a wife's duties.

My God, who *wouldn't* want a wife?[35]

5. CLASS DISCUSSION AND WRITING ASSIGNMENT: INTERNATIONAL ARGUMENT

Read the following article by the novelist and author Reiko Hatsumi in which he explains what "yes" (*hai*) means in Japanese. Are there other examples of words, gestures, customs, beliefs, or values like this one that could create confusion or distrust among people from different cultures? Draw on the experiences of international students both in and outside of class and on international news reports. Write a paper in which you explain one of the differences you have identified, along with what would be required to achieve common ground and better understanding.

Essay

A SIMPLE "HAI" WON'T DO

Reiko Hatsumi

Tokyo

When a TV announcer here reported Bill Clinton's comment to Boris Yeltsin that when the Japanese say yes they often mean no, he gave the news with an expression of mild disbelief.

---

[35]Judy Brady, "I Want a Wife." Reprinted by permission of the author.

Having spent my life between East and West, I can sympathize with those who find the Japanese yes unfathomable. However, the fact that it sometimes fails to correspond precisely with the Occidental yes does not necessarily signal intended deception. This was probably why the announcer looked bewildered, and it marks a cultural gap that can have serious repercussions.

I once knew an American who worked in Tokyo. He was a very nice man, but he suffered a nervous breakdown and went back to the U.S. tearing his hair and exclaiming, "All Japanese businessmen are liars." I hope this is not true. If it were, all Japanese businessmen would be driving each other mad, which does not seem to be the case. Nevertheless, since tragedies often arise from misunderstandings, an attempt at some explanation might not be amiss.

A Japanese yes in its primary context simply means the other has heard you and is contemplating a reply. This is because it would be rude to keep someone waiting for an answer without supplying him with an immediate response.

For example: a feudal warlord marries his sister to another warlord. (I am back to TV.) Then he decides to destroy his newly acquired brother-in-law and besieges his castle. Being human, though, the attacking warlord worries about his sister and sends a spy to look around. The spy returns and the lord inquires eagerly, "Well, is she safe?" The spy bows and answers "Hai," which means yes. We sigh with relief thinking, "Ah, the fair lady is still alive!" But then the spy continues, "To my regret she has fallen on her sword together with her husband."

Hai is also an expression of our willingness to comply with your intent even if your request is worded in the negative. This can cause complications. When I was at school, our English teacher, a British nun, would say, "Now children, you won't forget to do your homework, will you?" And we would all dutifully chorus, "Yes, mother," much to her consternation.

A variation of hai may mean, "I understand your wish and would like to make you happy but unfortunately . . ." Japanese being a language of implication, the latter part of this estimable thought is often left unsaid.

Is there, then, a Japanese yes that corresponds to the Western one? I think so, particularly when it is accompanied by phrases such as "sodesu" (It is so) and "soshimasu" (I will do so). A word of caution against the statement, "I will think about it." Though in Tokyo this can mean a willingness to give one's proposal serious thought, in Osaka, another business center, it means a definite no. This attitude probably stems from the belief that a straightforward no would sound too brusque.

When talking to a Japanese person it is perhaps best to remember that although he may be speaking English, he is reasoning in Japanese. And if he says "I will think about it," you should inquire as to which district of Japan he hails from before going on with your negotiations.[36]

---

[36]*New York Times*, April 15, 1992, Sec. A, p. 12.

6. QUESTIONS ON THE CHAPTER

a. What are some of the possible influences on individual styles of argument? Which of these are the most potent for you?

b. What are some of the differences researchers have identified between men's and women's styles of argument? Do you agree or disagree? What in your own experience has influenced your answer to this question?

c. Why might it be important to be aware of different argument styles in international or cross-cultural argument? Give some examples of problems that might arise along with some ideas of how to deal with them.

7. QUESTIONS ON THE ESSAYS FOR ANALYSIS

a. "We Knew What Glory Was," page 49. What makes this an effective argument? What do you visualize? How do you participate in this essay and identify with its characters?

b. "A View From Berkeley," page 52. What are the major reasons Chancellor Tien provides for retaining affirmative action in higher education? Do you share his views? Give reasons for your answer, and use some of your own experiences to support your reasons, just as he does.

c. "Giving People a Second Chance," page 55. Do you think this article might persuade businesspersons to hire ex-convicts? Would you be persuaded if you could hire? Why or why not? Give a detailed explanation of your views about hiring individuals who have been through a vocational training program in prison.

d. Why "I Want a Wife," page 56. What is Brady really saying when she says she wants a wife? What solutions would you propose for the problem of who should be responsible for all of the tasks and duties described in this essay?

e. "A Simple 'Hai' Won't Do," page 58. Give some examples of what Japanese persons may really mean when they say "yes" as described in this article. Do you ever say one thing and mean something else? Give an example. What effect does this have in your communication with others?

CHAPTER 3

A Process
for Reading Argument

This chapter focuses on how to identify an argumentative purpose in a text and also on how to employ active reading strategies to help you read argument. The next chapter focuses on employing active writing strategies to help you write argument. Reading and writing are artificially separated in these two chapters for the sake of instruction. In actual practice, however, they should be combined and used together as integrated activities. To get you started using reading and writing together, the "Write While You Read" box on the next page contains a simple idea that can have a huge impact on improving the quality of your reading. Look for other connections between the reading and writing processes while you read this and the next chapter.

You will need a variety of strategies to help you do the reading and writing required by this and your other college courses. These strategies will be most useful to you if you perceive them as processes. You will usually adapt your reading process to the relative level of difficulty and to your purpose for reading specific materials. For example, when the reading material is complex and unfamiliar and your purpose is to understand, analyze, evaluate, and perhaps to write about it, you will need a well-developed and strategic reading process to help you meet the requirements of these demanding tasks. At other times, a simpler process is required for simpler reading. Before we look at possible reading processes, however, let us first consider how you can recognize an argumentative purpose in the material you read.

RECOGNIZING WRITTEN ARGUMENT

Some texts are obviously intended as argument, and others conceal their argumentative purpose and make it more difficult to recognize. You will recognize an argumentative purpose more easily if you think of a continuum of six types of writing that ranges from obvious argument on one end through objective writing on the other. Each of the six types exhibits not only a different authorial intention but also a different relationship between the author and the audience.

Write While You Read

You are probably willing to admit, along with most students, that you sometimes read without thinking. You perhaps begin a reading assignment by counting the pages. Then you go back to stare at the words (or the computer screen) until you reach the end. During this process your mind is blank or focused elsewhere. The best and quickest way to change this blank reading pattern is to *write while you read*. As soon as you begin reading with a pencil or pen (not a highlighter) in hand—underlining, writing ideas in the margin (see the example on page 69), summarizing, writing responses—everything changes. *You have to think to write.*

Furthermore, writing while you read helps you with two types of thinking. First, you will *think about* the material you read and perhaps even rephrase it so that it makes better sense to you. Second, you will *think beyond* the material you read and use it to help you generate ideas for your own writing. Your reading, in other words, becomes a springboard for your original thoughts and ideas. So, pick up a pencil now and begin to write as you read. This process may take a little more time, but you will end up knowing far more than you would by "just reading," and your book with your annotations and ideas in it will be a valuable addition to your personal library.

---

1. **Exploratory or Multiple Perspective Argument.**   The author's purpose in exploratory articles, which are commonly found in newspapers and magazines, is to lay out and explain all of the major positions on a controversial issue but not to favor one particular position. The audience thus is invited to view an issue from several perspectives and to understand all of them better.

2. **Single Perspective Argument.**   The author's purpose is clearly and obviously to take a position and to change minds or to convince others. The author's point of view and purpose are clearly expressed along with reasons and supporting details that appeal to a wide audience. This is a pure form of argumentative writing.

3. **Extremist Argument.**   Authors who are "true believers" and who write about causes or special projects sometimes use strong values and emotional language to appeal to narrow audiences who already share their views. Imagine a labor union leader, for example, who is writing to workers to convince them to go on strike.

4. **Hidden Argument.**   Some ostensibly objective texts, on close examination, actually favor one position over another, but not in an obvious, overt manner. One sign that the text is not totally objective is selected and stacked supporting material that favors a particular point of view. Also, the presence of emotional language, vivid description, or emotional examples can be another sign that the author has strong opinions and intends not only to inform but also

to convince the audience. For example, an author who actually favors reducing student financial aid writes an "objective" report about students who have received aid. However, all the students described in the article either left college early or defaulted on their loans, and they are described as dropouts and parasites on society. No examples of successful students are reported. Even though the author does not state a position or write this article as an obvious argument, it is still clear that the author has a position and that it manifests itself in biased reporting. The intention, even though concealed, is to convince.

5. **Unconscious Argument.** Sometimes an author who is trying to write an objective report is influenced unconsciously by strong personal opinions about the subject, and the result is an unconscious intent to change people's minds. Imagine, for example, a strong pro-life newspaper reporter who is sent to write an objective expository article about an abortion clinic. It would be difficult for this individual to describe and explain the clinic without allowing negative perceptions to influence the way the facts are presented. Again, stacked or selected evidence, emotional language, quotes from authorities with well-known positions, or even pictures that establish a point of view may attest to an argumentative purpose while the author is unaware of it.

6. **Objective Reporting.** Sometimes authors simply describe, explain, or report facts and ideas that everyone would accept without controversy. The author's own point of view, opinions, or interpretations are deliberately omitted. This type is a pure form of expository writing. Examples include almanacs, data lists, weather reports, some news stories, and government, business, science, and technical reports. The audience reads such material to get information.

When you read and analyze argument, you will be studying and interpreting all these types of material with the exception of the last, objective reporting, and sometimes even their opinion creeps in. Now let's examine what you do at present when you read argument.

HOW DO YOU READ NOW?

You already have a reading process, but you may not have consciously adapted it to reading argument. You can improve your present reading process by analyzing what you do now and then acknowledging present habits that you will not want to give up. To that base you can add additional information and strategies to build further reading expertise. Analyze your present reading process by answering the following questions. At this point, think about reading in general rather than about reading argument.

What do you do . . .

- before you read?
- while you read?
- when the material is hard?
- when you finish reading?

Now change the focus to reading argument.

What do you do ...

- before you read argument?
- while you read argument?
- when the argumentative material is hard?
- when you finish reading argument?

Many students answer that they do nothing before they read, that they then just read, that they reread when the material is hard, and that they do nothing when they finish reading. That is a typical profile for students beginning an argument course. In answering the second question, "What do you do while you read argument," students new to argument class typically add one or more additional strategies to their usual reading process: They try to identify both sides of the issue, they try to keep an open mind, they decide whether to agree or disagree with the author, and they decide what stand to take.

What can you add to your present process to improve your reading of argument? Your goal is to become an active reader who concentrates and uses existing knowledge to construct new knowledge. Critical reading and thinking strategies will help you accomplish that.

HOW CAN YOU ORGANIZE A PROCESS FOR READING ARGUMENT?

The reading process for argument explained in the following pages and summarized in Box 3.1 integrates prereading, reading, and postreading strategies and incorporates writing at every stage. Before you examine this process, however, here are three cautionary notes:

1. Use your own reading process for most reading and add strategies either when you are not getting enough meaning or when your comprehension is breaking down altogether.
2. Be advised that no one uses all of the reading strategies described here all of the time. Instead, you should select those that are appropriate to the task, that is, appropriate for a particular type of material and for your reading purpose. You need to practice all of the strategies so that you are familiar with them, and you will be given an opportunity to do so in the exercises and activities. This is an artificial situation, however. Later, in real-life reading, you will be selective and use only those that apply to a particular situation.
3. There is no set order for employing active reading strategies even though the strategies will be laid out in an apparent order under the headings of prereading, reading, and postreading. In actuality, you may find yourself stopping to do some prereading in the middle of a difficult text, or you may

A Reading Process for Argument

PREREADING STRATEGIES

Read the title and first paragraph; background the issue. Identify the issue. Free-associate and write words and phrases that the issue brings to mind.

Evaluate and improve your background. Do you know enough? If not, read or discuss to get background. Look up a key word or two.

Survey the material. Locate the claim (the main assertion) and some of the subclaims (the ideas that support it); notice how they are organized. Do not slow down and read.

Write out your present position on the issue.

Make some predictions and write one big question. Jot down two or three ideas that you think the author may discuss and write one question you would like to have answered.

READING STRATEGIES

Use a pencil to underline and annotate the ideas that seem important.

Identify and **read** the information in the **introduction, body,** and **conclusion.**

Look for the claim, subclaims, and support. Box the **transitions** to highlight relationships between ideas and changes of subject.

Find the key words that represent major concepts and jot down meanings if necessary.

Analyze the rhetorical situation. Text, reader, author, constraints, exigence.

Read with an open mind and analyze the common ground between you and the author.

STRATEGIES FOR READING DIFFICULT MATERIAL

Read all the way through once without stopping.

Write a list of what you can understand.

Identify words and concepts you do not understand, look them up, and analyze how they are used in context.

Reread the material and add to your list of what you can understand.

Discuss the material with someone who understands it.

continued

BOX 3.1 A Summary of the Process for Reading Argument Explained in This Chapter.

POSTREADING STRATEGIES

Monitor your comprehension. Insist on understanding. Check the accuracy of your **predictions** and answer your **question.**

Analyze the organization and write either a **simplified outline** or a **summary** to help you understand and remember. Or make a **map.**

Write a response to help you think.

Compare your present position with your position before you read the argument.

Evaluate the argument and decide whether it is convincing or not.

Write what value this material has for you and **how you will use it.**

BOX 3.1 A Summary of the Process for Reading Argument Explained in This Chapter (*continued*)

stop to summarize a section of material, a postreading strategy, before you continue reading. The order here is simply to make these strategies easier to explain and use.

PREREADING STRATEGIES

You use what you already know to learn new material. It is all you have. To read better, learn to access what you know about a subject to help you interpret new, incoming material. If you know nothing about a subject, you will need to take special steps to learn more. Otherwise the new material will seem too difficult to read. The following sections present five prereading strategies to help you organize your prior knowledge about a subject, build background when you need it, and begin to analyze the material and make some predictions.

Read the Title and Background the Issue. Read the title and the first paragraph quickly to find out what is at issue. If you do not discover the issue there, read the last paragraph, where it is often stated, or read rapidly through the essay until you discover it. Then, access your background on the issue by writing, in phrases only, everything that comes to mind when you think of that issue. This process is called *backgrounding*. Here is an example: Suppose you read "Some College Costs Should Be Tax Deductible," the argument on page 22 in Chapter 1, and you have a negative initial reaction. You learn from the first paragraph that the issue is *tuition and tax deductions*. Your backgrounding might include

charity deductible
religious income deductible
tuition—not deductible

no college costs are deductible
students even pay taxes on scholarships
IRS reaction?

Here is a second example that refers back to the short argument entitled "We're Good Republicans—and Pro-Choice" that appears on page 23 in Chapter 1. The issue is *abortion*. Here is backgrounding by two different students who have different backgrounds and views:

Republicans	prochoice
against abortion	permit abortion
prolife	individual
abortion wrong	not political
conflict	Democrats

Evaluate and Improve Your Background Information. When attempts to background an issue are unsuccessful and it is clear that you lack information, use some special strategies to help you build background. Locate and read some other material on the subject that you can easily understand. An encyclopedia or easier books may be good sources of such information, or you can talk with someone who does understand the material, like a professor or a fellow student. Identify words that are used repeatedly and that you do not understand. Look them up in the glossary or dictionary.

Survey the Material. Survey a book or an article before you read it to get an introduction to the major ideas and a few of the supporting details.

Books. To survey a book (not a novel), follow these six steps in this order:

1. Read the *title* and focus on what it tells you about the contents of the book.
2. Read the *table of contents*. Notice how the content has been divided into chapters and organized.
3. Read the *introduction*. Look for background information about the subject and author and also for information to help you read the book.
4. Examine the special *features* of the book. Are these headings and subheadings in boldface type to highlight major ideas? Is there a glossary? An index? Charts? Other visuals? A bibliography?
5. Read the title and first paragraph of the *first* and *last chapters* to see how the book begins and ends.
6. Read the title and first paragraph of the *other chapters* to get a sense of the flow of ideas.

This procedure should take about half an hour. It will introduce you to the main issue and approaches in a book, and reading now will be much easier.

Articles and Chapters. To survey an article or chapter in a book, follow these six steps in this order:

1. Read the *title* and focus on the information in it.
2. Read the *introduction,* which is usually the first paragraph but can be several paragraphs long. Look for a claim and any forecasts of what is to come.
3. Read the *last paragraph* and look for the claim.
4. Read the *headings* and *subheadings,* if there are any, to get a sense of the ideas and their sequence. Read the first sentence of each paragraph, if there are no headings, to accomplish the same goal.
5. Study the *visuals:* pictures, charts, graphs. Read their captions. They often illustrate major ideas.
6. Identify the *key words* that represent the main concepts.

Surveying an article or chapter takes 10 to 15 minutes. It introduces you to the issue, the claim, and some of the subclaims and support. Survey before you read to make reading easier; survey when you do research to get a context for the material you quote; and survey when you review to help you focus on the important ideas.

Write Out Your Present Position on the Issue.   When you finish backgrounding and surveying, jot down your own current ideas and positions on the issue. This strategy will help guarantee your active interest as you read and will also promote an interaction between your ideas and the author's. Here are examples of such initial position statements; the first, on college costs, continues the initial negative reaction:

> There are too many tax breaks as it is—especially for the rich. Tuition does not fall into a tax-exempt category. The IRS would never allow this.

On the prochoice issue the two students might write:

> I'm prolife. Abortions are wrong. There should be some limits, laws, punishments against abortion. I'm not sure what or how to mandate them.

> I'm prochoice. Abortions are an individual not a political issue, and they should be readily available.

Make Some Predictions, and Write One Big Question.   Reading is a constant process of looking back at what you know and looking ahead to predict what you think may come next. Facilitate this natural process by linking what you know with what you predict will be in the text. Write your predictions and one big question to help focus your attention. Change your predictions as you read if they are off target and also stay open to the new ideas you did not predict. Finally, try to answer your big question when you finish reading.

Here are examples of predictions you might write about the tuition article:

> Will say that tuition is an unusual expense
> Will say that tuition is a sacrifice
> Will say tuition benefits society by educating people
> Will say tuition should be tax deductible

Here is an example of a big question you might ask before you read: How will the author justify a tax deduction for tuition?

Here are some predictions you might make about the abortion article:

Will say own experience causes them to be prochoice
Will need to reconcile that position with being Republicans

Here is a big question you might ask: How will these authors reconcile their politics with their experience?

READING STRATEGIES

Use a Pencil to Underline and Annotate Important Ideas.   Underlining with a pen or pencil and writing notes in the margin helps keep your mind on the material as you read. It also reduces the material you have read so that you can review it and find information more easily later. The key to successful marking is to do it very selectively. Do not color an entire paragraph with a yellow highlighter. Instead, underline only the words and phrases that help you reduce the content so that you can later reread only those parts while still getting a sense of the whole. To further reduce the text and make it even more useful, jot the major ideas in the margins, or summarize them at the end of sections. Write the big ideas along with your personal reactions on the flyleaves of a book or at the ends of chapters or articles. If you do not own the book, write on separate sheets of paper and keep them organized in a folder or in a section of your notebook that is set aside for reading notes.

Here is an example of the first two paragraphs of the essay about tuition and scholarships underlined and annotated as recommended. Note that this material is now easier to understand and review:

Tax breaks: tuition for scholarships

As the government spends increasingly less on financial aid, many leading colleges and universities are using a greater percentage of tuition revenues for scholarships. Just as income tax breaks are given for charitable contributions, this portion of tuition should be tax deductible.

Tuition for scholarships increasing

Statistics compiled by the Consortium on Financing Higher Education, which does research and analysis for 32 member colleges, show the growing importance of tuition for scholarships. In 1980, the consortium schools spent an average of 9.8 percent of tuition revenues on financial aid; last year, that figure rose to 15.9 percent. It will continue to rise as federal and state financing drops further.

Identify and Read the Information in the Introduction, Body, and Conclusion. The organization of ideas in argumentative texts is not very different from other texts. Much of what you read, for example, follows the easily recognizable introduction, main body, and conclusion format. The introduction may provide background information about the issue and the author, get attention, state the main point, or forecast some of the ideas to be developed in the main body. The main body will explain and develop the author's main point by giving reasons and support to prove it. The end or conclusion either summarizes by restating important points or concludes by stating the most important point, that is, what the author wants you to believe. Not all texts follow this pattern exactly, but enough of them do to justify your checking what you read against it.

Look for the Claims, Subclaims, Support, and Transitions. All arguments have the structural components you are familiar with from other kinds of discourse. The main difference is their names. The special characteristics of the components of argument will be described when the Toulmin model is discussed in Chapter 5. We start using Toulmin's terms here, however, to help you get used to them. The thesis of an argument, which shapes the thinking of the entire text and states what the author finally expects you to accept or believe, is called the *claim. Subclaims* are assertions or reasons that develop the claim. They are, however, almost meaningless without further explanation. *Support* in the form of facts, opinions, evidence, and examples is the most specific material that provides additional information and further explanation. Support makes the claim and subclaims clear, vivid, memorable, and, above all else, believable. *Transitions* lead the reader from one idea to another and also sometimes state the relationships among ideas. Furthermore, there is a constant movement between general and specific material in all texts, including argumentative texts, and this movement becomes apparent when the ideas are presented in various types of outline form.

Understand the Key Words. Sometimes figuring out the meaning of one word in a difficult passage will suddenly make the whole passage easier to understand. Most of us, unfortunately, do not even see many of the words we do not know unless we make the effort to look for them. Instead, our eyes slide over unfamiliar words because there is nothing in our background to help us make sense of them.

When reading material suddenly seems hard, go back and look for words you do not understand. Try to identify the key words, those that represent major concepts. In this chapter, "backgrounding" and "rhetorical situation" are examples of key words. First, read the context in which you find the word to help you understand it. A word may be defined in a sentence, a paragraph, or even several paragraphs. Major concepts in argument are often defined at length, and understanding their meaning will be essential to an understanding of the entire argument. If the context does not give you enough information, try the glossary, the dictionary, or another book on the subject. Remember that major concepts require longer explanations than a single synonym. Synonyms are useful for other minor words that are less critical to the understanding of the entire passage.

Analyze the Rhetorical Situation. "Rhetorical situation" is a term coined by Professor Lloyd Bitzer to describe the elements that combine to constitute a communication situation.[1] To understand these elements as they apply to argument helps us understand what motivates or causes the argument in the first place, who the author is, who the intended audience is, how they might react to it, and how we as readers might also respond. By analyzing and understanding the rhetorical situation, we gain critical insight into the entire context as well as the parts of an argument, and this insight ultimately helps us evaluate its final success or failure. Analyzing the rhetorical situation is an important critical reading strategy that can be initiated during the prereading stages but that should continue to be used as a tool for analysis throughout the reading process.

According to Bitzer, a rhetorical situation has five elements: the *exigence,* the *audience,* the *constraints,* the *author,* and the *text.* Let's look at these elements to see how they can help us understand and evaluate argumentative writing.

Exigence is the real-life, dramatic situation that signals individuals that something controversial has occurred and that they should try to make some sense of it. Exigence is a problem to be solved, a situation that requires some modifying response from an audience. Here are some examples of exigence for argument: Some scientists think they have discovered a new source of cheap energy but others cannot replicate it; several parents report that their children can access pornography on the Internet; a new medicine for AIDS doesn't seem to be working; too many homeless people are living in the streets and subways; politicians are questioning the welfare system; an abortion doctor is shot and killed; several African-American churches are burned to the ground by arsonists; human rights are being violated in another country. To bring the idea of exigence closer, here are some examples that might provide you with the exigence to engage in argument: You get a parking ticket; your registration is canceled for lack of payment but you know you paid; you and the person you live with are having trouble deciding who should do the household chores; you try to transfer in some past college credits and your current institution won't accept them; there is no day care provided on your campus for young children; athletics are draining campus resources and there aren't enough classes. In all cases, something is wrong, imperfect, defective, or in conflict. Exigence invites analysis and discussion, and sometimes also a written response to encourage both individual public awareness and discourse about problematic situations.

The *reader/audience* is the second element in the rhetorical situation. For argument to work, a potential audience must care enough to listen, read, and pay attention, to change its perceptions as a result of the argument, and, hopefully, even have the ability to mediate change or act in a new way. A rhetorical situation invites these special types of audience responses and outcomes. Most authors have a targeted or intended audience in mind, and, as you read a text, you may discover that your analysis and response vary considerably from the tar-

---

[1] Lloyd Bitzer, "The Rhetorical Situation," *Philosophy and Rhetoric,* 1 (January 1968): 1–14.

geted audience's probable response, particularly if different cultures or periods of time are involved. When you read, compare your perceptions of the argument with the perceptions you imagine the targeted or intended reading audience might have had. More information about audience is provided in Chapter 10.

Constraints make up the third element of the rhetorical situation. They include the existing people, events, values, beliefs, and traditions that constrain or limit the targeted audience and cause it to analyze the situation and react to it in a particular way. They also include the character, background, and style of the author that limit or influence him or her to write in a certain way. Constraints may bring people together or they may drive them apart. They certainly influence the amount of common ground that will be established between an author and an audience. Here are some examples of constraints: An audience feels constrained to mistrust the media because it thinks reporters exaggerate or lie; reporters believe it is their responsibility to expose character flaws in candidates running for office, so they feel constrained to do so at every opportunity; candidates think voters want to hear rousing platitudes, so they deliver rousing platitudes; voters have lost their faith in public leaders, so they do not want to vote; an audience is too disturbed by the severity of the environmental crisis to want to listen to information about it, so it shuts it out; people are too angry about destroyed property to consider peaceful solutions; some welfare recipients fear that changes in the system would deny food and shelter to them and their children. Or, to continue with the closer examples, you parked your car in a no-parking zone because you were late to class, but the police feel constrained by law to give you a ticket; you are angry because your college has made errors with your tuition payments before; you believe everyone should share the household chores but your partner disagrees; you must transfer credits to graduate on time; without child care you cannot attend classes; you do not particularly value college athletics and you do want classes available when you can take them. These constraining circumstances will influence the way you react to the issues and address your targeted audiences. The exigence, reader/audience, and constraints are in place before the author becomes a part of the rhetorical situation.

The *author* writes an argument in response to the exigence of the situation and usually with a particular audience in mind. The author ideally should consider any constraining circumstances or values as well.

The *text* is the written argument that has unique characteristics of its own that can be analyzed, such as the format, organization, argumentative strategies, language, style, and so on.

The following set of questions will help you analyze the rhetorical situation and get insight into its component parts. Note that *you as the reader* have been differentiated from the *original reader* to help with analysis.

1. **Exigence.**   What happened to cause this argument? Why is it perceived as a defect or problem? Is it new or recurring?

2. **Reader/Audience.**   Who is the targeted audience? What is the nature of this group? Can they be convinced? What are the anticipated outcomes? How do

you as a reader compare with the targeted audience? What are your constraints? How much common ground do you share with the author? What is your initial position? Are you motivated to change your mind or modify the situation?

3. **Constraints.**   What special constraining circumstances will influence the audience's and author's responses to the subject? What beliefs, attitudes, prejudices, people, habits, events, circumstances, or traditions are already in place that will limit or constrain their perceptions?

4. **Author.**   Who is the author? Consider background, experience, education, affiliations, and values. What is motivating the author to write?

5. **The Text.**   What kind of a text is it? What are its special qualities and features?

Here is a mnemonic to help you remember the five elements in the rhetorical situation. They have been arranged in a different order so that their first letters form a word: text, reader, author, constraints, exigence. Remember that there is a TRACE of the rhetorical situation in every argument that you read. Now, let's analyze the rhetorical situations of the two essays we have been using as examples in this chapter.

EXAMPLES OF ANALYSIS
OF THE RHETORICAL SITUATION

Example 1: "Some College Costs Should Be Tax Deductible"

Exigence.   The described situation is occurring in many colleges. Less government money is available for scholarships, so tuition money is being diverted to scholarships by the colleges. People who pay full tuition are helping to fund scholarship students but without the tax break they would get if they donated money directly to scholarship funds.

Reader/Audience.   Taxpayers and tuition payers who also can understand tax-deductible charitable contributions are potential audience members.

Constraints.   Some readers might feel constrained by tradition. Tax breaks for tuition are not usually given, and the IRS might balk. Also, changes in the tax structure would be required, and making such changes might be a lot of trouble. Readers might be constrained by the knowledge that tuition payments are required and charitable contributions are voluntary.

Author.   He advocates this change as a benefit to both scholarship and nonscholarship families. It is not clear which type of family he represents or what his personal stake is.

Type of Text.   This is a short newspaper opinion piece.

You as Reader.   What is your reaction? Where did you stand on this issue before you read? Where do you stand now? Why?

Example 2: "We're Good Republicans—and Pro-Choice"

Exigence.   Many Republicans across the country are by tradition prolife, and they support reversal of the *Roe* v. *Wade* Supreme Court ruling that protects abortion. The authors had an abortion and are in conflict because they are also Republicans.

Reader/Audience.   Both Republicans and Democrats with many different views on abortion are the potential audience. The authors want to modify the audience's perceptions of the issue.

Constraints.   The issue is perceived as black or white, with two sides only, by many people. The Republican party is prolife, and many of its members feel constrained to take a prolife position. The *Roe* v. *Wade* decision is in jeopardy. The authors hold a respected position in their community and that influences the way they write. Some audience members may be "true believers" and hold extreme views on this issue.

Authors.   These are high-profile people who announced their abortion in the newspaper. They seem to want to be role models for others. They need to reconcile their decision and values with their party loyalty and with their religious beliefs and values. They hope to convince others that there are more than two potential positions on the abortion issue.

Type of Text.   This is a short opinion piece in the newspaper.

You as Reader.   Where did you stand before? Where do you stand now? Why?

Read with an Open Mind and Analyze the Common Ground Between You and the Author.   Suppose you now begin to read the article on abortion that argues in favor of abortions in certain circumstances. Consider some unfortunately typical responses that readers of argument sometimes make at this point. Suppose you disagree strongly with the article, because you believe abortion is always wrong. You may be tempted not to read at all or to read hastily and carelessly, dismissing the author as a crackpot. Or, if your initial reaction has been different and you happen to agree with these authors' ideas, you might read carefully, marking the best passages and insisting on reading them aloud to someone else. If you are neutral on this issue, with opinions on either side, you might read with less interest and even permit your mind to wander. Your reading of the article about financial aid could be influenced in similar ways, depending on your perspective on that issue. These responses, as you can see, will distract you and interfere in very negative ways with your understanding of the article. Once you become aware of such unproductive responses, however, you can compensate for them by analyzing the common ground between you and the author and using this information to help you read more receptively and non-judgmentally, or with an open mind. In other words, try to generate interest or suspend major critical judgment until you have finished reading. Finally, reassess your original position to determine whether you now have reason to modify or change your perspective on the issue.

As you assess the common ground you think you share with the author, you can use written symbols to indicate how much or how little of it may exist: ◯ can mean you and the author are basically alike in your views and share common-ground; ⬭ can mean you are alike on some ideas but not on others and share some common ground; ◯◯ can mean your ideas are so different from the author's that there is no common ground; and X can mean that you are neutral in regard to the subject, that you consequently have little or no interest in it, and that you are not likely to agree, disagree, or establish common ground with the author. To avoid reading problems, you will now need to compensate for common ground differences that might interfere with comprehension. The symbols ◯◯, for disagreement and no common ground, and X, for neutral and no common ground should signal that you will have to use all of the active strategies for reading that you can muster to give these authors a fair hearing.

STRATEGIES FOR READING DIFFICULT MATERIAL

Read a difficult text all the way through once, to the end, without stopping. You will understand some of it, but not all. Then write brief lists of what you do and do not understand. Identify the words that are used repeatedly and that you do not understand. Look them up in the glossary or dictionary and analyze how they are used in context. Finally, reread the material, using active reading strategies to help you get meaning. Add more items to your list of material that you can understand. Finally, get together with a fellow classmate or someone else who does understand the material and discuss it.

POSTREADING STRATEGIES

Monitor Your Comprehension, Check the Accuracy of Your Predictions, Answer Your Questions. At this point insist on understanding. The results of reading are very much a private product that belongs to you and no one else. Only you can monitor and check your understanding of what you have read. One way to check is to look away to see if you can recite from memory the claim and some of the subclaims and support. If you cannot do this right after you have finished reading, you will probably not be able to do it later in discussion or on an exam. Reread, actively using reading strategies, and try again. Comprehension checks of this type help you concentrate and understand. Check your prereading predictions to see if they were accurate. You may need to change them. See if you can now answer the question you posed before you started reading.

Discover the Organization, and Write Summaries or Simplified Outlines. Here are summaries and simplified outlines of the two essays we are using as examples. The summaries condense and restate the material in a briefer form that will help you understand and remember it. The outlines lay out the ideas in these essays according to their levels of generality and specificity. Study these outlines to help you develop the ability to locate the most important ideas and understand their relationship to each other in any written text. The claim, the most general idea, is written at the left-hand margin, the subclaims are indented from the claim, and the support—the specific facts, opinions, examples, illustrations, and other data and statistics that ground the claim and subclaims in reality, the most specific material—is indented even further. Internalize the idea of a simplified outline and use it to help you find the claim and understand the ideas that support and develop it in the arguments you read.

EXAMPLES OF SUMMARIES AND SIMPLIFIED OUTLINES

Two types of summaries are illustrated: one written in paragraph form with complete sentences and the other written in phrases only. Use whichever form works best for you.

Example I.   Summaries and an Outline for "Some College Costs Should be Tax Deductible"

A Summary Written in Paragraph Form

The portion of tuition costs diverted to pay for scholarships for needy students should be tax deductible, like charitable contributions. Government funding for scholarships has diminished. Colleges are forced to use part of the tuition money for scholarships. Families who pay tuition sacrifice to do so. This plan would give them a break, and it would keep needy students in college.

A Summary Written in Phrases

Government funding for scholarships down—colleges using tuition money for scholarships—make part of tuition bill diverted to scholarships tax deductible—like charitable contributions—help those who pay full tuition—help those who need aid.

A Simplified Outline

Claim Tuition should be tax deductible like contributions to charities.

Support:	statistics, data, facts	• 32 colleges use tuition for scholarships. Increase from 9.8% in 1980 to 15.9% in 1990.
		• Median: $2,400 of $15,000 average tuition costs used for scholarships.
		• Chicago most (30.7%); Princeton least (1.4%).
		• Some families contribute $10,000 in 4 years and no tax relief.
Subclaims		• Scholarships good: create diversity.
		• Tax-deductible contributions voluntary and good: improve quality of life.
		• Tuition obligatory but improves life and is a charitable contribution when used for scholarships. Should have same tax treatment.

Example 2. Summaries and an Outline for "We're Good Republicans—and Pro-Choice"

A Summary Written in Paragraph Form

Authors are Republicans and prochoice. They had an abortion because the baby was deformed. Now the Republican party is favoring prolife, no abortions. It is trying to reverse the ruling that protects abortions, *Roe* v. *Wade*. Prochoice Republicans have to speak out. There are more than two positions on this. Two extreme positions cannot develop common ground. There is a need to embrace "uncommon ground" on this one and tolerate many views even when we do not agree.

A Summary Written in Phrases

Prochoice Republicans—need to speak out—party supporting prolife—trying to change legislation—party should not be pro or con but adopt third position—"uncommon ground"—tolerate many views because no simple solution.

A Simplified Outline

Support:	personal example	• Bad pregnancy problems with baby.
		• Decided on abortion.
		• Public decision—news release.
		• People sympathetic and understanding.

Subclaim	• Individual decision—no business of government or Republican party.
Support:	• *Roe* v. *Wade* protects this right.
Subclaims	• Prochoice Republicans need to speak out.
	• Not just two sides.
Claim:	• Look at from third side: uncommon ground that permits different perspectives.

Look back at the shape of the two simplified outlines. In the first, the claim is at the beginning, and in the second it is at the end. Now notice the types of support used by the authors. The first author relies on statistics and data, and the second on a personal example. The rhetorical situations for these essays are very different. The first deals with a relatively neutral issue, tuition and taxes, and most people will probably favor the claim, so it is placed first and supported with facts and data. The second deals with the difficult issue of abortion, so a story is told to create common ground, and the claim is deferred to the end, where more people will be likely to accept it. The positioning of the main points and the decision to use certain types of support are argumentative strategies. The authors have good reasons for using these strategies as they have. Chapters 5 to 7 will go into more detail about the special strategies of argument.

Make a Map. As an alternative to summaries or outlines, make a map of the ideas in a text. For many students, maps are the preferred way to reduce and reorganize the material they read. To make a map, write the most important idea, the claim, in a circle or on a line, and then attach major subclaims and support to it. Make your map in very brief form. Figures 3.1 and 3.2 are possible maps of the two essays we have been using as examples. You can be creative with map formats. Use whatever layout will give you a quick picture of the major ideas.

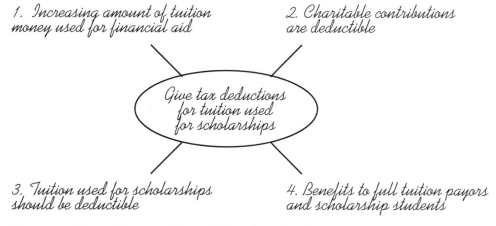

Figure 3.1 Map of Ideas for "Some College Costs Should Be Tax Deductible"

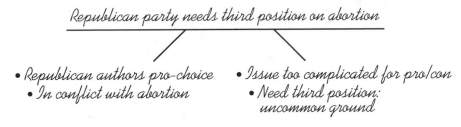

Republican party needs third position on abortion

- *Republican authors pro-choice*
  - *In conflict with abortion*

- *Issue too complicated for pro/con*
  - *Need third position: uncommon ground*

Figure 3.2 Map of Ideas for "We're Good Republicans—and Pro-Choice."

Write Some More to Help You Think. We made the observation at the beginning of this chapter that writing helps you concentrate and think while you read. You have been advised to use writing in a variety of ways while reading, and here are a few more suggestions of ways you can combine writing with reading. Write out all of the original ideas that are inspired by your reading immediately, as you read and when you finish reading, and before you forget them. When you finish reading, go back and look at your original position on the issue, the one that you wrote down before you began to read. Has it changed or been modified in any way as a result of your reading? If so, write out your new position. Write also a comparison of the author's position and your own. Write an evaluation of the author's argument in which you decide whether the author has been convincing or not. Provide some reasons for your opinion. Finally, jot down some ideas about what you can do with the material you have just read. What use can you make of it? Will you use it to think further, to add to your research, to learn more, to clarify something you did not understand? Almost everything one reads serves some useful purpose, and you can learn to reflect on what that purpose might be.

The reading strategies described in this chapter, such as backgrounding, predicting, asking questions, surveying, analyzing the rhetorical situation, summarizing, writing simple outlines, making maps, and writing ideas and reactions all work. They help you access what you already know, relate it to new material, see the parts as well as the whole, rephrase the material in your own words, reduce it to a manageable size, and think critically about it. Research studies have demonstrated that these activities help readers understand, analyze, remember, and think about the material they read.

EXERCISES AND ACTIVITIES

1. CLASS DISCUSSION: RECOGNIZING WRITTEN ARGUMENT
The following newspaper article was published on the front page of the *New York Times* as an objective story about some people in Los Angeles after riots in 1991 that were a reaction to the acquittal of four police who beat an African-American man named Rodney King. First, identify what seems to be at issue in

this article. It is not directly stated. Then, read the article carefully to see if you can recognize the author's attitudes, feelings, and opinions toward the subject at issue. What is the author's intention in this article? To explain? To convince? Or both? Justify your answer with specific examples from the article.

Essay

JOBS ILLUMINATE WHAT RIOTS HID: YOUNG IDEALS

Sara Rimer

When Disneyland came two weeks ago to the First A.M.E. Church in South-Central Los Angeles to hold interviews for 200 summer jobs, it was a good-will gesture born of the riots.

When more than 600 young men and women, many in coats and ties or dresses showed up, the Disney officials were taken aback.

America has been bombarded with television images of the youth of South-Central Los Angeles: throwing bricks, looting stores, beating up innocent motorists. The Disneyland staff who interviewed the applicants, ages 17 to 22, found a different neighborhood.

"They were wonderful kids, outstanding kids," said Greg Albrecht, a spokesman for Disneyland. "We didn't know they were there." Nor, Mr. Albrecht added, had they known that the young people of South-Central Los Angeles would be so eager to work at Disneyland.

Joe Fox, a spokesman for the First A.M.E. Church, said that had there been time to better publicize the Disneyland jobs, thousands would have applied. "People just want to work, period," he said. With hundreds of small businesses destroyed during the riots, jobs are harder to find than ever.

One of the 600 who wanted to work at Disneyland was Olivia Miles, at 18 the youngest of seven children of a nurse's aide and a disabled roofer. "My friend Lakesha's mother told us Disneyland was hiring," said Miss Miles, who has worked at McDonald's and Popeye's since she was 15. "I said: 'Disneyland! C'mon, let's go!'"

Miss Miles will graduate on June 30 from one of South-Central Los Angeles's public high schools, Washington Preparatory, where she has earned mostly A's and B's and was the co-captain of the drill team. Next fall, she will attend Grambling University in Louisiana.

Washington has 2,600 students; 70 percent are black, 30 percent are Hispanic. The principal, Marguerite LaMotte, says that as impressive as Olivia Miles is, she is not exceptional. "I have a lot of Olivia's," she said. Indeed, 118 seniors plan to attend four-year colleges and 131 will go to two-year colleges.

The world knows about the gang members; estimates put the number at 100,000 across Los Angeles County, and last year there were 771 gang-related homicides. No one has tried to count the young people like Olivia Miles. They are among the invisible people of South-Central Los Angeles.

In some ways, Miss Miles is just another high school senior. One of her favorite shows is "Beverly Hills 90210." She admires Bill Cosby and Oprah Winfrey. She enjoys reading books by Maya Angelou. And shopping. She loves soft-spoken, 17-year-old Damon Sewell, the defensive football captain at nearby Hawthorne High School. He will go on to Grambling with her.

Miss Miles and Mr. Sewell and their friends who live in the neighborhood pay a terrible price because of geography. They have to worry about simply staying alive. They have friends who have been shot and killed. They can't even get dressed in the morning without thinking, red and blue are gang colors; wearing them is dangerous. Then they have to confront the stigma that comes with being young and black and from Los Angeles.

"The neighborhood is famous now," Miss Miles said on Saturday as she and Mr. Sewell gave a tour of the devastation. They were just 15 minutes away from Beverly Hills and Hollywood. Miss Miles's tone was plaintive. "Why did it have to be famous for a riot? Why couldn't it be famous for people getting up in the world, or making money, or being actors?"

Getting ahead, despite enormous obstacles, is the story of the Miles family. Her parents, Aubrey and Willie Mae Miles, grew up in the South and migrated to Los Angeles. They started their lives together in an apartment in Watts and eventually bought a two-bedroom on 65th Street, in the heart of South-Central Los Angeles.

Olivia remembers playing softball on the block with another little girl, LaRonda Jones, who became her best friend and who will attend Santa Monica Community College next year. She also remembers how scared she was at night.

"I would lie in bed and hear the police helicopters overhead," she said.

Her four sisters and two brothers are all high school graduates. Except for 22-year-old Tracy, who is home with a 2-year-old daughter, they are all working. Shirley has a job in a school cafeteria. Cynthia is a mail carrier. Jacqueline is a cashier at Dodger Stadium. William is a custodian at police headquarters. Masad drives a school bus. Olivia visited Disneyland once, when she was 8. Jacqueline took her.

Mrs. Miles said she had never been there. Admission is $28.75 for adults, $23 for children 3 to 11. "Disneyland's a little high for me," she said.

Olivia Miles is tall and slim and walks with her head held high. "My mama tells me: 'Be the best of everything; be proud, be black, be beautiful,'" she said.

Miss Miles knew some white people when her family lived briefly in Long Beach, but that was years ago. She says she wishes there were white students at her high school. "I want to learn about different cultures," she said. She believes a job at Disneyland will give her that chance.

Aubrey Miles, who is 45, says he has taken pains to tell his daughter that there are good white people. They saved his life, he told her. He was putting a roof on an office building seven years ago when a vat of hot tar exploded. He was severely burned.

"The guys on the job, who were white, helped me," he said. "I was on the ground, on fire. They put the fire out. One guy sat me up and put his back against my back. I could feel the connection. Then, afterward in the hospital, it was the same thing with the doctors."

Mr. Miles was speaking by telephone from Gautier, Miss. He and his wife moved there last year to care for Mrs. Miles's mother. Olivia remained in Los Angeles with her sister Shirley so she could graduate with her friends.

By last September, she and Mr. Sewell were already talking about the prom. It was set for May 1 in Long Beach. To save money for the big night, Mr. Sewell, whose father was recently laid off from his machinist's job at McDonnell-Douglas, worked as many hours at McDonald's as he could get.

Two days before the prom, Miss Miles still needed shoes. After school, she caught the bus to the Payless store at Crenshaw Plaza. It was April 29, the day the four policemen who beat Rodney G. King were acquitted.

"This lady on the bus told me, 'Baby, you better hurry up and get in the house,'" she said. "I said, 'Why what's going on?' She said, 'The verdict was not guilty.'"

Miss Miles bought her shoes—"two pairs for $24.99"—and went home. The prom was postponed because of the riots. Watching the images of fire and violence engulf her neighborhood on television, she wept. "It hurt me when they beat that man in the truck up," she said. "I didn't know people could be that mean."

Her parents kept telephoning. "I was asking my Daddy, 'Why did this happen, why are they doing this?'" Miss Miles said. "He told me some people were just using it as an excuse, and some people were hurt that those cops didn't get any time."

Mr. Miles said the acquittal shattered his daughter. "She was about to lose it," he said. "She kept saying: 'Why am I working so hard? Why have you been telling me that I can achieve?' She had been sheltered. This was reality."

Mr. Miles, who grew up in a segregated Louisiana, said he had agonized over how to comfort her. "I didn't want her to just use it to sit on the curb and say, 'I'm black so I can't achieve,'" he said. "I told her: 'Don't let this stop you. You're going to college. Keep going on, even though you will be met with discrimination.'"

"I was praying, and talking to her," he said. "I was worried. I'm still worried. The summer's not over. . . ."

His daughter plans to be a lawyer. So does Mr. Sewell.

The riots presented Olivia Miles with the biggest ethical quandary of her life. "I saw people on television coming out with boxes of shoes and pretty furniture," she said. Her smile was embarrassed. "It was like Christmas. I wanted to get some. I was asking my sister if we could go. She said, 'No, you can't go out.' I thought: 'She's going to go to work. Should I get it, or shouldn't I get it? It's not fair that I can't. Everyone else is going to get stuff.'"

This, too, her father had foreseen. "I told her, 'There are going to be a lot of opportunities for you to get things, so just stay in the house,'" Mr. Miles said. "She knew automatically that stealing was a no-no. . . ."

That Sunday, Olivia was in her regular pew at the Mt. Sinai Baptist Church. "The pastor was saying, 'If you took something, shame on you. That's a sin,'" she said. She looked relieved all over again. "I was so happy."

Three weeks later, she and Mr. Sewell went to the prom in Long Beach. "We loved it," Mr. Sewell said. "We loved it." He was surprised, he said, when his classmates voted him prom king.

"I felt like a queen," Miss Miles said. Last Friday, Disneyland telephoned: She got the job. This summer, she will be selling balloons and popcorn at the amusement park, about 30 miles from her home, that calls itself "the happiest place on earth."

The job, which includes transportation furnished by Disneyland, will also be hers on holidays during the year. The pay is $5.25 an hour.

Miss Miles had made herself familiar with Disneyland's grooming code. "Good-bye, nails," she said exuberantly, holding out her long, manicured ones. "A job's a job! Disneyland's Disneyland. It's not like Popeye's or McDonald's. It's like 'Hey, girl, how'd you get that job at Disneyland?'"[2]

2. WRITING ASSIGNMENT: ANALYZE THE RHETORICAL SITUATION

Read "Don't Know Much About History" and discuss the rhetorical situation for this essay. What is the exigence for this essay? That is, what happened that motivated the author to write it? What are some of the characteristics of the audience that the author probably had in mind while writing? What do you learn about the author? What are some of the possible constraints of the author? Of the audience? How would you describe the text itself? Describe the rhetorical situation for this essay in one to two pages.

Essay

DON'T KNOW MUCH ABOUT HISTORY

Roberta Israeloff

EAST NORTHPORT, L.I.   Though I vowed, on graduation from high school in 1969, that I was leaving the suburbs forever, I now live in a town that is just 20 minutes from the one I grew up in. For all its problems and faults, suburbia offered me a superior public education, and I wanted my sons to have one, too.

Yet no sooner did we enroll them than I began to have misgivings. Their work did not seem to engage them, to challenge them as much as I remembered being challenged. It wasn't until last month that I was able to confirm my suspicions.

My eighth grader brought home a research paper assignment for his American history course. Thirty-one years ago, I took a similar course—and I saved my papers. Comparing the two assignments left no doubt: the older assignment was vastly superior.

---

[2] *New York Times*, June 18, 1992, Sec. A, pp. 1, 12. See Chapter 7, pp. 212–213 for additional analysis of this essay.

Back in 1965, we were given this quotation—from a turn-of-the-century commentator named Lloyd, in a book called "William Jennings Bryan and the Campaign of 1896"—and asked to agree or disagree with it:

"The Free Silver movement is a fake. Free Silver is the cow-bird of the reform movement. It waited until the nest had been built by the sacrifices and labour of others, and then laid its eggs in it. . . . The People's Party has been betrayed. No party that does not lead its leaders will ever succeed."

It took mind-splitting work just to decipher the quotation. And then, to fulfill the assignment, my classmates and I had to explore and understand three distinct phenomena. First, we had to digest gold and silver monetary standards. We had to research the reform movement, tracing the evolution of the People's Party from its origins. We had to sift through the politics of 1896, in which the Populists had to decide whether to field their own candidate and risk losing the election, or join the Democrats and risk annihilation.

After all this, we still had to figure out for which cause Lloyd was the mouthpiece. The passage, I finally realized, was an attempt to rally the Populists to take their own course—advice not taken. They nominated Bryan, who lost to William McKinley, thereby destroying the People's Party.

I concluded by urging Lloyd to grow up. The point is to have your issue prevail even if your party doesn't. The People's Party may have fallen on its sword, but it did so in a good cause.

In their assignment, my son and his classmates had to answer three questions. To the first, "Did we have to drop the bomb on Japan?," my son argued that Harry S. Truman, as well as many others, had no idea of the full devastation the atomic bomb would cause. On the second, whether it hastened a Japanese surrender, he equivocated. To the final question—"Is it fair to use the knowledge we have in 1996 to judge decisions made nearly 50 years ago?"—he wrote, "The simple answer is no."

We both received the same grade on our papers—100.

I do not intend to disparage my son, who has always been a highly conceptual thinker and an A student, or to exalt myself, for I was not alone in my high grade. But I think these two assignments illustrate a profound diminution of educational expectations.

When my classmates and I fulfilled our assignment, we couldn't help but learn that the world was much more complex than we could imagine; that we had to absorb reams of information before staking claim to an opinion; that objective "information" existed only within a context and issued from a point of view, both of which had to be fully understood.

From my son's paper, I see no evidence that he has absorbed any of these lessons. The newer assignment—three straightforward questions positing three answers—is premised on the modern view that we are all entitled to an opinion, no matter how little we may know.

To be honest, the ins and outs of the election of 1896 have not stayed with me. What has endured is the value I place on scholarship, argument and critical thinking. My teacher's high hopes for us, which at the time seemed far too ambitious to be fair, became the scaffolding upon which we built our careers and the ways we define ourselves.

As for my son and his classmates—the class of 2000—I'm not as hopeful. We expect terrifyingly little of today's students, and they are responding in kind.[3]

3. CLASS PROJECT: CREATE A COMPOSITE OF THE CLASS'S READING PROCESS

When all class members contribute their usual strategies to a composite reading process, the result is usually a very complete description of a possible reading process. Focus on developing a process for "Reading Argument," and write that title on the board. Under the title write the four headings *prereading, reading, reading difficult material,* and *postreading.* Class members should contribute both the strategies they use and those they would like to use to each of the four lists. When the activity is completed, students may freewrite for a few minutes on the reading process that they intend to use to read argument. Freewriting is described on page 99.

4. GROUP WORK: PRACTICE THE READING PROCESS

Read "The Road to Unreality," on page 86, practicing the active reading strategies described in this chapter. The strategies are listed below to help you remember and apply them. Do all of the prereading strategies together as a class. Then everyone should read, underline, and annotate the essay. Next, divide the class into five groups. Each group should select one of the reading strategies and one of the postreading strategies. Also, each group should appoint a scribe who takes notes on the group work and then reports to the class. Finally, discuss which strategies seemed to work best and which you personally might consider adding to your present reading process from time to time.

Active Reading Strategies

Prereading
1. Read the title and the first two to three paragraphs and identify the issue.
2. What background do you have on this issue?
3. Do you need to learn more before you begin reading?
4. Survey the essay (read the title, introduction, summary or conclusion, and the first sentence of each paragraph; identify key words). What have you learned?
5. What is your present position on the issue?
6. Predict one or two ideas in the essay.
7. Anticipate one question you think may be answered in the essay.

Reading
1. Find and label the introduction, body and conclusion. What information is in each of these parts?
2. Identify the claim, subclaims, support, and transitions.

---

[3] *New York Times*, June 15, 1996, Sec. A, p. 11.

3. Identify key words that represent the major concepts and try to define them from context.
4. Analyze the rhetorical situation.
5. Analyze the common ground between your group and the author.

Postreading

1. Monitor the group's comprehension. Recite the claim and a few of the ideas to each other without looking back. Check the accuracy of the class's predictions and decide whether or not the class's question was answered by the essay.
2. Write a group summary of the essay in a paragraph or in phrases, your choice.
3. Make a simple group outline and label the claim.
4. Make a group map of the ideas.
5. Write a group response. Include original examples, reactions, and ideas. Include an evaluation of whether or not the essay is convincing. Write some possible values of the essay for your group.

Essay

THE ROAD TO UNREALITY

Mark Slouka

In 1990, a reporter for the *New York Times*, following the famous case of a man accused of murdering his pregnant wife and then blaming the assault on an unknown black assailant, asked a neighbor of the couple for her thoughts on the tragedy. Do you accept his story? she was asked. Does it seem possible to you, knowing this man, that he made up the whole thing? "I don't know," the woman said, "I'm dying for the movie to come out so I can see how it ends.[1]

I don't think this woman was joking. Or being cynical. Or even evasive. I think she simply meant what she said. For her, a TV movie about the tragedy would tell her—more accurately than her own experience—what to believe. It would settle for her what was real. Less than a year later, the made-for-television movie "Good Night, Sweet Wife: A Murder in Boston" presumably did just that.

I bring up this episode for the light it sheds on an important cultural trend, a trend so pervasive as to be almost invisible: our growing separation from reality.[2] More and more of us, whether we realize it or not, accept the copy as the original. Increasingly removed from experience, overdependent on the representations of reality that come to us through television and the print media, we seem more and more willing to put our trust in intermediaries who "re-present" the world to us.

The problem with this is one of communication; intermediaries are notoriously unreliable. In the well-known children's game of telephone, a whispered message is passed along from person to person until it is garbled beyond recognition. If we think of that original message as truth, or reality, we stand today at the end of a long line of interpreters. It's a line that's been growing longer throughout the century. And now, accustomed to our place at the end of that line, we've begun to accept the fictions that reach us as the genuine article. This is not good news. For one thing, it threatens to make us stupid. For another, it makes us, collectively, gullible as children: we believe what we are told. Finally, it can make us dangerous.

When did we start accepting abstractions for the real thing? Most answers point roughly to the beginning of this century. Before 1900, daily life for the majority of individuals was agrarian, static, local—in other words, not that different from what it had been for centuries. The twentieth century, however, altered the pace and pattern of daily life forever. Within two generations, the old world (for better or worse) was gone. Its loss meant the loss of two things that had always grounded us: our place within an actual community and our connection to a particular physical landscape.[3]

What started us on the road to unreality? Though the catalog reads like a shopping list of many of the century's most dramatic trends—urbanization, consumerism, increasing mobility, loss of regionality, growing alienation from the landscape, and so on—technology, their common denominator, was the real force behind our journey toward abstraction.

A single example may make my point. As everyone knows, unreality increases with speed. Walking across a landscape at six miles an hour, we experience the particular reality of place: its smells, sounds, colors, textures, and so on. Driving at seventy miles an hour, the experience is very different. The car isolates us, distances us; the world beyond the windshield—whether desert mesa or rolling farmland—seems vaguely unreal. At supersonic speeds, the divorce is complete. A landscape at 30,000 feet is an abstraction, as unlike real life as a painting.

It's an unreality we've grown used to. Habit has dulled the strangeness of it. We're as comfortable with superhuman speed—and the level of abstraction it brings with it—as we are with, say, the telephone, which in a single stroke distanced us from a habit as old as our species: talking to one another face-to-face. We forget that initial users of the telephone (our grandmothers and grandfathers) found it nearly impossible to conceptualize another human being beyond the inanimate receiver; in order to communicate, they had to personify the receiver and speak *to* it, as to some mechanical pet, rather than *through* it to someone else. Today, that kind of instinctive attachment to physical reality seems quaint.

We've come a long way, very quickly. What surprises us now, increasingly, is the shock of the real: the nakedness of face-to-face communication, the rough force of the natural world. We can watch hours of nature programming, but place us in a forest or a meadow and we don't know quite what to do with ourselves. We look forward to hanging out at The Brick with Chris on *Northern Exposure* but dread running into our neighbor while putting out the trash. There has come to be something almost embarrassing about the unmediated event; the man or woman who takes out a musical instrument at a party and offers to play is likely to make everyone feel a bit awkward. It's so naked, somehow. We're more comfortable with its representation: Aerosmith on MTV, Isaac Stern or Eric Clapton on CD.

And now, as we close out the century, various computer technologies threaten to take our long journey from reality to its natural conclusion. They are to TV or videoconferencing what the Concorde is to the car. They have the capacity to make the partially synthetic environments we already inhabit complete—to remove us, once and for all, from reality.[4]

NOTES

1. Constance L. Hays, "Illusion and Tragedy Coexist After a Couple Dies," *New York Times*, 7 January 1990.
2. I am aware, of course, that the term *reality*, problematic since Plato, has lately become a political minefield. So as not to be misunderstood, then, let me be as clear as possible. I have no problem with those who argue that reality, like taste, is subjective—a product of one's race, gender, economic class, education, and so on. These qualifications strike me as good and true. At the same time, however, I believe that under the strata of subjectivity, of language and perspective, lies a bedrock of fact: neo-Nazis in Koln or California may define the Holocaust differently than I do, yet the historical *fact* stands firm. It is *this* kind of reality—immutable, empirical, neither historically nor culturally relative—that I refer to here.
3. The rapid acceleration of cultural change in the twentieth century, of course, is a historical truism. One of the most vivid documents recording this transformation in American culture (it originally appeared in 1929) is Robert S. and Helen M. Lynd, *Middletown: A Study in Contemporary American Culture* (New York: Harcourt Brace Jovanovich, 1959).

5. WRITING ASSIGNMENT: THE SUMMARY/RESPONSE PAPER

a. When you have finished reading the essay in Exercise 4, "The Road to Unreality" (p. 86), divide a piece of paper in half. On the top half write a summary of the essay. On the bottom half write your response to the essay. In your response you may show why you agree or disagree with the author, you may add additional examples, and/or you may describe other related ideas that the essay made you think about. Conclude what you finally think about the essay.

b. Read all of the essays related to one of the issue questions in "The Reader" and write summary/response papers on each of them.

c. Locate an article about "your issue" and write a summary/response paper on it.

6. GROUP WORK: CLASS MAPS

Some classes select an issue that all students will write about, others form groups around four or five issues that are selected by the groups, and some classes decide that each student will write on individual issues. Whether you are working with a group or alone, a map can often help you focus and clarify your issue, see its various aspects, and provide ideas for developing it.

---

[4] From Mark Slouka, *War of the Worlds* (New York: Basic Books, 1995) pp. 1–4.

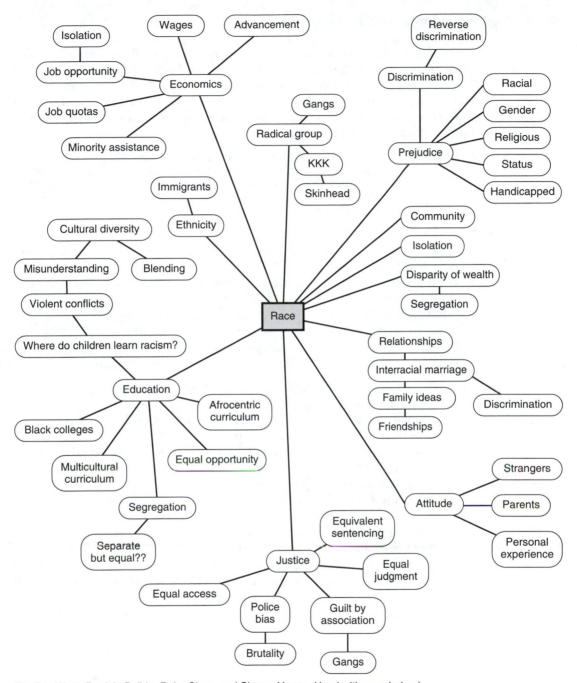

(By Eric West, Patricia Pulido, Ruby Chan, and Sharon Young. Used with permission.)

Figure 3.3 A Map That Answers the Question, What Are the Issues Related to Race? Use this map to discover specific related issues for paper topics.

To make a map, write the broad issue in a circle in the center of a page. Think of as many related aspects of that issue that you can and attach them to the broad issue. When you have completed the map, identify the aspect or aspects of the issue that interest you or your group. See if this aspect of the broad issue area can now be narrowed, expanded, or modified in some other way as a result of seeing it in this larger perspective.

> *Example:* Figure 3.3 is a map of the issue area *race* that was made by some of the students who test-read this book. They made this map after they had surveyed the articles about race in "The Reader." The map answers the question, What are the issues related to race?

7. QUESTIONS ON THE CHAPTER
a. What are some of the signs of a hidden argumentative purpose in an ostensibly objective essay?
b. What are the five elements in the rhetorical situation? Use TRACE to help you remember.
c. What are some prereading strategies that you will now want to use?
d. What are some reading strategies that you will now want to use?
e. What are some postreading strategies that you will now want to use?
f. What can you do when the material is difficult to understand?

8. QUESTIONS ON THE ESSAYS FOR ANALYSIS
a. "Jobs Illuminate What Riots Hid: Young Ideals," page 80. How does the description of "the kids" in South-Central Los Angeles in this essay contradict the usual stereotypes? What is the author trying to make you think about these young people? What new stereotypes are being developed? What do you think about these young people as a result of reading this essay? Have you modified any of your previous opinions?
b. "Don't Know Much About History," page 83. Agree or disagree with the author's statement, "We expect terrifyingly little of today's students, and they are responding in kind." Provide an example, just as the author did, to support your view.
c. "The Road to Unreality," page 86. Provide at least one example of your own to support the author's view that human beings are losing touch with reality and another example to support the opposing view. Do you, finally, agree or disagree with this author? Provide some reasons for your answer.

CHAPTER 4

A Process
for Writing Argument

This chapter will provide you with the expertise, confidence, and motivation that you will need to write arguments of your own on issues that are compellingly important to you. This chapter parallels Chapter 3, which covers the reading process, except that here the focus is on the writing process. First, you will be invited to analyze and describe your present individualistic writing process and adapt it for writing argument. Then, a possible process for writing argument will be laid out for your consideration. Next, you will think how you can incorporate elements of this process into your own present process while making it flexible and workable for you. Finally, you will practice the process by writing an exploratory paper in which you describe several perspectives on a single issue.

Chapter 3 introduced the concept that reading and writing should be integrated processes, and you were advised to write as part of your reading process. Writing while you read helps you understand a text better, and it helps you think beyond a text to develop ideas of your own. The "Read While You Write" box contains a corollary idea that can have a similarly powerful impact on the quality of your writing.

Read While You Write

You may at times "write" without thinking very much. That is, you find an idea, write something "off the top of your head," and turn it in, perhaps without even reading it yourself. Or you may try to write and find that you have nothing to say. One of the best ways to convert this blank writing to thoughtful writing is to read as part of your writing process. Reading while you write will provide you with background on your subject, new ideas to write about, fresh perspectives on your issue, and evidence and supporting details for your paper. It will at the same time suggest ways to solve writing problems as you read to understand how other writers have solved them.

You will usually adapt your writing process to the specific writing task at hand. When you are expected to write long, complicated papers that rely on research in outside sources, you will need a well-developed writing process composed of a variety of thinking and writing strategies. At other times you will need a less elaborate process for simpler papers. A writing process makes the most difficult writing tasks seem less difficult. It also helps you avoid procrastination and the discomforts of writer's block.

HOW DO YOU WRITE NOW?

You already have a writing process and, to make it useful for writing argument, you will need to adapt it to that purpose. Begin by thinking first about what you do when you write various other types of papers: lab reports, term papers, book reports, summaries of research, and so on.

What do you do . . .

- before you write the draft?
- while you are writing the draft?
- when you get stuck?
- when you finish writing the draft?

Many beginning college students, including those who test-read this book and who were asked to describe their writing processes during the first days of class, say they do nothing before they write unless the paper is long or difficult. They simply get some ideas, mentally organize them, and write the paper. When the paper is long or complicated, most students read, make some sort of outline, write what they can, read some more, and continue adding information until their paper is long enough to meet the requirements of the assignment.

Now change the focus of your writing process to describe how you would write argument.

What do you do . . .

- before you write the draft of an argument paper?
- while you are writing the draft of an argument paper?
- when you get stuck?
- when you finish writing the draft of an argument paper?

What can you add to your present process to improve your ability to write argument? One idea is to write at all stages of the process since writing helps you learn, and it also helps you think. Start writing ideas as soon as you begin thinking about your issue. Most people are especially creative and insightful during the early stages of a new writing project. Continue writing while you are thinking and gathering materials, organizing your ideas, and writing, rewriting, and revising your final copy. Notes and ideas on sheets of paper, on cards, and in notebooks are useful, as are lists, maps, various types of outlines, responses to re-search, drafts, and rewrites.

You must also be prepared to jot down ideas at any time during the process. Once your reading and thinking are under way, your subconscious mind takes over. At odd times you may suddenly see new connections or think of a new example, a new idea, a beginning sentence, or a good organizational sequence for the main ideas. Insights like these often come to writers when they first wake up. Plan to keep paper and pencil available so that you can take notes when good ideas occur to you.

HOW CAN YOU ORGANIZE A PROCESS FOR WRITING ARGUMENT?

The version of the writing process for argument explained in the following pages and summarized in Box 4.1 integrates reading and writing at every phase. Also, like the reading process in Chapter 3, the strategies are laid out here as prewriting, writing, strategies to use when you are stuck, and postwriting strategies. As you think about how you can adapt and use some of these ideas for writing argument, remember to keep the process flexible. That is, use your own present process, but add selected strategies as needed. It is unlikely that you will ever use all these strategies for one paper. Also, even though these strategies are explained here in an apparent order, you will not necessarily follow them in this order. You might write an entire section of your paper during the prewriting stage, or do some rewriting and revising while you are working on the initial draft. The strategies are not steps. They are suggestions to help you complete your paper. Integrate them with your present writing process and develop a way of writing argument papers that is uniquely yours.

The bare bones of the process can be stated simply. You need to

- select an issue, narrow it, take a tentative position, and write a claim
- do some reading and research
- create a structure
- write a draft
- revise and edit it

Prewriting Strategies

Prewriting is creative, and creativity is delicate to teach because it is individual. Still, like most writers, you will need directed prewriting strategies from time to time, either to help you get started on writing or to help you break through writer's blocks. Here are some suggestions to help you get organized, access what you already know, think about it, and plan what more you need to learn. You will not use all of these suggestions. Some, however, may become your favorite prewriting strategies.

A Writing Process for Argument

PREWRITING STRATEGIES

Get organized to write. Set up a place with materials. Get motivated.

Understand the writing assignment and schedule time. Break a complicated writing task into manageable parts and find the time to write.

Identify an issue and do some initial reading.

Analyze the rhetorical situation, particularly the exigence, the audience, and the constraints.

Focus on your issue and **freewrite.**

Brainstorm, make lists, map ideas.

Talk it through with a friend, your instructor, or members of a peer editing group.

Keep a journal, notebook, or folder of ideas.

Mentally visualize the major concepts.

Do some directed **reading and thinking.**

Use argument strategies.

Use reading strategies.

Use critical thinking prompts.

Plan and conduct **library research.**

Make an **expanded list or outline** to guide your writing.

Talk it through again.

WRITING STRATEGIES

Write the first draft. Get your ideas on paper so that you can work with them. Use your outline and notes to help you. Either write and rewrite as you go, or write the draft quickly with the knowledge that you can reread or rewrite later.

STRATEGIES TO USE WHEN YOU GET STUCK

Read more and **take more notes.**

Read your outline, rearrange parts, add more information to it.

Freewrite on the issue, **read some more,** and then **freewrite** some more.

Talk about your ideas with someone else.

Lower your expectations for your first draft. It does not have to be perfect at this point.

continued

BOX 4.1 A Summary of the Process for Writing Argument Explained in this Chapter.

POSTWRITING STRATEGIES

Read your draft critically, and also **have someone else read it.** Put it aside for 24 hours, if you can, to develop a better perspective for reading and improving.

Rewrite and revise. Make changes and additions until you think your paper is ready for other people to read. Move sections, cross out material, add other material, rephrase, as necessary.

Check your paper for final mechanical and spelling errors, **write the final title,** and **type or print it.**

BOX 4.1 A Summary of the Process for Writing Argument Explained in this Chapter. *(Continued)*

Get Organized to Write. Some people develop elaborate rituals like cleaning the house, sharpening the pencils, buying some special pens, putting on comfortable clothes, chewing a special flavor of gum, or making a cup of coffee to help them get ready to write. These rituals help them get their minds on the writing task, improve their motivation to write, and help them avoid procrastination and writer's block. A professional writer, describing what she does, says she takes a few moments before she writes to imagine her work as a completed and successful project. She visualizes it as finished, and she thinks about how she will feel at that time.[1]

Creating a place to write is an essential part of getting organized to write. A desk and a quiet place at home or in the library work best for most students. Still, if ideal conditions are not available, you can develop alternative places like a parked car on a quiet street, an empty classroom, the kitchen or dining room table, or a card table in an out-of-the-way corner of a room.

Writing projects usually require stacks of books and papers that, ideally, one can leave out and come back to at any time. If you cannot leave them out, however, use a folder, briefcase, or box to keep everything in one safe place. You can then quickly spread your work out again when it is time to write. You will need a system to keep these writing materials organized. You may have idea notes, research notes, lists and outlines, and drafts at various stages of completion to keep track of. Categorize this material, keep it in stacks, and arrange the material in each stack in the order in which you will probably use it.

Finally, make a decision about the writing equipment you will use. The major choices will be the computer, the typewriter, paper and pens or pencils, or some combination of these. Experiment with different methods and decide which is best for you. Most students prefer computers for the same reasons that many

---

[1]Barbara Neely, "Tools for the Part-Time Novelist," *The Writer,* June 1993, p. 17.

professional writers like them: writing is faster, and the copy is easier to read and revise. A disadvantage of computers is that some people write too much. They literally write everything that occurs to them, and some of it is undeveloped, poorly organized, or off the subject. If you tend to write too much, you can solve your problem by cutting ferociously when you revise.

Understand the Assignment and Schedule Time. You will need to analyze the writing assignment and find time to do it. Divide the assignment into small, manageable parts, assign a sufficient amount of time for each part, set deadlines for completing each part, and use the time when it becomes available. Below is an example.

Assignment. Write a five- to six-page, typed, double-spaced argument paper in which you identify an issue of your choice, take a position, make a claim, and support it so that it is convincing to an audience of your peers. Do as much reading as you need to do, but plan to draw material from at least five sources when you write your paper. Use MLA style (explained in Chapter 12) to document your sources and prepare your bibliography.

Analysis of Assignment

Week One

Read in "The Reader," get an issue, and write down some ideas.	2 hours Tuesday night.
Do some initial library research, including background reading, thinking, and note taking; write a first draft.	3 hours Thursday night.
Read the draft to a peer group in class and get ideas for additional research.	Friday's class.
Do research to fill in the needs of the first draft.	3 hours Saturday.

Week Two

Incorporate research and write a second draft.	3 hours Thursday night.
Read it to the peer editing group in class.	Friday's class.

Week Three

Rewrite, revise, and prepare final copy.	4 hours Tuesday night. Hand in on Wednesday.

Notice that the work on this paper has been spread out over two and a half weeks and that it is also broken down into manageable units. A student would be able to complete this paper successfully, on time, and without panic and discomfort if this schedule were followed. Notice that 15 hours have been set aside and protected for the various stages. The time is available even though the student may not need all of it. The student's focus should now be on finishing the paper as quickly as possible, and not on simply using all of this time.

Here is a professional writer who cautions about the importance of working to finish rather than working to put in time: "Don't set your goal as minutes or hours spent working; it's too easy to waste that time looking up one last fact, changing your margins, or, when desperate, searching for a new pen." Instead, she advises, set a realistic writing goal for each day and work until you complete it.[2] Another author advises that you avoid creating units of work that are so large or unmanageable that you won't want to do them, such as writing an entire paper in one day. It may sound good on the surface to write a whole paper in one day or one night, "but you'll soon feel overwhelmed," and "you'll start avoiding the work and won't get *anything* done." Remember, she says, "it's persistence that counts" in completing writing projects.[3]

Identify an Issue and Do Some Initial Reading. You may start with a broad issue area such as crime, education, health care, or tax reform. You will need to find a more narrow and specific issue within this broad area to write about, however. The map on page 89 shows one way to find more specific issues related to a broad issue area. Reading about your issue can also help you discover an aspect of an issue that you want to explore. When you have an issue you think you can work with, write it as a question and apply the twelve tests of an arguable issue that appear on page 26. You may also take a position on the issue and write a tentative claim. Additional information on how to write claims appears in Chapters 6 and 10.

Analyze the Rhetorical Situation. In Chapter 3 you learned to apply the elements of the rhetorical situation to help you read critically and analyze other authors' arguments. As a writer, you can now use the rhetorical situation to help you think critically and make decisions about your own writing.

All five elements of the rhetorical situation are important considerations for writers. Recall that three elements of the rhetorical situation are in place before you begin to write. They are the *exigence,* the *audience,* and the *constraints.* When you begin to write, two additional elements are added: you the *author,* and the *text* that you create. Figure 4.1 provides a diagram of these five elements to suggest some of the relationships among them.

Now consider the five elements from the writer's point of view:

Exigence. The exigence of the situation provides the motivation to write about the issue in the first place. Issues often emerge from real-life events that signal something is wrong. One student found a topic when a local jury appeared to

---

[2]Peggy Rynk, "Waiting for Inspiration," *The Writer,* September 1992, p. 10.
[3]Sue Grafton, "How to Find Time to Write When You Don't Have Time to Write," *The Writer's Handbook,* ed. Sylvia K. Burack (Boston: The Writer, 1991), p. 22.

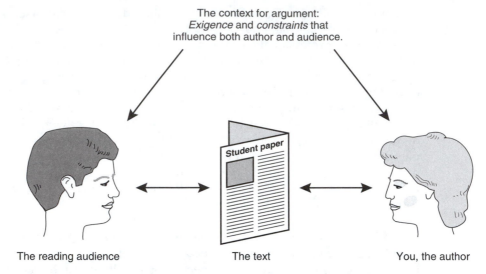

Figure 4.1 The Five Elements of the Rhetorical Situation That the Writer Considers While Planning and Writing Argument.

have made a mistake because it assigned probation to a murderer instead of prison time. Another student developed an exigence to write when she visited a national forest and discovered that acres and acres of trees had been cut down since the last time she was there. Yet another student discovered an exigence when he read a newspaper article about the assisted death of an old woman who was very ill, and he began to compare her situation with his grandmother's. Such occurrences can cause the writer to ask the questions associated with exigence: What issue is associated with each of these incidents? Are these new or recurring issues? Do they represent problems or defects? How and why?

Audience.   Now think about how potential reading audiences might regard the issues that emerge from these situations. Who are these people? Would they perceive these situations as problems or defects, as you do? Would they agree or disagree with you on the issues, or would they be neutral? What do they believe in? What are their values? Will you need to make a special effort with them to achieve common ground, or will you already share common ground? What audience outcomes can you anticipate? Will you be able to get the audience to agree and reach consensus, to take action, to agree on some points but not on others, or to agree to disagree? Or will they probably remain unconvinced and possibly even hostile?

Constraints.   Remember that constraints influence the ways in which both you and your audience think about the issues. What background, events, experiences, traditions, values, or associations are influencing both you and them? If you decide to write for an audience of lawyers to convince them to change the nature of jury trials, for instance, what are the constraints likely to be? How hard will it be to change the system? Or, if you are writing for forest service employees whose job it is to cut down trees, what constraints will you encounter with this group? If you are writing for a group of doctors who have been trained to preserve human life as long as possible, what constraints will you encounter with them? And how about you? What are your own constraints? How are your training, background, affiliations, and values either in harmony or in conflict with your audience? In other words, will your respective constraints drive you and your audience apart or will they bring you together and help you achieve common ground?

Author.   Other questions will help you think like an author of argument. Why am I interested in this issue? Why do I perceive it as a defect or problem? Is it a new or old issue for me? What is my personal background or experience with this issue? What makes me qualified to write about it? Which of my personal values are involved? How can I get more information? Refer to your direct experience if you have some. You may, for instance, be planning to go to law school, and you are interested in trial results, or you may have spent many happy childhood vacations camping in the forests, or maybe one of your relatives suffered many years before she died. Or you may have no direct experience, just an interest.

Text.   At this point, you can begin to plan your paper (the text). What strategies should you use? Should you employ Rogerian argument to build common ground? What types of support will work best? Should you state your claim right away or build up to it? What will your argumentative purpose be? What will your original approach or perspective be?

As you can see, the rhetorical situation can be employed to help you get ideas and plan, and you should actually keep it in mind throughout the writing process. It will be useful to you at every stage.

Focus and Freewrite.   Focus your attention, write a tentative title for your paper, and then freewrite for 10 or 15 minutes without stopping. Write about anything that occurs to you that is relevant to your title and your issue. Freewriting must be done quickly to capture the flow of thought. It may also be done sloppily, in incomplete sentences, with abbreviated words, even with errors.

Go back through your freewriting and find a phrase or sentence that you can turn into a claim. This freewriting is also your first partial manuscript. Later, you may use some or none of it in your paper. Its main value is to preserve the first creative ideas that flood your mind when you begin to work on a paper. Its other value is to focus and preserve your ideas so that they won't get lost when you later read the thoughts and opinions of others. If you start to freewrite and you find you do not have very many ideas, do some background reading in your issue area, and then try to freewrite again.

Brainstorm, Make Lists, Map Ideas.   Brainstorming is another way to get ideas down on paper in a hurry. The rules for brainstorming are to commit to a time limit, to write phrases only, to write quickly, and to make no judgments about what you or other members of a group are writing. Later you may go back to decide what is good or bad, useful or not useful. Brainstorming is like freewriting since it helps you get some ideas on paper quickly. It is also different from freewriting, since it usually produces only words and phrases, and it is often practiced as a group activity.

Listing is related to outlining. Insights may come at any time about how to divide a subject into parts, or how to set up three or four major headings for your paper. Write these ideas in list form. Or map your ideas to get a better sense of what they are and how they relate to each other (review Chapter 3, p. 78). You may also use a flowchart. Flowcharts are good for laying out processes or ideas and events that occur chronologically, over a period of time.

Talk It Through.   Many people find it easier to speak the first words than to write them. Typical audiences for an initial talk-through may include a peer editing group which is a small group of students in your class who will listen and read your paper at all stages; your instructor who, in conference, may ask a few questions and then just listen to you explore your ideas; or a writing center tutor who is trained to ask questions and then listen. Friends or family members can also become valued listeners. Some people like to tape-record the ideas they get from such sessions. Others prefer to end them with some rapid freewriting, listing, or brainstorming to preserve the good ideas that surfaced. If you do not tape-record or write, your good ideas may become lost forever. Security is writing your paper with a stack of notes and ideas already at hand and ready to use.

Keep a Journal, Notebook, or Folder of Ideas.   Instead of talking to others, some authors talk to themselves on a regular basis by writing in a journal or notebook or simply by writing on pieces of paper and sticking them in a folder. To help you gather material for an argument paper, you may clip articles, write summaries, and write out ideas and observations about your issue as they come to you. These materials will provide you with an excellent source of information for your paper when it is time to write it.

A professional writer describes this type of writing as a tool that helps one think. This author sets out some suggestions that could be particularly useful for the writer of argument:

Write quickly, so you don't know what's coming next.
Turn off the censor in your head.
Write from different points of view to broaden your sympathies.
Collect quotations that inspire you and jot down a few notes on why they do.
Write with a nonjudgmental friend in mind to listen to your angry or confused thoughts.
When words won't come, draw something—anything.
Don't worry about being nice, fair, or objective. Be selfish and biased; give your side of the story from the heart.

Write even what frightens you, *especially* what frightens you. It is the thought denied that is dangerous.

Don't worry about being consistent. You are large; you contain multitudes.[4]

You can write entire sections of material, ready to incorporate later into your paper. Or you can jot down phrases or examples to help you remember sudden insights. The object is to think and write on a regular basis while a paper is taking shape. Writing at all stages helps you discover what you know and learn about what you think.

Mentally Visualize. Create mental pictures related to your issue, and later describe what you see in your "mind's eye." For example, if you are writing about preserving forests, visualize them before any cutting has been done and then later after clear-cutting, which removes all trees in an area. Use these descriptions later in your paper to make your ideas more vivid and compelling.

Do Some Directed Reading and Thinking. Continue reading, thinking, and writing notes and ideas throughout the prewriting process. Read to get a sense of other people's perspectives on the issue and also to generate ideas of your own. As you read, you may find that you need to narrow and limit your issue even more, to one aspect or one approach. Try to think of an original perspective or "take" on the issue, a new way of looking at it. For example, the idea of "uncommon ground" and the personal example in "We're Good Republicans—and Pro-Choice" (p. 23), present an original approach to the abortion issue. As you continue reading and thinking, clarify your position on the issue, decide on your argumentative purpose (Chapters 6 and 10 will help), and revise your claim if you need to. When you have written your claim, write the word "because" and list some reasons. Or list some reasons and write the word "therefore," followed by your claim. This will help you decide, at least for now, whether your paper would be stronger with the claim at the beginning or at the end. Decide which words in your claim will need defining in your paper.

Use Argument Strategies. You will learn more about these in future chapters. The Toulmin model (Chapter 5) will help you plan the essential parts of your paper. Later, when you are revising, you can employ the Toulmin model to read and check the effectiveness of your argument. The claim questions in Chapter 6 will help you discover and write claims to focus your purpose for argument. The list of proofs from Chapter 7 will provide you with a variety of ways to develop your paper.

Use Reading Strategies. Use what you know about analyzing the organization of other authors' essays to help you organize your own paper. For exam-

---

[4]Marjorie Pellegrino, "Keeping a Writer's Journal," *The Writer,* June 1992, p. 27.

ple, you can plan an introduction, main body, and conclusion. You can make an outline composed of a claim, subclaims, support, and transitions. You can write a simplified outline to help you visualize the structure of your paper. When you have finished your draft, you can try to summarize it to test its unity and completeness. Or you can survey it. If you have problems with summarizing or surveying, you will probably need to revise more. Much of what you learned about reading in Chapter 3 can now be used not only to help you write argument of your own but also to read and evaluate it.

Use Critical Thinking Prompts.   You can get additional insight and ideas about your issue by using some well-established lines of thought that stimulate critical thinking. The "Critical Thinking Prompts" list provides some prompts that will cause you to think in a variety of ways. First, write out your issue, and then write your responses. You will be pleased by the quantity of new information these questions will generate for your paper.

Plan and Conduct Library Research.   To help you plan your research tasks, make a brief list or outline of the main sections of your paper. This list will help guide your research. Research takes a lot of time, and you will want to read only the materials in the library that are most relevant to the items on your research outline. Read and take notes on the materials you locate and relate them to your outline. Search for additional materials to fill in places on the outline where you need more information.

Make an Extended List or Outline to Guide Your Writing.   A written outline helps many people see the organization of ideas before they begin to write. Other people seem to be able to make a list or even work from a mental outline. Still others "just write" and move ideas around later to create order. There is, however, an implicit outline in most good writing. The outline is often referred to metaphorically as the skeleton or bare bones of the paper because it provides the internal structure that holds the paper together. An outline can be simple, a list of words written on a piece of scrap paper, or it can be elaborate, with essentially all major ideas, supporting details, major transitions, and even some of the sections written out in full. Some outlines actually end up looking like partial, sketchy manuscripts.

If you have never made outlines, try making one. Outlining requires intensive thinking and decision making. When it is finished, however, you will be able to turn your full attention to writing, and you will never have to stop to figure out what to write about next. Your outline will tell you what to do, and it will ultimately save you time and reduce much of the difficulty and frustration you would experience without it.

Talk It Through Again.   When you have completed your outline and are fairly satisfied with it, you can sharpen and improve it even more by reading it aloud and explaining its rationale to some good listeners. It is more and more

Critical Thinking Prompts

Use some, but not all of these each time.

1. **Associate it.** Consider other, related issues, big issues, or enduring issues. Also associate your issue with familiar subjects and ideas.
2. **Describe it.** Use detail. Make the description visual if you can.
3. **Compare it.** Think about items in the same or different categories. Compare it with things you know or understand well. Compare what you used to think about the issue and what you think now. Give reasons for your change of mind.
4. **Apply it.** Show practical uses or applications. Show how it can be used in a specific setting.
5. **Divide it.** Get insight into your issue by dividing it into related issues or into parts of the issue.
6. **Agree and disagree with it.** Identify the extreme pro and con positions and reasons for holding them. List other approaches and perspectives. Say why each position, including your own, might be plausible and in what circumstances.
7. **Consider it as it is, right now.** Think about your issue as it exists, right now, in contemporary time. What is its nature? What are its special characteristics?
8. **Consider it over a period of time.** Think about it in the past and how it might present itself in the future. Does it change? How? Why?
9. **Decide what it is a part of.** Put it in a larger category and consider the insights you gain as a result.
10. **Analyze it.** Break it into parts and get insight into each of its parts.
11. **Synthesize it.** Put it back together in new ways so that the new whole is different, and perhaps clearer and better, than the old whole.
12. **Evaluate it.** Decide whether it is good or bad, valuable or not valuable, moral or immoral. Give evidence to support your evaluation.
13. **Elaborate on it.** Add and continue to add explanation until you can understand it more easily. Give some examples to provide further elaboration.
14. **Project and predict.** Answer the question, "What would happen if …?" Think about further possibilities.
15. **Ask why, and keep on asking why.** Examine every aspect of your issue by asking why.

common to organize peer editing groups in writing classes to give students the opportunity to talk through outlines and to read drafts to fellow students who then act as critics who make recommendations for improvement. Reading and talking about your outline in the early stages helps clarify ideas, and it is easier to write about them later. At this stage, your student critics should explain to you what is clear and unclear and also what is convincing and not convincing.

Writing Strategies

Write the First Draft.   The objective of writing the first draft is to get your ideas in some kind of written form so that you can see them and work with them. Here is how a professional writer explains the drafting process:

> Writing a first draft should be easy because, in a sense, you can't get it wrong. You are bringing something completely new and strange into the world, something that did not exist before. You have nothing to prove in the first draft, nothing to defend, everything to imagine. And the first draft is yours alone, no one else sees it. You are not writing for an audience. Not yet. You write the draft in order to read what you have written and to determine what you still have to say.[5]

This author advises further that you "not even consider technical problems at this early stage." Nor should you "let your critical self sit at your desk with your creative self. The critic will stifle the writer within." The purpose, he says, is "not to get it right, but to get it written."[6]

Here is another writer, Stephen King, who advises putting aside reference books and dictionaries when concentrating on writing the first draft:

> Put away your dictionary. . . . You think you might have misspelled a word? O.K., so here is your choice: either look it up in the dictionary, thereby making sure you have it right—and breaking your train of thought and the writer's trance in the bargain—or just spell it phonetically and correct it later. Why not? Did you think it was going to go somewhere? And if you need to know the largest city in Brazil and you find you don't have it in your head, why not write in Miami or Cleveland? You can check it . . . but *later.* When you sit down to write, *write.* Don't do anything else except go to the bathroom, and only do that it if absolutely cannot be put off.[7]

You will be able to follow this advice if your outline and notes are available to guide you and keep you on track. If you occasionally get stuck, you can write some phrases, freewrite, or even skip a section that you cannot easily put into words. You will have another chance at your draft later. Right now, work only to capture the flow of ideas that is on the outline. You will discover, as you write, that many of the ideas that were only half formed on your outline will now become clear and complete as you get insight from writing.

---

[5]John Dufresne, "That Crucial First Draft," *The Writer,* October 1992, p. 9.

[6]Ibid., pp. 10–11.

[7]Stephen King, "Everything You Need to Know about Writing Successfully—in Ten Minutes," *The Writer's Handbook,* ed. Sylvia K. Burack (Boston: The Writer, 1991), pp. 30–31.

Use Special Strategies If You Get Stuck. Everyone suffers from writer's block from time to time, and there are a number of ways to get going again if you get stuck while writing your first draft. Many people read and take more notes at times like this. Since reading will make you think, you should write out all of the ideas and insights that come to you as you read. Soon you will have plenty of new material to add to your paper. You can also go back and reread your outline, lists, and other idea notes, rearrange them into new combinations, and add more information to them.

If you are so blocked that you simply cannot make yourself write the next words, try freewriting, that is simply writing fast in phrases or sentences on your topic. Then read some more, and follow that with additional freewriting. You may end up with a lot of material that doesn't make much sense and with a lot of unrelated bits and sentence fragments. You can go back through it later, however, cross out what you can't use, change phrases to sentences, add material in other places, and you will soon find that you are started again. Getting words on the page in any form is what it takes for some writers to break out of a block.

It is also extremely useful to talk about your ideas for your paper with someone else to get fresh insights and solve some of your writing problems. Or ask someone else to read a draft of your paper and to write some comments on it. This will provide you with fresh insights and ideas to get you moving again. Finally, give yourself permission to write a less than perfect first draft. You can paralyze yourself by trying to produce a finished draft on the first try. Lower your expectations for the first draft and remind yourself that you can always go back later and fix it.

Postwriting Strategies

Read Your Draft Critically and Submit It for Peer Review. When you can, put your draft aside for 24 hours, read it critically, and make all of the changes you can to improve it. It helps to read the paper aloud at this point to get an even better perspective on what can be improved. Then you can seek the opinion of other students once more in a class peer review session. The usual procedure for a peer editing session on a draft is to read the paper aloud to the group, or to do a round-robin reading session, where group members read all of the papers silently and make some notes before they discuss them one by one.

Peer groups make the writing task more sociable and provide you with immediate reactions from a real audience. They also help you become a more sensitive critic both of your own and of others' work. Most professional writers rely heavily upon other people's opinions at various stages of writing. Look at the prefaces of some of the books you are using this semester. Most authors acknowledge the help of several people who read their manuscript and made suggestions for improvement. Many individuals recommended improvements for this book. Some of these people were teachers, some were editors, some were friends and family members, some were colleagues, and many were students. The students who test-read this book have already been described. They wrote many good suggestions for improvement. In fact, these students were responsible for several of the major changes and special features in the book that make it easier to read and use. One student commented that she liked being a part of the writing process for this textbook because it helped her read her other textbooks more critically. If peer review groups are not part of your writing class, try to find someone else to read your draft. You need someone to make suggestions and give you ideas for improvement.

Rewrite and Revise.   Working with a rough draft is easier than outlining or drafting. It is, in fact, creative and fun to revise because you begin to see your work take shape and become readable. Skillfully revised material, incidentally, makes a good impression on the reader. It is worthwhile to finish your draft early enough so that you will have several hours to read and revise before you submit it in its final form to a reader.

Most writers have some ideas and rules about writing that come to their aid, from an inner voice, when it is time to revise. Listen to your inner voice so that you will know what to look for and what to change. If you do not have a strongly developed inner voice, you can strengthen it by learning to ask the following questions. Notice that these questions direct your attention to global revisions for improved clarity and organization, as well as to surface revisions for details.

1. **Is it clear?**   If you cannot understand your own writing, other people won't be able to, either. Be very critical of your own understanding as you read your draft. Make your writing clearer by establishing some key terms and using them throughout. Add transitions as well. Use those that are associated with the organizational patterns you have used. There is more information about these in Chapter 12. Or write a transitional paragraph to summarize one major part of your paper and introduce the next. If you stumble over a bad sentence, begin again and rewrite it in a new way. There are a dozen possible ways to write one sentence. Also, change all words that do not clearly communicate to you exactly what you want to say. This is no time to risk using words from the thesaurus that you are not sure about. Finally, apply this test: Can you state the claim or the main point of your paper and list the parts that develop it? Take a good look at these parts and rearrange them if necessary.

2. **What should I add?**   Sometimes in writing the first draft you will write such a sketchy version of an idea that it does not explain what you want to say. Add fuller explanations and examples, or do some extra research to improve the skimpy parts of your paper.

3. **What should I cut?**   Extra words, repeated ideas, and unnecessary material find their way into a typical first draft. Every writer cuts during revision. Stephen King, who made $7,000,000 in one year as a professional writer, describes how he learned to cut the extra words. His teacher was the newspaper editor John Gould who dealt with his first feature article as follows:

He started in on the feature piece with a large black pen and taught me all I ever needed to know about my craft. I wish I still had the piece—it deserves to be framed, editorial corrections and all—but I can remember pretty well how it looked when he had finished with it. Here's an example:

Last night, in the ~~well-loved~~
gymnasium ~~of~~ |Lisbon High School|, partisans
and Jay Hills fans alike were stunned by
an athletic performance unequalled in school
history: Bob Ransom, ~~known as "Bullet" Bob~~
~~for both his size and accuracy~~, scored
thirty-seven points. He did it with grace
and speed...and he did it with an odd courtesy
as well, committing only two personal fouls
in his ~~knight-like~~ quest for a record which
is basketball team
has eluded Lisbon ~~thinclads~~ since 1953...

When Gould finished marking up my copy in the manner I have indicated above, he looked up and must have seen something on my face. I think *he* must have thought it was horror, but it was not: it was revelation.

"I only took out the bad parts, you know," he said. "Most of it's pretty good."

"I know," I said, meaning both things: yes, most of it was good, and yes, he had only taken out the bad parts. "I won't do it again."

"If that's true," he said, "you'll never have to work again. You can do *this* for a living." Then he threw back his head and laughed.

And he was right: I *am* doing this for a living, and as long as I can keep on, I don't expect ever to have to work again.[8]

4. **Are the language and style consistent and appropriate throughout?** Edit out all words that create a conversational or informal tone in your paper. For example,

Change: And as for target shooting, well go purchase a BB gun or a set of darts.[9]

To read: A BB gun or set of darts serve as well for target shooting as a handgun.

---

[8]King., pp. 30–31.
[9]From a student paper by Blake Decker. Used with permission.

Also, edit out all cheerleading, slogans, clichés, needless repetition, and exhortations. You are not writing a political speech. For example,

Change: Violence! Why should we put up with it? Violence breeds violence, they say. America would be a better place if there were less violence.

To Read: Violent crime has begun to take over the United States, affecting everyone's life. Every day another story of tragedy unfolds where a man, a woman, or a child is senselessly killed by someone with a gun. Under the tremendous stress of this modern society, tempers flare at the drop of a hat, and people reach for a gun that was bought only for defense or safety. Then they make rash, deadly decisions.[10]

You will learn more about language and style in Chapter 7. In general, use formal, rational style in an argument paper unless you have a good reason to do otherwise. Use emotional language and examples that arouse feelings only where appropriate to back up logical argument.

5. **Is there enough variety?**   Use some variety in the way you write sentences by beginning some with clauses and others with a subject or even a verb. Vary the length of your sentences as well. Try to write not only simple sentences, but also compound and complex sentences. You can also vary the length of your paragraphs. The general rule is to begin a new paragraph every time you change the subject. Variety in sentences and paragraphs makes your writing more interesting to read. Do not sacrifice clarity for variety, however, by writing odd or unclear sentences.

6. **Have I used the active voice most of the time?**   The active voice is more direct, energetic, and interesting than the passive voice. Try to use it most of the time. Here is a sentence written in the active voice; it starts with the subject:

Virtual reality is an exciting new technology that will enhance nearly every aspect of our lives.[11]

Notice how it loses it directness and punch when it is written in the passive voice:

Nearly every aspect of our lives will be enhanced by virtual reality, an exciting new technology.

7. **Have I avoided sexist language?**   Try to avoid referring to all people in your paper as though they were either all male or all female. You can create as big a problem, however, by referring to everyone as "he or she" or "himself or herself." One way to solve this problem is to use plural pronouns, *they* or *them*, or occasionally rewrite a sentence in the passive voice. It is better to write, "The

---

[10]Decker.

[11]From a student essay by Greg Mathios. Used with permission.

pressure-sensitive glove is used in virtual reality," than to write, "He or she puts on a pressure-sensitive glove to enter the world of virtual reality."

8. **Have I followed the rules?** Learn the rules for grammar, usage, and punctuation, and follow them. No one can read a paper that is full of errors of this type. Make the following rules a part of that inner voice that guides your revision, and you will avoid the most common errors made by student writers:

- Write similar items in a *series,* separated by commas, and finally connected by *and.* **Example:** "The National Rifle Association, firearms manufacturers, and common citizens are all interested in gun control."[12]
- Use *parallel construction* for longer, more complicated elements that have a similar function in the sentence. **Example:** "Parents who fear for their children's safety at school, passengers who ride on urban public transit systems, clerks who work at convenience stores and gas stations, and policemen who try to carry out their jobs safely are all affected by national policy on gun control."
- Keep everything in the same *tense* throughout. Use the present tense to introduce quotes. **Example:** "As Sherrill *states,* 'The United States is said to be the greatest gun-toting nation in the world.' Millions of guns create problems in this country."
- Observe *sentence boundaries.* Start sentences with a capital letter and end them with a period or question mark. Make certain they express complete thoughts.
- Make *subjects agree with verbs.* **Example:** *"Restrictions* on gun control *interfere* [not *interferes*] with people's rights."
- Use *clear and appropriate pronoun referents.* **Example:** "The *group* is strongly in favor of gun control, and little is needed to convince *it* [not *them*] of the importance of this issue."
- Use commas to set off long initial clauses that are seven or more words long, to separate two independent clauses, to introduce quotes, and to separate words in a series. **Example:** "When one realizes that the authors of the Constitution could not look into the future and imagine current events, then one can see how irrational and irresponsible it is to believe that the right to bear arms should in these times still be considered a constitutional right, and, according to Smith, the groups that do so, 'are short-sighted, mistaken, and ignorant.'"

Check for final errors, add or adjust the title, type or print. Just before you submit your paper, check the spelling of every word you are not absolutely about. If spelling is a problem for you, buy a small spelling dictionary that contains only words and no meanings, or use the spell checker on the computer. If

---

[12]The examples in this list are drawn from a student paper by Blake Decker. I have revised his sentences for the sake of illustration.

you use a spell checker, you should still read your paper one last time since the computer might not find every error. At this point you should also correct all the typographical errors that remain and format your paper. Now either add a title or adjust your existing title if it needs it. Be sure that your title provides information about your paper that will help the reader understand what it is about.

Complete your revision process by reading your paper aloud one more time. Read slowly and listen. You will be surprised by the number of problems that bother your ears but that were not noticeable to your eyes. Your paper should be ready now to submit for evaluation. Either type it or print it out on a word processor.

PRACTICE THE PROCESS BY WRITING THE EXPLORATORY PAPER

In writing the exploratory paper,[13] the arguer identifies not just one opposing position, but as many of the major positions on an issue as possible, both past and present, and explains them through summaries and an analysis of the total rhetorical situation for the issue. The analysis of the rhetorical situation in these papers explains what caused the issue and what prompted past and present interest and concern with it, identifies who is interested in it and why, and examines the constraints of the inquiry and the various views in the ongoing conversation associated with it. The summaries of the positions not only explain each of the different perspectives on the issue, but also provide the usual reasons cited to establish the validity of each perspective. The writer's own opinions are not expressed at all, or are withheld until later in the paper.

There are a number of advantages of writing and reading exploratory papers. When writers and readers view an issue from many perspectives, they acquire a greater depth of understanding of it. They also acquire information and facts as well as opinion on all the various views. All these are beneficial because both the arguer and the reader become better educated and more fluent in their discussions of the issue. Exploratory papers also help establish common ground between writers and readers. Writers, by restating several opposing positions along with the usual reasons for accepting them, are forced to understand several opposing views. The reader is also interested because the exploratory paper explains all views, which usually includes the reader's as well. The reader feels that he or she has been heard and, consequently, is more willing to read and get information about the other positions on the issue. Exploratory papers provide the mutual understanding and common ground essential for the next stage in argument, the presentation of the writer's position and reasons for holding it. The ex-

---

[13]I am indebted to Professor James Kinneavy of the University of Texas at Austin for the basic notion of the exploratory paper.

ploratory paper thus paves the way for the writer to enter the conversation on an issue with a single-perspective argument.

Exploratory papers are a common genre in argumentative writing. You will encounter them in newspapers, news magazines, other popular magazines of opinion, and scholarly journals. They are easy to recognize because they take a broad view of an issue, and they explain multiple perspectives, instead of just one.

The following is an example of a short exploratory paper about single-sex classes in the public schools. The rhetorical situation, particularly the motivation for separating boys and girls into separate classes, is explained in the first paragraph. The author of this article then summarizes the different positions associated with this issue, including the reasons some schools give for separating the sexes, the arguments given by those who oppose this practice, and the requirements of federal law on the subject. Notice that the author does not take a side or express personal opinions directly. The reader gets a sense of the complexity of the issue and also of some new perspectives on it.

Essay

A ROOM OF THEIR OWN

LynNell Hancock and Claudia Kalb

What is the rhetorical situation?

Who can forget the pubescent pain of junior high? Boys sprout pimples, girls sprout attitude and both genders goad each other into a state of sexual confusion. Teachers in Manassas, Va., figured that all these colliding hormones were distracting students from their academic tasks. So officials at Marsteller Middle School decided to try something old: dividing girls and boys into separate academic classes. Eighth-grade girls say they prefer doing physics experiments without boys around to hog the equipment. Boys say they'd rather recite Shakespeare without girls around to make them feel "like geeks." An eerie return to the turn of the century, when boys and girls marched into public schools through separate doors? Yes, say education researchers. But will it work—and is it legal?

What is the position of the schools that have set up single-sex classes?

In districts across the country, public schools are experimenting with sexual segregation, in the name of school reform. There is no precise tally, in part because schools are wary of drawing attention to classes that may violate gender-bias laws. But, researchers say, in more than a dozen states—including Texas, Colorado, Michigan and Georgia—coed schools are creating single-sex classes. Some, like Marsteller, believe that separating the sexes will eliminate distractions. Others, like Robert Coleman Elementary in Baltimore, made the move primarily to get boys to work harder and tighten up discipline.

The great majority of the experiments are designed to boost girls' math and science scores. The stimulus for these efforts was a report four years ago from the American Association of University Women, which argued that girls were being shortchanged in public-school classrooms—particularly in math and science. The single-sex classroom, however, is not what the gender-equity researchers involved with AAUW had in mind as a remedy. Their report was meant to help improve coeducation, not dismantle it. Research shows single-sex schools tend to produce girls with more confidence and higher grades. But single-sex classrooms within coed schools? There are no long-term studies of that approach, only a smattering of skeptics and true believers. "It's a plan that misses two boats," charges David Sadker, coauthor of "Failing at Fairness"—the education of boys, and the reality that children need to learn how to cope in a coed world. In short, says University of Michigan researcher Valerie Lee, "these classes are a bogus answer to a complex problem."

What is the position of those who oppose single-sex classes?

Critics worry that segregated classes will set back the cause of gender equity just when girls are finally being integrated into all-male academics. Half a century ago, boys in advanced science classes learned, for example, that mold is used for penicillin while girls in home economics learned that mold is the gunk on the shower curtain. "It's not an era we're eager to return to," says Norma Cantu of the U.S. Office of Civil Rights.

What is the position of the federal law?

Miracles happen: As a general principle, federal law doesn't permit segregation by sex in the public schools. (Exceptions can be made for singing groups, contact sports and human-sexuality and remedial classes.) Some schools have survived legal challenges by claiming that their all-girl classes fill remedial needs. A middle school in Ventura, Calif., faced down a challenge by changing the name of its all-girl math class to Math PLUS (Power Learning for Underrepresented Students). Enrollment is open to boys, though none has registered yet.

What is the current trend?

Despite the skeptics, single-sex experiments continue to spread. Teachers and students believe they work. At the high school in Presque Isle, Maine, members of the popular all-girl algebra class go on to tackle the sciences. University of Maine professor Bonnie Wood found that girls who take the algebra course are twice as likely to enroll in advanced chemistry and college physics than their coed counterparts. Michigan's Rochester High School turns away 70 students every year from its girls-only science and engineering class. Marsteller boys raised their collective average in language arts by one grade after a single term. Girls boosted their science average by .4 of a point.

For the teachers involved, the progress is no mystery. Sheryl Quinlan, who teaches science at Marsteller, knows single-sex classes let her kids think with something besides their hormones. Impressing the opposite sex is a 14-year-old's reason for being. Take away that pressure, and miracles happen. Quinlan recalls the girl who took a "zero" on her oral report rather than deliver it in front of her boyfriend. Those days are over. Now, says Amanda Drobney, 14, "you can mess up in front of girls, and it's OK." We've come a long way, babies—or have we?[14]

> What is the authors' perspective as indicated in their final question?

Now, practice the process explained in this chapter by writing an exploratory paper of your own. Exercises at the end of this chapter will set up the assignment and help you complete it.

EXERCISES AND ACTIVITIES

1. **CLASS PROJECT: CREATE A COMPOSITE OF THE CLASS'S WRITING PROCESS**
   When all class members contribute their usual strategies to a composite writing process, the result is usually a very complete description of a possible writing process. Focus on developing a process for "Writing Argument," and write that title on the board. Under the title write the four headings *prewriting, writing, writing when you get stuck,* and *rewriting.* Class members should contribute both the strategies they use and those they would like to use to each of the four lists. When the activity is completed, students may freewrite for a few minutes on the writing process they intend to use to write argument.

2. **CLASS DISCUSSION: FINDING A FRESH PERSPECTIVE ON AN ISSUE**
   One of the purposes of an exploratory paper is to find a new way of looking at an issue, or a novel approach to it. It is often easy enough to identify the usual pro and con, yes or no positions on an issue. It takes some imagination and creative thinking to come up with new approaches that help people rethink their present positions.

   Read the following essay by John Paulos. Paulos is a mathematician who claims that a mathematical approach to issues can sometimes provide new perspectives on them. Identify the two issues he examines and the fresh approaches that he proposes.

   Now turn to the Table of Contents for "The Reader" and select one of the issue questions there. Identify the usual pro and con positions and then think of some other, novel approaches and positions on the issue that you might be able to argue in favor of.

---

[14]*Newsweek,* June 24, 1996, p. 76.

ABORTION ACTIVISTS BOMB CLINIC
Prohibitions and Arithmetical Arguments

John Allen Paulos

Controversial issues like gun control often lead powerful organizations to take inflexible positions, making it very difficult for novel approaches and arguments to be heard. Since they want to be valued by the group, members freely express opinions in line with what they perceive to be the group's attitudes and tend to suppress those that run counter to those of the group. A prejudicial breeze soon develops and brings with it leaders who are more extreme than the average member. One simpleminded way to resist such constriction of options is to put forward as many positions and arguments as one can in the hope of freeing discussion and allowing a middle ground to form. Because they tend to be abstract, arithmetical arguments are well suited to this purpose.

Thus, when I read of implacable opponents of abortion who terrorize women and doctors at abortion clinics, for example, I sometimes try to imagine scenarios that would undermine the belief of *some* of them in the absolute inviolability of the fetus's right to life. Pro-life groups sometimes employ extreme arguments in their verbal skirmishes with pro-choice groups (and vice versa). If an abortion at three months is okay, why not one at six? And if one at six months is acceptable, why not kill infants, or the very old for that matter? Again, such arguments have their place if they induce a fresh rethinking of positions. A brief sketch of one from a pro-choice perspective follows, in the form of an imaginary news story:

> Myrtle Jones, president of the pro-choice group Sense Not Sin, wondered at a rally yesterday what position abortion opponents might take if two facts about the world were to change. Ms. Jones asked her listeners to make two assumptions. The first is that, for some indeterminate reason—a virus, a hole in the ozone layer, some food additive or poison—women regularly become pregnant with thirty to fifty fetuses at a time. The second is that advances in neonatal technology make it possible to save easily some or all of these fetuses a few months after conception, but nonintervention at this time leads to the death of all the fetuses.
>
> Opponents of abortion who believe that all fetuses have an absolute right to life would presumably opt for intervention, argued Ms. Jones. Their choice would thus be either to adhere to their position and be overwhelmed by a population explosion of unprecedented magnitude or else to act to save only one or a few of the fetuses. The latter choice would, Ms. Jones stressed, be tantamount to abortion, since all the fetuses are viable: "It would, nevertheless, take someone quite doctrinaire to opt to have the birthrate increase, at least initially, by a factor of thirty to fifty."

This is obviously not a knock-down airtight argument (although delivered to the right audience, it might result in knock-downs). Since it might be described as coming from a leftish direction (assuming the idea of a political spectrum has any validity), let me offer a more rightish example of a harmful narrowing of the terms of debate. The offender is a segment of the antismoking movement. More than 400,000 Americans die annually from the effects of smoking, but there is some intriguing evidence that the number could be drastically reduced by the widespread use of smokeless chewing tobacco. Professors Brad Radu and Philip Cole recently published a note in *Nature* in which they claimed that the average life expectancy for a thirty-five-year-old smokeless tobacco user would be fifteen days shorter than that for a thirty-five-year-old nonsmoker. This is in contrast to 7.8 years lost by smokers. The authors estimate that a wholesale switch to smokeless tobacco would result in a 98 percent reduction in tobacco-related deaths.

Since a small amount of tobacco lasts all day, tobacco companies would likely oppose smokeless chewing tobacco. There has already been strong opposition to it from *some* antismoking groups because of an increase in the risk of oral cancer (which is much rarer than lung cancer, emphysema, and heart disease). I suspect that another reason is a certain misguided sense of moral purity—not unlike opposing the use of condoms because, unlike abstinence, they're not 100 percent effective. If the numbers presented here are confirmed, however, recommending a switch to smokeless tobacco for those smokers (and only those) who can't quit would seem like sound public policy.

Including such bits of unconventional, arithmetically flavored reporting more often would make newspaper coverage of abortion, smoking, and other contentious issues less tiresome and might even kindle a more thoughtful response to them. There is almost always a greater variety of positions on any issue than ever make it into newsprint.[15]

3. WRITING ASSIGNMENT: THE EXPLORATORY PAPER 1, EXPLORE AN ISSUE IN "THE READER."

Examine the Table of Contents for "The Reader" and select an issue question that is interesting to the class (or your group). Read the essays about it and take some notes on the various positions expressed in these essays. Now plan an exploratory paper by discussing the following questions. Take some notes on the discussion to help you write your paper later.

a. Describe the rhetorical situation for the issue. What has caused an interest in this issue in the first place? Who is interested and why? What are some of the constraints for the authors of the essays? For you?

b. Explain the different perspectives on the issue that emerge from the essays.

c. Map these perspectives and add some of your own. Write the issue question in the middle of a page (or on the board) and draw a circle around it. Write the specific perspectives identified in the essays and attach them to the circle (an example of a map appears on p. 78). Add original perspectives of your own and attach them as well. Use some of the critical thinking prompts on p. 103 to help you find other original perspectives. These prompts are effective prewriting strategies for exploratory papers.

---

[15]From John Allen Paulos, *A Mathematician Reads the Newspaper* (New York: Basic Books, 1995), pp. 69–71.

d. As an alternative to mapping, write brief summaries of the perspectives in the essays and also of the original perspectives that you and your classmates identify.

e. You now have the materials to write an exploratory paper. Here is the assignment:

1. Make a brief outline or list to organize at least three to five perspectives on the issue. Place them in the order in which you will present them.

2. Write a three-page paper in which you
   • explain the issue and the rhetorical situation;
   • summarize the various perspectives and positions on the issue;
   • state your position on the issue and indicate briefly why you hold it.

Use "A Room of Their Own" on p. 111 as a model to help you organize and write your paper.

4. **WRITING ASSIGNMENT: EXPLORATORY PAPER 2, EXPLORE YOUR ISSUE AND TAKE A POSITION FOR A FUTURE ARGUMENT PAPER**
Exploratory papers pave the way for position papers (taught in chapters 5 to 7 and 10 to 12). In position papers you take a position on an issue and defend it. An exploratory paper helps you find your position, understand others' positions, and even form rebuttals or counterarguments. Here is the assignment for an exploratory paper that is written as a preliminary exercise for a position paper.

a. Examine the Table of Contents for "The Reader" and select an issue question that is interesting to you. Read the set of essays that develop it. The essays in "The Reader" have been selected to represent a variety of perspectives on each issue question. Take some notes on the various perspectives you encounter. Do additional library research if you need to. Pages 354 to 364 in Chapter 11 will help you with library research.

   As an alternative, select your own issue, locate several articles or other sources of information about it, and examine them for different perspectives. You may want to select a campus issue, an issue from another class, an issue from home or work, or a public issue not represented in "The Reader." Take some notes.

   Think about the perspective on the issue that you may want to develop yourself in a later position paper.

b. Make certain you can identify and summarize at last three different perspectives on your issue: Examples: perspectives that are for, against, and in the middle; perspectives that represent three possible causes for a problematic situation; or perspectives that describe three possible solutions to a problem. You may add to these perspectives with ideas of your own. Your objective, however, is to identify at least three different ways of thinking about the issue you have selected to write about.

c. Write a three-page exploratory paper in which you
   • explain the issue;
   • describe the rhetorical situation;

- explain three (or more) positions on the issue along with some reasons for each of them;
- explain your interest in the issue and the position you will take;
- make a tentative claim and indicate how you will develop this claim in a future position paper.

The following is an example of an exploratory paper. It was written by a student in an argument class, Tanya Pierce. Her position paper on the same subject appears at the end of Chapter 12 on page 401. Read Tanya's paper and describe the issue, the rhetorical situation, the three positions she identifies, her interest in the issue, the position she takes, her claim, and her approach for developing her claim. You may want to use Tanya's paper as a model for your paper.

EXPLORATORY PAPER

TRIAL BY JURY, A FUNDAMENTAL RIGHT AND A FLAWED SYSTEM

Tanya Pierce

The right to a trial by jury is a fundamental part of the United States legal system. It is a right firmly entrenched in our democratic tradition. The jury system provides a buffer between the complex and often inflexible legal system and the average citizen on trial. The right to be judged by a jury of one's peers is a right that most Americans feel very strongly about. However, due to recent jury decisions, some critics are questioning the value of this institution.

Our jury system is by no means flawless. It is subject to constant scrutiny and debate concerning its merit and its downfalls. As is true in all institutions, juries are capable of making mistakes. Psychological studies have been done on many aspects of jury behavior. Political scientists are also intrigued by juries and the manner in which they arrive at important decisions. Although I believe most Americans believe in the jury system, there has been considerable controversy surrounding it lately. The public has become even more concerned about this institution recently. The outcomes of the Rodney King, the O. J. Simpson, and the Menendez brothers trials in Los Angeles and the outrage that followed the jurys' decisions are three examples of instances when the effectiveness of the jury system has come under fierce attack. From the public reaction to those decisions and others like them, it is very clear that the way in which juries reach their decisions is often as important to the American people as it is to the specific person on trial. Many people feel that the average jurist is not equipped to make the kinds of decisions they are faced with. These critics' suggestions range from restructuring the system to totally eliminating it.

Most average Americans, I believe, feel that the right to a jury trial is a fundamental one, and its guarantees should be honored. These people would argue that laws are inflexible. Statutes cannot deal with the individual circumstances in each case, but juries can take these into account. Still others believe that juries are favorable because they reflect the morals and values of the community they come from. Indeed, many proponents of the jury support the system because of a particular kind of jury bias, the tendency for jurors to place justice above the law (Goldberg 457).

Opponents of the system argue that juries are uneducated in legal procedures and should not be given the type of responsibility they have traditionally had. These people also argue that juries are biased. In fact, the psychological literature provides many examples of this bias. Jurors are less likely to punish a sad or distressed defendant, as opposed to a joyful one, apparently because the defendant is already being punished emotionally (Upshaw and Romer 162). Some opponents say that although juries are instructed not to pay attention to the media, they are more easily influenced by the news than judges. Critics of the jury system also point out that juries are expensive and are often unable to reach a consensus. They argue that the decision making should be left up to the people who know the law, judges and lawyers.

In between these two extremes are those people who agree with the jury system as a whole, but feel that some changes need to be implemented to improve its effectiveness. These people suggest that juries receive instruction prior to hearing testimony as well as before they begin deliberations. They argue that this would improve the system by providing some working legal knowledge for the jury as well as giving them an idea of what they are to listen for. Research has shown that in laboratory mock jury situations, exposing jurors to the laws involved in their decision making resulted in significantly fewer verdicts of guilty compared to not exposing jurors to the relevant laws (Cruse and Browne 131). This finding suggests that lawyers and judges should have the responsibility of insuring that the jury is adequately informed of the legal issues at hand and the laws and statutes available to handle those issues.

As a prospective law student, I am fascinated by this topic. I think it is incredible that juries, made up of ordinary citizens, make some of the most profound legal decisions in the world. I decided to write on this particular issue because of events such as the Rodney King verdict, the verdict in the Broskey case in Fort Worth, and the verdicts in the O. J. Simpson and Menendez brothers trials. These examples force me to evaluate the positive and negative aspects of jury trials. The rise in crime in this country and the question of what to do with the offenders makes the role of juries even more interesting. As a whole, though, I feel that the American guarantee of trial by jury is a valuable one. I do feel, however, that in order to improve its utility, judges and attorneys need to accept the responsibility for educating the jury on relevant legal issues. That is my claim. I will define the problem in detail and then explain how my solution of jury training can be implemented.[16]

---

[16]Used by permission.

Works Cited

Cruse, Donna, and Beverly A. Brown. "Reasoning in a Jury Trial: The Influence of Instructions." <u>Journal of General Psychology</u> 114 (1987): 129–133.

Goldberg, Janice C. "Memory, Magic, and Myth: The Timing of Jury Instructions." <u>Oregon Law Review</u> 59 (1981): 451–475.

Upshaw, Harry S., and Daniel Romer. "Punishments of One's Misdeeds as a Function of Having Suffered from Them." <u>Personality and Social Psychology Bulletin</u> 2 (1976): 162–169.

5. QUESTIONS ON THE CHAPTER

a. What are some of the benefits of including reading as part of the writing process?

b. What are some of the decisions writers need to make when they get physically organized to write?

c. How can the writer use the rhetorical situation during the prewriting phase of a paper?

d. What are some of the prewriting strategies you will use?

e. Describe your method for writing a first draft.

f. What would help you if you got stuck in the process of writing a paper?

g. What would you need to pay particular attention to in the rewriting and revising phase of the writing process?

6. QUESTIONS ON THE ESSAYS FOR ANALYSIS

a. "A Room of Their Own," page 111. Recall when you were in junior high school. Do you think you would have learned more effectively in a single-sex classroom? Why or why not? What do you think should be done to help junior high and high school students learn in public schools?

b. "Abortion Activists Bomb Clinic: Prohibitions and Arithmetical Arguments," page 114. The author presents new perspectives on the abortion and smoking issues to help people who are set in their views to look at these issues from fresh perspectives. What additional new approaches can you think of for these issues?

c. "Trial by Jury, a Fundamental Right and a Flawed System," page 117. What jury trial have you followed in recent years? Did you think the jury made a fair judgment? If you had been on the jury would you have agreed or disagreed? Why? Do you think the present jury system needs improvement? If so, what could be done to improve it?

PART TWO

Understanding the Nature of Argument for Reading and Writing

The purpose of Chapters 5, 6, and 7 is to explain the essential parts of an argument and show how they operate to convince an audience. Chapter 5 identifies and explains the parts of a traditional argument, Chapter 6 describes the types of claims and purposes in argument, and Chapter 7 presents the proofs for argument. Chapter 8 explains Rogerian argument, an alternative to traditional argument, that is particularly effective for building common ground. Chapter 8 ends with an assignment that synthesizes the critical reading and writing strategies taught in Chapters 1 to 8. Chapter 9 suggests some ways you can apply argument theory to literature. When you finish reading Part Two:

- You will understand and be able to identify the essential parts of an argument.
- You will know the key questions that arguments attempt to answer.
- You will be able to identify types of claims and purpose of argument.
- You will understand how argument can appeal to your reason, your emotion, and your sense of values about people's character in order to be convincing.
- You will know the major ways for developing the ideas in an argument and for making them convincing.
- You will have experience with three additional types of argument papers: the position paper, the Rogerian argument paper, and the critical analysis paper.
- You will know how to analyze arguments in literature and how to write your own arguments about literature.

CHAPTER 5

The Essential Parts of an Argument

The purpose of this and the next two chapters is to present some ideas from argument theory that will help you add additional strategies for reading and writing argument with confidence and expertise. Because people have been analyzing argument and writing theories of argument for 2,500 years, there is a considerable tradition of theory to draw on to help with this task. A theoretical background is useful because theory describes argument, and once you possess good descriptions, argument will be more familiar and consequently easier for you to read and write yourself.

As you acquire new understanding of argument, you will be adding to what you already know and gradually building a stronger and larger body of knowledge and understanding. Eventually, you will achieve "all-at-onceness," a quality Ann E. Berthoff describes in her book *The Sense of Learning* to describe the use of many ideas, bits of information, and strategies about reading and writing that finally come together so that you are able to use them unconsciously, simultaneously, and automatically.[1]

For now, however, you are still expanding your knowledge. Your goals in this chapter will be to get a better understanding of the usual anticipated outcomes of argument and to identify its component parts as they are identified by Stephen Toulmin in his model for argument.

THE OUTCOMES OF ARGUMENT: PROBABILITY VERSUS CERTAINTY

In Chapter 1 you learned that arguable issues require the possibility of at least two different views. It is the nature of argument to invite differing views and perspectives on issues. Outcomes can include achieving a closer agreement with a friendly audience or getting the attention and even perhaps some consensus from a neutral

---

[1]Ann E. Berthoff, *The Sense of Learning* (Portsmouth, NH: Boynton/Cook, 1990), pp. 86–91.

or hostile audience. Notice that these outcomes of argument are usually not described as establishing certainty or truth in the same sense that mathematics and science seek to establish certainty and truth. We do not argue about the fact that $2 + 3 = 5$ or that the area of a circle is πr^2. Mathematical proofs seek to establish such truths. Argument seeks to establish what is probably true as well as what might be expedient or desirable for the future. Arguers tell you what they think for now along with what they think should be done, given their present information. On that basis, you decide what you think for now, given your present information.

Throughout history, some thinkers have been drawn more to the idea of establishing truth and some have been drawn more to the idea of establishing probabilities. In ancient times the Greek philosopher Plato was interested in establishing truth. He employed dialectic, the question-and-answer method used in his dialogues, to help participants discover the Platonic ideas about truth. Aristotle, another Greek philosopher, was interested in probabilities. His *Rhetoric*, written somewhere between 360 and 334 B.C., is a key book in the history of argument theory, and its purpose is to train persuasive speakers to be convincing to audiences. Aristotle observed the orators of his time and described what they did. He noted that they were mainly concerned with matters and views concerning both the present and the future that were probably true instead of certainly true. The reason for their perspective lay in the audience. The ancient audience, like modern audiences, would disagree with many views that were stated as absolutely true. Those audiences could think of exceptions and reasons why certain views might not be true. Responsible persuaders, to communicate effectively, had to modify and qualify their views in order to make them acceptable to their audiences. They had to present probabilities instead of absolute truths. Thus views that are probably true comprise the realm of argument. To understand that realm better, it is useful to understand the parts that contribute to the whole argument.

THE PARTS OF AN ARGUMENT ACCORDING TO THE TOULMIN MODEL

Stephen Toulmin, a modern English philosopher, developed a six-part model of argument in his book *The Uses of Argument*, and this model has been useful to many people for explaining the essential parts of an argument.[2] At the time Toulmin wrote his book, his colleagues were logicians who were interested in discovering truth rather than probabilities. Toulmin tells us that his book had a chilly welcome among those English colleagues. His graduate adviser at Cambridge, he tells us, "was deeply pained by the book, and barely spoke to me for twenty years." Another colleague described it as "Toulmin's *anti*-logic book."[3] After that,

---

[2]Stephen Toulmin, *The Uses of Argument* (Cambridge: Cambridge University Press, 1958). I have adapted and added applications of the model to make it more useful for reading and writing.

[3]"Logic and the Criticism of Arguments," in James L. Golden, Goodwin F. Berquist, and William E. Coleman, *The Rhetoric of Western Thought*, 4th ed. (Dubuque, IA: Kendall Hunt, 1989), p. 375.

Toulmin expected his book to be a failure. But his editors assured him that people were buying it, and Toulmin found out who many of these people were when he visited the United States some time later. Professors in speech departments and departments of communication all over the United States were using his book to teach students to become better argumentative speakers. If you have ever taken a speech class, you may have already encountered the Toulmin model of argument. As time went by, the model was picked up by English departments to help students improve their reading and writing of argument. The Toulmin model has also been used in schools of law to help students learn to present legal argument. The Toulmin model is a very natural and practical model because it follows normal human thought processes. You will find that you have had experience with all its parts either in the everyday argument you carry on with your friends and family or in the arguments that you see on television.

The Toulmin model has six parts. The first three parts are essential to all argument. They include (1) the *claim,* (2) the *data* (which we are calling *support*), and (3) the *warrant.* Arguments may also contain one or more of three additional elements: (4) the *backing,* (5) the *rebuttal,* and (6) the *qualifier.* Figure 5.1 shows Toulmin's diagram of these three essential parts along with the three optional parts of the model.

Here is an example to illustrate how these parts work together in an actual argument: The narrator of a television program makes the *claim* that critical thinking is more important now than it was 60 years ago. This is followed by *support* that includes pictures of modern scientists launching space shuttles and air traffic controllers directing airplanes to land. These individuals seem intent and busy. It appears to be clear that if they do not think critically, there will be trouble. Then the camera switches to children riding on an old-fashioned school bus of 60 years ago. One is saying that he wants to grow up and be a farmer like his dad. This youngster is relaxed and bouncing along on the bus. He doesn't look like he is thinking critically or that he will ever need to. The unspoken part of this argument, the assumption that the author of this program hopes the audience will share, is the *warrant.* The author hopes the audience will agree, even though it is not explicitly stated, that farmers of 60 years ago did not have to think criti-

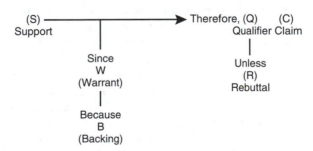

Figure 5.1 A Diagram of the Three Essential Parts of Toulmin's Model of Argument: Claim, Support, and Warrant; and the Three Optional Parts: Backing, Rebuttal, and Qualifier. From Stephen Toulmin, *The Uses of Argument* (Cambridge: Cambridge University Press, 1958), p. 104.

cally, that modern scientists and engineers do have to think critically, and that critical thinking was not so important then as now. The author hopes that the audience will look at the two bits of support, the scientist and the farmer's son, and make the leap necessary to accept the claim. That's right, the audience will think, those scientists and that young boy don't seem to share the same demands for critical thinking. Times have changed. Critical thinking *is* more important now than it was 60 years ago. Those three parts, the *claim*, the *support* and the *warrant*, are the three essential parts of an argument.

The other three parts, if present, might go like this: Suppose the camera then shifts to an old man who says, "Wait a minute. What makes you assume farmers didn't think? My daddy was a farmer, and he was the best critical thinker I ever knew. He had to think about weather, crops, growing seasons, fertilizer, finances, harvesting, and selling the crops. The thinking he had to do was as sophisticated as that of any modern scientist." This old fellow is indicating that he does not share the unstated warrant that farmers of 60 years ago had fewer demands on their thinking processes than modern scientists. In response to this rejoinder, the author, to make the argument convincing, provides *backing for the warrant*. This backing takes the form of additional support. The camera cuts to the narrator of the program: "At least two out of three of the farmers of 60 years ago had small farms. They grew food for their families and traded or sold the rest for whatever else they needed. The thinking and decision making required of them was not as complicated and demanding as that required by modern scientists. Your father was an exception." Notice that this backing takes the form of a smaller unit of argument within the argument. It is linked to the main argument, and it is used to back up the weakest part of the main argument. Furthermore, this smaller argument has a claim–support–warrant structure of its own: (1) the *claim* is that most farmers did not have to think; (2) the *support* is that two out of three did not have to think and that the old man's father was an exception; and (3) the *warrant*, again unstated, is that the old man will believe the statistics and accept the idea that his father was an exception. If he accepts this backing, the argument is on solid ground again. If he does not, if he asks for more backing for the new warrant by asking, "Hey, where did you get those statistics? They're not like any I ever heard," then another argument would need to be developed to cite the source of the figures and to convince the old man of their reliability. As you can see, the requests for backing, for more information to serve as further proof, can go on and on. But let's leave the old man and the narrator and look at what else might appear in this argument.

Suppose the camera now shifts to a modern science professor who wants to take exception with the claim itself by making a *rebuttal*. She makes her own claim, "The critical thinking required 60 years ago was demanding and sophisticated. Critical thinkers of that time had to figure out how to get the country out of a severe recession, and they had to develop the technology to win the Second World War." These opinions are then supported with factual evidence that includes pictures of individuals thinking.

After all of these challenges, exceptions, and requests for more information, the author at this point finds it necessary to *qualify* the original claim in order to make it acceptable to more of the audience members. Qualifying involves adding words and phrases to the claim like *sometimes, seems to be, maybe,* or *possibly* to make it more acceptable to the audience. In this case, the narrator now restates the qualified claim, "Critical thinking, because of modern science, seems to some people to be more important now than it was 60 years ago." Compare this with the original claim that critical thinking is more important now than it was 60 years ago. Figure 5.2 provides a diagram of this argument laid out according to the Toulmin model. You have probably never systematically used this or any other model to read or write argument. The model can serve as a kind of guide for reading and analyzing arguments and also for writing them. Authors do not usually use the model as an exact formula for writing, however. Rather, it describes what can be but not necessarily always is present in an argument. Consequently, when you read argument, you will at times easily locate some parts of the model and at other times you will not. Some arguments, in fact, may not contain one or more of the parts at all, like a rebuttal, for example. You are not getting it wrong if you read and do not find all of the parts. When you write, you do not need to make all parts explicit either. The following sections provide some details about each of the six parts that will help you understand them better.

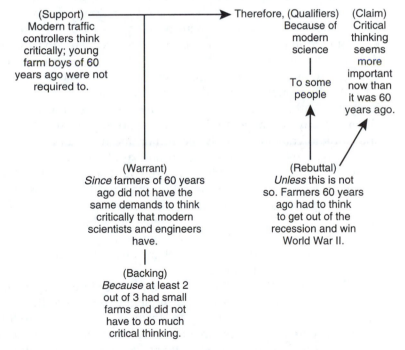

Figure 5.2 A Diagram of the Six Elements in the Toulmin Model.

Claim

Discover the claim of an argument by asking the question, What is the author trying to prove? Or plan a claim of your own by asking, What do I want to prove? The claim is the main point of the argument. Locating or identifying the claim as soon as possible helps you focus on what the argument is all about.

Synonyms for *claim* are *thesis, proposition, conclusion,* and *main point.* Sometimes an author of an argument in a newspaper or magazine will refer to "the proposition," or an individual arguing on television will ask, "What is your point?" They both are referring to the claim. When someone refers to the claim as the conclusion, don't confuse it with the conclusion, or final idea at the end of an argument. The claim can appear at the end, but it can also appear other places in the argument. The claim is sometimes stated in a sentence or sentences called the *statement of claim.* This sentence can also be called the *thesis statement,* the *purpose sentence,* the *statement of focus,* or the *statement of proposition.*

The terms used in this text to describe the main elements in argument along with some of their synonyms appear in Table 5.1. Become familiar with them so that you will understand other writers on the subject who may vary the terminology.

To locate the claim, what should you look for? The claim may be explicitly stated at the beginning of an argument, at the end, or even somewhere in the middle. Or, it may not be stated anywhere. It may sometimes be *implied,* in which case you will be expected to *infer* it. To infer an implicit claim, you will need to use what you already know about the subject along with what you have just read to formulate your own statement of it. In this case, the author is paying you a kind of compliment. The assumption is that you are smart enough to figure out the claim for yourself. You should probably make your own claims in your written arguments clear and explicit, however, at least at first.

Another interesting variation on the claim occurs in the case of irony. In irony the author says one thing but means something else. Usually the stated claim in irony is exaggerated, outrageous, or odd in some way. You may read it and think to yourself, "Surely the author doesn't *mean* this." The questions to ask at this point are "What does the author say?" and "What does the author really mean?" Again, you are expected to use your background and judgment to figure out what the author really means. Roberta Borkat in her essay "A Liberating Curriculum" (p. 478 in "The Reader") claims that she has decided to give all of her college students A's, but this assertion is not what she actually means. She uses this exaggerated ironic claim to get her audience's attention in hopes that they will pay more attention to the problems of grade inflation. This author says one thing but means something else.

The claim, whether implied or explicitly stated, organizes the entire argument, and everything else in the argument is related to it. The best way to identify it, if it is not obvious or easy to locate, is to complete the following statement as soon as you have finished reading: "This author wants to convince me to think that . . . ." When you have finished that statement, you have the claim. As a writer,

TABLE 5.1   Argument Terms Used in This Book and Some of Their Synonyms

CLAIM	STATEMENT OF CLAIM	SUBCLAIMS	SUPPORT	WARRANTS
Thesis Proposition Conclusion Main point Macro-argument Controlling idea	Thesis statement Purpose sentence Statement of focus Statement of proposition	Reasons Main ideas Micro-arguments Arguments Lines of argument Supporting arguments Specific issues	Evidence Opinions Reasons Examples Facts Data Grounds Proof Premise Statistics Explanations Information Personal narratives	Assumptions General principles Widely held values Commonly accepted beliefs Appeals to human motives Cultural values Presuppositions Unstated premises Generally accepted truths

you can check your own claim during revision by completing this statement: "I have convinced my audience to think that . . ."

Authors often make conscious decisions about where to place a claim and whether to make it explicit or implicit. Their decisions are related to their notions about the audience. A claim at the beginning is straightforward and draws the reader in right away, like the claim in "Some College Costs Should Be Tax Deductible" (p. 22). Both parties are thinking along the same lines, together, from the outset. Or an author may decide to lead up to the claim, in which case it may appear either in the middle or at the end. A delayed claim pulls the audience in even more and increases interest and attention, as in "We're Good Republicans— and Pro-Choice" (p. 23). "What is this author after?" the audience wonders, and reads to find out. The end of an essay is the most emphatic and memorable place for a claim. Many authors prefer to put the claim there to give it as much force as possible. There is some risk involved in putting the claim at the end. Students who use this strategy must be careful to cue their readers so that they understand where the argument is headed and do not feel they are being led through a random chain of topics. Both the unstated claim and the ironic claim require special attention on the part of the reader because, in these cases, the reader has to make an inference to figure them out. As a result of this effort, the reader may find an inferred claim especially convincing and memorable.

Argument, like any other discourse, has main ideas and ideas that support them, as was shown in Chapter 3. The claim is the main point of the entire piece, and the subclaims are the shorter supporting arguments or reasons for the claim. We will present two examples that illustrate the relationships among the issues, related issues, claims, and subclaims in argument. Included are the following:

1. **Two issue areas,** *racism* and the *environment,* that are at the most general level in these examples.
2. **Two of many possible specific related issues** in these issue areas that represent ideas *about* the general issue areas.
3. **Examples of claims** made in response to the specific related issues that are even more specific.
4. **Examples of some subclaims** used to support the claims. The subclaims are at the most specific level in this example because they represent ideas about the claims.

Example 1

Issue Area: Racism

Specific Related Issue: Where do racist attitudes come from?
  Claim: People are not born with racist attitudes; they have to be taught them.
    Subclaims: 1. Some parents transmit racist attitudes.
                2. The press can reinforce racist attitudes.
                3. Peer groups can also strengthen racist attitudes.
                4. Segregated schools and neighborhoods contribute to racist attitudes.

Example 2

Issue Area: The Environment

Specific Related Issue: How serious are the world's environmental problems?

  Claim: The environment is the single most serious problem the world faces today.

  Subclaims: 1. The rain forests are being destroyed, causing global warming.
  2. Increasing population is depleting resources in some parts of the world.
  3. Many important water sources are being polluted by industry.
  4. The ozone layer, which protects us from harmful sun rays, is being destroyed by chemicals.

Think for a moment about the two essays at the end of Chapter 1 that we have used as examples, "Some College Costs Should Be Tax Deductible" (p. 22) and "We're Good Republicans—and Pro-Choice" (p. 23). What are their claims? Complete these sentences: "The author of the essay about abortion wants me to believe that . . . ," and, "The author of the essay about tuition and taxes wants me to believe that . . ." Can you do it? If you can, you understand the concept of the claim, and you will be able to recognize the main controlling idea in the arguments you read and also use one to develop your own arguments.

Support

Discover the support in an argument by asking, What additional information does the author supply to convince me of this claim? Or, if you are the author, ask, What information do I need to supply to convince my audience? You can summarize the most essential elements of an argument as a *claim with support*. Aristotle wrote in his textbook the *Rhetoric* that the only necessary parts of an argument are the statement of proposition (the claim) and the proof (the support). There has been general agreement about those two essential parts of an argument for more than 2,300 years.

Support provides the evidence, opinions, reasoning, examples, and factual information about a claim that make it possible for us to accept it. Look back at the claims and subclaims on page 130. If you are to take these claims seriously, you will want some support to make them convincing.

The synonyms that Toulmin uses for support are *data* and *grounds*, the British equivalents. In the United States you will often read arguments in which the author says he (or she) is "grounding" a claim with particular support, and "data" is sometimes used as a synonym for facts and figures. Other synonyms for support are *proof, evidence,* and *reasons.* Sometimes authors refer to major evidence as *premises.* When you encounter that term in your reading, remember that premises lead to and support a conclusion (a claim). Don't confuse premises with the claim.

To locate support, what should you look for? One bit of good news: support is always explicitly stated, so you will not have to infer it as you sometimes have to infer the claim. Thus an understanding of the types of support is all you really need to help you recognize it. Here are some of the most common types:

Facts. In a court of law, factual support (the murder weapon, for example) is laid out on the table. In written argument it must be described. Factual support can include detailed reports of *observed events;* specific *examples* of real happenings; references to *events,* either *historical* or *recent;* and *statistical reports.* Factual support is vivid, real, and verifiable. Two people looking at it together would agree on its existence and what it looks like. They might not agree on what it *means* to each of them. That is, they might interpret it differently, but essentially they would agree on the facts themselves.

Opinions. When people start interpreting the facts, opinion enters the picture. The following quotation is an example of some statistics that have been interpreted. The author is a wildlife scientist who has studied wolves and other wild animals in Alaska for many years, and he is arguing against a plan by the state of Alaska to shoot wolves in order to protect herds of caribou.

> The state is portraying the wolf kill as an emergency measure to boost the size of what is called the "Delta caribou herd," which ranges east of Denali. But the herd's population decrease since 1989—from 11,000 to 4,000—represents little more than a return to the numbers that prevailed for decades until the mid-80's. The short-lived increase to 11,000 probably resulted largely from a temporary shift of caribou from a neighboring herd.
>
> The Delta herd didn't even exist until about 60 years ago; it is probably an offshoot of a much larger herd farther to the east. There is no major caribou-hunting tradition in this area, so the plan is not a matter of restoring something that hunters had enjoyed for generations. Over the past 12 months, most of the Delta herd has spent most of its time well outside the wolf-control area.
>
> In fact, the state's view that this and other caribou herds should be managed at stable or minimum sizes is a mistake. Virtually all of Alaska's caribou belong to a single population within which, over the span of decades, there are shifting centers of abundance. Thousands of caribou may abandon a range they have inhabited for decades and move to an area where numbers have traditionally been low. Despite recent declines in the Delta herd and in several nearby areas, other herds have increased dramatically. Statewide, the number of caribou has more then tripled over the past 15 years to about a million animals and is continuing to increase rapidly.[4]

Note that the raw data, the herd's decrease in numbers from 11,000 to 4,000, have been interpreted and explained. The author says the decrease in the caribou population has been caused by the herds moving around, and that actually there are now more caribou statewide than 15 years ago. Thus there is no need to slaughter wolves to protect caribou. State officials had interpreted the same data

---

[4]Excerpt from Gordon C. Haber, "The Great Alaska Wolf Kill," *New York Times,* October 2, 1993, Sec. A, Op-Ed.

to indicate that wolves should be killed to save the caribou. You need to distinguish between facts everyone would agree on and interpret in the same way and facts that are open to interpretation and opinion. We do not argue with the facts, as the saying goes, unless of course they are lies or they omit important information. We do, however, argue with interpretation and opinion.

Opinions may be the personal opinions of the author or the opinions of experts the author selects to quote. The quotes may be direct quotes, set off in quotation marks, or they may be summaries or paraphrases of what someone else thinks or has said. Furthermore, opinions may be informed, based on considerable knowledge and excellent judgment, or they may be ill-founded, based on hearsay and gossip. The most convincing opinions are those of experts, whether they be those of the author or of another person. Experts possess superior background, education, and experience on an issue. Contrast in your own mind the opinions of experts with the uninformed opinions of people on the evening news who are frequently cornered in the streets by reporters to give their opinions. Informed personal opinions and the opinions of experts can be more interesting and convincing than the facts themselves. Ill-founded, baseless opinion, on the other hand, is boring and rarely convincing.

Examples. Examples can be real or made up, long or short. They are used to clarify, to make material more memorable and interesting, and, in argument particularly, to prove. Examples that are real, such as instances of actual events or references to particular individuals, function in the same way that fact does in an argument. They are convincing because they are grounded in reality. Made-up or hypothetical examples are invented by the writer and, like opinions, can only demonstrate probabilities. Personal experience is one type of example that is frequently used in argument. Writers often go into considerable detail about the experiences that have influenced them to think and behave as they do. A combination of personal experience and the opinions and reasoning that have resulted from it is a common way to develop a claim.

There are no set rules about the placement of support in an argument. Support can appear *before* the claim, as in the following example: "The caribou have moved around and are alive [the support]; *therefore,* we do not need a wolf-kill policy [claim]." Or support can appear *after* the claim: "The wolf-kill policy should be abandoned [claim] *because* the caribou have moved around, and there are three times as many of them as 15 years ago [support]."

Different authors manage support in different ways depending on the requirements of the subject, their purpose, and their audience. When the issue is an abstract idea and the audience is informed, the author may present mainly opinions and few, if any, facts or examples. Such arguments include a claim and blocks of logical reasoning organized around subclaims to develop and prove the claim. If you were to outline the argument, you might not need more than two levels, as in the claim and subclaim examples on pages 130 and 131. When the subject requires more specific support or the audience needs more information to be convinced, specific materials at lower levels on an outline are required to ground the subclaims in facts, figures, quotations from others, or author opinions.

Here is an example that illustrates these levels. It includes (1) a general issue area, (2) one of many specific issues that could be generated by it, (3) a claim, (4) some subclaims, and (5) some support.

Example
Issue Area: Cities
Specific Related Issue: How should cities be planned so that people will live happily in them?
 Claim: Inner cities can be made more inhabitable.
  Subclaim: One way is to omit automobiles and encourage walking.
   Support: With no cars, people are forced to walk and interact, and interacting is pleasant. (opinion)
  Subclaim: Another way is to eliminate public housing projects.
   Support: More than half the poor are often in public housing. (fact)
   Support: Warehousing the poor is destructive to the neighborhood and occupants. (opinion)[5]

To summarize, support comprises all the explicitly stated explanations, information, facts, opinions, personal narratives, and examples that authors use to make their claims and subclaims convincing and believable. Notice that support may be true, as in the case of facts and real examples, or probable, as in the case of opinions and made-up stories and examples.

Readers and writers of argument should require that the support in an argument be acceptable and convincing. Factual evidence needs to be true and verifiable. All evidence needs to be clear, relevant, and understandable. It also should represent all of the significant information available; it must, in other words, be an adequate sample. The experts whose opinions are quoted should be experts, and their credentials should when necessary be identified by the author to show their degree of expertise. Personal opinion, to be convincing, should be original, impressive, interesting, and backed by factual knowledge, experience, good reasoning, and judgment. Support that meets these requirements is not only accepted but is often shared by the audience because they have had similar experiences and ideas themselves. Such quality support helps build common ground between the arguer and the audience. Rantings, unfounded personal opinions that no one else accepts, or feeble reasons like "because I said so" or "because everyone does it" are not effective support. Audiences usually do not believe such statements, they do not share experiences or ideas suggested by them, and they lose common ground with the arguer when they read or hear them.

When reading argument, to help you focus on and recognize the support, complete this sentence as soon as you finish. "The *author wants me to believe that* . . . [the claim] *because* . . . [list the support]." Now, try to complete this sen-

---

[5]Witold Rybczynski, "How to Rebuild Los Angeles," *New York Times*, June 6, 1992, Sec. A, p. 15.

tence as applied to "Some College Costs Should Be Tax Deductible" and "We're Good Republicans—and Pro-Choice" (Chapter 1): "The authors of the essay about abortion want me to believe that we need to consider more than two views on abortion because . . . ," and, "The author of the essay about tuition and taxes wants me to believe that the parts of tuition diverted for financial aid should be tax deductible because . . .". If you can list and summarize the support in these essays, you understand it. When you read to revise your own writing, you can complete this statement: "I have convinced my audience to believe [the claim] because [list your support]."

Warrants

Warrants are the assumptions, general principles, the conventions of specific disciplines, widely held values, commonly accepted beliefs, and appeals to human motives that are an important part of any argument. Even though they can be spelled out as part of the written argument, they usually are not. In many instances, it would be redundant and boring if they were. For example, an argument might go as follows: *Claim:* The president of the United States is doing a poor job. *Support:* The unemployment rate is the highest it has been in ten years. The unstated *warrants* in this argument might include the following **generally accepted beliefs:** The president is responsible for creating jobs; when unemployment is high, it is a sign that the president is doing a poor job; or, even though the president may be doing well in other areas, creating jobs is the main index to how well he is doing. You may be able to think of some other ways of expressing the warrants in this argument. Since individual audience members vary in their backgrounds and perspectives, not everyone will state the warrants in exactly the same way.

Here is another example, and this one relies on a **value warrant.** *Claim:* Business profits are adversely affected by environmental protection laws. *Support:* Obeying environmental protection laws that call for clean air, for example, costs industry money that could otherwise be realized as profit. The unstated *warrants* in this argument involve the relative value individuals place on the environment and on business profit, and might be stated thus: Profit is more important than clean air; businesses must make profit to survive; or, environmental protection laws are threatening the capitalistic system.

Finally, here is yet another example of a warrant that relies on a **commonly-accepted convention** of a specific discipline, which, in this case, is the discipline of writing. *Claim:* You have received a failing grade on this paper. *Support:* You have several sentence fragments and subject–verb agreement errors in your paper. The unstated *warrants* could be stated as follows: These types of errors result in a failing grade in college papers; or, the conventions of writing college papers do not allow for fragments and subject–verb agreement problems since these are errors and errors result in failing grades. When you encounter argument in your other college courses, try to identify the warrants that are implicit in these arguments and that are also part of the generally accepted knowledge or the conventions that inform these particular disciplines. Such warrants could include laws in physics, equations in mathematics, or theories in philosophy. Such information is not always spelled out in every argument, particularly if the people who are arguing share the same background information about these conventions, laws, equations, or theories. A physicist, for example, would not have to state the law of gravity to fill in the argument that an object dropped from a bridge will fall into the water below. Instead, the arguer assumes that the audience knows this material and will mentally fill it in to complete an argument. Toulmin called the warrants that are specific to particular disciplines *field dependent* because they are understood and accepted by individuals who have background and expertise in specific fields of knowledge. They can be differentiated from *field-independent* warrants that cut across disciplines and would be accepted by most people. The belief that the president should supply jobs is an example of a field independent warrant.

Warrants originate with the arguer. Note, however, that the warrants also exist in the minds of the audience. They can be *shared* by the arguer and the audience, or they can be *in conflict*. Furthermore, if the audience shares the warrants with the arguer, the audience will accept them, and the argument is convincing. If the warrants are in conflict and the audience does not accept them (they believe the president is not responsible for solving unemployment problems, or they believe sentence fragments are acceptable in academic writing because they have read writers who have used them), then the argument is not convincing to them.

Here is another example. A politician arguing that crimes are caused by a lack of family values expects the audience to supply the warrant that people with family values do not commit crime. The argument is strong and convincing for audiences who happen to share those same values and who thus share the warrant. It is not so convincing for audience members who believe there are other causes for crime that have nothing to do with family values. A conflicting warrant might be the belief that peer groups, not families, cause criminals to turn to crime.

Notice how warrants themselves, when they are recognized by the audience as either acceptable or not, can themselves become claims for new arguments. The examples of the two warrants in the previous paragraph about what causes crime can each be stated as new claims and supported as new arguments. Developing warrants as subjects for new arguments is called "chaining arguments." The process can go on indefinitely and can help direct an argument in a variety of interesting directions. For example, if one claims that peer groups cause crime and then supports that claim with the evidence that gangs are notorious for committing crimes, the shared warrant would be that gang members are criminals. That warrant could then become a claim for a new argument about the criminal records of gangs. A conflicting warrant, that many gang members are law-abiding citizens, could become the claim for a different argument that would provide an entirely different view of gang members.

Besides being related to what people commonly believe, value, want, or accept as background knowledge in a discipline, warrants are also culture-bound.

Since values, beliefs, and training vary from culture to culture, the warrants associated with them also differ from culture to culture. Some tension between Japan and the United States was caused by a Japanese official's claim that American workers are lazy and do not work hard enough. American workers were angry and countered with a rebuttal about how hard they think they work. Japanese and American workers have different work schedules, attitudes, and experience with leisure and work time. Consequently, the part of both arguments that was unstated, the warrant, described hard work in different ways for each culture. The lack of a shared warrant caused the tension. Furthermore, neither side was convinced by the other's argument.

You may be thinking at this point, How am I going to be able to understand warrants when they usually are not printed on the page, they exist in the minds of the author and the audience, and they may even differ from one individual or culture to another? You will not have the difficulty with warrants that you may be anticipating because you already know a great deal about people and the opinions and beliefs they are likely to hold. You may have never noticed warrants before. But, once you become aware of them, you will recognize them in every argument you read. Warrants are one of the most interesting features of argument. They represent the psychology of an argument in the sense that they reveal unspoken beliefs and values of the author and invite you to examine your own beliefs and make comparisons.

Finding warrants is not very different from "psyching people out," or trying to discover their "real reasons for saying things." Here is an example that might make finding warrants easier: Suppose your wife/husband/roommate makes the claim that you really should start sleeping at night, instead of staying up to study, because it is more beneficial to study in the daytime. As support, you are reminded that sunshine keeps people from getting depressed, that people sleep more soundly at night than in the day, and that you need to build daytime work habits because you probably will not get a nighttime job when you graduate.

To understand the warrants in this argument, you must try to figure out what else your roommate believes, values, and wants but has not said directly. The warrants might include these: Daytime people are better than nighttime people; you should be like other people and change your work habits to conform; you will get more done in the daytime because other people do; and you will have trouble switching from night to day if you ever have to. You might go a step further and ask, Why else is my roommate trying to change my work habits? What is the hidden agenda? Maybe it is because you leave the lights on and music playing all night. We figure out the subtexts or hidden agendas in our conversations with other people all the time. Warrants and hidden agendas are not the same, as you can see from these examples, but they are similar in the sense that neither are usually spelled out and that discovering them requires looking for what is left unstated in our communications with other people.

Some of the synonyms for warrants are *unstated assumptions, presuppositions of the author,* and *unstated premises.* Warrants are also sometimes described as generally accepted truths that the audience also will accept as true.

Warrants provide critical links in argument. For instance, they link the support to the claim by enabling an audience to accept particular support as proof of a particular claim. Without the linking warrant, the support may not be convincing. Here is an example:

The claim:	We no longer value human life.
The support:	Because we have legalized abortion.
The expected warrants:	Abortion destroys the fetus, which is human life. The author makes this assumption and expects you to also. If you make the link, the argument is convincing.
An alternative warrant:	Another individual believes the fetus is not a human life. This audience member does not share the author's warrant. The link is not made, and the argument is not convincing for that individual.

Here is another example:

The claim:	The appeal process for criminals should be shortened.
The support:	Because the appeals for criminals on death row can cost more than $2 million per criminal.
The expected warrants:	Spending more than $2 million to keep a convicted criminal alive a little longer is a waste of money. This individual shares the author's warrant, the link is made, and the argument is convincing.
An alternative warrant:	We are dealing with human life here, and we should spend whatever is necessary to make certain we have a fair conviction. This individual supplies an opposing warrant, the link between claim and support is not made, and the argument is not convincing.

Supply your own warrant in the following argument:

The claim:	The government should abolish loan funds for college students.
The support:	Because many students default on their loans, and the government cannot tolerate these bad debts.
The warrants:	Do you believe that evidence supports that claim? If yes, why? If no, why? Your answer provides the warrant. Is the argument convincing for you?

These examples demonstrate that the warrant links the evidence and the claim by justifying particular evidence as support for a particular claim. Notice also, however, how the warrant establishes or fails to establish a link between the author and the audience as well. Shared warrants result in successful arguments. When the warrant is not shared, or when there are conflicting warrants, the audience will question or disagree with the claim. When American workers argued with the Japanese about whether they are lazy or hardworking, a shared warrant was missing.

The Japanese claim:	American workers are lazy.
The support:	Because they only work 40 hours a week.
The Japanese warrant:	People who only work 40 hours a week are lazy.
The American rebuttal:	American workers are hardworking.
The support:	Because they work 40 hours a week.
The American warrant:	People who put in 40 hours a week are industrious and hardworking.

Perhaps now you can begin to appreciate the importance of shared warrants in argument. Shared warrants are critical to the success of an argument because they provide the most significant way that common ground is established between reader and writer in argument. Shared warrants and common ground, as you can imagine, are particularly important in international negotiations. Skillful negotiators take time to analyze warrants and to determine whether or not both parties are on common ground. If they are not, communication breaks down and argument fails.

At this point, you may wonder why authors do not spell out the warrants, since they are so critical to the success of the argument. There are two reasons for usually leaving warrants implicit, or unstated, so that the audience has to supply them. First, an audience who supplies the warrant is more likely to buy into the argument through a sense of participation. If there is potential for agreement and common ground, it will be strengthened by the audience supplying the warrant. Second, remember that audiences differ and that their views of the warrant also vary somewhat, depending on their past experiences and present perceptions. A stated warrant negates the rich and varied perceptions and responses of the audience by providing only the author's interpretation and articulation of the warrant. Less active participation is then required from the audience, and the argument is less powerful and convincing to them.

To help you discover warrants, ask questions like the following:

What is left out here?
Where is this author coming from?
What is causing this author to say these things?
Where am I coming from?
Do I believe that this evidence supports this claim? Why or why not?

As the author of argument, you should consider your audience and whether or not they will accept your warrants. More information will be provided in Chapter 10 to help you do so. Now let's look at the other three parts of the Toulmin model. Recall that these are optional. All or none might appear in a written argument.

Backing

You should have a sense by now that warrants, themselves, may require their own support to make them more acceptable to an audience, particularly if the audience does not happen to share them with the author. An author may provide backing, or additional evidence to "back up" a warrant, whenever the audience is in danger of rejecting it. When you are the author, you should provide backing also. In exchanges like debates or rebuttal letters to the editor, the author is sometimes asked to prove the warrant with additional support. Or the author may analyze the beliefs and values of the audience, anticipate a lack of common ground, and back the warrant with additional support explicitly in the text, just in case. For example, in the criminal appeals argument, the author might back the warrant that it is a waste of time to spend $2 million on a criminal appeal with additional statistical evidence that shows these appeals rarely result in a changed verdict. This additional backing would improve the likelihood that the audience would accept the claim.

Here is another example of backing for a warrant:

The claim: All immigrants should be allowed to come into the United States.

The support: Because immigration has benefited the U.S. economy in the past.

The warrant: Current economic conditions are similar to past conditions.

Backing for the warrant: Now, as in the past, immigrants are willing to perform necessary low-paying jobs that American citizens do not want, particularly in the service areas. Statistics could be supplied to show how many jobs of this type are available.

Look for backing in an argument by identifying the warrant and then determining whether or not you accept it. If you do not, try to anticipate additional information that would make it more acceptable. Then look to see if the author supplied that or similar additional support. For example, the author who assumed that a fetus is a human being would need to provide convincing backing for people not inclined to believe that it is.

Rebuttal

A rebuttal establishes what is wrong, invalid, or unacceptable about an argument and may also present counterarguments, or new arguments that represent entirely different perspectives or points of view on the issue. To attack the validity of the claim, an author may demonstrate that the support is faulty or that the warrants are faulty or unbelievable. Counterarguments start all over again, with a new set of claims, support, and warrants.

Here is an example of a rebuttal for the argument about immigration:

Rebuttal 1: Immigrants actually drain more resources in schooling, medical care, and other social services than they contribute in taxes and productivity.

Rebuttal 2: Modern immigrants are not so willing to perform menial, low-skilled jobs as they were in past generations.

Here is an example of a counterargument for the immigration argument:

The claim: Laws should be passed to limit immigration.

The support: Because we have our own unskilled laborers who need those jobs.

The warrant: These laborers are willing to hold these jobs.

Rebuttals may appear as answers to arguments that have already been stated, or the author may anticipate the reader's rebuttal and include answers to possible objections that might be raised. Thus an author might write a rebuttal to the claim that we should censor television by saying such a practice would violate the first amendment. Or, if no claim has been made, the arguer could anticipate what the objections to television violence *might* be (violence breeds violence, children become frightened, etc.) and refute them, usually early in the essay, before spelling out the reasons for leaving television alone.

Look for a rebuttal or plan for it in your own writing, by asking, What are the other possible views on this issue? When reading, ask, Are they represented here along with reasons? Or when writing, ask, How can I answer them? Phrases that might introduce refutation include, "some may disagree," "others may think," or "other commonly held opinions are," followed by opposing ideas.

Qualifiers

Remember that argument is not expected to demonstrate certainties. Instead, it usually only establishes probabilities. Consequently, the language of certainty (*always, never, the best, the worst,* and so on) promises too much when used in claims or in other parts of the argument. It is not uncommon for an author to make a claim, and in the midst of writing, to begin revising and qualifying it to meet the anticipated objections of an audience. Thus words like *always* and *never* change to *sometimes; is* or *are* change to *maybe* or *might; all* changes to *many* or *some; none* changes to a *few;* and *absolutely* changes to *probably* or *possibly.* Qualified language is safer for demonstrating the probabilities of an argument. Look to see if the author has stated the claim in other parts of the argument in probable or absolute terms, and then read the entire argument to figure out why.

The following is a qualified version of the claim that all immigrants should be allowed to come into the United States. These qualifications would make the original claim more acceptable to the people who offered the rebuttals and counterargument.

Immigrants should be allowed to enter the United States only if they can prove that they already have jobs yielding sufficient income to offset social services and that no American citizens are currently available to perform these jobs.

WHY IS THE TOULMIN MODEL VALUABLE FOR ANALYZING ARGUMENT?

The Toulmin model has some advantages that make it an excellent model for both reading and writing argument. Its most essential advantage is that it invites common ground and audience participation in the form of shared warrants, increasing the possibility of interaction between author and audience. The optional three parts of the Toulmin model also encourage an exchange of views and common ground because they require an arguer both to anticipate other perspectives and views and, at times, to acknowledge and answer them directly. The backing, for instance, requires additional evidence to satisfy audience concerns. The rebuttal requires answers to different or opposing views. The qualifier requires a modification of the claim to gain audience acceptance. The backing, rebuttal, and qualifier in the Toulmin model invite audience participation. They encourage dialogue, understanding, and agreement as argument outcomes. These features make it valuable for examining the multiple perspectives likely to be expressed in response to complex modern issues.

Thus the model works for reading or writing, not only in debate and single-perspective argument, but also in academic inquiry, negotiation, dialectic, or any other form of argument that requires exchange and attempts to reach agreement. It can even be a useful tool for one-on-one argument or personal decision making.

Writers of argument find the Toulmin model useful both as an invention strategy and as a revision strategy. It can be used to help an author come up with the essential parts of an argument in the first place, and later it can be used to check and evaluate the parts of a newly written argument. See page 237 for a writing assignment that relies on the Toulmin model as a tool to help the writer think about the parts of a position paper. See also page 240 for an example of a student-written position paper with its Toulmin elements labelled in the margins.

Readers of argument find the model useful for analyzing and describing the essential parts of a written argument. Listeners find it just as useful for analyzing and describing the essential parts of an argumentative speech. It can be used to write or to analyze both argument that aims at consensus or argument that aims at the establishment of winners. It accommodates all of the various forms of argument. The model is summarized in a handy chart for quick reference for the use of both readers and writers in the Summary Charts on page 409.

EXERCISES AND ACTIVITIES

1. **GROUP WORK AND CLASS DISCUSSION: TRUTH VERSUS PROBABILITY**
Each group should write one of these titles on the board: *television, health, graduation, recycling.* Now draw a vertical line under the title to establish two columns. Label them as follows:

Absolute Facts	**Probabilities**
(No argument)	(Possibility for argument)

Brainstorm the topic you selected and put each item you think of in one of the two columns. Take a look at the items and circle some that would be good topics for argument. As a class, discuss what is arguable and what is not arguable on each group's list.

2. **GROUP WORK AND CLASS DISCUSSION: APPLYING THE TOULMIN MODEL TO ADVERTISEMENTS.**
Study the automobile advertisement and also the statement by the Catholic League. The statement by the Catholic League was made in anticipation of the Fourth United Nations Conference on Women that was held in Beijing, China, in the fall of 1995. It is a response to the announced platform of ideas that was planned for discussion at the conference.
    Answer the following questions for each of these items:

- What is the claim?
- What is the support?
- What are the warrants?
- Do you share them?
- What types of rebuttal might you offer?
- Is the claim acceptable, or should it be qualified?

Will your

heart pound any

less because

it's safe? Will your

goose bumps care that it's practical?

Find your own road.™

9000 CS Turbo

Will that giddy feeling deep in your stomach diminish because the 9000 was ranked the safest car in Sweden three times in a row?* Will your exhilaration be dampened by the turbo's fuel efficiency? Will the guilty pleasure of driving it be compromised by its large interior and 56 cubic feet of cargo space? We don't think so. Experience turbo rush in the Saab 9000 CS. **For a free Saab Excursion Kit, call 1-800-582-SAAB, Ext. 222. www.saabusa.com**

SAAB

*For years 1990, 1992 and 1994. Based on a study of injuries sustained in auto accidents in Sweden. Data compiled by Folksam Insurance Institute between 1985 and 1993. To maximize safety benefits, you must wear seat belts. ©1996 SAAB CARS USA, INC.

When the Fourth United Nations Conference on Women begins tomorrow in Beijing, many eyes will focus on the Vatican. And well they should: the delegation from the Holy See stands in stark relief to those Western nations, the U.S. included, that seek to impose the politics of radical individualism on an increasingly resistant world.

The Holy See: Voice of Sanity in a Sea of Madness

- It is maddening to listen to the merits of alternative lifestyles when the institutions of marriage and the family are foundering.

- It is maddening to listen to discussions of "five genders" when every sane person knows there are but two sexes, both of which are rooted in nature.

- It is maddening to listen to the mantra of "pro-choice" when female mutilation, forced sterilizations and forced abortions go uncontested.

- It is maddening to listen to the glories of sexual liberation when we are left with the debris of illegitimacy, deadbeat dads and communicable diseases.

- It is maddening to listen to demands for quotas when female infanticide goes unchecked.

- It is maddening to listen to those who boycotted states that didn't pass the ERA now defend holding a human rights conference in a nation where torture and cannibalism (e.g., eating human embryos) are tolerated.

Against this madness is the Holy See. Its support for marriage, family, fatherhood and motherhood accords with its profound respect for the dignity of the human person. Its call for sexual restraint is more than good advice, it is a requisite of civilization.

Anyone is free to criticize the Holy See, but what we don't need is the kind of insult that Vatican delegates endured in Cairo. There is no role for Catholic bashing in any forum, and this is doubly true of U.N. venues.

Let the debate begin. If it's an honest one, we are confident that the sanity of the Holy See will triumph over the madness of its adversaries.

— *William A. Donohue*
President

Catholic League
for Religious and Civil Rights
1011 First Avenue, New York, New York 10022
(212) 371-3191

The Catholic League is the nation's largest Catholic civil rights organization, funded wholly through membership dues.

[6]*New York Times*, September 3, 1995, Sec. A, p. 11.

3. GROUP WORK AND CLASS DISCUSSION: APPLYING THE TOULMIN MODEL TO A CARTOON AND A SHORT ESSAY

Analyze the following cartoon and short article in small groups and then discuss the results of your analysis as a class. Use these questions to guide your analysis. You will need to infer some of the answers.

1. What is the claim? Is it explicitly stated, or did you have to infer it?
2. What is the support?
3. What are the warrants? Does the author back the warrants? If yes, how?
4. Do you share the warrants, or do you have conflicting warrants? If your warrants are in conflict, what are your warrants?
5. Is there a rebuttal in the article? What rebuttal might *you* offer?
6. Is the claim qualified? Is the qualifier effective? How could it be more effective?

WHAT'S HAPPENED TO DISNEY FILMS?

John Evans

Many of today's over-30 adults who grew up on a diet of Disney movies are now responsible, God-honoring parents. They want their children to experience the same magic in films and videos that they once enjoyed.

Does the name "Disney" still mean the same in the '90s that it did in the '60s? Not at all. Disney is now a huge conglomerate with such diverse subsidiaries as Miramax Films, Hollywood Pictures, and Touchstone Pictures. The films they produce range from the violent, degrading *Pulp Fiction,* a Miramax film, to the delightful *Beauty and the Beast,* a Walt Disney Co. film. In between these two extremes are a myriad of movies of varying degrees of decency and offensiveness.

Listed below are descriptions which illustrate the undesirable content included in some Walt Disney Pictures films intended for young children. These comments are based on reviews from the *Preview* Family Movie and TV Guide.

The Little Mermaid (1989), G-rated animated film. While Disney's villains in the past have simply been mean and nasty, Ursula, the wicked sea witch, is downright evil. Her bizarre appearance and morbid undersea abode exude images of witchcraft, and some scenes are likely to frighten small children. Also, offensive, sexually suggestive dialogue is uncalled for. In one scene the evil Ursula intimates that the mermaid will have to "let her body do her talking." In romantic song, Ariel sings to Eric, "You know you want to do it." Even more disturbing, however, is the picture on the video box that includes a very obvious phallic symbol.

Aladdin (1992), G-rated animated film. The panther head entrance to the cave and a volcanic eruption are violent, jolting, and intense. The Genie transforms the evil Jofar into a sorcerer who violently manipulates others. Jofar changes into a giant snake to fight Aladdin. Again, the evil characters are more than scary—they attack. Also, the video tape includes some suggestive dialogue whispered in the background during a balcony scene between Aladdin and Jasmine. The words, "Take off your—" can be heard, implying that the muffled word is "clothes."

Lion King (1994), G-rated animated film. New Age and occultic concepts appear to be introduced when it's said that the father lion is living on in the son. Also, a remark is made that dead kings are looking down on the young lion. These can be interpreted literally as the Hindu concept of the universality of the soul. Also, when the young lion talks to his dead father, this violates the biblical admonition against communicating with the spirits of the dead.

Lion King also includes intense violence, including a graphic stampede and clawing and biting among animals. This continues the trend to show hand-to-hand combat that inflicts severe injuries.

Pocahontas (1995), G-rated animated film. This brand new feature film favorably depicts Indian animism, the belief that every natural object, such as rocks and trees, have spirits. Also, it portrays communication with spirits of the dead as acceptable. "The producers give an exaggerated picture of the white colonists as greedy, bloodthirsty monsters who just want to rid the land of 'those savages.'"

The Walt Disney Pictures company continues to produce Disney's G-rated films as well as its more family oriented movies, such as *Iron Will, Angels in the Outfield, White Fang,* and the *Mighty Ducks* series. However, several years ago, the Disney organization decided to produce more "mature" films and established two wholly owned companies to produce them, Hollywood Pictures and Touchstone Pictures. Also, a few years ago, Disney acquired Miramax Films, which distributes some very offensive films, most of them produced in foreign countries.

A few examples of the most offensive films these companies have produced or distributed are given below.

Pulp Fiction (1994-Miramax Films). Disgusting R-rated adult film which contains over 320 obscenities and profanities, ongoing graphic and gratuitous violence, a homosexual rape, and much bizarre behavior.

Color of Night (1994-Hollywood Pictures). Gruesome R-rated murder mystery with bloody killings, stabbings, an impaling, and choking. Also, a sexual affair with graphic sexual content and nudity, and over 100 obscenities and profanities.

Priest (1995-Miramax Films). This controversial R-rated film sympathetically portrays a homosexual priest and depicts other Catholic priests as disreputable characters. Contains scenes of graphic homosexual lovemaking. Catholics nation-wide protested the film.

Who Framed Roger Rabbit? (1988-Touchstone Pictures). Suggestive, violent PG-rated cartoon film in which some characters are boiled in toxic waste and flattened by a steam roller. Also, features an implied extramarital affair, crude language, sexually suggestive humor, and a voluptuous, seductive female character.

For parents who want to select only wholesome, decent entertainment for their families, the *Preview* Family Movie and TV Guide publishes reviews of all current films twice a month. The reviews contain information on the desirable elements in a film as well as a detailed description of any offensive material.[7]

4. **CLASS DISCUSSION AND WRITING ASSIGNMENT: A TOULMIN ANALYSIS OF "LEARNING BY INTIMIDATION?"**
Do a Toulmin analysis of the following essay, "Learning by Intimidation?" In class discussion, identify the claim. Identify and discuss the effectiveness of the support. Describe the warrants, including the mother's warrants, the coach's warrants, and the young athletes' warrants, as well as any conflict regarding them.

Do not worry about finding the "right answers." There aren't any. Instead, use the model to help you read and analyze the essay, and then argue for your interpretation of it by writing about what it has helped you discover. Limit your paper to two to three pages.

LEARNING BY INTIMIDATION?

Rosemary Parker

His narrowed eyes burn like hot little coals, and he screams through clenched teeth, his face thrust into hers. She's young and scared and stands with head hung, eyebrows raised in an expression that, while failing to acknowledge his accusations, is careful not to challenge them. Even in her obvious distress she's practiced and automatically leans back a bit from time to time to avoid the spray of spit he spews as he spells it out for her: she's stupid, lazy and worthless, and if she doesn't shape up someone else will soon be doing her job.

The first time I witnessed it I was genuinely alarmed and thought of trying to intervene, or perhaps of calling in the authorities. But there were others there who knew these two better than I, and no one else batted an eye. He didn't hit her. I don't think he cursed. I tried to put myself in her mother's place—but her mother was there watching with me, and did nothing.

Then it was my daughter, and still I did nothing. Hey, if he were her boyfriend or her husband I like to think I'd be there in his face, or at least on the phone to social services trying to find counseling help. But this guy was my daughter's *coach.* And from what I hear from other parents, dads especially, this guy knows the game. He can teach her the skills she'll need, help her improve her game. And if he wants to, he can make her sit the bench. Which is why she beseeches me to mind my own business.

---

[7]*The Dallas/Fort Worth Heritage,* August 1995, p. 12.

And I do. Other mothers, once bothered as I, tell me it is better for our children to be screamed at than ignored. It's a sure sign of that nebulous desirable called potential, they say. I'll get used to it and so will the kids. Though it does seem to me that submissiveness is considered a part of that potential. The few girls with faces marked by defiance are more likely found near the end of the bench.

Besides, this guy's not alone. Why is that a comfort, knowing someone else has it worse? There's the coach at a neighboring school who takes it right down to a foot-stamping, bleacher-kicking tirade. And the boys get it worse than the girls. The boys' varsity-team players are a bunch of "f——pussies" when they falter; a band instructor preparing for competition screams threats of what will happen unless more precision is achieved, using words that shock even those kids whose language is an adolescent shade of blue.

What's going on here? In any other scenario, wouldn't this behavior be stopped? Haven't we agreed that abuse and humiliation are not appropriate instructional aids? And isn't it especially chilling to allow—to encourage—our daughters to accept such treatment at the hands of a man, to shrug it off as "part of the game"? After all, it wasn't that long ago when the playing field was much broader, when it was all "the game" and women were all required to put up with it if they wanted to keep their jobs or their marriages.

But somehow even women seem to see school competitions in a context all their own. Their daughters are at last competing and they'll need to learn to do their best to win. And if that means coaches using the traditional unkindnesses of pitting kids against their own teammates for playing time, yanking them out for a tongue-lashing in front of a gym full of their friends and relatives, or screaming out their mistakes as they try to play the game, well so be it.

In any case, isn't it necessary for kids to learn how to perform well under stress?

Actually not even the armed forces buys the old stress routine anymore, and drill instructors have been told to cool it a bit. Fraternity hazing is frowned upon and it's no longer tacitly acceptable to beat your wife or kids. I can't think of any other situation in which a collection of nice, middle-class parents would sit quietly by while an adult publicly reduced their children to tears. But short of corporal punishment or a technical foul (you can heap abuse on the children in your charge, but not on an adult referee), anything goes on the gym floor or the playing field.

I hate the way it works and I haven't gotten used to it. I still cringe along with the kids and sometimes can't bear to watch. I'm angry with myself for failing to challenge a wrong when my gut insists I should. I'm not sure I believe my children when they tell me they'd be the ones to pay for my speaking out, but I've not been willing to risk it, either. And when I witness the same thing in another sport or at another school, I tell myself it's none of my business, really. I recall the other arguments, too—that coaches are dedicated guys and that I am unable and unwilling to coach, so I should have no voice in how others do the job.

So while I wait for the answer to come to me I do silly little things, like yelling out "Good job!" to any player who exerts an effort, yelling it a little louder to the ones who screw up.

I tell myself it's not important anyway, that these are just children's games, after all, and that if their love of the game weren't enough to offset the guff, they'd quit. But I fume to think that those are the choices, and I wait for someone to take up the fight for our children's dignity.

Maybe one of the good coaches, one of the ones the kids adore, will step in. Maybe parents with more clout, whose kids are stars? But they have even more to lose. They may approve of these methods. It's gotten their kid further than the others, right? Maybe someone with kids who are not involved in sports, some outsider who could bring attention to the problem from a safer distance?

That's what I tell myself, but I'm not buying it. I know it's really my job, even though I am just an out-of-shape, over-40 mom with no credibility in this world of jocks. I know that with their eyes on the prize, their vision is different from mine. My children are the first to tell me that I just don't understand. But I thought I recognized harm when I saw it come a child's way—the least I can do is point to it.[8]

5. CLASS PROJECT: TOULMIN ANALYSES OF EXAMPLES SELECTED BY STUDENTS

Clip a short article, an advertisement, a cartoon, or a letter to the editor, and use the Toulmin model to analyze it. Identify the claim, support, and warrants. Identify also, if they are present, backing, rebuttals, or qualifiers. Circulate the clipping among classmates. Give a 2 to 3 minute oral report in which you describe the parts of the argument to the class.

6. WRITING ASSIGNMENT: TOULMIN ANALYSIS

Write a 200–300 word paper in which you identify the claim, support, and warrants in the clipping you brought for the class project (see exercise 5 above). Identify also, if they are present, backing, rebuttals, or qualifiers.

Examples of student-written Toulmin analysis papers of "What's Happened to Disney Films?" and the Hi and Lois cartoon (p. 146) follow. Read them to help you write your own Toulmin analysis. Also, see if you and your classmates agree with these analyses. Everyone does not apply the Toulmin model in exactly the same way. There are no absolutely correct answers because different readers' interpretations vary.

TOULMIN ANALYSIS OF "WHAT'S HAPPENED TO DISNEY FILMS?"

Beth Brunk

In "What's Happened to Disney Films?" John Evans claims that Disney is not making the same caliber of movies that it was in the past; the majority of recent Disney films are not suitable for young audiences. Evans supports his claim

---

[8]*Newsweek*, November 8, 1993, p. 14. Rosemary Parker is a mother of five who lives in Michigan.

through specific scenes and lines from recent Disney movies. *The Little Mermaid* and *Aladdin* contain sexual innuendoes. *The Lion King* presents New Age and occultic concepts and contains graphic violence. Disney's most recent film, *Pocahontas* "favorably depicts Indian animism" and portrays the white settlers in a bad light. Evans also frowns on Disney's ownership of Touchstone Pictures, Miramax Films and Hollywood Pictures which have produced movies such as *Who Framed Roger Rabbit?*, *Pulp Fiction* and *Color of Night,* all of which he believes tarnish the once wholesome Disney image.

Evan's argument has two warrants: Disney should only be making movies suitable for children regardless of the name it is produced under. Also, movies that are suitable for children are those which are based strictly on Christian ideologies and portray "the white man" in a positive light.

Evans prepares for rebuttal by naming some Disney movies such as *Iron Will, Angels in the Outfield* and *Mighty Ducks* which are considered to be suitable for children.

The backing for his warrants is Christian doctrines and the Bible. Although he does not appeal to either explicitly throughout much of the article, he does say that Simba's conversation with his dead father in *The Lion King* "violates the biblical admonition against communicating with the spirits of the dead." This world view underlies his entire argument.

His qualifier is a subtle one and is found at the end of the piece where he claims that there is information available, "for parents who want to select only wholesome, decent entertainment for their families." He allows that there may be some parents who do not care what their children watch and would therefore disagree with his claim.[9]

TOULMIN ANALYSIS: "HI & LOIS" COMIC STRIP

Rose M. Johnson

The argument in this comic strip consists of two stated items of support; both claims and warrants are implied. The two observed facts that serve as support are that Lou's Lawn Service will rake Mr. Thurston's lawn for $75 and that Mr. Thurston offers Mrs. Thurston $50 to do the same job. The implied claim may be either a broad generalization—women work cheaper than men—or a more specific conclusion—housewives work cheaper than men in business. Whether it is general or specific, this claim devalues the worth of women's work.

At least three warrants are implied, and they may be either general or specific. Stated generally, one warrant seems to be that women work for less than men; another, that women have the physical strength to do the same work as men; and another (implied from the picture of Mrs. Thurston sitting and read-

---

[9]Used with permission.

ing), that women do not have enough work to keep them busy and, therefore, have time on their hands. Each of these warrants could be qualified by limiting the logical inferences to housewives rather than to women as a whole.

Thurston's claim may be qualified by the phrasing of his second item of support as a question. That question may be equivalent to inserting a qualifying word like "probably" into the warrants and the claim. Also, Thurston's question may imply that he's expecting a rebuttal.[10]

---

[10]Used with permission.

(S) ——————————————— (Q) ———————————— (C)

- Lou's Lawn Service has offered to rake Mr. Thurston's lawn for $75.
- Mr. Thurston thinks that $75 is too much to rake his lawn. (Forget it!)
- Mr. Thurston thinks that his wife might rake the lawn for $50.
- Mr. Thurston doesn't want to rake the lawn himself.

(W)

- Probably
  - Thurston phrases his request to Mrs. Thurston as a question.
  - Thurston is holding the rake behind his back.
- Maybe only housewives will work for less.

- You can (probably) get a woman (or a housewife anyway) to do a business man's job for at least 1/3 less money.

- Women work for less than men do.
- Women can do the same work as men.
- Women do not have enough work to keep them busy.
- Housewives have too much time on their hands.

7. GROUP DISCUSSION: UNDERSTANDING VALUE WARRANTS
Warrants often come from the systems of values that people hold. The values will not be spelled out in an argument, yet they will still influence the arguer and be present as warrants in the argument. The following essay describes six American value systems. These systems are somewhat over-simplified, and they do not identify all American value systems. They are useful, however, to help you understand some of the values that people hold. Read the essay and then discuss which value systems you think may be operating in the selections you have analyzed. Provide reasons for your opinions. There are no correct answers. Use your imagination and have some fun with this exercise.

1. The Saab automobile ad, page 144.
2. The Catholic League ad, page 145.
3. The Hi and Lois cartoon, page 146.
4. "What's Happened to Disney Films?" page 146.
5. "Learning By Intimidation?" page 148.

AMERICAN VALUE SYSTEMS

Richard Rieke and Malcolm Sillars

As we have noted, by careful analysis individual values can be discovered in the arguments of ourselves and others. There is a difficulty, however, in attempting to define a whole system of values for a person or a group. And as difficult as that is, each of us, as a participant in argumentation, should have some concept of the broad systems that most frequently bring together certain values. For this purpose, it is useful for you to have an idea of some of the most commonly acknowledged value systems.

You must approach this study with a great deal of care, however, because even though the six basic value systems we are about to define provide a fair view of the standard American value systems, they do not provide convenient pigeonholes into which individuals can be placed. They represent broad social categories. Some individuals (even groups) will be found outside these systems. Many individuals and groups will cross over value systems, picking and choosing from several. Note how certain words appear as value terms in more than one value system. The purpose of this survey is to provide a beginning understanding of standard American values, not a complete catalog.[1]

THE PURITAN-PIONEER-PEASANT VALUE SYSTEM
This value system has been identified frequently as the *puritan morality* or the *Protestant ethic*. It also has been miscast frequently because of the excessive emphasis placed, by some of its adherents, on restrictions of personal acts such as smoking and consuming alcohol.[2] Consequently, over the years, this value system has come to stand for a narrow-minded attempt to interfere in other people's

business, particularly if those people are having fun. However, large numbers of people who do not share such beliefs follow this value system.

We have taken the liberty of expanding beyond the strong and perhaps too obvious religious implications of the terms *puritan* and *Protestant*. This value system is what most Americans refer to when they speak of the "pioneer spirit," which was not necessarily religious. It also extends, we are convinced, to a strain of values brought to this country by Southern and Eastern European Catholics, Greek Orthodox, and Jews who could hardly be held responsible for John Calvin's theology or even the term *Protestant ethic*. Thus, we have the added word *peasant*, which may not be particularly accurate. Despite the great friction that existed between these foreign-speaking immigrants from other religions and their native Protestant counterparts, they had a great deal in common as do their ideological descendants today. On many occasions after describing the puritan morality we have heard a Jewish student say, "That's the way my father thinks," or had a student of Italian or Polish descent say, "My grandmother talks that way all the time."

The Puritan-Pioneer-Peasant value system is rooted in the idea that persons have an obligation to themselves and those around them, and in some cases to their God, to work hard at whatever they do. In this system, people are limited in their abilities and must be prepared to fail. The great benefit is in the striving against an unknowable and frequently hostile universe. They have an obligation to others, must be selfless, and must not waste. Some believe this is the only way to gain happiness and success. Others see it as a means to salvation. In all cases it takes on a moral orientation. Obviously, one might work hard for a summer in order to buy a new car and not be labeled a "puritan." Frequently, in this value system, the instrumental values of selflessness, thrift, and hard work become terminal values where the work has value beyond the other benefits it can bring one. People who come from this value system often have difficulty with retirement, because their meaning in life, indeed their pleasure, came from work.

Likewise, because work, selflessness, and thrift are positive value terms in this value system, laziness, selfishness, and waste are negative value terms. One can see how some adherents to this value system object to smoking, drinking, dancing, or cardplaying. These activities are frivolous; they take one's mind off more serious matters and waste time.

Some of the words that are associated with the Puritan-Pioneer-Peasant value system are:

Positive: *activity, work, thrift, morality, dedication, selflessness, virtue, righteousness, duty, dependability, temperance, sobriety, savings, dignity*

Negative: *waste, immorality, dereliction, dissipation, infidelity, theft, vandalism, hunger, poverty, disgrace, vanity*

THE ENLIGHTENMENT VALUE SYSTEM

America became a nation in the period of the Enlightenment. It happened when a new intellectual era based on the scientific finding of men like Sir Isaac Newton and the philosophical systems of men like John Locke were dominant. The founders of our nation were particularly influenced by such men. The Declaration of Independence is the epitome of an enlightenment document. In many ways America is an enlightenment nation, and if enlightenment is not the predominant value system, it is surely first among equals.

The enlightenment position stems from the belief that we live in an ordered world in which all activity is governed by laws similar to the laws of physics. These "natural laws" may or may not come from God, depending on the particular orientation of the person examining them; but unlike many adherents to the Puritan value system just discussed, enlightenment persons theorized that people could discover these laws by themselves. Thus, they may worship God for God's greatness, even acknowledge that God created the universe and natural laws, but they find out about the universe because they have the power of reason. The laws of nature are harmonious, and one can use reason to discover them all. They can also be used to provide for a better life.

Because humans are basically good and capable of finding answers, restraints on them must be limited. Occasionally, people do foolish things and must be restrained by society. However, a person should never be restrained in matters of the mind. Reason must be free. Thus, government is an agreement among individuals to assist the society to protect rights. That government is a democracy. Certain rights are inalienable, and they may not be abridged; "among these are life, liberty and the pursuit of happiness." Arguments for academic freedom, against wiretaps, and for scientific inquiry come from this value system.

Some of the words that are associated with the Enlightenment value system are:

Positive: *freedom, science, nature, rationality, democracy, fact, liberty, individualism, knowledge, intelligence, reason, natural rights, natural laws, progress*

Negative: *ignorance, inattention, thoughtlessness, error, indecision, irrationality, dictatorship, fascism, bookburning, falsehood, regression*

THE PROGRESSIVE VALUE SYSTEM

Progress was a natural handmaiden of the Enlightenment. If these laws were available and if humans had the tool, reason, to discover them and use them to advantage, then progress would result. Things would continually get better. But although progress is probably an historical spin-off of the Enlightenment, it has become so important on its own that it deserves at times to be seen quite separate from the Enlightenment.

Richard Weaver, in 1953, found that "one would not go far wrong in naming progress" the "god term" of that age. It is, he said, the "expression about which all other expressions are ranked as subordinate. . . . Its force imparts to the others their lesser degrees of force, and fixes the scale by which degrees of comparison are understood."[3]

Today, the unmediated use of the progress value system is questioned, but progress is still a fundamental value in America. Most arguments against progress are usually arguments about the definition of progress. They are about what "true progress is."

Some of the key words of the Progressive value system are:

Positive: *practicality, efficiency, change, improvement, science, future, modern, progress, evolution*

Negative: *old-fashioned,[4] regressive, impossible, backward*

THE TRANSCENDENTAL VALUE SYSTEM

Another historical spin-off of the Enlightenment system was the development of the Transcendental movement of the early nineteenth century. It took from the Enlightenment all its optimism about people, freedom, and democracy, but rejected the emphasis on reason. It argued idealistically that there was a faculty higher than reason; let us call it, as many transcendentalists did, intuition. Thus, for the transcendentalist, there is a way of knowing that is better than reason, a way which *transcends* reason. Consequently, what might seem like the obvious solution to problems is not necessarily so. One must look, on important matters at least, to the intuition, to the feelings. Like the enlightenment thinker, the transcendentalist believes in a unified universe governed by natural laws. Thus all persons, by following their intuition will discover these laws, and universal harmony will take place. And, of course, little or no government will be necessary. The original American transcendentalists of the early nineteenth century drew their inspiration from Platonism, German idealism, and Oriental mysticism. The idea was also fairly well limited to the intellectuals. By and large, transcendentalism has been the view of a rather small group of people throughout our history, but at times it has been very important. It has always been somewhat more influential among younger people. James Truslow Adams once wrote that everyone should read Ralph Waldo Emerson at sixteen because his writings were a marvel for the buoyantly optimistic person of that age but that his transcendental writings did not have the same luster at twenty-one.[5] In the late 1960s and early 1970s, Henry David Thoreau's *Walden* was the popular reading of campus rebels. The emphasis of anti-establishment youth on Oriental mysticism, like Zen, should not be ignored either. The rejection of contemporary society and mores symbolized by what others considered "outlandish dress" and "hippie behavior" with its emphasis on emotional response and "do your own thing" indicated the adoption of a transcendental value system. Communal living is reminiscent of the transcendental "Brook Farm" experiments that were attempted in the early nineteenth century and described by Nathaniel Hawthorne in his novel *The Blithedale Romance.*

In all of these movements the emphasis on humanitarian values, the centrality of love for others, and the preference for quiet contemplation over activity has been important. Transcendentalism, however, rejects the common idea of progress. Inner light and knowledge of one's self is more important than material well-being. There is also some tendency to reject physical well-being because it takes one away from intuitive truth.

It should be noted that not everyone who argues for change is a transcendentalist. The transcendental white campus agitators of the late 1960s discovered that, despite all their concern for replacing racism and war with love and peace, their black counterparts were highly pragmatic and rationalistic about objectives and means. Black agitators and demonstrators were never "doing their thing" in the intuitive way of many whites.

It should also be noted that while a full adherence to transcendentalism has been limited to small groups, particularly among intellectuals and youth, many of the ideas are not limited to such persons. One can surely find strains of what we have labeled, for convenience, transcendentalism in the mysticism of some very devout older Roman Catholics, for instance. And perhaps many Americans become transcendental on particular issues, about the value to be derived from hiking in the mountains, for example.

Here are some of the terms that are characteristic of the Transcendental value system:

Positive: *humanitarian, individualism, respect, intuition, truth, equality, sympathetic, affection, feeling, love, sensitivity, emotion, personal kindness, compassion, brotherhood, friendship, mysticism*

Negative: *science,*[6] *reason, mechanical, hate, war, anger, insensitive, coldness, unemotional*

THE PERSONAL SUCCESS VALUE SYSTEM

The least social of the major American value systems is the one that moves people toward personal achievement and success. It can be related as a part of the Enlightenment value system, but it is more than that because it involves a highly pragmatic concern for the material happiness of the individual. To call it selfish would be to load the terms against it, although there would be some who accept this value system who would say "Yes, I'm selfish." "The Lord helps those who help themselves" has always been an acceptable adage by some of the most devout in our nation.

You might note that the Gallup poll, cited earlier in this chapter, is very heavily weighted toward personal values. Even "good family life" rated as the top value can be seen as an item of personal success. This survey includes only a few social values like "helping needy people" and "helping better America" and even those are phrased in personal terms. That is, the respondents were asked "how important you feel each of these is to you." The personal orientation of the survey may represent a bias of the Gallup poll, but we suspect it reflects much of American society. We are personal success-oriented in an individual way which would not be found in some other cultures (e.g., in the Japanese culture).

Here are some of the terms that tend to be characteristic of the Personal Success value system:

Positive: *career, family, friends, recreation, economic security, identity, health, individualism, affection, respect, enjoyment, dignity, consideration, fair play, personal*

Negative: *dullness, routine, hunger, poverty, disgrace, coercion, disease*

THE COLLECTIVIST VALUE SYSTEM

Although there are few actual members of various socialist and communist groups in the United States, one cannot ignore the strong attachment among some people for collective action. This is, in part, a product of the influx of social theories from Europe in the nineteenth century. It is also a natural outgrowth of a perceived need to control the excesses of freedom in a mass society. Its legitimacy is not limited to current history, however. There has always been a value placed on cooperative action. The same people today who would condemn welfare payments to unwed mothers would undoubtedly praise their ancestors for barnraising and taking care of the widow in a frontier community. Much rhetoric about our "pioneer ancestors" has to do with their cooperative action. And anticollectivist presidents and evangelists talk about "the team." At the same time many fervent advocates of collective action in the society argue vehemently for their freedom and independence. Certainly the civil rights movement constituted a collective action for freedom. Remember the link in Martin Luther King, Jr.'s speech between "freedom" and "brotherhood"?

But whether the Collectivist value system is used to defend socialist proposals or promote "law and order" there is no doubt that collectivism is a strong value system in this nation. Like transcendentalism, however, it is probably a value system that, at least in this day cannot work alone.

Here are some of the terms that tend to characterize the Collectivist value system:

Positive: *cooperation, joint action, unity, brotherhood, together, social good, order, humanitarian aid and comfort, equality*

Negative: *disorganization, selfishness, personal greed, inequality*

Clearly, these six do not constitute a complete catalog of all American value systems. Combinations and reorderings produce different systems. Two values deserve special attention because they are common in these systems and sometimes operate alone: *nature* and *patriotism*. Since the beginning of our nation the idea has prevailed that the natural is good and there for our use and preservation. Also, since John Winthrop first proclaimed that the New England Puritans would build "a city on the hill" for all the world to see and emulate, the idea has endured that America is a fundamentally great nation, perhaps God-chosen, to lead the world to a better life. This idea may be somewhat tarnished in some quarters today, but there is no doubt that it will revive as it has in the past. Linked to other value systems we have discussed, it will once more be a theme that will draw the adherence of others to arguments.[10]

---

[10]From Richard D. Reike and Malcolm O. Sillars, *Argumentation and the Decision Making Process,* 2nd ed. (Glenview, IL: Scott, Foresman, 1984).

NOTES

1. The following material draws from a wide variety of sources. The following is an illustrative cross section of sources from a variety of disciplines: Virgil I. Baker and Ralph T. Eubanks, *Speech in Personal and Public Affairs* (New York: David McKay, 1965), pp. 95–102; Clyde Kluckhohn, "An Anthropologist Looks at the United States," *Mirror for Man* (New York: McGraw-Hill, 1949), pp. 228–261; Stow Persons, *American Minds* (New York: Holt, Rinehart and Winston, 1958); Jurgen Ruesch, "Communication and American Values; A Psychological Approach," *Communication: The Social Matrix of Psychiatry*, Jurgen Ruesch and Gregory Bateson (New York: W. W. Norton, 1951), pp. 94–134; Edward D. Steele and W. Charles Redding, "The American Value System: Premises for Persuasion," *Western Speech,* 26 (Spring 1962), pp. 83–91; Richard Weaver, "Ultimate Terms in Contemporary Rhetoric," *The Ethics of Rhetoric* (Chicago: Henry Regnery, 1953), pp. 211–232; Robin M. Williams, Jr., *American Society,* 3rd ed. (New York: Alfred A. Knopf, 1970), pp. 438–504.
2. It is ironic that the original American Puritans did not have clear injunctions against such activity.
3. Weaver, p. 212.
4. Note that "old-fashioned" is frequently positive when we speak of morality and charm but not when we speak of our taste in music.
5. James Truslow Adams, "Emerson Re-read," *The Transcendental Revolt*, George F. Whicher, Ed. (Boston: D. C. Heath, 1949), pp. 31–39.
6. It is interesting to note, however, that one of the major organizations in the United States with transcendental origins, the Christian Science Church, combines transcendentalism with science.

8. QUESTIONS ON THE CHAPTER

a. Since people do not argue about the truth or facts that everyone accepts, what do they argue about? What are some examples?

b. Name and describe the three essential parts of the Toulmin model. Do the same for the three optional parts.

c. What are some synonyms for each of the three essential parts of the Toulmin model?

d. How does the warrant further the aims of argument? What is its value in making argument convincing?

e. Describe value warrants and field-dependent warrants.

9. QUESTIONS ON THE ESSAYS FOR ANALYSIS

a. "What's Happened to Disney Films?" page 146. What was the first Disney film that you saw? Did it have a disturbing effect on you? Drawing on your own experiences and those of other people you know, how important is it for parents to screen the movies and television that their children watch? Where would you draw the line if you were doing the screening? That is, would you agree with the author of this essay, or would you apply different criteria?

b. "Learning by Intimidation?" page 148. Is intimidation motivating for you? Why do you think coaches use intimidation to motivate athletes? Do you think intimidation is motivating in other contexts such as in the classroom or in the workplace? What else can be used to motivate people to achieve? If you had been the mother who wrote this article, what would you have done? Why?

CHAPTER 6

Types of Claims

This chapter and the one that follows it expand on and develop some of the ideas in Chapter 5. In Chapter 5 the claim, the support, and the warrants were identified as the three essential parts of an argument. This chapter, along with Chapter 7, provides additional information about these three parts. Claims are the subject of this chapter. Support and warrants, which constitute the proofs of an argument, are the subject of the next chapter.

Argument theorists categorize claims according to types, and these types suggest the fundamental purposes of given arguments. Knowing possible categories for claims and the special characteristics associated with each of them will help you better understand the purposes and special features of the arguments you read, and will also improve your writing of them. When reading, as soon as you identify the type of claim in an argument, you can predict and anticipate certain features of that type of argument. This technique helps you follow the author's line of thought more easily. When writing, knowing the types of claims can provide you with frameworks for developing your purpose and strategy.

When you begin to read argument with the idea of locating the claim and identifying it by type, your ability to identify and understand all the parts of an argument will increase. An understanding of proofs, the subject of Chapter 7, will improve your understanding further. As this chapter will demonstrate, certain proofs are often used to develop certain types of claims. Proofs are identified here and explained at length in the next chapter. Chapters 6 and 7, taken together, will teach you how to recognize and use both claims and proofs, the major components of argument. But first, here is a strategy for analyzing an argument to get a preliminary sense of its purpose and to identify its parts.

GET A SENSE OF THE PURPOSE AND PARTS
OF AN ARGUMENT

Survey.　Follow the procedure for surveying a book on page 67 or for surveying an article on pages 67–68. Your objective is to find the claim and some of the main subclaims or parts.

Divide the Argument into Its Parts.   Draw a line across the page (or make a light dot in the margin) each time the subject changes. This physical division of a written argument into its parts is called *chunking*. For example, in a policy paper that proposes a solution to a problem, the explanation of the problem would be a major chunk, as would be the explanation of the solution.

Ask Why the Parts Have Been Placed in the Particular Order.   Try to determine if the parts have been placed in a logical order to facilitate understanding, for instance, or whether they have been placed in a psychological order, leading up to the conclusion or action step at the end. There are other possibilities as well. Try to get a sense of how the author thought about and organized the parts.

Analyze the Relationships among the Parts.   When you have speculated about why the author put the parts in a particular order, go a step further and think about the relationships among these parts. Do they all contribute to a central idea, such as a specialized definition? Or are other relationships apparent, such as causes for effects or solutions for problems?

When you begin to write argument, write a claim, list a few supporting reasons that represent the tentative parts, and then think about the best sequence for these parts. The relationships among them will become clearer to you as you rearrange them in an order that is logical to you.

Once you have a sense of the overall purpose and shape of an argument, you can then identify the type of claim that predominates in it.

FIVE CATEGORIES OF CLAIMS

Virtually all arguments can be categorized according to one of five types of claims. You can identify each argument type by identifying the questions the argument answers. In general, certain types of organization and proof are associated with certain types of claims, as you will see in the following discussion. There are no hard-and-fast rules about using specific organizational strategies or types of proof to develop specific types of claims. Knowing common patterns and tendencies, however, helps readers make predictions about the course of an argument and helps writers plan and write their own arguments.

Here are the five categories of claims, along with the main questions that they answer:

1. *Claims of fact.* Did it happen? Is it true?
2. *Claims of definition.* What is it? How should we interpret it?
3. *Claims of cause.* What caused it? Or, what are the effects?
4. *Claims of value.* Is it good or bad? What criteria do we use to decide?
5. *Claims of policy.* What should we do about it? What should be our future course of action?

The sections that follow provide additional explanations of the five types of claims, along with the general questions they answer, some examples of actual claims, a list of the types of proof most typically associated with each type, the organizational strategies that one might expect for each type, and a short written argument that illustrates each type as it appears in practice.

Claims of Fact

Questions Answered by Claims of Fact.   Did it happen? Is it true? Does it exist? Is it a fact?

Examples of Claims of Fact.   (Note that all of the "facts" in these claims need to be proved as either absolutely or probably true in order to be acceptable to an audience. All of these claims, also, are controversial.) The ozone layer is becoming depleted. Increasing population threatens the environment. American drivers are becoming more responsible. America's military is prepared for any likely crisis. The abominable snowman exists in certain remote areas. Women are not as effective as men in combat. A mass murderer is evil and not insane. The American judicial system operates successfully.

Types of Proof Associated with Claims of Fact.   Factual proof, as you might guess, is especially appropriate for claims of fact. Such proof includes both past and present *facts, statistics, real examples,* and *quotations from reliable authorities. Inductive reasoning,* which cites several examples and then draws a probable conclusion from them, is also a common type of proof for claims of fact. *Analogies* that establish comparisons and similarities between the subject and something else that is commonly accepted as true are useful. *Signs* that present evidence of a past or present state of affairs are also useful to establish claims of fact. *Opinions* are used to support claims of fact and are usually also supported by factual data.

Possible Organizational Strategies.   Chronological order, which traces what has occurred over a period of time, usually in the order in which it occurred, can be used to develop claims of fact. For example, the history of the increase in population might be provided to show how it has happened over a period of time. Or topical order may be used. In topical order a group of reasons to support a fact may be identified and developed topic by topic. Thus reasons might be given for the existence of the abominable snowman, with each of them developed at length. This chapter is organized according to topics: the five types of claims.

The claim of fact itself is often stated at or near the beginning of the argument unless there is a psychological advantage for stating it at the end. Most authors make claims of fact clear from the outset, revealing early what they seek to establish.

An Example of an Argument That Contains a Claim of Fact.   The following are the opening paragraphs from a longer article that establishes the fact that the African-American community is in crisis and dysfunctional. This is controversial. Others might argue for a different view, that the African-American community is healthy and prospering.

Essay

BLACK AMERICA'S MOMENT OF TRUTH

Dinesh D'Souza

Claim of fact

The last few decades have witnessed nothing less than a breakdown of civilization within the African-American community. Vital institutions such as the small business, the church, and the family are now greatly weakened; in some areas, they are on the verge of collapsing altogether. And the symptoms of systemic decline are both numerous and ominous—extremely high rates of criminal activity, the normalization of illegitimacy, a preponderance of single-parent families, high levels of drug and alcohol addiction, a parasitic reliance on government provision, hostility to academic achievement, and a scarcity of independent enterprises. The next generation of young blacks is especially vulnerable. "We are in danger of becoming superfluous people in this society," says African-American scholar Anthony Walton. "We are not essential or even integral to the economy." Marian Wright Edelman of the Children's Defense Fund puts it more bluntly: "We have a black child crisis worse than any since slavery."

Examples of problems

Quote from authority

Statistics

This crisis did not exist a generation ago. In 1960, 78 percent of all black families were headed by married couples; today that figure is less than 40 percent. In the 1950s black crime rates, while higher than those for whites, were vastly lower than they are today. These figures suggest that the dire circumstances of the black community are not the result of genes or racism. The black gene pool has not changed substantially since mid-century, and racism then was far worse. The main problem facing African Americans is that they have developed a culture that represents an adaptation to past circumstances, but one that is now, in crucial respects, dysfunctional and pathological.[1]

Claims of Definition

Questions Answered by Claims of Definition. What is it? What is it like? How should it be classified? How should it be interpreted? How does its usual meaning change in a particular context?

---

[1]*The American Spectator*, October 1995, p. 35.

Examples of Claims of Definition.   (Note that here we are looking at definition claims that dominate the argument in the essay as a whole. Definition is also used as a type of support, often at the beginning, to establish the meaning of one or more key terms.) We need to define what constitutes a family before we talk about family values. In order to determine whether a publication is pornography or a work of art, we need to define what we mean by pornography in this context. To determine whether the police were doing their job or were engaging in brutality, we need to establish what we mean by police brutality. In order to determine whether a person is mentally competent, we need to define what we mean by that term. Should we describe what occurred during the 1992 Los Angeles riots as civil disobedience or vandalism? If we have established the fact that young men killed their parents, shall we define this killing as self-defense or premeditated murder?

Types of Proof Associated with Claims of Definition.   The main types of proof used to prove claims of definition are *references to reliable authorities and accepted sources* that can be used to establish clear definitions and meanings, such as the dictionary or a well-known work. Also useful are *analogies* and other comparisons, especially to other words or situations that are clearly understood and that can consequently be used to shed some light on what is being defined. *Examples,* both real and hypothetical, and *signs* can also be used to clarify or develop definitions.

Possible Organizational Strategies.   Comparison-and-contrast organization can dominate the development of a claim of definition and serve as the main structure. In this structure two or more objects are compared and contrasted throughout. For example, in an essay that expands the notion of crime to include white-collar crime, conventional crime would be compared with white-collar crime to prove that they are similar. In the previous chapter, we showed how some people compare abortion to murder to prove how they are similar.

Topical organization may also be used. Several special qualities, characteristics, or features of the word or concept are identified and explained as discrete topics. Thus, in an essay defining a criminal as mentally competent, the characteristics of mental competence would be explained as separate topics and applied to the criminal. Another strategy is to explain the controversy over the term and give reasons for accepting one view over another.

An Example of an Argument That Contains a Claim of Definition.   The following excerpt suggests the confusion that can be created if people do not agree on a definition for a term. William Safire writes a regular column on language for the *New York Times Magazine,* and his analysis in a column entitled "Family Values" identifies some of the arguments about the definition of family values during the 1992 political campaign when this concept was a political issue. Family values were again a political issue in the 1996 political campaign, this time identified by the Democrats as a positive value. Who possesses family values and who does not has been an enduring political issue in recent times.

FAMILY VALUES

William Safire

Essay

Quote from reliable authority and first definition

"Integrity, courage, strength"—those were the *family values* as defined by Barbara Bush at the Republican convention in Houston. She added "sharing, love of God and pride in being an American." Not much controversy in that definition.

Another authority and a second definition

But on "family values night," as Marilyn Quayle described the session dominated by Republican women, the values took on an accusatory edge: after recalling that many in the baby boom had not "joined the counterculture" or "dodged the draft," the Vice President's wife made clear to cheering conservatives what she felt was at the center of family values: "Commitment, marriage and fidelity are not just arbitrary arrangements."

Another authority and a third definition

Pat Robertson, the religious broadcaster who sought the Presidential nomination four years ago, eschewed such innuendo and slammed home the political point: "When Bill and Hillary Clinton talk about family values, they are not talking about either families or values. They are talking about a radical plan to destroy the traditional family."

Another authority and a fourth definition

We have here the G.O.P.'s political attack phrase of the 1992 campaign. When Mario Cuomo stressed the words *family* and *values* in his speech to the 1984 Democratic convention, he used them in a warmly positive sense. But *this year*, packaged in a single phrase, *the terms are an assertion of moral traditionalism* that carries an implicit charge: the other side seeks to undermine the institution of the family by taking a permissive line on (a) abortion rights, (b) homosexual rights and (c) the "character issue," code words for marital infidelity.

Claim of definition: the meaning that emerges this year

Signs of a lack of family values according to new definition

Sometimes pot smoking is included, but sex is most often the common denominator, and the pointing finger includes women who do not center their lives inside the home: the defeated candidate Pat Buchanan includes "radical feminists" in his angry denunciation of those who lack what he considers to be family values.[2]

Claims of Cause

Questions Answered by Claims of Cause.   What caused it? Where did it come from? Why did it happen? What are the effects? What probably will be the results both on a short-term and a long-term basis?

---

[2]*New York Times Magazine,* September 6, 1992, p. 14.

Examples of Claims of Cause. The United States champions human rights in foreign countries to further its own economic self-interests. Clear-cutting is the main cause of the destruction of ancient forests. Legalizing marijuana could have beneficial effects for medicine. The American people's current mood has been caused by a lack of faith in political leaders. The long-term effects of inadequate funding for AIDS research will be a disastrous worldwide epidemic. A lack of family values can lead to crime. Censorship can have good results by protecting children.

Types of Proof Associated with Claims of Cause. The argument must establish the probability of a cause-and-effect relationship. The best type of proof for this purpose is *factual data,* including *statistics* that are used to prove a cause or an effect. You can also expect *analogies,* including both *literal* and *historical analogies* that parallel cases in past history to show that the cause of one event could also be the cause of another similar event. You can, furthermore, expect *signs* of certain causes or effects, and you can also expect *induction.* Several examples cited as a cause will invite the inductive leap to a possible effect as the end result. *Deduction* is also used to develop claims of cause. Premises about effects are proposed, as in the Sherlock Holmes example in Chapter 7, page 197, and a conclusion about the possible cause is drawn.

Possible Organizational Strategies. One strategy is to describe causes and then effects. Thus clear-cutting would be described as a cause that would lead to the ultimate destruction of the forests, which would be the effect. Or effects may be described and then the cause or causes. The effects of censorship may be described before the public efforts that caused that censorship. You may also encounter refutation of other actual or possible causes or effects.

An Example of an Argument That Contains a Claim of Cause. The following article suggests that many of the world's economic problems are created by the way women are treated in some of the relatively impoverished nations of the world. Facts, quotations from authorities, and comparisons are used to establish that if women were treated differently, economic improvement would be the effect. Not all people in these countries would agree with this cause-effect argument.

Essay

Facts

PAYING THE PRICE OF FEMALE NEGLECT

Susan Dentzer

Call it the case of the missing women—*more than 100 million of them,* to be exact. It's a curiosity of human biology that women are hardier than men and thus outnumber their male counterparts in the United States, Europe and Japan. But in much of Asia, North

Quote from authority

Africa and parts of Latin America, the opposite is true: In all of South Asia, for example, females constitute less than 47 percent of the population, versus 52.2 percent in industrialized countries. The complex reasons, including poor health care and outright violence against women and girls, add up to pervasive neglect of females in many heavily populated nations. Harvard economist Amartya Sen concludes that well over 100 million women are in effect "missing" from the planet—the presumed victims of premature and preventable deaths. . . .

Claim

Effects if claim were adopted

The consequences for social justice are self-evident, but less well understood in the West are the global economic costs of such widespread female deprivation. Of the 1.3 billion people living in poverty worldwide, a staggering 70 percent are women, notes a recent report by the United Nations Development Program. Thus, the surest route to propelling nations out of poverty is to end the cycle of female neglect. . . . It may well be that giving women a leg up in education, entrepreneurship and political power could pay off in priceless benefits—ranging from slower population growth and higher incomes to healthier families.

Statistics

Vicious cycle. Women in developing nations clearly face a host of social and cultural obstacles, but they are also hurt by a simple economic calculus. On average, women worldwide earn 30 to 40 percent less than men; because their daughters will earn less, parents in poor countries often invest in them less than they do in their sons, especially in education and health care. The resulting vicious cycle of underinvestment exacts a huge toll, since research clearly shows that better-educated women are more likely to have fewer children, seek health care when needed, earn more money and plow more resources into educating their offspring. One recent World Bank analysis suggests that providing 1,000 girls in India with an extra year of primary schooling would cost a mere $32,000, yet would prevent the premature deaths of two women and 43 infants, as well as avert 300 births. Another concludes that if women in Kenya, who make up the majority of the nation's farmers, were educated on a par with Kenyan men, food-crop yields would increase by more than a fifth. . . .

Authority

Comparison

Most crucial may be increasing women's capacities to be agents of change rather than merely recipients of greater help from others, says economist Sen. He points to the Indian state of Kerala, where property inheritance among an elite group passes through the female line. Perhaps it is no coincidence that the state also has the most developed school system in India, and that the ratio of females to males approaches that of the United States and Europe. That lesson in the apparent consequences of women assuming more power may translate even to the United States, which ranks well down the roster of major industrialized countries in the number of women in the national legislature. And women themselves may owe it to the memories of more than 100 million of the missing to attempt no less.[3]

Claims of Value

Questions Answered by Claims of Value. Is it good or bad? How bad? How good? Of what worth is it? Is it moral or immoral? Who thinks so? What do those people value? What values or criteria should I use to determine its goodness or badness? Are my values different from other people's values or from the author's values?

Examples of Claims of Value. Computers are a valuable addition to modern society. School prayer has a moral function in the public schools. Viewing television is a wasteful activity. Mercy killing is immoral. The contributions of homemakers are as valuable as those of professional women. Animal rights are as important as human rights.

Types of Proof Associated with Claims of Value. *Value proofs* are important in developing claims of value. Value proofs appeal to what the audience is expected to value. Thus a sense of a common, shared system of values between the arguer and the audience is important for the argument to be convincing. These shared values must be established either explicitly or implicitly in the argument. *Motivational proofs* that appeal to what the audience wants are also important in establishing claims of value. People place value on the things that they work to achieve. Other types of proof used to establish claims of value include *analogies,* both *literal* and *figurative,* that establish links with other good or bad objects or qualities. Also, quotations from *authorities* who are admired help establish both expert criteria and judgments of good or bad, right or wrong. *Induction* is also used through the use of good examples to demonstrate that something is good, or through bad examples to show that something is bad. *Signs* that something is good or bad are sometimes cited. *Definitions* are used to clarify criteria for evaluation.

Possible Organizational Strategies. *Applied criteria* is one way to develop a claim of value. Criteria for evaluation are established and then applied to the subject that is at issue. For example, in arguing that a particular television series is the best on television, criteria for what makes a superior series would be identified and then applied to the series to defend it as best. The audience would have to agree with the criteria to make the argument effective. Or suppose the claim is made that toxic waste is the worst threat to the environment. A list of criteria for evaluating threats to the environment would be established and applied to toxic

---

[3]*U.S. News and World Report,* September 11, 1995, p. 45.

waste to show that it is the worst of all. Another possibility is to use *topical* organization by developing a list of reasons about why something is good or bad and
then developing each of the reasons as a separate topic. You may also expect that
narrative structure will sometimes be used to develop a claim of value. Narratives
are real or made-up stories that can illustrate values in action, with morals or
generalizations being noted either explicitly or implicitly along the way. An example of a narrative used to support a claim of value is the parable of the good
Samaritan who helped a fellow traveler. The claim is that helping one another in
such circumstances is valued and desirable behavior.

    An Example of an Argument That Contains a Claim of Value. The follow-
ing article examines the value of the men's movement from the author's point of
view. Notice the author's refutation of some of the opposing evidence. Also notice the author's conclusion and his major reasons for reaching this conclusion.

Essay

THE MEN'S MOVEMENT

Christopher Evans

Value proofs that are
ironic. He believes the
opposite.

The term pops up almost daily now, in print or on the air. The
"men's movement." The "Men's Movement."

    Either way, I wince. And it's not that we American men are
OK. We're not.

    Depending on the source, enough male-critical data are
around these days to justify shooting us all, or at least emasculating
all but the highest forms of us and sending us somewhere far away.

    We don't support our families, either when we're with them
or after we leave them. We do most of the killing, the chemical
abuse, the power abuse, and on and on. We can't feel or "emote" or
do any number of other things women can. So, the thinking goes,
we deserve being passed over in favor of women in the job market,
in the promotion derby.

    Does this make me mad? Absolutely. Does it make me feel like
a victim? To be honest, yes, at times.

    Yet when I think of a men's movement, I start to squirm. And
that's because the thought conjures the picture of a bunch of gun-
waving, jock-torching loonies hitting the streets to protest, and then
to litigate, on my behalf.

    It's not that I'm against men, privately or in groups, working
to remedy their inadequacies. I have no qualms with Wildman
Gatherings . . . [where] problemed males retreat to the wild to work,
play, grunt, spit, croon and hug in order to nurture such qualities as
compassion, sensitivity and all the rest.

Literal analogy; then compares the men's movement with other groups taken over by lunatic fringes

My problem with a men's movement is that I fear the various male-driven hate groups—whose underlying premise is always "Poor little me" and whose figurative finger is always pointed at other groups who have seized the American dream and done something with it—will latch onto it. And pretend to be speaking for me.

Then there is certain trivialization of the subgroup-advocacy phenomenon, something at the very heart of democracy and every human rights struggle worth its bloodshed. Subgroup-advocacy movements spring up when people with a common trait—in this case men, but it could be the one-legged transvestite plumbers of North America—band together to battle wrongs done them by somebody else.

If we have learned anything from subgroup-advocacies past, it is that the honorable and just causes behind most of them often are lost when sometimes self-serving folk join the movement to perpetuate their piece of the cause. What happens is that "the movement," be it civil rights, women's or anything else, becomes known by its most oddball and radical fringes, not by the masses within its mainstream.

Why bring this up now? Because there is growing evidence that suggests American men—heretofore known as the gender of power in the world's most opulent nation—are being preyed upon. And some of the evidence seems compelling. At first.

Farrell, the opposition, argues from signs and statistics that men lack power and need help

"If any other group—blacks, Jews, women or gays—were singled out to register for the draft based merely on characteristics at birth, we would immediately recognize it as genocide," writes Warren Farrell in the book *The Myth of Male Power*. "But when men are singled out based on their sex at birth, it is called power.

"What any other group would call powerlessness, men have been taught to call power. We don't call male-killing sexism, we call it glory. We don't call it a slaughter when 1 million men are killed or maimed in the battles of the Somme in World War I, we call it serving the country. We don't call those who selected only men to die murderers, we call them voters."

Farrell portrays American males as whipping boys—i.e. women commit one-third of domestic homicides, only 4 percent of custodial fathers in this country get child support, 94 percent of workplace fatalities are men, and so forth. Then he leads us to believe that American males suddenly are hapless, helpless wimps with no control over our own destiny.

Horse . . . feathers!

Refutation of Farrell

The problems most able-bodied American men face that are peculiar to males are by and large created by men. If child-support or child-custody laws or policies by which we draft people into the military are unfair, it's because men until recently not only made the laws and policies, but were responsible for carrying them out.

| | So, men, let's be concerned with our rights as a gender, sure. But first, let's shore up what we can without the hue and cry of a "movement," which surely sooner or later will become a refuge for the losers amongst us, namely the hate groups and their ilk, whose real forte is self-pity. |

Cause: Men caused these problems and can solve them

Motivational proofs: Men can be better people

Value claim: Negative reaction to men's movement

So, men, let's be concerned with our rights as a gender, sure. But first, let's shore up what we can without the hue and cry of a "movement," which surely sooner or later will become a refuge for the losers amongst us, namely the hate groups and their ilk, whose real forte is self-pity.

The rhetoric of the so-called "men's movement" can seem enticing. At first. We can blame testosterone for our woes. Or we can get on about the business of rectifying our part of the problem with the race—the human one.

If it means seeing a psychotherapist to find out who we are and how we can be better, so be it. If it means dropping our macho defense mechanisms and paying child support—or heading to the woods with a group of males to learn to communicate—let's get at it.

But a "men's movement?" Nah. Not for me.[4]

Claims of Policy

Questions Answered by Claims of Policy. What should we do? How should we act? What should future policy be? How can we solve this problem? What concrete course of action should we pursue to solve the problem? Notice that policy claims focus on the future more than the other types of claims, which tend to deal with the past or present.

Examples of Claims of Policy. The criminal should be sent to prison rather than to a mental institution. Everyone should be taught to recognize and report sexual harassment in the workplace. Every person in the United States should have access to health care regardless of cost. Small business loans must be made available to help people reestablish their businesses after a natural disaster. Both filmmakers and recording groups should make objectionable language and subject matter known to prospective consumers. Battered women who take revenge should not be placed in jail. Genetic engineering should be discouraged. Parents should have the right to choose the schools their children attend.

Types of Proof Associated with Claims of Policy. *Data* and *statistics* are used to support a policy claim, but so are moral and commonsense appeals to what people value and want. *Motivational appeals* are especially important for policy claims. The audience needs to become sufficiently motivated to think or even act in a different way. In order to accomplish this degree of motivation, the arguer must convince the audience that it wants to change. *Value* proofs are also used for motivation. The audience becomes convinced it should follow a policy to achieve important values. Also typical of policy claims is proof from *literal anal-*

---

[4]*Fort Worth Star-Telegram,* September 21, 1993, Sec. D, p. 1.

ogy. The arguer establishes what other similar people or groups have done and suggests the same thing can work in this case also. Or a successful effort is described, and the claim is made that it could work even better on a broader scale. This is another type of literal analogy, because it compares a small-scale effort to a large-scale, expanded effort. *Argument from authority* is also often used to establish claims of policy. The authorities quoted, however, must be trusted and must have good ethos. Effort is usually made to establish their credentials. *Cause* can be used to establish the origin of the problem, and *definition* can be used to clarify it. Finally, *deduction* can be used to reach a conclusion based on a general principle.

Possible Organizational Strategies. The problem-solution structure is typical of policy claims. The problem is first described in sufficient detail so that the audience will want a solution. Then the solution is spelled out. Furthermore, the solution suggested is usually shown to be superior to other solutions by anticipating and showing what is wrong with each of the others. Sometimes the problem and solution sections are followed by a visualization of how matters will be improved if the proposed solution is accepted and followed. Sometimes problem-solution arguments end with an action step that directs the audience to take a particular course of action (vote, buy, and so forth).

An Example of an Argument That Contains a Claim of Policy. The following argument identifies a problem, explains why on the surface it is not usually regarded as a problem, suggests how it could become one, and finally recommends a policy that can keep it from becoming a serious problem.

Essay

COMPUTERS IN CLASS

William Casey

Problem

Is this happening in your neighborhood? Sis and little brother Buddy, laptop computers nestled under their arms, await the yellow bus for the trip to middle school. This is not a recognizable scene in most places at the moment, but neither is it especially far-fetched. . . .

Historical perspective

On the surface, the question of computers in schools is a no-brainer. It would be nutty to insist that today's technology shouldn't be used to make the classroom experience more individualized, more effective, more immediate, more exciting. Computers have been in schools more than 20 years—and probably even do some good.

But the idea of a personal computer as a necessary daily tool for every American grammar school pupil is altogether a different

Example

thing. Beware the beguiling vision of 10-year-olds doing the bulk of their work—and homework—on a computer. It's another elusive silver bullet that promises to solve all of society's ills through technology. Regardless of whether parents or taxpayers buy the machinery, it's bad policy.

Who should decide

Determining the proper role of computers in schools is too important to be left to computer suppliers and educators. An educated public with clear and realistic expectations needs to help determine the right track for technology.

Educators add to problem

Educators, bless their hearts, forever seem to be casting about for the ultimate in curricular or teaching tools. They have a history of infatuation with innovation—junior high school, new math, whole language, open classrooms, mastery learning and phonics, to name a few. Some ideas turned out well and over time have earned permanent positions in our education systems. Others reflected change for change's sake and wound up in the trash bin, where they belong.

What are some solutions?

Exactly what is to be solved with computers in schools? Are we looking to improve instructional capacity and flexibility? Are we trying to make teachers and aides more productive by letting students take advantage of programmed learning tools? This all sounds good, and much has been accomplished with computer-assisted instruction.

Problems with over-doing it

But that's not the same as making the computer a symbol of well-tempered educational policy. There's danger in the message that a child is not fully educated if he or she can't surf the World Wide Web with dexterity, move around in Windows or the Finder, use a word processing program, or program in Logo or Basic.

Time problems

These skills can be learned outside the classroom. Worse, the time it takes students to acquire them is time stolen from the legitimate teaching schedule—and that's a bad trade.

Cost problems

And what kind of computers should be purchased? We're not talking brand names. Most school systems don't have the money to replace PCs or Macs on the two- to three-year cycle that shifting technologies demand. On the other hand, $2,500—the cost of just one computer—invested in books for the school library produces an asset that has, shall we say, a longer shelf life.

Personnel problems

And who changes the factory culture of schoolrooms to allow computers to be more effective? And who teaches the teachers? These are the really tough issues—the ones that more hardware won't solve.

Solution

Children are best served when schools contribute to shaping the solid foundations on which their future will be built. The student who can read with curiosity and understanding, who has mastered basic mathematical concepts, who can evaluate ideas critically

Claim

and who can communicate effectively is whom we're after. This is particularly the case in an era when skill sets have become so transitory. The role of personal computers in the educational mission can't be ignored, but it's also not central to it. . . .[5]

CLAIMS AND ARGUMENT IN REAL LIFE

In argument, one type of claim may predominate, but other types may be present as subclaims. It is not always easy to establish the predominant claim in an argument or to establish its type. You may find some disagreement in your class discussions when you try to categorize a claim according to type. The reason for this disagreement is that often two or more types of claim will be present in an argument. But close reading will usually reveal a predominant type with the other types serving as subclaims. For example, a value claim that the popular press creates harm by prying into the private lives of public figures may establish the fact that this is a pervasive practice, may define what should be public and what should not be public information, may examine the causes or, more likely, the effects of this type of reporting, and may suggest future policy for dealing with this problem. All may occur in the same article. Still, the dominant claim is one of value, that this practice of news writers is bad.

It is useful when reading argument to identify the predominant claim because doing so helps you identify (1) the predominant purpose of the argument, (2) the types of proofs that may be used, and (3) the possible organizational strategies. It is also useful, however, to identify other types of subclaims, and to analyze why they are used and how they contribute to the argumentative purpose. When planning and writing argument, you can, in turn, identify a predominant claim as well as other types of subclaims, proofs, and organization (see Table 11.1 on p. 353 and Table 12.1 on p. 380) to help you develop your main claim and purpose.

As you read and write argument, you will also notice that claims follow a predictable sequence when they originate in real-life situations. In fact, argument appears most vigorous in dramatic, life-and-death situations, or when a person's character is called into question. We see claims and rebuttals, many kinds of proofs, and every conceivable organizational strategy in these instances. For example, as juvenile crime in this country increased in recent years, the issues that emerged included these: What is causing young people to commit crimes? What can be done to protect the family unit? Is the educational system adequate? Should the criminal justice system treat young offenders differently from older criminals? Does racial discrimination contribute to juvenile crime? How can we make inner cities more livable? How can we improve social programs?

Such real-life situations, particularly when they are life-threatening as juvenile crime often is, not only generate issues; they also usually generate many ar-

---

[5]*Fort Worth Star-Telegram*, May 26, 1996, Sec. F, p. 8.

guments. Interestingly, the types of argument usually appear in a fairly predictable order. The first arguments made in response to a new issue-generating situation usually involve claims of fact and definition. People first have to come to terms with the fact that something significant has happened. Then they need to define what happened so that they can better understand it.

The next group of arguments that appear after fact and definition often inquire into cause. People need to figure out why the event happened. Multiple causes are often considered and debated. Next, people begin to evaluate the goodness or badness of what has happened. It is usually after all of these other matters have been dealt with that people turn their attention to future policy and how to solve the problems. Often the proofs associated with these claims are logical, but emotional proofs are frequently invoked as well because of the nature of the event.

We can use the Los Angeles riots as an example of this typical sequence of claims. The riots started quite suddenly in the spring of 1992 just hours after the court decision that allowed the police officers who had beaten Rodney King to go free. People around the country were caught off guard by the sudden rioting and looting in Los Angeles. The first newspaper article and even speeches by the president sought to establish and clarify what exactly was going on in that city. People asked, Is this a class riot? A race riot? War? Civil disobedience? Looting and lawbreaking? Civil demonstrations? Or what?

These initial fact and definition articles were followed by many others that speculated and argued about the causes of the riots. Were they caused by racial discrimination? Economic problems? Desire for power? A lack of home and community values? Anger at the court decision? One African-American civil rights leader argued that the cause was slavery, that people were still angry that their ancestors had been brought from Africa as slaves, and that the riots were an expression of their anger. Another African-American leader of an organization that fostered productive family life argued that civil rights leaders themselves incited the riots in order to keep their power base and government relief programs strong.

After much speculation about cause, people turned their attention to value and to argue about whether any good could be found in these riots. The president pointed out that not all people rioted and looted, and that some actually gave others a helping hand. But many bad or mixed good and bad results were identified as well. Racial tensions between African-Americans and Koreans surfaced during the riots and were regarded as bad. Considerable property was destroyed, and many people lost their homes or jobs.

It was not until most of these initial matters were analyzed and debated that discussion of future policy began to surface. Finally, headlines like "What Los Angeles Needs" began to appear. One individual recommended that the citizens of South-Central Los Angeles organize themselves as a Third World country and declare war on the United States. Other individuals outside of the area thought troops should be sent in to beat the rioters into submission. Other suggestions for dealing with the problems caused by the riots included new training and job programs, a retrial of the police officers, government loans to rebuild small businesses, a reconception of inner-city neighborhoods, and so on.

The same pattern of argument can be found in the sexual correctness issue that gathered speed after the Anita Hill–Clarence Thomas hearings, where Ms. Hill accused Mr. Thomas of sexual harassment, and the U.S. Navy Tailhook scandal, where male naval personnel harassed and abused women at an annual party. Articles written in response to such events often focus first on fact, or what happened. Were these actual incidents of sexual harassment, the authors ask, or were they just incidents of flirting, the type of thing that goes on all the time between men and women? Definitions of sexual harassment usually follow with attempts to define it in terms of actions, comments, or looks, and to distinguish it from generally cloddish, insensitive behavior. Once people establish that an incident of harassment has occurred and that it can be defined, cause next becomes an issue. Did the woman cause it by leading on the man? Was liquor at fault? Were hormones to blame, or perhaps the age-old war between the sexes? Value arguments surface next that focus on who has been harmed and whether that person has been badly or only mildly harmed. Policy issues, or what to do about it, come later. Should Clarence Thomas be denied a seat on the U.S. Supreme Court? Should the annual navy parties be discontinued? A few years ago policy to govern sexual correctness was established at Antioch College that required each person to obtain permission from the member of the opposite sex before making any advances of a sexual nature.

The set of articles arranged under the issue question, "What should be done with young offenders?" that appears on pages 517 to 531 of "The Reader" follows the same order just described. The first article establishes the fact that juvenile crime is a problem and that it will probably get worse. The next article establishes that poverty, not just bad character, is the principle cause of juvenile crime. The third article presents an example of juvenile crime to establish that it is bad and that its victims are hurt and angry. The last article in the section proposes solutions for dealing with the problem of juvenile crime.

You may be able to think of other issues that have inspired a variety of arguments and claims in this same roughly predictable order. It is useful to pay attention to the issues that come out of dramatic events, to the types of claims that are generated by them, and to the order in which these claims appear. Such analysis will help you anticipate the course an issue will take. It will also help you determine at what point in the ongoing conversation about an issue you happen to be at the present time. You can then speculate about the aspects of the issue that have already been argued and that are likely to be argued in the future.

HOW ARE THE CLAIMS AND THE CLAIM QUESTIONS VALUABLE FOR READING AND WRITING ARGUMENT?

Readers of argument find the list of the five types of claims and the questions that accompany them useful for identifying the claim and the main purpose in an argument: to establish fact, to define, to establish cause, to assign value, or to propose a solution. Claims and claim questions can also help readers identify minor purposes in an argument, those that are developed as subclaims. When a reader is able to discover the overall purpose of an argument, it is much easier to make predictions and to follow the argument.

Writers of argument find the list of the five types of claims and the questions that accompany them useful for analyzing an issue, writing a claim about it, and identifying both the controlling purpose for a paper and ideas that can be developed in the paper. Here is an example of how this can work. The author writes the issue in the form of a question, as in the example, Should high school students own cars? Then the author answers the claim questions by writing a paragraph in response to each of them: Did it happen? What is it? What caused it? Is it good or bad? and, What should we do about it? Finally, the author reads the paragraphs and selects the one that is most promising for formulating the major claim and purpose in the paper. The author also, however, uses the information in the other paragraphs as possible subclaims and support for the paper. See the essay "Hold Your Horsepower" on page 189 to see how one author accomplished this. See also the assignment on page 237 and the student-written model paper on page 240, both at the end of Chapter 7, to understand better how the claims and claim questions can be used as invention activities to generate a claim and other ideas and support for a position paper. The claims are summarized in a handy chart for quick reference for the use of both readers and writers in the Summary Charts on page 409.

EXERCISES AND ACTIVITIES

1. **CLASS DISCUSSION: PREDICTING TYPES OF CLAIMS**
   Bring in the front page of a current newspaper. Discuss headlines that suggest controversial topics. Anticipate from each headline the type of claim that you predict will be made.

2. **GROUP WORK: READING AND ANALYSIS OF TYPES OF CLAIMS**
   The class is divided into five groups, and each group is assigned one of the five articles that follow. Prepare for group work by reading the article assigned to your group. Then get in your groups and apply the new reading strategies described in this chapter by answering the following questions. Assign a person to report your answers to the class.

   a. How can you describe the organization of this argument? How might you chunk it into parts? Why are the parts in the order in which you find them? What are some of the relationships among the parts?
   b. What is the predominant type of claim?
   c. What other types of claims are present in the argument as subclaims?
   d. What are the major types of proofs? What are their effects on the audience?
   e. Where might you position this argument in an ongoing conversation about the issue? At the beginning, the middle, or the end? Why?

The articles:
"Gene Tests: What You Know Can Hurt You"
"We're Too Busy for Ideas"
"And a Purple Dinosaur Shall Lead Them"
"Rap's Embrace of 'Nigger' Fires Bitter Debate"
"A Fable for Tomorrow"

Essay

GENE TESTS: WHAT YOU KNOW CAN HURT YOU

Barbara Koenig

Last year, it was discovered that 1 percent of Ashkenazi Jewish women, those of Central or Eastern European ancestry, carry a mutated form of a gene that might predispose them to breast and ovarian cancer.

After this discovery, a surgeon who operates on women with breast cancer told me that a day rarely passes when a patient does not ask about "the gene test."

Even with this demand, however, almost all leading scientists and two major commercial testing laboratories agreed informally not to offer the test for the mutation to the general public because widespread testing would do more harm than good.

That consensus was broken recently by Dr. Joseph D. Schulman, director of the Genetics and I.V.F. Institute in Fairfax, Va. The doctor, who advertised the service on the World Wide Web, says it will give women access to valuable information. But in genetic testing, what you know won't necessarily help you—indeed, it might even hurt you.

As Alice Wexler points out in "Mapping Fate," her book about genetically determined Huntington's Disease, Americans' strong bias for information leads them to believe in genetic testing. Doing something, anything, to counter illness is considered the brave and correct approach.

But testing for the 185delAG mutation does not help most women. A positive test does not mean you will get cancer, and a negative test does not mean that you won't.

Most scientists agree that the mutation occurs in families in which many members have suffered from breast and ovarian cancer. But leaping to the conclusion that a mutation inevitably leads to cancer, especially for women without a family history, reflects a naïve genetic determinism and ignores the possible effects of the environment and other genes on one's health.

But let's assume that a woman from a high-risk family tests positive. What then? There is no guaranteed way to prevent cancer or detect it early. Some desperate women do resort to drastic measures such as surgically removing their breasts.

Paradoxically, this isn't the recommended treatment for many women already diagnosed with cancer. For a decade, more doctors have recommended and more women, especially those with small tumors, have chosen instead to have lumpectomies.

Knowing your genetic makeup can also create profound emotional and financial problems. For example, a spouse might use this information in a custody dispute. Or a woman might decide not to have children for fear of passing on the gene. But if she decides to adopt, will she be approved by an agency? And should a 9-year-old girl be tested for the mutation?

The test brings up other thorny questions that may be better left unexplored. For instance, with current technology, a woman could test a fetus for the gene and then abort it. In his ad, Dr. Schulman suggests that his Genetics and I.V.F. Institute may be able to screen embryos for the gene mutation.

There are also real economic repercussions. Women could face discrimination from employers and health insurers. And most physicians have little experience with ordering and interpreting genetic tests that determine a woman's cancer risk (and in guiding families through the turmoil generated by the results.)

Until basic research on the clinical significance of the 185delAG mutation is complete, there is no justification for widespread screening. Unfortunately, nothing prevents laboratories from offering genetic tests, nor are there any regulations to insure the quality of the tests.

In March, a Federal task force on testing suggested possible regulatory strategies, from requiring Food and Drug Administration approval for new tests to strengthening the laws that govern labs.

Either approach would slow down the premature commercialization of testing. Strict regulation may be unpopular among those who believe that women have a right to this information. But extreme caution should be the order of the day.[6]

WE'RE TOO BUSY FOR IDEAS

Michele McCormick

I recently became one of the last people in America to acquire a portable radio/headphone set. This delay was out of character—normally I ride the crest of every trend. But in this case I sensed a certain dangerous potential. So I put off the purchase for ages, feeling wary of such an inviting distraction. Too much headphone time, I worried, could easily impair my business performance, if not ruin my way of life completely.

As it turns out, my concerns were right on target.

---

[6]*New York Times*, April 6, 1996, p. 15. The author is associated with the Stanford University Center for Biomedical Ethics. She co-directs the program in genomics, ethics, and society.

The problem isn't the expense, or the constant exposure to musical drivel, or even the endangerment of my hearing—and I do like to keep the volume set on "blast." No, the problem is more subtle and insidious. It's simply that, once I was fully plugged in, things stopped occurring to me.

I get excited about good ideas. Especially my own. I used to have lists of them in all my regular haunts. My office desk, kitchen, car and even my gym bag were littered with bits of paper. Ideas ranging from a terrific brochure headline or a pitch to a new client for my public-relations agency to finding a new route to avoid the morning rush—each notion began as an unsummoned thought, mulled over and jotted down.

I'm convinced that such musings are the key to business and social vitality. They are the initial source of the innovative problem solving, creative solutions and even radical departures, without which success and progress are elusive. I've found that a lot of my better ideas originate in those times when I allow my mind to range freely.

The old story has it that Isaac Newton identified the concept and presence of gravity while sitting under an apple tree. One fruit fell and science gained a new dimension. While there may be some historic license in that tale, it's easy to see that if Newton had been wearing his Walkman, he probably would have overlooked the real impact of the apple's fall.

This is the problematic side of technological evolution. As tools become more compact, portable and inescapable, they begin to take away something they cannot replace. The car phone, battery-powered TV, portable fax and notepad-size computer do everything for accessibility. They make it easy to be in touch, to be productive, to avoid the tragedy of a wasted second. But there are worse things than empty time. A calendar packed to the max makes it easy to overlook what's missing. A dearth of good ideas isn't something that strikes like a lightning bolt. It's a far more gradual dawning, like the slow unwelcome recognition that one's memory has become less sharp.

If that dawning is slow, it's because our minds are fully occupied. It now takes an unprecedented depth of knowledge to stay on top of basic matters, from choosing sensible investments to keeping up on job skills to purchasing the healthiest food. There is literally no end to the information that has become essential.

When there is a chance to relax, we don't stop the input; we change channels. With earphones on our heads or televisions in our faces, we lock in to a steady barrage of news, views and videos that eliminate the likelihood of any spontaneous thought.

THWARTED INSIGHT

Still, we are not totally oblivious. We work hard to counter the mind-numbing impact of the river of information and factoidal jetsam we are forced to absorb. There is a deliberate emphasis on the importance of creative thought as a daily factor. Many businesses try to ensure that the workplace is conducive to clear thinking. They can provide employees with a comfortable environment and stimulating challenges, and summon them to brainstorming sessions. From seminars to smart drinks, from computer programs to yoga postures, there's no end to the strategies and products that claim to enhance creativity. It would be unfair to say that all of these methods are without value. But beyond a certain point they are, at best, superfluous. Trying too hard to reach for high-quality insight can thwart the process in the worst way.

The best ideas occur to me when my mind is otherwise unchallenged and there is no pressure to create. I have mentally composed whole articles while jogging, flashed upon the solution to a software dilemma while sitting in the steam room, come up with just the right opening line for a client's speech while pushing a vacuum. These were not problems I had set out to address at those particular times. Inventiveness came to my uncluttered mind in a random, unfocused moment.

Certainly not every idea that pops up during a quiet time is a winner. But a surprising number do set me on the path to fresh solutions. And I have found that a free flow of ideas builds its own momentum, leapfrogging me along to answers that work.

The bonus is that creative thought is joyful. It doesn't matter if the idea is for a clever party decoration, a better way to rearrange the living-room furniture or the definitive antigravity machine. When a fine idea emerges there is a moment of "Eureka!" that simply beats all.

The simple fact is that time spent lost in thought isn't really lost at all. That's why "unplugged time" is vital. It's when new directions, different approaches and exciting solutions emerge from a place that can't be tapped at will.

It is unwise to take this resource for granted. Better to recognize it, understand something about where it resides and thereby ensure it is not lost.

Clearly, this is far easier said than done. Technology is seductive. It chases us down, grabs hold and will not let us go. Nor do we want it to. The challenge is to keep it in its place and to remember that time spent unplugged brings unique rewards. This doesn't mean I will abandon my new radio headset toy. But I will take the precaution of leaving it in my dresser drawer on a regular basis.

Otherwise, unlike wise old Newton, I may see the fall but never grasp its meaning.[7]

AND A PURPLE DINOSAUR SHALL LEAD THEM

Adam Cadre

When I was very little, I had a reason to get up in the morning. The world was a scary place—stagflation, Three Mile Island, and scariest of all, disco—but I didn't care, because I knew that at four o'clock sharp I could sweep the clouds away and spend an hour where the air was sweet. That's right: Sesame Street. I was a

---

[7]*Newsweek*, March 29, 1993, p. 10. Michele McCormick is the owner of a small public relations firm in California.

"Sesame Street" freak. I watched it every single day. In fact, the one time I accidentally slept through it I was so distraught that I spent the next several days in a sort of existential despair (and if you think confronting the ultimate absurdity of existence is hard now, try it when you're four years old). Seriously, though, for a couple of years there my life really did revolve around "Sesame Street," and even after I grew out of it, it was always sort of heartwarming to know that Big Bird and friends were continuing to bring joy and enlightenment into the lives of generation after generation of little kids.

Now, suddenly, Big Bird is passe.

That's right—the powers that be seem to have decided that "Sesame Street" is not the ideal children's show it was once thought to be. Among the complaints that have been leveled against it by child psychologists and media watchdogs are: it's too fast; the world it presents is too unsettling for young children; most of the humor goes over the kids' heads; and so on. In the end, they conclude "Sesame Street" may be an effective educational tool, but it can also be quite harmful. After all, the first generation to grow up on "Sesame Street" has now come of age—and look how *they* turned out: alienated, cynical, completely devoid of any kind of attention span. And I suppose the critics have a point. "Sesame Street" *is* fast. It'll cut from the live-action storyline to an unrelated vignette between Bert and Ernie to a cartoon about the letter V to a quick documentary about dolphins to a news flash with Kermit the Frog to a cartoon about the number 7 and then back to the storyline, all in the space of a couple of minutes. You might even say that "Sesame Street" is a perfect primer for—no! not that! anything but that!—MTV. (Insert dramatic "DUM-DUM-dum" sound here.) So, yeah, it's fast. And true, while it may seem kind of hard to believe at first, the world of "Sesame Street" might well be a little unsettling. After all, Bert and Ernie are constantly squabbling, various muppets are collapsing from exhaustion or extreme pain every five minutes, and there's a nasty green guy lurking in the trash can. So it's not all bliss and harmony. And while I didn't realize this when I was four, a lot of the humor on "Sesame Street" *is* aimed at adults. A surprising amount of "Sesame Street" is satirical in nature. While the kids are learning about different kinds of animals, their parents are laughing at the Springsteen parody in "Barn in the USA"; while the kids are giggling at the sight of pigs with tennis rackets, it's for their parents' benefit that Old MacDonald mentions that the withdrawal of government subsidies has forced him to convert his farm into a condominium complex complete with health spa; and while the kids happily watch Oscar the Grouch groan in distress while some strange woman praises his candor, their parents (and college students doing research for "Bad Subjects" articles) are getting a kick out of the fact that the woman in question is Jodie Foster slumming on PBS between films. So it's true that "Sesame Street" isn't completely accessible to the kids. But people have been making these kinds of complaints for years now. Why are they suddenly gaining so much attention? Because now there's an alternative, one that's earned the praise of child psychologists and the undying love of little children everywhere: Barney. (Insert another dramatic "DUM-DUM-dum" sound here.)

Those of you who have spent the last year or so in a deep coma are probably wondering who or what Barney is. Well, Barney is a dinosaur from our imagination, and when he's tall he's what you'd call a dinosaur sensation. At least that's what the opening jingle says. It's a good thing they tell us, too, because otherwise it's kind of hard to tell. I suppose he does look vaguely reptilian, but then he's also purple, cuddly, and five feet tall, qualities not normally associated with your typical T. rex or velociraptor. But it's not his appearance that separates Barney from the "Sesame Street" crew—after all, if you can accept an eight-foot yellow talking bird, you can accept a five-foot purple talking dinosaur thing. No, what sets him apart from "Sesame Street" (and related programs like the dearly departed "Electric Company") is his disposition and the world he inhabits. In the world of "Barney & Friends," there is no conflict whatsoever. None. No one fights or disagrees, nothing bad ever happens. They just hang around and sing songs and learn how to count to ten over and over and over and play games and sing some more songs and then the credits roll. The songs themselves are also very different from those in "Sesame Street." The songs in "Sesame Street" are quite sophisticated, with complex melodies and often borrowing from rock, rap, music from other cultures, and in my day, disco. The songs in "Barney & Friends" are very, very simple, usually featuring tunes borrowed from other children's songs like "Yankee Doodle" and "This Old Man." And there is absolutely nothing in "Barney & Friends" that is not completely comprehensible to any three-year-old. So the child psychologists love Barney. And most little kids would gladly fall on a grenade for him. Why, then, does everybody else seem to hate him?

Barney, you see, has become the victim of one of the most vicious backlashes in recent memory. This backlash comes in two flavors. First, there are the parents of all the little Barneyphiles. Forced to buy every single scrap of Barney merchandise, forced to play the Barney videotapes over and over and over, and worst of all, forced to listen to the "I love you, you love me, we're a happy family" song roughly eighty thousand times a day, theirs is a classic case of backlash due to overexposure. (Others who have fallen prey to this phenomenon include Nirvana, the Energizer Bunny, and Ross Perot.) But then there's the curious case of all the people who hate Barney with a passion despite having never seen the show. Among these are the kids who quite literally beat the stuffing out of Barney in a Texas shopping mall. They haven't been forced to listen to the saccharine songs, they haven't had to suffer through the wretched acting, they haven't had to deal with Barney's grating voice clawing at their eardrums. So why does their hatred match, if not surpass, that of the parents who've had to deal with Barney firsthand? . . .

This, I think, is why [people] who have never ever seen the show hate Barney so much: he goes against all their values. The most important thing for a member of [the Sesame Street] generation to be is "cool"—and Barney is pretty much the definition of "uncool." Let's take a quick look at the kind of education Barney's legions are getting. First of all, it's much more structured. Every show is built around one theme, and sticks to it fairly faithfully—if the show's about how

to count to ten, ninety percent of the show is going to be about how to count to ten. Over and over and over. Secondly, unlike "Sesame Street," there is only one authority figure in "Barney & Friends": Barney himself. Barney has all the answers and the kids follow him without question. And what does Barney preach? Universal love, community, sincerity, friendship, team spirit; but also conformity, unquestioning adherence to authority, and enforced happiness. (One recent episode revolved around the attempts of Barney and some other kids to pester a little girl into cheering up—they simply *would not let* her be sad for a while.) These are the kind of values, both positive and negative, associated with [Barney]. . . .[8]

Essay

RAP'S EMBRACE OF "NIGGER" FIRES BITTER DEBATE

Michel Marriott

One of America's oldest and most searing epithets—"nigger"—is flooding into the nation's popular culture, giving rise to a bitter debate among blacks about its historically ugly power and its increasingly open use in an integrated society.

Whether thoughtlessly or by design, large numbers of a post–civil rights generation of blacks have turned to a conspicuous use of "nigger" just as they have gained considerable cultural influence through rap music and related genres.

Some blacks, mostly young people, argue that their open use of the word will eventually demystify it, strip it of its racist meaning. They liken it to the way some homosexuals have started referring to themselves as "queers" in a defiant slap at an old slur.

But other blacks—most of them older—say that "nigger," no matter who uses it, is such a hideous pejorative that it should be stricken from the national vocabulary. At a time when they perceive a deepening racial estrangement, they say its popular use can only make bigotry more socially acceptable.

"Nigger," of course, has long been an element of black vernacular, almost an honorific of the streets, strictly, and still, off limits to whites. But as the word has found voice in black music, dance and film, the role of black culture in popular culture has driven it into the mainstream.

For the last several years, rap artists have increasingly used "nigger" in their lyrics, repackaging it and selling it not just to their own inner-city neighborhoods but to the largely white suburbs. In his song "Straight Up Nigga," Ice-T

---

[8]*Bad Subjects: Political Education for Everyday Life,* 12 (1994). *Online.* Internet. Available bad subjects-request@uclink.berkeley.edu. Adam Cadre, who was born in 1974, wrote this while he was a senior English major at the University of California at Berkeley. This essay first appeared in a journal which is published monthly on the Internet. Its purpose is "to promote radical thinking and public education about the political implications of everyday life."

raps, "I'm a nigga in America, and that much I flaunt," and indeed, a large portion of his record sales are in white America.

In movies and on television, too, "nigger" is heard with unprecedented regularity these days. In "Trespass," a newly released major-studio film about an inner-city treasure hunt, black rappers portraying gang members call one another "nigger" almost as often as they call one another by their names.

And every Friday at midnight, Home Box Office televises "Russell Simmons' Def Comedy Jam," a half-hour featuring many black, cutting-edge comedians who frequently use "nigger" in their acts.

Sometimes, the use of the word is simply a flat-out repetition of the street vernacular. In rap and hip-hop music, a genre in which millions of its listeners adopt the artists' style and language, "nigger" is virtually interchangeable with words like "guy," "man" or "brother."

But often it is a discussion of the word's various uses and meanings in society, black or white. Not only is black popular culture the focus of the debate, it is often the medium for it.

"MAKES MY TEETH WHITE"

Paul Mooney, a veteran black stand-up comic and writer, recently released a comedy tape titled "Race." On the tape, which includes routines called "Nigger Vampire," "1-900-Blame-a-Nigger," "Niggerstein," "Nigger Raisins" and "Nigger History," Mr. Mooney explains why he uses the word so often.

"I say nigger all the time," he said. "I say nigger 100 times every morning. It makes my teeth white. Nigger-nigger-nigger-nigger-nigger-nigger-nigger-nigger-nigger. I say it. You think, 'What a small white world.'"

Blacks who say they should use the word more openly maintain that its casual use, especially in the company of whites, will shift the word's context and strip "nigger" of its ability to hurt. That is precisely what blacks have been doing for years, say linguists who study black vernacular. By using the word strictly among themselves, the linguists say, they change its context and in doing so dull its edge whenever whites use it.

Kris Parker, a leading rap artist known as KRS-One, predicts that through black culture's ability to affect popular American culture through the electronic media, "nigger" will be deracialized by its broader use and become just another word.

"In another 5 to 10 years, you're going to see youth in elementary school spelling it out in their vocabulary tests," he said. "It's going to be that accepted by the society."

But other blacks, especially members of the generation for whom Malcolm X and the Rev. Dr. Martin Luther King Jr. were living heroes, say no one should ever be permitted to forget what "nigger" has meant, and still means, in America.

"That term encapsulates so much of the indignities forced on our people," said the Rev. Benjamin F. Chavis Jr., a longtime civil-rights leader who is executive director of the United Church of Christ Commission for Racial Justice. "That term made us less than human, and that is why we must reject the usage of that term.

"We cannot let that term be trivialized," he said. "We cannot let that term be taken out of its historical context."

Some blacks say they are so traumatized by the oppressive legacy of "nigger," that they cannot even bring themselves to say the word. Instead, they choose linguistic dodges like "the N-word" or simply spelling the word out. Other blacks say they are "ambivalent" about the growing public use of "nigger."

"Does it signal a new progressive step forward toward a new level of understanding or a regressive step back into self-hate?" asked Christopher Cathcart, a black 29-year-old public relations specialist in New York. "I fear it is the latter."

Throughout history, nearly all minority groups have found themselves branded by hateful terms. Early in the century, such seemingly innocent words as "Irish" and "Jew" were considered pejoratives, said Edward Bendix, a professor of linguistic anthropology at the Graduate Center of the City University of New York.

In time the groups have used some of the same terms as passwords to their particular groups, which is what happened with "nigger" in the black vernacular. Indeed, Bob Guccione Jr., editor and publisher of the popular music magazine *Spin*—which reports extensively on the rap music scene—said that while whites are very reluctant to use "nigger" because it has "such an incredible weight of ugliness to it," blacks often use it in the presence of whites as a verbal demarcation point.

"In a sense, it empowers the black community in the white mainstream," said Mr. Guccione, who is white. "They can use a very powerful word like a passkey, and whites dare not, or should not, use it."

But seldom has a word like "nigger" been pushed into the mainstream while its negative connotations exist, said Dr. Robin Lakoff, a social linguist and author of the book *Talking Power* (Basic Books, 1990). "That's harder with 'nigger,' especially with so many people around who still use it in its racist meaning," said Dr. Lakoff, a professor of linguistics at the University of California at Berkeley.

Many of the blacks who defend their open use of the word acknowledge that whites still cannot publicly say "nigger" without stirring up old black-white antagonisms.

"Race in America is like herpes because you can never get rid of it," said James Bernard, who is black and senior editor of *The Source,* a magazine that covers the rap and hip-hop scene. "There is still a line."

"A HORRENDOUS WORD"

The magazine's multiracial staff recently published a story about Spike Lee and the basketball star Charles Barkley under a headline "NINETIES NIGGERS." Kris Parker, the rapper, said such uses represent progress. But to the white Chicago writer Studs Terkel, whose latest book, *Race* (The New Press, 1992), is a series of interviews with blacks and whites about race in America, the increased use of "nigger" represents anything but progress.

"It is a horrendous word," he said, adding that the new permissiveness may have more to do with the "wink and nod" of the Reagan-Bush years of dismantling civil rights gains than with rap artists naming themselves N.W.A., for Niggas With an Attitude.

Examples abound that "nigger" has not lost its wounding power when used by whites. Whether scratched into a restroom stall or scrawled on the house of a black family in a white neighborhood, "nigger" remains a graffito of hate—the most commonly heard epithet used during anti-black crimes, the authorities say.

When a black man from New Jersey was abducted and set ablaze by three white men in Florida on New Year's Day, one of the first things they said to him, according to the victim's mother, was "nigger."

BLURRING A LINE

The changing uses of the word have made for some curious situations on the white side of an increasingly blurred line.

Alex T. Noble, a white public relations intern in New York, said he has white friends who use "nigger" with one another as a term of endearment. Mr. Noble, who works with rappers, said when a black friend calls him a "nigger," "I feel flattered, like I'm part of something."

But, he adds, he is extremely reluctant to return the salutation.

"As a white person I would never go up to a black person and say, 'Yo, nigger,'" Mr. Noble said. "I think it's hard to outrun the legacy of oppression that word signifies. Anytime a white person says that word it is troublesome."

The attempts to demystify "nigger" are by no means new. One of the more publicized cases came in the early 1970's, when Richard Pryor used "nigger" in his stand-up comedy act with the express purpose of defanging its racist bite. He titled his seminal comedy album in 1974 "That Nigger's Crazy." Some years later, however, after a trip to Africa, Mr. Pryor told audiences he would never use the word again as a performer. While abroad, he said, he saw black people running governments and businesses. And in a moment of epiphany, he said he realized that he did not see any "niggers."[9]

Essay

A FABLE FOR TOMORROW

Rachel Carson

There was once a town in the heart of America where all life seemed to live in harmony with its surroundings. The town lay in the midst of a checkerboard of prosperous farms, with fields of grain and hillsides of orchards where, in spring, white clouds of bloom drifted above the green fields. In autumn, oak and maple and birch set up a blaze of color that flamed and flickered across a backdrop of

---

[9]*New York Times,* January 24, 1993, pp. 1, 11. Michel Marriott wrote this in response to the increasingly frequent use of the word "nigger" in new and different contexts.

pines. Then foxes barked in the hills and deer silently crossed the fields, half hidden in the mists of the fall mornings.

Along the roads, laurel, viburnum and alder, great ferns and wildflowers delighted the traveler's eye through much of the year. Even in winter the roadsides were places of beauty, where countless birds came to feed on the berries and on the seed heads of the dried weeds rising above the snow. The countryside was, in fact, famous for the abundance and variety of its bird life, and when the flood of migrants was pouring through in spring and fall people traveled from great distances to observe them. Others came to fish the streams, which flowed clear and cold out of the hills and contained shady pools where trout lay. So it had been from the days many years ago when the first settlers raised their houses, sank their wells, and built their barns.

Then a strange blight crept over the area and everything began to change. Some evil spell had settled on the community: mysterious maladies swept the flocks of chickens; the cattle and sheep sickened and died. Everywhere was a shadow of death. The farmers spoke of much illness among their families. In the town the doctors had become more and more puzzled by new kinds of sickness appearing among their patients. There had been several sudden and unexplained deaths, not only among adults but even among children, who would be stricken suddenly while at play and die within a few hours.

There was a strange stillness. The birds, for example—where had they gone? Many people spoke of them, puzzled and disturbed. The feeding stations in the backyards were deserted. The few birds seen anywhere were moribund; they trembled violently and could not fly. It was a spring without voices. On the mornings that had once throbbed with the dawn chorus of robins, catbirds, doves, jays, wrens, and scores of other bird voices there was now no sound; only silence lay over the fields and woods and marsh.

On the farms the hens brooded, but no chicks hatched. The farmers complained that they were unable to raise any pigs—the litters were small and the young survived only a few days. The apple trees were coming into bloom but no bees droned among the blossoms, so there was no pollination and there would be no fruit.

The roadsides, once so attractive, were now lined with browned and withered vegetation as though swept by fire. These, too, were silent, deserted by all living things. Even the streams were now lifeless. Anglers no longer visited them, for all the fish had died.

In the gutters under the eaves and between the shingles of the roofs, a white granular powder still showed a few patches; some weeks before it had fallen like snow upon the roofs and the lawns, the fields and streams.

No witchcraft, no enemy action had silenced the rebirth of new life in this stricken world. The people had done it themselves.

This town does not actually exist, but it might easily have a thousand counterparts in America or elsewhere in the world. I know of no community that has experienced all the misfortunes I describe. Yet every one of these disasters has actually happened somewhere, and many real communities have already suffered a substantial number of them. A grim specter has crept upon us almost unnoticed, and this imagined tragedy may easily become a stark reality we all shall know.

What has already silenced the voices of spring in countless towns in America? This book is an attempt to explain.[10]

3. GROUP WORK: READING AND ANALYSIS OF SEVERAL TYPES OF CLAIMS IN ONE ESSAY

The following essay is an example of several types of claims and associated purposes used in one essay. One type of claim, however, predominates in the essay and the other claims support and develop it. First divide the essay into "chunks" by drawing a line across the page each time the author changes the type of claim and purpose. Label the type of claim and predominant purpose of each chunk (example: fact, to establish the facts). Then establish the predominant claim and purpose of the entire essay. Speculate about the reasons the author had for placing the parts of this essay in this particular order. Discuss the relationship between the parts.

Much argumentative writing combines claims in this way, and you may want to study the pattern of claims used here as a possible model for one of your own argument papers.

Essay

HOLD YOUR HORSEPOWER

Lyla Fox

Folks in the small Michigan town where I grew up revere the work ethic. Our entire culture lauds those who are willing to work their tails off to get ahead. Though there's nothing wrong with hard work, I suggest that our youngsters may be starting too young—and for all the wrong reasons.

Increasingly I identify with Sisyphus trying to move that stone. There are more mornings than I would like to admit when many of my students sit with eyes glazed or heads slumped on their desks as I try to nurture a threatening-to-become-extinct interest in school. These are not lazy kids. Many are high-achieving 16- and 17-year-olds who find it tough to reconcile 7:30 A.M. classes with a job that winds down at 10:30 P.M. or later.

"What's wrong?" I asked a student who once diligently completed his homework assignments. He groggily grunted an answer. "I'm tired. I didn't get home until 11 P.M." Half the class nodded and joined in a discussion about how hard it is to try to balance schoolwork, sports and jobs. Since we end up working most of our adult life, my suggestion to the class was to forgo the job and partake of school—both intra- and extracurricular.

---

[10]*Silent Spring* (Boston: Houghton Mifflin, 1962), pp. 1–3. This is the first chapter of Rachel Carson's well-known book, *Silent Spring*. Carson was a marine biologist who is credited with starting the modern environmental movement with the publication of this book in 1962.

"Then how do I pay for my car?" the sleepy student, now more awake, asked. Click. The car. That's what all these bleary eyes and half-done papers are about. My students have a desperate need to drive their own vehicles proudly into the school parking lot. The car is the teenager's symbolic club membership. I know because I've seen the embarrassed looks on the faces of teens who must answer "No" to the frequently asked "Do you have a car?" National Merit finalists pale in importance beside the student who drives his friends around in a shiny new Ford Probe.

My own son (a senior at the University of Michigan) spent a good part of his high-school years lamenting our "no car in high school" dictate. When he needed to drive, we made sure he could always borrow our car. Our Oldsmobile 88, however, didn't convey the instant high-school popularity of a sporty Nissan or Honda. Our son's only job was to do as well as he could in school. The other work, we told him, would come later. Today I see students working more than the legally permitted number of hours to pay for their cars. I also see once committed students becoming less dedicated to schoolwork. Their commitment is to their cars and the jobs that will help them make those monthly car payments.

Once cars and jobs enter the picture, it is virtually impossible to get students focused on school. "My parents are letting me get a car," one of my brightest students enthused a few months ago. "They say all I have to do is get a job to make the payments." *All.* I winced, saying nothing because parents' views are sacrosanct for me. I bit my cheeks to keep from saying how wrong I thought they were and how worried I was for her schoolwork. Predictably, during the next few months, her grades and attitude took a plunge.

I say attitude because when students go to work for a car, their positive attitude frequently disappears. Teachers and parents are on the receiving end of curved-lip responses to the suggestion that they should knuckle down and do some schoolwork. A job and car payments are often a disastrous combination.

These kids are selling their one and only chance at adolescence for a car. Adults in their world must help them see what their children's starry eyes cannot: that students will have the rest of their lives to own an automobile and pay expenses.

Some parents, I know, breathe a sigh of relief when their children can finally drive themselves to orthodontist appointments and basketball practice. This trade-off could mean teens' losing touch with family life. Having a car makes it easy for kids to cut loose and take part in activities far from home. Needing that ride from Mom and Dad helps to keep a family connection. Chauffering teens another year or two might be a bargain after all.

What a remarkable experience a school day might be if it were the center of teens' lives, instead of that much-resented time that keeps them from their friends and their jobs. Although we may not have meant to, parents may have laid the groundwork for that resentment. By giving kids permission to work, parents are not encouraging them to study. Parents have allowed students to miss classes because of exhaustion from the previous night's work. By providing a hefty down payment on a $12,000 car and stressing the importance of keeping up the payments, they're sending a signal that schoolwork is secondary.

The kids I'm writing about are wonderful. But they are stressed and angry that their day has too few hours for too much work. Sound familiar? It should. It is the same description adults use to identify what's wrong with their lives.

After reading this, my students may want to hang me in effigy. But perhaps some of them are secretly hoping that someone will stop their world and help them get off. They might also concede that it's time to get out of the car and get on mass transit. For students in large metropolitan areas, public transportation is the only way to get around.

Adults should take the reins and let teens off the hook. We must say "no" when we're implored to "Please let me get a job so I can have a car." Peer pressure makes it hard for kids to turn away from the temptation of that shiny four-wheeled popularity magnet. It's up to the grown-ups to let kids stay kids a little longer.

The subject of teens and cars comes up in my home as well as in my classroom. My 15-year-old daughter gave me some bone-chilling news yesterday. "The Springers got Suzi her own car!" she announced. "All she has to do is make the payments."

I smiled and went back to correcting the essays that would have been lovely had their authors had some time to put into constructing them. The payment, I told myself after my daughter went grudgingly to begin her homework, may be greater than anyone in the Springer family could possibly imagine.[11]

4. GROUPS AND INDIVIDUALS, WRITING ASSIGNMENT: TYPES OF CLAIMS

Write a one-page paper organized around a single type of claim. Use the following claims as starter sentences for your paper, or think of your own based on an issue in "The Reader." Use the information about types of proofs and organizational strategies for each type of claim in this chapter to help you plan and write. Work in groups to generate the ideas and support for these papers.

a. Fact: Too many people own guns.
b. Definition: A definition of family values requires first a definition of a family.
c. Cause: Closing the college library on the weekends could have disastrous results.
d. Value: Computers are indispendable in modern education.
e. Policy: Parents should have the right to choose the schools their children attend.

5. QUESTIONS ON THE CHAPTER

a. What are the five types of claims?
b. What are the questions associated with each type?

---

[11]"My Turn," *Newsweek*, March 25, 1996, p. 16. Fox is a high school English teacher in Michigan.

c. What is a predictable sequence that claims follow when they originate in a dramatic, real-life situation?

d. How do claims typically appear in written argument, that is, do writers usually limit themselves to a single purpose and claim or not? Discuss.

6. **QUESTIONS ON THE ESSAYS FOR ANALYSIS**

a. "Black America's Moment of Truth," page 163. What was some of the evidence that the author presented to support his view that there is a breakdown of civilization within the African-American community? What evidence might someone use who wanted to refute this position? What is your own position? What evidence would you use to support your position?

b. "Family Values," page 165. Who are the four authorities on family values referred to in this article, and what are their views on this issue? What is the meaning of family values that emerges finally from this article? What, according to the author, are some signs of a lack of family values? What, in your opinion, are some signs of a lack of family values?

c. "Paying the Price of Female Neglect," page 166. Why is it important not to neglect women in a society? What are some examples in the article of efforts to change the trend of neglect in some countries? What else might be done? What would the results be?

d. "The Men's Movement," page 169. What, according to this author, seem to be the main problems that are addressed by the "men's movement?" What is the author's approach to these problems? Do you perceive these as problems? What is your approach for dealing with them?

e. "Computers in Class," page 172. What has your experience been with computers in school? Why were they used and how effective were they? If you were responsible for computerizing your campus and had the funds to do what you wanted, what would you do? How would you do it? Why would you do it?

f. "Gene Tests: What You Know Can Hurt You," page 178. What is the problem described in this article? What is the proposed solution? Can you think of other examples of information that might be controversial in the way that gene tests are? What is your opinion about communicating information of this sort to the people who are affected by it?

g. "We're Too Busy for Ideas," page 179. When and under what circumstances are you most likely to have creative thoughts? Do you think that technology helps you or hinders your creativity? How? What can you do to provide yourself with opportunities for more creative thinking?

h. "And a Purple Dinosaur Shall Lead Them," page 181. Describe the values the author claims are projected in "Sesame Street" and in "Barney and Friends." Do you agree or disagree with the author's assessment of the values in these programs? Why or why not? What values should be taught in children's programming?

i. "Rap's Embrace of 'Nigger' Fires Bitter Debate," page 184. What is the controversial issue in this essay? What are some of the positions taken by people quoted in the essay? What is your own position? What in your own experience has caused you to take this position?

j. "A Fable for Tomorrow," page 187. What is at issue in this essay? What is Rachel Carson's position? Is this still an issue? Who would disagree with Carson? Why? Where do you stand on this issue? Why? Are there examples from your own experience that influence your own position? What are they?

k. "Hold Your Horsepower," page 189. How people use their time is often controversial. How is it controversial in this essay? Can you think of other examples where time is controversial? In your opinion, is the problem the author identifies significant or not? Why do you think so?

CHAPTER 7

Types of Proofs

You learned in Chapter 5 that the claim, the support, and the warrants are the three essential parts of an argument. The last chapter helped you understand claims, and this chapter will help you understand the support and warrants that provide the proofs for the claim. The material in this chapter is organized to introduce you first to the different types of proofs, next to the language and style associated with each of them, and finally to some of the fallacies or pseudoproofs that sometimes occur in argument.

As you understand and begin to work with the proofs, you will discover that they are not simply uniform patterns that are obvious and easy to recognize. Rather, slippery and imperfect as they are, they represent an attempt to describe what goes on in the real world of argument and in the minds of writers and readers of argument. Understanding them can put you closer to an author, so that you may better understand how that individual thought about, interpreted, and developed a particular subject. Then, when you switch roles and become the author yourself, your knowledge of what can happen in argument will help you develop your own thoughts and create your own effective arguments.

THE TRADITIONAL CATEGORIES OF PROOF

The traditional categories of proof, like much of our most fundamental and useful argument theory, were first articulated by classical theorists, and they are still useful for describing what goes on in real-world argument today. Recall from chapter 5 that Aristotle, in the *Rhetoric,* said that an arguer must state a claim (or a proposition) and prove it. He also went into detail about the broad categories of proof that can be used to prove the probability of a claim. Aristotle's categories of proof are still useful either because they accurately describe what classical arguers did then and what modern arguers still do, or because Aristotle's ideas have become such an accepted part of our intellectual heritage that, like generations before us, we learn these methods and use them to observe, think about, and interpret reality. In either case, Aristotle's ideas and observations about argument still apply. They provide accurate descriptions of what goes on in argument.

Aristotle distinguishes between proofs that can be produced and laid on the table, so to speak, like a murder weapon, fingerprints, or a written contract, and proofs that are invented and represent the creative thinking and insights of clever and intelligent people.

Aristotle divides this second category of proof into three subcategories: proofs that appeal to logic and reason, proofs that establish *ethos* or the credibility of the source, and proofs that appeal to the emotions. The Greek words used to refer to the proofs are *logos* (logic), *ethos* (credibility), and *pathos* (emotion). *Logical proof* appeals to people's reason, understanding, and common sense. It is consistent with what we know and believe, and it gives us fresh insight and ideas about issues. As proof, it relies mainly on such support as reasoned opinion and factual data and also on warrants that suggest the soundness and truth of such support. Aristotle declared that logical proof is the most important type of proof in argument, and most modern theorists agree with him. Richard M. Weaver, a well-known modern rhetorician, for example, says that argument has its primary basis in reasoning and that it appeals primarily to the rational part of man. Logical proof, he says, provides, "the plot" of argument.[1] The other two types of proof are also present and important, however.

Proof that establishes ethos appeals to the audience's impressions, opinions, and judgments about the individual stating the argument. Arguers who demonstrate competence, good character, fair-mindedness, and goodwill toward the audience are more convincing than people who lack these qualities. Individuals who project such favorable qualities to an audience have established good *ethos*. Audiences are more likely to trust and believe individuals with good ethos than those without it. At times, arguers also need to establish the ethos of the experts whom they quote in their arguments. They usually accomplish this purpose by providing information about them so that audiences will appreciate these individuals' degree of expertise and, consequently, be more willing to accept what they say.

Emotional proof is used to appeal to and arouse the feelings of the audience. Audience's feelings are aroused primarily through emotional language, examples, personal narratives, and vivid descriptions of events that contain emotional elements and that arouse strong feelings in other people. Emotional proof is appropriate in an argument when it is used to develop the claim and when it contributes to the sense of logical conviction or agreement that are argument's intended outcomes. A well-reasoned set of logical proofs contributes to such outcomes. But emotion can also contribute to a strong acceptance of a logical conclusion. Imagine, for example, an argument in favor of increasing taxes to build housing for homeless people. The logical argument would describe reasons for these taxes, methods for levying them, and recommendations for spending them.

---

[1]Richard M. Weaver, "Language Is Sermonic," in Richard L. Johannesen, ed., *Contemporary Theories of Rhetoric: Selected Readings.* (New York: Harper & Row, 1971), pp. 163–179.

The argument would be strengthened, however, by a few vivid and emotional examples of homeless people who lead miserable lives.

The next three sections will introduce you to seven types of logical proof, one type of proof that builds *ethos,* and two types of emotional proof. All are commonly used in argument. The number and variety of logical proofs is greater than the others because logical thinking dominates and provides "the plot" for most argument. Most arguments rely on a variety of proofs because several types of proof usually provide a stronger argument than reliance on only one.

Each type of proof will be explained according to the following format so that you can understand each type as quickly and easily as possible:[2]

Description and Example. The proof is described and an example is provided.

Claim and Support. You are then told what to look for, or what types of support you can expect to find on the printed page and how to find the claim.

Warrant. You are told what you are expected to assume to make logical connections between the support and the claim. The warrants associated with types of proof suggest specific ways of thinking about support and its function in an argument.

Tests of Validity. You are provided with questions to ask to help you test the reliability and validity of the proof. These questions will focus your attention on both support and warrant and how they do or do not function together as effective proof. They will also help you locate the weaknesses in an argument which can help you plan rebuttal and formulate argument of your own.

At the end of the chapter, in the exercise section, some of the proofs in a short essay are identified and analyzed so that you can also see how they operate in a written argument.

SOME TYPES OF LOGICAL PROOF: *LOGOS*

Logical proofs (also called substantive proofs) include facts, reasons, and opinions that are based on reality. They rely on substantial factual information, data, and accounts of actual events, both past and present. The support used in logical proof is real and drawn from experience. Logical (or substantive) warrants guarantee the reliability and relevance of this support. Logical proofs represent common ways of thinking about and perceiving relationships among the events and data of the real world and then using those ideas and relationships as support for a line of argument.

---

[2]In this chapter I have drawn on some of Wayne Brockriede and Douglas Ehninger's ideas in "Toulmin on Argument: An Interpretation and Application," *Quarterly Journal of Speech,* 46, no. 1 (February 1969): 44–53. Specifically, I have expanded and adapted these authors' analysis of proofs to make it apply to the reading and writing of argument as explained in this book.

Argument from Deduction

Description and Examples. Deductive argument is also called argument from principle because its warrant is a general principle. Remember that the warrant may or may not be stated explicitly in an argument. Etymology can help you remember the special features of deductive argument. The prefix *de-* means "from" and the root *duc* means "lead." *A deductive argument leads from a general principle,* which is the warrant, applies it to an example or specific case, which is described in the support, and draws *a conclusion,* which is the claim.

In the last chapter you learned that argument deals with matters that are probably rather than certainly true. People do not argue about matters that are certainly true because they already agree about them. Here is an example of a deductive argument based on a general principle that people would agree with and accept as true. Thus, they would not argue about it.

General warrant:	Every person has a unique set of fingerprints.
Support:	The accused is a person.
Claim:	The accused has a unique set of fingerprints.

This example might be used as a minor argument to support a claim that someone is guilty of a crime. It would never be the main issue in an argument, however, because it is not arguable.

Most of the deduction you will encounter in argument, on the other hand, is arguable because it deals with probabilities rather than with certainties. Sherlock Holmes used deduction to reach his sometimes astonishing conclusions. Holmes examined the supporting evidence—footprints, for example—and deduced that the man who left them walked with a limp. The general principle, that most uneven footprints are left by people with limps, is an assumption that is important in Holmes's deductive thinking even though it is not stated in the argument. It does not need to be spelled out for readers who are able to supply that warrant themselves as they accept Holmes's conclusion. The Holmes deduction can be summarized as follows. The purpose of this argument is to establish the type of person who left these footprints.

Unstated warrant:	Most uneven footprints are left by people with limps.
Support:	These footprints are uneven.
Claim:	Thus the person who left these footprints walks with a limp.

Is there any part of that argument that you might challenge as only possibly or probably rather than as certainly true? If so, you can argue about it.

Claim and Support. Locate the claim by answering this question: "On the basis of a general principle (warrant), implied or stated, what does the author expect me to conclude about this specific example or case?"

Deductive Warrants. You are expected to assume that a general principle about a whole category of phenomena (people, places, events, and so forth) has been stated or implied in the argument and that it is accurate and acceptable. You are expected to decide that, since the general principle, or warrant, and the support for the specific case are both accurate and acceptable, then the conclusion also is acceptable and probably true.

Tests of Validity.   Ask, Is the warrant acceptable and believable? Does the warrant apply to the example or case? Is the support for the case accurate? How reliable, then, is the conclusion?

If the reader has a problem with either the warrant or the example in a deductive argument, the conclusion will not be acceptable. Consider Holmes's warrant that uneven footprints are left by people with limps. That may be convincing to some readers but not convincing to others. For instance, a reader who reflects that a person who pretends to limp or one who carries a heavy valise in one hand could also leave uneven footprints will also question the warrant and decide the proof is not even probably true.

Here is another example of a deductive argument that would not be equally successful with all audiences:

Unstated warrant:	Families cannot be happy when the mother works outside the home.
Support:	The mother in this family works outside the home
Claim:	This is an unhappy family.

For some readers who come from happy homes with working mothers the warrant in this example would seem faulty.

In the next example of a deductive argument, the support could be a problem for some readers who might have trouble accepting it because they think baby boomers are smart and responsible and would make excellent presidents. Thus they would reject the conclusion also.

Warrant:	People who are irresponsible and have materialistic lifestyles should not be president.
Support:	Baby boomers were irresponsible in the 1960s and are materialistic now.
Claim/conclusion:	A baby boomer should not be president.

All parts of a deductive argument need to be accurate and acceptable to the audience for it to be convincing.

Argument from Definition

Description and Examples.   Definition is extremely important in argument. It is difficult to argue about any subject unless there is general agreement about the meanings of the key terms, especially when they are part of the claim. Sometimes an entire argument is based on the audience's acceptance of a certain meaning of a key term. If the audience accepts the definition, then the arguer says that the claim should be accepted "by definition." For example, if abortion is defined as willful taking of human life, then, by definition, it is murder. Here is this argument laid out as deduction:

Unstated warrant: Willful taking of human life is murder.
Unstated support: Abortion is willful taking of human life.
Claim: Abortion is murder.

Here is another example:

Warrant: Family values characterize the good citizen.
Support: Radical feminists lack family values.
Claim: Radical feminist are not good citizens.

We will accept the claim that radical feminists, by definition, are poor citizens only if we also accept the warrants that define the good citizen as one who possesses family values and radical feminists as people who lack these values. (See the article "Family Values" on page 165 to see how this argument appears in print.)

Even though argument by definition takes the form of deductive argument, it is listed separately here to emphasize the important function of definitions in arguments that depend on it as major proof.

Claim and Support. Look for all definitions or explanations of words or concepts. These may be a sentence, several paragraphs, or an entire essay in length. Notice if the definition is used simply to define a word or if it is used as part of the proof in the argument. Look for a claim that you are expected to accept as a result of the definition.

Definition Warrants. You are expected to assume that the definition describes the fundamental properties and qualities of the term accurately so that it can be used to prove the claim.

Tests of Validity. Is this an accurate and complete definition? Is it convincing in this context? Are there exceptions or other definitions for this term that would make the final claim less reliable?

Argument from Cause

Description and Example. Argument from cause places the subject in a cause-effect relationship to show that it is either the cause of an effect or the effect of a cause. It is very common in argument to explain or to justify a claim with cause-effect reasoning. Here is an example. Notice in this example that the claim is stated first. This is to remind you that in actual argument there is no fixed order for the three parts of the argument.

> *Claim:* Children read better in school when their parents read to them at home.
>
> *Support:* Specific examples of parents reading to children who then read well at school.
>
> *Warrant:* The parents' reading caused the children to do better.

Claim and Support.   Look for examples, events, trends, and people that have caused certain things to happen. Look for the effects. For example, "Television violence causes children to become violent." Or turn it around and look for the effects first and then the causes: "Many children are violent as a result of watching too much violence on television." Look, also, for clue words such as *cause, effect, resulted in, as a result, as a consequence,* or *because* to indicate that cause-effect reasoning is being used. Finally, the claim states what you are expected to conclude as a result of this cause-effect reasoning: "Parents should be trained to read to their children," or, "Children should not watch violent television."

Causal Warrants.   You are expected to assume that the causes really do create the identified effects, or that the effects really are the results of the named causes.

Tests of Validity.   Are these causes alone sufficient to create these effects? Could these effects result from other causes? Can I think of exceptions to the cause-effect outcome that is claimed here?

Argument from Sign

Description and Example.   A specific visible sign is sometimes used to prove a claim. A sign can be used to prove with certainty: Someone breaks out in chicken pox, and the claim, based on that certain sign, is that the person has chicken pox. Or a sign can be used to prove the probability of a claim: A race riot, someone argues, is probably a sign of the claim that people think they are unfairly treated. Or the sign may turn out to be the pseudoproof of a false claim. A child asks, "Why should I believe in Santa Claus?" and the parent answers, "Look at all the toys under the tree that weren't there yesterday." That support is used as a sign for the claim that Santa Claus exists. Here is an example of a sign used to prove nationality. Would you say this is a certain or only probable sign?

> *Claim:* That person is Russian.
>
> *Support (sign):* She is speaking in Russian.
>
> *Warrant:* Speaking Russian is a sign of Russian nationality.

Claim and Support.   Look for visible clues, symptoms, and occurrences that are explained as obvious and clear signs of a certain belief or state of affairs. Look for the conclusion or claim that is made on the basis of these signs.

Sign Warrants.   You are expected to assume that the sign is actually a sign of what the author claims it to be.

Tests of Validity. Is this really a sign of what the author claims it to be? Is there another explanation for the sign?

Argument from Induction

Description and Example. Inductive argument provides a number of examples and draws a claim, in the form of a conclusion, from them. The audience is expected to accept the group of examples as adequate and accurate enough to make the inductive leap to the claim. Inductive argument is also called argument from generalization or argument from example because the claim is a generalization made on the basis of the examples. To help you remember the special features of inductive argument, learn its prefix *in-*, which means "in" or "into," and the root *duc*, which means "lead." *An inductive argument uses examples to lead into a claim or generalization about the examples.* Here is an example: Four different people take their cars to the same car repair shop and are overcharged. The claim is then made that anyone who takes a car to that repair shop will probably be overcharged.

Inductive reasoning is the basis of the scientific method. Most scientific conclusions are reached inductively. When a sufficient number of phenomena are observed repeatedly, then a generalization is made to explain them. Here is an example:

Claim:	The sun always comes up.
Support:	The sun has come up every day of recorded history.
Warrant:	That is a sufficient number of days to make that claim.

Induction demonstrates only probability when there is the possibility of an exceptional example. Someone may get a good deal at the repair shop. On the other hand, an apple always falls from a tree and thus demonstrates gravity, or the sun always comes up. No one has been able to find exceptional examples to disprove these generalizations.

To be effective, inductive argument requires a sufficient number of examples. When a generalization is made on the basis of only one, or a few, examples, it is called a "hasty generalization." To claim, for instance, that an office worker should always be able to enter a certain amount of data because he did it once may not be accurate. To make a broad generalization, such as *all* office workers ought to be able to enter a certain amount of data because *one* employee was able to, is called a "sweeping" generalization. An inadequate sample of cases weakens or invalidates an inductive argument.

Claim and Support. Look for a group of examples followed by a generalization (claim) based on the examples; or the generalization (claim) may be stated first and then be followed by several examples.

Inductive Warrants. You are expected to assume that the list of examples is representative and that it shows a definite trend. You are also expected to assume that if you added more examples of the same general type the resulting conclusion would not change.

Test of Validity. Is the sample adequate? Would more examples continue to show the trend? Are there examples that show an opposite trend, that provide an exception? (Was someone charged a reasonable amount at the repair shop?) Can we make the inductive leap from the examples to the generalization to demonstrate that it is probably true?

Argument from Statistics

Description and Example. Like other forms of logical proof, statistics describe relationships among data, people, occurrences, and events in the real world, only they do so in quantitative terms. Modern readers have considerable faith in numbers and statistics. They seem more "true" than other types of support to many people. It is more convincing to some people, for example, to make the claim that we should end draft registration because it costs $27.5 million per year than to simply claim that we should end it because we no longer need it.

Read statistical proofs carefully to determine where they come from and how reliable, accurate, and relevant they are. Note also whether the original figures have been *changed* or *interpreted* in some way. Figures are often *rounded off* or *stated in different terms,* such as percentages or graphs. They are also sometimes *compared* to other material that is familiar to the audience to make them more interesting or memorable.[3] Various types of graphs or charts, such as those used on page 349 to 352 also make data and statistics visual and even easier to grasp and remember.

Here is an example of a typical use of statistics in an article entitled "Child-Killing Increases in Rio."[4]

> *Claim:* Child-killing is increasing in Rio de Janeiro.
> *Support:* Forty percent more children may be killed this year than last year.
> *Warrant:* Forty percent represents an increase.

The source for these statistics is cited only as "preliminary statistics." On close reading, one realizes that 424 people under 18 were killed in one year in Rio compared with 348 who were killed in seven months of the next year. Thus the claim of a 40 percent increase is qualified to read "may be killed," since it is based on a projection of what might occur in the next five months. The figures are also converted to percentages. The author goes on to compare these figures with one that is more familiar to the reader, the number of child killings in the United States. It is claimed that 6,000 to 7,000 children, or 20 a day, died from gunshot wounds during the comparable period of time in the United States. Notice that these figures, also, are rounded off. The source for these last figures is cited as a news con-

---

[3]James Wood, *Speaking Effectively* (New York: Random House, 1988), pp. 121–127.
[4]James Brooke, "Child-Killing Increases in Rio," *Fort Worth Star-Telegram,* January 3, 1994, p. 7.

ference interview with the executive director of Unicef. You might have to read other sources on this subject to test the validity of these figures.

Claim and Support.   Look for numbers and data, in both their original and their converted form, graphs and charts of figures, as well as interpretations of them, including comparisons. Look for a claim based on the data.

Statistical Warrants.   You are expected to assume that the data have been gathered and reported accurately by competent people, that they are representative and complete unless stated otherwise, and that they have been interpreted fairly and truthfully.

Tests of Validity.   Where did these statistics come from? To what dates do the statistics apply? How reliable is the source? How accurate are they? How are they presented? Have they been rounded off, changed, or converted? How has the change affected their accuracy? Do they prove what they are supposed to prove? Have they been interpreted fairly, or are they exaggerated or skewed? Has enough backing been provided to prove their reliability? What are they compared to, and how does this comparison contribute to their final significance? Is any significant information left out?

Tests of Validity for Statistics Presented as Graphs.   Statistics are sometimes presented in graph form (see Chapter 11, pp. 349 to 352 for some examples of graphs). The tests of validity in this case include, where did the information come from? What information is included in the sample? How was it gathered? Is anything significant left out or ignored because it didn't fit? Are the charts and graphs accurately labelled? Are there any exaggerations?

Argument from Historical, Literal, or Figurative Analogy

Description and Examples.   *Historical and literal analogies* explore similarities and differences between items in the same general category, and figurative analogies do the same, only with items in very different categories. In drawing analogies, we show how something we may not know much about is like something we know in greater detail. In other words, we interpret what we do not know in the light of what we do know. We then supply the warrant that what happened in one case will happen in the other, we draw conclusions, and we make a claim based on the comparisons in the analogy.

Historical analogies explain what is going on *now* in terms of what went on in similar cases in the *past*. Future outcomes are also often projected from past cases. The idea is that what happened in the past will probably repeat itself in the present. Also, the two events are so similar that the results of the former will surely be the end result of the latter. For example:

Claim:	Many people will die of AIDS.
Support:	Many people died of the black death.
Warrant:	AIDS and the black death are similar.

Literal analogies compare two items in the same category: two school systems, two governments, two religions, two individuals. Outcomes are described as in historical analogies, that is, what happened in one case will happen in the other because of the similarities or the differences. For example:

Claim: The state should spend more money on education.
Support: Another state spent more money with good results.
Warrant: The two states are similar, and the results of one will be the results of the other.

Figurative analogies compare items from two different categories, as in metaphor, only the points of comparison in a figurative analogy are usually spelled out in more detail than they are in a metaphor. Many figurative analogies appeal to the emotions rather than to reason. Figurative analogies are only effective as logical proof when they are used to identify *real qualities* that are shared by both items and that can then be applied to help prove the claim logically. When the items in a figurative analogy are compared to add ornament or to stir up an emotional response, the analogy functions as emotional proof. It engages the emotions rather than the reason.

Here are some examples of figurative analogies used as logical proof. To prove that reading a difficult book should take time, Francis Bacon compares that activity with taking the time to chew and digest a large meal. The qualities of the two activities, rather than the activities themselves, are compared. Since these qualities are not spelled out, the audience must infer that both take time, and understanding, like digestion, benefits and becomes a permanent part of the individual. Here is this argument laid out so that you can see how it works:

Claim: Reading a difficult book should take time.
Support: Digesting a large meal takes time.
Warrant: Reading and eating are sufficiently alike that they can be compared.

Or, as another example of logical proof, the human fossil record is compared to an apple tree in early winter that has only a few apples on it. The quality that the fossil record and the tree have in common, which the reader must infer, is that both tree and fossil record have a complicated system of branches and limbs. Also, the few apples on the tree are like the few available fossils. At one time there were many of both. The qualities compared in these two instances improve a rational understanding of the fossil record.

Here is an example of a figurative analogy that is used as emotional proof and ornament rather than as logical proof: Warren Hinckle, in an article critical of political commentators, makes this statement about their writing: "Words such as 'Bonapartist,' even 'fascist,' run through their writing like beer through a fraternity boy."[5] The comparisons implied by that analogy do not result in logical

---

[5]Warren Hinckle, "Ross Perot: Hero of the Counterculture," *New York Times*, July 10, 1992, Sec. A, p. 29.

proof. The analogy is, however, striking and memorable, and would encourage a reader to adopt a certain emotional attitude toward such writers.

Claim and Support. Look for examples of items, events, people, and periods of times that are being compared. Whether these items are drawn from the past or present, as in the case of historical or literal analogies, they must be drawn from the same category: two types of disease, two types of school systems, two types of government, and so on. Look for the clue words *compare, contrast, like, similar to,* and *different from* to signal that comparisons are being made.

In the case of figurative analogies, look for two items being compared that are from totally different categories. Identify the qualities that they have in common. Look for the clue words *like, as, similar to,* or *compare.* Discover claims that are made as a result of comparing similarities or differences.

Comparison Warrants. You are expected to assume that the items being compared are similar as described, and that what happens in one case probably will occur in the other. For figurative analogies you are expected to assume that the qualities of the two items are similar and significant enough so that reference to one will help to explain the other and will serve as convincing proof.

Tests of Validity. Are the two items similar as claimed? Can I think of ways they are not similar or of other qualities they share that would change the claim? Are the outcomes really likely to be the same in both cases? Why? Or why not?

For figurative analogies, ask, Are the qualities of these two items similar, significant, and real enough to help prove a logical argument? Or are they so dissimilar, so far-fetched, or so trivial that the comparison does not prove anything? Does the analogy serve as an ornament, an emotional appeal, or a logical proof?

It is handy to be able to remember the logical proofs both when you are reading and when you are developing your paper so that you can use them more readily. Figure 6.1 provides a mnemonic device that will help you remember them. It shows the first letter of each proof rearranged to make a nonsense word, and a picture of that word to help you remember it. You can run through this mnemonic mentally when you are thinking about ways to develop the ideas in your paper.

Sign
Induction
Cause
Deduction
Analogies (literal, historical, figurative)
Definition
Statistics

Sic dads refuted by logical proof.

Figure 6.1 The Logical Proofs.

A TYPE OF PROOF THAT BUILDS CREDIBILITY: *ETHOS*

The materials provided in argument that help the audience gain a favorable impression of the arguer, the group the arguer represents, or the authorities and experts the arguer cites or quotes help create *ethos,* or the credibility of the author. The author may build credibility by referring to experience and credentials that establish his or her own expertise. Another way is to quote others, or to use arguments from authority.

Argument from Authority

Description and Example.   We are usually inclined to accept the opinions and factual evidence of people who are authorities and experts in their fields. In an article that claims California will have another earthquake, for example, the author describes and provides the professional credentials for several professors of geology from the major universities in southern California as well as scientists from the U.S. Geological Survey Office before quoting their opinions as support:

> *Claim:*   California will have an earthquake.
> *Support:*   Professors and scientists say so.
> *Warrant:*   These experts are reliable.

Authors themselves sometimes establish their own credentials by making references to various types of past experience that qualify them to write about their subject. They also sometimes establish the *ethos* of the group they represent, like "the great Republican Party."

Claim and Support.   Look for all references to the author's credentials, whether made by the author or by an editor. Look for references to the author's training, education, professional position, background, and experience. Notice, also, references to the audience's concerns, beliefs, and values that demonstrate the author's effort to establish common ground and to show fairness and goodwill toward the audience. Look for references to groups the author may represent, and notice how they are described. Look for direct or paraphrased quotations from experts. Differentiate between facts and statements of opinion. Look for credential statements about these experts. Look for claims that are made more valid as a consequence of this expert opinion.

Authoritative Warrants.   You are expected to assume that the information provided about the author, the group, or the expert is accurate, that these authorities are honorable, fair, reliable, knowledgeable, and experienced, and that they also exhibit goodwill toward the audience.

Tests of Validity.   Is there enough information to establish the true character and experience of the author? Is this information complete and accurate? Is there enough information about the group to believe what the author says about it? Are the credentials of the experts good enough to make their contributions reliable? Also, are the credentials relevant to the issue? (A star athlete may not be the best judge of soft drinks or fast food.) If a source is quoted, is it reliable? Argument based on authority is as good as the authorities themselves.

SOME TYPES OF EMOTIONAL PROOF: *PATHOS*

Some argument theorists would say that there should be no appeals to emotion or attempts to arouse the emotions of the audience in argument. The idea is that an argument should appeal only to reason. Emotion, they claim, clouds reasoning and judgment and gets the argument off course. Richard M. Weaver, quoted earlier in this chapter, would disagree. Weaver points out that people are not just austerely unemotional logic machines who are interested only in deduction, induction, and cause-effect reasoning. People also use language to communicate feelings, values, and motives.[6]

Furthermore, when we consider that the source of much argument lies in the dramatic, emotionally laden occurrences of everyday life, we realize how impossible it is to eliminate all emotion from argument. As you read the many argumentative essays included in this book, study the emotional material that is used by professional writers. Try to develop a sense of when emotion contributes to argument in effective and appropriate ways and when it does not. In general, emotional proofs are appropriate in argument when the subject itself is emotional and when it creates strong feelings in both the writer and the reader. For writers of argument, emotion leads to positions on issues, influences the tone of the writing, and informs some of the interpretations. For readers, emotion leads to a stronger engagement with the issue and influences the final outcomes. Emotional proof is appropriate when the occasion justifies it and when it strengthens logical conviction. It is inappropriate when it merely ventilates feelings, serves as an ornament, or distracts the audience from the logical conclusion of the argument. Types of emotional proof focus on *motivation*, or what all people want, and on *values*, or what we consider good or bad, favorable or unfavorable, acceptable or unacceptable.

Motivational Proofs

Description and Example. Some proofs appeal explicitly to what all audiences are supposed to want, such as food, drink, warmth and shelter, sex, security, belongingness, self-esteem, creativity, or self-expression. (See Box 10.1,

---

[6]Weaver elaborates on some of the distinctions between logic and emotion in "Language Is Sermonic."

p. 334, for a more complete list of human needs.) The purpose of motivational proof is to urge the audience to take prescribed steps to meet an identified need. Advertisements and speeches by political candidates provide obvious examples of motivational proof. Drink a certain beer or buy a brand of blue jeans, and you will be irresistible to others. Or support a particular candidate and you will gain job security and safe neighborhoods:

Claim: You should support this candidate.
Support: This candidate can help you get job security and safe neighborhoods.
Warrant: You want job security and safe neighborhoods.

Claim and Support. To find the claim, look for what you are asked to believe or do to get what you want.

Motivational Warrants. Look for references to items or qualities that you might need or want.

Tests of Validity. What am I supposed to need? Do I really need it? What am I supposed to do? Will doing what is recommended satisfy the need in the ways described?

Value Proofs

Description and Example. Some proofs appeal to what all audiences are expected to value, such as reliability, honesty, loyalty, industry, patriotism, courage, integrity, conviction, faithfulness, dependability, creativity, freedom, equality, devotion to duty, and so on. Here is an example that claims the curriculum can contribute to the values of equality and acceptance if it is multicultural:

Claim: The curriculum should be multicultural.
Support: A multicultural curriculum will contribute to equality and acceptance.
Warrant: You value equality and acceptance.

Claim and Support. Look for value statements that are generally accepted by everyone because they have been proved elsewhere many times. Examples include "Freedom of speech is our constitutional right" or "There should be no freedom without responsibility" or "Individuals who have the courage of conviction are to be trusted." Look for slogans that display such values as "Honest Abe," "The home of the free and the brave," or "Honesty is the best policy." Or look for narratives and examples that display values, such as the story of an industrious, thrifty, and ambitious mother who is on welfare. When the values are not directly stated, ask, What value or belief is causing the author to say this? Look for a claim that shows what will result if the recommended values are accepted.

Values Warrants.   You are expected to assume that you share the author's values and that they are as important as the author says they are.

Tests of Validity.   What are the values expressed or implicit in this argument? Do I share these values with the author? If not, how do we differ? What effect do these differences have on my final acceptance of the claim?

The mnemonic VAM (value, authority, and motivation) may help you remember and use the ethical and emotional proofs.

HOW ARE *LOGOS, ETHOS,* AND *PATHOS* COMMUNICATED THROUGH LANGUAGE AND STYLE?

You can learn to recognize logic, *ethos,* and emotion in argument not only by the use of proofs, but also by the language and style associated with each of these types of appeal. Actually, you will not often encounter pure examples of one of these styles, but instead you will encounter a mix, with one of the styles predominating. The same is true of writing. You may plan to write in logical style, but emotion and *ethos* creep in and actually help you create a richer and more varied style for your argument.

Language That Appeals to Logic

The language of logical argument, which is the language associated with reason, is sometimes called rational style. Words that carry mainly denotative meaning are favored in rational style over connotative and emotionally loaded language. The denotative meaning of a word is the commonly held meaning that most people would agree on and that is also found in the dictionary. Examples of words that have predominantly denotative meanings and that are emotionally neutral include *introduction, facts, information,* or *literal meaning.* Most people would agree on the meanings of those words and could produce synonyms. Words with strong connotative meaning may have many extra, unique, and personal meanings or associations attached to them that vary from person to person. Examples of words with connotative meaning, include *rock star, politician, mugger, family values,* or *human rights.* Several people, when asked to define such words, would usually provide a variety of personal meanings and examples that would not be exactly alike or match the denotative meanings of these words in a dictionary.

For support, rational style relies on opinion in the form of reasons, literal or historical analogies, explanations, and definitions, and also on factual data, quotations, and citations from experts and authorities. Furthermore, the reader is usually not required to make as many inferences as for other, more informal styles of writing. Most parts of the argument are spelled out explicitly for the sake of agreement and a better adherence of minds.

Slogans that elicit emotional response, such as "America is the greatest country," "The American people want change," or "Now is the time for healing," are also usually omitted in rational style. Slogans of this type substitute for logical thinking. Readers think better and draw better conclusions when provided with well-reasoned opinion, quotations from authorities, and facts.

For example, in the opening paragraph of an essay entitled "The Lost Art of Political Argument," Christopher Lasch argues in favor of argument and debate.

> Let us begin with a simple proposition: What democracy requires is public debate, not information. Of course it needs information too, but the kind of information it needs can be generated only by vigorous popular debate. We do not know what we need to know until we ask the right questions, and we can identify the right questions only by subjecting our own ideas about the world to the test of public controversy. Information, usually seen as the precondition of debate, is better understood as its by-product. When we get into arguments that focus and fully engage our attention, we become avid seekers of relevant information. Otherwise, we take in information passively—if we take it in at all.[7]

Rational style, you can see, evokes mainly a cognitive, rational response from its readers.

Language That Develops *Ethos*

Authors who seek to establish their own credentials and good character use language to provide a fair-minded view of reality that is restrained and accurate rather than exaggerated or overly opinionated. When language is used to create positive *ethos,* an audience will trust the author as a credible source of information and opinion.

Language that develops *ethos* has several specific characteristics. To begin with, the writer exhibits a consistent awareness of the audience's background and values by adopting a vocabulary level that is appropriate for the topic and the audience. The writer does not talk down, use technical jargon for an audience unfamiliar with it, or use slang or colloquial language unless the context allows for that. Rap music, for example, invites a different vocabulary level than does a scholarly paper.

Writers intent on establishing *ethos* are sensitive to different audiences and what they will admire, trust, and accept. They try to use language precisely, and to say exactly what they mean. They project an honest desire to communicate by avoiding ranting, using filler material that gets off the subject, or any other material that the audience would perceive as offensive or gross.

As you have probably figured out, an author can destroy *ethos* and alter an audience's favorable impression by changing the language. A student who uses colloquial, everyday expressions in a formal essay written for a professor, a commencement speaker who shouts obscenities at the student audience, or a father

---

[7]Christopher Lasch, "The Lost Art of Political Argument," *Harper's,* September 1990, p. 17.

who uses formal, abstract language to talk to his five-year-old all reflect inappropriate language for particular audiences and damage their *ethos* with those audiences.

When you read argument, notice how an author uses language to build connections and trust and also to establish reliability with the audience. When you write argument, use language that will help your audience regard you as sincere and reliable. Appropriate language is important when you write a college paper. The use of slang, slogans, and everyday language and expressions in otherwise formal writing damages your *ethos* and credibility. Writing errors, including mistakes in spelling, punctuation, and grammar, also damage *ethos* because they indicate a lack of concern and goodwill for your readers.

Here is an example of language that builds effective *ethos* with an audience. These excerpts come from Martin Luther King Jr.'s "Letter from Birmingham Jail." An explanation of the rhetorical situation for this letter and the full text of the letter appear on pages 268 to 286. Briefly, however, King was jailed because of his participation in the civil rights movement in Birmingham, Alabama, and he had been criticized publicly for his participation by eight of his fellow clergymen in that city. He wrote his letter to those clergymen. Notice how he deliberately uses language that is sincere and honest and that establishes his credibility as a trustworthy and responsible human being with values that his audience is likely to share. He does not come across as a crackpot, a troublemaker, or one who is angry at the system, which one might expect from someone who has been jailed for civil rights demonstrations.

> My Dear Fellow Clergymen:
>
> While confined here in the Birmingham city jail, I came across your recent statement calling my present activities "unwise and untimely." . . . Since I feel that you are men of genuine good will and that your criticisms are sincerely set forth, I want to try to answer your statement in what I hope will be patient and reasonable terms.
>
> I think I should indicate why I am here in Birmingham, since you have been influenced by the view which argues against "outsiders coming in." . . . I, along with several members of my staff, am here because I was invited here. I am here because I have organizational ties here.
>
> But more basically, I am in Birmingham because injustice is here. Just as the prophets of the eighth century B.C. left their villages and carried their "thus saith the Lord" far beyond the boundaries of their home towns, and just as the Apostle Paul left his village of Tarsus and carried the gospel of Jesus Christ to the far corners of the Greco-Roman world, so am I compelled to carry the gospel of freedom beyond my own home town. Like Paul, I must constantly respond to the Macedonian call for aid.
>
> Moreover, I am cognizant of the interrelatedness of all communities and states. I cannot sit idly by in Atlanta and not be concerned about what happens in Birmingham. Injustice anywhere is a threat to justice everywhere. We are caught in an inescapable network of mutuality, tied in a single garment of destiny. Whatever affects one directly, affects all indirectly. Never again can we afford to live with the narrow, provincial "outside agitator" idea. Anyone who lives inside the United States can never be considered an outsider anywhere within its bounds.

Underline the language in the above passages that you think King has used to establish good *ethos* with his audience of eight clergymen. Notice how King deliberately uses language to project sincerity and goodwill towards his audience.

He also selects examples and appeals to values that are compatible with his audience's interests and values. King's letter is a classic example of argument that establishes effective *ethos* with a particular audience.

Language That Appeals to Emotion

References to values and motives evoke feelings about what people regard as good and bad and about what they want, and authors use the language associated with emotional style in a variety of ways to express and evoke feelings about these matters. The following paragraphs describe a few special techniques that are characteristic of emotional style. Examples are drawn from the essay by Sara Rimer, "Jobs Illuminate What Riots Hid: Young Ideals," which appears in full in the exercise section of Chapter 3, pages 80 to 83.

Emotionally loaded language evokes connotative meaning and causes the audience to experience feelings and associations at a personal level that are not described in dictionaries. Underline the emotional language in this passage:

> America has been bombarded with television images of the youth of South-Central Los Angeles: throwing bricks, looting stores, beating up innocent motorists. The Disneyland staff who interviewed the job applicants, ages 17 to 22, found a different neighborhood.
>
> "They were wonderful kids, outstanding kids," said Greg Albrecht, a spokesman for Disneyland. "We didn't know they were there." Nor, Mr. Albrecht added, had they known that the young people of South-Central Los Angeles would be so eager to work at Disneyland.[8]

There are several examples of emotional language here. Did you, for example, underline the words used to describe the two types of kids the author claims live in South-Central Los Angeles: *throwing, looting,* and *beating up* in contrast to *wonderful* and *outstanding*?

Emotional examples engage the emotions, as in this example: "One of the 600 who wanted to work at Disneyland was Olivia Miles, at 18 the youngest of seven children of a nurse's aide and a disabled roofer." Miss Miles has humble origins but achieves success. Success stories of this type usually result in positive emotional responses from the reader.

Vivid description of an emotional scene creates an emotional reader response, as in this example:

> Aubrey Miles, who is 45, says he has taken pains to tell his daughter that there are good white people. They saved his life, he told her. He was putting a roof on an office building seven years ago when a vat of hot tar exploded. He was severely burned.
>
> "The guys on the job, who were white, helped me," he said. "I was on the ground, on fire. They put the fire out. One guy sat me up and put his back against my back. I could feel the connection. Then, afterward in the hospital, it was the same thing with the doctors."

---

[8]Sara Rimer, "Jobs Illuminate What Riots Hid: Young Ideals," *New York Times,* June 18, 1992, Sec. A, pp. 1, 12.

Notice how this description brings you into the scene, causes you to share the physical sensations and emotions of the individuals described, and then to share in the conclusion about the people who helped.

Narratives of emotional events draw readers into a scene just as vivid description does. Here is a story about Olivia Miles and her reaction to the looting during the riots in Los Angeles:

> The riots presented Olivia Miles with the biggest ethical quandary of her life. "I saw people on television coming out with boxes of shoes and pretty furniture," she said. Her smile was embarrassed. "It was like Christmas. I wanted to get some. I was asking my sister if we could go. She said, 'No, you can't go out.' I thought: 'She's going to go to work. Should I get it, or shouldn't I get it? It's not fair that I can't. Everyone else is going to get stuff.'"
>
> This, too, her father had foreseen. "I told her, 'There are going to be a lot of opportunities for you to get things, so just stay in the house,'" Mr. Miles said. "She knew automatically that stealing was a no-no."
>
> That Sunday, Olivia was in her regular pew at the Mt. Sinai Baptist Church. "The pastor was saying, 'If you took something, shame on you. That's a sin,'" she said. She looked relieved all over again. "I was so happy."

By describing the emotions of the characters in a narrative, the author invites the reader to share them also.

Emotional tone, created by emotional language and examples, indicates that the author has a strong feeling about the subject and wants the audience to share that feeling. Also, irony and sarcasm should always be viewed as examples of emotional tone. They indicate strong feeling and a desire for change.

Figurative analogies contribute to emotion in an argument, particularly when two emotional subjects are compared and the resulting effect appeals more to emotion than to reason.

Emotional style is the easiest of all the styles to recognize because it is emotionally charged, and it is often close to our own experiences. Do not commit the common reading error of noticing only emotional style, ignoring logic and *ethos,* and even missing the main point of the entire text because you become distracted by emotional material. Remember, in argument logic is the plot, and emotion and *ethos* add further support. Table 6.1 provides a summary of the characteristics of language used to appeal to reason, to establish *ethos,* and to appeal to emotion.

Ethics and Morality in Argument

A person's ability to argue persuasively has been recognized as a potentially powerful influence over other people for centuries. Thus, the classical argument theorists, Aristotle, Cicero, and Quintilian, all recognized that an arguer should be a good person with moral principles who is arguing for good causes. These writers criticized arguers who used their persuasive powers to manipulate people in order to achieve their own selfish ends. They stressed that an ethical arguer must have the courage and willingness to argue logically and honestly from a strong sense of personal integrity and values. Also, emotional and motivational appeals should be consistent with positive value systems that will benefit not

Table 6.1   A Summary of Language and Style in Argument

STYLE TO APPEAL TO LOGIC	STYLE TO DEVELOP *ETHOS*	STYLE TO APPEAL TO EMOTION
Theoretical, abstract language Denotative meanings Reasons Literal and historical analogies Explanations Definitions Factual data Quotations Citations from experts and authorities Informed opinion Explicit, spelled out Evokes a cognitive, rational response	Language appropriate to audience and to subject Restrained, sincere, fair-minded language Appropriate level of vocabulary Grammatically correct Demonstrates author's reliability, competency, and respect for audience's ideas and values through reliable and appropriate use of support and general accuracy	Vivid, concrete language Emotionally loaded language Connotative meanings Emotional examples Vivid descriptions Narratives of emotional events Emotional tone Figurative analogies Evokes an emotional response

only one individual but also society. Using emotions to cloud judgment or to persuade individuals to accept ideas that the arguer does not really believe in is clearly unethical. Basic standards of good judgment and common honesty have always been critical to ethical argument both in classical times and in the present.

People were struck by some letters discovered in Germany a few years ago that were perfect examples of excellent argument, but whose subject matter was totally immoral. These letters were the written orders for exterminating the Jews during World War II. Although Hitler was a convincing arguer, his values and his claims were immoral. In more recent years a political consultant working for the President of the United States was exposed as a person who had no core system of values and who was more interested in manipulating public opinion than in determining what was the best political course for the country. This individual was accused by the analysts at that time of believing in nothing.

Unethical individuals who argue mainly to manipulate public opinion often use unethical tactics to influence and gain adherence to their points of view. Such tactics include opinion polls that push for particular points of view, exaggerated or manipulated statistics, manufactured evidence, and deliberate fallacious reasoning. All of these techniques can be very effective in changing audience opinion even though they are based on false values and motives.

It is important that you learn to recognize the difference between ethical and unethical argument. You can begin by asking the two bottom-line questions: (1) *Am I convinced?* That is, does this argument change the way I think? Are the values honorable? Is the writer just and fair-minded? Is the support fair, accurate, and convincing? Can I accept the warrants? Should the claim be qualified if it isn't already? If you answer yes, that you are convinced, then you should also ask, (2) *Is this argument moral or immoral according to my values and standards of behavior?* You will need to judge the final moral worth of an argument by testing it against your own system of values.

The next section will help you learn to differentiate between honest, ethical argument and unethical, manipulative argument. The fallacies or pseudoproofs are often used by dishonest arguers to influence opinion.

THE FALLACIES OR PSEUDOPROOFS

In an advertisement for a health club, an attractive muscular man is embracing a beautiful slim woman. The caption reads, "Studies show diets don't work. This picture shows exercise does." No further evidence is provided. You do not have to be an expert in argument theory to sense that something is wrong with this proof.

Responsible and honest proof relies on skillful use of support and acceptable warrants to prove a claim. Since argument deals with probability instead of certainty, an argument may be perceived as very convincing, somewhat convincing, or not convincing at all. The success of the argument depends on the proofs. Weak support or a faulty or unacceptable warrant weakens an argument, but it is still an argument. The reader must ask the questions identified in this chapter to test the reliability and strength of the proofs and, ultimately, of the entire argument itself to decide whether it is well developed or underdeveloped, acceptable or unacceptable, moral or immoral.

Sometimes, as in the case of the advertisement just described, a reader will encounter material that may appear at first to be a proof, but really isn't a proof at all. It is a pseudoproof, which is commonly called a fallacy. Fallacies lead an audience astray, they distort and distract, they represent inadequate reasoning or nonreasoning, and they oversimplify a claim instead of proving it. Read "Love is a Fallacy" on pages 229 to 237 for an entertaining introduction to fallacies.

You will encounter fallacies in advertisements, letters to the editor, and other argumentative writings. Avoid using them in your own writing because they weaken your argument and damage your *ethos*. Recognize fallacies by asking, Is this material even relevant? Is it adequate? Do I agree? Does it support the claim? Learning some of the common types of fallacies will also help you recognize them. Here are some of the most common ones categorized under the same categories we have used for genuine proofs: logic, *ethos*, and emotion.

Some Fallacies in Logic

These fallacies pose as logical proof, but you will see that they are really pseudoproofs that prove nothing at all. You may have trouble remembering all of their names; many people do. Concentrate, instead, on the fallacious thinking characterized by each of them, such as introducing irrelevant material, providing wrong, unfair, inadequate, or even no support, drawing inappropriate conclusions, and oversimplifying the choices.

Begging the Question.   No support is provided by the arguer who begs the question, and the claim is simply restated, over and over again, in one form or another. For example "Capital punishment deters crime because it keeps criminals from committing murder," simply restates the same idea, only in other words. Or here are other familiar examples: "Why is this true? It's true because I know it's true." Or "Everyone knows that the president of the United States has done his best for the environment because he said so." You can remember the name of this fallacy, begging the question, by recalling that the arguer, when asked for support, begs off and simply restates the claim in the same or different words.

Red Herring.   A red herring provides irrelevant and misleading support that pulls the audience away from the real argument. For example, "I don't believe we should elect this individual as president of the United States because his wife does not cook, she does not stay home and care for her husband, and she does not meet the standards of an American housewife" is a red herring. Also, whether or not the police were racist in the O. J. Simpson trial was a red herring in the sense that even though their alleged racism might have provided a motive for planting evidence, their racism was finally unrelated to whether Simpson was innocent or guilty of murder. Another red herring in the O. J. Simpson case that influenced some people was the idea that O. J. is a great sports hero and that we should not attack and degrade great sports heros by trying them for murder. Authors of detective fiction sometimes use red herrings in their plots as false clues to divert the reader's attention from the real murderer. Remember the red herring fallacy by recalling that the fish, the red herring, was at one time used to train hunting dogs to follow a scent. It was not a true scent, however. The herring scent was irrelevant to the real smells of the real hunt, and the fallacy, the red herring, is irrelevant to an argument when it introduces such support as a wife's activities as an influence on the husband's qualifications for a job, or whether sports heros should be treated differently from other people.

Non Sequitur.   *Non sequitur* is Latin for "it does not follow." In this type of fallacy, the conclusion does not follow from the evidence and the warrant. In the example of the advertisement for the health club described at the beginning of this section, the statement "Studies show diets don't work. This picture shows exercise does" follows a picture of two slim, attractive people embracing. Most of us would agree that the picture, used as evidence, has little if anything to do with the claim that exercise works. The warrant, that exercise results in slimness, personal beauty, and romance, does not provide a convincing link between support and claim. Consequently, there is really no argument at all. Here is another example of a *non sequitur:* Women should not be placed in executive positions because they cannot drive cars as well as men.

Straw Man. A straw man involves attributing an argument to an opponent that the opponent never made and then refuting it in a devastating way. The arguer sets up an idea, refutes it, and appears to win, even though the idea has little or nothing to do with the issue being discussed. For example, a political candidate might set up a straw man by claiming that his opponent has said he is too old to do the job, when in fact the opponent has never mentioned age as an issue. Then the candidate refutes the age issue by detailing the advantages of age and appears to win even though this in not an issue at all. In fact, by refuting this false or non-issue, the candidate may give the impression that he could refute any other arguments put forth by the opposition as well. The use of a straw man suggests competency where it might not actually exist.

Stacked Evidence. Stacking evidence to represent only one side of an issue that clearly has two sides gives a distorted impression of the issue. For example, to prove that television is an inspiring and uplifting medium, the only evidence given is that "Sesame Street" is educational, "The Cosby Show" promotes family values, and news programs and documentaries keep audiences informed. The sex and violence programming is never mentioned.

Either-Or. Some arguments are oversimplified by the arguer and presented as black-or-white, either-or choices, when there are actually other alternatives. Some examples are "This country can either have a strong defense program or a strong social welfare program"; "We can either develop a strong space program or an urban development program"; "A woman can either be a mother or have a career"; and "A man can either go to graduate school or become a company man." No alternative, middle-ground, or compromise positions are acknowledged.

Post Hoc. This is short for *post hoc, ergo propter hoc,* a Latin phrase that translates, "after this, therefore because of this." To put it more simply, *post hoc* is the fallacy of faulty cause. For example, it is fallacious to claim in an advertisement that people will be more attractive and more popular if they buy and drive a certain make of car. Look at other advertisements on television or in magazines, and you will easily find other examples of *post hoc,* the claim that one thing causes another when there is actually no causal relationship between them. Think about the outdoor healthy virility of the Marlboro man, for example, and the suggestion that he got that way by smoking cigarettes. Another example is the person who finds romance by serving a particular spaghetti sauce or using a specific mouthwash.

Hasty generalization. Sometimes arguers "jump to conclusions," or draw a conclusion from too few examples. Thus, someone may conclude that the justice system is hopelessly flawed because someone is sent to jail by mistake; or, since some students in urban schools belong to gangs, then most urban students in those schools belong to gangs. Look back at the essay on page 80, "Jobs Illuminate What Riots Hid: Young Ideals." This author attempts to counter the stereotypical idea that young people in South-Central Los Angeles are rioters and hoodlums. The example of the young woman who was industrious and got a job at Disneyland can encourage an opposite type of hasty generalization and suggests that most of these young people are instead "wonderful kids, outstanding kids." Hasty generalizations often contribute to stereotyping.

Some Fallacies That Affect *Ethos*

Fallacies that are aimed at attacking character or at using character instead of evidence for proof are misleading and can damage *ethos*.

Ad Hominem.   An *ad hominem* argument attacks a person's character rather than a person's ideas. The press is notorious for such attacks during political campaigns, and so are some of the candidates themselves. The "character issue," for example, may receive more attention than more serious, substantive issues. Thus, negative information is provided about the candidates' personal lives rather than about their ideas and the issues that concern them. The purpose of *ad hominem* arguments is to discredit these individuals with the public. Here is another example of an *ad hominem* attack: Christianity is said to have no validity because of the careless personal and financial habits of some television evangelists. *Ad hominem* means "to the man" in Latin. An *ad hominem* argument directs attention away from the issues and to the man. Thus we become prejudiced and biased against an individual personally instead of evaluating that person's ideas.

Guilt by Association.   The fallacy of guilt by association suggests that people's character can be judged by examining the character of their associates. For example, an employee in a company that defrauds the government is declared dishonest because of his association with the company, even though he may have known nothing of the fraud. Or an observer is thrown into jail along with some political protesters simply because she was in the wrong place at the wrong time. Political figures are often judged as morally defective if they associate with people with questionable values and reputations. It is assumed that these individuals are members of these groups and guilty by association.

Using Authority instead of Evidence.   This is a variation of begging the question. The arguer relies on personal authority to prove a point rather than on evidence. For example, a salesman tells you to buy the used car because he is honest and trustworthy, and he knows your neighbor.

Some Emotional Fallacies

Irrelevant, unrelated, and distracting emotional materials are often introduced into argument to try to convince the audience. Here are some examples:

The Bandwagon Appeal.   The argument is that everyone is doing something, so you should also. For example, everyone is learning country-western dancing, so you should jump on the bandwagon and learn it also. Political and other public opinion polls are sometimes used to promote the bandwagon appeal. The suggestion is that since a majority of the people polled hold a certain opinion, you should adopt it also.

Slippery Slope.   The slippery-slope fallacy is a scare tactic that suggests that if we allow one thing to happen, we will immediately be sliding down the slippery slope to disaster. This fallacy is sometimes introduced into environment and abortion issues. Thus, if we allow loggers to cut a few trees, we will soon lose all the forests. Or, if a woman is required to wait 24 hours to reconsider her decision to have an abortion, soon no one will be permitted to have an abortion. This fallacy is similar to the saying about the camel that gets its nose into the tent. If we permit the nose today, we have the whole camel to deal with tomorrow. It is better not to start because disaster may result.

Creating False Needs.   Emotional proofs, as you have learned, appeal to what people value and think they need. Sometimes an arguer will create a false sense of need where none exists or will unrealistically heighten an existing need. The intent is to make the argument more convincing. Advertising provides excellent examples. The housewife is told she needs a shining kitchen floor with a high gloss that only a certain wax can provide. Parents are reminded that they want smart, successful children, so they should buy a set of encyclopedias.

These examples of fallacies provide you with a good sense of what constitutes fallacious reasoning. Armed with this list and with the tests of validity for genuine proofs listed under "Tests of Validity" on pages 198 to 209, you now have what you need to evaluate the strength and validity of the proofs in an argument. This information will help you make evaluations, form rebuttals to challenge weak arguments, and create arguments of your own.

HOW ARE THE PROOFS VALUABLE
FOR READING AND WRITING ARGUMENT?

Readers of argument find that by analyzing the proofs in an argument, it is then easier to answer the bottom line questions, Am I convinced? and, Is this argument moral or immoral? Analyzing the proofs in an argument focuses a reader's attention on the author's reasoning, use of supporting detail, and warrants. These are the elements in an argument that finally convince an audience. Applying the tests of validity to the proofs can also help a reader recognize fallacies, or faulty reasoning, which can reveal a manipulative or immoral purpose in the argument. Fallacies, as you have learned, are not convincing once you figure out how they work.

Writers of argument can use the proofs to help them think of ways to develop a claim. By running through the list of proofs and asking such questions as, What do I need to define? Should I use statistics? Can I generalize from some examples? What caused this? What can I compare this to? Who should I quote? and What audience values and motives can I appeal to? authors invent ideas and locate material that can be used at a specific level in a paper. The specific material is what makes a paper convincing. Also, thinking about the proofs makes authors more consciously aware of their own warrants and helps them decide whether to make them explicit in the argument or whether to leave them implicit so that the audience has to supply them. Finally, an awareness of proofs can help writers avoid fallacies in their writing.

The assignment on page 237 at the end of this chapter and the student-written model paper on page 240 will provide you with practice in using the proofs to invent support and warrants for a position paper. The proofs and the tests for validity are summarized in a handy chart for quick reference for the use of both readers and writers in the summary charts on page 409.

EXERCISES AND ACTIVITIES

1. **CLASS DISCUSSION: ANALYZING AND TESTING PROOFS, ASKING THE BOTTOM-LINE QUESTIONS, AND ANALYZING STYLE**
   a. Prepare for class discussion by reading the following essay, "The Two Nations," as well as the annotations in the margin that identify and describe the proofs in this essay.
   b. Test the validity of these proofs by asking the *test of validity questions:*
   Induction: Are the examples adequate? Would more examples continue to show the trend? Are there examples that show an opposite trend, that provide an exception? Can we make the inductive leap from the examples to the generalization to demonstrate that it is probably true?
   Authority: Are the credentials of the person quoted good enough to make this contribution reliable? Are the credentials relevant to the issue?
   Sign: Is this really a sign of what the author claims it to be? Is there another explanation for the sign?
   Cause: Do these causes create these effects? Do these effects result from these causes? Can I think of exceptions that would change or alter the cause-effect outcome that is claimed here?
   Historical analogy: Are the two items similar as claimed? Can I think of ways they are not similar or of other qualities they share that would change the claim? Will history repeat itself? Why? Why not?
   Deduction: Is the warrant acceptable and believable? Is there enough support, and is it fair and accurate? Is it an example of the generalization expressed in the warrant? Is the conclusion also probably true?

   c. Ask the bottom-line questions:
Are you convinced, or would you argue with one or more of the proofs?
Do you accept the claim? Why? Why not?
Is this argument moral or immoral by your standards?

   d. What is the predominant language style in this essay—does it feature primarily logic, *ethos*, or emotion? What other language and styles are also present? Explain your answer with examples.

Essay

THE TWO NATIONS

Anthony Lewis

Induction: Generalization that upper-income Americans live a better life than ordinary families, followed by examples in paragraphs 2 through 5.

1 Upper-income Americans generally, whether in public or private employment, live not just a better life but one quite removed from that of ordinary families. They hardly experience the problems that weigh so heavily today on American society. And that fact has dangerous political consequences.

Example: Health care

2 Health care, for example. The possibility of serious illness without insured care is now said to be the number one worry of Americans: not just the 40 million without any health insurance but the many millions more who have inadequate coverage or who are afraid to change jobs lest they lose protection.

3 The president does not have those concerns. He gets socialized medicine: care at public expense. Members of Congress and other top officials may also be treated in government hospitals. Nor is health insurance likely to be a concern for private Americans with incomes in the top 20 percent. Comprehensive coverage goes with the territory for them.

Example: Education

4 Or consider education. Public schools are among the most depressing features of contemporary life in this country, turning out young people unable to cope with the demands of a technological society—and culturally backward. Better-off families simply opt out of that problem. In large numbers, they send their children to private schools.

Example: Security

5 Crime is a menacing fact of daily life for millions of Americans; whole neighborhoods are unsafe. Of course the better-off may also be victims. But they increasingly protect themselves by living with alarm systems or in units with private security guards.

Induction: Generalization that top 20 percent is a varied group with examples of group members

6 All this refers not just to the super rich, the Lee Iacoccas whose inflated earnings have lately been so much discussed. The top-20-percent-income bracket includes business and financial people and professionals of all kinds: lawyers, doctors, journalists.

Authority: Establishes credentials of person quoted in next paragraph. Improves *ethos* of author because he is a friend of this writer and editor.

Sign: Food, hotels, etc. are signs of the sweet life.

Statistics: Summary and interpretation of who gets what.

Cause: Tax policies have caused the rich to become richer.

Historical analogy: The ancien regime in 1789 provided luxury for a few and was destroyed in the French Revolution.

Cause: The rich have the most political influence, which has caused or allowed them to create lower tax structures for themselves.

Deduction: *Warrant stated:* A democracy is not healthy when the top slice is isolated from the real problems.

Support: Twenty percent is isolated. (The rest of the essay proves this point.)

Conclusion (claim): We do not have a healthy democracy.

A friend of mine, a writer and editor, was at an economic conference in Switzerland recently. He is certainly not among the American rich. But he said he realized during that meeting how people of his professional class had come to have a qualitatively different life from most Americans. 7

For the elite, life really is sweeter than it used to be," he said. "Food is so much better. Hotels are more sumptuous. The variety of amusements available, the sports, the travel—it's a cornucopia. For the few." And there's the rub: it *is* for the few. The top 20 percent of Americans now get 47 percent of the country's total income. The bottom fifth get 3.9 percent. 8

The gap between rich and poor in America is far and away the widest in the developed world. It has widened dramatically in the last 10 years, both because real incomes have grown at the top and shrunk at the bottom and because tax and other policies have exacerbated the differential. 9

America is more like the ancien regime in France than ever before. But luxury is not just for royalty and a handful of nobles. It is for the top 20 percent. That is a lot of people. And therein lie political consequences. 10

The professionals, the rich and the upper-middle-class families in the top 20 percent have the most political influence in this country. They care, they vote, they contribute to politicians. And quite naturally, not out of evil, they will tend to favor their own interest. 11

No one should really be surprised then, that tax rates on upper incomes are so much lower in the United States than in Japan or European countries. It is not hard to understand why a president talks about the need to improve public education but puts no money where his mouth is. 12

In a democracy where a substantial top slice of the population is insulated from the country's most corrosive problems, it is politically very difficult to deal with those problems. And the rest of the people, the majority who live with them, become increasingly cynical about government and politics. 13

It is not a recipe for a healthy democratic society.[9] 14

2. WRITING ASSIGNMENT: EMPLOYING PROOFS

Write a two to three page argument of your own in which you state one of the following claims and prove it. Limit yourself to one subclaim as in "The Two Nations."

---

[9]*New York Times*, February 13, 1992, Sec. A, p. 15.

a. The United States is a healthy democracy.
b. The United States is not a healthy democracy.
c. My college puts the interest and concerns of it students first.
d. My college does not put the interests and concerns of its students first.

Discuss with the class or your small group some proofs that you could use to support the claim you select. Remember SICDADS (sign, induction, cause, deduction, analogy, definition, statistics) and VAM (value, authority, motivation). Include at least two types of proof in your paper, and label them in the margin.

3. **GROUP WORK AND DISCUSSION: EMOTIONAL PROOFS AND EMOTIONAL LANGUAGE AND STYLE**
   Prepare for group work and discussion by reading the following article, "The Whiny Generation." Focus on the emotional proofs and style in the essay. Answer the following questions, and have a member of your group report your findings to the class.

   a. Identify *motivational proofs* in the essay. Look for references to items or qualities that the author claims the twentysomething generation wants, and also the items or qualities that the author claims they should want.
   Tests of validity: What are twentysomethings supposed to need, according to the author? Do they really need those things? What are they supposed to do to get them? Will doing what is recommended satisfy the need in the ways described?
   b. Identify *value proofs* in the essay. Look for statements, stories, slogans, or examples that display the values that the author claims twentysomethings have. Look also for the values the author claims they should have. What does the author claim will result if twentysomethings accept the author's values?
   Tests of validity. Do you share the author's ideas about twentysomething values? Do you share the author's values? How do you differ? What effect do these differences have on your final acceptance of the claim?

THE WHINY GENERATION

David Martin

Essay

Ever since the publication of Douglas Coupland's book *Generation X,* we've been subjected to a barrage of essays, op-ed pieces and feature articles blaming us baby boomers for the sad face of the twentysomething generation: the boomers took all the good jobs; the boomers are destroying the planet, the media is boomer-dominated and boomer-obsessed. The litany is never-ending. If you believe the Generation X essayists, all the troubles of the world can be traced to us fortysomethings.

Well, enough is enough. As a baby boomer, I'm fed up with the ceaseless carping of a handful of spoiled, self-indulgent, overgrown adolescents. Generation Xers may like to call themselves the "Why Me?" generation, but they should be called the "Whiny" generation. If these pusillanimous purveyors of pseudo-angst would put as much effort into getting a life as they do into writing about their horrible fate, we'd be spared the weekly diatribes that pass for reasoned argument in newspapers and magazines.

Let's examine for a moment the horrible fate visited on Generation X. This is a generation that was raised with the highest standard of living in the history of the world. By the time they arrived on the scene, their parents were comfortably established in the middle class and could afford to satisfy their offspring's every whim. And they did, in spades.

Growing up in the '70s and '80s, the twentysomethings were indulged with every toy, game and electronic device available. They didn't even have to learn how to amuse themselves since Mom and Dad were always there to ferry them from one organized activity to another. If we baby boomers were spoiled, the Whiny Generation was left out to rot. They had it all.

That's the essence of the Generation X problem. We have a generation (or at least part of a generation) whose every need has been catered to since birth. Now, when they finally face adulthood, they expect the gift-giving to continue. I'm 28 and I'll never own a house, whines the Generation Xer. I'm 25 and I don't have a high-paying job, says another.

Are these realistic expectations? Of course not. It's the rare individual in the last 40 years who had a high-paying job and owned a home prior to his or her 30th birthday. But the Whiners want everything now. A generation raised on the principle of instant satisfaction simply can't understand the concepts of long-term planning and deferred gratification. What's their reaction when they don't get what they want? That's right—they throw a tantrum.

The Whiners' most common complaint is that they've been relegated to what Mr. Coupland calls McJobs—low-paying, low-end positions in the service industry. I don't doubt that many Whiners are stuck in such jobs. But whose fault is that? Here's a generation that had enormous educational opportunities. But many Whiners squandered those chances figuring that a good job was a right not a privilege.

My parents' generation provided a better shot at post-secondary education for their boomer children than they themselves had enjoyed. And we took advantage of that situation in droves as the number of college and university graduates soared. The Whiners were afforded even greater scope for educational success but many of them failed to maximize their opportunities. They had the chance to reach higher but often chose not to or chose foolishly or unwisely.

Those who pursued a liberal-arts degree with a view to obtaining a job were either wealthy or naive. Those who thought that fine arts or film studies would yield more than a subsistence living were only fooling themselves. And those who entered law school will find sympathy had to come by. More lawyers is one thing we definitely don't need.

The twentysomethings who planned their education wisely and spent the required years specializing in the technologies of the '90s now have the inside track in the job market. Those who chose to slide through high school to achieve semiliteracy are understandably unemployed or underemployed. Their cries of anguish do not now ring true. In fact, the youth unemployment rate is lower today than it was during the baby-boom recession of the early '80s. And despite the current recession, there are still plenty of positions available for highly skilled workers who exhibited the foresight and determination to achieve the necessary abilities.

The Whiners decry the lack of entry-level professional positions in the marketplace. Granted, during this current recession there are fewer such jobs. But that was also true in the early '80s. Instead of blaming everyone for this state of affairs, the Whiners should acquire more skills, education and specialized knowledge for the careers of the 21st century that will be awaiting those who have prepared themselves. Forget a career in law; start thinking about computers, telecommunications and health care.

POSITIONS OF POWER

As for the Whiners' complaint about the media being boomer-dominated and boomer-obsessed, that's nothing new. Once a generation has worked long and hard enough, it's only natural that some of its members become ensconced in positions of power. And once in power, it's not that surprising that they reflect the views, tastes and concerns of their contemporaries. Why should the media revolve around the lives of 25-year-olds? Remember, this is the generation whose biggest achievement to date is something called grunge rock. Once they've accomplished more, they'll get the media coverage.

So, I invite the Whiners to put aside their TV-generation values and accept cold, hard reality. Interesting, high-paying jobs and rich lifestyles are not automatic; they're not even commonplace. Most people live ordinary lives of quiet desperation stuck in uninteresting jobs that they're afraid to lose. If you want more than that, move out of your parents' houses, start working and, for heaven's sake, stop whining.[10]

   c. *Bottom line questions:*
      Are you convinced? Why, or why not?
      Is this argument moral or immoral by your standards? Why, or why not?
   d. *Language and style.*
      Identify examples of language that appeals to reason, to emotion, and that establishes *ethos.*
      Which, would you say, predominates?

---

[10]*Newsweek*, November 1, 1993, p. 10. David Martin, 43, is a lawyer and bureaucrat who lives in Ottawa.

4. WRITING ASSIGNMENT: USING EMOTIONAL PROOFS

Write a two-page reaction to "The Whiny Generation" in which you either agree or disagree with the author's emotional proofs and provide original proofs of your own. Experiment with emotional language and style.

5. CLASS DISCUSSION AND WRITING ASSIGNMENT: PROOFS AND STYLE IN THE DECLARATION OF INDEPENDENCE

The Declaration of Independence, a classic argument, was written by Thomas Jefferson in 1776 and was used to separate the American colonies from Great Britain. It established America as independent states, and thus it is a revolutionary document with a revolutionary purpose.

a. Read the Declaration of Independence, and to understand it better, divide it into its three major component parts. Draw a line at the end of part 1, which explains the general principles behind the revolutionary action. Then draw a line at the end of part 2, which lists the reasons for the action. Finally, identify the purpose of the third and last brief part of the document.

b. The document presents a deductive argument with the warrants in part 1, the support in part 2, and the conclusion in part 3. Summarize this structure as a deductive argument. Follow the examples in the chapter.

c. Test the argument by questioning the warrants and the support. If you accept them you accept the conclusion.

d. Identify other types of proof in the document.

e. Describe the predominant style in the document and give examples.

Essay

THE DECLARATION OF INDEPENDENCE

Thomas Jefferson

When in the course of human events, it becomes necessary for one people to dissolve the political bands which have connected them with another, and to assume among the Powers of the earth, the separate and equal station to which the Laws of Nature and of Nature's God entitle them, a decent respect to the opinions of mankind requires that they should declare the causes which impel them to the separation.

We hold these truths to be self-evident, that all men are created equal, that they are endowed by their Creator with certain unalienable Rights, that among these are Life, Liberty and the pursuit of Happiness.

That to secure these rights, Governments are instituted among Men, deriving their just powers from the consent of the governed.

That whenever any Form of Government becomes destructive of these ends, it is the Right of the People to alter or to abolish it, and to institute a new Government, laying its foundation on such principles and organizing its powers in such form, as to them shall seem most likely to effect their Safety and Happiness. Prudence, indeed, will dictate that Governments long established should not be changed for light and transient causes; and accordingly all experience hath shown that mankind are more disposed to suffer, while evils are sufferable, than to right themselves by abolishing the forms to which they are accustomed. But when a long train of abuses and usurpations pursuing invariably the same Object evinces a design to reduce them under absolute Despotism, it is their right, it is their duty, to throw off such government, and to provide new Guards for their future security.

Such has been the patient sufferance of these Colonies; and such is now the necessity which constrains them to alter their former Systems of Government. The history of the present King of Great Britain is a history of repeated injuries and usurpations, all having in direct object the establishment of an absolute Tyranny over these States. To prove this, let Facts be submitted to a candid world.

He has refused his Assent to Laws, the most wholesome and necessary for the public good.

He has forbidden his Governors to pass Laws of immediate and pressing importance, unless suspended in their operation till his Assent should be obtained; and when so suspended, he has utterly neglected to attend to them.

He has refused to pass over Laws for the accommodation of large districts of people, unless those people would relinquish the right of Representation in the Legislature, a right inestimable to them and formidable to tyrants only.

He has called together legislative bodies at places unusual, uncomfortable, and distant from the depository of their Public Records, for the sole purpose of fatiguing them into compliance with his measures.

He has dissolved Representative Houses repeatedly, for opposing with manly firmness his invasions on the rights of the people.

He has refused for a long time, after such dissolutions, to cause others to be elected; whereby the Legislative Powers, incapable of Annihiliation, have returned to the People at large for their exercise; the State remaining in the mean time exposed to all the dangers of invasion from without, and convulsions within.

He has endeavored to prevent the population of these States; for that purpose obstructing the Laws for Naturalization of Foreigners; refusing to pass others to encourage their migration hither, and raising the conditions of new Appropriations of Lands.

He has obstructed the Administration of Justice, by refusing his Assent to Laws for establishing Judiciary Powers.

He has made Judges dependent on his Will alone, for the tenure of their offices, and the amount and payment of their salaries.

He has erected a multitude of New Offices, and sent hither swarms of Officers to harass our People, and eat out their substance.

He has kept among us, in time of peace, Standing Armies without the consent of our legislatures.

He has affected to render the Military independent of and superior to the Civil Power.

He has combined with others to subject us to jurisdictions foreign to our constitution, and unacknowledged by our laws; giving his Assent to their acts of pretended Legislation:

For quartering large bodies of armed troops among us:

For protecting them, by a mock Trial, from Punishment for any Murders which they should commit on the Inhabitants of these States:

For cutting off our Trade with all parts of the world:

For imposing Taxes on us without or Consent:

For depriving us in many cases of the benefits of Trial by Jury:

For transporting us beyond Seas to be tried for pretended offenses:

For abolishing the free System of English Laws in a neighboring Province, establishing therein an Arbitrary government, and enlarging its Boundaries so as to render it at once an example and fit instrument for introducing the same absolute rule into these Colonies:

For taking away our Charters, abolishing our most valuable Laws, and altering fundamentally the Forms of our Governments.

For suspending our own Legislatures, and declaring themselves invested with Power to legislate for us in all cases whatsoever.

He has abdicated Government here, by declaring us out of his Protection and waging War against us.

He has plundered our seas, ravaged our Coasts, burnt our towns, and destroyed the Lives of our people.

He is at this time transporting large Armies of foreign Mercenaries to compleat the works of death, desolation and tyranny, already begun with circumstances of Cruelty & perfidy scarcely paralleled in the most barbarous ages, and totally unworthy the Head of a civilized nation.

He has constrained our fellow Citizens taken Captive on the high Seas to bear Arms against their Country, to become the executioners of their friends and Brethren, or to fall themselves by the Hands.

He has excited domestic insurrections amongst us, and has endeavored to bring on the inhabitants of our frontiers, the merciless Indian Savages, whose known rule of warfare, is an undistinguished destruction of all ages, sexes and conditions.

In every stage of these Oppressions We have Petitioned for Redress in the most humble terms: Our repeated Petitions have been answered only by repeated injury. A Prince, whose character is thus marked by every act which may define a Tyrant, is unfit to be the ruler of a free people.

Nor have We been wanting in attention to our British brethren. We have warned them from time to time of attempts by their legislature to extend an unwarrantable jurisdiction over us. We have reminded them of the circumstances of our emigration and settlement here. We have appealed to their native justice and magnanimity, and we have conjured them by the ties of our common kindred to disavow these usurpations, which would inevitably interrupt our connections and correspondence. They too have been deaf to the voice of justice and of consanguinity. We must, therefore, acquiesce in the necessity, which denounces our

Separation, and hold them, as we hold the rest of mankind, Enemies in War, in Peace Friends.

We, therefore, the Representatives of the *United States of America,* in General Congress, Assembled, appealing to the Supreme Judge of the world for the rectitude of our intentions, do, in the Name, and by authority of the good People of these Colonies, solemnly publish and declare, That these United Colonies are, and of Right ought to be Free and Independent States; that they are Absolved from all Allegiance to the British Crown, and that all political connection between them and the State of Great Britain, is and ought to be totally dissolved; and that as Free and Independent States, they have full power to levy War, conclude Peace, contract Alliances, establish Commerce, and to do all other Acts and Things which Independent States may of right do. And for the support of this Declaration, with a firm reliance on the protection of Divine Providence, we mutually pledge to each other our Lives, our Fortunes and our sacred Honor.

  f. Write a paper in which you explain the insights you now have about the structure, proofs, and style of the Declaration of Independence. Include an explanation of its parts, its deductive argument, its other types of proof, and its style.

6. GROUP WORK: FALLACIES

This exercise should help you understand, recognize, and remember some of the common fallacies. Read the following story and bring it up-to-date. Substitute a leather jacket or $200 athletic shoes for the raccoon coat. Each small group should take a fallacy. They are numbered in the margin. Change the slang and invent a modern example of each fallacy. (Note that there are some fallacies in this piece not mentioned in this chapter. You will be able to figure out why they are fallacies, however.) While you are at it, analyze some of the fallacies in the arguments of the three principal characters, the narrator, Petey, and Polly. Describe your analysis and updates to the class. Have fun with this exercise.

LOVE IS A FALLACY

Max Shulman

Cool was I and logical. Keen, calculating, perspicacious, acute, and astute—I was all of these. My brain was as powerful as a dynamo, as precise as a chemist's scales, as penetrating as a scalpel. And—think of it!—I was only eighteen.

It is not often that one so young has such a giant intellect. Take, for example, Petey Bellows, my roommate at the university. Same age, same background, but dumb as an ox. A nice enough fellow, you understand, but nothing upstairs. Emotional type. Unstable. Impressionable. Worst of all, a faddist. Fads, I submit, are the very negation of reason. To be swept up in every new craze that comes along, to surrender yourself to idiocy just because everybody else is doing it—this, to me, is the acme of mindlessness. Not, however, to Petey.

One afternoon I found Petey lying on his bed with an expression of such distress on his face that I immediately diagnosed appendicitis. "Don't move," I said. "Don't take a laxative. I'll get a doctor."

"Raccoon," he mumbled thickly.

"Raccoon?" I said, pausing in my flight.

"I want a raccoon coat," he wailed.

I perceived that his trouble was not physical, but mental. "Why do you want a raccoon coat?"

"I should have known it," he cried, pounding his temples. "I should have known they'd come back when the Charleston came back. Like a fool I spent all my money for textbooks, and now I can't get a raccoon coat."

"Can you mean," I said incredulously, "that people are actually wearing raccoon coats again?"

"All the Big Men on Campus are wearing them. Where've you been?"

"In the library," I said, naming a place not frequented by Big Men on Campus.

He leaped from the bed and paced the room. "I've got to have a raccoon coat," he said passionately. "I've got to!"

"Petey, why? Look at it rationally. Raccoon coats are unsanitary. They shed. They smell bad. They weigh too much. They're unsightly. They—"

"You don't understand," he interrupted impatiently. "It's the thing to do. Don't you want to be in the swim?"

"No," I said truthfully.

"Well, I do," he declared. "I'd give anything for a raccoon coat. Anything!"

My brain, that precision instrument, slipped into high gear. "Anything?" I asked, looking at him narrowly.

"Anything," he affirmed in ringing tones.

I stroked my chin thoughtfully. It so happened that I knew where to get my hands on a raccoon coat. My father had had one in his undergraduate days; it lay now in a trunk in the attic back home. It also happened that Petey had something I wanted. He didn't *have* it exactly, but at least he had first rights on it. I refer to his girl, Polly Espy.

I had long coveted Polly Espy. Let me emphasize that my desire for this young woman was not emotional in nature. She was, to be sure, a girl who excited the emotions, but I was not one to let my heart rule my head. I wanted Polly for a shrewdly calculated, entirely cerebral reason.

I was a freshman in law school. In a few years I would be out in practice. I was well aware of the importance of the right kind of wife in furthering a lawyer's career. The successful lawyers I had observed were, almost without exception, married to beautiful, gracious, intelligent women. With one omission, Polly fitted these specifications perfectly.

Beautiful she was. She was not yet of pin-up proportions, but I felt sure that time would supply the lack. She already had the makings.

Gracious she was. By gracious I mean full of graces. She had an erectness of carriage, an ease of bearing, a poise that clearly indicated the best of breeding. At table her manners were exquisite. I had seen her at the Kozy Kampus Korner eating the specialty of the house—a sandwich that contained scraps of pot roast, gravy, chopped nuts, and a dipper of sauerkraut—without even getting her fingers moist.

Intelligent she was not. In fact, she veered in the opposite direction. But I believed that under my guidance she would smarten up. At any rate, it was worth a try. It is, after all, easier to make a beautiful dumb girl smart that to make an ugly smart girl beautiful.

"Petey," I said, "are you in love with Polly Espy?"

"I think she's a keen kid," he replied, "but I don't know if you'd call it love. Why?"

"Do you," I asked, "have any kind of formal arrangement with her? I mean are you going steady or anything like that?"

"No. We see each other quite a bit, but we both have other dates. Why?"

"Is there," I asked, "any other man for whom she has a particular fondness?"

"Not that I know of. Why?"

I nodded with satisfaction. "In other words, if you were out of the picture, the field would be open. Is that right?"

"I guess so. What are you getting at?"

"Nothing, nothing," I said innocently, and took my suitcase out of the closet.

"Where you going?" asked Petey.

"Home for the week end." I threw a few things into the bag.

"Listen," he said clutching my arm eagerly, "while you're home, you couldn't get some money from your old man, could you, and lend it to me so I can buy a raccoon coat?"

"I may do better than that," I said with a mysterious wink and closed my bag and left.

"Look," I said to Petey when I got back Monday morning. I threw open the suitcase and revealed the huge, hairy, gamy object that my father had worn in his Stutz Bearcat in 1925.

"Holy Toledo!" said Petey reverently. He plunged his hands into the raccoon coat and then his face. "Holy Toledo!" he repeated fifteen or twenty times.

"Would you like it?" I asked.

"Oh yes!" he cried, clutching the greasy pelt to him. Then a canny look came into his eyes. "What do you want for it?"

"Your girl," I said, mincing no words.

"Polly?" he said in a horrified whisper. "You want Polly?"

"That's right."

He flung the coat from him. "Never," he said stoutly.

I shrugged. "Okay. If you don't want to be in the swim, I guess it's your business."

I sat down in a chair and pretended to read a book, but out of the corner of my eye I kept watching Petey. He was a torn man. First he looked at the coat with the expression of a waif at a bakery window. Then he turned away and set his jaw resolutely. Then he looked back at the coat, with even more longing in his face. Then he turned away, but with not so much resolution this time. Back and forth his head swiveled, desire waxing, resolution waning. Finally he didn't turn away at all; he just stood and stared with mad lust at the coat.

"It isn't as though I was in love with Polly," he said thickly. "Or going steady or anything like that."

"That's right," I murmured.

"What's Polly to me, or me to Polly?"

"Not a thing," said I.

"It's just been a casual kick—just a few laughs, that's all."

"Try on the coat," said I.

He complied. The coat bunched high over his ears and dropped all the way down to his shoe tops. He looked like a mound of dead raccoons. "Fits fine," he said happily.

I rose from my chair. "Is it a deal?" I asked, extending my hand.

He swallowed. "It's a deal," he said and shook my hand.

I had my first date with Polly the following evening. This was in the nature of a survey; I wanted to find out just how much work I had to do to get her mind up to the standard I required. I took her first to dinner. "Gee, that was a delish dinner," she said as we left the restaurant. Then I took her to a movie. "Gee, that was a marvy movie," she said as we left the theater. And then I took her home. "Gee, I had a sensaysh time," she said as she bade me good night.

I went back to my room with a heavy heart. I had gravely underestimated the size of my task. This girl's lack of information was terrifying. Nor would it be enough merely to supply her with information. First she had to be taught to *think*. This loomed as a project of no small dimensions, and at first I was tempted to give her back to Petey. But then I got to thinking about her abundant physical charms and about the way she entered a room and the way she handled a knife and fork, and I decided to make an effort.

I went about it, as in all things, systematically. I gave her a course in logic. It happened that I, as a law student, was taking a course in logic myself, so I had all the facts at my fingertips. "Polly," I said to her when I picked her up on our next date, "tonight we are going over to the Knoll and talk."

"Oo, terrif," she replied. One thing I will say for this girl: you would go far to find another so agreeable.

We went to the Knoll, the campus trysting place, and we sat down under an old oak, and she looked at me expectantly. "What are we going to talk about?" she asked.

"Logic."

She thought this over for a minute and decided she liked it. "Magnif," she said.

"Logic," I said, clearing my throat, "is the science of thinking. Before we can think correctly, we must first learn to recognize the common fallacies of logic. These we will take up tonight."

"Wow-dow!" she cried, clapping her hands delightedly.

I winced, but went bravely on. "First let us examine the fallacy called Dicto Simpliciter."   1

"By all means," she urged, batting lashes eagerly.

"Dicto Simpliciter means an argument based on an unqualified generalization. For example: Exercise is good. Therefore everybody should exercise."

"I agree," said Polly earnestly. "I mean exercise is wonderful. I mean it builds the body and everything."

"Polly," I said gently, "the argument is a fallacy. *Exercise is good* is an unqualified generalization. For instance, if you have heart disease, exercise is bad, not good. Many people are ordered by their doctors *not* to exercise. You must *qualify* the generalization. You must say exercise is *usually* good, or exercise is good *for most people*. Otherwise you have committed a Dicto Simpliciter. Do you see?"

"No," she confessed. "But this is marvy. Do more! Do more!"

"It will be better if you stop tugging at my sleeve," I told her, and when she   2 desisted, I continued. "Next we take up a fallacy called Hasty Generalization. Listen carefully: You can't speak French. I can't speak French. Petey Bellows can't speak French. I must therefore conclude that nobody at the University of Minnesota can speak French."

"Really?" said Polly, amazed. *"Nobody?"*

I hid my exasperation. "Polly, it's a fallacy. The generalization is reached too hastily. There are too few instances to support such a conclusion."

"Know any more fallacies?" she asked breathlessly. "This is more fun than dancing even."

I fought off a wave of despair. I was getting nowhere with this girl, absolutely nowhere. Still, I am nothing if not persistent. I continued. "Next comes   3 Post Hoc. Listen to this: Let's not take Bill on our picnic. Every time we take him out with us, it rains."

"I know somebody just like that," she exclaimed. "A girl back home—Eula Becker, her name is. It never fails. Every single time we take her on a picnic—"

"Polly," I said sharply, "it's a fallacy. Eula Becker doesn't *cause* the rain. She has no connection with the rain. You are guilty of Post Hoc if you blame Eula Becker."

"I'll never do it again," she promised contritely. "Are you mad at me?"

I sighed. "No, Polly, I'm not mad."

"Then tell me some more fallacies."

"All right. Let's try Contradictory Premises."   4

"Yes, let's," she chirped, blinking her eyes happily.

I frowned, but plunged ahead. "Here's an example of Contradictory Premises: If God can do anything, can He make a stone so heavy that He won't be able to lift it?"

"Of course," she replied promptly.

"But if He can do anything, He can lift the stone," I pointed out.

"Yeah," she said thoughtfully. "Well, then I guess He can't make the stone."

"But He can do anything," I reminded her.

She scratched her pretty, empty head. "I'm all confused," she admitted.

"Of course you are. Because when the premises of an argument contradict each other, there can be no argument. It there is an irresistible force, there can be no immovable object. If there is an immovable object, there can be no irresistible force. Get it?"

"Tell me some more of this keen stuff," she said eagerly.

I consulted my watch. "I think we'd better call it a night. I'll take you home now, and you go over all the things you've learned. We'll have another session tomorrow night."

I deposited her at the girl's dormitory, where she assured me that she had had a perfectly terrif evening, and I went glumly home to my room. Petey lay snoring in his bed, the raccoon coat huddled like a great hairy beast at his feet. For a moment I considered waking him and telling him that he could have his girl back. It seemed clear that my project was doomed to failure. The girl simply had a logic-proof head.

But then I reconsidered. I had wasted one evening; I might as well waste another. Who knew? Maybe somewhere in the extinct crater of her mind a few embers still smoldered. Maybe somehow I could fan them in flame. Admittedly it was not a prospect fraught with hope, but I decided to give it one more try.

Seated under the oak the next evening I said, "Our first fallacy tonight is called Ad Misericordiam." 5

She quivered with delight.

"Listen closely," I said. "A man applies for a job. When the boss asks him what his qualifications are, he replies that he has a wife and six children at home, the wife is a helpless cripple, the children have nothing to eat, no clothes to wear, no shoes on their feet, there are no beds in the house, no coal in the cellar, and winter is coming."

A tear rolled down each of Polly's pink cheeks. "Oh, this is awful, awful," she sobbed.

"Yes, it's awful," I agreed, "but it's no argument. The man never answered the boss's question about the qualifications. Instead he appealed to the boss's sympathy. He committed the fallacy of Ad Misericordiam. Do you understand?"

"Have you got a handkerchief?" she blubbered.

I handed her a handkerchief and tried to keep from screaming while 6 she wiped her eyes. "Next," I said in a carefully controlled tone, "we will discuss False Analogy. Here is an example: Students should be allowed to look at their textbooks during examinations. After all, surgeons have X rays to guide them during an operation, lawyers have briefs to guide them during a trial, carpenters have blueprints to guide them when they are building a house. Why, then, shouldn't students be allowed to look at their textbooks during an examination?"

"There now," she said enthusiastically, "is the most marvy idea I've heard in years."

"Polly," I said testily, "the argument is all wrong. Doctors, lawyers, and carpenters aren't taking a test to see how much they have learned, but students are. The situations are altogether different, and you can't make an analogy between them."

"I still think it's a good idea," said Polly.

"Nuts," I muttered. Doggedly I pressed on. "Next we'll try Hypothesis Contrary to Fact." 7

"Sounds yummy," was Polly's reaction.

"Listen: If Madame Curie had not happened to leave a photographic plate in a drawer with a chunk of pitchblende, the world today would not know about radium."

"True, true," said Polly, nodding her head. "Did you see the movie? Oh, it just knocked me out. That Walter Pidgeon is so dreamy. I mean he fractures me."

"If you can forget Mr. Pidgeon for a moment," I said coldly, "I would like to point out that the statement is a fallacy. Maybe Madame Curie would have discovered radium at some later date. Maybe somebody else would have discovered it. Maybe any number of things would have happened. You can't start with a hypothesis that is not true and then draw any supportable conclusions from it."

"They ought to put Walter Pidgeon in more pictures," said Polly. "I hardly ever see him any more."

One more chance, I decided. But just one more. There is a limit to what flesh and blood can bear. "The next fallacy is called Poisoning the Well." 8

"How cute!" she gurgled.

"Two men are having a debate. The first one gets up and says, 'My opponent is a notorious liar. You can't believe a word that he is going to say.' . . . Now, Polly, think. Think hard. What's wrong?"

I watched her closely as she knit her creamy brow in concentration. Suddenly a glimmer of intelligence—the first I had seen—came into her eyes. "It's not fair," she said with indignation. "It's not a bit fair. What chance has the second man got if the first man calls him a liar before he even begins talking?"

"Right!" I cried exultantly. "One hundred percent right. It's not fair. The first man has *poisoned the well* before anybody could drink from it. He has hamstrung his opponent before he could even start. . . . Polly, I'm proud of you."

"Pshaw," she murmured, blushing with pleasure.

"You see, my dear, these things aren't so hard. All you have to do is concentrate. Think—examine—evaluate. Come now, let's review everything we have learned."

"Fire away," she said with an airy wave of her hand.

Heartened by the knowledge that Polly was not altogether a cretin, I began a long, patient review of all I had told her. Over and over and over again I cited instances, pointed out flaws, kept hammering away without letup. It was like digging a tunnel. At first everything was work, sweat, and darkness. I had no idea when I would reach the light, or even *if* I would. But I persisted. I pounded and clawed and scraped, and finally I was rewarded. I saw a chink of light. And then the chink got bigger and the sun came pouring in and all was bright.

Five grueling nights this took, but it was worth it. I had made a logician out of Polly; I had taught her to think. My job was done. She was worthy of me at last. She was a fit wife for me, a proper hostess for my many mansions, a suitable mother for my well-heeled children.

It must not be thought that I was without love for this girl. Quite the contrary. Just as Pygmalion loved the perfect woman he had fashioned, so I loved mine. I decided to acquaint her with my feelings at our very next meeting. The time had come to change our relationship from academic to romantic.

"Polly," I said when next we sat beneath our oak, "tonight we will not discuss fallacies."

"Aw, gee," she said, disappointed.

"My dear," I said, favoring her with a smile, "we have now spent five evenings together. We have gotten along splendidly. It is clear that we are well matched."

"Hasty Generalization," said Polly brightly.   2

"I beg your pardon," said I.

"Hasty Generalization," she repeated. "How can you say that we are well matched on the basis of only five dates?"

I chuckled with amusement. The dear child had learned her lesson well. "My dear," I said, patting her hand in a tolerant manner, "five dates is plenty. After all, you don't have to eat a whole cake to know that it's good."

"False Analogy," said Polly promptly. "I'm not a cake. I'm a girl."   6

I chuckled with somewhat less amusement. The dear child had learned her lesson perhaps too well. I decided to change tactics. Obviously the best approach was a simple, strong, direct declaration of love. I paused for a moment while my massive brain chose the proper words. Then I began:

"Polly, I love you. You are the whole world to me, and the moon and the stars and the constellations of outer space. Please, my darling, say that you will go steady with me, for if you will not, life will be meaningless. I will languish. I will refuse my meals. I will wander the face of the earth, a shambling, hollow-eyed hulk."

There, I thought, folding my arms, that ought to do it.

"Ad Misericordiam," said Polly.   5

I ground my teeth. I was not Pygmalion; I was Frankenstein, and my monster had me by the throat. Frantically I fought back the tide of panic surging through me. At all costs I had to keep cool.

"Well, Polly," I said, forcing a smile, "you certainly have learned your fallacies."

"You're darn right," she said with a vigorous nod.

"And who taught them to you, Polly?"

"You did."

"That's right. So you do owe me something, don't you, my dear? If I hadn't come along you never would have learned about fallacies."

"Hypothesis Contrary to Fact," she said instantly.   7

I dashed perspiration from my brow. "Polly," I croaked, "you mustn't take all these things so literally. I mean this is just classroom stuff. You know that the things you learn in school don't have anything to do with life."

"Dicto Simpliciter," she said, wagging her finger at me playfully.   1

That did it. I leaped to my feet, bellowing like a bull. "Will you or will you not go steady with me?"

"I will not," she replied

"Why not?" I demanded.

"Because this afternoon I promised Petey Bellows that I would go steady with him."

I reeled back, overcome with the infamy of it. After he promised, after he made a deal, after he shook my hand! "That rat!" I shrieked, kicking up great chunks of turf. "You can't go with him, Polly. He's a liar. He's a cheat. He's a rat."

"Poisoning the Well," said Polly, "and stop shouting. I think shouting must   8
be a fallacy too."

With an immense effort of will, I modulated my voice. "All right," I said. "You're a logician. Let's look at this thing logically. How could you choose Petey Bellows over me? Look at me—a brilliant student, a tremendous intellectual, a man with an assured future. Look at Petey—a knothead, a jitterbug, a guy who'll never know where his next meal is coming from. Can you give me one logical reason why you should go steady with Petey Bellows?"

"I certainly can," declared Polly. "He's got a raccoon coat."[11]

7. WRITING ASSIGNMENT: A POSITION PAPER: NO RESEARCH

The purpose of this assignment is to practice using the Toulmin model, the claims, and the proofs to write a position paper in which you make a claim and prove it. This assignment does not require library research. It will require effective reasoning and specific information to make it convincing, however, so you will need information from some outside sources. You may select an issue question in "The Reader" as your topic and use the set of articles that accompanies it to provide information, or you may select a campus issue and use articles and interviews available on your campus for information. The instructions that follow assume that you will use a question from "The Reader." Change and adapt them if you are writing on an outside issue. Your paper should be about 1,000 words in length, or three to four pages, double-spaced.

a. Decide on a topic. Read the issue questions in "The Reader" and select one that interests you, that you know something about, and that you would like to learn more about.

b. Write an issue proposal, summary responses, and an exploratory paper to help you understand your topic and write a tentative claim. To help you

---

[11]Harold Matson Company, Inc., 1951. Renewed 1979 by Max Shulman.

understand the issue, write an issue proposal in which you explain your interest in the issue and also declare what you know along with what you still need to learn (see instructions and example, pp. 25 and 27). Then read the set of articles in "The Reader" and write brief summary responses for each of them. Finally, write an exploratory paper to help you understand the different perspectives on your issue and to help you find the perspective you will take. Write a tentative claim at the end of your exploratory paper (see instructions and example, pp. 115 and 117).

c. Use the claim questions to refine or revise your claim.

(1) Write out the issue question. Example: What should be done with young offenders?

(2) Apply the claim questions to the issue question and write a paragraph in response to each question.

Fact: Did it happen? Does it exist?
Definition: What is it? How can I define it?
Cause: What caused it?
Value: Is it good or bad?
Policy: What should we do about it?

Read the paragraphs you have written and select the one that is most promising for formulating the claim for your paper. Plan to use information from the other paragraphs to develop subclaims and support. Example: The material on what to do about the juvenile offenders issue seems most promising, so the policy claim becomes, "Juveniles convicted of serious crimes—including murder, rape, robbery, physical assault, and drug involvement—should face the same consequences as adults." Information from the other paragraphs can provide additional potential information for the paper, for example: how extensive juvenile crime is at present, how to define a "young offender," what possible causes can be identified for criminal behavior in young people, and what devastating effects it has on society.

d. Use the Toulmin model to identify the parts of your argument.

(1) Write the claim. All of the rest of your paper will support this claim.

(2) Write the support. Write two or three subclaims that you will develop in the paper. To help you do this, write the word "because" after your claim and list reasons that support it. Also, jot down ideas for specific support for these subclaims, such as examples, facts, and opinions, that come from your reading of the essays or from your own experience.

(3) Identify the warrants. Decide whether to spell out the warrants in your paper or to leave them implicit so that the reading audience will have to infer them.

(4) Decide on backing. Make some decisions about backing your warrants. Example: If one of your warrants is that harsh punishment is a deterrent to crime, you may have to back it with additional support since some readers may not agree.

(5) Plan rebuttal. Think about the positions held by others on this issue and write out some strategies for weakening their arguments. Example: You decide to allow that rehabilitation may work for young offenders who commit minor crimes, but you claim that more serious offenders will need more than rehabilitation.

(6) Decide whether to qualify your claim. Decide if you can make your paper more convincing to more people if you qualify your claim. Example: You limit adult punishment to young offenders who have committed serious crime.

e. Use the proofs to add specific material and make your paper more convincing. Ask the following questions to help you invent additional material for your paper. Use the acronyms SICDADS and VAM to help you run through the proofs. Write out your answers for those that are most promising.

(1) Signs: What symptoms or signs will demonstrate that this is so?

(2) Induction: What examples can I use and what conclusions can I draw from them? Are they convincing enough to help the reader make the "inductive leap"?

(3) Cause: What has caused this? Why is this happening? Think of explanations and examples of both cause and effect.

(4) Deduction: What concluding statements do I want to make? What general principles and examples (or cases) are they based on?

(5) Analogies: How can I show that what happened in one case will probably happen again in another case? Can I use a literal analogy to compare items in the same general category? Can I use a figurative analogy to compare items from different categories? Can I demonstrate that history repeats itself by citing an historical analogy?

(5) Definition: What words or concepts will I need to define?

(6) Statistics: What statistics can I use? Would they be more convincing in graph form?

(7) Values: What values can I appeal to? Should I spell them out or leave them implicit? Will narratives and emotional language make my appeals to values stronger?

(8) Authority: Who should I quote? What can I use from my own background and experience to establish my own expertise? How can I use language to create common ground and establish *ethos*?

(9) Motives: What does my audience need and want in regard to this topic? How can I appeal to those needs? Will emotional language help?

f. Write an outline, a draft, and a final copy (see suggestions in chapter 4, pp. 95 to 110). Use MLA documentation to cite in text references and to create a Works Cited page (see pp. 392 to 400)

The following is an example of a position paper based on the issue question in "The Reader," What should be done with young offenders? It was written by Kelly Dickerson, a student in an argument class. The type of claim, the elements of the Toulmin model, and the proofs are identified in the margins.

Student Paper

MINOR PROBLEMS?

Kelly Dickerson

Definition

Every time Americans tune into local news broadcasts or read daily papers, they are likely to be shocked at the increasing number of serious crimes committed by youths who are only sixteen years old or even younger. It is sometimes difficult to imagine these youngsters behaving like hardened criminals, but statistics continually prove that their crimes are often just as brutal as those committed by their adult counterparts. Inevitably, people begin questioning how successful the juvenile justice system is in reforming these youths and debating whether violent juveniles should be tried as adults in our legal system. After reading about this topic, I feel there is no question that juveniles convicted of serious crimes—including murder, rape, robbery, physical assault, and drug involvement—should face the same consequences as adults.

Policy claim

Subclaim the problem

Support

Statistics

While the teenage population in the United States has declined over the past decade, violent crimes committed by juveniles have sharply increased. Patricia Cohen in "Punishment" notes, "from 1988–1991 the youth murder-arrest rate climbed 80 percent" (518) and, at the time she wrote her article in 1996, 42 juveniles had been assigned to death row (518). According to Males and Docuyanan in "Crackdown on Kids: Giving Up on the Young," there were more than 200 teen murders in Central Los Angeles in 1993 (519), and another 459 teens were arrested there for murder in 1994 (520). Examples of teen crime are vivid and terrifying. Debra Dickerson in "Who Shot Johnny?" describes how a youth with no apparent motive shot and paralyzed her young nephew. The effect on both Johnny and his family have been devastating (523 to 526). Even Geoffrey Canada, who favors rehabilitation and other interventions over imprisonment for youthful offenders, suggests the need for a peace officer corps to keep youngsters from killing each other (528).

Induction

Authority

Warrant: the statistics and examples prove there is a problem.

Subclaim: the punishment does not always fit the crime.

Despite the staggering increase in serious crimes committed by young offenders, the punishment which juveniles receive has traditionally almost never fit the severity of the crimes. Since the system has historically viewed children as not being fully developed, physically or mentally, it has prevented them from being held accountable for their wrongdoing. Although many of these "children" commit horribly vicious crimes, they have been routinely treated as victims of society who are too delicate to receive the punishments which they deserve. Until very recently, lenient sentences and court proceedings have been the norm. The message they sent to serious juvenile criminals is that crime "pays" because there are no serious consequences for their actions. When the system lacks an

Warrant: the punishment should fit the crime.

Support: cause/effect

Warrant: Adult sentences are a deterrent to crime.

Appeal to value of justice

Rebuttal: Cost to society is the same, so young offenders should get same treatment as adults.

Support: cause/effect

Warrant: cost to society should determine punishment.

Subclaim: Use tougher measures

Support: sign

Warrant: Juveniles can still get off.

Backing: Authority
Support: comparison

Cause/effect

Qualifier

Restatement of *claim* and summary

element of fear, there is nothing to deter youthful offenders from committing future crimes. The current trend, as described by Males and Docuyanan (522), of assigning adult sentences to youths who commit serious crimes, is absolutely just if the punishment is to fit the crime.

Most pro-rehabilitation advocates argue that juvenile criminals are completely different from their adult counterparts and should, therefore, be treated differently in the justice system. However, the cost to society is the same regardless of the age of the criminal. What comfort does it give to the family of a slain or injured victim that the person who killed or maimed their loved one was a minor? Dickerson makes it clear that Johnny and his family suffer no less because Johnny was shot by a young offender. Instead of treating the loser who shot Johnny like a victim of society, this person should be treated like any other person who victimizes society and causes pain to individuals and communities.

Tougher measures must be taken to combat this growing problem of juvenile crime. In today's society, too many juveniles count on lenient sentences allotted by the juvenile justice system. As Dickerson says, a liberal lawyer can help a vicious criminal plea bargain the offense, receive a short sentence, and return to the streets to commit more crime (526). Furthermore, as Canada points out, many young offenders, who compare jail with staying on the streets, choose jail (528). When there are no harsh consequences of being caught, committing crimes can be perceived as having positive benefits. As a result, juveniles are continuing to become more violent and less concerned with the value of human life.

Although I agree with Males and Docuyanan that reduction of poverty along with rehabilitation can be very important in decreasing the amount of juvenile crime, I believe that these measures should be directed towards youths who have committed minor offenses. Conversely, I feel that juveniles like the one who shot Johnny, those who are convicted of serious crimes—including murder, rape, robbery, physical assault, and drug involvement—should be tried as adults. Their actions are obviously more serious than those who commit misdemeanor offenses, and they almost always result in greater direct harm to society. A message has to be sent that we will no longer tolerate brutal crimes simply because of the age of the criminal. These youths must be held completely accountable for their crimes, suffering harsh consequences and ultimately realizing that they are no longer protected by the law.[12]

---

[12]Used with permission.

WORKS CITED

Cohen, Patricia. "Punishment." George June/July 1996: 99. Rpt. in Perspectives on Argument. Nancy V. Wood. 2nd ed. Upper Saddle River, N.J.: Prentice Hall, 1998. 517–518.

Males, Mike and Faye Docuyanan. "Crackdown on Kids: Giving Up on the Young." The Progressive February 1996: 24–26. Rpt. in Perspectives on Argument. Nancy V. Wood. 2nd ed. Upper Saddle River, N.J.: Prentice Hall, 1998. 518– 523.

Dickerson, Debra, "Who Shot Johnny?" The New Republic 1 January 1996: 17–18. Rpt. in Perspectives on Argument. Nancy V. Wood. 2nd ed. Upper Saddle River, N.J.: Prentice Hall, 1998. 523–226.

Canada, Geoffrey, "Peace in the Streets." Utne Reader July/August 1995: 59–61. Rpt. in Perspectives on Argument. Nancy V. Wood. 2nd ed.Upper Saddle River, N.J.: Prentice Hall, 1998. 527–531.

8. CLASS PROJECT: CONDUCT A CLASS DEBATE

Debate is a traditional forum for argument, and your class can set up a debate in which everyone participates. A common model for debate is that two people on each side of the issue present their views and a judge declares who wins. For this class debate, however, we will use a somewhat different strategy that involves not only stating the opposing viewpoints but also working to find some common ground between the two opposing positions in order to create more productive argument and to avoid a standoff with no agreement and no resolution of the issue.

We draw on social-judgment theory to help organize the debate. Social-judgment theorists, who study the positions that individuals take on issues, plot positions on a continuum that range from extremely positive to extremely negative. They then describe these positions in terms of latitudes of acceptance. Individuals at the extremes of the continuum have narrow latitudes of acceptance and can usually only tolerate positions that are either the same as or very close to their own. Somewhere in the middle is a latitude of noncommitment. People in this area, who are close to the middle and who are not strongly ego-involved with the issue, have comparatively wide latitudes of acceptance and can tolerate a wide range of positions. The object of this debate is to increase everyones' latitudes of acceptance so that productive argument can take place.

PREPARING FOR THE DEBATES:

a. *Select an issue.* The class may nominate possible issues and then vote on one of them as a topic for debate. The issue should be written in statement form, like in the list below, so that individuals can either agree or disagree with it. Select one of the topics below or nominate one of your choice.

A List of Possible Topics for Debate

Articles in this book will provide background and some of the arguments for these issues. Page numbers are provided.

(1) Resolved: Men and women are not really different; they are, in fact, fundamentally the same. (pp. 426 to 434)

(2) Resolved: Computers are having a damaging effect on the quality of life in the world. (pp. 605 to 616)

(3) Resolved: Capital punishment should be used more frequently than it now is. (pp. 503 to 515)

(4) Resolved: Critically ill patients should have the option of seeking medical help to terminate their lives (pp. 644 to 654)

(5) Resolved: Abortion is wrong and should be against the law. (pp. 23 to 25)

(6) Resolved: Children should not have access to objectionable materials that might frighten them or subject them to immoral values. (pp. 547 to 550)

(7) Resolved: Traditional marriage is not necessary for happy and productive family life. (pp. 457 to 466)

(8) Resolved: Grades should be eliminated in college. (pp. 475 to 480)

(9) Resolved: Parents, not public institutions or industry, are responsible for child care. (pp. 628 to 633)

(10) Resolved: Racial differences no longer create significant problems. (pp. 561 to 571)

(11) Resolved: People should make more of an effort to pattern their lives after selected characters on television. (pp. 603 to 604)

b. *Create three groups.* The class will divide itself into three groups. Two groups are encouraged to take strong affirmative and negative positions and to argue from those points of view, presenting pro and con arguments, with presumably narrow latitudes of acceptance. A third, middle group with a wider latitude of acceptance will present suggestions for resolving some of the conflict. This group will look for common ground in the extreme positions, will try to reduce conflict, and will work to achieve better understanding and perhaps even a change of views in the opposing groups.

Group 1 is the affirmative group that is in favor of the subject for debate. Group 2 is the negative group that is against it. Group 3 is the critics/respondents who will attempt to resolve the conflict. The groups should be equal in size. To achieve this equality, some students may have to role-play positions that they do not, in fact, actually hold.

c. *Reading and writing.* All three groups should do some background reading on the subject for debate. The negative and affirmative teams will read to get ideas for their arguments and to develop ideas for refutation. The critics/respondents should read to understand the opposing positions. Students in groups 1 and 2 write one-page, 250-word papers outside of class that present some arguments to support their positions. After they have listened to the debate, the critic/respondents write 250-word papers that make an effort to resolve the conflict.

Conducting the Debate

Day one

a. *Begin with the opening papers* (10 minutes).   Two students from the affirmative group and two from the negative group agree to start the debate by reading their papers. The first affirmative, first negative, second affirmative, and second negative read their papers in that order.

b. *Others join in* (20 minutes).   Students may now raise their hands to be recognized by the instructor to give additional arguments from their papers. Each person should stand to speak. The speakers should represent each side in turn. The class should decide whether everyone should first be allowed to speak before anyone is permitted to speak a second time. The instructor should cut off speakers who are going on too long.

c. *Caucus and closing remarks* (15 minutes).   The affirmative and negative groups caucus for 5 minutes to prepare their closing arguments. Each group selects a spokesperson who then presents their final, strongest arguments in a 2-minute closing presentation.

d. *Critics/respondents prepare responses.*   The critics write one-page, 250-word responses outside of class that answer the following question: Now that you have heard both sides, how would you resolve the conflict?

Day Two

a. *Critics read* (20 minutes). All critics/respondents read their papers. Each paper should take about 2 minutes to read.

b. *Analyze outcomes* (30 minutes). The class should now discuss the outcomes of the debate by addressing the following questions:
   (1) What, in general, were some of the outcomes?
   (2) Who changed their opinions? Which ones? Why?
   (3) Who did not change? Why?
   (4) What are some of the outcomes of the attempts to reduce conflict and establish common ground?
   (5) What strategies have you learned from participating in debate that can help you in real-life arguments?

QUESTIONS ON THE CHAPTER

a. Describe logical proofs. Name the types of logical proof. Use the acronym SICDADS to help you remember them.

b. Describe proofs that build *ethos* or credibility. Name one type of proof that builds *ethos.*

c. Describe emotional proofs. Name two types of emotional support and explain why they appeal to the emotions.

d. Describe some of the features of the language and style associated with the three types of proof.

e. What is the difference between *ethos* in argument and ethics in argument?

f. What are fallacies? Why are they also described as pseudoproofs? Give some examples of fallacies.

QUESTIONS ON THE ESSAYS FOR ANALYSIS

a. "The Two Nations," page 221. What, in this author's view, is causing the majority of Americans to become "increasingly cynical about government and politics"? Are you satisfied with the level of benefits you have personally? Are there any benefits that you are lacking that cause you to be dissatisfied? What are they? Do you agree or disagree with this author's main point about the two nations? Why?

b. "The Whiny Generation," page 223. Who are included in Generation X and what are their characteristics? Are you a member of Generation X or some other group, like the baby boomers? What are the characteristics of your group? Why does the author refer to Generation X as the "whiny generation"? What does he think this generation should do to find their place in society? Do you agree or disagree? Why?

c. "The Declaration of Independence," page 226. Describe the rhetorical situation for "The Declaration of Independence." Why is it usually described as a "revolutionary document"? What are the four "self-evident" truths or human rights mentioned in this document? Do all people have equal claim to these rights, or can you think of constraining circumstances when certain individuals might be denied these rights? Do individuals pursue these rights, or do governments guarantee them? What is the difference? Discuss.

d. "Love is a Fallacy," page 229. Name and describe some of the fallacies described in this article. What special application does Polly make of these fallacies? Is there a fallacy involved in her choice of Petey as a boyfriend at the end? Is the narrator guilty of any fallacious thinking himself? Describe.

e. "Minor Problems?" page 240. Do you find this student paper convincing? Why or why not? What is your position on the issue of what to do with young offenders?

CHAPTER 8

Rogerian Argument and Common Ground

In the last three chapters, you have been studying traditional argument that has its origin in classical sources. It is the type of argument that predominates in American culture, and it is what you are used to when you listen to people argue on television or when you read arguments in many current periodicals or books. In traditional argument, the arguer states a claim and proves it by drawing on various types of proofs, including reasoning and evidence. The object is to convince an audience that the claim is valid and that the arguer is right. In this model of argument, the arguer uses the rebuttal to demonstrate how the opposition is wrong and to state why the audience should reject that position. The emphasis in traditional argument is on winning the argument. Debate, with participants on both sides trying to win by convincing a third-party judge, is one form of traditional argument, as is courtroom argument and all other single perspective argument in which one person argues to convince one or more people of a particular point of view.

As you know from your own experience and from reading about argument in this book, traditional argument does not always achieve its aims with the audience. In fact, in certain situations when strongly held opinions or entire value systems are challenged, traditional argument may not be effective with an audience at all. The audience may, in fact, simply stop listening or walk away. When that happens, it is useful to have another argumentative strategy to turn to, one that might work better in cases where there seems to be a stand-off and a lack of common ground among the arguing parties.

Rogerian argument is one such technique that is particularly useful for reducing conflict and establishing common ground between people who hold extremely divergent positions and who may even at times express hostility towards the opposition. We have seen that traditional argument encourages the arguer to use rebuttal to show how the opposition is wrong. By contrast, in Rogerian argument the arguer is obligated to spend at least some time at the outset of the argument explaining how the opposition is right, perhaps not in all, but at least in some circumstances. The description and examples of Rogerian argument in this chapter and in the practice exercises at the end of this chapter will demonstrate how various people achieve this aim.

You may find Rogerian argument frustrating at first, especially if you favor contention and agonistic debate in those situations where your important ideas and values seem to be under threat. Since Rogerian argument emphasizes making connections with the opposition and reducing hostility in such situations, you will need to curb your instincts to launch your argument by letting the opposition know how wrong you think they are. You can learn to use Rogerian argument, even if it is not your preferred or most natural style of arguing, in situations where traditional argument is no longer effective. It is a useful strategy when other strategies are failing. Here is an example of one situation in which the arguers involved in a public exchange about men's and women's issues decided to use a Rogerian approach.

ROGERIAN ARGUMENT AS A MEANS FOR ACHIEVING COMMON GROUND

"Where Are Men and Women Now?" was the title of a public performance staged in New York City in 1991 by Deborah Tannen, author of *You Just Don't Understand,* linguistics professor, and expert in male-female communication, and Robert Bly, author of *Iron John: A Book about Men* and leader of many "men's movement" workshops. The press publicized this exchange as a "face-to-face, word-to-word confrontation." An all-out "battle of the sexes" was predicted. The program was sold out to 1,000 people, half of whom were men and half women.

The audience and press expectations of open conflict and debate between these two were not realized, however. Instead, Bly and Tannen began the program by showing first what they agreed on. To establish a harmonious context for their exchange, Tannen began by reading a poem by Emily Dickenson and, while she read, Bly played a stringed instrument. Then, Bly showed his appreciation of Tannen by reading aloud from her book. Tannen, in turn, showed her appreciation of Bly by reading aloud from his book. Then the dialogue began as follows:

> ROBERT BLY: The first time I came in contact with your book, my wife and I were having dinner up in northern Minnesota, and someone started to read out of it. We both fell off our chairs laughing, because it illuminated every mistake we had made, including every misunderstanding. . . .

He continued by explaining how Tannen's book had helped him and his wife gain insight and communicate better. Bly explained how he had learned from Tannen to build rapport with his wife. He had learned to use a style that Tannen identified as a "woman's style."

Tannen then replied

> DEBORAH TANNEN: There's another side to this. You're assuming that it's good for men to learn to talk this way. And I always stop short of saying that be-

cause it's very important for me as a woman to say that men's styles are okay too.[1]

These two individuals, meeting for the first time at this special program, were determined not to fulfill the predictions of the press by providing a traditional war-between-the-sexes debate complete with the audience functioning as judge and trying to declare winners. Instead, they resorted to Rogerian argument, a special strategy that can be used at any time in argument to cool emotions, reduce conflict, and create sympathetic understanding. In their case their strategy involved demonstrating at the outset that they both understood and valued one another's ideas by reading from one another's books and then commenting on how they had valued them.

Another recent example of building common ground between disagreeing parties with each side demonstrating an understanding of the other's point of view was reported recently in the press. The "environmentalists," who typically want to protect the environment at all costs, often find themselves in opposition to individuals who make their living by exploiting the environment. Loggers, ranchers, mill owners, and other industrialists, for example, can fall into this second category. Individuals from both groups, stereotyped as "nature haters" and "eco-freaks" by the press, met in Idaho to discuss efforts for protecting endangered wildlife in the area. The environmentalists went to the meeting with some trepidation, but "as they joked and sparred over steak and beer, they discovered that neither side lived up to its stereotype. 'We found that we didn't hate each other,' said Alex Irby, a manager at the Konkolville sawmill. 'Turns out, we all like to do a lot of the same things. We love the outdoors.'" "Loggers in the back country sitting down with environmentalists is an astonishing change," reports Timothy Egan who wrote about the details of the meeting.[2] One can infer that the common ground established in this meeting was brought about by each side describing the value they placed on the environment and on outdoor activity in general. In such an exchange, both parties perceived that they had been heard and further dialogue was then possible.

As you can see, understanding the rhetorical situation in general and the audience in particular by analyzing what they think and value is of critical importance in Rogerian argument. In the two examples just cited, Tannen and Bly studied ahead of time and then demonstrated to the audience their understanding of one another's positions. The environmentalists, loggers, and mill workers discovered in conversation their shared values concerning the environment. In Chapter 10 you will learn in more detail how to analyze an audience yourself when you plan your researched position paper. As you read the rest of this chapter, however, including the examples of Rogerian argument, pay particular attention to how Rogerian arguers analyze their audiences' dissenting opinions and values and then respond to them as part of their overall strategy.

---

[1] Robert Bly and Deborah Tannen, "Where Are Men and Women Today?" transcript printed in *New Age Journal,* January/February 1992, pp. 28–33, 92–97.

[2] *New York Times Magazine,* July 7, 1996, p. 28.

ROGERIAN ARGUMENT AS STRATEGY

Carl Rogers was a psychotherapist who was well known for the empathetic listening techniques he used in psychological counseling. He later became interested in how these same techniques could be used to improve communication in other difficult, emotionally charged situations. Richard Young and his co-authors Alton Becker and Kenneth Pike built on Rogers's ideas to formulate Rogerian argument,[3] a method for helping people in difficult situations make connections, create common ground, and understand one another. The object was to avoid undue conflict or, even worse, a mutual standoff.

According to Young, Becker, and Pike, written Rogerian argument reduces the reader's sense of threat and conflict with the writer so that alternatives can be considered. Three things are accomplished by this strategy:

1. **Writers let readers know they have been understood.** To accomplish this purpose, the writer restates the opponent's position in summary form by using dispassionate, neutral language. Thus the writer demonstrates that the reader has been heard and that the writer understands the issue exactly as the reader does. Thus Tannen and Bly begin their special presentation by reading from one another's works to demonstrate that they are hearing one another.

2. **Writers show how readers' positions are valid in certain contexts and under certain conditions.** The writer thus demonstrates to the reader that at least part of the reader's position is acceptable, and thereby makes it easier for the reader to reciprocate and accept part of the writer's position. Notice how Bly says at the outset that Tannen's observations are valid and can be applied to conversations he has actually had with his wife. Tannen then points out that males' preferences in communicating are also okay. Thus they validate one another's positions.

3. **Writers get readers to believe that both of them share the same values, types of experience, attitudes, and perceptions, and are thus similar in significant ways.** Tannen and Bly accomplish this end by borrowing one another's theories and applying them to their own personal experiences. They make it clear that they both share the same values and types of experience.

The most important feature of Rogerian argument is listening empathetically and nonjudgmentally. Rogers says that people usually listen judgmentally and evaluatively. They are eager to jump in, point out what is right or wrong, and make corrections or refutations. Rogerian listening puts the writer in the reader's place by requiring the writer to provide neutral summaries of the reader's position that show sympathetic understanding. Thus the writer encourages a continued and open exchange of ideas with the reader. In Rogers's words, the writer "listens with" as opposed to "evaluating about."

---

[3] Richard Young, Alton Becker, and Kenneth Pike, *Rhetoric: Discovery and Change* (New York: Harcourt Brace and World, 1970), pp. 7–8, 274–290.

Table 8.1 is a chart that contrasts Rogerian argument, as explained by Young, Becker, and Pike, with the traditional pro-and-con model of argument associated with debate.

In Chapter 5 you learned about the Toulmin model for argument. The Toulmin model and Rogerian argument have one extremely important feature in common. Even though the Toulmin model includes rebuttal, it also provides for the creation of common ground in the shared warrants between arguer and audience

TABLE 8.1 Traditional and Rogerian Argument Compared

	TRADITIONAL ARGUMENT	ROGERIAN ARGUMENT
Basic Strategy	Writer states the claim and gives reasons to prove it. Writer refutes the opponent by showing what is wrong or invalid.	Writer states the opponent's claim and points out what is sound about the reasons used to prove it.
Ethos	Writer builds own character (*ethos*) by citing past experience and expertise.	Writer builds opponent's character perhaps at expense of his or her own.
Logos	Writer uses logic (all the proofs) as tools for presenting a case and refuting the opponent's case.	Writer proceeds in an explanatory fashion to analyze the conditions under which the position of either side is valid.
Pathos	Writer uses emotional language to strengthen the claim.	Writer uses descriptive, dispassionate language to cool emotions on both sides.
Goal	Writer tries to change opponent's mind and thereby win the argument.	Writer creates cooperation, the possibility that both sides might change, and a mutually advantageous outcome.
Use of Argumentative Techniques	Writer draws on the conventional structures and techniques taught in Chapters 5 to 7 of this book.	Writer throws out conventional structures and techniques because they may be threatening. Writer focuses, instead, on connecting empathetically.

(see pp. 135 to 139). Rogerian argument provides for common ground, as well, but this is accomplished through the shared values and assumptions established through the summary and restatement of the opponent's position.

WRITING ROGERIAN ARGUMENT

In order to write Rogerian argument, according to Young, Becker, and Pike, the writer proceeds in phases rather than following set organizational patterns or argumentative strategies. These phases are as follows:

1. The writer introduces the issue and shows that the opponent's position is understood by restating it.
2. The writer shows in which contexts and under what conditions the opponent's position may be valid. Note that the opponent is never made to feel completely wrong.
3. The writer then states his or her own position, including the contexts in which it is valid.
4. The writer states how the opponent's position would benefit if the opponent were to adopt elements of the writer's position. An attempt is finally made to show that the two positions complement each other and that each supplies what the other lacks.

VARIATIONS OF ROGERIAN ARGUMENT

Rogerian argument as described by Young, Becker, and Pike is rarely if ever written exactly according to their format. You can learn more about Rogerian argument by practicing according to their format, however, and the exercise section of this chapter provides four examples of Rogerian argument papers written by students who followed this format. You also will be invited to write a Rogerian argument paper by using this format.

As you read professionally written argument, however, you are much more likely to find elements or variations of Rogerian argument rather than arguments that include all of the parts of the Young, Becker, and Pike model. Here are some examples of variations of Rogerian argument that you may encounter in your academic reading:

1. **The report on past research at the beginning of an academic argument.** Authors of academic argument, as a matter of convention, very often begin their arguments with a report of how authors who have written before them have contributed to the subject. They provide these authors' names and summarize their contributions before they identify and develop their own contribution to the subject in the remaining part of the article. Thus, an ongoing conversation is established that acknowledges with appreciation what has gone before the new material that is the actual subject of the article.

2. **The research proposal.**   Research proposals that request funds and resources from granting agencies typically begin with a positive summary of the

contributions of past researchers. Only after this former work has been acknowledged does the researcher explain how the new proposed research will build on what has gone before.[4]

3. **The Rogerian response paper.**   This paper is written in response to an essay written by another person with whom the author disagrees. The author of a response paper typically rejects the position that the author of the other essay presents, but wants to create common ground and understanding with that person in order to keep a dialogue on the issue going. The goal is to make a connection with the author of the other essay and thus create a context of understanding so that both authors can continue exploring the issue. Such papers usually begin with a restatement of the other author's position along with an acknowledgment of what is valuable about that position before the author goes on to present a different view of the matter. In the exercise section of this chapter you will be invited to try writing a Rogerian response paper yourself.

As you read arguments written by other authors, look for additional examples of elements of Rogerian argument. The three examples just cited by no means exhaust the possibilities.

THE ADVANTAGES AND DISADVANTAGES OF ROGERIAN ARGUMENT

The advantages of Rogerian argument are clear. Such an approach helps release tension and disagreement and encourages negotiation and cooperation when values and aims are in conflict. Also, Rogerian argument has the potential of leveling or at least controlling uneven power relationships that may interfere with the peaceful resolution of conflicting issues.

There are also perceived disadvantages of Rogerian argument. It is sometimes difficult for the writer to understand and restate the reader's position, particularly when the reader/opponent is not present and no written material is available to explain the opposing position. Also, connecting with the reader/opponent by restating the opposing position may be extremely difficult if the writer is emotionally involved and strongly dislikes the opposing ideas. It takes courage, Rogers says, to listen and restate ideas that are strongly antithetical to your own. One has to want to make connections to succeed.

Rogerian argument has also been criticized as annoying to women. Some researchers claim that women have always been expected to understand others, sometimes even at the expense of understanding themselves. As one female critic puts it, Rogerian argument "feels too much like giving in."[5] Another critic finds

---

[4] I am indebted to Mary Stanley for alerting me to this use of Rogerian argument.

[5] See Catherine Lamb, "Beyond Argument in Feminist Composition," *College Composition and Communication,* February 1991, pp. 11–24. See also Phyllis Lassner, "Feminist Response to Rogerian Rhetoric," *Rhetoric Review,* 8 (1990): 220–232.

the advice that the writer should always use unemotional, dispassionate language to restate the opponent's argument unrealistic and constraining. Avoiding rude or insulting language is necessary, a matter of common sense. But to avoid all emotionally connotative language may be impossible.[6]

Rogerian argument persists as a viable model in spite of some of its shortcomings. Its central notion, that it is important to understand and see some validity in other people's opposing positions, is sometimes the only way to create common ground in difficult situations.

EXERCISES AND ACTIVITIES

1. CLASS DISCUSSION: UNDERSTANDING ROGERIAN ARGUMENT AS A STRATEGY FOR BUILDING COMMON GROUND

The following article describes an experiment to reduce hostility between Arab and Israeli teenagers as they talk, listen, and make friends in a summer camp in Maine. Analyze the Rogerian elements in this selection and answer the following questions:

a. Who are the parties, and why might they feel hostile?
b. What techniques are used to reduce hostility and create common ground at the camp? Are some of these techniques for reducing hostility Rogerian? If so, which of them are Rogerian?
c. How effective are the techniques described in this article for reducing hostility? What helps create productive argument? What problems remain to be solved?
d. How effective do you think Rogerian argument might be as one strategy for international argument that is aimed at negotiation and forming consensus between hostile participants?

A CAMP SOWS THE SEEDS OF PEACE

Sara Rimer

WAYNE, Maine, Aug. 26—Together again in the Maine woods, the two 16-year-old boys, one a Palestinian Arab, the other an Israeli Jew, took up the argument they began when they met at camp three years ago.

"In 1948, the U.N. gave the Jews the right to build their own country—what Israel is today," said one of the boys, Yehoyada Mande-el, who is known as Yo Yo and lives in Israel. "It's a fact. We were happy. We were ready to settle for this. But the Arabs said no."

---

[6] Doug Brent, "Young, Becker, and Pike's 'Rogerian' Rhetoric: A Twenty-Year Reassessment," *College English*, 53 (April 1991): 446–452.

Laith Arafeh is Palestinian and lives on the West Bank. "The U.N. resolution 181 was unfair," he countered. "It gave the Jews 56 percent of the land of Palestine when they were only 17 percent."

"O.K., let me finish," Yo Yo said, waving his arms, as he and his friend sat together on the dock by the lake. "Now, there was this war, the war of independence."

Laith rolled his eyes. "We call it the catastrophe, the '48 war." He looked at his watch. It was close to noon. History would have to wait.

"I have to pray now," he said.

"I'm coming with you," said Yo Yo, who would be celebrating the advent of the Jewish Sabbath the next night. He wanted to take pictures of his friend kneeling for Muslim prayers on the soccer field. They left the dock, arm in arm.

Laith and Yo Yo live less than 15 miles apart in the Middle East. But they had to travel thousands of miles, to the "Seeds of Peace" camp for Arab and Israeli boys and girls in Maine, to meet and argue and, with work, become friends. This is their third summer together in Maine. They are junior counselors now.

This is also the third summer of the nonprofit camp, which was founded by John Wallach, the former foreign editor of The Hearst Newspapers. He says he wanted to do what all the peace treaties could not—bring together young people who have been taught to hate.

The 130 campers, ages 13 to 16, who were selected with help from their governments, arrived here last Monday for two weeks at Camp Androscoggin just as the American campers had left. They came with adult escorts from their countries. The counselors are mostly young Americans. "Seeds of Peace," which operates on a shoestring budget with private contributions, does not have its own camp.

At other camps, drama and tension are created during the ritual "color war," in which campers compete on, say, the green and white teams. At "Seeds of Peace," the drama and tension are always present. No symbolic divisions are needed.

Like Yo Yo and Laith, Tamer Nagy, a 15-year-old Egyptian boy, is back for the third summer. "In the beginning, it wasn't easy," he said. "It wasn't like we said, 'Hi, we're friends.' All my life, what I've been growing up on, Israel is our enemy. Then we began to talk."

The task of getting along is complicated by sharp political, ethnic, cultural and religious differences. Nothing, not even swimming, is simple. Girls and boys must swim separately, in deference to the Muslims.

Mohamed Karim Bada, a 14-year-old Egyptian boy, said his Israeli bunkmate was angry that someone had drawn a Star of David on the floor of their cabin. "He said, 'That is our great sign; please don't walk on it,'" Mohamed said. Out of deference to his new friend, Mohamed said, he was very careful not to step on the Jewish symbol.

It is arguable whether bringing 130 young people together in the woods in Maine can change the situation back in their countries. But for a visitor to spend two days with Mohamed and Yo Yo and Laith, and the others, is to see something powerful. They play soccer, baseball, basketball and tennis together. They eat together. They sleep together in cabins. And they are changing.

When he heard about five Israelis dying in the latest suicide bombing of a bus, Laith told Yo Yo he was sorry.

Eighteen months before, after an Israeli settler blew up the mosque in Hebron, Yo Yo telephoned Laith to say that he was sorry. The boys talk regularly on the telephone.

Back in Jerusalem, Yo Yo has enrolled in an Arab study program. "I did a project on Arafat," he said, referring to the Palestinian leader. "Laith helped me." Looking at Laith, he grinned. "You have to do a project on Rabin."

Laith said: "Rabin is the one we have to deal with now. But I cannot forget that he used to be the minister of defense. I consider Rabin as a terrorist."

Yo Yo said: "The same thing goes for Arafat. He was the biggest terrorist."

Laith interrupted: "For you."

Yo Yo: "I'm saying for me."

Yo Yo changed the subject. "I've read the Koran in Hebrew. I memorized the first chapter." He began reciting it. "I could practically be a Muslim. Laith invited me for a Ramadan feast. It was great. I didn't even have to fast."

Laith said his parents, both doctors, like Yo Yo. He added: "His mother is a nice lady. She came to my house."

Laith asked: "Do you think your father would come to my house if I invite him?"

Yo Yo's voice was pained. "I don't think so."

"My father fought in the 1948 war, in '56 and '59," Yo Yo said. "He has no reason to trust them. When I go to visit Laith, he always says, 'Something bad is going to happen; they're going to do something.'"

When Laith visits, Yo Yo said, his father says hello, nothing more.

The silence hurts him, Laith said. But he added: "I can understand it."

In the evening, the campers meet with trained facilitators to talk about how they feel about each other. The discussions can get intense.

During one recent discussion, 15-year-old Sara Ababneh, Jordanian Muslim, talked angrily about her religion teacher back home. "He's antifeminist," she said. "He says, 'Women can't be judges, they can't do things to do with emotions because they're so emotionally sensitive,' I really hate this."

In another discussion, Laith recalled an incident on the bus the first summer, when he broke up a fight over a seat between two boys, one Israeli, the other Egyptian.

"You know what the Egyptian said to me?" he told the group. "He said, 'You Palestinians are all terrorists.' I was stunned. I heart it many times from Israelis, but you know something? I don't care. They're supposed to say something like that."

Everyone laughed. "But he's Arab," Laith said. "He's supposed to be my buddy. I despised him. I thought, 'He doesn't even deserve being punched.'"

That afternoon, Laith and Yo Yo had been talking about American teenagers. "They know a lot about basketball, baseball," Laith said.

Yo Yo said: "We both wish we could live like Americans. We would like to care about basketball and shoes—should we wear the red shoes or the black shoes?"

Yo Yo grew serious. "In two years I'm going to go into the Israeli Army. In two years, I'm going to have a gun in my hand. Naturally, it will be my nation first. Laith feels the same way."

Laith looked his friend in the eye. "If you were in a jeep, and I threw stones at the jeep, would you shoot me?"

Yo Yo did not hesitate. "I can't tell you I would not," he said.[7]

2. WRITING ASSIGNMENT: ROGERIAN ARGUMENT

The assignment is to write a three-page double-spaced Rogerian argument on an issue of your choice. There are several ways to set up this assignment. Read through the following options, select one that appeals to you, and proceed with the rest of the instructions for the assignment.

a. If you wrote an exploratory paper (as taught in Chapter 3), write a Rogerian argument in response to the position you discovered in that paper that is most unlike the position you defended.

b. Select any issue that you understand from at least two opposing points of view. It should be an issue that you feel strongly about, and you should also have strong negative feelings about the opposing viewpoint. Write a Rogerian argument in response to the opposing viewpoint.

c. Recall the last time you were in an argument in which you were angry and no one seemed to "win." Write a letter to the individual you were arguing with. Use Rogerian strategy.

d. Read a set of articles in "The Reader" that develop one of the subissues. Make a list of the ideas you disagree with and those you agree with. Write a Rogerian response to one of the ideas that you disagree with.

e. If you have participated in a classroom debate, team up with a member from the opposing side. Working in pairs, each of you should articulate the other student's position so that person feels "heard" and understood. Then write a Rogerian argument in response to that position.

f. Write a dialogue in which two people discuss an issue that they both feel strongly about. Write from two opposing points of view. Include Rogerian elements in this dialogue, like Tannen and Bly did in the example in the chapter, to show empathetic understanding of one another's positions.

Prewriting: To help you prepare to write this paper, in addition to the instructions provided above, write a one-paragraph summary of the opposing position and a one-paragraph summary of your position. Refer to these summaries when you write your paper.

---

[7] *New York Times,* September 3, 1995, p. 9.

Writing: Write your paper, and include all of the following parts:

(1) Introduce the issue and restate the opposing position to show you understand it.

(2) Show in which contexts and under what conditions the opposing position may be valid. State it so that it is acceptable to the opposition.

(3) Write a clear transition that moves the reader from the position you have just explained to the position that you favor and will now defend.

(4) State your own position and describe the context in which it is valid.

(5) Show how the opposing position would be strengthened if it added elements of your position, and try to reconcile the two positions.

Here are three examples of Rogerian argument written by students. The first example, entitled "Doctor-Assisted Suicide: Is It Ever an Option?" was written by a student who, as you will see, had a strong exigency for writing about doctor-assisted suicide. She found it extremely difficult to write this paper because she had to explain the opposition's position first in an open and fair-minded way. According to her, what she really wanted to do was say what she thought about the issue and be done with it. When she finished her paper, however, she reported that this approach had been very helpful. Because she could articulate the opposing position, she felt she could then make the argument for her own perspective with more confidence and force.

The second example, "Special Education's Best Intentions," was written by a student who had returned to school after several years and whose handicapped child required special education. The issue of how handicapped children are educated in the public schools was, understandably, a particularly compelling issue for her. She had often been frustrated by school officials who seemed more interested in procedures than in her child. Even though she felt hostility for some of these individuals, she still managed to state their point of view in a way that should be acceptable to them before she introduced her own. When she finished writing this paper, she commented that she usually feels powerless when talking with school officials. The approach taken here, she thought, would probably achieve better results than a confrontational argument that accused her audience of wrongdoing and neglect.

The third example, "Dear Mom," was written by a student whose parents wanted her to move out of her apartment and either come home, find a cheaper apartment, or move back into the dormitories. This student wrote her Rogerian argument as a letter addressed to her mother. She began by stating her mother's view, and even read this part to her mother to make certain she was stating it accurately. She then acknowledged the advantages of her mother's view but went on to show why her own views were also advantageous and valid. She finally gave this letter to both of her parents to read. The result was that her parents agreed to allow her to stay in her apartment.

At the end of the first paper on doctor-assisted suicide is a "Rogerian Argument Evaluation Sheet" that has been filled out by a reader. It lists the parts of the writing assignment for the Rogerian argument paper described in the assignment and shows how well this first paper met those requirements. When you have finished reading the other student papers, see if you can identify and describe the parts of those papers and complete evaluation sheets like the sample. This analysis will help you better understand how to write your own Rogerian argument.

READING 1

DOCTOR-ASSISTED SUICIDE: IS IT EVER AN OPTION?

Marion Duchac

Should doctor-assisted suicide ever be a legal option? It involves the extreme measure of taking the life of a terminally ill patient when the patient is in extreme pain and the chances for recovery appear to be hopeless. Those who argue against assisted suicide do so by considering the roles of the patient, the doctor, and God in these situations.   1

Should the patient take an active role in assisted suicide? When a patient is terminally ill and in great pain, those who oppose assisted suicide say that it should not be up to that patient to decide what his or her fate will be. There are greater powers at work that determine when a person dies: nature and God. Neither science nor personal preference should take precedence over these larger forces. An individual only has rights within the spheres of civil and criminal, not divine or natural law.   2

What role should the doctor have? Doctors, when taking the Hippocratic oath, swear to preserve life at all costs, and it is their ethical and legal duty to follow both the spirit and the letter of this oath. Their responsibility is to heal the sick, and in the cases when healing is not possible, then the doctor is obliged to make the dying person comfortable. Doctors are trained never to hasten death. Those who oppose assisted suicide believe that doctors who do help terminally ill patients die are committing a crime, and they should be dealt with accordingly. Doctors are also, by virtue of their humanness, capable of erring. Doctors could quite possibly say, for instance, that a cancer patient was terminal, and then the illness could go into remission forever. There is always an element of doubt concerning the future outcome of human affairs.   3

The third perspective to consider when thinking about assisted suicide is the role of God. Life is precious. Many people believe that it is not up to human beings to decide when to end their own or another's life. Only God knows when it is the right time for a person to die, and for humans to intervene in such a decision is *hubris*. Suicide is a crime against God, and to assist someone in this venture is not only to break criminal laws, but to break divine laws as well.   4

These general concerns of those who oppose assisted suicide are valid in certain contexts of the assisted-suicide question. For instance, patients are fallible. They cannot always be certain of their medical conditions. Pain clouds judgment, and so the patient should not be the sole arbiter of her or his own destiny.   5

Patients do not usually choose the course of their medical treatment, so they shouldn't be held completely responsible for decisions related to it. Doctors are also fallible, and it is understandable that they would not want to assume God's role and make the final decision about when death should occur. Since doctors are trained to prolong life, they usually do not elect to take it by prescribing assisted suicide. God is perhaps the final authority over life and death. God should have the final responsibility for taking life.

Another way to look at the issue of assisted suicide is to think less about the impaired judgment of the patient, the responsibility and authority of the physician, and the power of God, and more about the responsibilities of the people who are related to or who care for terminally ill patients in these painful and difficult times.   6

I have been one of those caregivers, and I am now a proponent of doctor-assisted suicide, especially in certain cases. I never thought about the issue much until my father begged my mother, brother, and me to hasten his death from terminal lung cancer. We were entirely unprepared for his request, and we had no intention of fulfilling it until his pain became so great that we simply could not stand by and watch him suffer. We ended up snowing him with morphine, which alleviated his pain and ultimately suppressed his bodily functions to the point where he could no longer survive. It was the most difficult thing I've ever done in my life, and I was never clear on the moral ramifications of our actions even as I took an active part in his death. It was only after the immediacy of the situation passed and the tension eased that I was able to think the issue through and decide how I felt.   7

My father was a patient who had finally refused additional aggressive, invasive medical treatment after having had multiple surgeries, chemotherapy treatments, and radiation treatments. He had the right to terminate his medical treatment. There is one decision that patients can make. Patients should and do have the right to discontinue medical treatment at any time for any reason. This course of action is within the civil rights of the patient, and it can be regarded as a form of suicide, but it is not assisted suicide. Once my father had decided to terminate treatment, however, we had no medical professionals guiding us through his inevitable death. At the time I wondered why a person who refuses medical *treatment*, even if this is a form of suicide, is then no longer eligible for medical *care*? In my father's case, once he refused treatment, then he no longer benefited from the comfort of having a medical professional involved in his dying and death. Death is a scary thing, and it is something people in this society are extremely unprepared for, so it would have been very comforting to have had the continued knowledgeable advice of a doctor even though my father had refused further invasive and aggressive treatment.   8

I now believe that blanketly opposing assisted suicide does no one a service. If someone is dying of cancer and begging to be put out of his or her misery, and someone gives that person a deadly dose of morphine, that seems merciful rather than criminal. If we can agree to this, then I think we could also agree that having a doctor close by measuring the dosage and advising the family and friends is a reasonable request. Without the doctor's previous treatment, the person would   9 surely be dead already. Doctors, in fact, tamper with God's wishes every day and think nothing of it. Even though Christian Scientists accept the argument that people should not be treated with medicine or in medical facilities because such treatment intrudes on God's domain, most people who get a strep throat, for instance, seek medical help, and the doctor gives them penicillin. Without the antibiotic, the patient could develop heart damage or even die. If doctors never intervened and let nature take its course, patients could die from conditions that we now consider merely bothersome inconveniences. In the case of cancer patients, it is often the case that only years of difficult and aggressive medical procedures keep such patients alive. The issue, in other words, has already been taken out of God's hands. Doctors have intervened for months or even years, so why not sanction this final, merciful intervention?

Life is indeed precious, but an inevitable part of life is death, and it should be precious, too. If life has become an intolerable litany of pain and intense suffering, and if the professional prognosis is one of death, then it seems that in order to preserve dignity and beauty, one should have the right to end her or his suffering quietly, surely, and with family and friends nearby.[8]

10

Evaluation Sheet for Rogerian Argument Paper

Requirements of Rogerian Argument	*What the Author Did*
1. Introduce the issue and state opposing position to show you understand it.	1. Introduced the issue in paragraph 1 and presented the opposing view from three perspectives with many good reasons in paragraphs 2 to 4.
2. Show how opposition might be right.	2. Showed the contexts in which these three perspectives might be right in paragraph 5.
3. Write a clear transition from the opposing position to your position.	3. Wrote a transition in paragraph 6 to move from opposing position to own position.
4. Give your position and show how you might be right.	4. Presented own position powerfully, using a single personal example in paragraphs 7 to 9.
5. Reconcile the two positions.	5. Reconciled the opposing views by valuing death as well as life in paragraph 10.

---

[8] Used with permission.

READING 2

SPECIAL EDUCATION'S BEST INTENTIONS

Lois Agnew

The American public's growing recognition of the educational rights of handi-   1
capped children culminated in the 1975 enactment of the Education for All Handicapped Children Act, Public Law 94–142. Once the need to provide quality education for all students was clearly established as a matter of public record, it also
became a need that would demand immediate action on the part of parents and
educators; the issue at hand shifted from a question of whether it should be done
to how it could be done.

It is natural in the midst of such change to turn to experts for guidance   2
about how to face the challenges that lie ahead. In the years following the passage
of PL 94–142, educators attempted to develop methods for identifying the needs
of handicapped students in a way which would allow for the development of educational programs designed to serve their individual needs. As time went on,
the methods for addressing students' goals became more carefully prescribed
and were implemented primarily through the agency of designated professionals
who were specially trained for dealing with such matters.

Of course developing a system for helping students whose needs are out of   3
the ordinary had been a necessary step in assimilating those students into the
world of public education. Hurling handicapped students into a regular education classroom without careful assessment of their needs would unquestionably
lead to frustration on all sides. The need to determine the level of each student's
skills clearly indicates the need for some type of testing program, and demands
the presence of individuals trained to administer and interpret those tests. The
entire process is obviously a crucial element in meeting the educational needs of
handicapped children.

However, the challenge of efficiently offering help to massive numbers of   4
students inevitably has resulted in the evolution of a bureaucratic network with
all of the disadvantages inherent in such a system. State education agencies and
local school districts alike have carefully allocated tremendous resources to carrying out the letter of PL 94–142; the assurance they have provided anxious parents
lies in their promise to find appropriate educational placement in the least restrictive environment possible for each child. The means for attempting such a mammoth task involves the use of a standard process of evaluation and diagnosis that
will enable the experts assigned to the task to assess not only each child's present
levels of performance educationally, but ultimately to make judgments about the
child's potential for classroom performance in the future.

It is in this respect that the bureaucratic nature of the special education pro-   5
gram falters in meeting the needs of the individual child. As necessary as such a
system may be to guarantee the efficient handling of large volumes of work, it becomes difficult in practice to maintain a focus on evaluation as the necessary

means to the worthwhile end of providing children with new educational opportunities; too often it becomes an end in itself, a source of a convenient label which in turn is used to predict where a child's limits will lie. It is a tragedy of our educational system that, in spite of the good intentions that have led us to emphasize test results and diagnosis for children with special needs, the machinelike efficiency of our program has achieved most of its goals without acknowledging that which is most important, addressing the needs of students as individuals. The idea of trained diagnosticians administering objective tests to students to determine their educational placement must be appealing to a society that values scientific method to the degree ours does; however, few real live children fall neatly into the categories that represent the conclusion of the process. Once their futures have been charted by the system, it becomes increasingly difficult for them to prove that they have potential beyond that which has been predicted by the experts.

I am the parent of such a child, and have on many occasions experienced   6
the frustration of watching well-meaning educators become so absorbed with finding an appropriate label for my son that they have apparently lost sight of the final goal of educating him. Although I share the interest they have in finding an appropriate educational placement for him, I have in the meantime grown weary of the process. I have seen my child through the ordeal of psychological, neurological, language, and educational evaluations, all conducted by authorities in their fields with an impressive assortment of credentials, and can state with certainty that the ability to help him is unrelated to the specialized training the system values most. Those who have made a significant difference in my son's life have been those rare people who have encountered him as an individual and have devoted their energies to bringing out his potential without reservation, and have been willing in the process to stop worrying about how he should be labeled. My contact with other parents of children with special needs tells me that my reaction to the process is quite common.

There is no question about the fact that the special education bureaucracy   7
serves a useful purpose in helping students find the classrooms and programs most suited to their needs. At the same time, it often appears to be a tendency for any bureaucratic system to become so absorbed with its own structure, so convinced of the infallibility of the experts it employs, that it fails to devote adequate attention to each person it attempts to serve. Because special education involves so many thousands of unique students, it seems almost impossible to find a balance between the efficiency that benefits everyone and the personal attention that is a crucial part of the process. Yet with children's lives at stake, it is critical that we never give up the effort to do so.[9]

---

[9] Used with permission.

READING 3

Student
Paper

DEAR MOM

Taryn Barnett

Dear Mom,

I wanted to write you a letter regarding the conversation we had yesterday. You said that you wanted me to do one of three things: move home, transfer to a cheaper complex, or move into the dorms. I understand that you believe these options would allow me to work less and save more money in order to concentrate on my studies. You think that this would be financially simpler for you and for me, and much less stressful for me.

I understand the logic behind your position in that the whole financial situation would be easier if I were living at home. First of all, we would not have as many expenses. Living at home would eliminate rent payments, cable bills, and electricity bills, but it would not eliminate phone bills, insurance bills, gas bills, or personal items. This would allow me to take some of the money that I am earning now and save it to give myself a strong financial foundation as I become more independent in the future. If I did not have a job and were under a lot of stress, I could see how it would make sense to move back home. If safety were not an issue I could see how it would save me money to move to a cheaper apartment complex. Also, moving into a cheaper apartment complex could eliminate the worries and the need for a roommate. For example, I have a roommate now and I have to worry about whether or not she will pay her share of the bills on time or whether I will have to cover for her until she has the money. Now, if I were going away to school I could see the advantages of living in the dorms. This would include not having to worry about the bills, meeting more people from school, and entering all of the social aspects of living on campus. It is also safer to live in a well-monitored environment. I see the ways your points are valid, so let us discuss those points and work together to find a good solution for both of us.

I believe that staying in school while working part-time in order to live in this complex is showing responsibility on my part. A big part of this for me is pride. I want to be able to prove to you and dad that I can do it on my own with as minimal help from you as possible. Having this independence is not only important to me, but it helps me learn about life through experience. To me, independence is learning to handle being responsible for myself and my actions, in which I figure out how to decide what to do, when to do it, and when to buckle down. Taking things into my hands and making sure everything that needs to get done does get done is a responsibility that I have learned how to prioritize. Now, in having this independence and showing my responsibility by keeping up with paying the bills on time (cable, phone, rent, and electricity) and getting my school work done for all four of my classes (Music Appreciation, Political Science, Psychology, and English) I am building up my credit and learning self-discipline. By self-discipline I mean teaching myself what is important to me and making sure I keep up with the work and reading in my classes. I pay $430 per month for rent in my apartment complex and, in comparison to some that are $395 per month all bills paid, I may not be in a cheap complex but I am in a safe complex. When a young woman lives alone, that is essential. It is a well-known fact that the cheaper the area of the apartment complex, the more prevalent is crime.

Since I am a full-time student and I get financial assistance from you and dad, I can work part-time and afford my apartment. If I were to move back home, I would not get the financial support from you and dad. So, I would still have to work the same number of hours in order to have any money because the only thing I would not have to worry about financially would be rent. While this offers less financial stress for you, it increases personal and operational stress between us. So, if we can keep our minds open we can see how our points complement each other.

Our points of view are very similar because any way you go I am saving the same amount of money. With your plan I have less income with less bills and work part-time to get by. With my plan I work the same number of hours and I get financial help from you and dad to help pay for the living expenses, but I have more expenses. So, you can see that either way I go to school, work, and save the same amount of money. Only if I stay in my apartment complex, I have all of the same benefits along with independence. So, unless I prove myself to be irresponsible, please do not ask me to give up my independence.

Sincerely,
Taryn[10]

3. WRITING ASSIGNMENT: THE ROGERIAN RESPONSE PAPER[11]

A Rogerian response paper is somewhat different from the examples of Rogerian argument presented in Exercise 2 since it is written in direct response to a particular essay. The process involves reading and understanding an essay with which you disagree and responding to it using Rogerian strategy. Here are some possible articles to respond to:

a. Write a response to the essay, "Cigarettes Make the Meal," printed below (this will work if you are a nonsmoker).
b. Write a response to "What's Happened to Disney Films?" (p. 146), to "Let Gays Marry" (p. 461), or to "Leave Marriage Alone," (p. 463).
c. Find a letter to the editor in your local or school newspaper that you disagree with and write a response to it.

Your paper should be at least two pages long.

Prewriting: Write a brief summary of the opposition's position and a brief summary of your position to make certain you understand them.

Writing: Include the following in your paper.

(1) State the opposition's position as presented in the article, and describe in what instances this position might work or be acceptable. As you

---

[10] Used with permission.
[11] I am indebted to Barbara Chiarello for the general concept of this assignment.

write, imagine that the author of the article will be reading your response. Write so that person will feel "heard."

(2) Write a clear transition to your position on the issue.

(3) State how your position would also work or be acceptable.

(4) Try to reconcile the two positions.

Essay

CIGARETTES MAKE THE MEAL

James Villas

For those victimized by the Draconian law forbidding smoking in New York City restaurants, there is hope for civilized dining. Two bills in the State Legislature would overturn the law. Then maybe the Europeans would stop snickering at us.

The year-old restriction, many restaurateurs tell me, has driven away customers, forced layoffs and cut deeply into profits. Above all, the law has made a mockery of one of life's most sybaritic pleasures—eating in the simplest bistro with the bonus of a good smoke. A bistro is simply not authentic without the mellow, stimulating, evocative, unique fragrance of smoke mingling with the intoxicating aromas and flavors of sweet onions, heady garlic, roasted meats, savory stews and racy wines.

To sip an aperitif without lighting up is indescribably boring. And the idea of lingering with friends over a fine brandy without a cigarette or cigar is ludicrous.

Anyone who doubts that smokers dine with greater gusto than their righteous counterparts need only ask Sirio Maccioni, the owner of Le Cirque. After the main course, they feel unfulfilled, he said: "The smokers are not even ordering dessert now, much less coffee. They even tell me where they are going for dessert."

The city law allows smoking in restaurants that have 35 or fewer seats. If you don't think smokers have more fun in these ridiculously few but blessed havens, observe how many abstainers, guzzling mineral water and fiddling with their silver, almost race through a meal with minimal conversation.

Compare them with relaxed smokers who gab endlessly, relishing their sinful cigarettes and wine long after the escargots, rack of lamb, cheese and tarts have been cleared. I often pity nonsmokers.

Hypocrisy is rampant. The worst offenders are travelers who return from Paris ecstatic about a romantic smoke-filled bistro and then adopt a politically correct attitude about "pollution" in our restaurants. But who can blame them? Most of the press, itself zealously antismoking, has ignored a study by the nonpartisan Congressional Research Service that found virtually no significant health risks from exposure to second-hand smoke.

Not long ago, a certain lady who gave up the habit a few years back dined with three smokers in a small Greenwich Village bistro. After a sumptuous, talkative, three-hour meal, while we were sipping espresso and marc de Bourgogne, she picked up my lighted Doral, took one long sensual draw and, tilting her head back with eyes closed, sighed wistfully and said: "God! I forgot just how wonderful that is! Now the dinner's complete." She was right.[12]

4. QUESTIONS ON THE CHAPTER
a. What are some of the special characteristics of Rogerian argument and how does it differ from traditional argument?
b. In what types of argumentative situations do you think you might find Rogerian argument more productive than traditional argument? Give examples of at least two issues where you might profitably resort to Rogerian argument.
c. What are some of the advantages and some of the disadvantages of Rogerian argument?
d. What difficulties, if any, do you contemplate in using Rogerian argument?

5. QUESTIONS ON THE ESSAYS FOR ANALYSIS
a. "A Camp Sows the Seeds of Peace," page 253. Describe some of the stereotypes that people are described as holding in this essay. What is being done to change them? How can stereotypical thinking best be changed in your judgment?
b. "Doctor-Assisted Suicide: Is It Ever an Option?" page 258. Have you known friends or relatives who might have been candidates for assisted suicide? Would you favor this course of action for them or not? Give your reasons.
c. "Special Education's Best Intentions," page 261. Provide some examples from your own experiences in school when you were treated as a member of the group and when you were treated as an individual. What are some measures that administrators and teachers could take to provide more individual attention for students?
d. "Dear Mom," page 263. The student who wrote this letter was at a stand-off with her parents on this issue. Why do you think the Rogerian approach helped her change her parents' minds? Describe what is effective in this letter. Could you write a Rogerian letter on a personal matter? What topics would you consider appropriate for a letter that employs this particular argument strategy?
e. "Cigarettes Make the Meal," page 265. Is the issue in this essay serious enough to motivate legislation to forbid smoking in public? Why do you think so? If you were arguing for or against a bill to outlaw smoking in public places, what reasons and evidence would you give for your position?

SYNTHESIS OF READING AND WRITING

WRITING ASSIGNMENT: THE CRITICAL ANALYSIS PAPER
This next assignment will help you synthesize the information you have learned in these first eight chapters and apply it to a well-known classic argument, "Letter from Birmingham Jail" by Martin Luther King, Jr. It will also

---

[12] *New York Times*, April 6, 1996, Sec. A, p. 15.

teach you to write the type of critical analysis paper sometimes required in other classes.

1. **Read the questions** entitled "Questions for Critical Reading." These questions can be employed to help you read and analyze any argument. You will practice answering them as you read the two letters printed here, the clergymen's letter and King's answer.
2. **Read the background information** that places these letters in their historical context. This information will help you analyze the rhetorical situation in which these letters were produced.
3. **Read the letters and answer the critical reading questions** as they appear in the margins in brief form.
4. **Participate in the class project** described on page 269 and take some notes.
5. **Write a critical analysis paper.** This paper should be four pages long, double-spaced, and it should present a critical analysis of the two letters by the clergymen and King. It should be based on the results of your group work and class discussion. Include the following in your paper, but do not necessarily limit yourself to these topics.
   a. Briefly summarize the rhetorical situation (context) for this argument. Include some of the circumstances that caused these letters to be written.
   b. Explain the issue and succinctly describe the positions taken by the clergymen and by King on this issue.
   c. Write summaries of the cores of the two arguments:
      Claims: The clergymen want to convince us to think that . . . King wants to convince us to think that . . .
      Support: Summarize the reasons and evidence in each letter. Cite specific examples of some of the proofs used in each letter. Explain why they are effective.
      Warrants: Explain the warrants. Where are the clergy coming from? Where is King coming from? Is there any attempt in the letters to establish common ground between the two parties?
   d. What is your final evaluation of the two arguments? Which is more convincing? Why? Which has greater moral value as judged by your personal standards and values?
   e. Why is King's letter considered a "classic" argument?

QUESTIONS FOR CRITICAL READING

1. What is the issue? State it as a question.
2. What is the author's particular perspective or "take" on the issue?
3. How would you describe the rhetorical situation?
4. Is this part of an ongoing conversation on this issue? What has gone before? What will come later?
5. Divide the material into its parts, and label the subject of each part. What are the subjects? Why are they in this order? How do they relate to each other?

6. What is the claim? It should be a statement. What type of claim is it?
7. What are the subclaims? What types of claims are they?
8. Is the argumentative intention clear, admitted, and straightforward, or is it concealed and presented under the guise of objective reporting?
9. Does the author use logical proofs? Describe them. What is the effect on the audience?
10. Does the author use emotional proofs? Describe them. What is the effect on the audience?
11. Does the author use proofs that build *ethos* or establish credibility? Describe them. What is the effect on the audience?
12. What type of language predominates, language that appeals to reason, language that appeals to emotion, or language that establishes credibility? In addition to the predominant language and style, are there examples of other types of language and style as well? Give examples and describe the effect on the audience.
13. What are the warrants? Do you share them? Do they need backing to make them more convincing to you? Do you share common ground with the author? Discuss the presence or lack of common ground and how it affects your acceptance of the claim.
14. Are rebuttal arguments used in the argument to point out how the opposition is wrong or in error on certain points? What are they? How effective are they?
15. Are Rogerian strategies used any place in the argument to point out how the opposition might also be correct on certain points? What are they? What is the effect?
16. Does the author exhibit a personal style of argument as discussed in Chapter 2? Describe it. What in the author's background has possibly contributed to this style?
17. Are there any fallacies in the argument? Or does the author complain of any fallacious thinking on the part of the opposition? Describe.
18. In the final evaluation, should the claim be qualified to make it more convincing to you? To the target audience? Or, is it acceptable as it is?
19. Are you convinced? Do you think others will be convinced? What do you perceive as the possible outcomes of this argument for yourself? For the target audience?
20. Is the argument moral and ethical or immoral and manipulative according to your standards and values? Why do you think so? Where are you coming from?

Background Information for Martin Luther King, Jr.'s "Letter from Birmingham Jail"

The two letters printed here were written in response to a dramatic situation that took place in Birmingham, Alabama, in 1963. Birmingham was a very strange place at that time. Black people were allowed to sit only in certain parts of buses and restaurants, they were required to drink out of separate water fountains, and they were not allowed in white churches, schools, or various other public places.

Martin Luther King, Jr., was a black Baptist minister who was a leader in the civil rights movement at that time. The purpose of the movement was to end segregation and discrimination and to create equal rights and access for black people.

King and others carefully prepared for demonstrations that would take place in Birmingham in the spring of 1963. The demonstrators began by sitting-in at lunch counters that had never served blacks before and by picketing stores. Twenty people were arrested the first day on charges of trespassing. Next, the civil rights leaders applied for permits to picket and hold parades against the injustices of discrimination and segregation. They were refused permission, but they demonstrated and picketed anyway. King was served an injunction by a circuit judge that said civil rights leaders could not protest, demonstrate, boycott, or sit-in. King and others decided that this was an unfair and unjust application of the law, and they decided to break it.

King, himself, decided to march on Good Friday, and he expected to go to jail. He was, in fact, arrested and jailed along with 50 other people before he had walked half a mile. King was in jail for eight days. During that time he wrote the "Letter from Birmingham Jail." It was written in response to the letter from eight white clergymen that had been published in the newspaper.

After King left jail, there were further demonstrations and some violence. Thousands of people demonstrated, and thousands were jailed. Finally, black and white leaders began to negotiate, and some final terms were announced May 10, 1963. All lunch counters, restrooms, fitting rooms, and drinking fountains in downtown stores were to be desegregated within 90 days; blacks were to be placed in clerical and sales jobs in stores within 60 days; the many people arrested during the demonstrations were to be released on low bail; and permanent lines of communication were to be established between black and white leaders. The demonstrations ended then, and the city settled down and began to implement the agreements.[13]

CLASS PROJECT: GROUP WORK AND DISCUSSION FOR CRITICAL READING AND CRITICAL ANALYSIS PAPER

Divide the class into seven groups and assign one of the focus topics below to each group. To prepare for the group work, all students read the two letters outside of class and make individual notes on the focus topics assigned to their groups. The brief questions in the margin will facilitate this reading and note taking. In class the groups will meet briefly to consolidate their views on the topic. Each group will then report out and other class members will discuss the results and take some notes. These notes will be used as prewriting materials for the critical analysis paper.

---

[13] This account is drawn from Lee E. Bains, Jr., "Birmingham, 1963: Confrontation over Civil Rights," in *Birmingham, Alabama, 1956–1963: The Black Struggle for Civil Rights*, ed. David J. Garrow (Brooklyn: Carlson, 1989), pp. 175–183.

Group 1. Focus: The rhetorical situation and Rogerian elements. Answer these questions:

1. What is the *exigence* for these two letters? What caused the authors to write them? What was the problem? Was it a new or recurring problem?
2. Who is the *audience* for the clergymen's letter? For King's letter? What is the nature of these audiences? Can they be convinced? What are the expected outcomes?
3. What are the *constraints*? Speculate about the beliefs, attitudes, habits, and traditions that were in place that limited or constrained both the clergymen and King. How did these constraining circumstances influence the audience at that time.
4. Think about the *authors* of both letters. Who are they? Speculate about their background, experience, affiliations, and values. What motivates them to write?
5. What kind of *text* is this? What effect do its special qualities and features have on the audience?
6. Think about *yourself as the reader*. What is your position on the issue? Do you experience constraints as you read? Do you perceive common ground with either the clergymen or King or both? Describe it. Are you influenced by these letters? How?
7. Are there any efforts to use Rogerian argument strategies and thereby build common ground by establishing that the opposition may at times be correct? If yes, provide some examples and analyze their effect.

Group 2. Focus: Organization and claims. Divide each letter into its main parts. What is the subject of each part? Why have the parts been placed in this particular order? What is the relationship between them? What is the main claim in each letter? What types of claims are they? What are some of the subclaims? What types of claims are they?

Group 3. Focus: Logical proofs; logical style. Analyze the use of logical proof in each of the letters. Provide examples. Describe their effect on the audience. Provide an example of the language of rational style in one of the letters.

Group 4. Focus: Emotional proofs; emotional style. Analyze the use of emotional proof in each of the letters. Provide examples. Describe their effect on the audience. Provide an example of the language of emotional style in one of the letters.

Group 5. Focus: Proofs that establish *ethos*; style that establishes *ethos*. Analyze the use of proofs that establish *ethos* or credibility in the letters. Provide examples. Describe their effect on the audience. Provide an example of language that establishes *ethos* in one of the letters.

Group 6. Focus: Warrants. Identify the warrants in each of the letters. How much common ground do you think exists between the authors of the letters? How much common ground do you share with the authors? As a result, which do you find more convincing? Why?

Group 7. Focus: Fallacious thinking and rebuttals. Provide examples of reasoning that is considered fallacious or wrong-headed by the opposing parties in each of the letters. What rebuttals are made in response to these? How effective are they?

Essay

LETTER FROM EIGHT WHITE CLERGYMEN

A Call for Unity

April 12, 1963

What is the issue?

We the undersigned clergymen are among those who, in January, issued "An Appeal for Law and Order and Common Sense," in dealing with racial problems in Alabama. We expressed understanding that honest convictions in racial matters could properly be

What is the clergymen's position?

pursued in the courts, but urged that decisions of those courts should in the meantime be peacefully obeyed.

What is the claim?

Since that time there had been some evidence of increased forebearance and a willingness to face facts. Responsible citizens have undertaken to work on various problems which cause racial friction

What type of claim is it?

and unrest. In Birmingham, recent public events have given indication that we all have opportunity for a new constructive and realistic approach to racial problems.

What are the rebuttals?

However, we are now confronted by a series of demonstrations by some of our Negro citizens, directed and led in part by outsiders. We recognize the natural impatience of people who feel that their hopes are slow in being realized. But we are convinced that these demonstrations are unwise and untimely.

How do the authors build *ethos*?

We agree rather with certain local Negro leadership which has called for honest and open negotiation of racial issues in our area. And we believe this kind of facing of issues can best be accomplished by citizens of our own metropolitan area, white and Negro, meeting with their knowledge and experience of the local situation. All of us need to face that responsibility and find proper channels for its accomplishment.

How do they appeal to logic?

Just as we formerly pointed out that "hatred and violence have no sanction in our religious and political traditions," we also point out that such actions as incite to hatred and violence, however technically

How do they appeal to emotion?

peaceful those actions may be, have not contributed to the resolution of our local problems. We do not believe that these days of new hope are days when extreme measures are justified in Birmingham.

What are the warrants?

We commend the community as a whole, and the local news media and law enforcement officials in particular, on the calm manner in which these demonstrations have been handled. We urge the public to continue to show restraint should the demonstrations continue, and the law enforcement officials to remain calm and continue to protect our city from violence.

Describe the predominant style.

We further strongly urge our own Negro community to withdraw support from these demonstrations, and to unite locally in working peacefully for a better Birmingham. When rights are consistently denied, a cause should be pressed in the courts and in negotiations among local leaders, and not in the streets. We appeal to both our white and Negro citizenry to observe the principles of law and order and common sense.

C.C.J. Carpenter, D.D., L.L.D, Bishop of Alabama; Joseph A. Durick, D.D., Auxiliary Bishop, Diocese of Mobile-Birmingham; Rabbi Milton L. Grafman, Temple Emanu-El, Birmingham, Alabama; Bishop Paul Hardin, Bishop of the Alabama–West Florida Conference of the Methodist Church; Bishop Nolan B. Harmon, Bishop of the North Alabama Conference of the Methodist Church; George M. Murray, D.D., L.L.D., Bishop Coadjutor, Episcopal Diocese of Alabama; Edward V. Ramage, Moderator, Synod of the Alabama Presbyterian Church in the United States; Earl Stallings, Pastor, First Baptist Church, Birmingham.

Essay

LETTER FROM BIRMINGHAM JAIL*

Martin Luther King, Jr.

April 16, 1963

What is the issue?

What is King's position?

My Dear Fellow Clergymen:

While confined here in the Birmingham city jail, I came across your recent statement calling my present activities "unwise and untimely." Seldom do I pause to answer criticism of my work and ideas. If I sought to answer all the criticisms that cross my desk, my secretaries would have little time for anything other than such correspondence in the course of the day, and I would have no time for constructive work. But since I feel that you are men of genuine good will and that your criticisms are sincerely set forth, I want to try to answer your statement in what I hope will be patient and reasonable terms.

Identify and describe the Rogerian elements and efforts to establish common ground throughout this letter.

I think I should indicate why I am here in Birmingham, since you have been influenced by the view which argues against "out-

1

2

Author's Note: This response to a published statement by eight fellow clergymen from Alabama (Bishop C.C.J. Carpenter, Bishop Joseph A. Durick, Rabbi Milton L. Grafman, Bishop Paul Hardin, Bishop Nolan B. Harmon, the Reverend George M. Murray, the Reverend Edward V. Ramage, and the Reverend Earl Stallings) was composed under somewhat constricting circumstances. Begun on the margins of the newspaper in which the statement appeared while I was in jail, the letter was continued on scraps of writing paper supplied by a friendly Negro trusty, and concluded on a pad my attorneys were eventually permitted to leave me. Although the text remains in substance unaltered, I have indulged in the author's perogative of polishing it for publication.

siders coming in." I have the honor of serving as president of the Southern Christian Leadership Conference, an organization operating in every southern state, with headquarters in Atlanta, Georgia. We have some eighty-five affiliated organizations across the South, and one of them is the Alabama Christian Movement for Human Rights. Frequently we share staff, educational and financial resources with our affiliates. Several months ago the affiliate here in Birmingham asked us to be on call to engage in a nonviolent direct-action program if such were deemed necessary. We readily consented, and when the hour came we lived up to our promise. So I, along with several members of my staff, am here because I was invited here. I am here because I have organizational ties here.

How does King build *ethos*?

But more basically, I am in Birmingham because injustice is here. Just as the prophets of the eighth century B.C. left their villages and carried their "thus saith the Lord" far beyond the boundaries of their home towns, and just as the Apostle Paul left his village of Tarsus and carried the gospel of Jesus Christ to the far corners of the Greco-Roman world, so am I compelled to carry the gospel of freedom beyond my own home town. Like Paul, I must constantly respond to the Macedonian call for aid.   3

What is the effect of the comparison with Paul?

Moreover, I am cognizant of the interrelatedness of all communities and states. I cannot sit idly by in Atlanta and not be concerned about what happens in Birmingham. Injustice anywhere is a threat to justice everywhere. We are caught in an inescapable network of mutuality, tied in a single garment of destiny. Whatever affects one directly, affects all indirectly. Never again can we afford to live with the narrow, provincial "outside agitator" idea. Anyone who lives inside the United States can never be considered an outsider anywhere within its bounds.   4

Draw a line at the end of the introduction.

Draw other lines at the end of each of the other major sections of material. Label the subject of each section in the margin.

You deplore the demonstrations taking place in Birmingham. But your statement, I am sorry to say, fails to express a similar concern for the conditions that brought about the demonstrations. I am sure that none of you would want to rest content with the superficial kind of social analysis that deals merely with effects and does not grapple with underlying causes. It is unfortunate that demonstrations are taking place in Birmingham, but it is even more unfortunate that the city's white power structure left the Negro community with no alternative.   5

What is the subject of this first section?

What is the claim?

What type of claim is it?

Is it qualified?

In any nonviolent campaign there are four basic steps: collection of the facts to determine whether injustices exist; negotiation; self-purification; and direct action. We have gone through all these steps in Birmingham. There can be no gain-saying the fact that racial injustice engulfs this community. Birmingham is probably the most thoroughly segregated city in the United States. Its ugly record of brutality is widely known. Negroes have experienced grossly unjust treatment in the courts. There have been more un-   6

Identify and analyze the effect of the emotional appeals.

solved bombings of Negro homes and churches in Birmingham than in any other city in the nation. These are the hard, brutal facts of the case. On the basis of these conditions, Negro leaders sought to negotiate with the city fathers. But the latter consistently refused to engage in good-faith negotiation.

Then, last September, came the opportunity to talk with leaders of Birmingham's economic community. In the course of the negotiations, certain promises were made by the merchants—for example, to remove the stores' humiliating racial signs. On the basis of these promises, the Reverend Fred Shuttlesworth and the leaders of the Alabama Christian Movement for Human Rights agreed to a moratorium on all demonstrations. As the weeks and months went by, we realized that we were the victims of a broken promise. A few signs, briefly removed, returned; the others remained.

7

As in so many past experiences, our hopes had been blasted, and the shadow of deep disappointment settled upon us. We had no alternative except to prepare for direct action, whereby we would present our very bodies as a means of laying our case before the conscience of the local and the national community. Mindful of the difficulties involved, we decided to undertake a process of self-purification. We began a series of workshops on nonviolence, and we repeatedly asked ourselves: "Are you able to accept blows without retaliating?" "Are you able to endure the ordeal of jail?" We decided to schedule our direct-action program for the Easter season, realizing that except for Christmas, this is the main shopping period of the year. Knowing that a strong economic-withdrawal program would be the by-product of direct action, we felt that this would be the best time to bring pressure to bear on the merchants for the needed change.

8

What are some of the values expressed in this argument?

Then it occurred to us that Birmingham's mayoral election was coming up in March, and we speedily decided to postpone action until after election day. When we discovered that the Commissioner of Public Safety, Eugene "Bull" Connor, had piled up enough votes to be in the runoff, we decided again to postpone action until the day after the runoff so that the demonstrations could not be used to cloud the issues. Like many others, we waited to see Mr. Connor defeated, and to this end we endured postponement after postponement. Having aided in this community need, we felt that our direct-action program could be delayed no longer.

9

Identify and describe the rebuttals.

You may well ask: "Why direct action? Why sit-ins, marches and so forth? Isn't negotiation a better path?" You are quite right in calling for negotiation. Indeed, this is the very purpose of direct action. Nonviolent direct action seeks to create such a crisis and foster such a tension that a community which has constantly refused to negotiate is forced to confront the issue. It seeks so to dramatize the

10

issue that it can no longer be ignored. My citing the creation of tension as part of the work of the nonviolent-resister may sound rather shocking. But I must confess that I am not afraid of the word "tension." I have earnestly opposed violent tension, but there is a type of constructive, nonviolent tension which is necessary for growth. Just as Socrates felt that it was necessary to create a tension in the mind so that individuals could rise from the bondage of myths and half-truths to the unfettered realm of creative analysis and objective appraisal, so must we see the need for nonviolent gadflies to create the kind of tension in society that will help men rise from the dark depths of prejudice and racism to the majestic heights of understanding and brotherhood.

What is the effect of the comparison with Socrates?

11 The purpose of our direct-action program is to create a situation so crisis-packed that it will inevitably open the door to negotiation. I therefore concur with you in your call for negotiation. Too long has our beloved Southland been bogged down in a tragic effort to live in monologue rather than dialogue.

What is King's planned argumentative strategy?

12 One of the basic points in your statement is that the action that I and my associates have taken in Birmingham is untimely. Some have asked: "Why didn't you give the new city administration time to act?" The only answer that I can give to this query is that the new Birmingham administration must be prodded about as much as the outgoing one, before it will act. We are sadly mistaken if we feel that the election of Albert Boutwell as mayor will bring the millennium to Birmingham. While Mr. Boutwell is a much more gentle person than Mr. Connor, they are both segregationists, dedicated to the maintenance of the status quo. I have hope that Mr. Boutwell will be reasonable enough to see the futility of massive resistance to desegregation. But he will not see this without pressure from devotees of civil rights. My friends, I must say to you that we have not made a single gain in civil rights without determined legal and nonviolent pressure. Lamentably, it is an historical fact that privileged groups seldom give up their privileges voluntarily. Individuals may see the moral light and voluntarily give up their unjust posture; but, as Reinhold Niebuhr has reminded us, groups tend to be more immoral than individuals.

Why does King refer to history?

Why does he refer to Niebuhr?

Identify and analyze the emotional proof.

13 We know through painful experience that freedom is never voluntarily given up by the oppressor; it must be demanded by the oppressed. Frankly, I have yet to engage in a direct-action campaign that was "well-timed" in the view of those who have not suffered unduly from the disease of segregation. For years now I have heard the word "Wait!" It rings in the ear of every Negro with piercing familiarity. This "Wait" has almost always meant "Never." We must come to see, with one of our distinguished jurists, that "justice too long delayed is justice denied."

What human motives and values does King appeal to?

Identify emotional
language, examples,
and vivid description.

We have waited for more than 340 years for our constitutional   14
and God-given rights. The nations of Asia and Africa are moving
with jetlike speed toward gaining political independence, but we
still creep at horse-and-buggy pace toward gaining a cup of coffee
at a lunch counter. Perhaps it is easy for those who have never felt
the stinging darts of segregation to say, "Wait." But when you have
seen vicious mobs lynch your mothers and fathers at will and
drown your sisters and brothers at whim; when you have seen hate-
filled policemen curse, kick and even kill your black brothers and
sisters; when you see the vast majority of your twenty million
Negro brothers smothering in an airtight cage of poverty in the
midst of an affluent society; when you suddenly find your tongue
twisted and your speech stammering as you seek to explain to your
six-year-old daughter why she can't go to the public amusement
park that has just been advertised on television, and see tears

What is the effect of the
emotional proof?

welling up in her eyes when she is told that Fun-town is closed to
colored children, and see ominous clouds of inferiority beginning to
form in her little mental sky, and see her beginning to distort her
personality by developing an unconscious bitterness toward white
people; when you have to concoct an answer for a five-year-old son
who is asking; "Daddy, why do white people treat colored people
so mean?"; when you take a cross-country drive and find it necessary to sleep night after night in the uncomfortable corners of your
automobile because no motel will accept you; when you are humiliated day in and day out by nagging signs reading "white" and "colored"; when your first name becomes "nigger," your middle name
becomes "boy" (however old you are) and your last name becomes
"John," and your wife and mother are never given the respected
title "Mrs."; when you are harried by day and haunted by night by
the fact that you are a Negro, living constantly at tiptoe stance,
never quite knowing what to expect next, and are plagued with
inner fears and outer resentments; when you are forever fighting a
degenerating sense of "nobodiness"—then you will understand

What is the predominant
type of proof in the first
section of the letter?

why we find it difficult to wait. There comes a time when the cup of
endurance runs over, and men are no longer willing to be plunged
into the abyss of despair. I hope, sirs, you can understand our legitimate and unavoidable impatience.

Draw a line where the
subject changes.
What is the subject of
the second section?

You express a great deal of anxiety over our willingness to   15
break laws. This is certainly a legitimate concern. Since we so diligently urge people to obey the Supreme Court's decision of 1954
outlawing segregation in the public schools, at first glance it may
seem rather paradoxical for us consciously to break laws. One may
well ask: "How can you advocate breaking some laws and obeying
others?" The answer lies in the fact that there are two types of laws:
just and unjust. I would be the first to advocate obeying just laws.

How and why does King use definition?

How does he support the definition?

What is the effect of the support?

Explain the example of just and unjust laws.

How does King further elaborate on this idea?

Conversely, one has a moral responsibility to disobey unjust laws. I would agree with St. Augustine that "an unjust law is no law at all."

Now, what is the difference between the two? How does one determine whether a law is just or unjust? A just law is a man-made code that squares with the moral law or the law of God. An unjust law is a code that is out of harmony with the moral law. To put it in the terms of St. Thomas Aquinas: An unjust law is a human law that is not rooted in eternal law and natural law. Any law that uplifts human personality is just. Any law that degrades human personality is unjust. All segregation statutes are unjust because segregation distorts the soul and damages the personality. It gives the segregator a false sense of superiority and the segregated a false sense of inferiority. Segregation, to use the terminology of the Jewish philosopher Martin Buber, substitutes an "I-it" relationship for an "I-thou" relationship and ends up relegating persons to the status of things. Hence segregation is not only politically, economically, and sociologically unsound, it is morally wrong and sinful. Paul Tillich has said that sin is separation. Is not segregation an existential expression of man's tragic separation, his awful estrangement, his terrible sinfulness? Thus it is that I can urge men to obey the 1954 decision of the Supreme Court, for it is morally right; and I can urge them to disobey segregation ordinances, for they are morally wrong.

Let us consider a more concrete example of just and unjust laws. An unjust law is a code that a numerical or power majority group compels a minority group to obey but does not make binding on itself. This is *difference* made legal. By the same token, a just law is a code that a majority compels a minority to follow and that it is willing to follow itself. This is *sameness* made legal.

Let me give another explanation. A law is unjust if it is inflicted on a minority that, as a result of being denied the right to vote, had no part in enacting or devising the law. Who can say that the legislature of Alabama which set up that state's segregation laws was democratically elected? Throughout Alabama all sorts of devious methods are used to prevent Negroes from becoming registered voters, and there are some counties in which, even though Negroes constitute a majority of the population, not a single Negro is registered. Can any law enacted under such circumstances be considered democratically structured?

Sometimes a law is just on its face and unjust in its application. For instance, I have been arrested on a charge of parading without a permit. Now, there is nothing wrong in having an ordinance which requires a permit for a parade. But such an ordinance becomes unjust when it is used to maintain segregation and to deny citizens the First-Amendment privilege of peaceful assembly and protest.

Analyze the deductive reasoning in this paragraph.

I hope you are able to see the distinction I am trying to point out. In no sense do I advocate evading or defying the law, as would the rabid segregationist. That would lead to anarchy. One who breaks an unjust law must do so openly, lovingly, and with a willingness to accept the penalty. I submit that an individual who breaks a law that conscience tells him is unjust, and who willingly accepts the penalty of imprisonment in order to arouse the conscience of the community over its injustice, is in reality expressing the highest respect for law.

20

Identify and describe the effect of the historical analogies.

Of course, there is nothing new about this kind of civil disobedience. It was evidenced sublimely in the refusal of Shadrach, Meshach and Abednego to obey the laws of Nebuchadnezzar, on the ground that a higher moral law was at stake. It was practiced superbly by the early Christians, who were willing to face hungry lions and the excruciating pain of chopping blocks rather than submit to certain unjust laws of the roman empire. To a degree, academic freedom is a reality today because Socrates practiced civil disobedience. In our own nation, the Boston Tea Party represented a massive act of civil disobedience.

21

What type of proof predominates in the second part of the letter?

We should never forget that everything Adolf Hitler did in Germany was "legal" and everything the Hungarian freedom fighters did in Hungary was "illegal." It was "illegal" to aid and comfort a Jew in Hitler's Germany. Even so, I am sure that, had I lived in Germany at the time, I would have aided and comforted my Jewish brothers. If today I lived in a Communist country where certain principles dear to the Christian faith are suppressed, I would openly advocate disobeying that country's antireligious laws.

22

Draw a line where the subject changes. What is the subject of the third section?

What are King's warrants in this passage?

I must make two honest confessions to you, my Christian and Jewish brothers. First, I must confess that over the past few years I have been gravely disappointed with the white moderate. I have almost reached the regrettable conclusion that the Negro's great stumbling block in his stride toward freedom is not the White Citizen's Counciler or the Ku Klux Klanner, but the white moderate, who is more devoted to "order" than to justice; who prefers a negative peace which is the absence of tension to a positive peace which is the presence of justice; who constantly says: "I agree with you in the goal you seek, but I cannot agree with your methods of direct action"; who paternalistically believes he can set the timetable for another man's freedom; who lives by a mythical concept of time and who constantly advises the Negro to wait for a "more convenient season." Shallow understanding from people of good will is more frustrating than absolute misunderstanding from people of ill will. Lukewarm acceptance is much more bewildering than outright rejection.

23

How do King's warrants differ from the clergymen's?

I had hoped that the white moderate would understand that law and order exist for the purpose of establishing justice and that

24

How and why does King use definition here?

when they fail in this purpose they become the dangerously structured dams that block the flow of social progress. I had hoped that the white moderate would understand that the present tension in the South is a necessary phase of the transition from an obnoxious negative peace, in which the Negro passively accepted his unjust plight, to a substantive and positive peace, in which all men will respect the dignity and worth of human personality. Actually, we who engage in nonviolent direct action are not the creators of tension. We merely bring to the surface the hidden tension that is already alive. We bring it out in the open, where it can be seen and dealt with. Like a boil that can never be cured so long as it is covered up but must be opened with all its ugliness to the natural medicines of air and light, injustice must be exposed, with all the tension its exposure creates, to the light of human conscience and the air of national opinion before it can be cured.

Identify and describe the effects of the analogies in these paragraphs.

In your statements you assert that our actions, even though peaceful, must be condemned because they precipitate violence. But is this a logical assertion? Isn't this like condemning a robbed man because his possession of money precipitated the evil act of robbery? Isn't this like condemning Socrates because his unswerving commitment to truth and his philosophical inquiries precipitated the act by the misguided populace in which they made him drink hemlock? Isn't this like condemning Jesus because his unique God-consciousness and never-ceasing devotion to God's will precipitated the evil act of crucifixion? We must come to see that, as the

What is the fallacious thinking King complains of?

federal courts have consistently affirmed, it is wrong to urge an individual to cease his efforts to gain his basic constitutional rights because the quest may precipitate violence. Society must protect the robbed and punish the robber. 25

I had also hoped that the white moderate would reject the myth concerning time in relation to the struggle for freedom. I have just received a letter from a white brother in Texas. He writes: "All Christians know that the colored people will receive equal rights eventually, but it is possible that you are in too great a religious hurry. It has taken Christianity almost two thousand years to accomplish what it has. The teachings of Christ take time to come to earth." Such an attitude stems from a tragic misconception of time, from the strangely irrational notion that there is something in the very flow of time that will inevitably cure all ills. Actually, time itself is neutral; it can be used either destructively or constructively. 26

Summarize King's reasoning about time.

More and more I feel that the people of ill will have used time much more effectively than have the people of good will. We will have to repent in this generation not merely for the hateful words and actions of the bad people but for the appalling silence of the good people. Human progress never rolls in on wheels of inevitability; it comes through the tireless efforts of men willing to be coworkers with God, and without this hard work, time itself becomes an ally of the forces of social stagnation. We must use time creatively, in the knowledge that the time is always right to do right. Now is the time to make real the promise of democracy and transform our pending national elegy into a creative psalm of brotherhood. Now is the time to lift our national policy from the quicksand of racial injustice to the solid rock of human dignity.

You speak of our activity in Birmingham as extreme. At first I was rather disappointed that fellow clergymen would see my nonviolent efforts as those of an extremist. I began thinking about the fact that I stand in the middle of two opposing forces in the Negro community. One is a force of complacency, made up in part of Negroes who, as a result of long years of oppression, are so drained of self-respect and a sense of "somebodiness" that they have adjusted to segregation; and in part of a few middle-class Negroes who, because of a degree of academic and economic security and because in some ways they profit by segregation, have become insensitive to the problems of the masses. The other force is one of bitterness and hatred, and it comes perilously close to advocating violence. It is expressed in the various black nationalist groups that are springing up across the nation, the largest and best-known being Elijah Muhammad's Muslim movement. Nourished by the Negro's frustration over the continued existence of racial discrimination, this movement is made up of people who have lost faith in America, who have absolutely repudiated Christianity, and who have concluded that the white man is an incorrigible "devil."

I have tried to stand between these two forces, saying that we need emulate neither the "do-nothingism" of the complacent nor the hatred and despair of the black nationalist. For there is the more excellent way of love and nonviolent protest. I am grateful to God that, through the influence of the Negro church, the way of nonviolence became an integral part of our struggle.

If this philosophy had not emerged, by now many streets of the South would, I am convinced, be flowing with blood. And I am further convinced that if our white brothers dismiss as "rabble-rousers" and "outside agitators" those of us who employ nonviolent direct action, and if they refuse to support our nonviolent efforts, millions of Negroes will, out of frustration and despair, seek solace and security in black-nationalist ideologies—a development that would inevitably lead to a frightening racial nightmare.

Oppressed people cannot remain oppressed forever. The yearning for freedom eventually manifests itself, and that is what has happened to the American Negro. Something within has reminded him of his birthright of freedom, and something without

27

28

29

30

Margin notes:

Describe the two opposing forces.

How and why does King attempt to reconcile the opposing forces?

Identify and describe the causal proof?

Summarize King's reasoning about the effects of oppression.

has reminded him that it can be gained. Consciously or unconsciously, he has been caught up by the *Zeitgeist*, and with his black brothers of Africa and his brown and yellow brothers of Asia, South America and the Caribbean, the United States Negro is moving with a sense of great urgency toward the promised land of racial justice. If one recognizes this vital urge that has engulfed the Negro community, one should readily understand why public demonstrations are taking place. The Negro has many pent-up resentments and latent frustrations, and he must release them. So let him march; let him make prayer pilgrimages to the city hall; let him go on freedom rides—and try to understand why he must do so. If his repressed emotions are not released in nonviolent ways, they will seek expression through violence; this is not a threat but a fact of history. So I have not said to my people: "Get rid of your discontent." Rather, I have tried to say that this normal and healthy discontent can be channeled into the creative outlet of nonviolent direct action. And now this approach is being termed extremist.

What is the effect of these comparisons?

But though I was initially disappointed at being categorized as an extremist, as I continued to think about the matter I gradually gained a measure of satisfaction from the label. Was not Jesus an extremist for love: "Love your enemies, bless them that curse you, do good to them that hate you, and pray for them which despitefully use you, and persecute you." Was not Amos an extremist for justice: "Let justice roll down like waters and righteousness like an everflowing stream." Was not Paul an extremist for the Christian gospel: "I bear in my body the marks of the Lord Jesus." Was not Martin Luther an extremist: "Here I stand; I cannot do otherwise, so help me God." And John Bunyan: "I will stay in jail to the end of my days before I make a butchery of my conscience." And Abraham Lincoln: "This nation cannot survive half slave and half free." And Thomas Jefferson: "We hold these truths to be self-evident, that all men are created equal. . . ." So the question is not whether we will be extremists, but what kind of extremists we will be. Will we be extremists for hate or for love? Will we be extremists for the preservation of injustice or for the extension of justice? In that dramatic scene on Calvary's hill three men were crucified. We must never forget that all three were crucified for the same crime—the crime of extremism. Two were extremists for immorality, and thus fell below their environment. The other, Jesus Christ, was an extremist for love, truth, and goodness, and thereby rose above his environment. Perhaps the South, the nation and the world are in dire need of creative extremists. 31

Summarize King's description of the oppressor race.

I had hoped that the white moderate would see this need. Perhaps I was too optimistic; perhaps I expected too much. I suppose I should have realized that few members of the oppressor race can 32 understand the deep groans and passionate yearnings of the op-pressed race, and still fewer have the vision to see that injustice must be rooted out by strong, persistent and determined action. I am thankful, however, that some of our white brothers in the South have grasped the meaning of this social revolution and committed themselves to it. They are still all too few in quantity, but they are big in quality. Some—such as Ralph McGill, Lillian Smith, Harry Golden, James McBride Dabbs, Ann Braden and Sarah Patton Boyle—have written about our struggle in eloquent and prophetic terms. Others have marched with us down nameless streets of the South. They have languished in filthy, roach-infested jails, suffering the abuse and brutality of policemen who view them as "dirty nigger-lovers." Unlike so many of their moderate brothers and sis-ters, they have recognized the urgency of the moment and sensed the need for powerful "action" antidotes to combat the disease of segregation.

33   Let me take note of my other major disappointment. I have been so greatly disappointed with the white church and its leader-ship. Of course, there are some notable exceptions. I am not un-mindful of the fact that each of you has taken some significant stands on this issue. I commend you, Reverend Stallings, for your Christian stand on this past Sunday, in welcoming Negroes to your worship service on a non-segregated basis. I commend the Catholic leaders of this state for integrating Spring Hill College several years ago.

34   But despite these notable exceptions, I must honestly reiterate that I have been disappointed with the church. I do not say this as one of those negative critics who can always find something wrong with the church. I say this as a minister of the gospel, who loves the church; who was nurtured in its bosom; who has been sustained by its spiritual blessings and who will remain true to it as long as the cord of life shall lengthen.

35   When I was suddenly catapulted into the leadership of the bus protest in Montgomery, Alabama, a few years ago, I felt we would be supported by the white church. I felt that the white ministers, priests and rabbis of the South would be among our strongest allies. Instead, some have been outright opponents, refusing to under-stand the freedom movement and misrepresenting its leaders; all too many others have been more cautious than courageous and have remained silent behind the anesthetizing security of stained-glass windows.

36   In spite of my shattered dreams, I came to Birmingham with the hope that the white religious leadership of this community would see the justice of our cause and, with deep moral concern, would serve as the channel through which our just grievances

Margin notes:

What types of proof are used in this third section?

Draw a line where the subject changes. What is the subject of the fourth section?

Reconsider the rhetorical situation: What went before? What will come later?

How does King build *ethos* in this fourth section?

What common ground did King hope for? How was he disappointed?

could reach the power structure. I had hoped that each of you would understand. But again I have been disappointed.

I have heard numerous southern religious leaders admonish their worshipers to comply with a desegregation decision because it is the law, but I have longed to hear white ministers declare: "Follow this decree because integration is morally right and because the Negro is your brother." In the midst of blatant injustices inflicted upon the Negro, I have watched white churchmen stand on the sideline and mouth pious irrelevancies and sanctimonious trivialities. In the midst of a mighty struggle to rid our nation of racial and economic injustice, I have heard many ministers say: "Those are social issues, with which the gospel has no real concern." And I have watched many churches commit themselves to a completely other-worldly religion which makes a strange, un-Biblical distinction between body and soul, between the sacred and the secular.

How and why does King use vivid description?

I have traveled the length and breadth of Alabama, Mississippi and all the other southern states. On sweltering summer days and crisp autumn mornings I have looked at the South's beautiful churches with their lofty spires pointing heavenward. I have beheld the impressive outlines of her massive religious-education buildings. Over and over I have found myself asking: "What kind of people worship here? Who is their God? Where were their voices when the lips of Governor Barnett dripped with words of interposition and nullification? Where were they when Governor Wallace gave a clarion call for defiance and hatred? Where were their voices of support when bruised and weary Negro men and women decided to rise from the dark dungeons of complacency to the bright hills of creative protest?"

Yes, these questions are still in my mind. In deep disappointment I have wept over the laxity of the church. But be assured that my tears have been tears of love. There can be no deep disappointment where there is not deep love. Yes, I love the church. How could I do otherwise? I am in the rather unique position of being the son, the grandson and the great-grandson of preachers. Yes, I see the church as the body of Christ. But, oh! How we have blemished and scarred that body through social neglect and through fear of being nonconformists.

What is the effect of the historical analogy?

There was a time when the church was very powerful—in the time when the early Christians rejoiced at being deemed worthy to suffer for what they believed. In those days the church was not merely a thermometer that recorded the ideas and principles of popular opinion; it was a thermostat that transformed the mores of society. Whenever the early Christians entered a town, the people in power became disturbed and immediately sought to convict the Christians for being "disturbers of the peace" and "outside agita-

37

38

39

40

tors." But the Christians pressed on, in the conviction that they were "a colony of heaven," called to obey God rather than man. Small in number, they were big in commitment. They were too God-intoxicated to be "astronomically intimidated." By their effort and example they brought an end to such ancient evils as infanticide and gladiatorial contests.

Things are different now. So often the contemporary church is a weak, ineffectual voice with an uncertain sound. So often it is an arch-defender of the status quo. Far from being disturbed by the presence of the church, the power structure of the average community is consoled by the church's silent—and often even vocal—sanction of things as they are.   41

But the judgment of God is upon the church as never before. If today's church does not recapture the sacrificial spirit of the early church, it will lose its authenticity, forfeit the loyalty of millions, and be dismissed as an irrelevant social club with no meaning for the twentieth century. Every day I meet young people whose disappointment with the Church has turned into outright disgust.   42

How does King contrast organized religion and the inner church? What is the effect?

Perhaps I have once again been too optimistic. Is organized religion too inextricably bound to the status quo to save our nation and the world? Perhaps I must turn my faith to the inner spiritual church, the church within the church, as the true *ekklesia* and the hope of the world. But again I am thankful to God that some noble souls from the ranks of organized religion have broken loose from the paralyzing chains of conformity and joined us as active partners in the struggle for freedom. They have left their secure congregations and walked the streets of Albany, Georgia, with us. They have gone down the highways of the South on tortuous rides for freedom. Yes, they have gone to jail with us. Some have been dismissed from their churches, have lost the support of their bishops and fellow ministers. But they have acted in the faith that right defeated is stronger than evil triumphant. Their witness has been the spiritual salt that has preserved the true meaning of the gospel in these troubled times. They have carved a tunnel of hope through the dark mountain of disappointment.   43

Why does King use historical analogies here?

I hope the church as a whole will meet the challenge of this decisive hour. But even if the church does not come to the aid of justice, I have no despair about the future. I have no fear about the outcome of our struggle in Birmingham, even if our motives are at present misunderstood. We will reach the goal of freedom in Birmingham and all over the nation, because the goal of America is freedom. Abused and scorned though we may be, our destiny is tied up with America's destiny. Before the pilgrims landed at Plymouth, we were here. Before the pen of Jefferson etched the majestic words of the Declaration of Independence across the pages of   44

What types of proof are used in the fourth section?

history, we were here. For more than two centuries our forebears labored in this country without wages; they made cotton king; they built the homes of their masters while suffering gross injustice and shameful humiliation—and yet out of a bottomless vitality they continued to thrive and develop. If the inexpressible cruelties of slavery could not stop us, the opposition we now face will surely fail. We will win our freedom because the sacred heritage of our nation and the eternal will of God are embodied in our echoing demands.

Before closing I feel impelled to mention one other point in your statement that has troubled me profoundly. You warmly commended the Birmingham police force for keeping "order" and "preventing violence." I doubt that you would have so warmly commended the police force if you had seen its dogs sinking their teeth into unarmed, nonviolent Negroes. I doubt that you would so quickly commend the policemen if you were to observe their ugly and inhumane treatment of Negroes here in the city jail; if you were to watch them push and curse old Negro women and young Negro girls; if you were to see them slap and kick old Negro men and young boys; if you were to observe them, as they did on two occasions, refuse to give us food because we wanted to sing our grace together. I cannot join you in your praise of the Birmingham police department.

It is true that the police have exercised a degree of discipline in handling the demonstrators. In this sense they have conducted themselves rather "nonviolently" in public. But for what purpose? To preserve the evil system of segregation. Over the past few years I have consistently preached that nonviolence demands that the means we use must be as pure as the ends we seek. I have tried to make clear that it is wrong to use immoral means to attain moral ends. But now I must affirm that it is just as wrong, or perhaps ever more so, to use moral means to preserve immoral ends. Perhaps Mr. Connor and his policemen have been rather nonviolent in public, as was Chief Pritchett in Albany, Georgia, but they have used the moral means of nonviolence to maintain the immoral end of racial injustice. As T. S. Eliot has said: "The last temptation is the greatest treason: To do the right deed for the wrong reason."

I wish you had commended the Negro sit-inners and the demonstrators of Birmingham for their sublime courage, their willingness to suffer and their amazing discipline in the midst of great provocation. One day the South will recognize its real heroes. They will be the James Merediths, with the noble sense of purpose that enables them to face jeering and hostile mobs, and with the agonizing loneliness that characterizes the life of the pioneer. They will be old, oppressed, battered Negro women, symbolized in a seventy-

45

46

47

Draw a line where the subject changes. What is the subject of section five?

What is the predominant type of proof in this fifth section?

Provide some examples.

Describe the effect.

two-year-old woman in Montgomery, Alabama, who rose up with a sense of dignity and with her people decided not to ride segregated buses, and who responded with ungrammatical profundity to one who inquired about her weariness: "My feets is tired, but my soul is at rest." They will be the young high school and college students, the young ministers of the gospel and a host of their elders, courageously and nonviolently sitting in at lunch counters and willingly going to jail for conscience' sake. One day the South will know that when these disinherited children of God sat down at lunch counters, they were in reality standing up for what is best in the American dream and for the most sacred values in our Judaeo-Christian heritage, thereby bringing our nation back to those great wells of democracy which were dug deep by the founding fathers in their formulation of the Constitution and the Declaration of Independence.

Draw a line to set off the conclusion. What is the concluding idea?

What is King's purpose in this conclusion?

Do you find the two letters convincing? Why, or why not?

Never before have I written so long a letter. I'm afraid it is much too long to take your precious time. I can assure you that it would have been much shorter if I had been writing from a comfortable desk, but what else can one do when he is alone in a narrow jail cell, other than write long letters, think long thoughts and pray long prayers? 48

If I have said anything in this letter that overstates the truth and indicates an unreasonable impatience, I beg you to forgive me. If I have said anything that understates the truth and indicates my having a patience that allows me to settle for anything less than brotherhood, I beg God to forgive me. 49

Are the clergymen's and King's arguments moral or immoral according to your values and standards?

I hope this letter finds you strong in the faith. I also hope that circumstances will soon make it possible for me to meet each of you, not as an integrationist or a civil-rights leader but as a fellow clergyman and a Christian brother. Let us all hope that the dark clouds of racial prejudice will soon pass away and the deep fog of misunderstanding will be lifted from our fear-drenched communities, and in some not too distant tomorrow the radiant stars of love and brotherhood will shine over our great nation with all their scintillating beauty. 50

Yours for the cause of Peace and Brotherhood,
MARTIN LUTHER KING, JR.

CHAPTER 9

Argument and Literature

The purpose of this chapter is to extend the applications of the argument theory that you have studied in the first eight chapters of this book and to suggest that you apply this theory both when you read imaginative literature and when you write papers about literature, including poetry, short stories, plays, and novels. Any theory that is applied to literature can help you look at it in whole new ways. Argument theory works this way also. Argument theory is useful for speculating about the ideas and themes in literature, especially when there is no general agreement about what these ideas are exactly, and it can also provide insight into literary characters, particularly into how they argue and interact with one another. Finally, argument theory can help you write papers about literature and argue in favor of your own understandings and insights.

A basic idea in this book has been that argument can be found everywhere and particularly where people are. Creative writers, along with the imaginative characters they create, are as argumentative as any other people. It should not surprise you that argument is as pervasive in literature as it is in real life. In fact, literature often raises issues, takes positions on them, and even changes people's views about them. Literature can be convincing because it invites readers to identify with its characters, which creates common ground, and because it almost always employs effective emotional appeal. Literature has high interest appeal as well. Argument achieved through literary narrative can be one of the most convincing forms of argument.

The rest of this chapter will provide you with examples and focus questions to help you apply argument theory to literature. The exercises at the end of this chapter will furnish you with sufficient practice to get you started. Note, also, that in the introductory material to each of the eight issues in "The Reader," the suggestion is made to expand your perspective on "The Reader" issues through literature and film. Specific examples of relevant literature and film are provided. Film, like literature, raises issues, makes claims, and changes people's views about controversial subjects. You can analyze arguments in film and write arguments about film just as you would a piece of literature.

FINDING AND ANALYZING ARGUMENTS IN LITERATURE

When you apply argument theory to the reading of literature, you will be "inside the text," so to speak, analyzing what is there and working to understand it. Your focus may be on the main argument made by the text, or it may be on one or more of the characters and the arguments they make. Let's consider first how to analyze the main argument.

What Is At Issue? What Is the Claim?

To use argument theory to read a literary text and analyze the main argument, focus on the issues raised in the work, on the perspectives that are expressed, and on the claims that are made. The claims may be explicit, overtly and openly expressed, or they may be implicit, covert and merely suggested, so that you will need to infer them yourself. There may also be conflicting claims in a single work that seem at times to contradict each other. The Toulmin model is useful for analyzing and understanding the main line of argument in a literary work.

For example, here is a poem that makes an explicit argument:

To the Virgins to Make Much of Time
Robert Herrick (1591–1674)

Gather ye rosebuds while ye may:
   Old Time is still a-flying;
And this same flower that smiles today,
   Tomorrow will be dying.

The glorious lamp of heaven, the sun,
   The higher he's a-getting,
The sooner will his race be run,
   And nearer he's to setting.

That age is best which is the first,
   When youth and blood are warmer;
But being spent, the worse, and worst
   Times still succeed the former.

Then be not coy, but use your time;
   And while ye may, go marry:
For having lost but once your prime,
   You may for ever tarry.

In applying the Toulmin model to this poem, most readers would agree that a policy claim is stated in the first line and restated in different language in the last stanza. There would not be much disagreement, furthermore, about that claim: young women should marry in their prime and not later, would be one way of putting it. Or, the poet's first line, "Gather ye rosebuds while ye may," serves as well to express the claim of this poem. The support is supplied in the form of reasons: time is flying, and it is better to marry when one is young than when one is old. The warrant that connects the support to the claim is that women will want to marry in the first place. Women who accept this warrant may be persuaded that they should, indeed, seize the day and wait no longer.

The claims in imaginative literature are not always this easy to identify. Sometimes it is necessary to ask some questions to identify what is at issue and to formulate the claim. Here are some questions to help you make these determinations:

1. What is most of this work about? This will help you identify the subject of the work.
2. Can the subject be regarded as controversial? That is, would it invite more than one perspective? This will help you discover the issues.
3. What positions are taken on the issue, and who takes them? This will help you discover both explicit and implicit claims along with who is making them: the author, a narrator, or various characters in the text.
4. If the claim is not stated, what evidence can I use from the text to help me state it myself? Draw on such evidence to help you make the claim explicit.
5. Will everyone agree that this is a viable claim, or will I need to make a case for it? Paper topics often come from disagreements over how to state the main argument in a literary work.

In her poem "The Mother," Gwendolyn Brooks begins, "Abortions will not let you forget." She continues by saying that she has never forgotten her "killed children," she ends the poem,

> oh, what shall I say, how is the truth to be said?
> You were born, you had body, you died.
> It is just that you never giggled or planned or cried.
>
> Believe me, I loved you all.
> Believe me, I knew you, though faintly, and I loved,
> I loved you all.

One could argue that the claim of the poem is in the first sentence, "Abortions will not let you forget," a claim of fact. However, by the time one has read the entire poem, one can also infer and make a case for a value claim, that abortions cause the mothers who seek them considerable psychological pain and are difficult for them to endure as time goes on. There is sufficient evidence in the poem to make an argument for that second claim as well.

Still other literary texts may express conflicting claims about an issue. In Frost's "Mending Wall," two claims are made about the issue concerning the value of fences. The two claims are, "Something there is that doesn't love a wall" and "Good fences make good neighbors." These claims contradict each other. Furthermore, careful readers have pointed out that convincing arguments are made for both of these positions in the poem. In the case of "Mending Wall," the poem tends to start an argument rather than deliver one.[1] Once again, paper top-

---

[1]Tim Morris provided me with some of the examples and insights in this chapter as well as with some of the literary examples in "The Reader."

ics come out of such disagreements and can provide you with material to write papers about. You can always take a position yourself on any argument started by a literary work.

In other literary texts arguments are made entirely through metaphor, as in Frost's poem "Birches," where swinging on birch trees becomes a way of escaping from the cares of life, or in another Frost poem, "The Road Not Taken," where the two roads in the poem become metaphors for two possible life choices. Metaphors are comparisons of items from two different categories. They work like figurative analogies since they invite readers to make unique mental connections and to expand their perspective on a subject in new and original ways. The meanings of metaphors in a literary work are often difficult to pin down exactly. Thus they become the subject of controversy and are often open to a variety of interpretations. The disputed meaning of a key metaphor in a literary work can become a fruitful paper topic.

Characters Making Arguments

The second way to employ argument theory to analyze literature is to apply it to specific arguments that are made by literary characters in the context of a literary text. Also enlightening is to consider how these individual characters' arguments contribute to the main argument of the text. The rhetorical situation, the modes of appeal, the identification of fallacies, and an application of the Toulmin model all help with this type of analysis.

It is further useful to identify the form that the argument takes in the work. Possibilities are listed in Chapter 1, pages 6 to 8. For example, a character may argue internally with himself as Hamlet does when he asks, "To be or not to be, that is the question . . ." in Shakespeare's *Hamlet*. A character may also argue with an imaginary audience as does the woman who constructs an imaginary argument with her child's counselor in the short story, "I Stand Here Ironing" by Tillie Olsen. Two individuals may argue one-on-one, both trying to convince the other, as in the poem "Myth" by Muriel Rukeyser; or, the character may make a single perspective argument to convince a mass audience as Marc Antony does in his speech that begins, "Friends, Romans, Countrymen, lend me your ears" in Shakespeare's *Julius Caesar*. The characters may argue in front of a third-party judge as they do in the play *Inherit the Wind*, which is about the Scopes "monkey trial." Identifying the form of the argument will help you understand the rhetorical situation in which it takes place. It will focus your attention on who is arguing, with whom they are arguing, and to what end.

A famous literary argument is Satan's persuasion of Eve in John Milton's seventeenth-century epic *Paradise Lost*. The story is familiar. Adam and Eve have been placed in the garden of Eden by God and have been told they may eat anything in the garden except the fruit from the tree of knowledge. The rhetorical situation goes like this: Satan is the arguer. He sneaks into the garden, enters the serpent, and in that guise, tempts Eve, his audience, to eat the forbidden fruit. This is a one-on-one argument with Satan trying to convince Eve. The exigence of Satan's argument is that he needs to get a foothold on earth so that he can spend more time there and less time in Hell, a very unpleasant place in this poem. Satan's constraints are that he must get Eve alone because he's afraid he cannot persuade Adam, Eve is a bit vain as he has discovered, and there are good angels around who could frustrate his plan. Thus, he decides to hide in the serpent. Satan's persuasive argument, full of fallacies as it is, is successful with Eve. She eats the fruit, she gets Adam to eat it also, and, as a result, they are expelled from the garden forever.

In the poem we witness the entire persuasive process that involves Satan and Eve, from the audience analysis carried on by Satan as he hides in the garden, watching Eve and analyzing her weaknesses, to the final changes in Eve's thought and action brought about by Satan's argumentative speeches. As part of this process, we overhear Satan's initial planning of his argument and, as he schemes and plans, we observe that there is a vast difference between his private feelings and beliefs and the "parts" he puts on in order to establish *ethos* with Eve. Satan is not an ethical arguer. He is an immoral manipulator. We also watch Satan deliberately plant a highly emotional version of the temptation in Eve's mind in the form of a dream. The remembered pleasure and emotional appeal of this dream will help make the later logical argument even more readily acceptable to Eve.

When Satan in the serpent delivers the speeches in Book 9 of the poem that finally convince Eve that she should eat the apple, he employs *ethos, pathos,* and *logos* to strengthen his argument. He flatters Eve, he appeals to her desire to be more powerful, he refutes what God has told her with fallacious reasoning, he uses induction to show that he ate the fruit and did not die so Eve will not die either, he points to himself as a sign of the intelligence and power that can come from eating the fruit, and he uses a deductive argument that can be summarized as follows:

> Eve should know evil in order to recognize good.
> Eating the fruit will help Eve know evil.
> Thus, Eve should eat the fruit in order to recognize good.

There are other examples of logical and emotional appeal in this argument that are not detailed here. Furthermore, if the Toulmin model is also employed to analyze Satan's argument, his purpose and strategy become even clearer, particularly as we examine some of his warrants. One of these, for example, is that humans want to become gods. Satan himself envies God and assumes that humans will also.

Another unique feature of the argument in *Paradise Lost* is that we are allowed to witness the argument outcomes. Not only do we observe Eve's outward actions, but we are also a party to her inner thoughts following Satan's speech. We see her eat the fruit. We also learn from her private musings how her reasoning, her emotional state, and the credibility she places in the serpent have been changed by Satan's speeches. We have a full explanation of what has convinced Eve to disobey God, and why the argument has been successful.

If you become interested in analyzing the argument in *Paradise Lost*, you might also like to know that Satan makes no fewer than twenty public addresses in the poem, and that his audiences range in size from the single Eve to the multitudes of the fallen angels. Furthermore, Adam, Eve, God, the Son, and some of the angels in the poem make arguments of their own that can be profitably analyzed with argument theory.

Here is a list of questions that you can use to help you analyze the arguments of fictional characters in literature. Note that these questions are only slightly changed from those listed on pages 267 to 268 that are provided there to help you analyze a prose reading such as Martin Luther King, Jr.'s "Letter from Birmingham Jail."

1. What is at issue in the literary work?
2. Who is the character taking a position on this issue, and what is the character's position on the issue?
3. What is the rhetorical situation for the argument?
4. What is the claim made by the character? Is it stated overtly? Or is it implied? Write it yourself as a statement and identify its type.
5. How does the character establish credibility? What logical and emotional proofs does the character use?
6. What type of language predominates: language that appeals to reason, language that appeals to emotion, or language that establishes credibility? Describe the language.
7. What are the warrants?
8. How does the character establish common ground? Through warrants? Through Rogerian argument? What else?
9. Are rebuttals used? How effective are they?
10. Are there fallacies? How do they distort the argument?
11. What are the outcomes of the argument? Is it convincing? To whom? What happens as a result?
12. Is the argument moral or immoral according to the standards established in the literary text itself? How would you evaluate the argument according to your own standards and values?
13. How does the argument made by the character contribute to the main argument of the text?

To help you learn to do an analysis of a literary argument, try analyzing Marc Antony's famous speech that begins, "Friends, Romans, Countrymen . . . ," from Shakespeare's *Julius Caesar.* It appears on page 312 of the Exercises and Activities section. A student-written analysis of this speech is provided as an example on page 316.

WRITING ARGUMENTS ABOUT LITERATURE

Argument theory can also be used to help you formulate your own argument about your insights and understanding of a literary text. At this point you will move "outside of the text," you will identify an issue about the text on which there is no general agreement, you will take a position on that issue, you will state your position in a claim, and you will present evidence from the text to prove it. Argument theory can be extremely beneficial in writing scholarly argument of this type. The Toulmin model will help you the most. It can help you identify an issue to write about in the first place, and it can also help you set up the elements of your argument.

Your first challenge will be to move from reading literature to writing about it. First, you will need to find an issue to write about. To help you find an issue, ask, *What is unclear about this text that I think I can explain?* or, *What is left out by the author that I think I can explain?* Focus on the main argument of the text, on the characters themselves, on what the narrator says about the characters, or on the meaning of metaphors to help you discover possible issues to write about. Controversy often resides in those locations. Also, issues may emerge in class discussion, or issues may come from the questions in your literature anthology. If all else fails, write a summary of a literary text along with your reaction to it. Then read your reaction and circle the most promising idea in it. It should be an idea that you think you can make a claim about and defend with evidence from the text.

Here are some examples of issues that appear in literary texts. In Henry James's novel *The Turn of the Screw* there is an unresolved question about whether the ghosts are real or not. One student actually went through the novel and highlighted all of the evidence in one color that suggests they are real and then highlighted all of the evidence in another color that suggests they are imaginary. According to this student, the quantity of evidence for both explanations was roughly comparable in the novel. If you decided to write about that issue, you could argue for either position and find plenty of people who would agree with you. Your instructor would evaluate your paper on the quality of its argument rather than whether or not you had resolved the controversy. Some literary controversies cannot be finally resolved any more than many issues in life can be finally resolved. Here is another example of a literary issue. At the end of Ernest Hemingway's short story "The Short Happy Life of Francis Macomber" a wounded and enraged buffalo charges the main character who is on an African safari. His wife shoots, but the bullet kills her husband instead of the buffalo. The "great white hunter" who is leading this expedition assumes the wife meant to kill her husband instead of the buffalo, and there is plenty of evidence in the story to suggest this might have been her intent. On the other hand, it is equally possible to argue that she was really shooting at the buffalo and hit her husband by mistake. You could write a paper in which you argue for either position just so long as you provide plenty of evidence from the story to support your position. In other words, you could make either position convincing. One student wrote a paper about a poem by William Butler Yeats in which she argued in favor of one interpretation, and she got an A. The next year, in another class, she argued in favor of a completely different interpretation of the same poem, and she got another A. In both cases she provided plenty of evidence from the poem itself to support the claims she made. Both of her arguments were convincing.

Here are some questions to help you make a claim about a literary work and write a convincing argument to support it:

1. What is an issue raised by this text that needs clarification?
2. What are the different perspectives that can be taken on this issue?
3. Which perspective will I take?
4. What support from the text will I use to defend my position?
5. What warrants are implicit in my argument, and will they be acceptable to the person who will evaluate this paper? Should I use backing for any of these warrants?
6. Would my paper be more convincing if I included a rebuttal of the opposing positions?
7. Will my claim be more acceptable to my audience if I qualify it?

Once you have read and thought about a literary text and you have answered these questions, you will write your paper just like you would write any other position paper in which your aim is to state what you think and provide evidence to support it. You can use suggestions from the other chapters in this book to help you meet this aim. The next three chapters will be particularly useful to you since they provide detailed information on how to write position papers, particularly those requiring research.

EXERCISES AND ACTIVITIES

1. WRITING ASSIGNMENT: ANALYZE THE ARGUMENT IN A POEM
The following poem was written by Langston Hughes in 1926 while he was a student at Columbia University in New York City. Read it, summarize it briefly, and write your reaction to it. Discuss it, using the questions at the end to guide your discussion.

THEME FOR ENGLISH B

Langston Hughes

The instructor said,

> Go home and write
> a page tonight.
> And let that page come out of you—
> Then, it will be true.

I wonder if it's that simple?

I am twenty-two, colored, born in Winston-Salem.
I went to school there, then Durham, then here
to this college on the hill above Harlem.
I am the only colored student in my class.

The steps from the hill lead down to Harlem,
through a park, then I cross St. Nicholas,
Eighth Avenue, Seventh, and I come to the Y,
the Harlem Branch Y, where I take the elevator
up to my room, sit down, and write this page:
It's not easy to know what is true for you or me
at twenty-two, my age. But I guess I'm what

I feel and see and hear. Harlem, I hear you:
hear you, hear me—we two—you, me talk on this page.
(I hear New York, too.) Me—who?

Well, I like to eat, sleep, drink, and be in love.
I like to work, read, learn, and understand life.
I like a pipe for a Christmas present,
or records—Bessie, bop, or Bach.

I guess being colored doesn't make me not like
the same things other folks like who are other races.
So will my page be colored that I write?
Being me, it will not be white.
But it will be
a part of you, instructor.
You are white—
yet a part of me, as I am a part of you.
That's American.

Sometimes perhaps you don't want to be a part of me.
Nor do I often want to be a part of you.
But we are, that's true!
As I learn from you,
I guess you learn from me—
although you're older—and white—
and somewhat more free.

This is my page for English B.

DISCUSSION QUESTIONS FOR "THEME FOR ENGLISH B"

a. What issues are raised in this poem? State them as questions.
b. What is the rhetorical situation?
c. Are any claims made? Are they explicit or implied? If implied, how would you put them into words?
d. What is the perspective in this poem? What other perspectives might be taken?
e. What support is offered for the position in the poem?
f. How does the author create common ground?
g. What are some of the warrants?

Write a 300–400 word paper about the main argument in this poem and how it is developed.

2. **WRITING ASSIGNMENT: AN ARGUMENT ABOUT A LITERARY WORK**
The purpose of this assignment is to discover an issue, make a claim, and write about your interpretation of a story. The author of the following story has said that she was prompted to write the story by a remark she came across in

William James's "The Moral Philosopher and the Moral Life." In it, James suggests that if multitudes of people could be "kept permanently happy on the one simple condition that a certain lost soul on the far-off edge of things should lead a life of lonely torment," our moral sense "would make us immediately feel" it would be an unequivocally unacceptable bargain. The story is written as a parable, that is, it is written to illustrate a principle. Think about these things as you read the story. Then answer the questions and follow the instructions for writing at the end.

THE ONES WHO WALK AWAY FROM OMELAS

Ursula K. LeGuin

With a clamor of bells that set the swallows soaring, the Festival of Summer came to the city Omelas, bright-towered by the sea. The rigging of the boats in harbor sparkled with flags. In the streets between houses with red roofs and painted walls, between old moss-grown gardens and under avenues of trees, past great parks and public buildings, processions moved. Some were decorous: old people in long stiff robes of mauve and gray, grave master workmen, quiet, merry women carrying their babies and chatting as they walked. In other streets the music beat faster, a shimmering of gong and tambourine, and the people went dancing, the procession was a dance. Children dodged in and out, their high calls rising like the swallows' crossing flights over the music and the singing. All the processions wound towards the north side of the city, where on the great water-meadow called the Green Fields boys and girls, naked in the bright air, with mudstained feet and ankles and long, lithe arms, exercised their restive horses before the race. The horses wore no gear at all but a halter without bit. Their manes were braided with streamers of silver, gold, and green. They flared their nostrils and pranced and boasted to one another; they were vastly excited, the horse being the only animal who has adopted our ceremonies as his own. Far off to the north and west the mountains stood up half encircling Omelas on her bay. The air of morning was so clear that the snow still crowning the Eighteen Peaks burned with white-gold fire across the miles of sunlit air, under the dark blue of the sky. There was just enough wind to make the banners that marked the racecourse snap and flutter now and then. In the silence of the broad green meadows one could hear the music winding through the city streets, farther and nearer and ever approaching, a cheerful faint sweetness of the air that from time to time trembled and gathered together and broke out into the great joyous clanging of the bells.

Joyous! How is one to tell about joy? How describe the citizens of Omelas?

They were not simple folk, you see, though they were happy. But we do not say the words of cheer much any more. All smiles have become archaic. Given a description such as this one tends to make certain assumptions. Given a description such as this one tends to look next for the King, mounted on a splendid stallion and surrounded by his noble knights, or perhaps in a golden litter borne by great-muscled slaves. But there was no king. They did not use swords, or keep slaves. They were not barbarians. I do not know the rules and laws of their society, but I suspect that they were singularly few. As they did without monarchy and slavery, so they also got on without the stock exchange, the advertisement, the secret police, and the bomb. Yet I repeat that these were not simple folk, not dulcet shepherds, noble savages, bland utopians. They were not less complex than us. The trouble is that we have a bad habit, encouraged by pedants and sophisticates, of considering happiness as something rather stupid. Only pain is intellectual, only evil interesting. This is the treason of the artist: a refusal to admit the banality of evil and the terrible boredom of pain. If you can't lick 'em, join 'em. If it hurts, repeat it. But to praise despair is to condemn delight, to embrace violence is to lose hold of everything else. We have almost lost hold, we can no longer describe a happy man, nor make any celebration of joy. How can I tell you about the people of Omelas? They were not naïve and happy children—though their children were, in fact, happy. They were mature, intelligent, passionate adults whose lives were not wretched. O miracle! but I wish I could describe it better. I wish I could convince you. Omelas sounds in my words like a city in a fairy tale, long ago and far away, once upon a time. Perhaps it would be best if you imagined it as your own fancy bids, assuming it will rise to the occasion, for certainly I cannot suit you all. For instance, how about technology? I think that there would be no cars or helicopters in and above the streets; this follows from the fact that the people of Omelas are happy people. Happiness is based on a just discrimination of what is necessary, what is neither necessary nor destructive, and what is destructive. In the middle category, however—that of the unnecessary but undestructive, that of comfort, luxury, exuberance, etc.—they could perfectly well have central heating, subway trains, washing machines, and all kinds of marvelous devices not yet invented here, floating light-sources, fuelless power, a cure for the common cold. Or they could have none of that: it doesn't matter. As you like it. I incline to think that people from towns up and down the coast have been coming in to Omelas during the last days before the Festival on very fast little trains and double-decked trams, and that the train station of Omelas is actually the handsomest building in town, though plainer than the magnificent Farmer's Market. But even granted trains, I fear that Omelas so far strikes some of you as goody-goody. Smiles, bells, parades, horses, bleh. If so, please add an orgy. If an orgy would help, don't hesitate. Let us not, however, have temples from which issue beautiful nude priests and priestesses already half in ecstasy and ready to copulate with any man or woman, lover or stranger, who desires union with the deep godhead of the blood, although that was my first idea. But really it would be better not to have any temples in Omelas—at least, not manned temples. Religion yes, clergy no. Surely the beautiful nudes can just wander about, offering themselves like divine soufflés to the hunger of the needy and the rapture of the flesh. Let them join the processions. Let tambourines be struck above the copulations, and the glory of desire be proclaimed upon the gongs, and (a not unimportant point) let the offspring of these delightful rituals be beloved and looked after by all. One thing I know there is none of in Omelas is guilt. But what else should there be? I thought that first there were no drugs, but that is puritanical. For those who like it, the faint insistent sweetness of *drooz* may perfume the ways of the city, *drooz* which first brings a great lightness and brilliance to the mind and limbs, and then after some hours a dreamy languor, and wonderful visions at last of the very arcana and inmost secrets of the Universe, as well as exciting the pleasure of sex beyond all belief; and it is not habit-forming. For more modest tastes I think there ought to be beer. What else, what else belongs in the joyous city? The sense of victory, surely, the celebration of courage. But as we did without clergy, let us do without soldiers. The joy built upon successful slaughter is not the right kind of joy; it will not do; it is fearful and it is trivial. A boundless and generous contentment, a magnanimous triumph felt not against some outer enemy but in communion with the finest and fairest in the souls of all men everywhere and the splendor of the world's summer: this is what swells the hearts of the people of Omelas, and the victory they celebrate is that of life. I really don't think many of them need to take *drooz*.

Most of the processions have reached the Green Fields by now. A marvelous smell of cooking goes forth from the red and blue tents of the provisioners. The faces of small children are amiably sticky; in the benign grey beard of a man a couple of crumbs of rich pastry are entangled. The youths and girls have mounted their horses and are beginning to group around the starting line of the course. An old woman, small, fat, and laughing, is passing out flowers from a basket, and tall young men wear her flowers in their shining hair. A child of nine or ten sits at the edge of the crowd, alone, playing on a wooden flute. People pause to listen, and they smile, but they do not speak to him, for he never ceases playing and never sees them, his dark eyes wholly rapt in the sweet, thin magic of the tune.

He finishes, and slowly lowers his hands holding the wooden flute.

As if that little private silence were the signal, all at once a trumpet sounds from the pavilion near the starting line: imperious, melancholy, piercing. The horses rear on their slender legs, and some of them neigh in answer. Sober-faced, the young riders stroke the horses' necks and soothe them, whispering, "Quiet, quiet, there my beauty, my hope. . . ." They begin to form in rank along the straight line. The crowds along the racecourse are like a field of grass and flowers in the wind. The Festival of Summer has begun.

Do you believe? Do you accept the festival, the city, the joy? No? Then let me describe one more thing.

In a basement under one of the beautiful public buildings of Omelas, or perhaps in the cellar of one of its spacious private homes, there is a room. It has one locked door, and no window. A little light seeps in dustily between cracks in the boards, secondhand from a cobwebbed window somewhere across the cellar. In one corner of the little room a couple of mops, with stiff, clotted, foul-smelling heads, stand near a rusty bucket. The floor is dirt, a little damp to the touch, as cellar dirt usually is. The room is about three paces long and two wide: a mere broom closet or disused tool room. In the room a child is sitting. It could be a boy or a girl. It looks about six, but actually is nearly ten. It is feeble-minded. Perhaps it was born defective, or perhaps it has become imbecile through fear, malnutrition, and neglect. It picks its nose and occasionally fumbles vaguely with its toes or genitals, as it sits hunched in the corner farthest from the bucket and the two mops. It is afraid of the mops. It finds them horrible. It shuts its eyes, but it knows the mops are still standing there; and the door is locked; and nobody will come. The door is always locked; and nobody ever comes, except that sometimes—the child has no understanding of time or interval—sometimes the door rattles terribly and opens, and a person, or several people, are there. One of them may come in and kick the child to make it stand up. The others never come close, but peer in at it with frightened, disgusted eyes. The food bowl and the water jug are hastily filled, the door is locked, the eyes disappear. The people at the door never say anything, but the child, who has not always lived in the tool room, and can remember sunlight and its mother's voice, sometimes speaks. "I will be good," it says. "Please let me out. I will be good!" They never answer. The child used to scream for help at night, and cry a good deal, but now it only makes a kind of whining, "eh-haa, eh-haa," and it speaks less and less often. It is so thin there are no calves to its legs; its belly protrudes; it lives on a half-bowl of corn meal and grease a day. It is naked. Its buttocks and thighs are a mass of festered sores, as it sits in its own excrement continually.

They all know it is there, all the people of Omelas. Some of them have come to see it, others are content merely to know it is there. They all know that it has to be there. Some of them understand why, and some do not, but they all understand that their happiness, the beauty of their city, the tenderness of their friendships, the health of their children, the wisdom of their scholars, the skill of their makers, even the abundance of their harvest and the kindly weathers of their skies, depend wholly on this child's abominable misery.

This is usually explained to children when they are between eight and twelve, whenever they seem capable of understanding; and most of those who come to see the child are young people, though often enough an adult comes, or comes back, to see the child. No matter how well the matter has been explained to them, these young spectators are always shocked and sickened at the sight. They feel disgust, which they had thought themselves superior to. They feel anger, outrage, impotence, despite all the explanations. They would like to do something for the child. But there is nothing they can do. If the child were brought up into the sunlight out of that vile place, if it were cleaned and fed and comforted, that would be a good thing, indeed; but if it were done, in that day and hour all the prosperity and beauty and delight of Omelas would wither and be destroyed. Those are the terms. To exchange all the goodness and grace of every life in Omelas for that single, small improvement: to throw away the happiness of thousands for the chance of the happiness of one: that would be to let guilt within the walls indeed.

The terms are strict and absolute; there may not even be a kind word spoken to the child.

Often the young people go home in tears, or in a tearless rage, when they have seen the child and faced this terrible paradox. They may brood over it for weeks or years. But as time goes on they begin to realize that even if the child could be released, it would not get much good of its freedom: a little vague pleasure of warmth and food, no doubt, but little more. It is too degraded and imbecile to know any real joy. It has been afraid too long ever to be free of fear. Its habits are too uncouth for it to respond to humane treatment. Indeed, after so long it would probably be wretched without walls about it to protect it, and darkness for its eyes, and its own excrement to sit in. Their tears at the bitter injustice dry when they begin to perceive the terrible justice of reality, and to accept it. Yet it is their tears and anger, the trying of their generosity and the acceptance of their helplessness, which are perhaps the true source of the splendor of their lives. Theirs is no vapid, irresponsible happiness. They know that they, like the child, are not free. They know compassion. It is the existence of the child, and their knowledge of its existence, that makes possible the nobility of their architecture, the poignancy of their music, the profundity of their science. It is because of the child that they are so gentle with children. They know that if the wretched one were not there sniveling in the dark, the other one, the flute-player, could make no joyful music as the young riders line up in their beauty for the race in the sunlight of the first morning of summer.

Now do you believe in them? Are they not more credible? But there is one more thing to tell, and this is quite incredible.

At times one of the adolescent girls or boys who go to see the child does not go home to weep or rage, does not, in fact, go home at all. Sometimes also a man or woman much older falls silent for a day or two, and then leaves home. These people go out into the street, and walk down the street alone. They keep walking, and walk straight out of the city of Omelas, through the beautiful gates. They keep walking across the farmlands of Omelas. Each one goes alone, youth or girl, man or woman. Night falls; the traveler must pass down village streets, between the houses with yellow-lit windows, and on out into the darkness of the fields. Each alone, they go west or north, towards the mountains. They go on. They leave Omelas, they walk ahead into the darkness, and they do not come back. The place they go towards is a place even less imaginable to most of us than the city of happiness. I cannot describe it at all. It is possible that it does not exist. But they seem to know where they are going, the ones who walk away from Omelas.[2]

DISCUSSION QUESTIONS: ANALYZE THE ARGUMENT IN "THE ONES WHO WALK AWAY FROM OMELAS":

a. What is this story about? What is the issue (or issues) raised by this story?
b. What are some of the perspectives in the story? Who takes them?
c. Write your version of a claim made by this story and put a few of these claims on the board. Which of these are viable claims that could be supported with evidence from the text, and which are not?

Discover an issue; make a claim; write a paper. Write answers to the following questions to help you think.

a. Build on your answers to the first three questions above: What still needs clarification about the issues raised in the story? For instance, what is un-

---

[2]Ursula K. LeGuin, Copyright 1973.

clear? What is left out or not wholly explained? Identify an issue for your paper and write it in question form.

b. What are the different perspectives that can be taken on this issue?

c. Which perspective will you take? Write a claim in the form of a statement.

d. What support from the text will you use to defend your claim?

e. What warrants are implicit in your argument? Will they be acceptable to the person who will evaluate this paper? Should you use backing for any of these warrants?

f. Would your paper be more convincing if you included a rebuttal of the opposing positions?

g. Will your claim be more acceptable to your audience if you qualify it?

h. Write a 500-word position paper defending the claim you have made about this story.

3. **CLASS PROJECT: CONDUCT A LITERARY DEBATE IN AN IMAGINARY COURTROOM ON AN ISSUE IN A PLAY**

The following play was later written as a short story entitled "A Jury of Her Peers." In 1916 the author wrote the play for the Provincetown Playhouse which she and her husband founded in Massachusetts in the early 1900s. The assignment that is detailed at the end will call on you to imagine the trial that might follow this play. Would you rather become a member of the prosecution, a member of the defense, or a member of the jury? Think about your answer as you read.

Play

TRIFLES

Susan Glaspell

Characters

GEORGE HENDERSON, *Country Attorney*
HENRY PETERS, *Sheriff*
LEWIS HALE, *A Neighboring Farmer*
MRS. PETERS
MRS. HALE

Scene: *The kitchen in the now abandoned farmhouse of* John Wright, *a gloomy kitchen, and left without having been put in order—unwashed pans under the sink, a loaf of bread outside the breadbox, a dish-towel on the table—other signs of incompleted work. At the rear the outer door opens and the* Sheriff *comes in followed by the* County Attorney *and* Hale. *The* Sheriff *and* Hale *are men in middle life, the* County Attorney *is a young man; all are much bundled up and go at once to the stove. They are followed by the two women—the* Sheriff's *wife first; she is a slight wiry woman, a thin nervous face.* Mrs. Hale *is larger and would ordinarily be called more comfortable looking, but she is dis-*

turbed now and looks fearfully about as she enters. The women have come in slowly, and stand close together near the door.

County Attorney: *(Rubbing his hands.)* This feels good. Come up to the fire, ladies.

Mrs. Peters: *(After taking a step forward.)* I'm not—cold.

Sheriff *(unbuttoning his overcoat and stepping away from the stove as if to the beginning of official business):* Now, Mr. Hale, before we move things about, you explain to Mr. Henderson just what you saw when you came here yesterday morning.

County Attorney: By the way, has anything been moved? Are things just as you left them yesterday?

Sheriff *(looking about):* It's just the same. When it dropped below zero last night, I thought I'd better send Frank out this morning to make a fire for us—no use getting pneumonia with a big case on; but I told him not to touch anything except the stove—and you know Frank.

County Attorney: Somebody should have been left here yesterday.

Sheriff: Oh—yesterday. When I had to send Frank to Morris Center for that man who went crazy—I want you to know I had my hands full yesterday. I knew you could get back from Omaha by today, and as long as I went over everything here myself—

County Attorney: Well, Mr. Hale, tell just what happened when you came here yesterday morning.

Hale: Harry and I had started to town with a load of potatoes. We came along the road from my place; and as I got here, I said, "I'm going to see if I can't get John Wright to go in with me on a party telephone." I spoke to Wright about it once before, and he put me off, saying folks talked too much anyway, and all he asked was peace and quiet—I guess you know about how much he talked himself; but I thought maybe if I went to the house and talked about it before his wife, though I said to Harry that I didn't know as what his wife wanted made much difference to John—

County Attorney: Let's talk about that later, Mr. Hale. I do want to talk about that, but tell now just what happened when you got to the house.

Hale: I didn't hear or see anything; I knocked at the door, and still it was all quiet inside. I knew they must be up, it was past eight o'clock. So I knocked again, and I thought I heard somebody say, "Come in." I wasn't sure, I'm not sure yet, but I opened the door—this door *(indicating the door by which the two women are still standing),* and there in that rocker—*(pointing to it)* sat Mrs. Wright. *(They all look at the rocker.)*

County Attorney: What—was she doing?

Hale: She was rockin' back and forth. She had her apron in her hand and was kind of—pleating it.

Country Attorney: And how did she—look?

Hale: Well, she looked queer.

Country Attorney: How do you mean—queer?

Hale: Well, as if she didn't know what she was going to do next. And kind of done up.

Country Attorney: How did she seem to feel about your coming?

Hale: Why, I don't think she minded—one way or other. She didn't pay much attention. I said, "How do, Mrs. Wright, it's cold, ain't it?" And she said, "Is it?"—and went on kind of pleating at her apron. Well, I was surprised; she didn't ask me to come up to the stove, or to set down, but just sat there, not even looking at me, so I said, "I want to see John." And then she—laughed. I guess you would call it a laugh. I thought of Harry and the team outside, so I said a little sharp: "Can't I see John?" "No," she says, kind o' dull like. "Ain't he home?" says I. "Yes," says she, "he's home." "Then why can't I see him?" I asked her, out of patience. "'Cause he's dead," says she. *"Dead?"* says I. She just nodded her head, not getting a bit excited, but rockin' back and forth. "Why—where is he?" says I, not knowing what to say. She just pointed upstairs—like that *(himself pointing to the room above).* I got up, with the idea of going up there. I walked from there to here—then I says, "Why, what did he die of?" "He died of a rope around his neck," says she, and just went on pleatin' at her apron. Well, I went out and called Harry. I thought I might—need help. We went upstairs, and there he was lyin'—

Country Attorney: I think I'd rather have you go into that upstairs, where you can point it all out. Just go on now with the rest of the story.

Hale: Well, my first thought was to get that rope off. I looked . . . *(Stops, his face twitches.)* . . . but Harry, he went up to him, and he said, "No, he's dead all right, and we'd better not touch anything." So we went back downstairs. She was still sitting that same way. "Has anybody been notified?" I asked. "No," says she, unconcerned. "Who did this, Mrs. Wright?" said Harry. He said it businesslike— and she stopped pleatin' of her apron. "I don't know," she says. "You don't *know*?" says Harry. "No," says she, "Weren't you sleepin' in the bed with him?" says Harry. "Yes," says she, "but I was on the inside." "Somebody slipped a rope round his neck and strangled him, and you didn't wake up?" says Harry. "I didn't wake up," she said after him. We must 'a looked as if we didn't see how that could be, for after a minute she said, "I sleep sound." Harry was going to ask her more questions, but I said maybe we ought to let her tell her story first to the coroner, or the sheriff, so Harry went fast as he could to Rivers' place, where there's a telephone.

County Attorney: And what did Mrs. Wright do when she knew that you had gone for the coroner?

Hale: She moved from that chair to this over here . . . *(Pointing to a small chair in the corner.)* . . . and just sat there with her hands held together and looking down. I got a feeling that I ought to make some conversation, so I said I had come in to see if John wanted to put in a telephone, and at that she started to laugh, and then she stopped and looked at me—scared. *(The County Attorney, who has had his notebook out, makes a note.)* I dunno, maybe it wasn't scared. I wouldn't like to say it was. Soon Harry got back, and then Dr. Lloyd came, and you, Mr. Peters, and so I guess that's all I know that you don't.

County Attorney (looking around): I guess we'll go upstairs first—and then out to the barn and around there. *(To the Sheriff.)* You're convinced that there was nothing important here—nothing that would point to any motive?

Sheriff: Nothing here but kitchen things. *(The County Attorney, after again looking around the kitchen, opens the door of a cupboard closet. He gets up on a chair and looks on a shelf. Pulls his hand away, sticky.)*

County Attorney: Here's a nice mess. *(The women draw nearer.)*

Mrs. Peters (to the other woman): Oh, her fruit; it did freeze. *(To the Lawyer.)* She worried about that when it turned so cold. She said the fire'd go out and her jars would break.

Sheriff: Well, can you beat the women! Held for murder and worryin' about her preserves.

County Attorney: I guess before we're through she may have something more serious than preserves to worry about.

Hale: Well, women are used to worrying over trifles. *(The two women move a little closer together.)*

County Attorney (with the gallantry of a young politician): And yet, for all their worries, what would we do without the ladies? *(The women do not unbend. He goes to the sink, takes a dipperful of water from the pail and, pouring it into a basin, washes his hands. Starts to wipe them on the roller towel, turns it for a cleaner place.)* Dirty towels! *(Kicks his foot against the pans under the sink.)* Not much of a housekeeper, would you say, ladies?

Mrs. Hale (stiffly): There's a great deal of work to be done on a farm.

County Attorney: To be sure. And yet . . . *(With a little bow to her.)* . . . I know there are some Dickson county farmhouses which do not have such roller towels. *(He gives it a pull to expose its full length again.)*

Mrs. Hale: Those towels get dirty awful quick. Men's hands aren't always as clean as they might be.

County Attorney: Ah, loyal to your sex. I see. But you and Mrs. Wright were neighbors. I suppose you were friends, too.

Mrs. Hale (shaking her head): I've not seen much of her of late years. I've not been in this house—it's more than a year.

County Attorney: And why was that? You didn't like her?

Mrs. Hale: I liked her well enough. Farmers' wives have their hands full, Mr. Henderson. And then—

County Attorney: Yes—?

Mrs. Hale (looking about): It never seemed a very cheerful place.

County Attorney: No—it's not cheerful. I shouldn't say she had the home-making instinct.

Mrs. Hale: Well, I don't know as Wright had, either.

County Attorney: You mean they didn't get on very well?

Mrs. Hale: No, I don't mean anything. But I don't think a place'd be any cheerfuller for John Wright's being in it.

County Attorney: I'd like to talk more of that a little later. I want to get the lay of things upstairs now. *(He goes to the left, where three steps lead to a stair door.)*

Sheriff: I suppose anything Mrs. Peters does'll be all right. She was to take in some clothes for her, you know, and a few little things. We left in such a hurry yesterday.

County Attorney: Yes, but I would like to see what you take, Mrs. Peters, and keep an eye out for anything that might be of use to us.

Mrs. Peters: Yes, Mr. Henderson. *(The women listen to the men's steps on the stairs, then look about the kitchen.)*

Mrs. Hale: I'd hate to have men coming into my kitchen, snooping around and criticizing. *(She arranges the pans under the sink which the Lawyer had shoved out of place.)*

Mrs. Peters: Of course it's no more than their duty.

Mrs. Hale: Duty's all right, but I guess that deputy sheriff that came out to make the fire might have got a little of this on. *(Gives the roller towel a pull.)* Wish I'd thought of that sooner. Seems mean to talk about her for not having things slicked up when she had to come away in such a hurry.

Mrs. Peters (who has gone to a small table in the left rear corner of the room, and lifted one end of a towel that cover a pan): She had bread set. *(Stands still.)*

Mrs. Hale (eyes fixed on a loaf of bread beside the breadbox, which is on a low shelf at the other side of the room. Moves slowly toward it): She was going to put this in there. *(Picks up loaf, then abruptly drops it. In a manner of returning to familiar things.)* It's a shame about her fruit. I wonder if it's all gone. *(Gets up on the chair and looks.)* I think there's some here that's all right, Mrs. Peters. Yes—here; *(Holding it toward the window.)* this is cherries, too. *(Looking again.)* I declare I believe that's the only one. *(Gets down, bottle in her hand. Goes to the sink and wipes it off on the outside.)* She'll feel awful bad after all her hard work in the hot weather. I remember the afternoon I put up my cherries last summer. *(She puts the bottle on the big kitchen table, center of the room. With a sigh, is about to sit down in the rocking chair. Before she is seated realizes what chair it is; with a slow look at it, steps back. The chair, which she has touched, rocks back and forth.)*

Mrs. Peters: Well, I must get those things from the front room closet. *(She goes to the door at the right, but after looking into the other room steps back.)* You coming with me, Mrs. Hale? You could help me carry them. *(They go into the other room; reappear, Mrs. Peters carrying a dress and skirt, Mrs. Hale following with a pair of shoes.)*

Mrs. Peters: My, it's cold in there. *(She puts the cloth on the big table, and hurries to the stove.)*

Mrs. Hale (examining the skirt): Wright was close. I think maybe that's why she kept so much to herself. She didn't even belong to the Ladies' Aid. I suppose she felt she couldn't do her part, and then you don't enjoy things when you feel shabby. She used to wear pretty clothes and be lively, when she was Minnie Foster, one of the town girls singing in the choir. But that—oh, that was thirty years ago. This all you was to take in?

Mrs. Peters: She said she wanted an apron. Funny thing to want, for there isn't much to get you dirty in jail, goodness knows. But I suppose just to make her feel more natural. She said they was in the top drawer in this cupboard. Yes, here. And then her little shawl that always hung behind the door. *(Opens stair door and looks.)* Yes, here it is. *(Quickly shuts door leading upstairs.)*

Mrs. Hale (abruptly moving toward her): Mrs. Peters?

Mrs. Peters: Yes, Mrs. Hale?

Mrs. Hale: Do you think she did it?

Mrs. Peters (in a frightened voice): Oh, I don't know.

Mrs. Hale: Well, I don't think she did. Asking for an apron and her little shawl. Worrying about her fruit.

Mrs. Peters (starts to speak, glances up, where footsteps are heard in the room above. In a low voice): Mr. Peters says it looks bad for her. Mr. Henderson is awful sarcastic in speech, and he'll make fun of her sayin' she didn't wake up.

Mrs. Hale: Well, I guess John Wright didn't wake when they was slipping that rope under his neck.

Mrs. Peters: No, it's strange. It must have been done awful crafty and still. They say it was such a—funny way to kill a man, rigging it all up like that.

Mrs. Hale: That's just what Mr. Hale said. There was a gun in the house. He says that's what he can't understand.

Mrs. Peters: Mr. Henderson said coming out that what was needed for the case was a motive; something to show anger or—sudden feeling.

Mrs. Hale (who is standing by the table): Well, I don't see any signs of anger around here. *(She puts her hand on the dish towel which lies on the table, stands looking down at the table, one half of which is clean, the other half messy.)* It's wiped here. *(Makes a move as if to finish work, then turns and looks at loaf of bread outside the breadbox. Drops towel. In that voice of coming back to familiar things.)* Wonder how they are finding things upstairs? I hope she had it a little more red-up there. You know, it seems kind of *sneaking.* Locking her up in town and then coming out here and trying to get her own house to turn against her!

Mrs. Peters: But, Mrs. Hale, the law is the law.

Mrs. Hale: I s'pose 'tis. *(Unbuttoning her coat.)* Better loosen up your things, Mrs. Peters. You won't feel them when you go out. *(Mrs. Peters takes off her fur tippet, goes to hang it on hook at the back of room, stands looking at the under part of the small corner table.)*

Mrs. Peters: She was piecing a quilt. *(She brings the large sewing basket, and they look at the bright pieces.)*

Mrs. Hale: It's log cabin pattern. Pretty, isn't it? I wonder if she was goin' to quilt or just knot it? *(Footsteps have been heard coming down the stairs. The Sheriff enters, followed by Hale and the County Attorney.)*

Sheriff: They wonder if she was going to quilt it or just knot it. *(The men laugh, the women look abashed.)*

County Attorney (rubbing his hands over the stove): Frank's fire didn't do much up there, did it? Well, let's go out to the barn and get that cleared up. *(The men go outside.)*

Mrs. Hale (resentfully): I don't know as there's anything so strange, our takin' up our time with little things while we're waiting for them to get the evidence. *(She sits down at the big table, smoothing out a block with decision.)* I don't see as it's anything to laugh about.

Mrs. Peters (apologetically): Of course they've got awful important things on their minds. *(Pulls up a chair and joins Mrs. Hale at the table.)*

Mrs. Hale (examining another block): Mrs. Peters, look at this one. Here, this is the one she was working on, and look at the sewing! All the rest of it has been so nice and even. And look at this! It's all over the place! Why, it looks as if she didn't know what she was about! *(After she has said this, they look at each other, then start to glance back at the door. After an instant Mrs. Hale has pulled at a knot and ripped the sewing.)*

Mrs. Peters: Oh, what are you doing, Mrs. Hale?

Mrs. Hale (mildly): Just pulling out a stitch or two that's not sewed very good. *(Threading a needle.)* Bad sewing always made me fidgety.

Mrs. Peters (nervously): I don't think we ought to touch things.

Mrs. Hale: I'll just finish up this end. *(Suddenly stopping and leaning forward.)* Mrs. Peters?

Mrs. Peters: Yes, Mrs. Hale?

Mrs. Hale: What do you suppose she was so nervous about?

Mrs. Peters: Oh—I don't know. I don't know as she was nervous. I sometimes sew awful queer when I'm just tired. *(Mrs. Hale starts to say something, looks at Mrs. Peters, then goes on sewing.)* Well, I must get these things wrapped up. They may be through sooner than we think. *(Putting apron and other things together.)* I wonder where I can find a piece of paper, and string.

Mrs. Hale: In that cupboard, maybe.

Mrs. Peters (looking in cupboard): Why, here's a birdcage. *(Holds it up.)* Did she have a bird, Mrs. Hale?

Mrs. Hale: Why, I don't know whether she did or not—I've not been here for so long. There was a man around last year selling canaries cheap, but I don't know as she took one; maybe she did. She used to sing real pretty herself.

Mrs. Peters (glancing around): Seems funny to think of a bird here. But she must have had one, or why should she have a cage? I wonder what happened to it?

Mrs. Hale: I s'pose maybe the cat got it.

Mrs. Peters: No, she didn't have a cat. She's got that feeling some people have about cats—being afraid of them. My cat got in her room, and she was real upset and asked me to take it out.

Mrs. Hale: My sister Bessie was like that. Queer, ain't it?

Mrs. Peters (examining the cage): Why, look, at this door. It's broke. One hinge is pulled apart.

Mrs. Hale (looking, too): Looks as if someone must have been rough with it.

Mrs. Peters: Why, yes. *(She brings the cage forward and puts it on the table.)*

Mrs. Hale: I wish if they're going to find any evidence they'd be about it. I don't like this place.

Mrs. Peters: But I'm awful glad you came with me, Mrs. Hale. It would be lonesome for me sitting here alone.

Mrs. Hale: It would, wouldn't it? *(Dropping her sewing.)* But I tell you what I do wish, Mrs. Peters. I wish I had come over sometimes when *she* was here. I— *(Looking around the room)*—wish I had.

Mrs. Peters: But of course you were awful busy, Mrs. Hale—your house and your children.

Mrs. Hale: I could've come. I stayed away because it weren't cheerful—and that's why I ought to have come. I—I've never liked this place. Maybe because it's down in a hollow, and you don't see the road. I dunno what it is, but it's a lonesome place and always was. I wish I had come over to see Minnie Foster sometimes. I can see now—*(Shakes her head.)*

Mrs. Peters: Well, you musn't reproach yourself, Mrs. Hale. Somehow we just don't see how it is with other folks until—something comes up.

Mrs. Hale: Not having children makes less work—but it makes a quiet house, and Wright out to work all day, and no company when he did come in. Did you know John Wright, Mrs. Peters?

Mrs. Peters: Not to know him; I've seen him in town. They say he was a good man.

Mrs. Hale: Yes—good; he didn't drink, and kept his word as well as most, I guess, and paid his debts. But he was a hard man, Mrs. Peters. Just to pass the time of day with him. *(Shivers.)* Like a raw wind that gets to the bone. *(Pauses, her eye falling on the cage.)* I should think she would 'a' wanted a bird. But what do you suppose went with it?

Mrs. Peters: I don't know, unless it got sick and died. *(She reaches over and swings the broken door, swings it again; both women watch it.)*

Mrs. Hale: You weren't raised around here, were you? *(Mrs. Peters shakes her head.)* You didn't know—her?

Mrs. Peters: Not till they brought her yesterday.

Mrs. Hale: She—come to think of it, she was kind of like a bird herself—real sweet and pretty, but kind of timid and—fluttery. How—she—did—change. *(Silence; then as if struck by a happy thought and relieved to get back to everyday things.)* Tell you what, Mrs. Peters, why don't you take the quilt in with you? It might take up her mind.

Mrs. Peters: Why, I think that's a real nice idea, Mrs. Hale. There couldn't possibly be any objection to it, could there? Now, just what would I take? I wonder if her patches are in here—and her things. *(They look in the sewing basket.)*

Mrs. Hale: Here's some red. I expect this has got sewing things in it. *(Brings out a fancy box.)* What a pretty box. Looks like something somebody would give you. Maybe her scissors are in here. *(Opens box. Suddenly puts her hand to her nose.)* Why—*(Mrs. Peters bends nearer, then turns her face away.)* There's something wrapped up in this piece of silk.

Mrs. Peters: Why, this isn't her scissors.

Mrs. Hale (lifting the silk): Oh, Mrs. Peters—it's—*(Mrs. Peters bends closer.)*

Mrs. Peters: It's the bird.

Mrs. Hale (jumping up): But, Mrs. Peters—look at it. Its neck! Look at its neck! It's all—other side to.

Mrs. Peters: Somebody—wrung—its neck. *(Their eyes meet. A look of growing comprehension of horror. Steps are heard outside. Mrs. Hale slips box under quilt pieces, and sinks into her chair. Enter Sheriff and County Attorney, Mrs. Peters rises.)*

County Attorney (as one turning from serious things to little pleasantries): Well, ladies, have you decided whether she was going to quilt it or knot it?

Mrs. Peters: We think she was going to—knot it.

County Attorney: Well, that's interesting, I'm sure. *(Seeing the birdcage.)* Has the bird flown?

Mrs. Hale (putting more quilt pieces over the box): We think the—cat got it.

County Attorney (preoccupied): Is there a cat? *(Mrs. Hale glances in a quick covert way at Mrs. Peters.)*

Mrs. Peters: Well, not now. They're superstitious, you know. They leave.

County Attorney (to Sheriff Peters, continuing an interrupted conversation): No sign at all of anyone having come from the outside. Their own rope. Now let's go up again and go over it piece by piece. *(They start upstairs.)* It would have to have been someone who knew just the—(Mrs. Peters sits down. The two women sit there not looking at one another, but as if peering into something and at the same time holding back. When they talk now, it is the manner of feeling their way over strange ground, as if afraid of what they are saying, but as if they cannot help saying it.)*

Mrs. Hale: She liked the bird. She was going to bury it in that pretty box.

Mrs. Peters (in a whisper): When I was a girl—my kitten—there was a boy took a hatchet, and before my eyes—and before I could get there—(Covers her face an instant.)* If they hadn't held me back, I would have—(Catches herself, looks upstairs where steps are heard, falters weakly.)—hurt him.

Mrs. Hale (with a slow look around her): I wonder how it would seem never to have had any children around. *(Pause.)* No, Wright wouldn't like the bird—a thing that sang. She used to sing. He killed that, too.

Mrs. Peters (moving uneasily): We don't know who killed the bird.

Mrs. Hale: I knew John Wright.

Mrs. Peters: It was an awful thing was done in this house that night, Mrs. Hale. Killing a man while he slept, slipping a rope around his neck that choked the life out of him.

Mrs. Hale: His neck. Choked the life out of him. *(Her hand goes out and rests on the birdcage.)*

Mrs. Peters (with a rising voice): We don't know who killed him. We don't know.

Mrs. Hale (her own feeling not interrupted): If there'd been years and years of nothing, then a bird to sing to you, it would be awful—still, after the bird was still.

Mrs. Peters (something within her speaking): I know what stillness is. When we homesteaded in Dakota, and my first baby died—after he was two years old, and me with no other then—

Mrs. Hale (moving): How soon do you suppose they'll be through, looking for evidence?

Mrs. Peters: I know what stillness is. *(Pulling herself back.)* The law has got to punish crime, Mrs. Hale.

Mrs. Hale (not as if answering that): I wish you'd seen Minnie Foster when she wore a white dress with blue ribbons and stood up there in the choir and sang.

(*A look around the room.*) Oh, I *wish* I'd come over here once in a while! That was a crime! That was a crime! Who's going to punish that?

Mrs. Peters (looking upstairs): We mustn't—take on.

Mrs. Hale: I might have known she needed help! I know how things can be—for women. I tell you, it's queer, Mrs. Peters. We live close together and we live far apart. We all go through the same things—it's all just a different kind of the same thing. (*Brushes her eyes, noticing the bottle of fruit, reaches out for it.*) If I was you, I wouldn't tell her her fruit was gone. Tell her it *ain't.* Tell her it's all right. Take this in to prove it to her. She—she may never know whether it was broke or not.

Mrs. Peters (takes the bottle, looks about for something to wrap it in; takes petticoat from the clothes brought from the other room, very nervously begins winding this around the bottle. In a false voice): My, it's a good thing the men couldn't hear us. Wouldn't they just laugh! Getting all stirred up over a little thing like a—dead canary. As if that could have anything to with—with—wouldn't they *laugh!* (*The men are heard coming downstairs.*)

Mrs. Hale (under her breath): Maybe they would—maybe they wouldn't.

County Attorney: No, Peters, it's all perfectly clear except a reason for doing it. But you know juries when it comes to women. If there was some definite thing. Something to show—something to make a story about—a thing that would connect up with this strange way of doing it. (*The women's eyes meet for an instant. Enter Hale from outer door.*)

Hale: Well, I've got the team around. Pretty cold out there.

County Attorney: I'm going to stay here a while by myself. (*To the Sheriff.*) You can send Frank out for me, can't you? I want to go over everything. I'm not satisfied that we can't do better.

Sheriff: Do you want to see what Mrs. Peters is going to take in? (*The Lawyer goes to the table, picks up the apron, laughs.*)

County Attorney: Oh I guess they're not very dangerous things the ladies have picked up. (*Moves a few things about, disturbing the quilt pieces which cover the box. Steps back.*) No, Mrs. Peters doesn't need supervising. For that matter, a sheriff's wife is married to the law. Ever think of it that way, Mrs. Peters?

Mrs. Peters: Not—just that way.

Sheriff (chuckling): Married to the law. (*Moves toward the other room.*) I just want you to come in here a minute, George. We ought to take a look at these windows.

County Attorney (scoffingly): Oh, windows!

Sheriff: We'll be right out, Mr. Hale.

(*Hale goes outside. The Sheriff follows the County Attorney into the other room. Then Mrs. Hale rises, hands tight together, looking intensely at Mrs. Peters, whose eyes take a slow turn, finally meeting Mrs. Hale's. A moment Mrs. Hale holds her, then her own eyes point the way to where the box is concealed. Suddenly Mrs. Peters throws back quilt pieces and tries to put the box in the bag she is wearing. It is too big. She opens box, starts to take the bird out, cannot touch it, goes to pieces, stands there helpless. Sound of a knob turning in the other room. Mrs. Hale snatches the box and puts it in the pocket of her big coat. Enter County Attorney and Sheriff.*)

County Attorney (facetiously): Well, Henry, at least we found out that she was not going to quilt it. She was going to—what is it you call it, ladies?

Mrs. Hale (her hand against her pocket): We call it—knot it, Mr. Henderson.

ASSIGNMENT FOR A LITERARY DEBATE[3] ON *TRIFLES*

a. **Set the scene and create some groups.** Imagine that the classroom is a courtroom. Mrs. Wright will be on trial. The birdcage, the box with the bird in it, and the rope used to strangle Mr. Wright will be placed on the table as evidence. One third of the class will identify themselves as members of the prosecution whose role is to prove Mrs. Wright guilty of the murder of her husband. One third of the class will identify themselves as members of the defense who will come up with a strategy for defending Mrs. Wright. Options are to argue that she is not guilty, that she is not guilty by reason of insanity, or that she is guilty but should be extended leniency. The members of the defense should meet briefly at the end of the class that precedes the trial to decide on the strategy they will use to defend Mrs. Wright. The final third of the class will become the jury who will write critiques of the prosecution and the defense and make a decision about whether Mrs. Wright should or should not be found guilty of murder. The instructor is the judge whose role is to keep things moving along.

The day before the trial, the class should divide themselves into these three groups. Each member of the prosecution and each member of the defense should then prepare written arguments of approximately 250 words for the next class period. They should express a clear position and provide plenty of evidence and reasons as support. Class members should get as much evidence from the text as possible. The evidence may also be related to personal experience and knowledge from other classes. A psychology class, for example, may provide evidence about probable human behavior. Class members may draw on character, cause, factual evidence, and the values of those involved. They should remember that value systems can contradict each other. They should be aware of warrants that the jury is likely to hold. Each student should present a case as clearly and logically as possible.

b. **Conduct the trial.** The prosecution and defense meet as groups at the beginning of class to decide on speaking order. The first speaker should read and the others may add additional evidence and arguments from their papers. During this time the jury should assemble and elect a jury foreman who will later deliver the verdict.

The format is as follows:

Each side has ten minutes to present their case. This presentation will be followed by a ten-minute break during which each side will formulate rebuttals to the points that their opponents have made. Each side will have five minutes to rebut their opponent's arguments. No one may interrupt the other side at any time. The jury then meets briefly, votes, and gives the decision of the majority.

---

[3]I am indebted to Audrey Wick for this assignment.

Each member of the jury writes a 250-word paper outside of class giving reasons for voting either in favor of the defense or in favor of the prosecution.

4. **WRITING ASSIGNMENT: ANALYZE THE ARGUMENT OF A LITERARY CHARACTER**

The following speeches are made by Marc Antony in Shakespeare's *Julius Caesar*. The rhetorical situation is as follows: Caesar has been stabbed to death by Brutus and other conspirators and denounced as an unfit ruler of Rome. Antony, loyal to Caesar, has been allowed to give the funeral oration. Brutus has told Antony that he is not to say anything that would reflect badly on any of the conspirators. See what Antony does instead. Then answer the questions at the end of these speeches and follow the instructions for the writing assignment.

ANTONY'S FUNERAL SPEECH FOR CAESAR

from Shakespeare's *Julius Caesar*

Speech

Antony: Friends, Romans, countrymen, lend me your ears.
I come to bury Caesar, not to praise him.
The evil that men do lives after them:
The good is oft interred with their bones.
So let it be with Caesar. The nobles Brutus
Hath told you Caesar was ambitious.
If it were so, it was a grievous fault,
And grievously hath Caesar answered it.
Here, under leave of Brutus and the rest—
For Brutus is an honorable man,
So are they all, all honorable men—
Come I to speak in Caesar's funeral.
He was my friend, faithful and just to me;
But Brutus says he was ambitious,
And Brutus is an honorable man.
He hath brought many captives home to Rome,
Whose ransoms did the general coffers fill.
Did this in Caesar seem ambitious?
When that the poor have cried, Caesar hath wept;
Ambition should be made of stronger stuff.
Yet Brutus says he was ambitious,
And Brutus is an honorable man.
You all did see that on the Lupercal
I thrice presented him a kingly crown,
Which he did thrice refuse. Was this ambition?
Yet Brutus says he was ambitious,
And sure he is an honorable man.
I speak not to disprove what Brutus spoke,

> But here I am to speak of what I do know.
> You all did love him once, not without cause.
> What cause withholds you then to mourn for him?
> O judgment! Thou art fled to brutish beasts,
> And men have lost their reason. Bear with me;
> My heart is in the coffin there with Caesar,
> And I must pause till it come back to me.

The audience here makes a few comments about the passion in Antony's speaking, and Antony speaks again.

Antony: But yesterday the word of Caesar might
     Have stood against the world. Now lies her there,
     And none so poor to do him reverence.
     O masters! If I were disposed to stir
     Your hearts and minds to mutiny and rage,
     I should do Brutus wrong, and Cassius wrong,
     Who, you all know, are honorable men.
     I will not do them wrong; I rather choose
     To wrong the dead, to wrong myself and you,
     Than I will wrong such honorable men.
     But here's a parchment with the seal of Caesar.
     I found it in his closet; 'tis his will. *(He shows the will).*
     Let but the commons hear this testament—
     Which, pardon me, I do not mean to read—
     And they would go and kiss dead Caesar's wounds
     And dip their napkins in his sacred blood,
     Yea, beg a hair of him for memory,
     And dying, mention it within their wills,
     Bequeathing it as a rich legacy
     Unto their issue.

All: The will, the will! We will hear Caesar's will!

Antony: Have patience, gentle friends: I must not read it.
     It is not meet you know how Caesar loved you.
     You are not wood, you are not stones, but men;
     And being men, hearing the word of Caesar,
     It will inflame you, it will make you mad.
     'Tis good you know not that you are his heirs,
     For if you should, O, what would come of it?

Antony steps off the podium and stands by Caesar's body.

Antony: If you have tears, prepare to shed them now.
     You all do know this mantle. I remember
     The first time ever Caesar put it on;
     'Twas on a summer's evening in his tent,
     That day he overcame the Nervii.

Look, in this place ran Cassius' dagger through.
See what a rent the envious Casca made.
Through this the well-beloved Brutus stabbed,
And as he plucked his cursed steel away,
Mark how the blood of Caesar followed it,
As rushing out of doors to be resolved
If Brutus so unkindly knocked or no—
For Brutus, as you know, was Caesar's angel.
Judge, O you gods, how dearly Caesar loved him!
This was the most unkindest cut of all;
For when the noble Caesar saw him stab,
Ingratitude, more strong than traitors' arms,
Quite vanquished him. Then burst his mighty heart,
And in his mantle muffling up his face,
Even at the base of Pompey's statue,
Which all the while ran blood, great Caesar fell.
O, what a fall was there, my countrymen!
Then I, and you, and all of us fell down,
Whilst bloody treason flourished over us.
O, now you weep, and I perceive you feel
The dint of pit. These are gracious drops.
Kind souls, what, weep you when you but behold
Our Caesar's vesture wounded? Look you here,
Here is himself, marred as you see with traitors.
(He lifts Caesar's mantle)

Antony finally reads Caesar's will which proves Caesar's generosity towards the citizens of Rome. The audience is inflamed by Antony's speech.

QUESTIONS ON ANTONY'S FUNERAL ORATION.

Break the class into five groups. Each group will take one of the questions below, work for ten minutes, and then report back to the class.

a. What is the issue? What is Antony's ostensible purpose in this speech to the Roman people? What is his actual purpose? How does the rhetorical situation constrain Antony? How does Antony build common ground with his audience?

b. Use the Toulmin model and state Antony's claim, support, and warrants. Are there any rebuttals? Qualifiers?

c. How does Antony use emotional appeal and incite *pathos* in his audience? Cite examples in the speech that cause the audience to feel emotion.

d. What are some examples of logical appeal that Antony uses to persuade the audience?

e. How does Antony destroy the *ethos* of the conspirators? How does he develop a positive *ethos* for himself? Would you say that Antony is a moral or immoral speaker in the context of the play?

Writing Assignment

Write a 500 to 750 word paper in which you draw on the answers to the above questions to explain Antony's argumentative strategy in his speech to the Roman people. At the end of your paper, write your responses to the following questions: Did Marc Antony accomplish his purpose? What do you think were the most persuasive parts of the speech?

When you have written your paper, you may want to read the student example that appears on page 316.

5. **QUESTIONS ON THE CHAPTER**
   a. How can argument theory be used in the study of literature? Name and describe the three approaches described in the chapter.
   b. What are some of the questions the reader can ask to arrive at a claim in a work of literature? What are some of the ways in which claims are expressed in literature?
   c. Describe the argument theory you would employ to help you analyze an argument that a character makes in a literary work.
   d. What are some of the suggestions made in this chapter to help you find a topic for a position paper you might write about an issue in literature?
   e. What is your main responsibility as a writer when you argue on one side or the other of a literary issue?

6. **QUESTIONS ON THE LITERATURE**
   a. "Theme for English B," page 294. What is the relationship established between the teacher and the student in this poem? Think about similarities, differences, and common ground between them. How does the student in the poem interpret the writing assignment? How does he respond to it? What do you think of his version of this assignment?
   b. "The Ones Who Walk Away From Omelas," page 296. How is happiness defined in this poem? Who gets to define it? Why? Why do some walk away? Make some connections: what actual societies or organized groups of people existing either now or in history might be suggested by this parable? Why do you think so?
   c. *Trifles*, page 301. Characterize the men and the women in this play. What is the relationship between them? What contributes to this relationship? What are the results of it in the play? How do you think Mr. Wright died? What evidence is there in the play to support your answer? Why is the play called *Trifles*?
   d. "Friends, Romans, Countrymen," page 312. Visualize the scene for this speech. What do you see? How does the audience act before Antony begins to speak? How are they affected by the speech? What is the effect of repeating the refrain, "For Brutus is an honorable man"? What historical evidence does Antony draw on? What physical evidence does he point to? What is the effect of his evidence?

MARC ANTONY'S ARGUMENT

Sara Orr

In William Shakespeare's *Julius Caesar*, Marc Antony delivers a very persuasive argument to the commoners of Rome. On March 15, Marcus Brutus and several other conspirators joined together and murdered Julius Caesar. Following this ghastly attack, Marcus Brutus spoke to the commoners and convinced them that what he had done was for the good of Rome. Brutus described Caesar as an overly ambitious ruler, who had to be stopped before he gained too much power. Brutus was very successful in persuading the commoners to see and support his side of the situation. When Marc Antony was allowed to speak, Brutus' only stipulation was that Antony could not in any way blame the conspirators for their act. He was only to deliver a funeral speech for Julius Caesar. Marc Antony took this opportunity to speak to the audience and present his own argument about Caesar's death. It is in this famous speech that many elements of argument prove to be successful tools in effectively changing an audience's perspective.

Marc Antony first states his purpose to his audience. He claims to be there to bury Caesar, not to praise him in any way. This enables the audience to open up their minds to what Antony is going to say. His true purpose though evolves during the speech. His goal is to convince the audience that the act that Brutus and the conspirators did was not honorable, and therefore, they were wrong in murdering Caesar. Because Marc Antony promised not to blame the conspirators, he must reach this goal deceptively. He uses the modes of classical appeal: *logos, pathos,* and *ethos.* These elements enable Antony to persuade the crowd to change their view of Brutus and the death of Caesar.

Antony uses several examples of logical appeal in his speech to the Romans. He gives them hard evidence to prove that Caesar was not too ambitious, nor was he cruel and ruthless. Antony details events such as the offer of the crown at the Feast of Lupercal which Caesar denied three times. This surely did not seem ambitious. Antony also reminds the audience of the many ransoms Caesar has brought home to Rome that have filled the coffers. Again, this does not seem ambitious. Antony also produces Caesar's will, and tempts the audience into forcing him to read it. This tangible piece of Caesar's generosity helps persuade the common crowd to see that Caesar was not as ambitious as Brutus had said.

Marc Antony destroys the *ethos* or character of the conspirators while promoting his own *ethos* to the crowd. One of the ways he destroys the *ethos* of the conspirators is through the repetition of the lines, "For Brutus is an honorable man, So are they all honorable men." It is soon clear that Antony is being satirical in using these lines. In repeating these "honorable" lines, Marc Antony soon causes the Roman crowd to question the idea of whether or not these men were truly honorable. Antony's persuasive strategy depends on the warrant that the act of murder is not honorable, so these men could not be honorable. If the crowd can see this through his repetition of these lines about honor, he will be successful in destroying the *ethos* of the conspirators. He creates his own positive *ethos* by being very humble and mournful for Caesar. He claims he must pause because he is so overcome with grief that he can no longer speak. This causes the audience to sympathize with Antony. He continues to build this positive view of himself when he produces the will. He tells the commoners that he should not read it to them because it would hurt them to know how much Caesar loved them. He speaks as though his first concern is the people's feelings, and this adds to his positive *ethos*.

However, Antony's most persuasive technique is his ability to incite *pathos* or emotion in the audience. He is capable of changing the anger the commoners have for Caesar to tears of sadness for their ruler and revenge for his death. He begins by disclaiming the idea that Caesar was ambitious. This lures the crowd into Antony's speech so that he can incite emotion in them. When he produces the will, he begs the crowd not to make him read it. It would make them angry to know how much Caesar loved them. "And being men, hearing the word of Caesar/It will inflame you, it will make you mad." The temptation is too great, and the crowd forces Antony to read the will. He then leads the audience to tears as he recreates the murder scene. He points to each of the stab wounds seen in Caesar's cloak. Antony gives a name to each stab wound making it much more personal to the crowd. When he shows where the beloved Brutus stabbed, it is almost too much for the commoners to bear. He calls it the "most unkindest cut of all" since Brutus was Caesar's favorite, his angel. Even after the crowd is shedding tears, Antony goes one step further: he removes Caesar's mantle so that his bare, bloody body is there for the crowd to witness. "Here is himself, marred as you see with traitors." By this time, the crowd is so angry and sorrowful, they are driven to riot and rage, just as Marc Antony planned.

Marc Antony was definitely successful in moving the audience. Although he never states his true claim or purpose, it becomes quite evident through his support what his feelings are about this murderous event. The challenge laid before Antony was great, but he overcame it through the powerful uses of argument. His ability to maneuver the crowd from one side completely to the other was done through the use of argument. Had Brutus known the power of argument that Antony commanded, he may not have allowed Antony to speak to the crowd of Romans in the first place.[4]

---

[4]Used with permission.

PART THREE

Writing a Research Paper That Presents an Argument

The purpose of these last three chapters is to teach you to write an argument paper from your own perspective that incorporates research materials from outside sources. Since other professors or even employers may also ask you to produce such papers, this instruction should be useful to you not only now but in the future as well. Chapter 10 teaches you to write a claim, clarify the purpose for your paper, and analyze your audience. Chapter 11 teaches you various creative strategies for inventing and gathering research material for your paper. Chapter 12 teaches ways to organize this material, write and revise the paper, and prepare the final copy. Methods for locating and using resource materials from the library are also included in Chapters 11 and 12. When you finish reading Part Three:

- You will know how to write your claim and determine the main argumentative purpose of your paper.
- You will know how to analyze your audience and predict how it might change.
- You will know how to think about your claim and gather material from your own background and experience to support it.
- You will know how to organize and conduct library and computer research to support your claim further.
- You will know a variety of possible ways to organize the ideas for your paper.
- You will know how to incorporate research materials into your paper and prepare the final copy.

CHAPTER 10

Clarifying Purpose and Understanding the Audience

This chapter and the two that follow will help you plan, research, and write an argument paper, referred to from now on as a "position paper," in which you state your claim and prove it. Chaim Perelman's definition of argument quoted in Chapter 1 will help you focus on your final objective in writing this paper: you will seek "to create or increase the adherence of minds to the theses presented for their [the audience's] assent."[1] In other words, you will try to get your reading audience to agree, at least to some extent, with your claim and the ideas you use to support it.

UNDERSTANDING THE ASSIGNMENT AND GETTING STARTED

The position paper will be completed in stages as you work your way through this and the next two chapters. The final assignment for writing the position paper appears on page 390. You may want to read it now so that you will know the final goal of these three chapters.

To get started on your paper you need to select an issue. There is advice on how to do that in Chapter 1. Any issue that you consider using should be submitted to the twelve tests for an arguable issue that appear on page 26. These tests will help you ascertain whether or not your issue is potentially arguable. You may also want to write an issue proposal, also taught in Chapter 1, to help you clarify your initial thinking. As a reminder, here is an example of an issue proposal written by a student interested in finding creative ways of using prisoners' time while they are in jail. Note how the issue proposal helped him focus his issue, think about the context for it, articulate his own interest in it, recall what he already knew about it, and plan what else he needed to learn.

---

[1]Chaim Perelman and L. Olbrechts-Tyteca, *The New Rhetoric: A Treatise on Argumentation* (Notre Dame, IN: Notre Dame Press, 1969), p. 45.

ISSUE PROPOSAL: PRISON LABOR

Shawn Farnsworth

Everyone is aware of criminal activity, and it has some psychological or emotional impact on every person. There must be some way to ease the mental burden crime places on the general public and, further, to find a way in which criminals might repay their social debt in a way that would benefit both them and society. The purpose of criminal punishment is not solely to incarcerate criminals, but also to rehabilitate them. Is it possible to make significant advances toward rehabilitation and repayment of the social debt incurred by criminals through the use of prison labor? Perhaps under the proper conditions, this is a possible solution.

Every year, Americans pay thousands of dollars in taxes just to support one prisoner. It seems almost abusive to spend so much tax money to maintain the simple life of a person whose actions are immobilized through incarceration. Additionally, the apparent lack of use of such an enormous amount of manpower borders on wastefulness. I find the concept of prison labor compelling because not only does the possibility of a reduction in taxes exist, but there is the opportunity for prisoners to acquire new skills and abilities, thus benefitting themselves as well as society. After all, skilled laborers are an asset to society, and jail might provide a splendid opportunity to change negative forces in society to positive ones.

I know that prison labor is used in many states to make everything from license plates to designer jeans. However, while many people support prison labor, there are those who oppose it, saying that it is slave labor and that it has a bad effect on competing businesses. The way in which prison labor is conducted and the results of its use also vary from state to state. In some cases, prisoners are contracted by organizations outside of the prisons, and in other instances, work may be done for the government or for the prison itself. In some places the prisoners are paid for the work they do, although the wages are low and much of the money goes to the prison.

In order to make a fair assessment in support of prison labor, clearly I will need to know more about how prison labor is currently being used. Furthermore, I will need to accumulate information about labor laws, criminal laws, and the effects of prison labor on other businesses. It would also be crucial to study how labor affects rehabilitation and how the general public perceives it. I would like, finally, to be able to propose ways to make the use of prison labor more uniformly accepted and more consistently practiced. In a sincere effort to develop and refine prison labor programs, we may discover the rehabilitative benefits to the prisoner of good hard work.[2]

---

[2]Used with permission.

After writing the issue proposal, you may also want to explore your issue further by doing some initial reading about it and writing an exploratory paper. The exploratory paper, which is taught in Chapter 4, pages 110 and 113, invites you to look at three or more existing perspectives on your issue. Writing this paper helps you find your perspective on your issue, and it also helps you understand other perspectives so that you can refute them better.

The student who wrote the issue proposal on prison labor followed it with an exploratory paper in which he identified the following three perspectives on his issue: (1) Some people believe that the status quo is fine, and there should be no changes. These people argue that prisoners provide labor that other people don't want to do. To expand the prison labor system might create harmful competition with outside labor. (2) Other people oppose prison labor. They argue that prison is punishment, not job training, that it creates inequalities in the prison system, and that it violates the rights of outside businesses. (3) Still other people think that the prison labor system needs some changes and that it can be employed in a way that does not violate human rights or conflict with outside businesses. People who take this position say that prison labor can be organized and maintained like regular businesses, and that to be good, it should be competitive.

The assignment for the exploratory paper calls for a tentative claim at the end of the paper. This student's tentative claim was, With some reform of the present system, prison labor can become a smoothly operating industry that benefits society.

WRITE A CLAIM AND CLARIFY YOUR PURPOSE

Whether you write an issue proposal and an exploratory paper or not, you will want to write your claim for your position paper as early in the process as possible. Your claim is important because it provides purpose, control, and direction for everything else that you include in your paper. Information to help you write a claim appears in some of the earlier chapters. Mapping your issue (see pp. 78 and 88) or freewriting about it (see p. 99) can help you narrow and focus an issue so that you can finally write a claim about it. A number of examples of claims appear in Chapter 6 (starting on p. 162). The claim questions in Chapter 6 can also be used to help you write a claim and establish the fundamental purpose for your paper. You can freewrite in response to each of the five claim questions to get a sense of the best purpose and claim for your paper. Thus, your main purpose will be either to establish fact (What happened?), to define (What is it?), to show cause (What caused it?), to establish value (Is it good or bad?), or to propose policy (What should we do?). The claim about prison labor is a policy claim that focuses on what we should do. Other examples in the following list demonstrate how the claim questions can be used to establish purpose for your claim and your paper. But first, here is a detailed explanation of a rhetorical situation for an issue on crime and the treatment of criminals that will be used as an example in this chapter and that could serve as motivation for a written argument: A teenage white supremacist murdered a black middle-class family man. This crime was committed in Texas, where juries are impaneled both to decide guilt and to sentence the criminal. The jury decided the white supremacist was guilty and, in ignorance, sentenced him both to probation and a jail term. The law does not permit both sentences, and so the murderer ended up with probation. As you can imagine, there was public concern, and issues surfaced. Here is how the claim questions can be used in this situation to decide on a purpose and a claim.

Using Claim Questions to Plan Purpose and Claim

1. To establish a claim of fact, ask: What happened? Does it exist? Is it a fact? Is it true?

> *Example:* You and the audience know about the murder and have just learned about the probationary sentence. Something seems very wrong. Your purpose is to analyze what is wrong, especially since some people are satisfied and others are dissatisfied with the sentence. Your claim is a claim of fact, *The murderer escaped an appropriate sentence.* Your strategy will be to organize the paper chronologically, giving a history of what has happened, and quoting both facts and expert opinion to prove your claim.

2. To establish a claim of definition, ask: What is it? What is it like? How should we interpret it? How does its usual meaning change in this context?

> *Example:* You think there was a definition problem in the sentencing procedure. The jury was supposed to assign an appropriate sentence for a murder. You decide your audience needs a definition of an appropriate sentence for a murder. Your claim is, *Probation is not an appropriate sentence for murder.* Your argument relies on expert opinion and the citation of similar cases to illustrate what an appropriate sentence for murder should be.

3. To establish a claim of cause, ask: What caused it? Where did it come from? Why did it happen? What are the effects? What will the short-term and long-term results be?

> *Example:* Personal conversations and media reports indicate considerable confusion over the cause of the sentence. Some people think the jury was racially prejudiced, others think the murderer was assigned probation because he is young, and others are baffled. You decide the cause was the jury's lack of information, and your claim is, *The jury did not know and did not receive information about how to sentence murderers, and as a result it recommended an inappropriate sentence.* To prove this claim, you examine the training provided to jurors. You interview people who have served on juries. You try to learn what training was available for this particular jury.

4. To establish a claim of value, ask: Is it good or bad? How bad? How good? Of what worth is it? Is it moral or immoral? Who thinks so? What criteria should I use to decide goodness or badness? Are these the same criteria the audience would apply?

Example: There seems to be some disagreement about whether this sentence was good or bad, and you decide to declare it a bad sentence. Your claim is, *It was wrong of the jury to assign the murderer probation and no jail sentence.* To prove this, you appeal to the standard needs and values you assume your audience holds, including a desire for physical safety, a sense of fairness and justness, and a respect for the jury system which, you argue, has failed in this case.

5. To establish a claim of policy, ask: What should we do about it? What should be our future course of action? How can we solve the problem?

Example: By the time you write your paper, everyone has decided that the jury has made a mistake. In fact, the criminal is back in jail on another charge waiting for a new trial. You decide to write a policy paper in which you recommend jury training so that this same problem will not recur. Your claim is, *Juries need pretrial training in order to make competent judgments.* An example of a policy paper organized around this claim and written in response to this actual rhetorical situation appears at the end of Chapter 12 in the Exercise section.

When you have decided on your main purpose and written your claim, you can now begin to think about ways to develop your claim.

SOME PRELIMINARY QUESTIONS TO HELP YOU DEVELOP YOUR CLAIM

Ask the following questions to further clarify and develop your claim. Some tentative answers to these questions now can help you stay on track and avoid problems with the development of your paper later.

Is the Claim Narrow and Focused? You may have started with a broad issue area, such as technology or education, that suggests many specific related issues. You may have participated in mapping sessions in class to discover some of the specific issues related to an issue area, and this work may have helped you narrow your issue. You may now need to narrow your issue even further by focusing on one prong or aspect of it. Here is an example:

Issue area: The environment
   Specific related issue:
   What problems are associated with nuclear energy?
      Aspects of that issue:
      What should be done with nuclear waste?
      How hazardous is it, and how can we control the hazards?
      What are the alternatives to nuclear energy?

In selecting a narrowed issue to write about, you may want to focus on only one of the three aspects of the nuclear energy problem. You might, for instance, decide to make this claim: Solar power is better than nuclear energy. Later, as you write, you may need to narrow this topic even further and revise your claim:

Solar power is best for certain specified purposes. Any topic can turn out to be too broad or complicated when you begin to write about it.

You may also need to change your focus or perspective to narrow your claim. You may, for example, begin to research the claim you have made in response to your issue, but while doing research, discover that the real issue is something else. As a result, you decide to change your claim. For example, suppose you decide to write a policy paper about freedom of speech. Your claim is, Freedom of speech should be protected in all situations. As you read and research, however, you discover that an issue for many people is a narrower one related to freedom of speech specifically as it relates to violence on television and children's behavior. In fact, you encounter an article that claims, Television violence should be censored even if doing so violates free-speech rights. You decide to refocus your paper and write a value paper that claims, Television violence is harmful and not subject to the protection of free-speech rights.

Which Controversial Words in Your Claim Will You Need to Define? Identify the words in your claim that may need defining. In the example just used, you would need to be clear about what you mean by *television violence, censorship,* and *free-speech rights.*

Can You Learn Enough to Cover the Claim Fully?   If the information for an effective paper is unavailable or too complicated, write another claim, one that you know more about and can research more successfully. Or narrow the claim further to an aspect that you can understand and develop.

What Are the Different Perspectives on Your Issue?   Make certain that your issue invites two or more perspectives. If you have written an exploratory paper on your issue, you already know what several views are. If you have not written such a paper, explore your issue by writing several claims that represent several points of view, and then select the one you want to prove. For example:

- Solar power is better than nuclear power.
- Solar power is worse than nuclear power.
- Solar power has some advantages and some disadvantages when compared to nuclear power.
- Solar power is better than nuclear power for certain specified purposes.

As you identify the different perspectives on your issue, you can also begin to plan some refutation that will not alienate your audience. An angry or insulted audience is not likely to change.

How Can You Make Your Claim Both Interesting and Compelling to Yourself and Your Audience?   Develop a fresh perspective or "take" on your issue when writing your claim. Suppose, for example, you are writing a policy paper that claims public education should be changed. You get bored with it. You keep running into old reasons that everyone already knows. Then you discover a couple of new aspects of the issue that you could cover with more original ideas and material. You learn that some people think parents should be able to choose their children's school, and you learn that competition among schools might lead to improvement. You also learn that contractors can take over schools and manage them in order to improve them. You refocus your issue and your perspective. Your new fact claim is, Competition among schools, like competition in business, leads to improvement. The issue and your claim now have new interest for you and your audience because you are looking at them in a whole new way. (See page 113 for additional information on developing an original perspective.)

At What Point Are You and the Audience Entering the Conversation on the Issue? Consider your audience's background and initial views on the issue to decide how to write a claim about it. If both you and your audience are new to the issue, you may decide to stick with claims of fact and definition. If they partially understand it, but need more analysis, you may decide on claims of cause or value. If both you and your audience have adequate background on the issue, you may want to write a policy claim and try to solve the problems associated with it. Keep in mind, also, that issues and audiences are dynamic. As soon as audiences engage with issues, both begin to change. So you need to be constantly aware of the current status of the issue and the audience's current stand on it.

What Secondary Purpose Do I Want to Address in My Paper? Even though you establish your predominant purpose as policy or cause, you may still want to answer the other claim questions, particularly if you think your audience needs that information. You may need to explain what happened or speculate on causes as part of the background information you provide. You may need to provide definitions for the key words in your claim. You may want to address value questions in order to engage your audience's motives and values. Finally, you may want to suggest policy briefly even though your paper has another predominant purpose.

MAKE A PRELIMINARY OUTLINE

Make a preliminary outline to guide your future thinking and research and to help you maintain the focus and direction you have already established. Even though you may not know very much about your issue and your claim at this point, it can be valuable, nevertheless, to write what you want to learn. Attach to your outline a preliminary research plan and some ideas to help you get started on a first draft. See the box on page 328 as an example.

You now have the beginning of an argument paper: a claim, some reasons, and some ideas to explore further. Your claim may change, and your reasons will probably change as you think, read, and do research. Before you go further, however, you need to think more about the audience. The nature of your audience can have a major influence on how you will finally write your argument paper.

A Preliminary Outline

VALUE CLAIM

Television violence is harmful and should not be subject to the protection of free speech rights, because

1. Violence on television and in life seem to be related.
2. Children do not always differentiate between television and reality.
3. Parents do not supervise their children's television viewing.
4. Even though free speech is a constitutional right, it should not be invoked to protect what is harmful to society.

RESEARCH NEEDS

I need to find out how free speech is usually defined. Does it include all freedom of expression, including violence on television? Also, I will need to find the latest studies on television violence and violent behavior, particularly in children. Will there be a cause-effect relationship? Even though I want to focus mainly on value and show that violent television is bad, I will also need to include definition and cause in this paper.

DRAFT PLAN

I will define television violence and free speech. I need to do some background reading on censorship and freedom of speech, and summarize some of this information for my readers. My strongest material will probably be on the relationship between violence on television and in real life. I think now I'll begin with that and end with the idea that the Constitution should not be invoked to protect harmful elements like television violence. I'm going to write for an audience that either has children or that values children. I will use examples from an article I clipped about how children imitate what they see on television.

UNDERSTAND THE AUDIENCE TO HELP YOU ACHIEVE SUCCESSFUL ARGUMENT OUTCOMES

Why is it important to understand your audience? Why not just argue for what you think is important? Some definitions and descriptions of effective argument emphasize the techniques of argument rather than the outcomes. They encourage the arguer to focus on what he or she thinks is important. For example, an argument with a clear claim, clear logic and reasoning, and good evidence will be described by some theorists as a good argument. The position in this book, however, has been different. If the argument does not reach the audience and create some common ground in order to convince or change it in some way, then the argument, no matter how skillfully crafted, is not productive. Productive argument, according to the definitions we used in Chapter 1, must create common ground and achieve some definable audience outcomes.

In order for the writer of argument to reach the audience, create common ground, and bring about change, two essential requirements need to be met. First, the audience must be willing to listen and perhaps also be willing to change. Second, the author must be willing to study, understand, and appeal to the audience. Such analysis will enable the author to appeal to the audience's present opinions, values, and motives, and to show as often as possible that the author shares them to achieve the common ground essential for effective argument. Thus both audience and author need to cooperate to a certain degree for argument to achieve any outcomes at all.

Here are four strategies to help you begin the process of understanding and appealing to your audience:

1. Assess the audience's size and familiarity to you.
2. Determine how much you have in common with your audience.
3. Determine the audience's initial position and what changes in views or actions might occur as a result of your argument.
4. Identify the audience's discourse community.

Assess the Audience's Size and Familiarity. Audiences come in all sizes and may or may not include people you know. The smallest and most familiar audience is always yourself; you must convince yourself in internal argument. The next smallest audience is one other person. Larger audiences may include specific, known groups such as family members, classmates, work associates, or members of an organization you belong to. You may also at times write for a large unfamiliar audience composed of either local, national, or international members. And, of course, some audiences are mixed, including both people you do and do not know. Your techniques will vary for building common ground with both large and small, familiar and unfamiliar audiences, but your argumentative aim will not change.

Determine What You and the Audience Have in Common. You may or may not consider yourself a member of your audience, depending on how closely you identify with it and share its views. For example, if you are a member of a union, you will probably identify and agree with its official position, particularly on work-related issues. If you work with management, you will hold other views about work-related issues. Your methods of achieving common ground with either of these audiences will be somewhat different, depending on whether you consider yourself a member of the group or not.

Determine the Audience's Initial Position and How It Might Change. As part of your planning, project what you would regard as acceptable audience outcomes for your argument. Think about the degree of common ground you initially share with your audience, because it is then easier to imagine audience change. There are several possibilities of initial audience positions and possible changes or outcomes.

You may be writing for a *friendly* audience that is in near or total agreement with you from the outset. The planned outcome is to *confirm this audience's beliefs and strengthen its commitment.* You can be straightforward with this audience, addressing it directly and openly with the claim at the beginning, supported with evidence and warrants that it can accept. Political rallies, religious sermons, and public demonstrations by special interest groups, such as civil rights or prolife groups, all serve to make members more strongly committed to their original beliefs. When you write for a friendly audience, you will achieve the same effect.

Another type of audience either *mildly agrees* with you or *mildly opposes you.* This audience may possess no clear reasons for its tendencies or beliefs. Possible outcomes in this case usually include (1) *final agreement* with you, (2) *a new interest* in the issue and a commitment to work out a position on it, or (3) *a tentative decision* to accept what seems to be true for now. To establish common ground with this type of audience, get to the point quickly and use support and warrants that will establish connections.

Other audiences may be *neutral* on your issue, uncommitted and uninterested in how an issue is resolved one way or another. Your aim will be to *change the level of their indifference* and encourage them to take a position. You may only be able to get their attention or raise their level of consciousness. As with other audiences, you will establish common ground with a neutral audience by analyzing its needs and by appealing to those needs.

A *hostile* audience that disagrees with you may be closed to the idea of change, at least at first. Anticipated outcomes for such audiences might include *avoiding more hostility* and *getting them to listen* and *consider possible alternative views.* Rogerian argument or a delayed claim may be necessary to get such an audience to listen at all. It is always possible that a hostile audience might *change its mind,* or at least *compromise.* If all else fails, sometimes you can get a hostile audience to *agree to disagree,* which is much better than increasing the hostility.

Think of your relationship with your audience as if it were plotted on a sliding scale. At one end are those who agree with you, and at the other end are those who disagree. In the middle is the neutral audience. Other mildly hostile or mildly favorable audiences are positioned at various points in between. Your knowledge of human nature and argument theory will help you plan strategies of argument that will address all these audience types.

Identify the Audience's Discourse Community. An audience's affiliations can help define its nature. Specialized groups that share subject matter, background, experience, values, and a common language (including specialized and technical vocabulary, jargon, or slang) are known as *discourse communities.* Common ground automatically exists among members of a discourse community because they understand one another easily.

Consider discourse communities composed of all scientists, all engineers, or all mathematicians. Their common background, training, language, and knowledge make it easier for them to connect, achieve common ground, and work toward conclusions. The discourse community itself, in fact, creates some of the common ground necessary for successful academic inquiry or for other types of argument.

You are a member of the university or college discourse community where you attend classes. This community is characterized by reasonable and educated people who share common background and interests that enable them to inquire into matters that are still at issue. You are also a member of the discourse community in your argument class, which has a common vocabulary and common tasks and assignments. Outsiders visiting your class would not be members of this community in the same way that you and your classmates are.

What other discourse communities do you belong to? How do the discourse communities in your home, among your friends, and at work differ from your university and argument class discourse communities? For some students, the differences are considerable. The strategies for connecting with others, building common ground, and arguing within the context of each of your discourse communities can vary considerably. With some reflection, you will be able to think of examples of the ways you have analyzed and adapted to each of them already. You can improve your natural ability to analyze and adapt to audiences by learning some conscious strategies for analyzing and adapting to both familiar and unfamiliar audiences.

SOME WAYS TO ANALYZE A FAMILIAR AUDIENCE

At an early stage in the writing process, you need to answer certain key questions about your audience. To get this information you may simply ask members of your audience some questions. Asking questions isn't always possible or advisable, however. More often, you will have to answer for your audience by studying them and even doing research.

The following list presents a set of 13 questions to ask about a familiar audience. You do not have to answer every question about every audience. You may need to add a question or two, depending on your audience. Answer questions that are suggested by the particular rhetorical situation for your argument. For example, the age range of the audience might be a factor to consider if you are writing about how to live a successful life; the diversity of the class might be important if you are writing about racial issues; or class interests, particularly outdoor interests, might be useful to know if you are writing about the environment.

As you read through the audience analysis questions, imagine that you are continuing to work on the argument paper on the topic of jury trials. Recall that your claim is, *Juries need pretrial training in order to make competent judgments.* The information that you uncover about your audience follows each question.

1. Describe the audience in general. Who are they? What do you have in common with them?

> *Example:* My audience is my argument class. We have common educational goals, language, assignments, campus interests, and experiences.

2. What are some of the demographics of the group? Consider size, age, gender, nationality, education, and professional status.

Example: Two-thirds of the 25 students are 18 to 20 years old, and one-third are over 30. Fifty-six percent are female, and 44 percent are male. Slightly less than half are white; about a third are black, Hispanic, and Asian; and the rest are international students. About three-fourths are freshman and sophomores, and the rest are upperclassmen. More than half of the class works at part-time outside jobs. Two have full-time professions in insurance and sales.

3. What are some of their organizational affiliations? Consider political parties, religion, social and living groups, and economic status.

Example: Roughly half say they are Democrat, and half Republican. Three say they are Libertarians. Fifty percent say they attend Christian churches, 20 percent are Jewish, and the rest either are Islamic or Hindu or say they are not religious. Four belong to fraternities or sororities, a few live in the dorms, and the rest live at home or in apartments. Most are in the middle or lower-middle class with aspirations to graduate, get better jobs, and move up.

4. What are their interests? Include outside interests, reading material, and perhaps majors.

Example: The group lists the following interests and activities: sports, movies, television, exercise and fitness, camping and hiking, attending lectures, repairing and driving cars, listening to music, reading local newspapers, and reading news magazines. They are all college students. Five are in engineering, six are in business, one is in nursing, and the rest are in humanities and social sciences.

5. What is their present position on your issue? What audience outcomes can you anticipate?

Example: My issue is jury trials, and my claim is, Juries need pretrial training in order to make competent judgments. Most of the class have not thought about this issue and either are neutral or mildly agree. A show of hands reveals that five think juries need more training, fifteen don't know, and five favor the status quo. I can expect the neutral and status quo members to become interested and perhaps even agree. I can expect the others to agree more strongly than they do now.

6. Will they interpret the issue in the same way you have?

Example: This issue comes from a local event, and some class members may see a double-jeopardy issue or some other issue emerging from it. I will have to focus their attention on my issue and make it important to them.

7. How significant is your issue to the audience? Will it touch their lives or remain theoretical for them?

Example: This is a personally significant issue for the people planning to be lawyers. It has some personal significance for most of the others, also, because everyone who votes is a potential jury member. The international students will have interest in it, depending upon their background and experience. I need to find out what their experiences have been.

8 Are there any obstacles that will prevent your audience from accepting your claim as soon as you state it?

Example: Part of this audience believes that juries are always effective and need no improvement. I will have to challenge that idea.

9. At what point are they in the ongoing conversation about the issue? Will they require background and definitions? Are they knowledgeable enough to contemplate policy change?

Example: Ninety percent know about the recent local case in which the jury made a poor judgment because of ignorance of procedures. Half of the class have been called for jury duty, and two have served. Three intend to go to law school and have considerable background and interest in juries. This audience knows enough to think about policy changes.

10. What is the attitude of your audience toward you?

Example: I think I have a friendly audience, and I am an insider, a part of it. We have established an open atmosphere in this class, and there are no personal hostilities that I can see. We share the same discourse community.

11. What beliefs and values do you and your audience share?

Example: In regard to my issue, they value trial by jury, they value a job well done, and they value education.

12. What motivates your audience? What are their goals and aims?

Example: My audience would be personally motivated to do a good job if they were on a jury.

13. What argument style will work best with your audience?

Example: I don't want to debate this issue. I would like to get consensus and a sense of cooperation instead. In fact, I picked this issue because it is one that people will probably not fight about. I want to use examples that will appeal to my audience's experiences. I am willing to negotiate or qualify my conclusion if the class members who critique my paper have trouble with it.

Go through these questions and try to answer them for a potential audience, as has been done here, at an early stage of the writing process. To help you answer questions 11 and 12 about values and motives, refer to Box 10.1.

CONSTRUCT AN UNFAMILIAR AUDIENCE

Sometimes you will not be able to gather direct information about your audience because it will be unfamiliar to you and unavailable for study. In this case, you will need to draw on your past experience for audience analysis. To do so you will have to imagine a particular kind of audience, a *universal audience,* and write for it when you cannot get direct audience information.

Chaim Perelman, who has written exclusively about the difficulty of identifying the qualities of audiences with certainty, has developed the concept of the

1. Survival needs: food, warmth, and shelter; physical safety.
2. Health: physical well-being, strength, endurance, energy; mental stability, optimism.
3. Financial well-being: accumulation of wealth; increased earning capacity; lower costs and expenses; financial security.
4. Affection and friendship: identification in a group; being accepted, liked, loved; being attractive to others; having others as friends or objects of affection.
5. Respect and esteem of others: having the approval of others, having status in a group, being admired, fame.
6. Self-esteem: meeting one's own standards in such virtues as courage, fairness, honesty, generosity, good judgment, and compassion; meeting self-accepted obligations of one's role as employee, child or parent, citizen, member of an organization.
7. New experience: travel; change in employment or location; new hobbies or leisure activities; new food or consumer products; variety in friends and acquaintances.
8. Self-actualization: developing one's potential in skills and abilities; achieving ambitions; being creative; gaining the power to influence events and other people.
9. Convenience: conserving time or energy; the ease with which the other motives can be satisfied.

BOX 10.1   Needs and Values That Motivate Most Audiences[3]

universal audience.[4] He suggests planning an argument for a composite audience that has individual differences but also important common qualities. This universal audience is educated, reasonable, normal, adult, and willing to listen. Every arguer constructs the universal audience from his or her own past experience, and, consequently, the concept of the universal audience varies somewhat from individual to individual and culture to culture.

The construct of the universal audience can be useful when you write argument and other papers for your other college classes. It is especially useful when the audience is largely unknown and you cannot obtain much information about it. Imagine writing for a universal audience on those occasions. Your professors and classmates as a group possess the general qualities of this audience.

---

[3]This list is based on Abraham Maslow's hierarchy of needs and motives from his book *Motion and Personality*, expanded by James A. Wood in *Speaking Effectively* (New York: Random House, 1988), pp. 203–204. Reproduced with permission.

[4]See Perelman and Olbrechts-Tyteca, *The New Rhetoric*, for additional details on the universal audience.

It is also useful to try to construct an unfamiliar audience's possible initial position on your issue. When you do not know your audience's position, it is best to imagine it as neutral to mildly opposed to your views and direct your argument with that in mind. Imagining an unfamiliar audience as either hostile or friendly can lead to extreme positions that may cause the argument to fail. Imagining the audience as neutral or mildly opposed ensures an even tone to the argument that promotes audience interest and receptivity. The following excerpt from a speech report illustrates some of the problems that were created when the speaker assumed total agreement from the audience. Notice that the author, who describes himself as an audience member, is obviously different from the audience members imagined by the speaker. How is he different? What is the effect? What changes could this speaker make to create better common ground with all of her audience members? Consider what this speaker might have done differently if she had imagined a neutral or mildly opposed audience, instead of a strongly friendly audience.

> I am listening to a lecture by Helen Caldicott, the environmental activist. Dr. Caldicott is in top form, holding forth with her usual bracing mixture of caustic wit and prophetical urgency. All around me, an audience of the faithful is responding with camp-meeting fervor, cheering her on as she itemizes a familiar checklist of impending calamities: acid rain, global warming, endangered species.
>
> She has even come up with a fresh wrinkle on one of the standard environmental horrors: nuclear energy. Did we know, she asks, that nuclear energy is producing scores of anencephalic births in the industrial shanty-towns along the Mexican border? "Every time you turn on an electric light," she admonishes us, "you are making another brainless baby."
>
> Dr. Caldicott's presentation is meant to instill unease. In my case, she is succeeding, though not in the way she intends. She is making me worry, as so many of my fellow environmentalists have begun to make me worry—not simply for the fate of the Earth, but for the fate of this movement on which so much depends. As much as I want to endorse what I hear, Dr. Caldicott's effort to shock and shame just isn't taking. I am as sympathetic a listener as she can expect to find, yet rather than collapsing into self-castigation, as I once might have, I find myself going numb.
>
> Is it possible that green guilt, the mainstay of the movement has lost its ethical sting?
>
> Despite my reservations, I do my best to go along with what Dr. Caldicott has to say—even though I suspect (as I think most of her audience does) that there is no connection between light bulbs and brainless babies.[5]

USING INFORMATION ABOUT YOUR AUDIENCE

When you complete your analysis of your audience, you need to go back through the information you have gathered and consciously decide which audience characteristics to appeal to in your paper. As an example, look back through the audi-

---

[5]Theodore Roszak, "Green Guilt and Ecological Overload," *New York Times,* June 9, 1992, Sec. A, p. 13.

ence analysis of the argument class that was done for you. Suppose that you are the student who is planning to write the paper about jury training. You decide that the general questions about the makeup of the group suggest that you have a fairly typical college audience. They are varied enough in their background and experience so that you know they will not all share common opinions on all matters. They do have in common, however, their status as college students. Furthermore, all of you belong to the same group, so you can assume some common values and goals. All of them, you assume, want to be successful, to graduate, and to improve themselves and society; you can appeal to these common motives. All or most of them read local newspapers or watch local news programs, so they will have common background on the rhetorical situation for your issue. You have asked about their present views on jury training, and you know that many are neutral. Your strategy will be to break through this neutrality and get commitment for change.

You decide, furthermore, that you may have to focus the issue for them because they are not likely to see it your way without help. They should also, you decide, know enough to contemplate policy change. You can appeal to their potential common experience as jurors and their need for physical safety, fairness, and good judgment in dealing with criminals. You can further assume that your audience values competence, expertise, and reasonableness, all important outcomes of the training system you intend to advocate. Your argument style will work with the group because you have already analyzed styles, and yours is familiar to them. They either share your style or are flexible enough to adapt to it. You are now in a position to gather materials for your paper that will be convincing to this particular audience. You will develop reasoning, including support and warrants, that they can link to their personal values, motives, beliefs, knowledge, and experience.

You need to show the same care in adapting to the needs of a universal audience. Since this audience is reasonable, educated, and adult, support and warrants must be on its level and should also have broad applicability and acceptance. Odd or extreme perspectives or support will usually not be acceptable. An example is the electric light causing brainless babies in "Green Guilt and Ecological Overload." This example does not have universal appeal. Notice, also, that the universal audience, as a reasonable and educated audience, should inspire a high level of argumentative writing. Careful research, intelligent reasoning, and clear style are requirements for this audience.

EXERCISES AND ACTIVITIES

1. THE POSITION PAPER: WRITE A CLAIM AND CLARIFY YOUR PURPOSE

Complete the following worksheet by writing answers to the questions. They will help you focus on your claim and ways to develop it. Discuss your answers with the other members in your writing group, or discuss some of your answers with the whole class.

Claim Development Worksheet

1. Freewrite in response to the claim questions, decide on a purpose, and write your claim in a complete sentence (refer to page 238 for help).
2. Which will be your predominant argumentative purpose in developing the claim? Fact? Definition? Cause? Value? Policy?
3. What is your original slant on the issue, and is it evident in the claim?
4. Is the claim too broad, too narrow, or okay for now?
5. How will you define the controversial words in your claim?
6. Do you predict at this point that you may have to qualify your claim to make it acceptable to the audience? How?

2. THE POSITION PAPER: MAKE A PRELIMINARY OUTLINE

Use the following worksheet to help you construct a preliminary outline and a guide for thinking and research:

Preliminary Outline Worksheet

TYPE OF CLAIM AND CLAIM

1. Identify the type of claim, write the claim, and write the word *because* after the claim. List three to five possible reasons or subclaims that you might develop in your paper. What minor purposes do they add to your paper? Fact? Definition? Cause? Value? Policy?

RESEARCH

2. Anticipate your research needs. Which reasons can you develop with your present knowledge and information? Which will you need to think about and research further? Can you learn enough to develop the claim, or should you modify it so that you can learn enough? What types of research materials will you seek?
3. How much additional background reading do you need to do, and where should you do it? Is an encyclopedia sufficient, or should you ask your professor or a librarian for a better source? What other readings and research will you need to do?

DRAFT PLAN

4. How much background will you need to provide your readers? What terms will you need to define?
5. What are your strongest opinions? Your best reasons?
6. What is a tentative way to begin your paper? What is a tentitive way to end it?
7. What original examples, descriptions, or comparisons occur to you now?

3. **CLASS DISCUSSION: THE CLASS AS AN AUDIENCE**
   Conduct an audience analysis of your class. Answer questions 1 through 4 (p. 324) to get a general idea of the nature of your group. These questions have to do with the audience in general, its demographic makeup, its organizational affiliations, and its interests. Follow the model provided by the examples. Make a list of additional audience factors that class members might keep in mind when they narrow their issues, define their purposes, and state their claims.

4. **THE POSITION PAPER: AUDIENCE ANALYSIS OF YOUR WRITING GROUP**
   Do an analysis of the small group of four or five individuals in your class who will serve as readers and critics of your paper from now until you hand it in. Your aim is to get an idea of how your audience regards your issue before you write. Your aim is to help your audience members become interested in reading your paper and perhaps even to change their minds. Do this as a group project, with each group member, in turn, interviewing the others and jotting down answers to the following questions:

Audience Analysis Worksheet

1. Describe your issue. What is your audience's present position on your issue? Describe some other perspectives on your issue, and ask for their reactions to those ideas. State your claim and ask if there is anyone who cannot accept it as stated. If there is, ask why.
2. How significant is your issue to the audience? If it is not considered significant, describe why it is significant to you and talk about ways you can make it more significant to them.
3. At what point are they in the ongoing conversation about the issue? What do they already know about your issue?
4. How will you build common ground? What beliefs and values do you and your audience share about your issue? What motivates them in regard to your issue?
5. What argument style will work best with them? A direct adversarial style? A Rogerian consensual style? Why?
6. Write what you have learned from this analysis to help you plan your appeal to this audience. Include values and motives in your discussion.

---

5. **ORAL REPORTS: WRITING FOR AN AUDIENCE**
   Clip and bring to class either an advertisement, cartoon, or a letter to the editor from any magazine or newspaper. In a two- to three-minute report, describe it, read it, or show it to the class; describe in as much detail as possible the audience to whom it is addressed; and point out some ways the author has worked to establish common ground with the audience. Analyze the following cartoon

*"I'll tell you what this election is about. It's about homework,
and pitiful allowances, and having to clean your room. It's
also about candy, and ice cream, and staying up late."*[6]

to get you started. Who is the audience for this cartoon? How does the speaker establish common ground with the audience?

6. **SMALL GROUP WORK AND WRITING ASSIGNMENTS: ADAPTING TO AN AUDIENCE AND ACHIEVING OUTCOMES**
Prepare for group work by reading the following written transcript of a public speech. It is accompanied by a description of the rhetorical situation and an account of the immediate audience outcomes.

   a. *Small group work.* In groups, analyze and describe what the speaker did to achieve particular audience outcomes.
   b. *Writing assignment.* Write a two-page paper on your discussion of the speech.

---

[6]*The New Yorker*, May 27, 1996, p. 115.

PRESIDENT BILL CLINTON'S MEMORIAL DAY SPEECH
AT THE VIETNAM VETERANS MEMORIAL, MAY 31, 1993

Rhetorical situation: President Clinton has been perceived as a draft dodger by some people, and when he spoke at the Vietnam Memorial on Memorial Day in 1993, he faced a mixed audience of overtly hostile to mildly hostile people. Here is the account in the *New York Times* that describes the audience: "As Mr. Clinton rose to speak on this balmy Washington afternoon on Memorial Day, he was greeted with a cacophony of enthusiastic applause, peppered by catcalls of 'Draft dodger!' 'Liar!' and 'Shut up, coward!' Many veterans in the audience, some wearing their green war fatigues and crumpled jungle hats, turned their backs when Mr. Clinton began his remarks."[7] Clinton made some special efforts to adapt to this hostile audience, and there was a mixed response at the end. Some people praised him, and others remained angry. Read the speech and analyze what Clinton did to make his audience more friendly and accepting of him and his views.

Essay

TEXT OF CLINTON SPEECH AT VIETNAM MEMORIAL

Bill Clinton

Thank you, thank you very much. General Powell, General McCaffrey and my good friend Lou Puller, whom I did not know was coming here today, I thank you so much.

To all of you who are shouting, I have heard you. I ask you now to hear me. I have heard you.

Some have suggested that it is wrong for me to be here with you today because I did not agree a quarter of a century ago with the decision made to send the young men and women to battle in Vietnam. Well, so much the better. Here we are celebrating America today. Just as war is freedom's cost, disagreement is freedom's privilege. And we honor it here today.

But I ask all of you to remember the words that have been said here today, and I ask you at this monument, Can any American be out of place? And can any Commander in Chief be in any other place but here on this day? I think not.

Many volumes have been written about this war and those complicated times, but the message of this memorial is quite simple: These men and women fought for freedom, brought honor to their communities, loved their country and died for it.

They were known to all of us. There's not a person in this crowd today who did not know someone on this wall. Four of my high school classmates are there, four who shared with me the joys and trials of childhood and did not live to see the three score and 10 years the Scripture says we are entitled to.

Let us continue to disagree if we must about the war, but let us not let it divide us as a people any longer.

---

[7]*New York Times*, June 1, 1993, Sec. A, p. 1.

No one has come here today to disagree about the heroism of those whom we honor. But the only way we can really honor their memory is to resolve to live and serve today and tomorrow as best we can and to make America the best that she can be. Surely that is what we owe to all those whose names are etched in this beautiful memorial.

As we all resolve to keep the finest military in the world, let us remember some of the lessons that all agree on. If the day should come when our service men and women must again go into combat, let us all resolve they will go with the training, the equipment, the support necessary to win, and, most important of all, with a clear mission to win.

Let us do what is necessary to regain control over our destiny as a people here at home, to strengthen our economy and to develop the capacities of all of our people, to rebuild our communities and our families where children are raised and character is developed. Let us keep the American dream alive.

Today let us also renew a pledge to the families whose names are not on this wall because their sons and daughters did not come home. We will do all we can to give you not only the attention you have asked for but the answers you deserve.

Today I have ordered that by Veterans Day we will have declassified all United States Government records related to P.O.W.'s and M.I.A.'s from the Vietnam War—all those records except for a tiny fraction which could still affect our national security or invade the privacy of their families.

As we allow the American public to have access to what our Government knows, we will press harder to find out what other governments know. We are pressing the Vietnamese to provide this accounting not only because it is the central outstanding issue in our relationship with Vietnam, but because it is a central commitment made by the American Government to our people. And I intend to keep it.

You heard General Powell quoting President Lincoln: "With malice toward none and charity for all, let us bind up the nation's wounds."

Lincoln speaks to us today across the years. Let us resolve to take from this haunting and beautiful memorial a renewed sense of our national unity and purpose, a deepened gratitude for the sacrifice of those whose names we touched and whose memories we revere and a finer dedication to making America a better place for their children and for our children, too.

Thank you all for coming here today. God bless you, and God bless America.[8]

7. QUESTIONS ON THE CHAPTER

    a. What are the claim questions and how can they be used to establish major and minor purposes in your position paper?

    b. What are some additional preliminary questions that you can ask to help you develop your claim?

---

[8]*New York Times,* June 1, 1993, Sec. A, p. 10.

    c. What is the purpose of the preliminary outline? What three main types of information are included on it?

    d. What would you need to consider about an audience to discover how much common ground you share?

    e. What is a discourse community? How does it help establish common ground?

    f. What are a few items described in this chapter that you consider particularly important in conducting an audience analysis?

    g. What is the universal audience? What are its special qualities? Why is it a useful idea?

8. QUESTIONS ON THE ESSAYS FOR ANALYSIS

    a. Clinton's Memorial Day Speech, page 340. What is the purpose and occasion for this speech? Describe the audience. What argument style does Clinton employ with this audience? How does Clinton try to establish common ground with the audience? What particular experiences, values, and motives does he want to appear to have in common with the audience? Why does he mention General Powell and Lincoln? How successful is this speech in establishing common ground?

CHAPTER 11

Invention and Research

The writing process is both creative and critical. For example, invention and research are creative, and rewriting and revision are critical. This chapter is about creativity. It encourages you to think about what you already know and believe before you seek the opinions of others. As a result, your voice will become the major voice in your paper, and your ideas will predominate over those of others. Information and ideas from other sources will be brought in later to back up what you finally think.

The invention strategies presented here are appropriate for helping you think about and develop your ideas for your position paper. Use them along with the prewriting invention strategies that appear in Chapter 4. All of the invention strategies from both chapters are summarized on the invention worksheet on page 367.

The first two strategies described here are logical thinking methods to help you expand on your topic. These are followed by some strategies for using argument theory from earlier chapters to help you invent ideas and identify the parts of your paper. The last sections of the chapter will help you do library research, another creative source of information and opinion for your paper.

USE BURKE'S PENTAD TO ESTABLISH CAUSE

Asking the question *why* will help you establish cause for controversial incidents and human motives. So will a systematic application of Kenneth Burke's pentad as he describes it in his book *A Grammar of Motives*.[1] In his first sentence, Burke poses the question "What is involved when we say what people are doing and why they are doing it?" Burke identified five terms and associated questions that can be used to examine possible causes for human action and events. Since establishing cause is an important part of many arguments, and especially of fact, cause, and policy arguments, the pentad is potentially very useful to the writer of argument. Here are

---

[1] Kenneth Burke, *A Grammar of Motives* (New York: Prentice Hall, 1945), p. xv. James Wood pointed out to me the value of Burke's pentad in attributing cause in argument.

Burke's terms and questions along with some examples to demonstrate application. These examples, by the way, are intended to be controversial. As you read the examples drawn from the Los Angeles riots of 1992 and the U.S. budget deficit, go a step further and apply these questions to your own issue to help you think about cause. Burke's pentad, by the way, is similar to the journalist's questions *who, what, where, when,* and *why* except that it yields even more information than they do.

1. **Act. What was done?** What took place in thought or deed?

Example: The rioting in L.A. got out of control, and, like many big riots, it could not be controlled by the police.
Example: Lowered taxes and undisciplined spending occurred over a period of time and contributed to the national debt.

2. **Scene. When or where was it done?** What is the background or scene in which it occurred?

Example: The L.A. ghettos were the scene for the riots in 1992. Racial tension, anger at the police over the Rodney King beating, and gangs are all part of the scene.
Example: The entire U.S. economy, including government and private spending, is the scene. The 1980s are usually cited as the time when spending was particularly uncontrolled.

3. **Agent. Who did it?** What person or kind of person performed the act?

Example: The people who rioted, stole, broke into buildings, burned them, and fought are agents. So are the police. Peer pressure, or the predisposition to riot because others are doing it, is a characteristic of the agent in this case.
Example: Politicians, particularly the Republicans in the 1980s, are agents. So are greedy, wealthy American citizens.

4. **Agency. How did he (she) do it?** What means or instruments were used?

Example: Guns were available that provided the means. Television news coverage was also part of the agency because it allowed rioters to know what was going on and communicate with one another.
Example: Lower taxes for the wealthy were used to increase private spending but also to increase government debt.

5. **Purpose. Why did it happen?** What was the main motivation?

Example: The purpose was to protest the King verdict and the racism behind it.
Example: The purpose was to reduce the income tax and protect wealthy people.

Notice that you can focus on the answer to any one of the five questions and argue that it is the main cause of what happened. Also, each of the five questions provides a different perspective on the cause of the problem. Furthermore, the answers to these questions stir controversy. You may, in fact, have found yourself disagreeing with the answers in the examples. As Burke puts it, "Men may violently disagree about the purposes behind a given act, or about the character of the person who did it, or how he did it, or in what kind of situation he acted; or they may even insist upon totally different words to name the act itself."[2] Still, he goes on to say, one can begin with some kind of answers to these questions, which then provide a starting point for inquiry and argument. Apply Burke's pentad to every issue you write about to provide you with a deeper perspective on the causes or motives behind it.

USE CHAINS OF REASONS TO DEVELOP GREATER DEPTH OF ANALYSIS AND DETAIL

Another method of developing a claim or subclaim in your paper is to use chains of reasons to help you get a line of thinking going. You use this method quite naturally in verbal argument when you make a claim, someone asks you questions like "Why?" or "What for?" and you give additional reasons and evidence as support. For example:

You claim:	The university should be more student-friendly.
Someone asks:	Why do you think so? I think it's okay.
You answer:	Because students are its customers, and without us it would not exist.
Someone asks:	Why wouldn't it?
You answer:	Because we pay the money to keep it going.
Someone asks:	Why do students keep it going? There are other sources of income.
You answer:	Because our tuition is much more than all of the other sources combined.

You get the idea. Imagining that you are in a dialogue with another person who keeps asking why enables you to create quantities of additional support and detailed development for your claim. Also, by laying out your argument in this way you can see where you need more support. In the preceding example, you need to provide support to show what portion of the operating budget is funded by student tuition. You might also give examples of insensitive treatment of students and explain what students have in common with customers.

To chain an argument, repeat the *why . . . because* sequence three or four times, both for your main claim and also for each of your subclaims. Add evidence in all the places where your argument is sketchy. You will end up with a detailed analysis and support for your claim that will make it much less vulnerable to attack.

---

[2]Burke.

USE ARGUMENT THEORY TO THINK SYSTEMATICALLY ABOUT YOUR ISSUE

Use what you have learned about argument in earlier chapters to help you think about your claim and some ways to develop it.

Analyze the Rhetorical Situation. Focus your attention on the total context for your argument, including the motivation for the issue, how you will write about it, and how your reader-audience will react to it. Use the rhetorical situation questions, and apply them to your paper:

1. What is the *exigence* (context, dramatic real-life situation) that makes me and others perceive this issue as controversial?
2. Who is the *audience;* that is, who besides me thinks the issue is a problem? How do they view it?
3. What are the *constraints* (other people, events, affiliations, organizations, values, beliefs, or traditions) that influence the audience's perceptions of this issue, and will they bring us together or drive us apart?
4. What is motivating *me,* the *author,* to write about this issue; what makes me qualified?
5. What will be the purpose and strategies of the text I produce?

Use the Toulmin Model. The following paragraphs present a brief review of the six parts of the Toulmin model with suggestions to help you use them as guides for thinking and planning the parts of your argument paper. They are written as questions, and by the time you have answered them, you will have the essential parts of your paper.

What Is My Claim? What type of claim is it? What are my subclaims, or reasons? If you used the claim development worksheet on page 337, your claim will be well developed. Your claim is the thesis statement of your paper. It tells your readers what you are trying to prove. Decide whether it will be stronger to place it at the beginning, in the middle, or at the end. Classify your claim as fact, definition, cause, value, or policy to establish your fundamental purpose and help you plan support and organization. You will also need to invent subclaims or reasons that will develop your claim. Take another look at the brief outlines of claims and subclaims on pages 130 and 131 for some examples. Your reasons should be "good" reasons, or ones that are acceptable to your audience.

What Support Should I Use? You will need to develop the subclaims in your paper with support. Research is a necessity for many argument papers because support (facts, opinions, reasoning, examples) creates convincing argument. When you think about *facts,* consider using descriptions of events you or others you know have observed, or specific examples or accounts of other real happenings. You may also use narratives of both historical and recent events and statistical reports. Facts should be vivid, real, and verifiable to be convincing. Plan also to include *opinion.* Opinions and reasoning are your interpretations, explanations, and ideas about factual information. While facts, by themselves, are comparatively lifeless and boring, they become interesting and convincing when they are presented along with explanations about their significance and relevance. Besides your own opinions, you may also want to include expert opinion that can be summarized, paraphrased, or quoted directly in your paper. You must also tell your reader in the text who these experts are and where you found their ideas. The next chapter provides you with details on these techniques. When you quote opinions, select those that seem to you to be "informed," that is, based on knowledge, experience, and good judgment. Think also of some *examples.* They clarify points, make them interesting and easier to remember and, in argument, help prove the claim. Remember that examples can be real or made up, long or short; and real examples are more convincing than hypothetical examples.

What Are My Warrants? Remember that support and warrants, taken together, constitute the proofs or lines of argument for your paper. Every time you use a particular piece of support, a warrant, usually implicit, will cause your audience either to accept or reject it as appropriate support for the claim. Write down the warrants that are working in your paper, and answer three questions about them: (1) Do they link the evidence and the claim? You want the audience to think, "Ah, yes, I see how that evidence supports that claim and makes it convincing." (2) Do you believe your own warrants? If you do not, make some changes. Argument from personal conviction is the most convincing argument. (3) Will your audience share your warrants or reject them? If you think they will reject them, consider the possibility of stating them and providing some backing for them.

What Backing Might I Provide to Make My Warrants More Acceptable and Convincing? You may use additional support, including facts, expert opinion, reports, studies, and polls, to back up your warrants. You can do the same to back up evidence when necessary. Add material, in other words, to make your paper more convincing whenever you think your audience requires it.

How Should I Handle Rebuttal? Not all argument papers include rebuttal. You will usually strengthen your own position, however, if you decide to include rebuttal. It is particularly important to identify the arguments on the other side and point out what is wrong with them when the issue is familiar and obviously controversial. Your audience will be familiar with the other views and will expect your opinion on them in your paper.

When you plan rebuttal, here are some specific strategies to consider: Use your exploratory paper or do some background research to get a sense of the different perspectives on your issue. Then write your own claim and state reasons in favor of it; next, write an opposing claim and state reasons to support it; and finally, write a claim that represents a middle or neutral view and write reasons for it. Now, study the claims and reasons that are different from your own and attack their weakest features. Is it the support, the warrants, or the claims themselves that are the most vulnerable? Name some of the weakest features of these other perspectives, and point out the problems associated with them in your paper.

Another strategy for rebuttal is to build a strong case of your own that undercuts an opposing position but does not specifically acknowledge it. State and demonstrate that yours is the strongest position available. Or you can always examine the opposition's major proofs and apply the tests of validity explained in Chapter 7. In your paper, point out all problems with these proofs. Finally, for a hostile audience, use Rogerian argument to restate one or more opposing positions and show the special circumstances in which they might be valid. Then present your own position as better than all of the others. Remember that rebuttal should not offend the audience. Angry people won't pay serious attention or change their minds. Watch members of the U.S. Congress on C-SPAN television for examples of cordial rebuttal. They constantly engage in rebuttal, but they are polite and usually compliment the opposition while they disagree with them. This courtesy reduces hostility both in the opposition and the audience.

Will I Need to Qualify My Claim? If you believe strongly in your claim, you may want to state it as absolutely true. You must realize, however, that absolute positions will only be acceptable to people who already agree with you. To gain the adherence of more members of your audience, you may need to qualify your claim by using such words as *usually, often, probably, sometimes,* or *almost always.*

Plan Your Proofs.   Here is a review of the types of proof. A variety of types in your paper will make it more interesting and convincing. Refer to Chapter 7 or the summary chart (p. 409) for explanations as needed.

Logical Proofs. Logical proofs are convincing because they are real and drawn from experience. Here they are for quick reference:

1. *Deduction,* or applying a general principle or premise to a specific case or example and reaching a conclusion.
2. *Definitions,* which can be very short, a word or phrase only, or very long, from several sentences to several paragraphs to the entire essay.
3. *Cause,* or attributing cause or effect to your claim.
4. *Sign,* or pointing out the symptoms or signs that something is so.
5. *Induction,* or drawing a conclusion based on representative cases or examples.
6. *Statistics,* or numbers, data, graphs, and charts along with your interpretations of them.
7. *Analogies* (figurative, historical, and literal), or explaining what we do not understand in terms of what we do understand.

Proofs that Affect Ethos. Ethical proofs provide opinion and establish the *ethos* or authority of the quoted individuals. Mention the professions and affiliations of the people you quote along with their background, education, or experience to show that they are particularly qualified to provide information and opinions about your issue. Recall that ethical proofs include *your own opinions* as well as the *opinions of experts and authorities.*

Emotional Proofs. When the subject itself is emotional, when the audience will accept it, and when the occasion justifies it, emotional proofs are appropriate. As a general rule, use emotion to strengthen logical conviction rather than for its own sake. You can introduce feeling into your argument by using emotionally loaded language, emotional examples, personal narratives with an emotional impact, and vivid descriptions of emotional scenes. Two specific types of emotional proof are *motivational proofs,* or appealing to what your audience needs or wants and showing them how to get it; and *value proofs,* or establishing what your audience values and showing them how to achieve it. Keep in mind that the audience will be convinced only by appeals to specific needs or values that they can accept or agree with.

CONSIDER PRESENTING STATISTICAL PROOF IN GRAPHS AND CHARTS

As you gather your proofs for your paper, you may want to think about presenting any statistics you intend to use in the form of graphs and charts, particularly since computer software now makes this relatively easy to do. Graphs and charts can be especially useful when the statistical information is too cumbersome to include in the written body of your paper. There are many different kinds of graphs, but the most commonly used are the line, bar, and circle (or pie) graphs. These three kinds of graphs can be easily generated through common word processing packages such as Microsoft Word™ or WordPerfect™. The examples that follow present graphs of data from the *World Almanac,* an excellent source for up-to-date statistics on many subjects. **Bar graphs** are usually used when you want to compare measurements of some kind. The numbers used in the measurements are often large, and the bar graph offers a picture that makes the numbers easily understood. **Line graphs** are most often used to show a change in a measurement over time. Some of the different measurements associated with line graphs are temperature, height and weight, test scores, population changes, and profits. **Circle graphs** are ordinarily used to show how something is divided. For instance, a circle graph would be an effective way to show where the government spent its money over a specific period of time. Whatever kind of graph you use, however, you must be sure that it is correctly and clearly titled and labeled, that the units of measurement are noted, and that you report the source of the statistical information used in the graph.

If you are writing a paper arguing the ineffectiveness of AIDS education in America (including North and South America and the Caribbean) and Africa, and you want to give your audience some background concerning the number of AIDS cases reported in these parts of the world over the past ten years, a bar graph might be the best way to present this information. Figure 11.1 provides an example.

A line graph is most effective when showing change over a period of time. If you are writing a paper arguing that the United States needs to take care of its debt, you might want to show the change in the deficit over a number of years to let your reader better understand the growth pattern of the debt. The line graph in Figure 11.2 shows this information.

A circle or pie graph can quickly show how something is divided up. If you are writing a paper arguing that people are largely ignoring the depletion of the ozone caused by automobile emissions, you might want to sum the percentage of the different sizes of cars sold in the United States during a recent year. A circle graph would be an effective way to present this information. An example is provided in Figure 11.3.

Sometimes the statistical information you need to include in your paper is very detailed and too lengthy for a graph. In this case, a chart or a table is recommended. For instance, if you wanted to argue for ZPG (Zero Population Growth), you might want to give some of the projected figures for populations of major countries. A chart would probably be the most effective way of presenting this material. See the example in Figure 11.4.

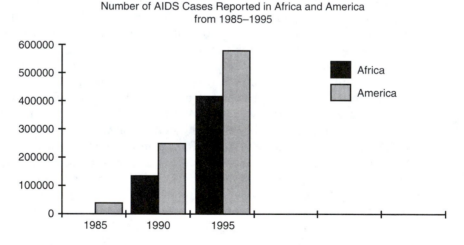

Number of AIDS Cases Reported in Africa and America
from 1985–1995

Figure 11.1 An Example of a Bar Graph that Compares Large Numbers. Source: The World Health Organization.[3]

---

[3]"Estimated HIV Infection and Reported AIDS Cases," *The World Almanac and Book of Facts*. Mahwah, N.J.: Funk and Wagnalls, 1996, p. 840.

Public Debt of the United States

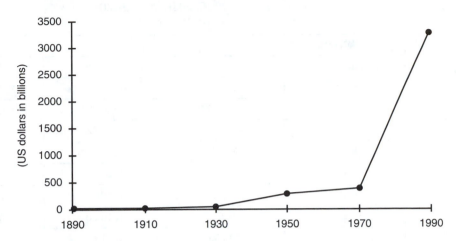

Figure 11.2 An Example of a Line Graph Showing Change Over a Period of Time. Source: Bureau of Public Debt, U.S. Department of the Treasury.[4]

Sales of US Cars by Size (1994)

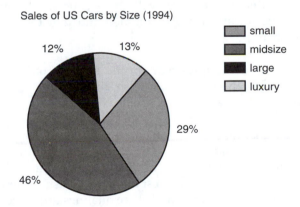

Figure 11.3 An Example of a Circle Graph Showing How Something Is Divided Up. Source: American Automobile Manufacturers Association.[5]

[4]"Public Debt of the U.S.," *The World Almanac and Book of Facts*. Mahwah, N.J.: Funk and Wagnalls, 1996, p. 112.

[5]"U.S. Car Sales by Vehicle Size and Type, 1984–94," *The World Almanac and Book of Facts*. Mahwah, N.J.: Funk and Wagnalls, 1996, p. 211.

Current Population and Projections for Selected Countries: 1995, 2010, and 2020
(in thousands)

COUNTRY	1995	2010	2020
Bangladesh	128,095	176,902	210,248
Brazil	160,737	183,742	197,466
China	1,203,097	1,348,429	1,424,725
India	936,546	1,173,621	1,320,746
Japan	125,506	129,361	126,062
Mexico	93,986	120,115	136,096
Nigeria	101,232	161,969	215,893
Russia	149,909	155,933	159,263
Saudi Arabia	18,730	31,198	43,255
United States	263,814	300,811	326,322

Figure 11.4 An Example of a Table That Presents Comparison Data. Source: Bureau of the Census, U.S. Department of Commerce.[6]

As a final check on the validity of your graphs and tables, check to see that nothing significant has been omitted and that the charts and graphs are accurately labelled.[7]

Use Proofs Appropriate for the Purpose or Type of Claim. Some proofs work better than others to establish different types of claims.[8] The following are not rules, just suggestions for you to consider.

Fact and Cause. Fact and cause papers call for substantive, factual support, including data and statistics. In developing either a fact or a cause paper, consider naming specific *causes* and *effects*, naming and describing *symptoms* and *signs*, using *induction* to suggest that if one exists others do also, using *analogies* to suggest that items coexist and share qualities and outcomes, and using *definitions* that place items in classes or categories. Also, consider quoting an *authority* to demonstrate that a reputable person says something is a fact or can identify what

---

[6]"Current Population and Projections for All Countries: 1995, 2010, and 2020," *The World Almanac and Book of Facts.* Mahwah, N.J.: Funk and Wagnalls, 1996, pp. 838–839.

[7]I am indebted to Samantha Masterton for generating these graphs and explanations.

[8]I am indebted to Wayne E. Brockriede and Douglas Ehninger for some of the suggestions in this section. They identify some types of proof as appropriate for different sorts of claims in their article "Toulmin on Argument: An Interpretation and Application," *Quarterly Journal of Speech,* 46 (February 1960): 44–53.

caused it. Emotional proofs are less valuable than *logical* and *ethical* proofs in establishing fact or cause.

Definition. Definition papers can be developed with *literal analogies* that invite comparisons of similar items, with *historical analogies* that suggest that if one thing happens, another thing will also, and with *classification,* or putting the item in a category with known characteristics. *Authorities* can be used to define it or support a particular view or interpretation of it. *Emotional proofs* are only relevant if the subject is emotional and you want the audience to accept an emotional definition—for example, abortion is a bloodbath.

Value Argument. Value arguments require *motivational proofs* and *value proofs,* and they must be connected to the needs and values of the audience. *Authorities* may also be used to establish the value of something. *Definition* can be used to put an item in a good or bad category or class. *Analogies* that compare good or bad items or outcomes may also be used. Value arguments also require criteria for making value judgments. You will need to establish these criteria and describe where they came from. They may be your own, society's, a particular group's, or those of the universal audience.

Policy. Policy papers can be developed with *literal analogies* showing that what worked in one case will also work in another. *Authorities* can be used to establish either the severity of the problem or the efficacy of the solution. *Motivational proofs* may be used to demonstrate how certain solutions or policies meet the needs of the audience. Table 11.1 summarizes the proofs that are appropriate for developing specific types of claims.

TABLE 11.1   Proofs That Are Particularly Appropriate for Developing Specific Types of Claims

CLAIMS OF FACT	CLAIMS OF DEFINITION	CLAIMS OF CAUSE	CLAIMS OF VALUE	CLAIMS OF POLICY
Facts	Reliable authorities	Facts	Value proofs	Data
Statistics	Accepted sources	Statistics	Motivational proofs	Motivational proofs
Real examples	Analogies with the familiar	Historical analogies	Literal analogies	Value proofs
Quotes from reliable authorities	Examples	Literal analogies	Figurative analogies	Literal analogies
Inductions	Real	Signs	Quotes from reliable authorities	Reliable authorities
Literal and historical analogies	Made up	Induction	Induction	Deduction
Signs	Signs	Deduction	Signs	Definition
Informed opinion		Quotes from reliable authorities	Definitions	Statistics
			Cause	Cause

USE ORGANIZATIONAL PATTERNS
TO HELP YOU THINK

Organizational patterns represent established ways of thinking about, developing, and organizing ideas. Chapter 12 will teach you to use organizational patterns to help you shape your paper when you are ready to write it. Now, however, during the early inventional stages of your paper, organizational patterns can also be used to help you discover material for your paper and to help you think about it. Here are some of the most commonly used organizational patterns for argumentative writing:

1. **Claim With Reasons.**   Write your claim and think of some reasons that will support it. Add various types of examples and other evidence.

2. **Problem-solution.**   This is a pattern commonly used for policy papers. If you find yourself thinking of your topic in policy terms, that is, what should be done, consider describing the problem first and then proposing a solution that should solve it.

3. **Cause-effect.**   If you are trying to establish cause in your paper, you will find it useful to think both in terms of causes and their effects.

4. **Chronological/narrative.**   You may find it useful to consider your topic as it evolves over a period of time. This is a useful pattern to use for fact arguments especially when you are trying to establish what happened.

5. **Comparison-contrast.**   If you are thinking about definition, it is useful to compare and contrast to show what your subject is like, but also what it is not like.

When you have worked through a few of the invention strategies described so far, you will be ready to do some research and get additional information from outside sources for your paper. Research is much easier to perform when you are fairly certain about your own thoughts and feelings on your particular issue. However, continue to interweave inventional strategies with library or computer research as you go along. All of the strategies in this chapter, although described separately, should be integrated to maintain a high level of creativity through the information-gathering phase.

SOME SUGGESTIONS TO HELP YOU WITH
LIBRARY AND COMPUTER RESEARCH

Library and computer research is a creative process that allows you to expand your ideas. Here are some suggestions to streamline your research:

Get Organized for Research.   First, get acquainted with the library itself. Locate the card or computer catalogs and indexes to books and articles, the books and articles themselves (including those on microfilm), and the government documents and reference books. Locate your library's computer lab. If you are unfamiliar with accessing the Internet, then see if your library offers free classes or printed material to help you get started. Also, find out where the copy center or copy machines are located in your library. Finally, find the reference desk and the reference librarians who will answer your questions when you get stuck. Now get prepared to write. Bring pens, sheets of paper, 3×5 cards, and something to keep them in. Think about buying three different colors of cards to color code the three types of information you will write on them: white for bibliography, yellow for all material you will cite in your paper, and blue for your own ideas. Also, bring money for the copy machine.

Use Your Preliminary Outline and Tentative Research Plan. Be specific about the material you seek in the library so that you do not get off course and waste time reading aimlessly. Once you begin research, you quite possibly will change some of your ideas about your topic. When you have new ideas, change your outline so that it continues to focus and guide your research. Every piece of research material that you examine should be related to an item on your outline unless you are reading creatively to get ideas.

Start with the Bibliography. The bibliography is the list of sources you will locate and read to add information to your paper. Search for books and for articles in magazines, journals, newspapers, and on the computer. Locate books by consulting the card catalog or the computer index. If your library still maintains a card catalog, you will find that each book is represented in it with three different cards: the first, with the author's name printed at the top, is filed in the *author section* of the catalog; the second, with the title of the book printed at the top, is filed in the *title section;* and the third, with the subject of the book printed at the top, is filed in the *subject section* of the catalog. The subject section will be particularly useful to you in the early stages of research because all of the library's books on your subject will be cataloged there in one place. You can often read the titles and decide which books might be useful.

Your library has probably closed down the card catalog and now stores the same information in a computer index. You will use a computer terminal to call up the same information you would find in the card catalog. That is, you may search for a book by looking for its author, title, or subject. Computer indexes also permit you to search by "key word." Enter a key word that represents your topic, such as "clear-cutting," and the computer will display all titles of books and articles that contain that word. Key-word searches are the quickest way to build a bibliography, as the key-word search is a powerful and effective research tool. Read the titles of the books and articles as they appear on the screen to locate those that might be useful. When you have found a book title that looks promising, move to the screen that gives complete information about that book. There you will find all of the other subject headings under which that book is listed in the index. Use those subject headings, or key words extracted from them, to expand your search. For instance, you might move from the original key word of "clear-cutting" to a new key word, "erosion," in order to access more varied material. Computer indexes are "user-friendly" and will tell you on the screen how to use them. Follow the directions exactly and ask for help if you get frustrated.

To find articles in the library you will need to consult indexes to periodical literature, such as *The Reader's Guide to Periodical Literature, The Social Sciences Index, The Humanities Index, The Education Index,* and *The Engineering Index.* There are quite a few of these indexes, representing a variety of subject areas. They are usually shelved together in one area of the library. Take some time to read their titles and browse in them. Browsing will help you discover the ones that will be most useful for directing you to articles on your issue.

Many periodical indexes are available on the computer. They are called databases. Two of the most common are Infotrac and Firstsearch. You can use these databases by typing in subjects or key words and executing a search. A list of associated articles in periodicals and scholarly journals will be displayed on the screen with the most current appearing first. Many of the entries include an **annotation** or a brief explanation of what the article contains. (See the example of an annotated bibliography on p. 369). By reading the annotations, you can save time and be more certain which articles will be important for you to locate and read. The computer databases will also indicate which periodicals and journals your library holds, and they will enable you to capture and print a list of the articles that you are interested in and will want to find later in the library.

One of the most helpful databases available through the Internet is called PAR (Periodical Abstracts Research). PAR enables you to limit your search to full-text articles only. In other words, you may actually access and print entire periodical articles without ever leaving your computer. This is a very useful service, and it is worth learning if your library offers it.

Newspapers, such as the *New York Times,* the *Wall Street Journal,* the *Christian Science Monitor,* or the *London Times,* along with news magazines like *Time* and *Newsweek,* are kept on microfilm in a special section of the library. Some books and many other journals are kept in this form also. When you encounter the abbreviations *mic, mf, mc,* or *mfc* as part of the catalog information for a book or magazine, you will need to locate it in the microfilm section. Machines are available there that enlarge the tiny images so that you can read them. Other machines enable you to print copies of microfilm material.

Indexes to newspapers and some magazines are available in the microfilm section as well. *Newsbank* is a particularly useful index for authors of argument papers. Check if your library has it. It collects newspaper articles from 150 urban newspapers starting from 1970 on almost any contemporary issue you can think of. Look up your issue in the *Newsbank* index, and it will lead you to a microfiche card that may contain 15 to 20 articles on your issue. Indexes to large daily newspapers and news magazines are also available in the microfilm section. Look up your subject in one of them, and then locate the articles they identify in the microfilm files.

You may also want to do research in other areas of the library, such as the reference room or the government documents area. Or you may decide to do a computer search. The reference room contains a variety of volumes that provide biographical information. If you need to establish the credibility of one of your authorities, you can get biographical information from the *Biography Index, Current Biography*, or the various editions of *Who's Who*.

Government documents contain considerable data and other factual information useful for argument. Indexes to consult to help you locate material in government documents include the *Public Affairs Information Bulletin*, the *Monthly Catalog*, and the *Index to U.S. Government Periodicals*. Look up your issue in each of them. Your librarian will help you locate the actual materials among the government documents.

Your school library may offer you free access to a computer lab and the Internet. Some of the software titles your library may make available for your use include Lynx, Gopher, Netscape, and Yahoo. You must be wary, however. The material posted on the Internet does not usually go through a publisher or editor, so anyone familiar with computers can create a Website and put articles or other writings on it. You cannot always be certain of a writer's authority or credibility, so you must be careful. Not all of the information available on the Internet is fully reliable. Also, you should use the online articles and information sparingly unless directed otherwise by your instructor. Your credibility as a writer partially depends on the variety and quality of the sources you use in your paper, and you should aim to have a solid representation of print sources in addition to any Internet sources you might use. An exception would be for a topic that is only discussed on the Internet and not elsewhere. The annotated bibliography on page 369 provides a reasonable balance of printed and Internet materials. Use it as a guide to the types of sources you might find for your paper unless you are instructed to do otherwise.

One of the most common and easy Web browsers to use to surf the Internet is called Netscape. If your library has Netscape software available, you will find it extremely user-friendly. Very basically, Netscape offers a text line in which you may type an Internet address (known as a URL or a Uniform Research Locator) or a key word. Once you have typed in the information, all you need to do is use the mouse to click on the "search" button in order to find the particular site of the URL or the related sites of the key word.

Surfing the Internet can be an excellent way to find out the up-to-date dialogue surrounding your issue. The Internet offers a forum for you to discuss your issue with other interested people: you can send e-mail to addresses made available on Websites, and you can take part in "live" chats in discussion rooms. If you are taking an English class in a computer classroom, your instructor might be able to give you the opportunity to discuss your issue anonymously on the computer with your classmates. Remember that e-mail and chatting are potential sources for your paper, so always generate a print copy of any exchanges you think are particularly interesting or pertinent. Your instructor may want you to submit print copies of electronic material you quote or paraphrase in your final paper.

You should make a bibliography card for any site on the Internet that you want to visit again or that contains information you want to use in your paper.

Make a note of the author's name (if known), the title of the document (in quotes), the title of the complete work (underlined if applicable), the date of publication (if available), the number of pages or paragraphs (if given, or n. pag. "no pagination"), the publication medium (Online), the name of the computer network, and the date you visited the address. Add, finally, the word "Available," and write out the full http address (URL). You will need this information later when you assemble the bibliography for your paper. Add an annotation that includes a brief summary of the site's content and how you intend to use it in your paper. Figure 11.5 offers an example.

Also, you should make a separate bibliography card for every print book, article, or pamphlet that looks useful and that you want to locate. A bibliography card for a book must include the author, title, place of publication, publisher, date of publication, and call number so that you can find it later in the library. Add an annotation or explanation of how you will use the source in your paper. Figure 11.6 provides an example.

A bibliography card for an article must include the author's name (if there is one), the title of the article, name of the publication, volume (if there is one), the date of publication, the page numbers, and the call number or other description of location in the library. Add an annotation to each card about how you will use the source in your paper. Figure 11.7 provides an example.

The call numbers for periodicals will be easy to find if they are listed in the computer. If they are not, ask the librarian. Often, a library's list of periodicals and corresponding call numbers are printed in books that are located throughout the library. Be forewarned. Some of the older issues of a periodical may be in bound volumes in the book stacks, some of the newer ones may be on microfilm, and the newest issues may be stacked on shelves in the current-periodicals section of the library. You may have to look for a while to find what you want.

Emal Russ. "Jury Nullification." <u>The Eagle</u> 1995. 3 pp. Online. Internet. 11 July 1996. Available. <http://www.pacific.net/~dglaser/EAGLE/ISSUES/ISSUE 23-9/07juryNullification. html>

Use to define and explain jury nullification. An example of why it is crucial that juries understand their rights and duties. This has great appeal because it discusses the little known power of a jury to nullify a law if the jurors believe the law is unjust.

Figure 11.5 A Bibliography Card for an Article from the Internet with http Address

Wishman, Seymour. <u>Anatomy of a Jury:</u> <u>The System</u> <u>on Trial</u>.

New York: Times Books, 1986.

| Annotation | Use to demonstrate problems with present system. Author has been trial lawyer for 20 years and has tried hundreds of cases. Objective, but with some lawyer's bias. Wide audience appeal. | KF 8972 .W57 Stacks | Call number |

Figure 11.6 A Bibliography Card for a Book with Annotation and Call Number[9]

When you complete your bibliography search, you will have a card for each item you want to find along with its location in the library or on the Internet. You will also have written on the card how you now think you will use each source in your paper. You can add author information and a general evaluation to this annotation later when you get your hands on the source itself.

Now you are ready to go find the books and articles. Be prepared for a certain amount of frustration. If your book is checked out, for example, look at the other books shelved in the same area. They will also be on your subject and may

Robinson, Archie S. "We the Jury: Who Serves, Who Doesn't." <u>U.S.A. Today:</u> <u>The Magazine of the American Scene</u>. 120 (January 1992): 62–63.

| Annotation | Use for background information on characteristics of juries. Author has examined current surveys of data. Very objective source. Wide appeal. | L11 S36 | Call number and location |

Figure 11.7 A Bibliography Card for an Article in a Magazine with Annotation and Location in Library

---

[9]I am indebted to Peggy Kulesz for the idea of adding annotations.

be as useful as the one you can't find. Also, make enough bibliography cards for articles so that if you cannot find some of them, you will be able to find others.

Survey and Skim. When you have located your research material, do not try to completely read through all of it. You will never finish. It is important, however, to understand the context of the material you quote and to learn something about the author. Survey rather than read books and articles (see Chapter 3). Use this technique to locate information quickly. It is especially important to read the preface to a book to learn the author's position on the issue. Then use the table of contents and index to find specific information. After you have surveyed, you can then skim relevant parts to find the specific information you need. To skim, read quickly every fourth or fifth line, or sweep your eyes across the page in large diagonal movements. If you know what you are looking for and you are concentrating on finding it, you will be able to use these means to locate information quickly and successfully.

Read Creatively to Generate Ideas. Surveying and skimming may not always yield the understanding that you require, particularly if the material is difficult or dense or if you do not know exactly what information you are looking for. In these situations, switch from surveying or skimming to creative reading to help you think and get additional ideas for your paper.

Creative reading is different from some of the other types of reading that you do. For example, *leisure reading* is done for relaxation and pleasure. *Study reading* requires you to read, understand, learn, and remember material so that you can pass a test. *Critical reading,* which you learned to do in Parts One and Two of this book, has you identify and analyze the parts of an argument within an overall context. *Creative reading* enables you to get ideas and think critically. Here are some questions that you can keep in mind to guide creative reading.

1. What strikes me in this text? What interests me? Why?
2. What new ideas and answers are occurring to me as I read?
3. How can I relate (compare, elaborate, apply, associate) this new material with what I already know?
4. Do these new ideas challenge any of my existing ideas? How? Can I reconcile the differences?
5. What are the implications of these new ideas?
6. How can I use these new ideas in my paper?

Remember to use the Toulmin model to read all argument. It will help you focus on the important parts: the claim, the support, and the warrants. It will also call your attention to the different ways that other authors handle rebuttal. You may want to follow someone's example when you write your own.

Take Some Notes and Fill In Your Outline. Keep your preliminary outline handy as you read and take notes, and then take notes to fill in your outline. Revise your outline as needed.

Either write notes on cards or copy the material you intend to use on one of the copy machines. Whichever system you use, you must differentiate among the material you quote, the material you write in your own words (paraphrase), the material you summarize, and your own ideas. Code the different types of information by using different colors of cards, by writing with different colors of pens, or by labeling the type of information on each card. Place all of your own ideas in square brackets [ ], and always indicate directly quoted material by placing it in quotation marks.

If you decide to use the copy machine instead of writing note cards, make sure to copy the entire article or entire section of a book and write source information on it: the name of the publication, the volume, and the date for an article, and the author, title, city of publication, publisher, and date for a book. Consider copying the first couple of pages of each periodical or book so you do not have to write down all of the publication information by hand. Also, if you generated and printed search lists from your library's computer databases, they will usually contain all of the publication information you need. If you printed these lists, then be sure not to throw them away. They can prove to be valuable. However you obtain the publication information, get it the first time so that you will not have to go back to find this material again.

Indicate at the top of the card or in the margin of copied material where you intend to use it in your paper. Use a brief version of a heading on your preliminary outline for this cross-referencing.

Write only brief source information on your note cards because complete information is available on your bibliography cards. The author's name is usually enough, unless you are using two books by the same author. Then write the author's name and a short title at the top of each note card. Copy quoted material exactly, and place it in quotes so that it will go into your paper that way. Add the page number at the end. See Figure 11.8 for an example of a note card with a direct quote.

Problems—current system

Wishman.

"Jury instructions are often incomprehensible because they are drafted by lawyers and judges who do not realize how much of their 'legalese' vocabulary and syntax was acquired in law school… little effort is made to write clear and simple language for those not legally trained." p. 224

Figure 11.8 A Note Card with Quoted Material

Introduction—statistics

Robinson.

He quotes survey done by defense trial lawyers assoc.
45% adult Americans have been called for jury duty.
17% have served through a trial.

p. 62

Figure 11.9 A Paraphrased Note Card

Paraphrased material should also be recorded carefully and accurately with the page number at the end. Since you are condensing or changing the wording of this material, do not place it in quotation marks. You will still have to let your reader know where you got it when you write your paper, so include on the card the author's name and page number. Also indicate where you will use it in your paper. Figure 11.9 provides an example. Figure 11.10 provides an example of a note card with the student essayist's original idea on it.

Arrange these cards as you go along according to the categories that are written at the top. Then place the categories in the sequence you think you will follow in your paper. The cards are now ready to work into your paper when you write the first draft.

---

need for change

mine.

If the judge gives instructions to the jury only once and in unfamiliar legal language, the jury will forget or confuse them. The current system needs to be improved.

Figure 11.10 A Note Card with an Original Idea or Reaction on It

EVALUATE YOUR RESEARCH MATERIALS

Your main concern in evaluating research materials is to determine that it is relevant to the particular points you are making in your paper. Research materials, when worked into a paper, can clarify, prove, justify, elaborate on, illustrate, and add interest to the major ideas. But before they can function in any of those ways, they must first be relevant and related to the topics they support.

You will also discover that each book or article you locate for research will fit into categories similar to those described at the beginning of Chapter 3. Identifying this material by category will make you more aware of what you are using and will also help you interpret it for your audience.

Extremist, Biased, True-Believer Writing.   Recognize biased material by the emotional language, extreme examples, and implicit value systems that are associated with extremist rather than mainstream groups. One student doing research on changing the two-party system in the United States encountered so much odd, extreme material that she almost had to change to a new issue. She knew that if she used only the extremist material in her paper, she would appeal to a very small audience.

Deliberate Argumentative Writing with Wider Audience Appeal.   Recognize argumentative material by its obvious position on a controversial issue and, specifically, by its claim, support, and warrants. Learn what you can about the author's credentials and about the sources consulted to provide support. The purpose will be clear, and the reasons and support will have appeal for a specific audience. Discover which audience, and decide whether the material has sufficiently wide appeal so that it might even be acceptable to a universal audience.

Exploratory Writing.   Recognize exploratory material by its objective explanation of several different views or perspectives on any issue. Use this material to help you define your own position and plan ways to refute others.

Objective Writing with a Hidden or Unconscious Argumentative Purpose.   An unusual amount of emotional language, carefully selected or stacked evidence, and quotes from biased sources and authorities characterize this material. Use such material to support your own position if the audience will accept it. Or attack the obvious bias in this material if you want to refute it.

Objective, Factual Writing.   Genuinely objective writing contains facts and information that do not change from one source to another. It may include surveys, almanacs, data lists, polls, reports (including scientific reports), and some news articles. It will be acceptable as proof to your audience if you convince them also that the data were compiled, interpreted, and reported by objective, unbiased, responsible, and experienced researchers.

You can further evaluate each research source by comparing it with other sources on the same subject, by analyzing the warrants, by applying the tests for the validity of the proofs, by determining whether or not the source in which you found it is biased, by looking up reviews, and by asking your professor for an opinion about it. Finally, you should also judge whether a source is moral or immoral, ethical or unethical according to your standard of values.

EXERCISES AND ACTIVITIES

1. SMALL GROUPS: PRACTICE DEVELOPING PROOFS FOR DIFFERENT TYPES OF CLAIMS

Each group works on one of the five tasks in the following lettered list. Use a claim that a group member has already written, or make a claim about a familiar campus issue such as parking, registration, overloaded classes, or opportunities for social life. Write this claim in five different ways, for example:

Fact: Social life on this campus is nonexistent.
Definition: To determine whether social life exists on this campus, we need to define and describe an acceptable social life for college students.
Cause: The lack of social life on campus is caused by programming plans that have failed.
Value: Social life on this campus is worse than it was in high school.
Policy: Social life needs to be improved through direct action by students, faculty, and administration.

Note that all of these claims are controversial. See other examples of claims in Chapter 6, pp. 162 to 171.

a. *Write a claim of fact.* Develop it with one-sentence proofs of the following types:
  (1) Causes and/or effects
  (2) Symptoms and signs
  (3) Induction
  (4) Analogies or comparisons
  (5) Definition
b. *Write a claim of definition.* Develop it with one-sentence proofs of the following types:
  (1) Comparison to a similar case
  (2) Literal or historical analogy
  (3) Figurative analogy
  (4) Classifying or placing it in a category with known characteristics
c. *Write a claim of cause.* Develop it with one-sentence proofs of the same types used above for claim of fact.
d. *Write a value claim.* Develop it with one-sentence proofs of the following types:
  (1) A value proof
  (2) A motivational proof

(3) A quotation from an authority

(4) A definition

(5) A comparison

e. *Write a policy claim.* Develop it with one-sentence proofs of the following types:

(1) Literal analogies

(2) A quotation from an authority

(3) A motivational proof

Number or arrange your proofs in the best logical order and read your brief arguments aloud to the class.

2. PRACTICE BURKE'S PENTAD AND WRITE A PAPER

Use Burke's pentad to analyze the whole context and particularly the cause either of the claim you have written for your paper or a claim generated in response to a recent event that is stirring controversy on the national or local scene: a change in policy, a crime, a riot or demonstration, a diplomatic visit, a political appointment, job layoffs, and so on. Check the newspaper. Then answer the following questions:

a. *Act:* What was done?

b. *Scene:* When or where was it done?

c. *Agent:* Who did it?

d. *Agency:* How did he (she, they) do it?

e. *Purpose:* Why did it happen?

Decide which of the five perspectives provides the strongest and most easily defensible cause. Express it in the form of a causal claim. Read your claims to the class, and write a one-page paper in which you explain the cause you selected.

3. PAIRS OF STUDENTS: INVENTION STRATEGY FOR POSITION PAPER USING BURKE'S PENTAD AND CHAINS OF REASONS

a. On your own, answer each of the five questions in Burke's pentad as it applies to your issue: What was done? When or where was it done? Who did it? How did he (she, they) do it? And why did it happen? Write a paragraph of at least 100 words in which you synthesize your responses.

b. Exchange your synthesis with a classmate. Read each other's syntheses and write a thought-provoking question that asks for additional information about the topic or about the author's point of view. Return the paper to its author. Each author should read the question and write a reasoned response of two or three sentences. Exchange papers again, read the responses, and ask another question. Continue this questioning and answering until time is called.

c. When the time is up, read over the chain of reasons you developed for your issue. What surprised you? What do you need to research more? Where do you think your answers were the strongest? Once you have examined this particular chain of reasons closely, write a two-page paper analyzing the line of thinking that developed and how it might apply when you write your paper.[10]

4. THE POSITION PAPER: INVENTION OF IDEAS

Read through the list of invention strategies on the worksheet on the next page. They represent a composite of those described in this chapter and in Chapter 4. Some of them will be "hot spots" for you. That is, they will immediately suggest profitable activity for developing your paper. Check those that you want to use at this point and complete them. There may be only two or three. Include the Toulmin model, however. It is one of the best invention strategies for argument.

5. PAIRS OF STUDENTS: BECOMING FAMILIAR WITH THE LIBRARY

Visit your library with a partner and begin to do research. This exercise will take roughly one class period if you and your partner work quickly.

You and your partner should explore the issues you have selected to write about in your position papers. Or select an issue from the following list. Use the library to practice finding sources. To find your sources, work through the six library stations until you have completed the assignment. If you need help locating a source, ask a librarian for assistance.

Gun control
Violence on television
Death penalty
Sex education
Pollution
Censorship
Gang violence
The ozone layer

Library Stations

Station 1—On-line catalog or card catalog and periodical indexes.
At this station, locate books and articles about your subject by using the computer to do a key-word or subject search; or use the card catalog to find books about your subject, and one of the periodical indexes to find articles. Determine also how to find the call numbers for the periodicals if they are not listed in the computer. You will need to find a variety of sources that focus on your topic. Write down the call numbers of a book about your subject, a current periodical (one that has not yet been bound), a bound periodical, and an article that has been preserved on microfilm or microfiche, such as a weekly news magazine.
Station 2—The stacks.
Next, go to the stacks and use the call number to locate the book about your subject. When you find it, locate a copy machine, and make a copy of the

---

[10]I am indebted to Corri Wells for this class exercise.

Invention Worksheet

Write your claim _____ .

Begin to develop your claim by using some of the following invention strategies. If you cannot generate information and ideas, do some background reading and then come back to these.

1. Freewrite for five minutes.
2. Brainstorm additional ideas and details in brief phrases for another five minutes.
3. Make a list or map that shows the parts of your paper.
4. Explain to someone in your class or group what you expect to accomplish in your paper, or talk into a tape recorder about it.
5. Write your insights in a journal or on sheets of paper filed in a folder.
6. Mentally visualize and write a description of a scene related to your claim.
7. Make a preliminary outline. Add research and draft plans.
   a. Write a claim and some subclaims.
   b. Plan definitions for all controversial terms in your claim.
   c. Plan background reading and research.
   d. Plan background information for the reader.
   e. Identify your strongest opinions and best reasons.
   f. Think of tentative ways to begin and end your paper.
   g. Think of original examples, descriptions, or comparisons.
8. Think through the rhetorical situation. Remember TRACE: text, reader, author, constraints, exigence.
9. Use the Toulmin model to come up with the key parts of your paper.
   a. Classify your claim according to its type.
   b. Describe the support you will need.
   c. Describe one or more of your warrants.
   d. Decide on backing for your warrants.
   e. Plan your rebuttal strategy.
   f. Plan qualifiers if necessary.
10. Decide on some proofs that are appropriate for your type of claim. Remember SICDADS and VAM: sign, induction, cause, deduction, analogies (literal, figurative, historical), definition, and sign; and also value, authoritative, and motivational proofs.
11. Apply critical thinking prompts. Start with your claim, but then make these recursive; that is, apply them at any point and more than once during the process.

Associate it.	Think about it as it is now.	Evaluate it.
Describe it.	Think about it over time.	Elaborate on it.
Compare it.	Decide what it is a part of.	Project and predict.
Apply it.	Analyze its parts.	Ask why.
Divide it.	Synthesize it.	

12. Use Burke's pentad to establish cause: act, scene, agent, agency, purpose.
13. Use chains of reasons to develop your claim through five repetitions of *claim, why, because*: Describe where you need to add evidence.

title page or of the title page and the pages you will quote, paraphrase, or summarize in your paper. Bring the copy to your next class meeting.

Station 3—Bound periodicals.

Locate the bound periodicals in your library, and find the magazine article you selected. Make a copy of the first page of the article or of the entire article if you intend to draw information from it for your paper. (If for some reason the volume you need is not on the shelf, find another article in a bound volume and make a copy of the first page of it to demonstrate that you located these volumes.)

Station 4—Current periodicals.

Locate the current periodicals and find the article you selected. Make a copy of the first page of the article or of the entire article if you intend to use it. (Again, if you can't find the particular issue of the periodical you need, make a copy from another current periodical. Remember, the main goal of this orientation exercise is to familiarize you with the library. It is desirable to locate specific articles you can use.)

Station 5—Microfilm/microfiche.

Next, go to the part of your library that houses the microforms. Using the viewer, find your article and write down one interesting quote from the article. Bring the quote to class with you along with the name of the source, the date, and the page number where you found your quote.

Station 6—Reference desk.

Find the reference desk at your library. Ask the assistant working there to sign your assignment sheet. Now you will know where to go to receive assistance from reference librarians.[11]

6. THE POSITION PAPER: RESEARCH

Research Worksheet

1. Get organized for research: gather cards, pencils, money for the copy machine, paper, and a big envelope or folder. Review your preliminary outline and research plan.
2. Create a bibliography of ten to twelve sources. Plan to locate and use at least four to six for your paper. Include both books and articles, and write pertinent information on cards. Add annotations to the cards about possible use, author, and evaluation of evidence.
3. Survey and skim for specific information. Take notes.
4. Read creatively for original ideas. Take notes.
5. Make evaluative judgments about each source.

---

[11]This exercise was prepared by Leslie Snow.

7. THE POSITION PAPER: WRITE AN ANNOTATED BIBLIOGRAPHY

Go to the library and find ten quality sources that you think will be valuable for your position paper. Copy all the information you will need to cite your sources in the MLA or APA format (see pp. 392 to 400 for information on how to do this). Use separate cards or sheets of paper for each item so that you can later place them in alphabetical order. Do not read each item; instead, survey and skim the contents thoroughly enough to get a good idea of the general content. Summarize this information in a short paragraph for each item. Add a short explanation of how you might use the source in your paper. Alphabetize the ten sources and type them. An example of an annotated bibliography appears on below.

Student Paper

ANNOTATED BIBLIOGRAPHY

Back, Anthony L., Jeffrey I. Wallace, Helene E. Starks, and Robert E. Perlman. "Physician-Assisted Suicide and Euthanasia in Washington State: Patient Requests and Physician Responses." Journal of the American Medical Association 275 (1996): 919–24.

The objective of this study was to estimate how often physicians receive requests for physician-assisted suicide and euthanasia. The conclusion of the study is that requests for physician-assisted suicide and euthanasia are not rare. Another conclusion is that patients are more concerned with becoming a burden or suffering a loss of personal dignity and control than they are concerned with pain and personal physical suffering.

I will use this study to show that the issues surrounding assisted suicide and euthanasia are not isolated. The results shown in this study, however, clearly describe that the exigence is (or should be) equally present for all people.

Beauchamp, Tom L., ed. Intending Death: The Ethics of Assisted Suicide and Euthanasia. Upper Saddle River, NJ: Prentice Hall, 1996.

This book includes many perspectives on the ethical questions raised by assisted suicide and euthanasia. Many of the essays offer historical and even personal perspectives concerning the issues. The introduction (written by the editor) is excellent, as it lays the groundwork for the assisted suicide/euthanasia issues by exploring definitions, language, morality, and the current state of affairs.

I will use this book by choosing two or three of the essays that express different slants on the issues. I will also use the introduction to help me set up some of my definitions.

Cowley, Geoffrey, and Mary Hager. "Terminal Care: Too Painful, Too Prolonged." Newsweek. 4 Dec. 1995: 74–75.

This article reports on a study conducted by the American Medical Association that found that many patients, even if they have living wills, are not having their last wishes honored by doctors and are dying in ICU units across the country.

The article uses the example of a 92-year-old woman who arrived at an emergency room with an exploded digestive tract. She specifically refused surgery, but the doctors continued with the surgery anyway. She died, in pain, three weeks later. The article says that doctors do not accept death as a part of life, and that "every one of us is currently at risk of dying on someone else's terms" (75).

I particularly liked the conclusion of this article, and so I will probably quote more heavily from it than from the rest of the article. It seems clear that American patients and their doctors need to arrive at a place where personal wishes can be discussed, recorded, and honored.

DeathNET. 10 Sept. 1996 <http://www.rights.org/~deathnet/bridge.html>.

DeathNET is an international information service dealing with the end-of-life issues and the rights of the terminally ill. This site offers a web conference area, although registration is required to participate. The conference area is reportedly devoted to the intelligent discussion of end-of-life issues and problems. This site claims to sincerely consider all aspects of the end-of-life issues, but it is clearly sympathetic to the right of the individual to choose his or her means of death.

I might use this site by downloading specific up-to-date articles that will help to illustrate exigence. Since the site is updated with all of the latest news concerning Kevorkian and others involved in litigation, I might use it to show the very latest developments in the areas of assisted suicide and euthanasia.

Euthanasia World Directory. 10 Sept. 1996 <http://www.efn.org/~ergo/>.

The Euthanasia World Directory is a non-profit listing of all right-to-die groups. This site also includes information on suicide, assisted suicide, euthanasia laws, living wills, Dr. Kevorkian, Hemlock Society, Derek Humphry, and more. This site offers lots of links to almost every conceivable topic related to death and dying. Although certainly pro-choice in matters of death and dying, this site offers more than propaganda. One of the links even recommends movies that deal sensitively with issues concerning death and dying.

Since this site has a more personal slant, I might use it to gain personal examples and illustrations to help humanize the issues. It is important that these issues are not abstracted to the point where people forget that real lives are involved, and there is ample information at this site that can be used to remind my audience of that.

Fein, Esther B. "The Right to Suicide: Some Worry Could Evolve Into a Duty to Die." New York Times 7 Apr. 1996: L24.

In this article, Fein argues that many of the terminally ill will not want to become burdens to their families, and if society allows assisted suicide as a legal option, many of these people will think it is their duty to commit suicide. Fein also presents some of the arguments for and against assisted suicide from a financial viewpoint. Assisted suicide can save money in terms of cutting short prolonged and inevitably useless care and treatment of terminally ill patients, but financial problems might also prompt someone to take the route of assisted suicide even though he or she might not really want to die.

I will use this article to give voice to the opposition and to use for my rebuttal. Fein's concerns are valid in some contexts, but I think she is taking a "slippery-slope" attitude. I believe that if assisted suicide is regulated (meaning that each terminally ill person must meet specific and stringent guidelines before becoming eligible for assisted suicide) and that if a terminally ill person uses financial concerns to determine his or her ultimate decision, that is a legitimate basis for choosing to exit this world early. Fein seems to think that is unreasonable. I don't.

Gutmann, Stephanie. "Death and the Maiden." <u>New Republic</u>. 24 June 1996: 20–28.

This article points out that the first eight of Dr. Kevorkian's early clients were women and that their medical complaints were questionable. For instance, the first woman that Kevorkian assisted to kill herself suffered from very early-stage Alzheimer's. She was still able to beat her grown son at tennis, and her memory was generally fine except for slight lapses. Gutmann raises serious questions concerning the ethics of Dr. Kevorkian's actions, and she hints that he preys on what might be the most emotionally vulnerable person in society—the middle-aged woman.

I might use this article in a rebuttal. One of the main questions brought up by end-of-life issues is who is responsible for deciding when assisted suicide should be performed?

Hawkes, Edward. Personal interview. 30 June 1996.

Dr. Hawkes is a general practitioner against active assisted suicide for ethical and religious reasons, and he discusses the different kinds of advice he offers his patients who seek his assistance to end their lives (counseling, hospice, and further treatment). Dr. Hawkes is not against passive euthanasia, however, and he tells about some of the situations in which he is certain that he hastened the dying process through the use of morphine and other pain-inhibiting drugs. Dr. Hawkes' argument is based on a claim of definition, as he makes a clear distinction between active and passive euthanasia.

I might use Dr. Hawkes' comments to help make the distinction between active and passive euthanasia. The more I read, the more I realize what an important distinction this is for proponents as well as opponents of assisted suicide and euthanasia. Dr. Hawkes makes comments that are personal *and* professional, so I think that excerpts will make a greater impact than a dry definition would.

Kevorkian, Jack. "A Modern Inquisition." <u>Humanist</u>. Nov.–Dec. 1994: 7–9.

This article is adapted from a speech Dr. Kevorkian delivered upon receiving the 1994 Humanist Hero Award from the American Humanist Association at its annual conference in Detroit, Michigan. In this article, Kevorkian argues that our society is not civilized and that we have not progressed much beyond the Dark

Ages. Kevorkian argues that money is the impetus that keeps assisted suicide from becoming law. He also argues that religious and secular hospitals should operate separately with religious hospitals able to "perform any insanity they wish" (8). Although this article is rather rambling, it offers a clear glimpse into Kevorkian's personal and ethical motivations for what he does.

Since Kevorkian is the leading figure in terms of the assisted suicide question, I will be using quotes from this article to represent his voice as well as to give justification for Kevorkian's actions and for the practice of assisted suicide in general. Kevorkian is extremely outspoken, so his rhetoric lends itself to effective quotes.

United States Committee on Finance. 103rd Cong., 2nd sess. Hearings on End of Life Issues and Implementation of Advance Directives under Health Care Reform. Washington: GPO, 1994.

This hearing deals with the implications of death and dying to the economy in general, and to the health care reform issue in particular. Many doctors were in attendance, and their prepared and extemporaneous statements reflect more ethical concerns than they do economic ones. The issues brought up in this hearing are many, and the minutes are an excellent source for understanding the concerns and stands of the different U.S. government officials on the issues related to death and dying.

I might use this document to explore the problems of bureaucratic involvement in issues that I think are best dealt with on an individual and private basis.[8]

8. QUESTIONS ON THE CHAPTER
a. What three inventional strategies discussed in this chapter particularly appeal to you? Describe them and explain how you might use them.
b. What are the five elements of Burke's pentad? How is the pentad useful in argument? What, in particular, does it help to establish?
c. What method is suggested in this chapter to help you create a chain of reasons about your issue?
d. Several argument theories and models were reviewed in this chapter to help you review your ideas and think about them. Choose two that will be particularly useful to you. Why are they useful?
e. What is the value of making bibliography cards, writing annotations, and writing how you might use the source? How can this activity help you as you research and write your paper?
f. What three types of information might you write on note cards?
g. What should you take into consideration when you evaluate your research sources?

---

[8]Prepared by Samantha Masterton.

CHAPTER 12

Organizing, Writing, and Revising

This chapter will provide you with the information you need to create some order in the material you have gathered so that you can now write your argument paper. Specifically, you will be taught some ways to organize and outline, to incorporate research into your first draft, and to revise and prepare the final copy. Organization, or deciding on a framework of ideas for your paper, will be dealt with first.

HOW DOES ORGANIZATION HELP YOU AND YOUR READER?

Everyone has a natural tendency to associate or group ideas and to place them in an order so that they make sense and are easier to remember. You have probably already begun to do this with the materials for your paper. You may have made a preliminary outline, labeled note cards, and written some lists. Eventually, these activities will help your reader, who will understand organized ideas far more easily than disorganized ones. To illustrate this fact, here are two examples. The ideas and information in Example 1 are a collection of ideas for a value paper that have not yet been organized.

Example 1. *Claim: Women have more opportunities for variety in their lives now than they had 50 years ago.*

Women's movement.
Several causes for changes in women's opportunities.
Comparison between women at mid-twentieth and at end of twentieth century.
Some women are dysfunctional.
Examples of three contemporary women.
Not all changes are good—signs of stress in women, men, children.

Women are now self-actualized.
Statistical data suggesting the variety of positions occupied by women in 1990s and in 1950s.
Labor-saving devices, education, economy, and women's ambitions contribute to change.
A review of human needs and motivation and how they relate to women.
Improved opportunities for women.
The effects of the changes on men and children.
Analysis of the causes for the changes in opportunities for women.
Donna Reed and Murphy Brown.

How can this jumble of ideas and information be organized for an effective argument paper? Thinking about organization requires that you identify the *parts*, place them in an *order*, and establish some *relationships* among them. In other words, you must establish reasons for discussing one idea before another.

In Example 2 the parts have been rearranged. The same items appear in both examples, but they have been organized in Example 2 according to the following rationale:

1. The issue is introduced as a fact, that women have more opportunity now. This fact is illustrated with examples and statistics to focus the issue and get attention and interest.
2. Burke's pentad is used to explore causes for the changes: agency (labor-saving devices), scene (education and economy), agent (women and women's movement), and purpose (to satisfy personal needs) are cited as causes.
3. The effects of the changes are explained and illustrated with examples.
4. The opposition is refuted and negative perceptions are changed to positive values.
5. The value claim, that the changes are good, is stated and made more convincing with a quote.

Example 2. *Title: Improved Opportunities for Women*

Introduction: Women now have a wide range of opportunities.

A comparison between women at mid-twentieth and end of twentieth century. Example, two television characters who reflect social mores: Donna Reed (1950s) and Murphy Brown (1990s).
Statistical data suggesting the variety of roles occupied by women in the 1990s and in the 1950s.

I. Analysis of the causes for the changes in women's roles.

Labor-saving devices—freed-up time.
Education—improved competencies.
Economy—requires two incomes.
Women's movement—made women more aware of human needs and motivation and how they relate to women.

II. Effects of the changes.

Women now able to meet needs for self-actualization in a variety of ways, some of which were formerly reserved for men.
Examples of three contemporary women who are satisfied with their lives: professional, military, homemaker.

III. Rebuttal: Some people argue that not all changes have been good and that there are signs of stress in women, men, and children. Actually, the effects they perceive as bad are good.

The stress for women is good stress because they now choose what they want to do.
Men are closer to their children because they share responsibility.
Children learn to take more initiative and shoulder more responsibility.
People made dysfunctional by the changes would probably have problems in any setting.

IV. Conclusion: *Claim: Women have more opportunities for variety in their lives now than they had 50 years ago.*

The benefits outweigh the problems.
Quote from an authority about women's current satisfaction.
No one would want to go back.

This is not the only organizational strategy that could have been used for this paper. The rebuttal, for example, could have been placed first. The effects could have been described before the causes. The value claim could have been placed at the beginning instead of at the end. Any one of these alternatives might have worked as well as another, provided they made sense to the author and were convincing to the audience.

Read the materials you have gathered for your own paper and think about (1) how they can be divided into *parts*, (2) how these parts can be placed in an *order*, and (3) what the logical *relationships* are among them. List the parts, tentatively number them to reflect order, and explain the rationale for your decisions.

To help you plan the *parts*, keep the Toulmin model in mind. Your parts should include a claim, support, and warrants, and possibly also backing for the warrants, a rebuttal, and a qualifier for the claim. Think also about the subclaims that represent the major sections of the paper and the facts, examples, and opinions that support them. Tentatively plan the introduction and conclusion and what to include in them. The usual functions of the introduction are to focus and introduce the topic, provide some background, and get the attention of the audience. The conclusion usually refocuses the claim through restatement and final, compelling reasons.

To help you think about *order*, keep in mind that the beginning of your paper is a strong position for arguments, but that the end is even stronger. Put your strongest material at or near the end, other strong material at the beginning, and the less impressive material in the middle. Also, think about your audience when determining order. For instance, for a hostile audience you might argue about women's roles by admitting that the 1950s were a good time for women, but adding that times have changed, and finally showing how the 1950s way of life is now impractical. For a neutral audience, you might want to present strong and interesting examples at the beginning to get attention and create interest. For a friendly audience, you can show how things are better right away and thus confirm an already favorable opinion.

To focus on *relationships*, use words that name the relationships you have worked out. As in Example 2, write the words *causes, effects,* and *rebuttals* into your plan to clarify the main sections and suggest the relationships among them.

HOW CAN ORGANIZATIONAL PATTERNS HELP YOU THINK AND ORGANIZE?

For centuries, authors have used certain established patterns of thought to help them think about, develop, and organize ideas. This practice benefits both authors and readers who, as a result, are able to follow and understand the material more easily. Some of these patterns of thought are particularly helpful for organizing the ideas in argument. The following list describes those most commonly used. These patterns, by the way, can dominate your paper as the dominant pattern or can combine as minor patterns within the dominant pattern to organize some of the sections.

1. **Claim-with-reasons (or reasons-followed-by-claim) pattern.** This pattern takes the following form:

> Statement of claim
>> Reason 1
>> Reason 2
>> Reason 3, and so forth

Set this pattern up by writing the claim, following it with the word *because,* and listing some reasons. Or list some reasons, follow them with the word *therefore,* and write the claim. For example, you may present the claim that we need a national health care program, which is followed by reasons: the unemployed have no insurance, the elderly cannot afford medicine, many children do not receive adequate health care. The reasons may be distinct and different from one another and set up like separate topics in your paper. Or you may have created a chain of related reasons by asking *why* and answering *because* five or six times. Also, some of your reasons may be used to refute, others to prove, and still others to show how your claim will meet the needs and values of the audience. Support all reasons with facts, examples, and opinions. You may use transitional phrases such as *one reason, another reason, a related reason,* or a *final reason* to emphasize your reasons and make them stand out in your paper.

2. **Cause-effect (or effect-cause) pattern.** The cause-effect pattern may be used to identify one or more causes followed by one or more effects or results. Or you may reverse this sequence and describe effects first and then the cause(s). For example, the causes of water pollution might be followed by its effects on both humans and animals. You may use obvious transitions to clarify cause-effect, such as "What are the results? Here are some of them," or simply the words *cause, effect,* or *result.*

3. **Applied criteria pattern.** This pattern establishes criteria or standards for evaluation and judgment and then shows how the claim meets them. For example, in an argument about children in day care, the criteria of physical safety, psychological security, sociability, and creativity are established as successful criteria for day-care centers. Then the claim is made that day care meets those criteria as well as or even better than home care, and support is provided. Or criteria for great poems are established, and the claim and evidence demonstrate how a particular poem meets those criteria. The applied criteria pattern is obviously useful for value arguments. It is also useful in policy arguments to establish a way of evaluating a proposed solution. You may want to use the words and phrases *criteria, standards, needs,* and *meets those criteria or needs* to clarify the parts of your paper.

4. **Problem-solution pattern.** The problem-solution pattern is commonly used in policy papers. There are at least three ways to organize these papers. The problem is described followed by the solution. In this case, the claim is the solution, and it may be stated at the beginning of the solution section or at the end of the paper. An alternative is to propose the solution first and describe the problems that motivated it last. Or a problem may be followed by several solutions, one of which is selected as the best. When the solution/claim is stated at the end of the paper, the pattern is sometimes called the delayed proposal. For a hostile audience, it may be effective to describe the problem, show why other solutions do not work, and finally suggest the favored solution. For example, you may want to claim that labor unions are the best solution for reducing unemployment. First, you describe the unemployment problem in vivid detail so that the audience really wants a solution. Then you show how government mandates and individual company initiatives have not worked. Finally, you show how labor unions guarantee employment for workers. You may use the words *problem* and *solution* to signal the main sections of your paper for your reader.

5. **Chronological/narrative pattern.** Material arranged chronologically is explained as it occurs in time. This pattern may be used to establish what happened for an argument of fact. For example, you may want to give a history of childhood traumas to account for an individual's current criminal behavior. Or you may want to tell a story to develop one or more points in your argument. Use transitional words like *then, next,* or *finally* to make the parts of the chronology clear.

6. **Deductive pattern.** Recall that deductive reasoning involves reasoning from a generalization, applying it to cases or examples, and drawing a conclu-

sion. For example, you may generalize that the open land in the west is becoming overgrazed; follow this assertion with examples of erosion, threatened wildlife, and other environmental harms; and conclude that the government must restrict grazing to designated areas. The conclusion is the claim. You may use such transitional phrases as *for instance, for example,* or *to clarify* to set your examples off from the rest of the argument, and *therefore, thus, consequently,* or *in conclusion* to lead into your claim.

7. **Inductive pattern.** The inductive pattern involves citing one or more examples and then making the "inductive leap" to the conclusion. For instance, five or six examples of boatloads of illegal immigrants landing in the United States who require expensive social services lead some people to conclude that they should be sent home. Others may conclude that they should be allowed to stay. No matter which claim/conclusion is chosen, it can be stated at the beginning or at the end of the paper. The only requirement is that it be based on the examples. The same transitional words used for the deductive pattern are also useful for the inductive: *for instance, for example,* or *some examples* to emphasize the examples, and *therefore, thus,* or *consequently* to lead into the claim.

8. **Comparison-contrast pattern.** This pattern is particularly useful in definition arguments and in other arguments that show how a subject is like or unlike other similar subjects. It is also often used to demonstrate a variety of similarities or differences. For example, the claim is made that drug abuse is a medical problem instead of a criminal justice problem. The proof consists of literal analogies that compare drug abuse to AIDS, cancer, and heart disease in a number of areas to redefine it as a medical problem. The transitional words *by contrast, in comparison, while, some* and *others* are sometimes used to clarify the ideas in this pattern.

9. **Rogerian pattern.** You were introduced to Rogerian argument in Chapter 8. Here is a review of the recommended strategy for this pattern of argument: You first introduce the issue and state the opponent's position on it. Then you show that it is understood, valued, and viable in certain contexts or conditions. Next, you state your own position and show the contexts in which it is valid. Finally, you show how the opponent's position would be improved by adopting all or at least some elements of your position. In other words, you finally show how the positions complement one another.

For example, the issue of gays in the military, each time it surfaces, results in particularly adamant positions on either side. Military leaders oppose openly gay behavior in the military, and gay service personnel want the same rights and opportunities as other people, including the right to be open about their sexual preferences. Rogerian strategy aimed at convincing military leaders to change their minds requires an opening statement that explains their position and gives reasons and evidence to show that it is understood and considered valid in certain circumstances. Next, the counterposition that gays should be allowed to be openly gay is offered along with reminders that gay military personnel have served well in the past and that their gay behavior has not been harmful. Finally, the claim is made that the military is improved by allowing gays and lesbians to serve as openly gay personnel because they are happier and better-adjusted employees.

10. **Motivated sequence pattern.** A common distinction between argument and persuasion is that argument results in agreement or conviction and persuasion results in action or changed behavior. The motivated sequence is a persuasive pattern that is used to motivate an audience to do something. You may find it useful when you want to persuade your audience to act. There are five steps. We will use, as an example, the campus issue that is a problem at some schools: insufficient numbers of classes for all the students who want to enroll.

a. *Attention.* First, create some interest and desire.

   Example: How often have you tried to register for a class only to be told that it is closed and you must try again next semester?

b. *Need.* Now, heighten the audience's need to do something about this situation.

   Example: A problem arises because you, like many other students, had planned to graduate at the end of this semester. If you cannot get into the classes you need to graduate, once again you put your life on hold for another half year. And what guarantee exists that the needed classes will be available to you next semester? The frustration may continue.

c. *Satisfaction.* Next, show that your proposed plan of action will solve the problem and satisfy the audience's needs.

   Example: There is a way of dealing with this problem. Enroll in the nearby college, take the course there, and transfer it back here to be counted as credit toward your graduation. You will complete your course work on schedule, learn just as much, and be ready to take that job you lined up at the time you agreed to start. You may have to drive more and complete some extra paperwork, but it will finally be worth it.

d. *Visualization.* Describe how things will be if the plan is put into action. Be positive.

   Example: Imagine yourself six months from now with your diploma in hand, ready to tackle the real world, take on an interesting job, and make some money for a change. You'll be able to make car payments, get into a nice apartment, and put aside the pressures of school, including trying to get into closed classes.

e. *Action.* Finally, tell the audience what it needs to do to satisfy its needs and create the desired outcomes.

   Example: It's easy to enroll at the other college. Call the registrar and start the necessary paperwork today.

Note that the motivated sequence includes the introduction and conclusion in its total structure. The other organizational patterns do not.[1]

---

[1]The motivated sequence pattern is popularized by Alan Monroe in his public speaking textbooks.

11. **Exploratory pattern.** The pattern you used to write your exploratory paper can be expanded for a single-perspective argument paper. Recall that you explained the positions of those in favor of the issue, those against it, and those with various views in between. Your objective was to explain the range of different perspectives on the issue. Having stated these positions, you can now expand your exploratory paper by refuting some of them, and by stating and supporting your own. You may want to use another pattern, such as the claim with reasons, to organize your own position on the issue.

Some of these organizational patterns are particularly appropriate for specific types of claims. Table 12.1 suggests patterns you might want to consider as promising for particular argumentative purposes. You may, of course, combine more than one pattern to develop a paper. For example, you may begin with a narrative of what happened, then describe its causes and effects, and finally propose a solution for dealing with the problems created by the effects.

Use organizational patterns to help you think and organize your ideas. The patterns may be too constraining if you start with one and try to fill it in with your own material. You may prefer to work with your ideas first, without the conscious constraints of a pattern to guide you. At some point, however, when you are finished or nearly finished organizing your ideas, move out of the creative mode and into the critical mode to analyze what you have done. You may find that you have arranged your ideas according to one or more of the patterns without being consciously aware of it. This is a common discovery. Now use what you know about the patterns to improve and sharpen the divisions among your ideas and to clarify these ideas with transitions. You will ultimately improve the readability of your paper by making it conform more closely to one or more specific patterns of organization.

TABLE 12.1 Appropriate Patterns for Developing Types of Claims (The first in each list is the one most commonly used.)

CLAIM OF FACT	CLAIM OF DEFINITION	CLAIM OF CAUSE	CLAIM OF VALUE	CLAIM OF POLICY
Claim + reasons	Deductive	Cause-effect	Applied criteria	Problem-solution
Inductive	Claim + reasons	Claim + reasons	Cause-effect	Applied criteria
Chronological/ narrative	Comparison	Rogerian	Claim + reasons	Motivated sequence
	Rogerian	Deductive	Chronological/ narrative	Cause-effect
Cause-effect	Exploratory	Exploratory	Rogerian	Claim + reasons
Rogerian	Inductive		Inductive	Rogerian
Exploratory			Deductive	Exploratory
			Comparison	
			Exploratory	

OUTLINE THE PAPER AND CROSS REFERENCE NOTE CARDS

You have already been provided with a rationale and some ideas for outlining in Chapter 4. Most people need some sort of outline to guide their writing when they are working not only with their own ideas but also with outside sources. Make the kind of outline that works best for you. Think of it as a guide that will help you write later. At the very least, indicate on your outline the major ideas or headings, and list under them the ideas and research you will use for support and development. Read through your invention and research notes, and check to make certain that all are cross-referenced in some way to the outline. Identify the places where you need more information and research. If you have gathered research material on cards, paperclip the cards to the places on the outline where they will be used later. Or if you have copied material, use numbers to cross-reference the passages you intend to quote to your outline. Work with your outline until it flows logically and makes sense.

If you have the opportunity, discuss your outline with your instructor, a peer editing group, or a friend. Someone else can often tell you if the organization is clear and logical, point out places where you will need more support and evidence, and also tell you whether or not the warrants will be generally acceptable.

Here is an example. The following outline is more complete than a preliminary outline to guide research. It would be complete enough to guide writing for some people. Other people might want to add more detail to it before attempting the first draft. It is the sort of outline one might take to a peer editing group to discuss and get suggestions for the actual writing of the paper.

Outline: **Working title for paper: Is Technology Good or Bad? The Technophobic Perspective**

Introduction: Value claim: Even though most people claim to be technophiles, many are really closet technophobes, and that may represent a desirable state of affairs.

(Define technophobia as a fundamental distrust of modern technology, and give some examples, like getting the answering machine when you need to talk with a human, the old typewriter that was updated to a computer on "Murder, She Wrote," and automated teller machines and credit cards that cause some people to lose control over their financial resources.)

Reasons:

I. Technology is advancing too rapidly, which causes some people to lag behind and resent it.
- It's hard to learn the new ways and give up the old ones.
- It's hard to adjust to constant change.

continued

II. Technology is perceived as dehumanizing by many people.
- Technology reduces human initiative.
- New machines sometimes have a higher profile than individual people.

III. Technology changes the way many of us use our time, and we resent it.
- We spend less time thinking and reflecting and more time engaged with machines (Example: People who spend hours a day on the Internet).
- We spend less time outdoors communing with nature and more time inside watching movies and television.
- We are losing our sense of what is "real."

IV. Many people become nostalgic for the way things were.

Conclusion: It is time for technophobes to declare themselves, and they should not be ashamed of their technophobia. It may lead to a healthy skepticism about technology that will help humans maintain their humanity while they objectively evaluate what technology can and cannot contribute to their lives.

Note that this outline is worked out in detail in some areas but not in others. The ideas in it so far, however, belong to the author. The peer group that critiques it at this stage would be able to identify the areas in which this paper is likely to need more development and would suggest areas for research. The author goes to the library and finds three relevant articles about: (1) students who spend too much time on the Internet, (2) a professor who will not give up his old typewriter for a computer, and (3) a teacher who likes her old bicycle.

The following are some examples of notes that this author has taken to use in the rough draft of the paper (see Figures 12.1 to 12.5). They have been taken from the essay about the old bicycle that appears on page 384.

Mednick, Johanne. "The Highs of Low Technology." *Toronto Globe and Mail.* 23 July 1993:

Use as an example of 4, nostalgia.

Figure 12.1 The Bibliography Card for the Article by Mednick with Annotation.

> <u>4. Nostalgia</u>
>
> Mednick
>
> "Perhaps my bike is representative of a world gone by, . . . My bike is certainly not built for speed. . . . It's built for taking time. It makes people feel relaxed." p. 16

Figure 12.2 A Direct Quote. The ellipsis (. . .) indicate that material has been omitted from the material quoted in paragraph 6 of Mednick's article

> <u>2. Dehumanizing</u>
>
> Mednick
>
> She says that her microwave and her computer make her feel that life is getting too complicated and out of control. p. 16

Figure 12.3 A Paraphrase of the Ideas in Paragraph 7 of Mednick's Article.

> <u>4. Nostalgia</u>
>
> Mednick
>
> She claims that people still long for the older, simpler machines like her old bicyle and the simpler way of life they represented. p. 16

Figure 12.4 A Summary of the Article by Mednick.

4. Nostalgia

mine

Examples of nostalgia for the old, besides Mednick's bicycle: wood stoves, old typewriters, old cash registers. People save these because of the ways of life they represent — they are still attractive to them.

Figure 12.5   A Card with the Author's Original Insight Written on It.

Essay

THE HIGHS OF LOW TECHNOLOGY

Johanne Mednick

I have a wonderful bicycle. Most people refer to is as "the old clunker," an an-   1
cient piece of metal the likes of which can be found in the dump or, if you're
lucky, at garage sales.

In other words, people trashed these things a long time ago. Mine is a   2
souped-up version of the basic "no-speeder," vintage 1930 or '40—two large
wheels, seat, handle bars, basket, bell and the simple mechanism that allows me
to pedal my way to wherever I'm going. I go uphill and downhill, easily gliding
past all the riders on racers and mountain bikes intent on engaging the right gear
for the occasion.

It's not that I'm an Amazon bike rider or anything. In fact, I won't make it   3
up those hills if I don't get the necessary run at the start. But I have confidence in
my bike. It gives me power, and I cherish its simplicity.

What intrigues me, in this age of technological innovation (which is   4
nowhere more apparent than in the bicycle world), is the number of people who
stop me and comment on my bike. It's a regular conversation piece. "Where did
you get that thing?" "I haven't seen one of those in ages." "What a great bike." I
get all kinds of comments—the best one being from a motorcycle gang who cornered me while I was locking it up. They politely suggested to me that I wear
gloves while riding to protect my hands. Maybe I should also don a leather
jacket.

But really, what is it that people are admiring? Are they admiring me for re-   5
sisting the lure toward mass bicycle consumerism? I must look like an eyesore
pedalling behind my family, who all ride the latest model of designer-coloured
mountain bike. (To them, I'm some sort of anomaly, an embarrassment not fit to

be on the road.) On the other hand, maybe people are just genuinely curious, as they would be if confronted with a dinosaur bone. I never get the feeling that they think I'm crazy for riding something archaic when I could be fiddling with gears and having a presumably easier time of things. I believe that this curiosity runs deeper. My bike seems to touch a sensitive chord in people, and I'm not quite sure what or why that is.

Perhaps my bike is representative of a world gone by, the world before gim- 6
micks and gadgets, accessories and attachments. A time when people thought in terms of settling into a cushioned seat, stopping the movement with their heel and travelling a bit slower than we are travelling now. My bike is certainly not built for speed, but who needs speed when I can coast along the streets, hold my head high and deliciously feel the wind on my face? It's built for taking time. It makes people feel relaxed.

When I'm riding my bike, I feel as though I have control. And I don't feel 7
that way about most things these days. I don't deny that my computer or my microwave make my life a lot easier. I use these things, but they also make me feel rather small and, in a strange way, inadequate. What if I press the wrong button? What if something goes wrong? Maybe if I learned to understand these appliances I'd feel better, more secure about my relationship with technology. But frankly, I'm not comforted by manuals and how-to courses. Of course there are always "experts" I could go to who seem to know everything about anything. Relative, friend or salesperson, these people seem to breathe the latest invention and revel in ingenuity.

I just don't get excited over yet another thing I could do if I pulled the right 8
lever or set the right program. Nervous and unsure in the beginning, I eventually adapt to these so-called conveniences and accept them as a part of life, but I'm not entirely convinced of their merit. I crave simplicity and I have a sneaking suspicion that many people feel the same way. That's why they admire my bike. It comforts them and gives them a sense of something manageable, not too complicated.

I'm not suggesting that we go back to a pioneer-village mentality. But I do 9
think it's important to respect that which is simple and manageable—no doubt difficult in a time when more is better and new is best. I'm proud that my clunker makes me and others feel good. It allows me the opportunity to relax and, at best when I'm heading down the road, escape what I don't understand.[2]

Now look back at the note cards on pages 382 to 384 and the outline on page 381. Note that at the top of each card the number and a short title of the relevant subidea on the outline are recorded. Thus "4. Nostalgia" refers to *point IV* on the outline. Note also that the quoted material is placed in quotation marks to remind the author that these are the essayist's exact words. The paraphrase, or rephrasing of the ideas in paragraph 7, is written in the author's words and thus is

---

[2] *Toronto Globe and Mail,* July 23, 1993, p. A16. Johanne Mednick is a teacher who lives in Canada. She wrote this article in 1993.

without quotes. The summary, also in the author's words and without quotes, states the main point of the article. When all of the notes have been taken on all of the articles, they can be stacked in the order in which they will be used in the paper and placed next to the outline. The author is now ready to begin the draft. Most of the material in the paper will be the insights, observations, ideas, and examples of the author. Some other material from the cards, however, will be incorporated into the paper to add interest and improve the clarity and credibility of the final paper.

HOW TO INCORPORATE RESEARCH INTO THE FIRST DRAFT

Use your common sense in working your research materials into your draft. Your objective is to create a smooth document that can be easily read while at the same time demonstrating to your readers exactly which materials are yours and which are drawn from outside sources. Introduce each quote as you write it into the draft, so that it is clear where your words and ideas leave off and where someone else's begin. Then write all quoted and paraphrased material into the context of the draft so that your entire paper will be in place for smooth reading. The following are three paragraphs that show the quoted, paraphrased, and summarized material from the Mednick article worked into the first draft so that it is absolutely clear what is the author's and what is Mednick's.

An Example of Incorporating Research Material

Many people become nostalgic for the ways things were. Some people keep old cash registers at their businesses to remind customers of days gone by. Other people fire up wood stoves to help them remember earlier times. Johanna Mednick, a teacher in Canada, claims that many people still long for older, simpler machines and also for the way of life they represent (16).

Mednick uses her old bicycle as an example. "Perhaps my bike is representative of a world gone by . . . ," she says. "My bike is certainly not built for speed . . . It's built for taking time. It makes people feel relaxed" (16).

New computers and microwave ovens, by contrast, make people feel that life is getting too complicated and out of control (Mednick 16).

Notice that in the first two paragraphs Mednick's name is used in the text to introduce the material that is attributed to her. Since it is clear from the context where her material begins and where it leaves off, it is only necessary to insert the page number of her article at the end of the borrowed material. In the third paragraph, Mednick's name is not included in the text and it is less clear whose idea this is. To make it absolutely clear to the reader that this is another idea of Mednick's, her last name along with the page number is placed at the end of the borrowed idea. The full information about this source and where it was first located will be placed on final bibliography pages at the end of the paper. The reader who wants to know when and where Mednick published her article can refer to those pages.

A Common Student Error

Avoid mixing your words with those of another author while neglecting to put the quoted words in quotation marks. Sometimes it is obvious to the reader where your words leave off and those of another author's begin since individual authors commonly differ in their style and voice. However, this creates a problem for the reader who cannot sort out your ideas from those of others. Example 1 shows what students often do without realizing they are mismanaging quoted material. Example 2 shows how to correct the problem. Read the first two paragraphs of the Mednick article first and then read Examples 1 and 2 below.

Example 1: The wrong way to incorporate research.

Low technology can be a high for many people. A wonderful bicycle that most people would refer to as an old clunker might bring its owner considerable pleasure. Its two large wheels, seats, handle bars, basket, bell, and pedals help its owner glide past all of the riders on racers and mountain bikes who are intent on engaging the right gear for the occasion (Mednick 16).

The problem with that paragraph is that the author has simply copied much of Mednick's original language without putting it in quotation marks to indicate which of it is her own and which has been supplied by the author. Example 2 shows the acceptable way of writing this same material. Notice how in this second example it is absolutely clear which of this paragraph belongs to Mednick and which belongs to the author.

Example 2: The right way to incorporate research.

"Low technology," according to Johanna Mednick, can be a "high" for many people. She owns a "wonderful bicycle" and says that "most people refer to it as an 'old clunker.'" Still, it brings its owner considerable pleasure. What she likes best about it are its "two large wheels, seat, handle bars, basket, bell, and pedals," which help its owner pass up other riders who are on more modern bikes (16).

Avoid Plagiarism

As you add quoted, paraphrased, and summarized material from other sources to your paper, you must indicate where your words leave off and someone else's begin, and you must also indicate the original source for all borrowed material. The next sections of this chapter will teach you how.

To simply use other people's ideas or words in your paper without acknowledging where they came from or to whom they belong is a form of academic theft called *plagiarism.* Although some students might think that they had not committed plagiarism in Example 1, above, because they quoted the source at the end of the paragraph, they actually have because they have used a considerable amount of Mednick's language verbatim without indicating that is hers. Penalties for plagiarism can be severe and range from a failing grade to probation or suspension from college. Avoid plagiarism by differentiating between your ideas and those of others at all stages of the paper-writing process. In fact, you were advised to color code your note cards to keep your ideas separate from the direct quotes, paraphrases, and summaries that you draw from other people's works. If you use the color-coding method, you will be less likely to confuse your work with that of others.

Cite Your Sources

Some of the main features of source acknowledgment appear at the end of the Exercise section in this chapter. Use this material as a handy reference guide when you are working borrowed material into your paper and also when you are preparing the final list of the works you have used. These methods will inform your reader exactly what material in your paper is yours, what belongs to other people, and where you found the material in the first place. You will first be shown a number of examples of ways to incorporate borrowed material into the text of your paper and to use intext citations (page numbers in parentheses) to show in brief form where it originally appeared. You will then be shown how to prepare entries for the list of sources that you have used. This list will appear at the end of your paper. Read through the types of sources that might appear on your list, beginning on page 395. They may suggest examples of resources for your paper that you have not thought of.

As you incorporate borrowed material from other sources, you will need to follow a system and a set of conventions that has been prescribed for this purpose. There are several such systems. The two that are taught at the end of this chapter are MLA style, which is recommended by the Modern Language Association for papers written in the humanities, and APA style, recommended by the American Psychological Association for papers written in the social sciences. Both give advice on how to acknowledge the work of other individuals in your paper and also how to give full information about these sources in a list of "Works Cited" (MLA) of "References" (APA) at the end of the paper. The Council of Biology Editors publishes the *CBE Manual,* now in a fifth edition, which shows how to document sources in scientific papers in such areas as the natural sciences, chemistry, geography, and geology. No matter which system you use, be consistent throughout your paper.

Additional examples of incorporating quoted, paraphrased, and summarized material along with lists of works cited and references appear in the two student argument papers that begin on page 401. Study the annotations in the margins of these papers. They demonstrate how quoted and summarized material can be incorporated into papers and acknowledged according to MLA style in the first paper and APA style in the second.

MAKE FINAL REVISIONS AND PREPARE THE FINAL COPY

There is considerable additional information in Chapter 4 that you can review to help you write and rewrite your paper. It may take several tries, but you will eventually get a version of your paper that you are content to show to other readers. Seek the help of your peer editing group, a tutor, your instructor, or other readers once again, when you have improved your paper as much as possible on your own. When you get to this point, you will think your paper is pretty good. Now is the time, however, to put aside your pride and let others take a final look at it. During this final revision process, you and your readers can use the Toulmin model to help you identify and revise the major elements in your paper.

1. Find your claim. Is it clear? Is it well positioned?
2. Check the quantity and quality of your support.
3. Check to see if your warrants are acceptable to your audience.
4. Decide if backing for your warrants would make them stronger.
5. Focus on your rebuttal, if you have one. Does it address all of the opposing arguments, and does it do so effectively?
6. Would it make your argument stronger to qualify your claim?

As you go through your paper these final times, make all the remaining changes, large and small. Write a meaningful title that reflects the content of your paper, if you haven't already. Rewrite parts by using better, different words; cut out anything that doesn't contribute to the meaning; add where necessary; re-arrange if you have a good reason to do so; and make all final corrections. You will finally reach a point where you are satisfied and ready to quit. Now it is time to prepare the final copy.

Type your paper on 8 1/2 × 11 inch paper, and double space it. Leave one-inch margins all around. One inch from the top of the first page, by the left margin, type and double space your name, your instructor's name, the course number, and the date. Double space again and type the title. Skip four spaces and begin typing your paper. You do not need to number the first page. Number all other pages, however, at the top right-hand corner with your last name before the page number. Attach the "Works Cited" or "References" page(s). Spell check it if you are using a computer and proofread it one last time. Your paper is now ready for submission.

EXERCISES AND ACTIVITIES

1. SMALL GROUPS, POSITION PAPER: PEER CRITIQUE OF OUTLINE

Make some sort of an outline or write a partial manuscript that will serve as a plan for your paper and bring it to class. Organize peer editing groups of three or four students. Explain to the group what your paper is about and how you plan to develop it. Get ideas from the others to help with drafting and possibly also with adding research.

2. WHOLE CLASS, POSITION PAPER: CREATE A PEER CRITIQUE SHEET

The peer critique sheet is a worksheet that provides a guide for revision. Make a list on the board of all of the special requirements for a good argument paper: clear claim, acceptable warrants, etc. Select five to ten items from this list that you believe are essential elements to consider during revision. Organize them on a peer critique sheet. The peer editing groups can now use these sheets to critique individual student papers and make recommendations for revision.

3. **SMALL GROUPS, POSITION PAPER: PEER CRITIQUE OF DRAFT**
   Draft and revise your paper and bring it to class. In your group, read all of the papers either silently or aloud, and make observations and recommendations about each of them on the peer critique sheets you created in Exercise 2. Discuss each paper in turn, giving strengths, weaknesses, and recommendations for improvement. Give the filled-in peer critique sheets to the student authors for further guidance.

4. **POSITION PAPER: ASSIGNMENT FOR PREPARING FINAL COPY**
   Make final revisions and prepare the final copy. Your paper should be five or six pages long, be double-spaced, and use approximately four or five outside sources. Use MLA format throughout unless advised to use APA or some other format. The two student papers on pages 401 to 407 can be used as examples. The first demonstrates general format, in-text citations, and the "Works Cited" page required for MLA style. The second demonstrates similar requirements for APA style. Notice, also, that in both papers the ideas that control the papers are the authors' original ideas and opinions and that the quoted and paraphrased material provides support for their ideas.

5. **POSITION PAPER: TOULMIN ANALYSIS**
   Write a one-page Toulmin analysis of your paper and submit it with your paper.

6. **POSITION PAPER: SUBMISSION LETTER**
   Write a letter to your instructor and submit it with your final paper. Describe what you like about your paper and what still dissatisfies you. Identify problems or passages where you would like some opinion.

7. **CLASS PROJECT: CONDUCT A SYMPOSIUM**
   You had the opportunity to practice debate at the end of Chapter 7. Some issues lend themselves to inquiry much more readily than to debate. Recall from Chapter 1 that the purpose of inquiry is to discover new views, knowledge, and truths about a complex issue. There are no clear-cut pro and con positions, no judges, and no emphasis on winning, as there often are in debate. Instead, there are potentially as many views as there are participants, and each participant contributes new insights, new reasons, new examples, or new perspectives that the other participants may or may not have considered. Everyone achieves better understanding of the issue through mutual feedback, and sometimes individuals are even persuaded to change their minds. One way to display a variety of perspectives on an issue of common concern is in the symposium format.

   a. Assignment 1.   Whole Class: Conduct a Symposium of Position Papers
      (1) Present one set of argument papers written during the semester by members of the class in a symposium format. Each student writes a

250-word abstract of his or her paper, which states the claim, the main points made about it, and some of the evidence. Each paper will take about two minutes to read.

(2) Organize groups around the same or related topics. The best group size is six or seven students with a moderator. The moderator calls on each student who in turn presents a paper. Each set of papers is followed by a five to ten minute question-and-answer period. Two sets of papers can usually be presented in a class period. Thus, most classes can complete the symposium activity in two class periods.

b. Assignment 2.   Class Project: Conduct a Symposium on a Selected Issue
The procedure for this assignment is (1) to select an issue, (2) to identify different perspectives on it, (3) to form groups of students who will brainstorm ideas about each of the different perspectives; (4) to assign all students to write one-page, 250-word papers on the perspective that their group has discussed, and (5) to select one member from each group to read his or her paper in a symposium, which is followed by a class question-and-answer session. The object is to cooperate in discovering new views and knowledge on a difficult question that is still open to inquiry.

Day One: Preparing for the Symposium

(1) *Select an issue.* The class should vote on an issue for inquiry. Some suggestions for issues and accompanying essays that would invite a variety of perspectives for a symposium topic include:

Do People in Their Twenties Have Unrealistic Expectations?

See "The Whiny Generation," p. 223.

How Can People Better Set Priorities and Manage Their Time?

See "We're Too Busy for Ideas," p. 179.

Do Men Teach and Learn Differently Than Women?

See "Teaching and Learning as a Man," p. 431

Should Freedom of Speech Be Limited on the Internet?

See "The Next Front in the Book Wars," p. 547.

What Should Be Done With Young Offenders?

See "Peace in the Streets," p. 527.

What Effect Does Television Have on Its Viewers?

See "The Age of Show Business," p. 593.

Any of the issue questions that are related to the seven issue areas in "The Reader" would provide productive topics for a symposium. Read through the table of contents to see which of these questions and groups of essays would be of interest to your class.

(2) *Read.* Read the essay(s) relevant to the selected issue. Mark the passages that suggest original perspectives on the issue to you.

(3) *Brainstorm ideas.* Class members as a whole group should brainstorm the different perspectives on the issue and list them on the board. They can refer to their reading notes to help them.

(4) *Form groups, select topics, and invent ideas.* Students should work in groups of three or four. Each group selects a different perspective on the issue from the list on the board, makes a claim about it, and brainstorms ideas and support. Each group member makes notes for the one-page, 250-word paper that each student will write outside of class. Each group also selects one of its members to read his or her paper in the symposium.

Day Two: The Symposium.

(1) *Conduct the symposium.* The class selects a moderator to sit with the speakers in the front of the room, preferably at a table. The moderator introduces the speakers and gives the titles of their papers. The speakers read their papers.

(2) *Question-and-answer session.* Class members who have functioned as the audience ask the speakers questions and also contribute their own views on the subject.

(3) *Conclusions.* Students spend ten minutes writing their own conclusions about the symposium.

8. **QUESTIONS ON THE CHAPTER**
   a. Why is it important to organize the ideas in a paper? How does it help the reader? How does it help the writer?
   b. What advice was given in the chapter to help you organize the ideas in your paper?
   c. What are some examples of organizational patterns that you might use in a position paper? Name five and describe their main features or rationale.
   d. How might making an outline or fairly complete list of ideas help you write the first draft of your paper?
   e. What are some of the potential values of a peer editing session?
   f. Describe the first draft. What should you probably include in it?
   g. What are some of the things you should keep in mind when you revise your paper?
   h. What is the purpose of in-text citations and the final list of sources?

HOW TO DOCUMENT SOURCES USING MLA AND APA STYLES

The following material will demonstrate how to use in-text citations and lists of works cited (MLA) or references (APA) to indicate where borrowed source material first appeared. For additional detail on how to use MLA style, consult *the*

MLA Handbook for Writers of Research Papers (4th ed., 1995), published by the Modern Language Association, and the *Publication Manual of the American Psychological Association* (4th ed., 1994), published by the American Psychological Association.

How to Write In-Text Parenthetical Citations

Both the MLA and APA systems of documentation ask that you show where you originally found a direct quote, a paraphrase, or a summary by inserting a brief parenthetical citation at the end of the borrowed material in your written text. The MLA system requires that you provide the author and the page number: (Jones 13). APA requires that you provide the author, the date of publication, and the page numbers, which are introduced by "p." or "pp.": (Jones, 1983, p. 5). If, however, you mention the name of the author in the text, you do not need to include the author's name in the parenthetical material. The following are examples.

1. **Direct quote with the author mentioned in the text.**

   MLA: As Howard Rheingold describes his first trip into virtual reality, "My body wasn't in the computer world" (15–16).

   APA: As Howard Rheingold (1991) describes his first trip into virtual reality, "My body wasn't in the computer world" (pp. 15–16).

2. **Direct quote with the author not mentioned in the text.**

   MLA: Virtual reality changes perceptions radically. As one participant explains it, "My body wasn't in the computer world. I could see around me, but one of my hands had accompanied my point of view onto the vast electronic plain that seemed to surround me" (Rheingold 15–16).

   APA: As one participant explains it, "My body wasn't in the computer world. I could see around me" (Rheingold, 1991, pp. 15–16).

3. **Paraphrase or summary with the author mentioned in the text.**

   MLA: Howard Rheingold describes his first trip into virtual reality as one that involved his hand and arm but not his whole body (15–16).

   APA: Howard Rheingold (1991) describes his first trip into virtual reality as one that involved his hand and arm but not his whole body (pp. 15–16).

4. **Paraphrase or summary with the author not mentioned the text.**

   MLA: One's whole body is not always a part of the virtual reality experience. Sometimes only a hand and arm enter that reality (Rheingold 15–16).

   APA: One's whole body is not always a part of the virtual reality experience. Sometimes only a hand and arm enter that reality (Rheingold, 1991, pp. 15–16).

5. **Two or more authors.** If two or three authors have written the material you have borrowed, include all of their names either in the introductory material or the citation.

> **MLA:** "Virtual reality is all about illusion" (Pimentel and Teixeira 7).
> **APA:** Pimental and Teixeira (1993) remind us, "Virtual reality is all about illusion" (p. 7).

For more than three authors, use only the first author's name and add "et al." to the citation for MLA. For APA, list all of the authors' names for the first reference, but use the first name and et al. for subsequent references.

6. **Corporate author.** Sometimes written materials are attributed to a corporate rather than to an individual author. In this case, use the name of the corporation or group, preferably in the material that precedes the quote.

> **MLA:** According to the <u>Notebook</u> published by the Network Project, "The quote" (7).

Or you can mention the corporate author at the end:

> **APA:** "The quote" (Network Project, 1992, p. 7).

7. **Title only.** When no author is listed for either a book or an article, use the title or the first words of an abbreviated title in your citation.

> **MLA:** Article: ("Creativity and Television" 14).
>   Book: (<u>Neilsen Television</u> 17).
> **APA:** Article: (Creativity and Television," 1973, p. 14).
>   Book: (<u>Neilsen television,</u> 1975, p. 17).

8. **Article in a book.** If you quote an article that appears in a book such as this one, use the name of the author of the article in your citation, not the author or editor of the book.

The following is one additional tip to help you work borrowed material into your paper:

Typing short and long quotations. Type short quotes (four lines or less for MLA or forty words or less for APA) right into your paper. Make them visually part of it by double spacing, running them out to the margins, and putting them in quotation marks. Longer quotes should be indented ten spaces (five for APA) from the left-hand margin and printed as a block. The parenthetical citations for long quotes appear right after the final period and are positioned in the same way for both the MLA and APA systems.

How to Write the List of "Works Cited" (MLA) or "References" (APA)

Attach to your draft a list of all of the works you have quoted or paraphrased in your paper. This list is entitled either "Works Cited" (MLA) or "References" (APA). Look also at the examples of the student papers beginning on page 401. The first of them follows MLA format, and the second follows APA. Include on your list only the works you have actually used in your paper. The easiest way to prepare this list is to alphabetize your bibliography cards according to the authors' last names or, if no author is listed, by the title of the work. Omit *a, an,* and *the* in alphabetizing. **Type the bibliography by double spacing** it throughout and by indenting the second line of each citation five spaces for MLA, or three spaces of the first line for APA.

Basic Format for Books and Articles

	MLA	*APA*
For a book:	Author, <u>Title of Book.</u> City: <u>Publisher</u>, date.	Author. (Date). <u>Title of book.</u> City: Publisher.
For an article:	Author. "Title of Article." <u>Name of Periodical</u> <u>volume number</u> (year of publication): page numbers.	Author. (Date). Title of article. <u>Name of Periodical,</u> p. or pp.

Note that MLA capitalizes all important nouns in a title, headline style, even if the original does not, and that APA capitalizes only the first word in a title, sentence style. Also, for articles, MLA uses quotation marks and APA does not. The titles of magazines and journals, however, are written in headline style for both MLA and APA. Note, also, the difference in indenting.

Here are some examples of the types of sources that are most commonly cited for argument papers. Examples of both MLA and APA styles are provided.

How to List Books

1. *Book by One Author*

   MLA: Rheingold, Howard. <u>Virtual Reality.</u> New York: Simon, 1991.
   APA: Rheingold, H. (1991). <u>Virtual reality.</u> New York: Simon & Schuster.

2. *Book by Two or Three Authors*

   MLA: Pimentel, Ken, and Kevin Teixeira. <u>Virtual Reality: Through the New Looking Glass.</u> New York: McGraw Hill, 1993.
   APA: Pimentel, K., & Teixeira, K. (1993). <u>Virtual reality: Through the new looking glass.</u> New York: McGraw Hill.

   Use the same format to add a third author.

3. *Book by More Than Three Authors*

   MLA: Comstock, George, et al. <u>Television and Human Behavior.</u> New York: Columbia UP, 1978.
   APA: Comstock, G., Chaffee, S., Katzman N., McCombs, M., & Roberts, D. (1978). <u>Television and human behavior.</u> New York: C Columbia University Press.

4. *How to List Two or More Books by the Same Author*

MLA: Rheingold, Howard. Tools for Thought. New York: Simon, 1985.
--- . Virtual Reality. New York: Simon, 1991.
APA: Rheingold, H. (1985). Tools for thought. New York: Simon & Schuster.
Rheingold, H. (1991). Virtual reality. New York: Simon & Schuster.

5. *Books by a Corporate Author*

MLA: VPL Research. Inc. Virtual Reality at Texpo '89. Redwood City, CA: VPL Research, 1989.
APA: VPL Research, Inc. (1989). Virtual reality at Texpo '89. Redwood City, CA: VPL Research, Inc.

6. *Book with No Author Named*

MLA: Virtual Reality Marketplace. Westport: Meckler, 1992.
APA: Virtual reality marketplace. (1992). Westport: Meckler.

7. *Book Reprinted in a Later Edition*

MLA: Malthus, Thomas R. An Essay on the Principle of Population. 1798. London: William Pickering, 1986.
APA: Malthus, T. R. (1986). An essay on the principle of population. London: William Pickering. (Original work published in 1798).

8. *Translation*

MLA: Rousseau, Jean-Jacques. La Nouvelle Héloïse. 1761. Trans. Judith H. McDowell. University Park: Pennsylvania State UP, 1968.
APA: Rousseau, J.-J. (1968). La Nouvelle Héloïse. (J. H. McDowell, Trans.). University Park: Pennsylvania State University Press. (Original work published in 1761).

9. *Subsequent Editions*

MLA: Thompson, Warren S. Population Problems. 4th ed. New York: McGraw Hill, 1953.
APA: Thompson, W. S. (1953). Population problems. (4th ed.). New York: McGraw Hill.

10. *Proceedings from Conference or Symposium*

MLA: McKerrow, Raymie E., ed. Argument and the Postmodern Challenge: Proceedings of the Eighth SCA/AFA Conference on Argumentation. 5–8 Aug. 1993. Annandale, VA: Speech Communication Assn., 1993.

APA: McKerrow, R. E. (Ed.). (1993). Argument and the postmodern challenge: Proceedings of the eighth SCA/AFA conference on argumentation. Annandale, VA: Speech Communication Association.

11. *Introduction, Preface, Foreword, or Afterword*

MLA: Schneiderman, Ben. Foreword. Interacting with Virtual Environments. Ed. Lindsay MacDonald and John Vince. Chichester, NY: J. Wiley, 1994. x – xi.

APA: Schneiderman, B. (1994). Foreword. In L. MacDonald and J. Vince (Eds.), Interacting with virtual environments. Chichester, NY: Wiley.

12. *Government Documents*

MLA: United States. F.B.I. U.S. Dept. of Justice. Uniform Crime Reports for the United States. Washington: GPO, 1990.

APA: Federal Bureau of Investigation, U.S. Department of Justice. (1990). Uniform crime reports for the United States. Washington, DC: U.S. Government Printing Office.

How to List Articles

13. *Article from a Periodical*

MLA: Monastersky, Richard. "The Deforestation Debate." Science News 10 July 1993 :#26–27.

APA: Monastersky, R. (1993, July 10). The deforestation debate. Science News, pp. 26–27.

14. *Article from a Newspaper*

MLA: Weinstein, Jack B. "The War on Drugs Is Self-Defeating." New York Times 8 July 1993: A11.

APA: Weinstein, J. B. (1993, July 8). The war on drugs is self-defeating. New York Times, p. A11.

15. *Article with No Author Listed*

MLA: "A Democratic Army." The New Yorker 28 June 1993: 4+.
For MLA, use a plus sign when the pages are interrupted with ads and other material in the magazine. For APA, list all pages on which the article is printed.

APA: A democratic army. (1993, June 28). The New Yorker, pp. 4, 6.

16. *Article in a Journal with Continuous Pagination from January to December*

MLA: Jasinski, James. "Rhetoric and Judgment in the Constitutional Ratification Debate of 1787–1788: An Exploration of the Relationship between Theory and Critical Practice." Quarterly Journal of Speech 78 (1992): 197–218.

APA: Jasinski, J. (1992). Rhetoric and judgment in the constitutional ratification debate of 1787–1788: An exploration of the relationship between theory and critical practice. Quarterly Journal of Speech, 78, 197–218.

17. *Article in a Journal That Pages Each Issue Separately*

MLA: Rosenbloom, Nancy J. "In Defense of the Moving Pictures: The People's Institute, The National Board of Censorship and the Problem of Leisure in Urban America." American Studies 33.2 (1992): 41–60.

APA: Rosenbloom, N. J. (1992). In defense of the moving pictures: The people's institute, the National Board of Censorship and the problem of leisure in urban America. American Studies, 33(2), 41–60.

18. *Edited Collection of Articles or an Anthology*

MLA: Forester, Tom, ed. The Information Technology Revolution. Cambridge, MA: MIT UP, 1985.

APA: Forester, T. (Ed.). (1985). The information technology revolution. Cambridge, MA: MIT Press.

19. *Article in an Edited Collection or an Anthology*

MLA: Boden, Margaret A. "The Social Impact of Thinking Machines." The Information Technology Revolution. Ed. Tom Foster. Cambridge, MA: MIT Press, 1985. 95–103.

APA: Boden, M. A. (1985). The social impact of thinking machines. In T. Foster (Ed.), The information technology revolution (pp. 95–103). Cambridge, MA: MIT Press.

20. *Reprinted Article in an Edited Volume or Collection (like "The Reader" in this book)*

MLA: Fox, Lyla. "Hold Your Horsepower." Newsweek 25 March 1996: 16. Rpt. in Perspectives on Argument. Nancy V. Wood. 2nd ed. Upper Saddle River, NJ: Prentice Hall, 1998. 189–91.

APA: Fox, L. (1998). Hold your horsepower. In N. Wood, Perspectives on argument (2nd ed.). (pp. 189–91). Upper Saddle River, NJ: Prentice Hall.

21. *Signed Article in a Reference Work*

MLA: Davidson II, W. S. "Crime." Encyclopedia of Psychology. Ed. Raymond J. Corsini. 4 vols. New York: Wiley, 1984. 310–12.

APA: Davidson II, W. S. (1984). Crime. In R. J. Corsini (Ed.), Encyclopedia of psychology (pp. 310–12). New York: Wiley.

22. *Unsigned Article in a Reference Work*

MLA: "Quindlen, Anna." Current Biography. Apr. 1993.
APA: Anna Quindlen (1993, April). In Current Biography.

23. *Review*

MLA: Watts, Steven. "Sinners in the Hands of an Angry Critic: Christopher Lasch's Struggle with Progressive America." Rev. of The True and Only Heaven: Progress and Its Critics, by Christopher Lasch. American Studies 33.2 (1992): 113–20.
APA: Watts, S. (1992). Sinners in the hands of an angry critic: Christopher Lasch's struggle with progressive America. [Review of The true and only heaven: Progress and its critics]. American Studies, 33 (2), 113–120.

24. *Letter to the Editor*

MLA: McCaffrey, Mark. Letter. Utne Reader July–Aug. 1993: 10.
APA: McCaffrey, M. (1993, July/August). [Letter to the editor.] Utne Reader, p. 10.

25. *Editorial*

MLA: "A Touch of Class for the Court." Editorial. New York Times 25 July 1993: E16.
APA: A touch of class for the court. (1993, July 25). [Editorial.] New York Times, p. E16.

How to List Electronic Sources

26. *Article in an Electronic Journal*

MLA: Herring, Susan. "Gender and Democracy in Computer-Mediated Communication." Electronic Journal of Communication. 3.2 (1993): 17 pp. 30 Sept. 1996.
http://dc.smu.edu/dc/classroom/Gender.txt.
APA: Herring, S. (1993). Gender and democracy in computer-mediated communication [32 paragraphs]. Electronic Journal of Communication, 3 (2). Retrievd September 30, 1996 from the World Wide Web: http://dc.smu.edu/dc/classroom/Gender.txt.

27. *CD-ROMs*

MLA: The Oxford English Dictionary. 2nd ed. CD-ROM. Oxford: Oxford UP, 1992.
APA: The Oxford English Dictionary (1992). [CD-ROM]. Oxford: Oxford UP.

28. *Electronic Mail (E-MAIL)*

MLA: Rieder, David. E-mail to the author. 4 Oct. 1995.
APA: Do not cite in References. Cite in text as D. Rieder (personal communication, October 4, 1995).

How to List Media: Microforms, Video, Television, Film

29. *ERIC Information Service (Microform)*

MLA: Land, Warren A., and Elizabeth R. Land. The Effect of Changing a Professional Educational Program on National Teacher Education Test Scores. ERIC ED 365 729.

APA: Land, W. A., & Land, E. R. The effect of changing a professional educational program on national teacher education test scores. (ERIC Document Reproduction Service No. ED 365 729).

30. *Videotapes*

MLA: Composition. Prod. ABC/Prentice Hall Video Library. Videocassette Prentice Hall, 1993.

APA: ABC/Prentice Hall Video Library (Producer). (1993). Composition [Video]. Englewood Cliffs, NJ: Prentice Hall.

31. *Radio and Television Programs*

MLA: Resolved: Political Correctness Is a Menace and a Bore. Prod. and dir. Warren Steibel. With William F. Buckley, Jr., Firing Line. PBS. KDTN, Dallas. 2 December 1993.

APA: Steibel, W. (Producer and Director), Buckley, Jr., W. F. (Moderator). (1993, December 2). Resolved: Political correctness is a menace and a bore. [Television program]. Dallas: KDTN, PBS Firing Line.

32. *Film*

MLA: JFK. Dir. Oliver Stone. Warner, 1991

APA: Stone, O. (Director). (1991). JFK [film]. Los Angeles: Warner.

How to List Interviews and Speeches

33. *Published Interviews*

MLA: Hardin, Garrett. Interview with Cathy Spencer. Omni June, 1992: 55–63.

APA: Hardin, G. (1992, June). [Personal interview with C. Spencer]. Omni, pp. 55–63.

34. *Personal Interview*

MLA: Wick, Audrey. Personal interview. 27 May 1994.

APA: Wick, A. (1994, May 27). [Personal interview].

35. *Lectures, Speeches, Addresses*

MLA: Yeltsin, Boris. Address to the U.S. Congress. Washington, DC June 18. 1992.

APA: Yeltsin, B. (1992, June 18). Address. Speech presented to the U.S. Congress. Washington, DC.

MLA STYLE

Student Paper

Tanya Pierce
Professor Snow
English 3102
10 February 1995

The Importance Of Jury Instructions

Author speaking: Summaries of different perspectives on issue drawn from exploratory paper.

The right to a trial by jury is a fundamental right guaranteed by our United States Constitution. The Supreme Court has consistently protected this right and has extended it to all but the most trivial of cases. However, our jury system is not without flaws. On the contrary, many critics of the jury system argue that juries are simply uneducated in the basic concepts of law necessary to intelligently decide cases. Others claim that juries are too biased, and this taints the judicial process. These criticisms are not totally unfounded in many cases. In spite of its problems, however, the jury system is a valuable institution. It provides a buffer between our often harsh and inflexible legal system and the average citizen on trial. It is critical to our democratic society. In fact, one conclusion of a recent survey on jury service conducted by an association of defense trial lawyers is that

Direct quote cited: Author of quote not mentioned in text. Author speaking: Introduction to policy claim.

"the more involvement people have in the jury process, the more they seem to take to heart their responsibilities as citizens in our democratic society" (Robinson 62). Still because of recent mistakes made by juries and the growing scrutiny of the decisions made by juries, it is necessary to improve our jury system.

Problems: Time, exemptions.

Serving on a jury takes a great deal of time. Because jury service does require one to spend a lot of time, many Americans will do just about anything to get out of jury duty. In addition, many segments of the population are exempt from jury duty either by permissible judicial rule, by law, or by custom. Among the occupational groups generally exempt in the vast majority of jurisdictions

Summary cited.

are professionals such as lawyers, licensed physicians and dentists, members of the armed forces, officers of all three branches of government, police officers, fire fighters, clergy, and teachers (Abraham 117). The average jury in America consists of housewives or househusbands, retirees, blue-collar workers, and the unemployed. Ac-

Summary cited.

cording to the survey quoted above, only forty-five percent of all adult Americans have been called for jury duty, and only seventeen percent have served through an actual trial (Robinson 62). These people often are not indispensable in their jobs and are not as limited by time constraints as are the exempt groups. Critics of the jury system argue that these juries are often not educated enough to handle the responsibility of deciding important cases.

Author speaking: More problems: Unprepared jurors.

It is sad to say but in many cases the jurists are ignorant of the legal issues surrounding a given case. In many instances they do not understand the facts in the case, and they often do not understand the consequences of their decisions. For example, the jury in the recent Brosky hate crime case thought that it was sentencing Brosky to five years in jail plus ten years probation. It is an either-or situation. Because of this lack of understanding by the jury and the ineffective instructions given by the judge and attorneys involved in the case, a grave and irreversible injustice was done. Brosky was given only ten years probation for the murder of another human being. This is just one of numerous cases where the jury's lack of knowledge has led to disastrous decisions.

Supported by specific example.

Transition: Current solutions and their problems.

Something clearly needs to be done to educate these jurors. Current practice requires the judge to give instructions, called a charge, to the jury before it begins deliberations. According to Henry Abraham, who has written extensively on the judicial process, "Much thought goes—or should go—into this charge, which is intended as an exposition of the law and is delivered orally in most, although not all, cases" (131).

Direct quote cited. Author in text.

One of the problems with the judge's charge, however, is that most states do not permit the jury to take either a copy or a tape recording of it with them when they leave the courtroom to make their deliberations. Seymour Wishman, a criminal lawyer who has tried hundreds of cases before juries, quotes one judge who supports the idea of allowing jurors to take written or audiotaped instructions with them. According to this judge, we expect people to listen to instructions once and remember them well enough to make "monumental decisions" (224).

Summary cited. Author in text.

Transition.

The judge's instructions are not only difficult to remember; they are also sometimes difficult for the jury to understand. Wishman goes on to claim, "Jury instructions are often incomprehensible because they are drafted by lawyers and judges who do not realize how much of their 'legalese' vocabulary and syntax was acquired in law school. . . . little effort is made to write clear and simple language for those not legally trained" (224). Abraham, agreeing that there can be significant problems with the judge's charge, says, "Many a charge has, ultimately, been instrumental in causing a mistrial; many another has been found to be defective on points of law by appellate courts" (131).

Direct quotes cited. Authors in text.

Transition.

Obviously, the educational process for jurors needs to be improved, and judges and lawyers need to become active participants in this educational process. They need to take the responsibility for informing jurors about the relevant legal issues in each case. They must educate jurors on the rules of law applicable to the cases at hand and in language they can understand. Some may argue that this system may be abused by lawyers who want to bias a jury in

Author speaking.

Solution: Establish new policy.
Refutation of those who may disagree.

Author speaking.

their favor. This is, of course, possible. But one must realize that juries are inherently biased. Each jurist walks in with his or her own distinct set of values and beliefs. The lawyers are always trying to influence them to see their side. I would argue, however, that it is better to risk the possibility of some additional bias in order for the juries to be better informed. It is more desirable to have a knowledgeable jury, even at the risk of some bias, rather than to have a jury that is totally in the dark about the legal issues surrounding a particular case.

Support for solution.

Summary cited.

Some research suggests that juries should be given lessons in the law before the trial begins and also at various points during the trial. Psychological studies have consistently shown that early exposure and frequent exposure to legal principles correlate with juries that are more likely to presume innocence in a case until sufficient evidence is provided to decide otherwise. Experimental mock juries questioned midway through testimony showed a significantly higher indecision rate when they had been informed about the legal issues involved before the start of testimony than those who had not been instructed earlier (Heuer and Penrod 429). This suggests that juries instructed prior to the presentation of evidence are more likely to consider all of the evidence of a case before arriving at a decision of guilt or innocence.

Author speaking: More refutation and benefits of solution.

Summary cited.

Although some may interpret this psychological data as suggesting that informing juries early and frequently would delay the judicial process, I believe the opposite is true. Instructing juries on the basic legal concepts will help them be more open-minded. They will have more intelligent discussions during deliberations because they will know what issues to concentrate on. Psychological tests have also demonstrated that juries who are informed on legal concepts frequently are less likely to result in a hung jury (Goldberg 456). This latter finding is especially valuable since so much government money in the form of our tax dollars is wasted when juries are unable to arrive at a unanimous decision.

Author speaking: Summary of perspective in paper.

Policy claim in last sentence.

The right to be judged by a group of one's peers is a right most Americans value highly. It helps ensure that all citizens will be given a fair chance in our legal system. It is valuable because it allows the American public to play an active role in our judicial process. However, like all institutions our jury system is not without its flaws. It is important for us to recognize the shortcomings in this process and try to improve it. A positive start towards improving the jury system would be for judges and lawyers to take a more active role in educating jurors at several crucial points during the course of a trial.[3]

---

[3]Used by permission.

Works Cited

Abraham, Henry J. The Judicial Process: An Introductory Analysis of the Courts of the United States, England, and France. 5th ed. New York: Oxford UP, 1986.

Goldberg, Janice C. "Memory, Magic, and Myth: The Timing of Jury Instructions." Oregon Law Review 59 (1981): 451–75.

Heuer, Larry, and Steven Penrod. "A Field Experiment with Written and Preliminary Instructions." Law and Human Behavior 13 (1989): 409–30.

Robinson, Archie S. "We the Jury: Who Serves, Who Doesn't." USA Today: The Magazine of the American Scene 120 (Jan. 1992): 62–63.

Wishman, Seymour. Anatomy of a Jury: The System on Trial. New York: Times Books. 1986.

APA STYLE

Student Paper

Darrell D. Greer
Professor Snow
English 1302
10 February 1995

Alaskan Wolf Management

Introduction and background of problem. Quotes from authorities and statistics to establish extent of problem.

In the past few years Alaska has been witnessing a decline in the populations of caribou and moose in the Fortymile, Delta, and Nelchina Basin areas. This decline in the caribou and moose populations is due mainly to the uprising of the wolf populations in these three areas. Robert Stephenson of the Alaska Department of Fish and Game claims, "Wolf packs will kill one caribou every two days or so, and one moose every three to ten days" (Keszler, 1993, p. 65). The Delta caribou herd alone declined from about eleven thousand in 1989 to less than four thousand this spring ("Alaska Wolf," 1993, p. 6). With statistics like these the caribou and moose population in Alaska is clearly a problem that needs immediate attention.

This rapid decline in caribou and moose populations is devastating to the state. Not only are they a valuable resource for Alaska in terms of nonresident hunting and tourist sight-seeing, but for many remote residents, caribou and moose are their main source of food. The way of life for many Alaskans is one that the average American cannot vaguely understand. Max Peterson, the executive director of the International Association of Wildlife Agencies, says that in Alaska, "People interact as another predator in the ecosys-

Quotations worked into text that suggest the unique character of the problem in Alaska.

tem," and, as a result, "the interest in Alaska by people outside Alaska certainly is greater than their knowledge of Alaska" (Keszler, 1993, p. 67). Ted Williams (1993) clarifies the lifestyle that many rural Alaskans lead:

> Genuine subsistence is the most environmentally benign of all possible lifestyles. Subsisters do not—indeed cannot—deplete fish and wildlife because if they do, they will subsist no more. But even in the remotest native villages, Alaska as trackless wilderness where people blend with nature is just an old dream. Many villagers are now on social welfare programs and are therefore cash dependent. (p. 49)

Failing to protect existing caribou and moose populations could lower the subsistence level for some Alaskans, even more than it is at present.

The biologists of the state of Alaska believe that wolf populations are nowhere close to being endangered. They estimate the total wolf population in Alaska to be between 5,900 and 7,200. In the three areas up for wildlife management (about 3.5 percent of the state), Rodney Boertje, an Alaskan Department of Fish and Game wildlife biologist, says, "Wolf populations can sustain harvest rates of twenty-five to forty percent. So sixty to eighty-five percent of wolves must be removed for control efforts to be effective" (Keszler, 1993, p. 66). This amount totals between three hundred and four hundred wolves in these three areas. Wildlife management experts believe the most humane and efficient way of accomplishing this task is through aerial shootings of wolves.

With the announcement of the wolf management plan proposed by Alaska Governor Walter Hickel and the Alaska Department of Fish and Game involving aerial shootings of wolves, the animal rights groups started an all-out war with the state. They organized widespread mailings to the governor and threatened massive boycotts of tourism in Alaska if the plan was not repealed (Keszler, 1993, p. 65). The animal rights groups believe that other methods of management could increase caribou and moose populations. One such method is reducing bag limits, shortening hunting seasons, or totally eliminating hunting in these three areas. This type of management will not be effective in this situation, however, since hunters are not the real cause of the problem. Pete Buist, a Fairbanks, Alaska, resident, says, "In control areas, hunters are taking less than five percent of the annual production of meat animals. Predators are taking more than seventy-five percent" (1993, p. 12). Animal rights groups commonly point to hunters as the culprits in animal conservation efforts. According to Arms (1994), however, "Nowadays in developed countries, groups representing hunting and fishing interests are the most active conservationists. They understand that their sport and, sometimes, their livelihood depend

---

A long quotation of more than 40 words is indented and written in block form. No quotation marks are necessary for indented quotes. The source is indicated at the end. Note that the author is mentioned in the text.

Statistics and quotations from authorities to strengthen the solution preferred by this author.

Refutation of the animal rights groups and their solutions to the problem.

on sustained or increasing populations of the organisms they hunt or fish" (p. 347). As mentioned earlier, rural Alaskans who depend on caribou and moose for subsistence are some of these hunters who continue to take these animals but not in dangerously large numbers.

Another alternative management method that has been brought up by the animal rights groups is tranquilizing and capturing the wolves and chemically sterilizing them or using some other sort of contraception. This method has not been scientifically proven to work. Even if it did work, this method would take entirely too long to be effective for this situation. Contraception only deals with the wolf numbers down the road, and not with existing numbers, which would remain the same for now. Existing wolves in the immediate future may devastate the caribou and moose populations so drastically that they will not be able to recover.

Evaluation and refutation of other solutions.

In the United States Constitution the management of fish and wildlife is left up to the individual states. When Alaska made the professional decision that the best way to control their wolf population was by aerial shootings, the animal rights groups picked only that part of a larger plan to attack. In media reports activists "portrayed the plan simply as a mass extermination of wolves designed to increase game numbers for out-of-state hunters and wildlife watchers" (Keszler, 1993, p. 39). They showed through commercials "visions of helicopter gunships slaughtering wolves by the hundreds" (Keszler, 1993, p. 39) when, in fact, the aerial shooting of wolves is just one small part of the plan. The animal rights groups did not focus on the parts of the plan that dealt with the restrictions to help the wolves in other areas. In Denali National Park and Preserve, Alaskan conservationists plan to do away with all hunting and trapping to give the wolves a sanctuary with no outside pressure (Keszler, 1993, p. 65). Other laws and bans on hunting and trapping to protect wolves would take place in areas around Anchorage and Fairbanks. The practice of land-and-shoot hunting (a practice used by many trappers to locate game by helicopter, land the helicopter, and start hunting) would be banned statewide (Keszler, 1993, p. 65). But none of these efforts to protect the wolf population were even discussed by the animal rights activists.

Establishment of the *ethos* of conservationists in Alaska to make their plan acceptable.

Author has identified a problem, evaluated several solutions, and arrived at this solution as the best possible. This is a value argument because it claims one of several considered solutions is the best.

The professional wildlife biologists at the Alaska Department of Fish and Game have taken a lot of heat from the animal rights media reports on their decision to go ahead with the original plan to manage wolf populations through aerial shooting and other methods not mentioned by the media. The biologists of the state of Alaska have devoted their lives to the preservation of wildlife. They know Alaska and Alaska's wildlife better than anyone else. After researching and trying other methods, they believe the best solution

Problem solution and
policy are also strong
features in this
argument.

Claim in last sentence.

to their problem is through aerial shooting. Their main concern is to protect the wildlife population as a whole, and not just to wage a "war on wolves." While the animal rightists are sitting around in their offices wondering which animals to save, the biologists at Alaska's Department of Fish and Game are in the field researching the range conditions and overall population conditions to better manage the wildlife community as a whole. As inhumane and immoral as it might seem, the aerial shooting of wolves is still the best solution for game management in this situation.[4]

References

Alaska wolf update. (1993, August). American Hunter, p. 6.

Arms, K. (1994). Environmental science (2nd ed.). Forth Worth, TX: Harcourt Brace.

Buist, P. (1993, September). Letter to the editor. American Hunter. p. 12.

Keszler, E. (1993, May). Wolves and big game: Searching for balance in Alaska. American Hunter, pp. 38–39, 65–67.

Williams, T. (1993, May/June). Alaska's war on the wolves. Audubon, pp. 44–47, 49–50.

---

[4]Used by permission.

SYNTHESIS OF CHAPTERS 1–12: SUMMARY CHARTS

TRACE

The Rhetorical Situation

For You as the Reader

Text. What kind of text is it? What are its qualities and features?

Reader. Are you one of the readers the writer anticipated? Do you share common ground with the author and other audience members? Are you open to change?

Author. Who is the author? How is the author influenced by background, experience, education, affiliations, values? What is the author's motivation to write?

Constraints. What beliefs, attitudes, habits, affiliations, or traditions will influence the way you and the author view the argument?

Exigence. What caused the argument, and do you perceive it as a defect or problem?

For the Targeted Reader at the Time It Was Written

Text. What kind of text is it? Is it unique to its time?

Reader. What was the nature of the targeted readers? Were they convinced? How are they different from other or modern readers?

Author. Who is the author? What influenced the author? Why was the author motivated to write?

Constraints. What beliefs, attitudes, habits, affiliations, or traditions influenced the author's and the readers' views in this argument?

Exigence. What happened to cause the argument? Why was it a problem? Has it recurred?

For You as the Writer

Text. What is your argumentative strategy? What is your purpose and perspective? How will you make you paper convincing?

Reader. Who are your readers? Where do they stand on the issue? How can you establish common ground? Can they change?

Constraints. How are your training, background, affiliations, and values either in harmony or conflict with your audience? Will they drive you apart or help build common ground?

Exigence. What happened? What is motivating you to write on this issue? Why is it compelling to you?

THE PROCESS

(Be selective and flexible in using the strategies, and remember there is no best order. You will backtrack and repeat.)

When You Are the Reader

Prereading Strategies

- **Read the title and first paragraph; background the issue.** Identify the issue. Free-associate and write words and phrases that the issue brings to mind.
- **Evaluate and improve your background.** Do you know enough? If not, read or discuss to get background. Look up a key word or two.
- **Survey the material.** Locate the claim (the main assertion) and some of the subclaims (the ideas that support it); notice how they are organized. Do not slow down and read.
- **Write out your present position on the issue.**
- **Make some predictions and write one big question.** Jot down two or three ideas that you think the author may discuss and write one question you would like to have answered.

Reading Strategies

- **Pick up a pencil, underline, and annotate** the ideas that seem important.
- **Identify** and **read** the information in the **introduction, body,** and **conclusion.**
- **Look for the claim, subclaims, and support.** Box the **transitions** to highlight relationships between ideas and changes of subject.
- **Find the key words** that represent major concepts and jot down meanings if necessary.
- **Analyze the rhetorical situation.** Text, reader, author, constraints, exigence.
- **Read with an open mind and analyze the common ground** between you and the author.

Strategies for Reading When the Material is Difficult

- **Read all the way** through once without stopping.
- **Write a list** of what you can understand.
- **Identify words and concepts** you do not understand, look them up, and analyze how they are used in context.
- **Reread the material** and add to your list of what you can understand.
- **Discuss the material** with someone who understands it.

When You Are the Writer

Prewriting Strategies

- **Get organized to write.** Set up a place with materials. Get motivated.
- **Understand the writing assignment and schedule time.** Break a complicated writing task into manageable parts and find the time to write.
- **Identify an issue and do some initial reading.** Use the twelve tests (p. 26) to make certain you have an arguable issue.
- **Analyze the rhetorical situation,** particularly the exigence, the audience, and the constraints.
- **Focus** on your issue and **freewrite.**
- **Brainstorm, make lists, map ideas.**
- **Talk it through** with a friend, your instructor, or members of a peer editing group.
- **Keep a journal, notebook, or folder of ideas.**
- **Mentally visualize** the major concepts.
- Do some directed **reading and thinking.**
- Use **argument strategies.**
- Use **reading strategies.**
- Use **critical thinking prompts.**
- Plan and conduct **library research.**
- Make an **expanded list or outline** to guide your writing.
- **Talk it through again.**

Writing Strategies

- **Write the first draft.** Get your ideas on paper so that you can work with them. Use your outline and notes to help you. Either write and rewrite as you go, or write the draft quickly with the knowledge that you can reread or rewrite later.

Strategies to Use When You Get Stuck

- **Read more** and **take more notes.**
- **Read your outline, rearrange parts, add more information** to it.
- **Freewrite** on the issue, **read some more,** and then **freewrite** some more.
- **Talk about your ideas** with someone else.
- **Lower your expectations for your first draft.** It does not have to be perfect at this point.

continued

THE PROCESS *(continued)*

When You Are the Reader

Postreading Strategies
- **Monitor your comprehension.** Insist on understanding. Check the accuracy of your **predictions** and answer your **question.**
- **Analyze the organization** and write either a **simplified outline** or a **summary** to help you understand and remember. Or make a MAP.
- **Write a response** to help you think.
- **Compare your present position** with your position before you began to read.
- **Evaluate the argument** and decide whether it is convincing or not.
- **Write what value** this material has for you and **how you will use it.**

When You Are the Writer

Postwriting Strategies
- **Read your draft critically,** and also **have someone else read it.** Put it aside for 24 hours, if you can, to develop a better perspective for reading and improving.
- **Rewrite and revise.** Make changes and additions until you think your paper is ready for other people to read. Move sections, cross out material, add other material, rephrase, as necessary.
- **Check your paper** for final mechanical and spelling errors, **write the final title,** and **type or print it.**

THE TOULMIN MODEL

When You Are the Reader

1. *What is the claim?* What is this author trying to prove? Look for the claim at the beginning or at the end, or infer it.
2. *What is the support?* What information does the author use to convince you of the claim? Look for reasons, explanations, facts, opinions, personal narratives, and examples.
3. *What are the warrants?* What assumptions, general principles, values, beliefs, and appeals to human motives are implicit in the argument? Where is the author coming from? Does the support develop the claim? Are the warrants stated, or must they be inferred?
4. *Is backing supplied for the warrants?* See if additional support is provided to make the warrants more acceptable to the reader.
5. *Is there a rebuttal?* Are other perspectives on the issue stated in the argument? Are they refuted? Are counterarguments given?
6. *Has the claim been qualified?* Look for qualifying words like *sometimes, most, probably, possibly.* Decide what is probably the best position to take on the issue, for now.

When You Are the Writer

1. *What is my claim?* Decide on the type of claim and the subclaims. Decide where to put the claim in your paper.
2. *What support will I use?* Invent reasons, opinions, and examples. Research and quote authorities and facts.
3. *What are my warrants?* Write out the warrants. Do they strengthen the argument by linking the support to the claim? Do you believe them yourself? Will the audience share them or reject them?
4. *What backing for the warrants should I provide?* Add polls, studies, reports, expert opinion, or facts to make your warrants convincing.
5. *How should I handle rebuttal?* Include other perspectives and point out what is wrong with them. Make counterarguments.
6. *Will I need to qualify my claim?* Decide if you can strengthen your claim by adding qualifying words like *usually, often, probably.*

TYPES OF PROOF AND TESTS OF VALIDITY

Logical Proofs (7)

(Rearrange the logical proofs to form the mnemonic SICDADS: sign, induction, cause, deduction, analogies, definition, statistics.)

When You Are the Reader		When You Are the Writer
Locate or infer the general principle (warrant). Apply it to the example or case. Draw a conclusion/claim.	**I. *Deduction*.** Applying a general principle (warrant) to an example or a case and drawing a conclusion. *Example:* Warrant: Most uneven footprints are left by people with limps. Support: These footprints are uneven. Claim: The person who left these footprints walks with a limp. **Test of Validity.** Ask if the general principle (warrant) and the support are probably true, because then the claim is also probably true.	Make a general statement. Apply it to an example or a case. Draw a conclusion. Decide whether to make the general statement (warrant) explicit or implicit.
Look for definitions of key words or concepts. They can be short, a word or sentence, or long, several paragraphs or an entire essay. Notice if the reader is supposed to accept the claim "by definition" because it has been placed in an established category.	**II. *Definition*.** Describing the fundamental properties and qualities of a term or placing an item in a category and proving it "by definition." *Example:* Warrant: Family values characterize the good citizen. Support: Radical feminists lack family values. Claim: Radical feminists are not good citizens.	Isolate the key terms and concepts, especially those in your claim. Define all terms that you and your reader must agree on for the argument to work. Place some ideas or items in established categories and argue that they are so "by definition."

continued

413

TYPES OF PROOF AND TESTS OF VALIDITY (continued)

When You Are the Reader		When You Are the Writer
	Tests of Validity. Ask if the definition is accurate and reliable, or if there are exceptions or other definitions that would make it less reliable. Ask if the item belongs in the category in which it has been placed.	
Look for examples, trends, people, events that are cited as causes for the claim. Look for effects of the claim.	III. *Cause.* Placing the claim in a cause-effect relationship to show that it is either the cause of an effect or an effect of a cause. *Example:* Claim: Children read better in school when their parents read to them at home. Support: There are specific examples of parents reading to children who then read well at school. Warrant: The parents' reading caused the children to do better. **Tests of Validity.** Ask if these causes alone are sufficient to create these effects or could these effects result from other causes. Try to think of exceptions to the cause-effect outcome.	Make a claim and ask what caused it. Apply Burke's pentad to focus the main cause: What was done? Where was it done? Who did it? How did he/she do it? Why did it happen?
Look for clues, symptoms, occurrences that are explained as signs or symptoms that something is so.	IV. *Sign.* Pointing out the symptoms or signs that something is so. *Example:* Claim: The child has chicken pox. Support: The child had spots. Warrant: Those spots are a sign of chicken pox. **Test of Validity.** Ask if this is really a sign of what the author claims, or if there is another explanation.	Think of symptoms or signs that you can use to demonstrate that something is so.

continued

TYPES OF PROOF AND TESTS OF VALIDITY *(continued)*

When You Are the Reader	When You Are the Writer
Look for a conclusion/claim based on examples or cases.	Give some examples and draw a conclusion/claim based on them; *or* make the claim and back it up with a series of examples.

V. *Induction.* Drawing a conclusion (claim) from a number of representative cases or examples.

Example:

Claim: Everyone liked that movie.

Support: know three people who liked it.

Warrant: Three examples are enough.

Tests of Validity. Ask if there are enough examples, or if this is a "hasty" conclusion/claim? Try to think of an exception that would change the conclusion/claim. See if you can make the "inductive leap" from the examples to the conclusion/claim and accept it as probably true.

When You Are the Reader	When You Are the Writer
Look for numbers, data, tables of figures along with interpretations of them.	Find data, statistics, and tables of figures to use as evidence to back up your claim. Make clear where you get the statistics, and add interpretations of experts.

VI. *Statistics.* Using figures or data to prove a claim.

Example:

Claim: We should end draft registration.

Support: It costs 27.5 million dollars per year.

Warrant: This is too much; it proves we should end it.

Tests of Validity. Ask where the statistics came from, to what dates they apply, and if they are fair and accurate. Ask if they have been exaggerated or skewed. Ask if they prove what they are supposed to prove.

continued

TYPES OF PROOF AND TESTS OF VALIDITY (continued)

When You Are the Reader

Literal and historical analogy:
Look for items, events, people, or periods of time that are being compared.

VII. *Analogies: literal, historical, and figurative.* Interpreting what we do not understand by comparing it with something we do. Literal and historical analogies compare similar items, and figurative analogies compare items from radically different categories.

Example of historical analogy:

Claim: Many people will die of AIDS.

Support: Many people died of the black death.

Warrant: AIDS and the black death are similar.

Example of literal analogy:

Claim: The state should spend more money on education.

Support: Another state spent more money with good results.

Warrant: The two states are similar, and the results of one will be the results of the other.

Example of figurative analogy:

Claim: Reading a difficult book should take time.

Support: Digesting a large meal takes time.

Warrant: Reading and eating are sufficiently alike that they can be compared.

When You Are the Writer

Literal and historical analogy:
Think of items in the same category that can be compared. Show that what happened in one case will also happen in the other. Or demonstrate that history repeats itself.

continued

TYPES OF PROOF AND TESTS OF VALIDITY *(continued)*

When You Are the Reader	When You Are the Writer
Figurative analogy: Look for extended metaphors or items compared that are from totally different categories.	*Figurative analogy:* Think of comparisons with items from other categories. Try to compare items that have similar qualities, characteristics, or outcomes.
Tests of Validity. For literal analogies, ask if the cases are so similar that the results of one will be the results of the other. For historical analogies, ask if history will repeat itself. For figurative analogies, ask if the qualities of the items being compared are real enough to provide logical support, or if they are so dissimilar that they do not prove anything.	

Proof That Establishes *Ethos* (1)

When You Are the Reader	When You Are the Writer
Look for references to the author's credentials, background, and training. Look for credential statements about quoted authorities.	1. *Authority.* Quoting established authorities or experts or establishing one's own authority and credibility. *Example:* Claim: California will have an earthquake. Support: Professors and scientists say so. Warrant: These experts are reliable. **Test of Validity.** Ask if the experts, including both outside authorities and the author, are really experts. Remember that argument from authority is only as good as the authorities themselves.	Refer to your own experience and background to establish expertise. Quote the best and most reliable authorities. Establish common ground and respect by using appropriate language and tone.

Emotional Proofs (2)

When You Are the Reader	When You Are the Writer
Look for references to items or qualities you might need or want and advice on how to get them. Look for emotional language, description, and tone.	1. *Motives.* Appealing to what all audiences are supposed to need, such as food, drink, warmth and shelter, sex, security, belonging, self-esteem, creativity, and self-expression. Urging audiences to take steps to meet their needs.	Think about what your audience needs, and show how your ideas will help them. Use emotional language and tone where appropriate.

continued

TYPES OF PROOF AND TESTS OF VALIDITY *(continued)*

When You Are the Reader		When You Are the Writer

Example:

Claim: You should support this candidate.

Support: The candidate can help you get job security and safe neighborhoods.

Warrant: You want job security and safe neighborhoods.

Tests of Validity. Ask if you really need what the author assumes you need. Ask if doing what is recommended will satisfy the need as described.

II. *Values.* Appealing to what all audiences are supposed to value, such as reliability, honesty, loyalty, industry, patriotism, courage, integrity, conviction, faithfulness, dependability, creativity, freedom, equality, devotion to duty, and acceptance by others.

Example:

Claim: The curriculum should be multicultural.

Support: A multicultural curriculum will contribute to equality and acceptance.

Warrant: You value equality and acceptance.

Tests of Validity. Ask if you share the author's values. Ask about the effect that differences in values will have on the argument.

Look for value statements generally accepted by most people.

Look for examples or narratives that display values.

Infer values (warrants) that are not explicitly stated.

Look for emotional language and tone.

Appeal to your audience's values through warrants, explicit value statements, and narratives that illustrate values.

Use emotional language and tone where appropriate.

TYPES OF CLAIMS (5)

I. ***Claims of fact.*** What happened? Is it true? Does it exist? Is it a fact?

Examples:

> Increasing population threatens the environment.
> Television content promotes violence.
> Women are not as effective as men in combat.

Readers	Writers
• Look for claims that state facts. • Look for facts, statistics, real examples, quotes from reliable authorities. • Anticipate induction, analogies, and signs. • Look for chronological or topical organization or a claim plus reasons.	• State the claim as a fact even though it is controversial. • Use factual evidence and expert opinion. • Use induction, historical and literal analogies, and signs. • Consider arranging your material as a claim with reasons.

II. ***Claims of definition.*** What is it? What is it like? How should it be classified? How should it be interpreted? How does its usual meaning change in a particular context?

Examples:

> We need to define what constitutes a family before we discuss family values.
> A definition will demonstrate that the riots were an instance of civil disobedience.

Readers	Writers
• Look for a claim that contains or is followed by a definition. • Look for a reliable authorities and sources for definitions. • Look for comparisons and examples. • Look for comparison-and-contrast, topical, or deductive organization.	• State your claim and define the key term/terms. • Quote authorities, or go to dictionaries, encyclopedias, or other reliable sources for definitions. • If you are comparing to help define, use comparison-contrast and organization. • Use deductive organization.

III. ***Claims of cause.*** What caused it? Where did it come from? Why did it happen? What are the effects? What probably will be the results on a short-term and long-term basis?

Examples:

> Clear-cutting is the main cause of the destruction of ancient forests.
> Censorship can result in limits on freedom of speech.
> The American people's current mood has been caused by a faltering economy.

Readers	Writers
• Look for a claim that states or implies cause or effect.	• Make a claim that states or implies cause or effect.

continued

TYPES OF CLAIMS (5) *(continued)*

Readers	Writers
• Look for facts and statistics, comparisons, such as historical analogies, signs, induction, deduction, and causal arguments. • Look for cause-effect or effect-cause organization.	• Use facts and statistics. • Apply Burke's pentad to focus the main cause. • Use historical analogies, signs, induction, deduction. • Consider using cause-effect or effect-cause organization.

IV. *Claims of value.* Is it good or bad? How good? How bad? Of what worth is it? Is it moral or immoral? Who thinks so? What do those people value? What values or criteria should I use to determine its goodness or badness? Are my values different from other people's or the author's?

Examples:

Computers are a valuable addition to modern education.

School prayer has a moral function in the public schools.

Mercy killing is immoral.

Readers	Writers
• Look for claims that make a value statement. • Look for value proofs, motivational proofs, analogies, both literal and figurative, quotes from authorities, signs, and definitions. • Expect emotional language. • Look for applied-criteria, topical, and narrative patterns of organization.	• State your claim as a judgment or value statement. • Analyze your audience's needs and values, and appeal to them. • Use literal and figurative analogies, quotes from authorities, signs, and definitions. • Use emotional language appropriately. • Consider the applied-criteria, claim-and-reasons, or narrative organizational patterns.

V. *Claims of policy.* What should we do? How should we act? What should future policy be? How can we solve this problem? What course of action should we pursue?

Examples:

The criminal should be sent to prison rather than to a mental hospital.

Sex education should be part of the public school curriculum.

Battered women who take revenge should not be placed in jail.

Readers	Writers
• Look for claims that state that something should be done. • Look for data, motivational appeals, literal analogies, and argument from authority. • Anticipate the problem-solution pattern of organization.	• State the claim as something that should be done. • Use data, motivational appeals, analogies, and authorities as proof. • Use emotional language appropriately. • Consider the problem-solution pattern of organization.

PART FOUR

The Reader

Introduction to "The Reader": Reading and Writing About Issue Areas

"T he Reader" contains seven sections that introduce you to broad issue areas that engage modern society: men's and women's roles, education, crime and the treatment of criminals, freedom of speech, racism in America, the electronic media, and social and personal responsibility. Articles are then organized under specific related issues in each broad category. "The Reader" contains both classical and contemporary essays. These explore some of the individual perspectives and positions people have taken in regard to issues both now and in the past. You may quickly bring them up to date by reading what is being written about them now as you read this book.

You may also expand your perspective on each of these issues through film and literature. In the introduction to each issue area, a list of related films and literary works that treat these issues in interesting ways is provided. The films are available on videotape, and the literature is available in anthologies and in the library.

THE PURPOSE OF "THE READER"

"The Reader" serves three main purposes:

1. It introduces you to big issue areas and a few of their specific related issues. It also helps you build background and provides you with information to quote in your papers.
2. It provides you with models of different types of arguments and thus gives you a better idea of how argument works in general. It provides you with examples and strategies for improving your own written arguments.
3. It helps you think and invent arguments and ideas of your own by providing you with essays that function as springboards for your own thoughts and reactions.

HOW TO USE "THE READER"

See chapters for details or review.

1. Select an issue that is compelling for you. Background it. Anticipate ways to build common ground with those who oppose you. (Chapters 1 and 8)
2. Survey it: Read the titles and summaries of the articles in the table of contents; read the introductory material and "The Rhetorical Situation" at the beginning of the issue area; read the introductions to the articles. (Chapter 3)
3. Select the related issue area that interests you the most. (Chapters 1 and 3)
4. Read the articles in the related issue area and jot down the claim and some of the major support and warrants for each. (Chapters 3 and 5)
5. Make a map or write a list of all of the smaller related issues that you can think of that are related to the issue you have read about. (Chapter 3)
6. Write an exploratory paper in which you explain the perspectives presented by the articles in "The Reader." You may also want to do outside research. Explain at least three perspectives on your issue. (Chapter 4)
7. Take a position on your issue, and phrase it as a question. Apply the 12 tests on page 26 to make certain you have an arguable issue. (Chapter 1)
8. State your claim, clarify your purpose, plan, and write an argument paper that presents your position on the issue. (Chapters 10, 11, and 12)

QUESTIONS TO HELP YOU READ CRITICALLY AND ANALYTICALLY

1. What is at issue?
2. What is the claim? What type of claim is it?
3. What is the support?
4. What are the warrants?
5. What are the weaknesses in the argument, and how can I refute them?
6. What are some other perspectives on the issue?
7. Where do I stand now?

QUESTIONS TO HELP YOU READ CREATIVELY AND MOVE FROM READING TO WRITING

1. What is my exigence for writing about this topic?
2. What is my general position compared to the author's?
3. Which specific ideas do I agree or disagree with?
4. Do the essays confirm what I think, or do they cause me to change my mind?
5. What original or related ideas are occurring to me as I read?
6. What original perspective can I take?
7. What type of claim do I want to make?
8. What can I quote, paraphrase, or summarize?

SECTION I
Issues Concerning Men's and Women's Roles

WHAT ARE THE ISSUES?

1. Do Men and Women Students Learn Differently in the Classroom?

Of course, men and women are different. The authors of the essays in this section argue about how great these differences are as they occur in the classroom. A related issue is whether men and women should expect different or special treatment from teachers and each other. See also "Love is a Fallacy," page 229.

2. What Do Women Expect of Themselves in Society?

Two feminists give their views on women's roles. Friedan, writing in the 1960s, explains some of the motivation for the most recent women's movement that began in the 1960s. Faludi examines recent opinions regarding the outcomes and value of this movement. The final article, written by a man, argues that women enjoy considerable advantages in modern society. See also "Paying the Price of Female Neglect," page 166, and "Why I Want a Wife," page 56.

3. What Do Men Expect of Themselves in Society?

Rotundo explores contemporary roles for men and contrasts modern men's roles with those of men in the nineteenth century. Theroux complains about the traditional male roles and Adler describes a "new" role for the '90s male. See also "The Men's Movement," page 169.

4. What Is a Family? Does It Have to Be Traditional?

Who should marry, who shouldn't marry, and who should stay married are some of the issues discussed in this section. The pros and cons of family life is also a major theme. See also "Family Values," page 165.

Extend Your Perspective with Film and Literature Related to Men's and Women's Roles

Films: Discloure, 1996; *Annie Hall,* 1977; *The Birdcage,* 1996.
Literature: poem: "Myth" by Muriel Rukeyser; short story: "The Chrysanthemums" by John Steinbeck; plays: *The Doll's House* by Henrik Ibsen and *M. Butterfly* by David Henry Hwang; novel: *Persuasion* by Jane Austen.

THE RHETORICAL SITUATION

The roles that men and women should assume in the home, at work, and in society have been debated since humans first organized themselves into societies. Every age has produced writings on this subject, and the issues associated with it are some of the most enduring. The world's religions, along with societal customs and traditions, provide both the constraints and many of the warrants. In this section, current authors give their perspectives on men's and women's roles, beginning with Betty Friedan, whose book *The Feminine Mystique*, published in 1963, provided much of the energy for the women's movement in the second half of the twentieth century.

The basic questions that are raised in the writings in this section include: Are men and women really different in the ways they learn, or are they fundamentally the same? Do they have equal opportunity and treatment at home, at school, in the public sphere, and in the workplace? What types of roles should men and women assume? How are these roles reflected in the family unit? Is the basic family unit changing?

Men's and women's issues touch everyone's lives eventually, so there is a constant exigency. Look at the best-seller list. Browse in the magazine section of a bookstore. What are the related issues on this subject now? Which of them affect you? Men's and women's issues are intensely personal, and you will probably want to consult your own experience as you read and write about them.

1. Do Men and Women Students Learn Differently in the Classroom?

TEACHERS' CLASSROOM STRATEGIES SHOULD RECOGNIZE THAT MEN AND WOMEN USE LANGUAGE DIFFERENTLY

Deborah Tannen

The author of You Just Don't Understand: Men and Women in Conversation *describes how her research for that book has made her sensitive to the differences in men and women students' class discussion patterns in her classrooms. Tannen is a professor of linguistics at Georgetown University.*

When I researched and wrote my latest book, *You Just Don't Understand: Women and Men in Conversation*, the furthest thing from my mind was reevaluating my teaching strategies. But that has been one of the direct benefits of having written the book.

Chronicle of Higher Education, June 19, 1991, pp. B1, B3.

The primary focus of my linguistic research always has been the language of everyday conversation. One facet of this is conversational style: how different regional, ethnic, and class backgrounds, as well as age and gender, result in different ways of using language to communicate. *You Just Don't Understand* is about the conversational styles of women and men. As I gained more insight into typically male and female ways of using language, I began to suspect some of the causes of the troubling facts that women who go to single-sex schools do better in later life, and that when young women sit next to young men in classrooms, the males talk more. This is not to say that all men talk in class, nor that no women do. It is simply that a greater percentage of discussion time is taken by men's voices.

The research of sociologists and anthropologists such as Janet Lever, Marjorie Harness Goodwin, and Donna Eder has shown that girls and boys learn to use language differently in their sex-separate peer groups. Typically, a girl has a best friend with whom she sits and talks, frequently telling secrets. It's the telling of secrets, the fact and the way that they talk to each other, that makes them best friends. For boys, activities are central: Their best friends are the ones they do things with. Boys also tend to play in larger groups that are hierarchical. High-status boys give orders and push low-status boys around. So boys are expected to use language to seize center stage: by exhibiting their skill, displaying their knowledge, and challenging and resisting challenges.

These patterns have stunning implications for classroom interaction. Most faculty members assume that participating in class discussion is a necessary part of successful performance. Yet speaking in a classroom is more congenial to boys' language experience than to girls', since it entails putting oneself forward in front of a large group of people, many of whom are strangers and at least one of whom is sure to judge speakers' knowledge and intelligence by their verbal display.

Another aspect of many classrooms that makes them more hospitable to most men than to most women is the use of debate-like formats as a learning tool. Our educational system, as Walter Ong argues persuasively in his book *Fighting for Life* (Cornell University Press, 1981), is fundamentally male in that the pursuit of knowledge is believed to be achieved by ritual opposition: public display followed by argument and challenge. Father Ong demonstrates that ritual opposition—what he calls "adversativeness" or "agonism"—is fundamental to the way most males approach almost any activity. (Consider, for example, the little boy who shows he likes a little girl by pulling her braids and shoving her.) But ritual opposition is antithetical to the way most females learn and like to interact. It is not that females don't fight, but that they don't fight for fun. They don't *ritualize* opposition.

Anthropologists working in widely disparate parts of the world have found contrasting verbal rituals for women and men. Women in completely unrelated cultures (for example, Greece and Bali) engage in ritual laments: spontaneously produced rhyming couplets that express their pain, for example, over the loss of loved ones. Men do not take part in laments. They have their own, very different verbal ritual: a contest, a war of words in which they vie with each other to devise clever insults.

When discussing these phenomena with a colleague, I commented that I see these two styles in American conversation: Many women bond by talking about troubles, and many men bond by exchanging playful insults and put-downs, and other sorts of verbal sparring. He exclaimed: "I never thought of this, but that's the way I teach: I have students read an article, and then I invite them to tear it apart. After we've torn it to shreds, we talk about how to build a better model."

This contrasts sharply with the way I teach: I open the discussion of readings by asking, "What did you find useful in this? What can we use in our own theory building and our own methods?" I note what I see as weaknesses in the author's approach, but I also point out that the writer's discipline and purposes might be different from ours. Finally, I offer personal anecdotes illustrating the phenomena under discussion and praise students' anecdotes as well as their critical acumen.

These different teaching styles must make our classrooms wildly different places and hospitable to different students. Male students are more likely to be comfortable attacking the readings and might find the inclusion of personal anecdotes irrelevant and "soft." Women are more likely to resist discussion they perceive as hostile, and, indeed, it is women in my classes who are most likely to offer personal anecdotes.

A colleague who read my book commented that he had always taken for granted that the best way to deal with students' comments is to challenge them; this, he felt it was self-evident, sharpens their minds and helps them develop debating skills. But he had noticed that women were relatively silent in his classes, so he decided to try beginning discussion with relatively open-ended questions and letting comments go unchallenged. He found, to his amazement and satisfaction, that more women began to speak up.

Though some of the women in his class clearly liked this better, perhaps some of the men liked it less. One young man in my class wrote in a questionnaire about a history professor who gave students questions to think about and called on people to answer them: "He would then play devil's advocate . . . *i.e.*, he debated us. . . . That class *really* sharpened me intellectually. . . . We as students do need to know how to defend ourselves." This young man valued the experience of being attacked and challenged publicly. Many, if not most, women would shrink from such "challenge," experiencing it as public humiliation.

A professor at Hamilton College told me of a young man who was upset because he felt his class presentation had been a failure. The professor was puzzled because he had observed that class members had listened attentively and agreed with the student's observations. It turned out that it was this very agreement that the student interpreted as failure: Since no one had engaged his ideas by arguing with him, he felt they had found them unworthy of attention.

So one reason men speak in class more than women is that many of them find the "public" classroom setting more conducive to speaking, whereas most women are more comfortable speaking in private to a small group of people they know well. A second reason is that men are more likely to be comfortable with the debate-like form that discussion may take. Yet another reason is the different attitudes toward speaking in class that typify women and men.

Students who speak frequently in class, many of whom are men, assume that it is their job to think of contributions and try to get the floor to express them. But many women monitor their participation not only to get the floor but to avoid getting it. Women students in my class tell me that if they have spoken up once or twice, they hold back for the rest of the class because they don't want to dominate. If they have spoken a lot one week, they will remain silent the next. These different ethics of participation are, of course, unstated, so those who speak freely assume that those who remain silent have nothing to say, and those who are reining themselves in assume that the big talkers are selfish and hoggish.

When I looked around my classes, I could see these differing ethics and habits at work. For example, my graduate class in analyzing conversation had 20 students, 11 women and 9 men. Of the men, four were foreign students: two Japanese, one Chinese, and one Syrian. With the exception of the three Asian men, all the men spoke in class at least occasionally. The biggest talker in the class was a woman, but there were also five women who never spoke at all, only one of whom was Japanese. I decided to try something different.

I broke the class into small groups to discuss the issues raised in the readings and to analyze their own conversational transcripts. I devised three ways of dividing the students into groups: one by the degree program they were in, one by gender, and one by conversational style, as closely as I could guess it. This meant that when the class was grouped according to conversational style, I put Asian students together, fast talkers together, and quiet students together. The class split into groups six times during the semester, so they met in each grouping twice. I told students to regard the groups as examples of interactional data and to note the different ways they participated in the different groups. Toward the end of the term, I gave them a questionnaire asking about their class and group participation.

I could see plainly from my observation of the groups at work that women who never opened their mouths in class were talking away in the small groups. In fact, the Japanese woman commented that she found it particularly hard to contribute to the all-woman group she was in because "I was overwhelmed by how talkative the female students were in the female-only group." This is particularly revealing because it highlights that the same person who can be "oppressed" into silence in one context can become the talkative "oppressor" in another. No one's conversational style is absolute; everyone's style changes in response to the context and others' styles.

Some of the students (seven) said they preferred the same-gender groups; other preferred the same-style groups. In answer to the question "Would you have liked to speak in class more than you did?" six of the seven who said Yes were women; the one man was Japanese. Most startlingly, this response did not come only from quiet women; it came from women who had indicated they had spoken in class never, rarely, sometimes, and often. Of the 11 students who said the amount they had spoken was fine, 7 were men. Of the four women who checked "fine," two added qualifications indicating it wasn't completely fine. One wrote in "maybe more," and one wrote, "I have an urge to participate but often feel I should have something more interesting/relevant/wonderful/intelligent to say!!"

I counted my experiment a success. Everyone in the class found the small groups interesting, and no one indicated he or she would have preferred that the class not break into groups. Perhaps most instructive, however, was the fact that the experience of breaking into groups, and of talking about participation in class, raised everyone's awareness about classroom participation. After we had talked about it, some of the quietest women in the class made a few voluntary contributions, though sometimes I had to insure their participation by interrupting the students who were exuberantly speaking out.

Americans are often proud that they discount the significance of cultural differences: "We are all individuals," many people boast. Ignoring such issues as gender and ethnicity becomes a source of pride: "I treat everyone the same." But treating people the same is not equal treatment if they are not the same.

The classroom is a different environment for those who feel comfortable putting themselves forward in a group than it is for those who find the prospect of doing so chastening, or even terrifying. When a professor asks, "Are there any questions?," students who can formulate statements the fastest have the greatest opportunity to respond. Those who need significant time to do so have not really been given a chance at all, since by the time they are ready to speak, someone else has the floor.

In a class where some students speak out without raising hands, those who feel they must raise their hands and wait to be recognized do not have equal opportunity to speak. Telling them to feel free to jump in will not make them feel free; one's sense of timing, of one's rights and obligations in a classroom, are automatic, learned over years of interaction. They may be changed over time, with motivation and effort, but they cannot be changed on the spot. And everyone assumes his or her own way is best. When I asked my students how the class could be changed to make it easier for them to speak more, the most talkative woman said she would prefer it if no one had to raise hands, and a foreign student said he wished people would raise their hands and wait to be recognized.

My experience in this class has convinced me that small-group interaction should be part of any class that is not a small seminar. I also am convinced that having the students become observers of their own interaction is a crucial part of their education. Talking about ways of talking in class makes students aware that their ways of talking affect other students, that the motivations they impute to others may not truly reflect others' motives, and that the behaviors they assume to be self-evidently right are not universal norms.

The goal of complete equal opportunity in class may not be attainable, but realizing that one monolithic classroom-participation structure is not equal opportunity is itself a powerful motivation to find more-diverse methods to serve diverse students—and every classroom is diverse.

TEACHING AND LEARNING AS A MAN

Robert J. Connors

Connors is Professor of English and Director of the Writing Center at the University of New Hampshire. He has written numerous articles on rhetorical history and theory. In this article, Connors explores some of the specific needs of men in learning and teaching situations.

. . . Does teaching young men effectively call for pedagogical techniques different from those effective with young women? Teaching interventions in a writing course must finally, of course, be individualized if they are to be useful. Typing all male students as barbarians, or aggressive strivers, or brown-nosers is not useful; like female students, each one is different. But I have not been able to keep from noticing that men and women often react differently to different sorts of pedagogies.

This difference is very clear in the ways that men and women relate to pedagogies based on collaboration. In distinguishing between "hierarchical" and "dialogic" methods of collaboration on writing tasks, Lisa Ede and Andrea Lunsford in *Singular Texts, Plural Authors* avoid gender stereotypes as much as they can (132–35). Even so, it is impossible for the reader not to associate dialogic collaboration, in which "the group effort is seen as an essential part of the production" (133), with feminism and women's ways of knowing, and hierarchical collaboration, with its product-based goals and clearly defined subordinate and superordinate roles, with the ways men do things. Ede and Lunsford's discussion of these two collaborative methods is sensitive and subtle; they do not demonize hierarchical collaboration in spite of their admiration for (and use of) dialogic collaboration. But because it *is* dialogic, feminist, and "subversive," dialogic work clearly seems more valuable to them, as it does to many teachers of writing. The problem for male students is that many do not come to dialogic collaboration easily, or come to it at all, and if egalitarian, communitarian, consensus-based collaboration is part of a teacher's expectations of group work, male students will consistently disappoint. It is not how men have been trained to do business, and expecting that we can blunt the aggressive individualism that *is* their cultural training in a few weeks is unrealistic.

Young men are simply more drawn to individual work and to hierarchies. Indeed, any writing teacher can illustrate this gender differential by setting up workshop groups segregated by gender. My experience is that the all-women's groups may or may not collaborate dialogically, but that the all-men's groups will certainly proceed hierarchically. A leader will emerge, roles in the project will be assigned, methods will be set up—the whole mechanism of rationalistic Western problem-solving will appear before your eyes. Even the careless or absent member who just "mails it in" in terms of group work is performing a role,

College English, February 1996, pp. 154–157.

and all of us have seen the phenomenon of the "male star" student, one who consistently goes out of his way to create an image, to impress us with his charisma and abilities.

I have also noticed that young men usually want clearly defined individualized credit for the work they do and the roles they play in groups. "Group credit" often seems to them unfair. This cultural training in individualism appears in many forms—and many of them serve young men badly in school settings. The "star" role does not work for everyone. . . . Some of our male students have evolved a serf mentality: to act inexpressive, to take orders for as long as they have to, to give as little as they can, and to rebel in the ways available to them. Newly minted as "adults," they are naturally conflicted by school roles, since the tacit code of male honor they are taught in this culture demands pride, individuality, and resistance, but most find themselves in situations of dependence, powerlessness, and servitude to goals they may not understand or accept.

One of the results of this conflict is that men lag far behind women in educational achievement. Though we hear more in the popular press about the self-esteem problems of young girls in school settings, in fact girls consistently do better in most school subjects than boys. Women's mean high school class rank has been higher than men's (by a minimum of ten percentage points) at least since the early seventies (Adelman 3). In the 1992 NAEP, twelfth-grade girls outperformed boys by 10.2 points in reading and 21 points in writing on a 500-point scale (National Center for Education Statistics *Report* 462, 486). Since 1978, more women than men have completed bachelor's degrees each year, and today men are a minority—around 46 percent—of both bachelor's and master's degrees awarded (National Center for Education Statistics, *Digest* 245). Honors Programs are even more clearly split, with the one at my own school over 65 percent women (and as much as 80 percent in humanities disciplines). Women's GPAs at my university average 2.90, while men's average 2.65. Men are simply falling behind in college education.

Why is this happening? As Willard Gaylin puts it in *The Male Ego,* the cultural signals that young girls are given to be cooperative rather than physically aggressive often result in more flexible social and interpersonal abilities:

> In many ways this better prepares women for modern life than male biology does. We do not live in a world in which power is measured by grip, height, or size of biceps, but by position, accomplishment, intellectual achievement, and the like. The early lessons the little boys learn about becoming men may tragically become the spears on which their self-respect will be impaled in modern adult life. But the lesson of those early days persists, and men will be trapped testing themselves on an obsolete power basis throughout their lives, if only in symbolic language and metaphorical actions. (35)

The power of these conflicts to harm young men can be seen in the tacit attitudes that many teachers have about their male students. Many have no idea who to *be* in their relations with their students. Most of us have stories about our most disgusting brown-nosers (or were they really just wonderful enthusiasts?), but many are also familiar with what Mary Hiatt calls "the student at bay," usually male,

who feverishly agrees with everything a teacher says and takes directions grate-
fully, does as little as he can, never volunteers, and who leaves the course having
given as little of his real self as possible.

How do we get through this serf mentality, break through into the underlife
of students? It will probably not be possible until we admit that our young men
have different attitudinal responses to teaching and learning than our young
women students. Since men's studies and the men's movement are both concerned with the structures that culture uses to construct manhood, it seems natural that we might look to these movements for help in understanding the struggles our students undergo as they submit themselves to the complex institutional
structure of higher education.

We must thus ask ourselves: what are male learning styles? As Carol Gilligan and Belenky et al. have suggested, women seem to learn more happily and
naturally in related, collaborative, and nurturing environments. Academic feminism has tended to extrapolate that data into a pedagogy that assumes that female learning styles should be normative, but an honest inquiry into the success
of this project reveals serious problems, at least for young men. Inexpressivity,
for instance, is a learned behavior in men that serves several functions, but we
often tend to read it as simple coldness and write off the students as insensitive
(Sattel 355). Our readings of male students are often too simple; males simply do
not respond in situations involving motivation, self-disclosure, or collaboration
the way that female students do, and to assume that they must learn to in a single
semester is unrealistic. Whatever our critique may be of the cultural assignments
our young men have received, punishing them as individuals because they don't
meet our new standards is unfair. Our job must include understanding them.

These are only a few of the issues we face that men's studies can help us
shed light on. If we are to grapple effectively with the attitudes of young men, we
cannot continue to view them merely as order-takers, or sulky vandals, or cultural naïfs who can be easily reformed with a dose of cultural studies. The fact is
that we are still struggling today with the meaning of the shift away from all-
male education that took place 150 years ago, and at this point we have not fore-
grounded gender issues equally for men and women. The feminism within and
the feminization of composition pedagogy that have become such powerful parts
of composition studies today have not yet made much room for male students—
or male teachers. Although it is understandable why male attitudes, fears, and
psychological structures have been either ignored or subjected to offhand dis-
missal in the discourse of contemporary composition, the result has not been
more effective understanding of our students. As writing teachers, we have a
unique opportunity to assist or thwart our students' searches. It will require,
however, more than our current assumptions that we want to turn out seemingly
genderless "writers," or that pedagogies that make collaboration and subordination of the individual normative will work equally well for all. Like it or not, we
will produce writers who are young women and young men. We need to confront directly what this means to us as older women and older men. We need, for
the first time, to confront gender issues wholly.

Works Cited

Adelman, Clifford. *Women at Thirtysomething: Paradoxes of Attainment.* Washington, D.C.: U.S. Dept. of Education, 1991.

Belenky, Mary Field, Blythe McVicker Clinchy, Nancy Rule Goldberger, and Jill Mattuck Tarule. *Women's Ways of Knowing.* New York: Basic Books, 1986.

Ede, Lisa, and Andrea Lunsford. *Singular Texts, Plural Authors: Perspectives on Collaborative Writing.* Carbondale: Southern Illinois UP, 1990.

Gaylin, Willard. *The Male Ego.* New York: Penguin, 1992.

Gilligan, Carol. *In a Different Voice: Psychological Theory and Women's Development.* Cambridge: Harvard UP, 1982.

Harris, Joseph. Letter to author, 2 March 1995.

Hiatt, Mary P. "Students at Bay: The Myth of the Student Conference." *CCC* 26 (Feb. 1975): 38–41.

Kimmel, Michael S., and Michael A. Messner, eds. <u>Men's Lives</u>. 2nd ed. New York: Macmillan, 1992.

National Center for Education Statistics. *Digest of Education Statistics 1994.* Washington, D.C.: U.S. Dept. of Education, 1994.

———. *The NAEP 1992 Technical Report.* Washington, D.C.: U.S. Dept. of Education, 1994.

Sattel, Jack W. "The Inexpressive Male: Tragedy or Sexual Politics?" Kimmel and Messner. 350–57.

2. What Do Women Expect of Themselves in Society?

THE PROBLEM THAT HAS NO NAME
Betty Friedan

This is an excerpt from The Feminine Mystique, *published in 1963, a book that explains the reasons for the current women's movement.*

The problem lay buried, unspoken, for many years in the minds of American women. It was a strange stirring, a sense of dissatisfaction, a yearning that women suffered in the middle of the twentieth century in the United States. Each suburban wife struggled with it alone. As she made the beds, shopped for groceries, matched slipcover material, ate peanut butter sandwiches with her children, chauffered Cub Scouts and Brownies, lay beside her husband at night—she was afraid to ask even of herself the silent question—"Is this all?"

For over fifteen years there was no word of this yearning in the millions of words written about women, for women, in all the columns, books and articles by experts telling women their role was to seek fulfillment as wives and mothers. Over and over women heard in voices of tradition and of Freudian sophistication

From Betty Friedan, *The Feminine Mystique* (New York: W. W. Norton, 1963), pp. 15–16, 22, 23–24, 30–31, 32.

that they could desire no greater destiny than to glory in their own femininity. Experts told them how to catch a man and keep him, how to breastfeed children and handle their toilet training, how to cope with sibling rivalry and adolescent rebellion; how to buy a dishwasher, bake bread, cook gourmet snails, and build a swimming pool with their own hands; how to dress, look, and act more feminine and make marriage more exciting; how to keep their husbands from dying young and their sons from growing into delinquents. They were taught to pity the neurotic, unfeminine, unhappy women who wanted to be poets or physicists or presidents. They learned that truly feminine women do not want careers, higher education, political rights—the independence and the opportunities that the old-fashioned feminists fought for. Some women, in their forties and fifties, still remembered painfully giving up those dreams, but most of the younger women no longer even thought about them. A thousand expert voices applauded their femininity, their adjustment, their new maturity. All they had to do was devote their lives from earliest girlhood to finding a husband and bearing children.

By the end of the nineteen-fifties, the average marriage age of women in America dropped to 20, and was still dropping, into the teens. Fourteen million girls were engaged by 17. The proportion of women attending college in comparison with men dropped from 47 per cent in 1920 to 35 per cent in 1958. A century earlier, women had fought for higher education; now girls went to college to get a husband. By the mid-fifties, 60 per cent dropped out of college to marry, or because they were afraid too much education would be a marriage bar. Colleges built dormitories for "married students," but the students were almost always the husbands. A new degree was instituted for the wives—"Ph.T." (Putting Husband Through).

In 1960, the problem that has no name burst like a boil through the image of the happy American housewife. In the television commercials the pretty housewives still beamed over their foaming dishpans and *Time*'s cover story on "The Suburban Wife, an American Phenomenon" protested: "Having too good a time . . . to believe that they should be unhappy." But the actual unhappiness of the American housewife was suddenly being reported—from the *New York Times* and *Newsweek* to *Good Housekeeping* and CBS Television ("The Trapped Housewife"), although almost everybody who talked about it found some superficial reason to dismiss it. It was attributed to incompetent appliance repairmen (*New York Times*), or the distances children must be chauffered in the suburbs (*Time*), or too much PTA (*Redbook*). Some said it was the old problem—education: more and more women had education, which naturally made them unhappy in their role as housewives. "The road from Freud to Frigidaire, from Sophocles to Spock, has turned out to be a bumpy one," reported the *New York Times* (June 28, 1960). "Many young women—certainly not all—whose education plunged them into a world of ideas feel stifled in their homes. They find their routine lives out of joint with their training. Like shut-ins, they feel left out. In the last year, the problem of the educated housewife has provided the meat of dozens of speeches made by troubled presidents of women's colleges who maintain, in the face of complaints, that sixteen years of academic training is realistic preparation for wifehood and motherhood." [. . .]

A number of educators suggested seriously that women no longer be admitted to the four-year colleges and universities: in the growing college crisis, the education which girls could not use as housewives was more urgently needed than ever by boys to do the work of the atomic age.

The problem was also dismissed with drastic solutions no one could take seriously. (A woman writer proposed in *Harper's* that women be drafted for compulsory service as nurses' aides and baby-sitters.) And it was smoothed over with the age-old panaceas: "love is their answer," "the only answer is inner help," "the secret of completeness—children," "a private means of intellectual fulfillment," "to cure this toothache of the spirit—the simple formula of handing one's self and one's will over to God."[1]

The problem was dismissed by telling the housewife she doesn't realize how lucky she is—her own boss, no time clock, no junior executive gunning for her job. What if she isn't happy—does she think men are happy in this world? Does she really, secretly, still want to be a man? Doesn't she know yet how lucky she is to be a woman? [. . .]

Can the problem that has no name be somehow related to the domestic routine of the housewife? When a woman tries to put the problem into words, she often merely describes the daily life she leads. What is there in this recital of comfortable domestic detail that could possibly cause such a feeling of desperation? Is she trapped simply by the enormous demands of her role as modern housewife: wife, mistress, mother, nurse, consumer, cook, chauffeur; expert on interior decoration, child care, appliance repair, furniture refinishing, nutrition, and education? Her day is fragmented as she rushes from dishwasher to washing machine to telephone to dryer to station wagon to supermarket, and delivers Johnny to the Little League field, takes Janey to dancing class, gets the lawnmower fixed and meets the 6:45. She can never spend more than 15 minutes on any one thing; she has no time to read books, only magazines; even if she had time, she has lost the power to concentrate. At the end of the day, she is so terribly tired that sometimes her husband has to take over and put the children to bed.

This terrible tiredness took so many women to doctors in the 1950's that one decided to investigate it. He found, surprisingly, that his patients suffering from "housewife's fatigue" slept more than an adult needed to sleep—as much as ten hours a day—and that the actual energy they expended on housework did not tax their capacity. The real problem must be something else, he decided—perhaps boredom. Some doctors told their women patients they must get out of the house for a day, treat themselves to a movie in town. Others prescribed tranquilizers. Many suburban housewives were taking tranquilizers like cough drops. "You wake up in the morning, and you feel as if there's no point in going on another day like this. So you take a tranquilizer because it makes you not care so much that it's pointless."

---

[1]See the seventy-fifth anniversary issue of *Good Housekeeping*, May, 1960, "The Gift of Self," a symposium by Margaret Mead, Jessamyn West, *et al.*

It is easy to see the concrete details that trap the suburban housewife, the continual demands on her time. But the chains that bind her in her trap are chains in her own mind and spirit. They are chains made up of mistaken ideas and misinterpreted facts, of incomplete truths and unreal choices. They are not easily seen and not easily shaken off.[. . .]

If I am right, the problem that has no name stirring in the minds of so many American women today is not a matter of loss of femininity or too much education, or the demands of domesticity. It is far more important than anyone recognizes. It is the key to these other new and old problems which have been torturing women and their husbands and children, and puzzling their doctors and educators for years. It may well be the key to our future as a nation and a culture. We can no longer ignore that voice within women that says: "I want something more than my husband and my children and my home."

BACKLASH: BLAME IT ON FEMINISM

Susan Faludi

This is an excerpt from Backlash: The Undeclared War against American Women, *published in 1991, which provides a defense for the women's movement.*

To be a woman in America at the close of the 20th century—what good fortune. That's what we keep hearing, anyway. The barricades have fallen, politicians assure us. Women have "made it," Madison Avenue cheers. Women's fight for equality has "largely been won," *Time* magazine announces. Enroll at any university, join any law firm, apply for credit at any bank. Women have so many opportunities now, corporate leaders say, that we don't really need equal opportunity policies. Women are so equal now, lawmakers say, that we no longer need an Equal Rights Amendment. Women have "so much," former President Ronald Reagan says, that the White House no longer needs to appoint them to higher office. Even American Express ads are saluting a woman's freedom to charge it. At last, women have received their full citizenship papers.

And yet . . .

Behind this celebration of the American woman's victory, behind the news, cheerfully and endlessly repeated, that the struggle for women's rights is won, another message flashes. You may be free and equal now, it says to women, but you have never been more miserable.

This bulletin of despair is posted everywhere—at the newsstand, on the TV set, at the movies, in advertisements and doctors' offices and academic journals.

From Susan Faludi, *Backlash: The Undeclared War against American Women* (New York: Doubleday, 1991), pp. ix–xv, xxiii.

Professional women are suffering "burnout" and succumbing to an "infertility epidemic." Single women are grieving from a "man shortage." The *New York Times* reports: Childless women are "depressed and confused" and their ranks are swelling. *Newsweek* says: Unwed women are "hysterical" and crumbling under a "profound crisis of confidence." The health advice manuals inform: High-powered career women are stricken with unprecedented outbreaks of "stress-induced disorders," hair loss, bad nerves, alcoholism, and even heart attacks. The psychology books advise: Independent women's loneliness represents "a major mental health problem today." Even founding feminist Betty Friedan has been spreading the word: she warns that women now suffer from a new identity crisis and "new 'problems that have no name.'"

How can American women be in so much trouble at the same time that they are supposed to be so blessed? If the status of women has never been higher, why is their emotional state so low? If women got what they asked for, what could possibly be the matter now?

The prevailing wisdom of the past decade has supported one, and only one, answer to this riddle: it must be all that equality that's causing all that pain. Women are unhappy precisely *because* they are free. Women are enslaved by their own liberation. They have grabbed at the gold ring of independence, only to miss the one ring that really matters. They have gained control of their fertility, only to destroy it. They have pursued their own professional dreams—and lost out on the greatest female adventure. The women's movement, as we are told time and again, has proved women's own worst enemy.

"In dispensing its spoils, women's liberation has given my generation high incomes, our own cigarette, the option of single parenthood, rape crisis centers, personal lines of credit, free love, and female gynecologists," Mona Charen, a young law student, writes in the *National Review*, in an article titled "The Feminist Mistake." "In return it has effectively robbed us of one thing upon which the happiness of most women rests—men." The *National Review* is a conservative publication, but such charges against the women's movement are not confined to its pages. "Our generation was the human sacrifice" to the women's movement, *Los Angeles Times* feature writer Elizabeth Mehren contends in a *Time* cover story. Baby-boom women like her, she says, have been duped by feminism: "We believed the rhetoric." In *Newsweek,* writer Kay Ebeling dubs feminism "the Great Experiment That Failed" and asserts "women in my generation, its perpetrators, are the casualties." Even the beauty magazines are saying it: *Harper's Bazaar* accuses the women's movement of having "lost us [women] ground instead of gaining it."

In the last decade, publications from the *New York Times* to *Vanity Fair* to the *Nation* have issued a steady stream of indictments against the women's movement, with such headlines as WHEN FEMINISM FAILED or THE AWFUL TRUTH ABOUT WOMEN'S LIB. They hold the campaign for women's equality responsible for nearly every woe besetting women, from mental depression to meager savings accounts, from teenage suicides to eating disorders to bad complexions. The "Today" show says women's liberation is to blame for bag ladies. A guest columnist in the *Baltimore Sun* even proposes that feminists produced the rise in slasher movies. By making the "violence" of abortion more acceptable, the author reasons, women's rights activists have made it all right to show graphic murders on screen.[. . .]

Some "liberated" women themselves have joined the lamentations. In confessional accounts, works that invariably receive a hearty greeting from the publishing industry, "recovering Superwomen" tell all. In *The Cost of Loving: Women and the New Fear of Intimacy*, Megan Marshall, a Harvard-pedigreed writer, asserts that the feminist "Myth of Independence" has turned her generation into unloved and unhappy fast-trackers, "dehumanized" by careers and "uncertain of their gender identity." Other diaries of mad Superwomen charge that "the hardcore feminist viewpoint," as one of them puts it, has relegated educated executive achievers to solitary nights of frozen dinners and closet drinking. The triumph of equality, they report, has merely given women hives, stomach cramps, eyetwitching disorders, even comas.

But what "equality" are all these authorities talking about?

If American women are so equal, why do they represent two-thirds of all poor adults? Why are nearly 75 percent of full-time working women making less than $20,000 a year, nearly double the male rate? Why are they still far more likely than men to live in poor housing and receive no health insurance, and twice as likely to draw no pension? Why does the average working woman's salary still lag as far behind the average man's as it did twenty years ago? Why does the average female college graduate today earn less than a man with no more than a high school diploma (just as she did in the '50s)—and why does the average female high school graduate today earn less than a male high school dropout? Why do American women, in fact, face one of the worst gender-based pay gaps in the developed world?

If women have "made it," then why are nearly 80 percent of working women still stuck in traditional "female" jobs—as secretaries, administrative "support" workers and salesclerks? And, conversely, why are they less than 8 percent of all federal and state judges, less than 6 percent of all law partners, and less than one half of 1 percent of top corporate managers? Why are there only three female state governors, two female U.S. senators, and two Fortune 500 chief executives? Why are only nineteen of the four thousand corporate officers and directors women—and why do more than half the boards of Fortune companies still lack even one female member?

If women "have it all," then why don't they have the most basic requirements to achieve equality in the work force? Unlike virtually all other industrialized nations, the U.S. government still has no family-leave and child care programs—and more than 99 percent of American private employers don't offer child care either. Though business leaders say they are aware of and deplore sex discrimination, corporate America has yet to make an honest effort toward eradicating it. In a 1990 national poll of chief executives at Fortune 1000 companies, more than 80 percent acknowledged that discrimination impedes female employees' progress—yet, less than 1 percent of these same companies regarded *remedying* sex discrimination as a goal that their personnel departments should pursue. In fact, when the companies' human resource officers were asked to rate their department's priorities, women's advancement ranked last.

If women are so "free," why are their reproductive freedoms in greater jeopardy today than a decade earlier? Why do women who want to postpone childbearing now have fewer options than ten years ago? The availability of different forms of contraception has declined, research for new birth control has virtually halted, new laws restricting abortion—or even *information* about abortion—for young and poor women have been passed, and the U.S. Supreme Court has shown little ardor in defending the right it granted in 1973.

Nor is women's struggle for equal education over; as a 1989 study found, three-fourths of all high schools still violate the federal law banning sex discrimination in education. In colleges, undergraduate women receive only 70 percent of the aid undergraduate men get in grants and work-study jobs—and women's sports programs receive a pittance compared with men's. A review of state equal-education laws in the late '80s found that only thirteen states had adopted the minimum provisions required by the federal Title IX law—and only seven states had anti-discrimination regulations that covered all education levels.

Nor do women enjoy equality in their own homes, where they still shoulder 70 percent of the household duties—and the only major change in the last fifteen years is that now middle-class men *think* they do more around the house. (In fact, a national poll finds the ranks of women saying their husbands share equally in child care shrunk to 31 percent in 1987 from 40 percent three years earlier.) Furthermore, in thirty states, it is still generally legal for husbands to rape their wives; and only ten states have laws mandating arrest for domestic violence—even though battering was the leading cause of injury of women in the late '80s. Women who have no other option but to flee find that isn't much of an alternative either. Federal funding for battered women's shelters have been withheld and one third of the 1 million battered women who seek emergency shelter each year can find none. Blows from men contributed far more to the rising number of "bag ladies" than the ill effects of feminism. In the '80s, almost half of all homeless women (the fastest growing segment of the homeless) were refugees of domestic violence.

The word may be that women have been "liberated," but women themselves seem to feel otherwise. Repeatedly in national surveys, majorities of women say they are still far from equality. Nearly 70 percent of women polled by the *New York Times* in 1989 said the movement for women's rights had only just begun. Most women in the 1990 Virginia Slims opinion poll agreed with the statement that conditions for their sex in American society had improved "a little, not a lot." In poll after poll in the decade, overwhelming majorities of women said they needed equal pay and equal job opportunities, they needed an Equal Rights Amendment, they needed the right to an abortion without government interference, they needed a federal law guaranteeing maternity leave, they needed decent child care services. They have none of these. So how exactly have we "won" the war for women's rights?

Seen against this background, the much ballyhooed claim that feminism is responsible for making women miserable becomes absurd—and irrelevant. [. . .] The afflictions ascribed to feminism are all myths. From "the man shortage" to "the infertility epidemic" to "female burnout" to "toxic day care," these so-called female crises have had their origins not in the actual conditions of women's lives but rather in a closed system that starts and ends in the media, popular culture, and advertising—an endless feedback loop that perpetuates and exaggerates its own false images of womanhood.

Women themselves don't single out the women's movement as the source of their misery. To the contrary, in national surveys 75 to 95 percent of women credit the feminist campaign with *improving* their lives, and a similar proportion say that the women's movement should keep pushing for change. Less than 8 percent think the women's movement might have actually made their lot worse.[. . .]

To blame feminism for women's "lesser life" is to miss entirely the point of feminism, which is to win women a wider range of experience. Feminism remains a pretty simple concept, despite repeated—and enormously effective—efforts to dress it up in greasepaint and turn its proponents into gargoyles. As Rebecca West wrote sardonically in 1913, "I myself have never been able to find out precisely what feminism is: I only know that people call me a feminist whenever I express sentiments that differentiate me from a doormat."

The meaning of the word "feminist" has not really changed since it first appeared in a book review in the *Athenaeum* of April 27, 1895, describing a woman who "has in her the capacity of fighting her way back to independence." It is the basic proposition that, as Nora put it in Ibsen's *A Doll's House* a century ago, "Before everything else I'm a human being." It is the simply worded sign hoisted by a little girl in the 1970 Women's Strike for Equality: I AM NOT A BARBIE DOLL. Feminism asks the world to recognize at long last that women aren't decorative ornaments, worthy vessels, members of a "special-interest group." They are half (in fact, now more than half) of the national population, and just as deserving of rights and opportunities, just as capable of participating in the world's events, as the other half. Feminism's agenda is basic: It asks that women not be forced to "choose" between public justice and private happiness. It asks that women be free to define themselves—instead of having their identity defined for them, time and again, by their culture and their men.

The fact that these are still such incendiary notions should tell us that American women have a way to go before they enter the promised land of equality.

CAN WOMEN "HAVE IT ALL?"

William A. Henry III

William A. Henry III is a Pulitzer Prize winner. In his book, In Defense of Elitism, Henry comments on some basic, fundamentally ingrained ideas about women in the 1990s.

Whenever the feminist movement gets a bit captious or silly—as in the 1993 fuss over whether there were enough statues of women in public parks and plazas in

From William A. Henry, III, *In Defense of Elitism* (New York: Anchor–Doubleday, 1994), pp. 102–109.

New York City—it is surely useful to remind oneself that many women, especially the best educated and most historically aware among them, are ablaze with rage over the way things used to be. To be born female was, by and large, to be born with limited horizons and few options. That was true not only in the eighteenth century and the ones that preceded it, but in the nineteenth and indeed the twentieth. I have seen the warping effects of frustration in the mothers of my friends; these women married and gave birth to successful men but found no place in the public world themselves, and their dammed-up drive often went into oversteering the careers of their husbands and children. My own mother regretted all her adult life that she had majored in English rather than her true love, physics, because she had been convinced by older women (including her aunt, a pioneer college dean) that the sciences were not "ladylike." Katharine Graham, perhaps the most powerful woman in America, has observed, "Power is neither male nor female." But Graham came to power the way almost every woman in history got there, up to virtually the present moment: through inheritance and marriage. Power may be neutral, but the road to it has been signposted by gender.

Having said all that, a dispassionate observer must still find it curious that women, a literary majority of the American population and holders of a large majority of its private wealth, have managed to get themselves classified as a minority group. They continue to enjoy advantages in recruitment and promotion long after the doors once closed to them have been flung wide open. It may still be hard for a woman to become a firefighter or steelworker; taunting or outright harassment of those who do crash the barrier is frequent and disgraceful (although reflective, for good or ill, of how male locker room louts also treat each other). In terms of jobs that matter in the formation of thought and allocation of resources, however—in other words, jobs for the elite—the evidence proving access for women is incontrovertible. Barely a quarter of a century after the women's movement began to make its mark, a third or more of all medical school, law school, and business school graduates are women, according to Census Bureau figures published in *The Washington Post.* By the same count, forty-six percent of the nation's financial managers are women, and so are forty-two percent of biologists and thirty-nine percent of mathematics professors—to name just three fields considered resistant to women and in which women traditionally were thought not to excel. In psychology, public relations, and my own niche of journalism, women now appear to be an absolute majority. While women still feel underrepresented in elective government (in part because they will not vote as a block for a fellow female in anything like the same percentages that, say, blacks will give to a fellow black), the gender ratio in the managerial ranks of the civil service is nearly fifty-fifty. Few women run major corporations, but many in the middle management generation seem to be well on their way.

Quotas, by whatever euphemism they are known, have become superfluous. Their primary effect, as with blacks, is to de-credential candidates who could have succeeded without help. Whenever quotas are operating, a woman who gets a good job is apt to be viewed as having arrived there solely because she is a woman—and in her heart of hearts is apt to ask herself if that might really be true.

The moral rationale for affirmative action on behalf of women is even weaker than the political and economic one. When blacks point to the cumulative effects of slavery and racial discrimination as a basis for giving them special advantages, they are speaking as an identifiable community. Both they themselves and the larger society around them have viewed them as a collective entity. In every generation up to the present one, and to a distressing extent even today, blacks have been born into families apt to be disadvantaged socially, educationally, and economically, have grown up in neighborhoods where similar disadvantages were the norm, and have entered schools and workplaces prone to perceive them as automatically inferior. It does not take much imagination to trace a clear hereditary line from the injustices of the past to the inadequacies of the present. Even so, the time must come when affirmative action gives way to open competition. . . . When it comes to elite jobs, that time is already here.

Women, by contrast, can claim no such hereditary burden. Their sense of historical grievance is largely irrelevant and almost entirely self-imposed. Whatever happened to women in the past, it is only minimally visited upon women of today. Feminist anger is primarily a theoretical and ideological, not a practical, construct. Novelist Michael Crichton summed up the absurdity of much such posturing by privileged women in his latest socially astute best seller *Disclosure*. A careworn husband whose wife starts running a feminist guilt trip on him says in reply, "You're a partner in a law firm, for Christ's sake. You're about as oppressed as Leona Helmsley."

Yes, women are descended from a long line of thwarted women. They are equally descended from a long line of admittedly unthwarted men. The spiritual connection with female forebears may seem stronger, but the biological link is exactly the same. The distribution of children by gender remains roughly fifty-fifty no matter the social class of the parents, so women cannot claim, as blacks can, to have been born into comparative economic privation.

It is true that adult women tend to be paid less than men and to be grouped disproportionately on the lower rungs of the economic ladder. Susan Faludi's *Backlash* and its ideological kin notwithstanding, that variance is attributable to many other factors besides overt prejudice. Women are often less educated or credentialed. They tend to be employed in fields that society rewards less extravagantly (some women, ill versed in the workings of the free market or temperamentally inclined to the folly of Marxism, see that fact of life as some sort of conspiracy). In no-nonsense economic terms, women tend to be less committed to their careers. They take time away to have children. They are ready to stay home or leave work abruptly when one of those children is sick or when an aging parent is in trouble. They often object on family grounds to long and irregular hours or abruptly scheduled travel and other normal, male-accepted demands of a job. All these outside concerns are socially valid, but they get in the way of work. Many women who also see themselves as caregivers want the rules of the workplace rewritten to suit their personal needs. Indeed, they want their relative lack of commitment (or, as they would phrase it, alternative set of priorities) treated as something admirable and reward-worthy in a business setting. That attitude almost never wins appreciation from an employer and has rarely if ever led men to success; still, women argue that past and proven ways of doing business are irredeemably commingled with "sexism." In personal style, moreover, women tend to be less aggressive and confrontational than men while performing in an economy that seeks and compensates those go-getter qualities. . . .

Even among women prepared to accept the reality of the past, one finds a widespread yearning to rewrite the rules of the present so that women may enjoy a more glorious future.

The overt goal of these feminists is to change ground rules of working life so that wives and mothers can, as the boast runs, "have it all." They argue that society benefits by giving special privileges to mothers in the marketplace. Is that so? Let me admit here that I think children are better off when their mothers (or fathers) stay home full-time, at least until the children enter school. I believe that much of the perceived educational decline of children has very little to do with the favorite whipping boy, television, and a great deal to do with a phenomenon that more closely fits the time frame of the decline—the two-income household, which in practice generally means employment for the mothers of young children. If this causal relationship holds true (and I readily concede that it is opinion rather than fact—if shared, albeit reluctantly, by virtually every working mother I know), then any benefit to society from the mother's working has to be weighed against the developmental loss to the next generation. Day care, the common solution, is usually merely custodial. The yuppie alternative, a live-in nanny, clearly represents an intellectual step down for the child. Of the ten parental couples to whom my wife and I are closest, eight have used live-ins, of whom not one had attended college (although the biological parents were mostly Ivy Leaguers) and only three were native speakers of English.

3. What Do Men Expect of Themselves in Society?

MANHOOD IN THE TWENTIETH CENTURY

E. Anthony Rotundo

These excerpts about some of the possible role models for modern males are taken from Rotundo's book American Manhood: Transformations in Masculinity from the Revolution to the Modern Era. *It was published in 1993.*

From the late eighteenth century to the late twentieth, "manhood" has changed along with its environment. Two centuries ago, the town and the extended family formed the matrix of life in the Northern states. For some, the church con-

From E. Anthony Rotundo, *American Manhood: Transformations in Masculinity from the Revolution to the Modern Era* (New York: Basic Books, 1993), pp. 284–287, 289, 362–363.

gregation also provided a society in which a man (or woman) might develop an identity. Now, at the end of the 1900s, those institutions have faded in importance for most middle-class folk. Our primary community is the nuclear family, which is an isolated unit under the best of circumstances—and current circumstances are not the best, for a large proportion of nuclear families are riven by divorce. The large bureaucratic institutions where so many middle-class men work resemble eighteenth-century communities in certain ways: they are hierarchical, and they make elaborate demands on the individual. Unlike the more genuine communities of the colonial and revolutionary eras, however, the great corporate bodies of our time do not provide the individual with security, nor with any sense of organized connection to other people or to the flow of human history.

In the twentieth century, some of our most engaging experiences of community come from our participation in communities of consumption.[1] To be moved as part of a concert audience or to discover someone who shares one's tastes can be exciting experiences, but neither of them guarantees the sense of personal connection or support that a human community can provide.

An many social critics have recently noted, we lack even the rudiments of a language to discuss community and connection.[2] This point is starkly illustrated when a president of the United States, trying to praise the voluntary help that some people give to others, resorts again and again to the image of "a thousand points of light" to describe what he praises. Surely, a society that valued connectedness would be able to produce a more accurate image of human help and kindness than this vision of separation in a vast, cold darkness.

Of course, in losing a strong sense of community, we have gained something else vitally important. Once, men had their positions in society ascribed to them largely by birth; now, those positions are a matter of individual achievement. The weight of the community and the dead hand of the past rest more lightly upon the individual—especially the male individual—than they once did. Individual initiative, as a principle, has been applied far beyond matters of social status. Middle-class men of the last two centuries have had profoundly individualistic experiences; each one must earn approval, win love, attain power, make friendship, mold an identity.[3] Since the early 1800s, these have all become individual quests. They are (as we like to think of it) detached from social necessity in a way that was not possible two hundred or more years ago. Even where we have genuine communities in our own time (be it in the nuclear family, in friendship groups, or in small, informal organizations), they are created by individual effort. We cherish our belief in individual initiative, our sense that the fate of each person lies in that person's hands.

We also cherish our modern notion that the core of each individual is an inner essence, a unique combination of temperament, passion, and personal experience untouched by society. This idea of a deep, true passionate self has been with us for at least two centuries, but not until the turn of the twentieth century did middle-class men and women begin to rethink the relationship between the self and the molding efforts of the individual. For the American bourgeoisie, the nineteenth century was a time of self-making, both in the economic sense and in the sense of shaping the desires and talents of the inner self to fit the proper moral and social forms. The twentieth century, by contrast, has been increasingly a time of self-realization, when individuals have worked to let their impulses and personal potentials flourish. In little more than a hundred years, the balance of bourgeois values has tipped from self-discipline to self-expression, from self-denial to self-enjoyment.

The true male nature is thought to deserve the same thing that any other portion of the deepest self deserves—an outlet in the real world. Men are still perceived as more aggressive, more primitive, more lustful, more dominating, and more independent than women—but how can these manly passions fit into the organized civilization of the twentieth century? This is nearly the same question that men and women asked at the start of the nineteenth century, when men's aggressive ambitions were set loose from the restraints of hierarchy and communal opinion; but the context for asking the question is very different today.

Middle-class observers at the dawn of the nineteenth century treated "male" passions—assertive and competitive drives—with fearful condemnation. The cultural structure of separate spheres was erected to allow expression of those drives for the greater economic and political good in a way that would also isolate them from sanctuaries of civilization and provide their male carriers with a source of constant purification. In the twentieth century, the competitive, aggressive drives—though still defined as male—are seen with less fear and more reverence. We think of them as vital contents of a man's true self in an era when the true self is regarded as sacrosanct. Although impulses to dominance and assertion are still viewed with some suspicion, there is general agreement that they can be productive and that they deserve a social outlet without stigma. This, in turn, raises an important question for twentieth-century men: What are the best outlets for the "male" passions in the twentieth century?

Men have developed several ideals of manhood that have offered answers to this question. One ideal is the "team player." Based on an ethic of sublimation, this ideal takes competitive athletics as a model for fitting aggression and rivalry into the new bureaucratic work settings of the twentieth century.[4] While a man struggles to reach the top within his own organization through fierce competition with his teammates, he also cooperates with them in the contest between his organization and others. In this way, the old investment of aggressive, selfish passions in economic competition has gained new life in the modern world.

Another strategy for establishing a relationship between male passion and modern life is represented by the "existential hero." This ideal grows out of a belief that there is, in fact, no proper place for true masculine impulse within modern society. The hero who lives by this belief is suspicious of authority, wary of women, and disgusted with corrupt civilization. If he would be true to the purity of his male passions and principles, he must—and can only—live at the margins of society. This romantic ideal has been embodied in such popular figures as Humphrey Bogart, Ernest Hemingway, and John Wayne.[5] It has an economic counterpart in the cult of the entrepreneur who pursues his vision outside the contaminating influence of corporate institutions.

A third approach is signified by the ideal of the "pleasure seeker." This is a man who works hard at his job so that he can afford as much satisfaction of his passions after work as possible. Some men might find such outlets in exciting, dangerous sports like skydiving or rock climbing. They may seek adventure through risky drugs, risky driving, and risky games with money (speculation and other forms of high-stakes gambling). A pleasure-seeking middle-class man can become a consumer connoisseur, pursuing the finest clothes, the finest cars, the finest art and entertainment, or the finest women. One form of this ideal has found expression in *Playboy* magazine. Its pages make explicit what is only implied in other commercial media—that sex and beautiful women are consumer products, accoutrements to the good life. They are one outlet for the masculine passions of the pleasure seeker.[6]

In the late twentieth century, one more symbolic ideal of manhood has emerged, the "spiritual warrior." Conjured up in the teaching of Robert Bly and other leaders of the mythopoeic men's movement, this ideal was born of dissatisfaction with the other ideals and images of men that have recently dominated American culture. It grows from a direct, conscious focus on the passions that its advocates assume are naturally male.[7] The spiritual warrior believes he has lost touch with those passions and lost his ability to connect directly with other men. In the process, he has been prevented from fulfilling his deepest spiritual needs as well.[8]

This understanding of manhood appeals intensely to many men because of its focus on fatherhood. Bly and others lament the growing distance between fathers and sons in the modern world. The teachers of the spiritual warrior ideal see the disconnection of sons from their fathers repeating itself in the disconnection of men from passion, from the spirit, from their fellow men. Here begins a striking series of parallels with the movement toward primitive masculinity at the turn of the twentieth century. For the spokesmen of that movement voiced the same concerns about the absence of fathers that men are voicing today. They also expressed the same anxiety about the dangers of a boy learning his vision of manhood through the eyes of mothers and other women.[9][. . .]

There is one important trait that all four ideals share.[. . .] Each of them signifies a turning away from women. The ideal of the spiritual warrior represents a ritual quest for manhood in an all-male setting. The ideal of the pleasure seeker may treat women as objects of pleasure or as accessory companions in his pursuit of enjoyment, but considers them largely irrelevant to the fulfillment of his yearnings. The ideal of the existential hero endorses separation from the confinement of civilization and the halter of permanent, personal commitment—and, given our cultural associations between women and the bonds of civilization, it is no surprise that adherents of this ideal view women's world with suspicion.

The world of the team player is less intrinsically exclusive of women than that of the other ideals. Pristine in its blindness to personal history, the great contest for success is technically open to anyone who can play and win according to its competitive rules. As we have seen historically, however, the middle-class male workplace was constructed by men according to shared male values and customs that are culturally alien to women. In recent years, women have made statistical inroads in the world of the team player, but as yet there is little change—culturally or statistically—at the level where most power is wielded.[13] In reality, the ideal of the team player posits a world where women have difficulty surviving even though they are not explicitly forbidden to enter.

NOTES

1. The term "communities of consumption" is Daniel Boorstin's. See Boorstin, *The Americans: The Democratic Experience* (New York, 1973), 89–164.
2. The central text here is Robert N. Bellah et al., *Habits of the Heart: Individualism and Commitment in American Life* (New York, 1985). For an earlier statement of this theme, see Philip Slater, *The Pursuit of Loneliness: American Culture at the Breaking Point* (Boston, 1970).
3. Alexis de Tocqueville in *Democracy in America* (trans. Henry Reeve [New York, 1945]) described much of this and anticipated its consequences. Most poignantly, see vol. 2, 144–47.
4. In his study of male heroes in magazines, Theodore P. Greene (*America's Heroes: The Changing Models of Success in American Magazines* [New York, 1970]) notes the rise of "Idols of Organization" in the mid-1910s. Greene describes these men as hard-working, efficient organizers who brought nineteenth-century persistence and industry into a bureaucratic work setting. The new hero was a team player who believed deeply in efficient organization and cooperation. As Greene depicts him, "the new 'Idol of Organization' was neither the creator nor the owner of the enterprise which he ran. The new demand was for men who could take over existing organizations and run them with a minimum of human friction and a maximum of practical results" (Greene, *America's Heroes*, 333–34).
5. On Hemingway as a model of manhood, see Leonard Kriegel, *On Men and Masculinity* (New York, 1979), 89–112. The existential hero—and variations on the ideal—in American movies are treated in Donald Spoto, *Camerado: Hollywood and the American Man* (New York, 1978). See also an essay on Clint Eastwood as a late twentieth-century hero: Robert Mazzacco, "The Supply-Side Star," *New York Review of Books*, Apr. 1, 1982.
6. The very term *playboy* shows how old standards of manhood have been turned on their heads. The idea that a man should aspire to be a boy would have been sufficiently shocking to an eighteenth-century Yankee. The idea that this boy-man's goal in life was to play would have seemed downright effeminate. For an analysis of *Playboy* that stresses rebellion against domesticity rather than regression, see Barbara Ehrenreich, *The Hearts of Men: The American Dream and the Flight from Commitment* (New York, 1984), 42–51. See also her analysis of the Beat movement of the 1950s as another reaction to twentieth-century middle-class concepts of home and family (52–67). Harvey Cox, looking at the surface of the magazine more than its underlying philosophy, has described *Playboy* as a guide to a style of manhood (based largely on consumption) that emphasizes the pursuit of pleasure. See Harvey Cox, *The Secular City: Secularization and Urbanization in Theological Perspective* (New York, 1966), 172–78.
7. The mythopoeic men's movement differs with this book in its basic assumptions about gender. Its stance is "essentialism": manhood begins with a timeless, unchanging core of qualities that all men ultimately possess. The stance of this book is one of "cultural construction": manhood is a mental category created and recreated by cultures as they, and their social and physical environments, change.
8. For a useful summary of what the men's movement is about, see Jack Thomas, "The New Man: Finding Another Way to Be Male," *Boston Globe*, Aug. 21, 1991, 43, 46–47;

"Following the Beat of a Different Drum," Aug. 21, 1991, 43, 46; and "The Bible of the Men's Movement," Aug. 21, 1991, 43, 47.

9. These concerns are summarized in Edward S. Martin, "The Use of Fathers," *Harper's New Monthly Magazine,* 117 (1908); G. Stanley Hall, "Feminization in Schools and Home: The Undue Influence of Women Teachers—The Need of Different Training for the Sexes," *World's Work,* 16 (1908); and C. P. Seldon, "Rule of Mother," *North American Review* (1895). Joe L. Dubbert explores the turn-of-the-century literature on absent fathers in *A Man's Place: Masculinity in Transition* (Englewood Cliffs, N.J., 1979), 140–44.

. . .

13. Some of the changes and the roadblocks are summarized in Lisa Belkin, "Bars to Equality of Sexes Seen as Eroding, Slowly," *New York Times,* Aug. 20, 1989, 1, 26; Alison Leigh Cowan, "Women's Gains on the Job: Not without a Heavy Toll," *New York Times,* Aug. 21, 1989, 1, 14.

BEING A MAN

Paul Theroux

This author was born in 1941 and writes travel literature. He first published this essay in Sunrise with Seamonsters *in 1985.*

There is a pathetic sentence in the chapter "Fetishism" in Dr. Norman Cameron's book *Personality Development and Psychopathology.* It goes, "Fetishists are nearly always men; and the commonest fetish is a woman's shoe." I cannot read that sentence without thinking that it is just one more awful thing about being a man—and perhaps it is an important thing to know about us.

I have always disliked being a man. The whole idea of manhood in America is pitiful, in my opinion. This version of masculinity is a little like having to wear an ill-fitting coat for one's entire life (by contrast, I imagine femininity to be an oppressive sense of nakedness). Even the expression "Be a man!" strikes me as insulting and abusive. It means: Be stupid, be unfeeling, obedient, soldierly and stop thinking. Man means "manly"—how can one think about men without considering the terrible ambition of manliness? And yet it is part of every man's life. It is a hideous and crippling lie; it not only insists on difference and connives at superiority, it is also by its very nature destructive—emotionally damaging and socially harmful.

The youth who is subverted, as most are, into believing in the masculine ideal is effectively separated from women and he spends the rest of his life finding women a riddle and a nuisance. Of course, there is a female version of this male affliction. It begins with mothers encouraging little girls to say (to other adults) "Do you like my new dress?" In a sense, little girls are traditionally urged to please adults with a kind of coquettishness, while boys are enjoined to behave

Excerpts from Paul Theroux, "Being a Man," *Sunrise with Seamonsters: Travels and Discoveries* (Boston: Houghton Mifflin, 1985).

like monkeys towards each other. The nine-year-old coquette proceeds to become womanish in a subtle power game in which she learns to be sexually indispensable, socially decorative and always alert to a man's sense of inadequacy.

Femininity—being lady-like—implies needing a man as witness and seducer; but masculinity celebrates the exclusive company of men. That is why it is so grotesque; and that is also why there is no manliness without inadequacy—because it denies men the natural friendship of women.

It is very hard to imagine any concept of manliness that does not belittle women, and it begins very early. At an age when I wanted to meet girls—let's say the treacherous years of thirteen to sixteen—I was told to take up a sport, get more fresh air, join the Boy Scouts, and I was urged not to read so much. It was the 1950s and if you asked too many questions about sex you were sent to camp—boy's camp, of course: the nightmare. Nothing is more unnatural or prisonlike than a boy's camp, but if it were not for them we would have no Elk's Lodges, no pool rooms, no boxing matches, no Marines.

And perhaps no sports as we know them. Everyone is aware of how few in number are the athletes who behave like gentlemen. Just as high school basketball teaches you how to be a poor loser, the manly attitude towards sports seems to be little more than a recipe for creating bad marriages, social misfits, moral degenerates, sadists, latent rapists and just plain louts. I regard high school sports as a drug far worse than marijuana, and it is the reason that the average tennis champion, say, is a pathetic oaf.

Any objective study would find the quest for manliness essentially right-wing, puritanical, cowardly, neurotic and fueled largely by a fear of women. It is also certainly philistine. There is no book-hater like a Little League coach. But indeed all the creative arts are obnoxious to the manly ideal, because at their best the arts are pursued by uncompetitive and essentially solitary people. It makes it very hard for a creative youngster, for any boy who expresses the desire to be alone seems to be saying that there is something wrong with him.

It ought to be clear by now that I have something of an objection to the way we turn boys into men. It does not surprise me that when the President of the United States has his customary weekend off he dresses like a cowboy—it is both a measure of his insecurity and his willingness to please. In many ways, American culture does little more for a man than prepare him for modeling clothes in the L. L. Bean catalogue. I take this as a personal insult because for many years I found it impossible to admit to myself that I wanted to be a writer. It was my guilty secret, because being a writer was incompatible with being a man.

There are people who might deny this, but that is because the American writer, typically, has been so at pains to prove his manliness that we have come to see literariness and manliness as mingled qualities. But first there was a fear that writing was not a manly profession—indeed, not a profession at all. (The paradox in American letters is that it has always been easier for a woman to write and for a man to be published.) Growing up, I had thought of sports as wasteful and humiliating, and the idea of manliness was a bore. My wanting to become a writer was not a flight from that oppressive role-playing, but I quickly saw that it was at odds with it. Everything in stereotyped manliness goes against the life of the mind. The Hemingway personality is too tedious to go into here, and in any case his exertions are well-known, but certainly it was not until this aberrant behavior was examined by feminists in the 1960s that any male writer dared question the pugnacity in Hemingway's fiction. All the bullfighting and arm wrestling and elephant shooting diminished Hemingway as a writer, but it is consistent with a prevailing attitude in American writing: one cannot be a male writer without first proving that one is a man.

It is normal in America for a man to be dismissive or even somewhat apologetic about being a writer. Various factors make it easier. There is a heartiness about journalism that makes it acceptable—journalism is the manliest form of American writing and, therefore, the profession the most independent-minded women seek (yes, it is an illusion, but that is my point). Fiction-writing is equated with a kind of dispirited failure and is only manly when it produces wealth—money is masculinity. So is drinking. Being a drunkard is another assertion, if misplaced, of manliness. The American male writer is traditionally proud of his heavy drinking. But we are also a very literal-minded people. A man proves his manhood in America in old-fashioned ways. He kills lions, like Hemingway; or he hunts ducks, like Nathanael West; or he makes pronouncements like, "A man should carry enough knife to defend himself with," as James Jones once said to a *Life* interviewer. Or he says he can drink you under the table. But even tiny drunken William Faulkner loved to mount a horse and go fox hunting, and Jack Kerouac roistered up and down Manhattan in a lumberjack shirt (and spent every night of *The Subterraneans* with his mother in Queens). And we are familiar with the lengths to which Norman Mailer is prepared, in his endearing way, to prove that he is just as much a monster as the next man.

When the novelist John Irving was revealed as a wrestler, people took him to be a very serious writer; and even a bubble reputation like Eric (*Love Story*) Segal's was enhanced by the news that he ran the marathon in a respectable time. How surprised we would be if Joyce Carol Oates were revealed as a sumo wrestler or Joan Didion active in pumping iron. "Lives in New York City with her three children" is the typical woman writer's biographical note, for just as the male writer must prove he has achieved a sort of muscular manhood, the woman writer—or rather her publicists—must prove her motherhood.

There would be no point in saying any of this if it were not generally accepted that to be a man is somehow—even now in feminist-influenced America—a privilege. It is on the contrary an unmerciful and punishing burden. Being a man is bad enough; being manly is appalling (in this sense, women's lib has done much more for men than for women). It is the sinister silliness of men's fashions, and a clubby attitude in the arts. It is the subversion of good students. It is the so-called "Dress Code" of the Ritz-Carlton Hotel in Boston, and it is the institutionalized cheating in college sports. It is the most primitive insecurity.

And this is also why men often object to feminism but are afraid to explain why: of course women have a justified grievance, but most men believe—and with reason—that their lives are just as bad.

BUILDING A BETTER DAD

Jerry Adler

Jerry Adler is a frequent writer for Newsweek *magazine.*

How do we assess a man's life? The late William S. Paley, founder and longtime chairman of CBS, devoted his life to the pursuit of wealth, power, fame and worldly pleasure—just like me, come to think of it, except he was very much luckier at it. But what I remember best about him is a telling remark in one of his many fulsome obituaries. Paley, said a friend, wasn't the kind of guy to attend his kids' Little League games, but when they needed him, he was there for them. And I thought, gee, how could one of the great visionaries of American industry be such a putz? Little League games are precisely when your kids need you the most. I accept that I will never own a Cézanne or sleep with a starlet, but nobody will say anything so dumb about me when I die, because *I've been to more goddam ball games in the past eight years than Cal Ripken Jr.*

Ha-ha. Just kidding, guys. I love Little League games, the earlier on Saturday morning the better. They remind me that it's always been hard to be a man. That was true even for my father, in the heyday of American malehood, the 1950s, when he would haul his weary suitbound hide off the bus every day at 6 P.M. and, responding to the invariable question, mutter, "Every day is hard when you're trying to make a living." By the standards then in effect, he was a model father, without once taking his kid backpacking, helping them sew costumes for their Kwanzaa pageant or making marinara sauce from scratch for their dinners. These are just a few of the ways in which men of my generation have redefined their roles beyond the business of making a living. Of course, most men still have to make a living, too, so in a single generation, fatherhood (like motherhood) has gotten twice as hard. I don't want to take anything away from Paley's achievements, but as far as I'm concerned, creating CBS would have been a more impressive feat if he'd done it while lugging his kids to the office in a Snugli.

Which he might actually do, if he were alive today. Men today "have permission to care for their children that they didn't have a generation ago," says Betty Thomson of the Center for Demography and Ecology at the University of Wisconsin. It's no coincidence that society gave men this permission just when they were needed to watch the kids so their wives could go to law school. By 1991, 20 percent of American fathers were taking care of young children in the home. (Two years later, as the economy improved, that proportion dropped to 16 percent.) But this cultural shift goes deeper than home economics. Baby boomers have transformed paternity, as they have every other institution they have touched, into an all-consuming vocation and never-ending quest for improvement and self-fulfillment. An outpouring of books, tapes, magazines and seminars—especially

Newsweek, June 17, 1996, pp. 58–64.

notable in the weeks leading up to Father's Day—both celebrates the pleasures of fatherhood and exhorts men to improve their performance in it.

Family responsibility was a major theme of the Million Man March in Washington last year, as it is of the revival-style meetings of the Promise Keepers, an evangelical group that has been filling stadiums all over the country. Executives quit lucrative jobs to spend more time with their families, a phrase that used to mean "he couldn't find his way out of the men's room." Jeffrey E. Stiefler, the 49-year-old president of American Express, resigned last year to become a consultant and "watch his sons grow up." "How many presidents of Fortune 500 companies get to do that?" his former wife remarked in The Wall Street Journal. Bill Galston, President Clinton's domestic-policy adviser, quit to return to teaching after his 10-year-old son told him "baseball's not fun when there's no one there to applaud you." I say go for it, Bill—*and don't even think of bringing that laptop to the game Saturday.*

Just kidding, Bill; you wouldn't do that. You know that fathering today demands far more concentration and effort than it did when you were growing up in the 1950s, that discredited era of emotionally distant, conformist, workaholic dads. To an astonishing extent, today's fathers define themselves in opposition to the generation that raised them. There is "a substantial gulf between the boomer generation and their fathers," says Don Eberley of the National Fatherhood Initiative. "There is disappointment, a sense of loss, regret bordering on anger."

This, of course, was the seminal kvetch of the men's movement: the alienation of fathers from their families, dating from the Industrial Revolution, which separated the worlds of work and home. A son who feels let down by his father carries a lifelong grievance. How could he have been so blind, so indifferent to my needs, so absorbed in the stupid newspaper? At the age of 49, Robert Blumenfeld, a San Francisco businessman, recalls exactly how many times his father played ball with him (once) and what his father said when he graduated from high school *cum laude:* that some other 18-year-old had just signed with a baseball team for $100,000. Dan Koenigshofer, a 46-year-old engineer in Chapel Hill, N.C., "can't ever recall that my dad said he loved me" (although he's sure that he did love him, in his taciturn 1950s way). David Weinstein, a Harvard economist, even knows where his father was when he was born, 32 years ago. He was in his office. Back then, the next day was soon enough for a new father to visit his son; Weinstein's dad was presumably in no hurry to learn how to change a diaper, since most men in those years didn't expect they would ever need to know.

Something changed in the culture when these men grew up, and sociologists are still trying to figure out exactly what it was. Somehow, out of the poignancy of memories such as these, men forged a determination to do better. There was new research: around 1980 psychologists discovered that attachment to the father—previously assumed to commence around the time a child began drawing a weekly allowance—actually forms at the same time as the maternal bond, six to eight months. Weinstein, taking no chances, made sure that he was the very first thing his son, Jeremy, saw when he poked his head into the world almost two years ago. But the most profound changes didn't grow out of a laboratory. Koenigshofer tells his kids—ages 4 and 1—he loves them "a dozen times a day." "You no longer see families where the dad says, upon finding that a kid has a dirty diaper, 'Go find your mother'," says Michael Lamb, a psychologist at the National Institutes of Health and a leading authority on American family structure. "But it was universal 20 years ago." A *Newsweek* Poll found that seven out of 10 American fathers spend more time with their children than their own fathers did; nearly half think they are doing a better job and only 3 percent think they're worse. What other area of American life has shown such improvement in just a generation?

Of course, *Newsweek* didn't poll the kids. Their wives, for what it's worth, tended to agree with them. But proving that men are actually being better fathers—as opposed to talking and writing books about it—is one of the great unsolved problems of contemporary sociology. "We all think there's been a change," says Thomson, "but I haven't seen any data that convinces me it's true." Part of the problem is that the same quest for self-realization that has led men to seek fulfillment in nurturing and sacrifice has also led them in increasing numbers to pursue their destiny with a sexy divorcée from their aerobics class. More than half of all American children born in the 1970s and 1980s are expected to spend part of their childhoods with just their mothers. A Census Bureau study found that 16.3 million American children were living with just a mother in 1994—and 40 percent of those hadn't seen their father in at least a year. It would take an awful lot of millionaire executives quitting the rat race to offset that statistic. "Men today are better fathers when they're around—and worse when they're not," says Andrew Cherlin, a Johns Hopkins sociologist who studies American families.

True, some studies have shown that fathers today are more involved with their children. But even those researchers admit that the demonstrable changes are small compared with what you'd expect from watching Donahue over the years. Studies of different nations show that American fathers are about average in parental involvement, spending on average 45 minutes a day caring for their children by themselves; American mothers, by the way, spend the most among women of any nation studied, more than 10 hours daily. (The least-involved fathers: Japanese, averaging three minutes a day.) "Women are still doing twice as much [child care] as men, although 20 years ago they were doing three times as much," says James A. Levine, director of the Fatherhood Project of the Families and Work Institute. "Progress has been slow, and it will continue to be slow."

Levine's assumption, clearly, is that it is desirable—for children, for society and for fathers themselves—for men to spend more time with their children. This seems obvious at first glance, although advocacy groups for fatherhood can also summon up reams of statistics to demonstrate it. "What reduces crime, child poverty, teen pregnancy AND requires no new taxes?" asks a handout from the National Fatherhood Initiative. The answer, of course, is responsible fatherhood (although like many panaceas, this one is vulnerable to the counterexample: if fathers can prevent all these social ills, how has Japan escaped them?). This organization was founded in 1994 to "reinstate fatherhood as a national priority," and it focuses mostly on public-policy issues related to divorce, abandonment and unwed motherhood. Its materials are thick with sound-bite-size statistics asserting, for instance, that "Fatherless children are twice as likely to drop out of school" or that "Seventy percent of the juveniles in state reform institutions grew up in single- or no-parent institutions." The National Center for Fathering, by contrast, has a more evangelical approach, exhorting individual fathers to greater "commitment" and to enhancement of their fathering "skills." Levine's organization promotes the compatibility of family life and work for men who may still feel guilty about sneaking out on, say, a half-written magazine story on the remote chance that this will be the day someone hits a ball right to where their kids are standing in right field.

Most married parents would agree that one grown-up is not enough to raise a child, although if pressed they would probably admit that two grown-ups are not nearly enough either. But when sociologists began studying the long-term effects of fathers' involvement, they didn't find what they'd expected. A few studies, mostly with highly educated and motivated fathers who displayed a superhuman threshold of boredom, did indeed show a correspondence between the time fathers spent with their children and such desirable traits as "increased cognitive competence" and "a more internal locus of control." But in an influential review of the research Lamb concluded dolefully that in general "there is little evidence and no coherent reason to expect that increased paternal involvement in itself has any clear-cut or direct effects." *So tell your coach Daddy had to work really, really hard this week and he's too tired to pitch batting practice Saturday, OK?*

Just kidding. This is so counterintuitive, so potentially dangerous and subversive, that not even the experts want to believe it. Instead, they're trying to prove that what counts is the quality of the father's involvement. To do this requires a statistically useful standard for judging fathers. Lamb's collaborator, Joseph Pleck of the University of Illinois, describes "positive paternal involvement" as being "high in interaction, accessibility and responsibility, and within the engagement component, performing positive activities and possessing positive stylistic characteristics." Before you get too worked up about this discovery, though, Pleck cautions that "to date, no research has directly tested this perhaps obvious prediction."

There is, however, one undisputed benefit to "paternal involvement," according to psychologists: it's better for the fathers. The effects of taking care of one's children include enhanced self-esteem, increased marital happiness and the quality psychoanalyst Erik Erikson called "generativity," referring to the ability to sacrifice and take responsibility for others. There are other ways to achieve this, such as devoting one's life to the betterment of humanity. But fatherhood is by far the most common test of selflessness, and in some ways the most exacting.

That's right: all those high-powered executives who are dropping out so they never have to miss another Little League game are in for a shock: their new career requires just as much intensity, focus and mastery of technique as business or war. That is the message of Ken Canfield, an educator who founded the National Center for Fathering in 1990. "There are rising expectations for fathers," warns Canfield, whose column in Today's Father magazine is ominously titled

"In the Trenches." In the 1950s, good fathers paid the bills and handed out discipline. Now, he says, "you have to be sensitive, you have to be emotionally involved, you have to forgo job advancement to be a good dad." Books like Canfield's "Seven Secrets of Effective Fathers" or "The Five Key Habits of Smart Dads," by Paul Lewis, bring to bear on fatherhood the same management-by-objective insight that has inspired 10,000 business best sellers. ("Effective fathers have a task orientation toward fathering" . . . "Without some simple guidelines to help them win at being dads, most men lack the confidence that breeds success.") Other books focus on developing specific skills, like making a popping sound with your finger in your mouth. ("Keep your cheek taut and your forefinger stiff and hooked," advise John Boswell and Ron Barrett in "How to Dad.") "Men want things summarized," says Canfield. "They want orientation. They want to know: 'What should I be doing?'"

And dads are doing it! Dads like Blumenfeld, who gets up every morning at 6:30 to make breakfast for his 13-year-old son, Bryan. Blumenfeld craftily sets the sports section next to Bryan's cereal bowl, and in that way, he says, "I guess I trick him into doing 20 more minutes of reading before school." How's that for task orientation? Or Robert Jones, a Birmingham, Ala., lawyer, who came into four tickets to a baseball game, and told his then 10-year-old son to invite two friends. When Jones got home, there were three friends instead of two, so Jones taught his son a lesson; he left him home and took the other boys to the game. That's how you win at being a dad—especially if, like Jones, you then demonstrate your sensitivity by getting all teary at the game and bringing everyone home after the first inning.

The analogy between fathering and managing a corporation breaks down, though, at one critical point. The return on investment is outside your control. The limits of possible success are set, more or less arbitrarily, at the moment of conception. You can do everything the books say and your kid still won't develop enough "increased cognitive competence" to get into Harvard.

And, naturally, you don't get paid for being a father—quite the contrary, as everyone knows—which explains the persistence of the myth that it's actually tremendous fun. There is a whole literature of fathers' lush, almost sensuous tributes to their own kids, the smell of their scalps after their baths, the secret pleasure of tiptoeing into their rooms to watch them sleep. People who have experienced only romantic love may find it hard to believe that the parental kind can turn one's brain to mush just as readily.

Boston TV producer Michael Greene likes to put some Aretha Franklin on the stereo, crank it up real high, and dance with his 5-year-old daughter, an experience that moves him to unparsable rhapsodies about "getting connected back to some basic essence of my life." Sitting quietly late at night with his infant son dreamily gumming a bottle was "like falling in love again," says Weinstein. In "Father's Day: Notes From a New Dad in the Real World," Bill McCoy, an editor of Parents magazine, describes how during softball games his mind would wander to "the way my daughter pushes me over when I'm sitting cross-legged on the carpet, then tumbles into my arms as I fall." His solution was to give up softball.

Art Perlman, a writer and lyricist who works from his New York apartment, looks after 6-year-old Jason while his wife puts in long days in her law office. Father and son fill their afternoons discussing topics Perlman lists as "colonial history, U.S. presidents, dinosaurs, space and science and animals in general." I don't think I'd given dinosaurs more than five minutes' thought in the year before my first son was born—and then, suddenly, my life opened up to a menagerie of fascinating, exotic creatures *that I wish had stayed buried for another 200 million years.*

Just kidding. I love dinosaurs, Barney especially. I don't want to sound like my own father, who frankly disdained them—a typical attitude of 1950s-era dads. Yet I detect a paradox in this frantic rejection of the values of the Eisenhower era. At the time, the postwar years in America were actually regarded as a remarkable experiment in family togetherness. Much of the iconography of American domestic life—the Saturday Little League games, the Sunday barbecues, the backyard birthday parties—dates from just that despised era. Parents, after all, moved to the suburbs for their children, not in order to work late at the office or eat out more often. And, as David Blankenhorn pointedly observes in "Fatherless America," fathers of the 1950s overwhelmingly stayed married and supported their families with their paychecks—an example that seems lost on all too many of their offspring.

And for me, Lord, if I can do no more, at least help me do no less: to come home to my family each night, to take care of them to the best of my ability, to raise my children with the certainty that no matter how much they screw up the rest of their lives, one person loved them unconditionally. Like millions of other men, I have made my choice. We will never know what greatness might have lain within our reach, not to mention starlets. And we will find satisfaction in knowing we did what was right, *without expecting any gratitude for it.*

Just kidding.

4. What Is a Family? Does It Have to Be Traditional?

GET MARRIED, MADONNA

Jonathan Alter

Alter wrote this piece for Newsweek *soon after the news of Madonna's pregnancy was publicized. How serious do you think Alter's claim is?*

Dear Madonna:

Congratulations on becoming pregnant. Some of us are looking forward to the inevitable "Madonna With Child" video, not to mention watching "Evita" breast-feed live at next year's Oscars. That would be you, Madonna: always peering over the hype horizon, pushing the edge of the predictable. The world pop *provocateur.*

Newsweek, April 29, 1996, p. 51.

But I'm writing out of concern that you're losing your touch. You told the press last week that you and the father of your baby, the now noted personal trainer Carlos Leon, won't be getting married. How conventional! How predictable! How uncool! You've now joined celebrities like *Farrah Fawcett,* not to mention nearly a third of the rest of the country. (Twenty-two percent of white babies are born to unwed mothers; 69 percent of African-American babies.) You call this getting ahead of the curve? Mariah Carey's married. She's also at the top of the charts. A coincidence? I don't think so.

If not Carlos, maybe you could marry a woman. Strike a blow against the right-wingers. They keep pushing family values but condemn gay marriage, which is inconsistent. If they believe that commitment is better than promiscuity, they need to back gay unions. Gay, straight—the important thing is to just get married.

Yes, we all understand your reluctance. When asked about marriage, you had a cogent two-word answer: Sean Penn. Been there, done that. Marriage is especially complicated for you: any prenuptial agreement with Carlos would weigh more than his barbells. And people seem so shortsighted, don't they? Years spent living with Carlos under the same roof without being married would be better for the child than if a forced wedding gave way to a predictably messy Hollywood divorce.

But will Carlos be under the same roof? It's not entirely clear. You've implied that you are prepared to raise your baby alone. Part of your message seems to be that you don't *need* men, except for sex, reproduction and maybe an occasional stroll in the park with the kid. Again, this puts you sadly in the bourgeois mainstream. This is now an extraordinarily common view, and it's substantiated by a long and sordid record of mistreatment of women by men. The problem is that it's also an extraordinarily destructive view.

A confession here, Madonna. I'm married and the father of three. Married people want others in the pool with them. But this papa will not try to preach, except to say that you should read. You know that already. You fancy yourself a bit of an intellectual. So why haven't you absorbed more about the causes of American social pathology? The research is quite definitive, actually. A little quiz: the most accurate predictor for whether a child will drop out of school, face unemployment and commit crime is . . . what? Poverty? No. Race? No. Neighborhood? Nope. The answer is growing up in a single-parent family. It's the only killer correlation.

Obviously there are millions of exceptions, and your child—born with plenty of advantages—may be one of them. Material Girls can provide. But what's "freedom" for the rich like you can spell disaster for the disadvantaged. When you're Madonna, you have to take account of your influence on them. You've said you want your art to touch people. Your life is a large part of your art. Ergo, your choices—and the messages they send—have consequences that you can't in good conscience ignore. How about all of those teenagers who even today want to dress like you, sing like you, be like you? What are you signaling to them?

It's one thing to advise teenagers, as you do in your music, to keep their babies if they want. But now you seem to be going further, conveying that the marriage contract itself is not important for raising kids. This is apparently also the view of Susan Sarandon, Tim Robbins, Kurt Russell, Goldie Hawn and other unmarried celebrity parents.

But, again, the research—and the point telegraphed to younger people—is unambiguous. For all its flaws, marriage continues to be the pathway to responsible fatherhood. Married men, as David Blankenhorn, author of "Fatherless America," puts it, are "less likely to do bad, and more likely to do good, in any area you measure," from supporting their children to holding a job. We're talking here about taming men, Madonna, socializing them so they don't wreck the culture. If you can't manage to get married yourself, the least you can do is speak up for the idea, the way you speak up for tolerance, sexual freedom and artistic expression.

Being in show business, you understand the significance of contracts. They impose reciprocal responsibilities that make completing a project (be it cutting an album or raising a child) easier. The contract must sometimes be broken, obviously, and there's a hot debate going on now about whether divorce should be made harder to obtain as a way to strengthen marriage. But the bond itself is more than a piece of paper. It's a measure of the commitment necessary to properly shepherd children toward adulthood.

The fact that any of this has to be explained is a sign of how much American values have changed since the day when Ingrid Bergman's career was almost ruined because she had a baby out of wedlock. I'm not advocating a return to those days, though a little stigma directed at errant role models wouldn't hurt. What I'm suggesting is that artists like you who claim to be interested in divining the future of American culture need to readjust your vision. The next wave is restoring the family, and with it, the country itself. Ride it, Madonna.

MARRIAGE AS WE SEE IT

Chris Glaser

Chris Glaser is the author of Uncommon Calling—A Gay Christian's Struggle to Serve the Church. *He describes how exchanging vows with his partner in a church ceremony made him feel transformed.*

Between my own Presbyterian church's vote rejecting ordination of gays and lesbians and the House vote against same-sex marriages, I feel beaten up. The one-two punch came early in July. Had I been the victim of a street gay-bashing, I would be able to seek comfort from my church and legal redress from the government. When the gay-bashers are my own church and government, I'm bewildered, wondering where to turn.

Newsweek, September 16, 1996, p. 19.

The two most sacred commitments in my life—my calling to the ministry and my same-gender marriage—are under attack because they are deemed threatening to a church and a society troubled by the lack of family cohesion, so-called "traditional family values." Our culture fails to see this as a largely heterosexual problem but instead scapegoats homosexuals, just as we who are gay and lesbian attempt to maintain relationships within our biological families and establish our own family units. Our birth families often come under attack for supporting us; our chosen families are refused recognition. Our families of faith treat us as society once treated illegitimate children. In the body politic, rights taken for granted by heterosexuals are called "special" when applied to us.

I've lived long enough in the gay movement to witness those who oppose us come full circle in their reasons that we should be outcasts from church and society. Twenty years ago, gay love was opposed because it supposedly didn't lead to long-term relationships and the rearing of children. Today gay love is attacked because gay people in committed relationships and gay couples with children are coming out. In the past, gays were denounced because we supposedly were "selfish" and "irresponsible." Now we're denounced if our selfless service—from the ministry to the military—is revealed. This damned-if-we-don't-and-damned-if-we-do syndrome should offer a clue to our opponents that their basis for being anti-gay is not reason.

From 1976 to 1978 I served on a national Presbyterian task force whose mandate was to lead our denomination in a study of homosexuality, particularly as it related to ordination. During one regional hearing, a minister testified that homosexuals shouldn't be ordained because we didn't form lasting relationships. Another pastor spoke proudly of leading a female couple in his church to see the "error" of their ways, thus breaking up their 20-year relationship. During these hearings, when anyone mentioned the possibility of sanctioning gay marriages, audible gasps came from the crowd. We could talk about gay ordination, but marriage was more sacrosanct!

In 1991 a Presbyterian committee on human sexuality endorsed a sexual ethic of "justice-love" for sexual relationships, including heterosexual marriage and homosexual unions. Fellow churchgoers went ballistic. To suggest that heterosexual marriage was not the bastion of all that is good and sacred about sexuality was too radical a concept for most of the church. The committee's report pointed out that heterosexual marriage as a holy paradigm had clay feet, mentioning the subjugation of women in most marriages, the problems of marital rape and parent-child incest, as well as adultery. The study also clearly affirmed gays and lesbians and our relationships. During the assembly that rejected the report, some opponents seemed to be saying to gay people, "We'll give you ordination—just give us back marriage."

Resistance to calling same-sex unions marriages is beyond my understanding. In no way does it lessen the sacred or civil nature of marriage. Indeed, its value is bolstered by the recognition that both homosexuals and heterosexuals wish to enter into such a covenant. Commonly, both procreation and companionship are viewed as independent satisfactory goals of marriage. Gay and lesbian couples enjoy companionship; some lesbians bear children; many lesbian and gay couples rear them.

It's true that the most ancient Biblical sexual ethic is procreation-obsessed. That's why the Bible accepts practices we now find unacceptable, such as polygamy, concubinage and required sexual intercourse with the childless wife of a dead brother. It is also true that Jesus, the source of Christianity, saw fidelity, not gender, as the central issue in marriage and redefined family as fellow believers rather than blood relatives. Until a few centuries ago in Western culture, marriage was primarily an economic institution that ensured inheritance rights, protected political arrangements and produced offspring. Only relatively recently did the ideal of romantic love supplant these reasons. That change redefined marriage far more dramatically than will the inclusion of same-gender couples under the rubric.

When my partner's and my relationship was blessed two years ago by our Presbyterian church in Atlanta, I felt transformed by our exchange of vows before God and a supportive community of family, friends and church members. I felt even more tenderly toward my partner and I understood more profoundly the sacred nature of our commitment. But when the local newspaper ran a notice of our ceremony, other Presbyterians demanded that our pastor be reprimanded and our blessing "undone."

Another male couple attending the ceremony expressed regret that they had never had such a ceremony. Less than two weeks later, one was killed in a traffic accident. Because most members of their congregation was unaware of the significance of their relationship, the surviving partner did not receive the support that might have otherwise been offered by fellow churchgoers.

Even as the position on anti-gay ordination goes to presbyteries for ratification and the marriage bill is taken up by the Senate, I'm grateful to know that if something were to happen to me or my partner, our congregation, family and neighborhood would be there for us, caring for us in trouble, challenging us to keep faith in God and one another. I grieve that the same cannot be said of all congregations, families and communities throughout this land.

LET GAYS MARRY

Andrew Sullivan

Andrew Sullivan is the senior editor of The New Republic *and the author of* Virtually Normal: An Argument about Homosexuality. *William Bennett, in the essay following this one, answers Sullivan's claims.*

"A state cannot deem a class of persons a stranger to its laws," declared the Supreme Court last week. It was a monumental statement. Gay men and lesbians, the conservative court said, are no longer strangers in America. They are citizens,

Newsweek, June 3, 1996, p. 26.

entitled, like everyone else, to equal protection—no special rights, but simple equality.

For the first time in Supreme Court history, gay men and women were seen not as some powerful lobby trying to subvert America, but as the people we truly are—the sons and daughters of countless mothers and fathers, with all the weaknesses and strengths and hopes of everybody else. And what we seek is not some special place in America but merely to be a full and equal part of America, to give back to our society without being forced to lie or hide or live as second-class citizens.

That is why marriage is so central to our hopes. People ask us why we want the right to marry, but the answer is obvious. It's the same reason anyone wants the right to marry. At some point in our lives, some of us are lucky enough to meet the person we truly love. And we want to commit to that person in front of our family and country for the rest of our lives. It's the most simple, the most natural, the most human instinct in the world. How could anyone seek to oppose that?

Yes, at first blush, it seems like a radical proposal, but, when you think about it some more, it's actually the opposite. Throughout American history, to be sure, marriage has been between a man and a woman, and in many ways our society is built upon that institution. But none of that need change in the slightest. After all, no one is seeking to take away anybody's right to marry, and no one is seeking to force any church to change any doctrine in any way. Particular religious arguments against same-sex marriage are rightly debated within the churches and faiths themselves. That is not the issue here: there is a separation between church and state in this country. We are only asking that when the government gives out *civil* marriage licenses, those of us who are gay should be treated like anybody else.

Of course, some argue that marriage is *by definition* between a man and a woman. But for centuries, marriage was *by definition* a contract in which the wife was her husband's legal property. And we changed that. For centuries, marriage was *by definition* between two people of the same race. And we changed that. We changed these things because we recognized that human dignity is the same whether you are a man or a woman, black or white. And no one has any more of a choice to be gay than to be black or white or male or female.

Some say that marriage is only about raising children, but we let childless heterosexual couples be married (Bob and Elizabeth Dole, Pat and Shelley Buchanan, for instance). Why should gay couples be treated differently? Others fear that there is no logical difference between allowing same-sex marriage and sanctioning polygamy and other horrors. But the issue of whether to sanction multiple spouses (gay or straight) is completely separate from whether, in the existing institution between two unrelated adults, the government should discriminate between its citizens.

This is, in fact, if only Bill Bennett could see it, a deeply conservative cause. It seeks to change no one else's rights or marriages in any way. It seems merely to promote monogamy, fidelity and the disciplines of family life among people who have long been cast to the margins of society. And what could be a more conservative project than that? Why indeed would any conservative seek to oppose those very family values for gay people that he or she supports for everybody else? Except, of course, to make gay men and lesbians strangers in their own country, to forbid them ever to come home.

LEAVE MARRIAGE ALONE

William Bennett

William Bennett is the editor of The Book of Virtues, *and he is a codirector of Empower America. This article is a response to the preceding one. Which argument do you find more compelling? Why?*

There are at least two key issues that divide proponents and opponents of same-sex marriage. The first is whether legally recognizing same-sex unions would strengthen or weaken the institution. The second has to do with the basic understanding of marriage itself.

The advocates of same-sex marriage say that they seek to strengthen and celebrate marriage. That may be what some intend. But I am certain that it will not be the reality. Consider: the legal union of same-sex couples would shatter the conventional definition of marriage, change the rules which govern behavior, endorse practices which are completely antithetical to the tenets of all of the world's major religions, send conflicting signals about marriage and sexuality, particularly to the young, and obscure marriage's enormously consequential function—procreation and child-rearing.

Broadening the definition of marriage to include same-sex unions would stretch it almost beyond recognition—and new attempts to expand the definition still further would surely follow. On what *principled* ground can Andrew Sullivan exclude others who most desperately want what he wants, legal recognition and social acceptance? Why on earth would Sullivan exclude from marriage a bisexual who wants to marry two other people? After all, exclusion would be a denial of that person's sexuality. The same holds true of a father and daughter who want to marry. Or two sisters. Or men who want (consensual) polygamous arrangements. Sullivan may think some of these arrangements are unwise. But having employed sexual relativism in his own defense, he has effectively lost the capacity to draw any lines and make moral distinctions.

Forsaking all others is an essential component of marriage. Obviously it is not always honored in practice. But it is the ideal to which we rightly aspire, and in most marriages the ideal is in fact the norm. Many advocates of same-sex mar-

Newsweek, June 3, 1996, p. 27

riage simply do not share this ideal; promiscuity among homosexual males is well known. Sullivan himself has written that gay male relationships are served by the "openness of the contract" and that homosexuals should resist allowing their "varied and complicated lives" to be flattened into a "single, moralistic model." But that "single, moralistic model" has served society exceedingly well. The burden of proof ought to be on those who propose untested arrangements for our most important institution.

A second key difference I have with Sullivan goes to the very heart of marriage itself. I believe that marriage is not an arbitrary construct which can be redefined simply by those who lay claim to it. It is an honorable estate, instituted of God and built on moral, religious, sexual and human realities. Marriage is based on a natural teleology, on the different, complementary nature of men and women—and how they refine, support, encourage and complete one another. It is the institution through which we propagate, nurture, educate and sustain our species.

That we have to engage in this debate at all is an indication of how steep our moral slide has been. Worse, those who defend the traditional understanding of marriage are routinely referred to (though not to my knowledge by Sullivan) as "homophobes," "gay-bashers," "intolerant" and "bigoted." Can one defend an honorable, 4,000-year-old tradition and not be called these names?

This is a large, tolerant, diverse country. In America people are free to do as they wish, within broad parameters. It is also a country in sore need of shoring up some of its most crucial institutions: marriage and the family, schools, neighborhoods, communities. But marriage and family are the greatest of these. That is why they are elevated and revered. We should keep them so.

GAY MARRIAGE? DON'T SAY I DIDN'T WARN YOU

Katha Pollitt

Pollitt wrote this piece for The Nation. *How does Pollitt support her claim that gay marriages should be legalized? Note and examine the different types of proofs Pollitt employs in this essay.*

When gay friends argue in favor of same-sex marriage, I always agree and offer them the one my husband and I are leaving. Why should straights be the only ones to have their unenforceable promise to love, honor and cherish trap them like houseflies in the web of law? Marriage will not only open up to gay men and lesbians whole new vistas of guilt, frustration, claustrophobia, bewilderment, declining self-esteem, unfairness and sorrow, it will offer them the opportunity to

The Nation, April 29, 1996, p. 9.

prolong this misery by tormenting each other in court. I know one pair of exes who spent in legal fees the entire value of the property in dispute, and another who took five years and six lawyers to untie the knot. Had these couples merely lived together they would have thrown each other's record collections out the window and called it a day. Clearly something about marriage drives a lot of people round the bend. Why shouldn't some of those people be gay?

Legalizing gay marriage would be a good idea even if all it did was to chasten conservative enthusiasts like Andrew Sullivan and Bruce Bawer, who imagine that wedlock would do for gays what it is less and less able to do for straights—encourage monogamy, sobriety and settled habits. Gay conservatives are quick to criticize hetero offenders against the socio-marital order, like divorced and single parents and poor women who nonetheless have children. Legalizing gay marriage will do a lot to open these men's eyes: Soon they'll be divorcing, single parenting and bankrupting each other like the rest of us. Maybe we'll hear less about restoring the stigma of "illegitimacy" and divorce over at *The New Republic* when gay men find themselves raising kids with no help from a deadbeat co-dad.

I'm for same-sex marriage because I'd be a hypocrite not to be: I married, after all, for reasons that apply to gay couples—a mix of love, convention and a practical concern for safeguarding children, property, my husband and myself from unforeseen circumstances and strange legal quirks. I don't see why gays shouldn't be able to make the same choice, but I've yet to see an argument on the other side that doesn't dissolve into bias and prejudice and thinly disguised religious folderol. In a recent *New York Times* Op-Ed, former Quayle speechwriter Lisa Schiffren attacked the idea of gay marriage by defining marriage as about procreation, with the many non-procreating couples—infertile, voluntarily childless, middle-aged and elderly—included out of politeness. (It was a banner weekend for Schiffren at the *Times*—the very next day the *Magazine* published her essay claiming that the legalization of abortion explains why no one offered her a subway seat when she was pregnant.) In a particularly overwrought 1991 *Commonweal* essay, Jena Bethke Elshtain depicted gay marriage as "antinatal—hostile to the regenerative female body." Haven't these writers ever heard of Heather's two mommies and Daddy's roommate? *Lots* of gay and lesbian couples are raising children together these days. Interestingly, neither of these defenders of the hearth mentions love—maybe gays are the last romantics, after all.

For social conservatives like Elshtain and Schiffren, opposition to gay marriage is more than homophobia: It's a move in a larger, high-stakes policy struggle over the family. The kernel of truth grasped by anti-gay-marriage conservatives is that same-sex wedlock is part of the modern transformation of marriage from a hierarchical, gender-polarized relationship whose permanence was enforced by God, law, family and community into a more equal, fluid and optional relationship whose permanence depends on the mutual wishes of the partners. Whatever its conservative champions think, gay marriage could never have become a realistic political issue, with considerable popular support from straights, without the breakdown of traditional family values—widespread divorce, non-marital births, cohabitation, blended families, double-income couples, interracial and interfaith and no-faith unions, abortion, feminism. When it becomes legal, as I believe it will, same-sex marriage will be the result, not the cause, of a change in the meaning of marriage. The reason arguments against it sound so prudish and dated and irrational is that they are.

Proponents of same-sex marriage make much of the unfairness of denying gay couples the many rights and privileges awarded husbands and wives—health insurance, survivors' rights, mutual custody of children, job protection under the Family and Medical Leave Act and so on. Far be it from me to pooh-pooh as a motive for marriage a system that has saved me literally thousands of dollars in dental bills. But even as we support legalizing same-sex unions, we might ask whether we want to distribute these rights and privileges according to marital status. Why should access to health care be a byproduct of a legalized sexual connection, gay or straight? Wouldn't it make more sense to give everyone his or her own health insurance? Similarly, gays and lesbians rightly resent the ways in which their inability to marry leaves them vulnerable to parental interference: The case of Sharon Kowalski, whose parents took custody after she suffered brain damage in a crash and for many years denied visitation to her lover, is a notorious example but hardly unique; the annals of the AIDS crisis are full of parents who cut their child's lover off from contact, participation in medical decisions and property—including shared property. But all unmarrieds are potentially subject to this kind of hostile takeover, not just gays. What's wrong is the legal mindset that regards unmarried 40-year-olds as the wards of Mom and Dad.

The truth is, we are moving toward a society in which the old forms of human relationships are being disrupted or reshaped, and sooner or later the law must accommodate that reality. Legalizing gay marriage is part of the process, but so is diminishing the increasingly outmoded privileged status of marriage and sharing out its benefits along different, more egalitarian lines. Andrew Sullivan and Bruce Bawer may have more in common with single mothers than they would like to think.

QUESTIONS TO HELP YOU THINK AND WRITE
ABOUT MEN'S AND WOMEN'S ROLES

1. Do you agree or disagree with Tannen and Connors about the differences in conversation and learning styles of men and women? Have some of your instructors in the past been better teachers of one gender than the other? Why? Support your answer with evidence and ideas from Tannen's and Connors' articles as well as with examples and narratives from your own experience. What would improve the environment in your argument class and make it easier for you to contribute to class discussion? How can classrooms be made equitable and inclusive for all students?

2. Read Friedan's essay and answer the question, What is the problem that has no name? Seek the perspective of students in class who remember the 1950s. Or interview parents. Was it a problem then for all women? For a few? Bring it up to date. Is it a problem now? How severe a problem? How do those who perceive it as a problem try to solve it? Are the solutions good or bad? Evaluate them from a personal and a societal perspective.

3. What does Faludi mean by a "backlash" in feminism? What is your position on feminism as it is described in this article? Think of some reasons to support Faludi's position. Think of other reasons why she might be wrong. Describe some personal examples to support both of the following claims: women are more equal now than they were before; women are less equal now than they were before. Which do you agree with? Why?

4. Imagine Friedan, Faludi, and Henry in conversation about women's roles. On which points about women's roles as wife, mother, and worker outside of the home would they agree and on which would they disagree? Now join this conversation yourself. Which of these authors best represents your views about contemporary women's roles at home, at work, and in society?

5. Consider the four roles described for modern man in Rotundo's article. Are they sufficient? How would Adler add to the list? Why? Evaluate these roles. Why are they good? Why are they bad? Is a mix possible? What would be a good mix? Why?

6. Theroux challenges some of the male stereotypes. What do you think his exigence was for writing on this subject? Do you share this exigence? Why or why not?

7. Examine your and your classmates' views on marriage. Why is marriage necessary (or unnecessary)? What should change in the personal and societal realms concerning the expectations and allowances of marriage? What should stay the same? What problems can you identify with the institutions of marriage? How can these problems be solved?

8. Have the opinions of Glaser, Sullivan, Bennett, and Pollitt influenced your views about same-sex marriages? What were your views before you read these essays? What are your views now? If your views have changed, how have they changed?

SECTION II
Issues in Education

WHAT ARE THE ISSUES?

1. What Should Schools Teach?

The enduring argument about what students should learn is introduced in this section with an essay written in 1625 and is brought up-to-date by two contemporary authors writing in the 1990s. The modern authors focus both on areas that are and are not traditionally associated with the traditional curriculum. See also "Don't Know Much About History," page 83 and "Special Education's Best Intentions," page 261.

2. What Are Some of the Problems with Grading/Evaluating Learning?

The articles in this section explore the problems associated with grading, grade inflation, and standardized testing.

3. How Much Should Schools Change to Help Students Succeed?

The authors of three articles provide suggestions for school reform that have student success as their final goal. You probably will not disagree with this goal, but you may disagree with some of the methods these authors propose for reaching it. See also "Learning by Intimidation," page 148, and "A Room of Their Own," page 111.

4. Extend Your Perspective with Film and Literature Related to Education?

Films: Stand and Deliver, 1987 and *Back to School,* 1986.
Literature: poems: "The Student" by Marianne Moore, "Theme for English B" by Langston Hughes, and "Learning to Read" by Frances E. W. Harper; essay: "Education" by E. B. White; short story: "The Lesson" by Toni Cade Bambara; novel: *The Chosen* by Chaim Potok.

THE RHETORICAL SITUATION

In classical times, Plato argued that students should not be allowed to read poetry because it appealed to emotion and warped the perception of truth. In the seventeenth century, Milton made a strong case for introducing writing instruction late in students' careers, after they had read widely and deeply on many subjects. What students should learn, when and under what conditions they should learn it, and who should teach it are enduring issues that continue to receive lively attention.

For example, some people argue that traditional public schools need radical reform. They also argue that the curriculum that focuses mainly on the European cultural heritage should be broadened to include the study of minority and third world cultural heritages. Another issue, what schools should and should not teach in addition to the traditional subjects, is familiar to all of you. For some people, athletics, art, and music are unnecessary additions that threaten the essential core of instruction. For others, personal values, training in emotions, character building, and self-esteem are considered essential additions to the traditional core. What students should know and be able to do when they leave school and take their places as workers and citizens is at the heart of this issue. Successful education, in most people's minds, leads to successful lives and a successful society. What constitutes a successful life and a successful society provide some of the warrants for this issue.

Because everyone in the United States is expected to attend school, there is a constant exigency for a wide variety of education issues. Only a few of them are represented here. They include what schools should teach, some problems with grading and other forms of evaluation, and how much schools should change in order to help students succeed. As a student yourself, you will undoubtedly be able to add your own related issues to this list.

1. What Should Schools Teach?

OF STUDIES

Francis Bacon

> *This well-known essay comes from Bacon's collection of short essays published in 1625. As you read it, identify the major points that Bacon makes about education, including what schools of his time should teach and how they should teach it.*

Studies[1] serve for delight, for ornament, and for ability. Their chief use for delight is in privateness and retiring;[2] for ornament, is in discourse; and for ability, is in the judgment and disposition of business. For expert[3] men can execute, and perhaps judge of particulars, one by one; but the general counsels, and the plots and marshaling of affairs come best from those that are learned. To spend too much time in studies is sloth; to use them too much for ornament, is affectation; to make judgment wholly by their rules, is the humor[4] of a scholar. They perfect nature, and are perfected by experience, for natural abilities are like natural plants that need pruning by study; and studies themselves do give forth directions too much at large, except they be bounded in by experience. Crafty men contemn studies, simple men admire them, and wise men use them; for they teach not their own

---

Selected Essays of Francis Bacon Ed. J. Max Patrick. New York: Appleton Century Crofts, 1948.

use, but that is a wisdom without them and above them, won by observation. Read not to contradict and confute; nor to believe and take for granted; nor to find talk and discourse; but to weigh and consider. Some books are to be tasted, others to be swallowed, and some few to be chewed and digested; that is, some books are to read only in parts; others to be read, but not curiously;[5] and some few to be read wholly and with diligence and attention. Some books also may be read by deputy, and extracts made of them by others, but that would[6] be only in the less important arguments and the meaner sort of books; else distilled books are like common distilled waters, flashy[7] things. Reading maketh a full man; conference a ready man; and writing an exact man. And therefore, if a man write little, he had need have a great memory; if he confer little, he had need have a present wit: and if he read little, he had need have much cunning, to seem to know that he doth not. Histories make men wise, poets witty,[8] the mathematics subtile, natural philosophy deep, moral grave, logic and rhetoric able to contend. . . .

NOTES

1. Used in a broad sense, including reading.
2. Privacy and retirement.
3. Experienced in practical affairs (but with little book-learning).
4. Eccentricity.
5. Attentively.
6. Should.
7. Insipid or specious.
8. Wise, ingenious.

READING, WRITING, NARCISSISM

Lilian G. Katz

Lilian Katz is a professor of early childhood education at the University of Illinois. This article first appeared in the American Educator, *and it was later adapted for the* New York Times *Op-Ed page.*

Developing and strengthening children's self-esteem has become a major goal of our schools. Although it is true that many children, especially the youngest students, have low self-esteem, our practice of lavishing praise for the mildest accomplishments is not likely to have much success. Feelings cannot be learned from direct instruction, and constant reminders about how wonderful one is may raise doubts about the credibility of the message and the messenger.

A project by a first grade class in an affluent Middle Western suburb that I recently observed showed how self-esteem and narcissism can be confused. Working from copied pages prepared by the teacher, each student produced a booklet called "All About Me." The first page asked for basic information about

New York Times, July 15, 1993, Op-Ed.

the child's home and family. The second page was titled "what I like to eat," the third was "what I like to watch on TV," the next was "what I want for a present" and another was "where I want to go on vacation."

The booklet, like thousands of others I have encountered around the country, had no page headings such as "what I want to know more about," "what I am curious about," "what I want to solve" or even "to make."

Each page was directed toward the child's basest inner gratifications. Each topic put the child in the role of consumer—of food, entertainment, gifts and recreation. Not once was the child asked to play the role of producer, investigator, initiator, explorer, experimenter or problem-solver.

It is perhaps this kind of literature that accounts for a poster I saw in a school entrance hall. Pictures of clapping hands surround the title "We Applaud Ourselves." While the sign's probable purpose was to help children feel good about themselves, it did so by directing their attention inward. The poster urged self-congratulation; it made no reference to possible ways of earning applause— by considering the feelings or needs of others.

Another common type of exercise was a display of kindergartners' work I saw recently that consisted of large paper-doll figures, each having a balloon containing a sentence stem that began "I am special because. . ." The children completed the sentence with the phrases such as, "I can color," "I can ride a bike," and "I like to play with my friends." But these children are not likely to believe for very long that they are special because they can color or ride a bike. What are they going to think when they discover just how trivial these criteria for being special are?

This overemphasizing self-esteem and self-congratulation stems from a legitimate desire to correct previous generations' traditions of avoiding compliments for fear of making children conceited. But the current practices are vast over-corrections. The idea of specialness they express is contradictory: If everybody is special, nobody is special.

Adults can show their approval for children in more significant ways than awarding gold stars and happy faces. Esteem is conveyed to students when adults and peers treat them with respect, ask for their views and preferences and provide opportunities for decisions and choices about things that matter to them. Children are born natural and social scientists. They devote much time and energy to investigating and making sense of their environments. During the preschool and early school years, teachers can capitalize on this disposition by engaging children in investigations and projects.

Several years ago, I saw this kind of project at a rural British school for 5- to 7-year-olds. A large display on the bulletin board read: "We Are a Class Full of Bodies. Here Are the Details." The display space was filled with bar graphs showing birth dates, weights and heights, eye colors, number of lost teeth, shoe sizes and other data of the entire class. As the children worked in small groups to take measurements, prepare graphs and help one another post displays of their analyses, the teacher was able to create an atmosphere of a community of researchers looking for averages, trends and ranges.

Compare this to the American kindergarten I visited recently in which the comments made by the children about a visit to a dairy farm were displayed on

the bulletin board. Each sentence began with the words "I liked." For example, "I liked the cows" and "I liked the milking machine." No sentences began "What surprised me was. . ." and "What I want to know more about is. . ."

Of course children benefit from positive feedback. But praise and rewards are not the only methods of reinforcement. More emphasis should be placed on appreciation—reinforcement related explicitly and directly to the *content* of the child's interest and effort. For example, if a child poses a thoughtful question, the teacher might come to class the next day with a new reference book on the same subject. It is important that the teacher shows appreciation for pupils' concerns without taking their minds off the subjects at hand or directing their attention inward.

When children see that their concerns and interests are taken seriously they are more likely to raise them in discussion and to take their own ideas seriously. Teachers can strengthen children's disposition to wonder, reflect, raise questions and generate alternative solutions to practical and intellectual problems. Of course, when children are engaged in challenging and significant activities, they are bound to experience failures and rebuffs. But as long as the teacher accepts the child's feelings and responds respectfully—"I know you're disappointed, but you can try again tomorrow"—the child is more likely to learn from the incident than be harmed by it.

Learning to deal with setbacks, and maintaining the persistence and optimism necessary for childhood's long road to mastery are the real foundations of lasting self-esteem. Children who are helped to develop these qualities will surely respect themselves—though they probably will have better things to think about.

THE HOLLOW CURRICULUM

Robert N. Sollod

Robert Sollod teaches psychology at Cleveland State University. This argument first appeared in The Chronicle of Higher Education.

The past decade in academe has seen widespread controversy over curricular reform. We have explored many of the deeply rooted, core assumptions that have guided past decisions about which subjects should be emphasized in the curriculum and how they should be approached. Yet I have found myself repeatedly disappointed by the lack of significant discussion concerning the place of religion and spirituality in colleges' curricula and in the lives of educated persons.

I do not mean to suggest that universities should indoctrinate students with specific viewpoints or approaches to life; that is not their proper function. But American universities now largely ignore religion and spirituality, rather than considering what aspects of religious and spiritual teachings should enter the

The Chronicle of Higher Education, March 18, 1992, p. A60.

curriculum and how those subjects should be taught. The curricula that most undergraduates study do little to rectify the fact that many Americans are ignorant of religious and spiritual teachings, of their significance in the history of this and other civilizations, and of their significance in contemporary society. Omitting this major facet of human experience and thought contributes to a continuing shallowness and imbalance in much of university life today.

Let us take the current discussions of multiculturalism as one example. It is hardly arguable that an educated person should approach life with knowledge of several cultures or patterns of experience. Appreciation and understanding of human diversity are worthy educational ideals. Should such an appreciation exclude the religious and spiritually based concepts of reality that are the backbone upon which entire cultures have been based?

Multiculturalism that does not include appreciation of the deepest visions of reality reminds me of the travelogues that I saw in the cinema as a child—full of details of quaint and somewhat mysterious behavior that evoked some superficial empathy but no real, in-depth understanding. Implicit in a multicultural approach that ignores spiritual factors is a kind of critical and patronizing attitude. It assumes that we can understand and evaluate the experiences of other cultures without comprehension of their deepest beliefs.

Incomprehensibly, traditionalists who oppose adding multicultural content to the curriculum also ignore the religious and theological bases of the Western civilization that they seek to defend. Today's advocates of Western traditionalism focus, for the most part, on conveying a type of rationalism that is only a single strain in Western thought. Their approach does not demonstrate sufficient awareness of the contributions of Western religions and spirituality to philosophy and literature, to moral and legal codes, to the development of governmental and political institutions, and to the mores of our society.

Nor is the lack of attention to religion and spirituality new. I recall taking undergraduate philosophy classes in the 1960's in which Plato and Socrates were taught without reference to the fact that they were contemplative mystics who believed in immortality and reincarnation. Everything that I learned in my formal undergraduate education about Christianity came through studying a little Thomas Aquinas in a philosophy course, and even there we focused more on the logical sequence of his arguments than on the fundamentals of the Christian doctrine that he espoused.

I recall that Dostoyevsky was presented as an existentialist, with hardly a nod given to the fervent Christian beliefs so clearly apparent in his writings. I even recall my professors referring to their Christian colleagues, somewhat disparagingly, as "Christers." I learned about mystical and spiritual interpretations of Shakespeare's sonnets and plays many years after taking college English courses.

We can see the significance of omitting teaching about religion and spirituality in the discipline of psychology and, in particular, in my own field of clinical psychology. I am a member of the Task Force on Religious Issues in Graduate Education and Training in Division 36 of the American Psychological Association, a panel chaired by Edward Shafranske of Pepperdine University. In this work, I have discovered that graduate programs generally do not require students to learn anything about the role of religion in people's lives.

Almost no courses are available to teach psychologists how to deal with the religious values or concerns expressed by their clients. Nor are such courses required or generally available at the undergraduate level for psychology majors. Allusions to religion and spirituality often are completely missing in textbooks on introductory psychology, personality theory, concepts of psychotherapy, and developmental psychology.

Recent attempts to add a multicultural perspective to clinical training almost completely ignore the role of religion and spirituality as core elements of many racial, ethnic, and national identities. Prayer is widely practiced, yet poorly understood and rarely studied by psychologists. When presented, religious ideas are usually found in case histories of patients manifesting severe psychopathology.

Yet spiritual and mystical experiences are not unusual in our culture. And research has shown that religion is an important factor in the lives of many Americans; some studies have suggested that a client's religious identification may affect the psychotherapeutic relationship, as well as the course and outcome of therapy. Some patterns of religious commitment have been found to be associated with high levels of mental health and ego strength. A small number of psychologists are beginning to actively challenge the field's inertia and indifference by researching and writing on topics related to religion and spirituality. Their efforts have not as yet, however, markedly affected the climate or curricula in most psychology departments.

Is it any wonder that religion for the typical psychotherapist is a mysterious and taboo topic? It should not be surprising that therapists are not equipped even to ask the appropriate questions regarding a person's religious or spiritual life—much less deal with psychological aspects of spiritual crises.

Or consider the field of political science. Our scholars and policy makers have been unable to predict or understand the major social and political movements that produced upheavals around the world during the last decade. That is at least partly because many significant events—the remarkable rise of Islamic fundamentalism, the victory of Afghanistan over the Soviet Union, the unanticipated velvet revolutions in Eastern Europe and in the Soviet Union, and the continuing conflicts in Cyprus, Israel, Lebanon, Northern Ireland, Pakistan, Sri Lanka, Tibet, and Yugoslavia—can hardly be appreciated without a deep understanding of the religious views of those involved. The tender wisdom of our contemporary political scientists cannot seem to comprehend the deep spirituality inherent in many of today's important social movements.

Far from being an anachronism, religious conviction has proved to be a more potent contemporary force than most, if not all, secular ideologies. Too often, however, people with strong religious sentiments are simply dismissed as "zealots" or "fanatics"—whether they be Jewish settlers on the West Bank, Iranian demonstrators, Russian Baptists, Shiite leaders, anti-abortion activists, or evangelical Christians.

Most sadly, the continuing neglect of spirituality and religion by colleges and universities also results in a kind of segregation of the life of the spirit from the life of the mind in American culture. This situation is far from the ideals of Thoreau, Emerson, or William James. Spirituality in our society too often represents a retreat from the world of intellectual discourse, and spiritual pursuits are often cloaked in a reflexive anti-intellectualism, which mirrors the view in academe of spirituality as an irrational cultural residue. Students with spiritual interests and concerns learn that the university will not validate or feed their interests. They learn either to suppress their spiritual life or to split their spiritual life apart from their formal education.

Much has been written about the loss of ethics, a sense of decency, moderation, and fair play in American society. I would submit that much of this loss is a result of the increasing ignorance, in circles of presumably educated people, of religious and spiritual world views. It is difficult to imagine, for example, how ethical issues can be intelligently approached and discussed or how wise ethical decisions can be reached without either knowledge or reference to those religious and spiritual principles that underlie our legal system and moral codes.

Our colleges and universities should reclaim one of their earliest purposes—to educate and inform students concerning the spiritual and religious underpinnings of thought and society. To the extent that such education is lacking, our colleges and universities are presenting a narrow and fragmented view of human experience.

Both core curricula and more advanced courses in the humanities and social sciences should be evaluated for their coverage of religious topics. Active leadership at the university, college, and departmental levels is needed to encourage and carry out needed additions and changes in course content. Campus organizations should develop forums and committees to examine the issue, exchange information, and develop specific proposals.

National debate and discussion about the best way to educate students concerning religion and spirituality are long overdue.

2. What Are Some of the Problems with Grading/Evaluating Learning?

MAKING THE GRADE

Kurt Wiesenfeld

Wiesenfeld is a physicist, and he teaches at Georgia Tech in Atlanta.

It was a rookie error. After 10 years I should have known better, but I went to my office the day after final grades were posted. There was a tentative knock on the door. "Professor Wiesenfeld? I took your Physics 2121 class? I flunked it? I wonder if there's anything I can do to improve my grade?" I thought: "Why are you

Newsweek, June 17, 1996, p. 16.

asking me? Isn't it too late to worry about it? Do you dislike making declarative statements?"

After the student gave his tale of woe and left, the phone rang. "I got a D in your class. Is there any way you can change it to 'Incomplete'?" Then the e-mail assault began: "I'm shy about coming in to talk to you, but I'm not shy about asking for a better grade. Anyway, it's worth a try." The next day I had three phone messages from students asking *me* to call *them*. I didn't.

Time was, when you received a grade, that was it. You might groan and moan, but you accepted it as the outcome of your efforts or lack thereof (and, yes, sometimes a tough grader). In the last few years, however, some students have developed a disgruntled-consumer approach. If they don't like their grade, they go to the "return" counter to trade it in for something better.

What alarms me is their indifference toward grades as an indication of personal effort and performance. Many, when pressed about why they think they deserve a better grade, admit they don't deserve one but would like one anyway. Having been raised on gold stars for effort and smiley faces for self-esteem, they've learned that they can get by without hard work and real talent if they can talk the professor into giving them a break. This attitude is beyond cynicism. There's a weird innocence to the assumption that one expects (even deserves) a better grade simply by begging for it. With that outlook, I guess I shouldn't be as flabbergasted as I was that 12 students asked me to change their grades *after* final grades were posted.

That's 10 percent of my class who let three months of midterms, quizzes and lab reports slide until long past remedy. My graduate student calls it hyperrational thinking: if effort and intelligence don't matter, why should deadlines? What matters is getting a better grade through an unearned bonus, the academic equivalent of a freebie T shirt or toaster giveaway. Rewards are disconnected from the quality of one's work. An act and its consequences are unrelated, random events.

Their arguments for wheedling better grades often ignore academic performance. Perhaps they feel it's not relevant. "If my grade isn't raised to a D I'll lose my scholarship." "If you don't give me a C, I'll flunk out." One sincerely overwrought student pleaded, "If I don't pass, my life is over." This is tough stuff to deal with. Apparently, I'm responsible for someone's losing a scholarship, flunking out or deciding whether life has meaning. Perhaps these students see me as a commodities broker with something they want—a grade. Though intrinsically worthless, grades, if properly manipulated, can be traded for what has value: a degree, which means a job, which means money. The one thing college actually offers—a chance to learn—is considered irrelevant, even less than worthless, because of the long hours and hard work required.

In a society saturated with surface values, love of knowledge for its own sake does sound eccentric. The benefits of fame and wealth are more obvious. So is it right to blame students for reflecting the superficial values saturating our society?

Yes, of course it's right. These guys had better take themselves seriously now, because our country will be forced to take them seriously later, when the stakes are much higher. They must recognize that their attitude is not only self-destructive, but socially destructive. The erosion of quality control—giving appropriate grades for actual accomplishments—is a major concern in my department. One colleague noted that a physics major could obtain a degree without ever answering a written exam question completely. How? By pulling in enough partial credit and extra credit. And by getting breaks on grades.

But what happens once she or he graduates and gets a job? That's when the misfortunes of eroding academic standards multiply. We lament that schoolchildren get "kicked upstairs" until they graduate from high school despite being illiterate and mathematically inept, but we seem unconcerned with college graduates whose less blatant deficiencies are far more harmful if their accreditation exceeds their qualifications.

Most of my students are science and engineering majors. If they're good at getting partial credit but not at getting the answer right, then the new bridge breaks or the new drug doesn't work. One finds examples here in Atlanta. Last year a light tower in the Olympic Stadium collapsed, killing a worker. It collapsed because an engineer miscalculated how much weight it could hold. A new 12-story dormitory could develop dangerous cracks due to a foundation that's uneven by more than six inches. The error resulted from incorrect data being fed into a computer. I drive past that dorm daily on my way to work, wondering if a foundation crushed under kilotons of weight is repairable or if this structure will have to be demolished. Two 10,000-pound steel beams at the new natatorium collapsed in March, crashing into the student athletic complex. (Should we give partial credit since no one was hurt?) Those are real-world consequences of errors and lack of expertise.

But the lesson is lost on the grade-grousing 10 percent. Say that you won't (not can't, but won't) change the grade they deserve to what they want, and they're frequently bewildered or angry. They don't think it's fair that they're judged according to their performance, not their desires or "potential." They don't think it's fair that they should jeopardize their scholarships or be in danger of flunking out simply because they could not or did not do their work. But it's more than fair; it's necessary to help preserve a minimum standard of quality that our society needs to maintain safety and integrity. I don't know if the 13th-hour students will learn that lesson, but I've learned mine. From now on, after final grades are posted, I'll lie low until the next quarter starts.

A LIBERATING CURRICULUM

Roberta F. Borkat

Roberta Borkat is a professor of English and comparative literature at San Diego State University. Use what you learned about claims on pages 128 to 131 to help you establish the claim of this essay.

A blessed change has come over me. Events of recent months have revealed to me that I have been laboring as a university professor for more than 20 years under a misguided theory of teaching. I humbly regret that during all those years I have caused distress and inconvenience to thousands of students while providing some amusement to my more practical colleagues. Enlightenment came to me in a sublime moment of clarity while I was being verbally attacked by a student whose paper I had just proved to have been plagiarized from "The Norton Anthology of English Literature." Suddenly, I understood the true purpose of my profession, and I devised a plan to embody that revelation. Every moment since then has been filled with delight about the advantages to students, professors and universities from my Plan to Increase Student Happiness.

The plan is simplicity itself: at the end of the second week of the semester, all students enrolled in each course will receive a final grade of A. Then their minds will be relieved of anxiety, and they will be free to do whatever they want for the rest of the term.

The benefits are immediately evident. Students will be assured of high grade-point averages and an absence of obstacles in their march toward graduation. Professors will be relieved of useless burdens and will have time to pursue their real interests. Universities will have achieved the long-desired goal of molding individual professors into interchangeable parts of a smoothly operating machine. Even the environment will be improved because education will no longer consume vast quantities of paper for books, compositions and examinations.

Although this scheme will instantly solve countless problems that have plagued education, a few people may raise trivial objections and even urge universities not to adopt it. Some of my colleagues may protest that we have an obligation to uphold the integrity of our profession. Poor fools, I understand their delusion, for I formerly shared it. To them, I say: "Hey, lighten up! Why make life difficult?"

Those who believe that we have a duty to increase the knowledge of our students may also object. I, too, used to think that knowledge was important and that we should encourage hard work and perseverance. Now I realize that the concept of rewards for merit is elitist and, therefore, wrong in a society that aims for equality in all things. We are a democracy. What could be more democratic than to give exactly the same grade to every single student?

Newsweek, April 12, 1993, p. 11.

One or two forlorn colleagues may even protest that we have a responsibility to significant works of the past because the writings of such authors as Chaucer, Shakespeare, Milton and Swift are intrinsically valuable. I can empathize with these misguided souls, for I once labored under the illusion that I was giving my students a precious gift by introducing them to works by great poets, playwrights and satirists. Now I recognize the error of my ways. The writings of such authors may have seemed meaningful to our ancestors, who had nothing better to do, but we are living in a time of wonderful improvements. The writers of bygone eras have been made irrelevant, replaced by MTV and *People* magazine. After all, their bodies are dead. Why shouldn't their ideas be dead, too?

JOYOUS SMILES

If any colleagues persist in protesting that we should try to convey knowledge to students and preserve our cultural heritage, I offer this suggestion: honestly consider what students really want. As one young man graciously explained to me, he had no desire to take my course but had enrolled in it merely to fulfill a requirement that he resented. His job schedule made it impossible for him to attend at least 30 percent of my class sessions, and he wouldn't have time to do much of the reading. Nevertheless, he wanted a good grade. Another student consulted me after the first exam, upset because she had not studied and had earned only 14 points out of a possible 100. I told her that, if she studied hard and attended class more regularly, she could do well enough on the remaining tests to pass the course. This encouragement did not satisfy her. What she wanted was an assurance that she would receive at least a B. Under my plan both students would be guaranteed an A. Why not? They have good looks and self-esteem. What more could anyone ever need in life?

I do not ask for thanks from the many people who will benefit. I'm grateful to my colleagues who for decades have tried to help me realize that seriousness about teaching is not the path to professorial prestige, rapid promotion and frequent sabbaticals. Alas, I was stubborn. Not until I heard the illuminating explanation of the student who had plagiarized from the anthology's introduction to Jonathan Swift did I fully grasp the wisdom that others had been generously offering to me for years—learning is just too hard. Now, with a light heart, I await the plan's adoption. In my mind's eye, I can see the happy faces of university administrators and professors, released at last from the irksome chore of dealing with students. I can imagine the joyous smiles of thousands of students, all with straight-A averages and plenty of free time.

My only regret is that I wasted so much time. For nearly 30 years, I threw away numerous hours annually on trivia: writing, grading and explaining examinations; grading hundred of papers a semester; holding private conferences with students; reading countless books; buying extra materials to give students a feeling for the music, art and clothing of past centuries; endlessly worrying about how to improve my teaching. At last I see the folly of grubbing away in meaningless efforts. I wish that I had faced facts earlier and had not lost years because of old-fashioned notions. But such are the penalties for those who do not understand the true purpose of education.

WHAT'S WRONG WITH STANDARD TESTS?

Ted Sizer

Ted Sizer, an education professor at Brown University, is chairman of the Coalition for Essential Schools and director of the Annenberg Institute for School Reform.

Over the years I have listened to many parents talk about their children and their children's schools. Thoughtful parents want us teachers to know and to respect their youngsters and their specialness: the talents and weaknesses, the volatility, the vulnerability, the poignant hope. They want their kids to be cared for, understood, and thereby judged, as *individuals*—and as individuals of promise and potential.

At the same time there *are* patterns to growth and development, patterns that transcend the individual, which teachers (and parents too) should ponder and understand. But the patterns are just that—tendencies, generalized expectations, useful guideposts.

An intensely painful reality for American educators is that we have turned these well-intentioned testing guideposts into hitching posts, into benevolent "systems" through which children can predictably move. Students are judged by norms based on chronological age. They are taught with a common pedagogy, at a common pace within their assigned groupings.

One of American educators' greatest conceits is the belief that people can be pigeonholed, in effect sorted by some scientific mechanism, usually the standardized test.

The results of even the most carefully and sensitively crafted tests cannot be used fairly for high-stakes purposes for individuals; the belief that they can persists stubbornly in the educational community, in spite of an avalanche of research that challenges the tests' precision—and in spite of parents' common sense.

All of us who have taught for a while know "low testers" who became wonderfully resourceful and imaginative adults and "high testers" who as adults are, sadly, brittle and shallow people. We cringe as we remember how we so unfairly characterized them. . . .

Danny Algrant's writing and directing of the 1994 film, "Naked in New York," certainly was not completely evident when I taught him. Danny was an ebullient itch, even as a high school senior, a trial—but a worthy one—for his teacher. All that ebullient itchiness I gather now has been focused in successful

New York Times Magazine, January 8, 1995, p. 58.

film making. And so on: the awkward adolescent who now juggles the myriad demands of an inner-city school as principal, or the "low tester" who is now a successful writer.

As a high-school principal, I sadly experienced a conversation with a highly placed education official who spun out for me both colorful descriptions of his own *very* special, *very* talented and *very* particular children and in the same breath admiring testimony about his state's narrowly standardized testing program and the student assignments that would arise from it. This elaborate system, of course, was for other people's children. His children needed the special attention of a private school. To this day, the irony eludes him.

There is tremendous public reluctance to question the usage and values of such tests. Being against conventional "testing" makes one appear to be against "standards." Test scores both give those in charge a device to move large numbers of students around and provide a fig leaf to justify labeling and tracking them in one way or another. How can we, they say, accept each little person as complicated, changeable, special? Impossible. It would take too much time. (Then privately, But not for *my* child. Let me tell you about her.)

It would be silly, however, to dismiss all standardized testing. If carefully crafted and interpreted, these tests can reveal certain broad trends, even if they tell us only a bit about individual children. Such testing is helpful at the margins: it can signal the possibility of a troubled or especially gifted or otherwise "special" youngster. It can signal competence at immediate and comparable work if the classroom task to be completed (effective close reading of a text) is similar to the test (made up of prose passages and related questions) and if the task is attempted shortly after taking the test.

But none of the major tests used in American elementary and secondary education correlates well with long-term success or failure. S.A.T. scores, for example, suggest likely grades in the freshman year at college; they do not predict much thereafter.

On the contrary, conventional tests can distort and thereby corrupt schooling. Most do not measure long-term intellectual habits. Indeed, many undermine the value of such by excessively emphasizing immediate, particular facts and skills considered out of context.

Those characteristics that we most value fail to be "tested": the qualities of mind and heart upon which we count for a healthy culture.

And a competitive work force. Send me, says the business leader, young employees who know something about using important knowledge, who learn readily and independently, who think for themselves and are dependable in the deepest sense. The college teacher says much the same, perhaps describing the qualities somewhat differently. Unfortunately, when classifying students, schools still peg kids by brief paper records and scores. "If the combined S. A. T. scores are below 1100, we will not consider the student," the admissions staff says, knowing full well that some high scorers are less worthy potential students than some low scorers.

Assessment and accountability are worthy goals. The task is to create a system that usefully and fairly assesses what we care about and that does not distort the process of learning. Such a system cannot be done on the cheap. There is no shortcut to a fair and full understanding of a human being.

An accountable system should depend largely on students' real work rather than on data emerging from test booklets duly recorded on a transcript. It should not only "look at" this work—an essay or an evolved mathematical proof—but ask the student to defend it. If defense of a conclusion were a part of the expected assessment, students would work hard to go deeper than the mere recollection of particular answers.

For each student, a variety of assessments should be in constant development, with no fixed assignment of merit. Schools should accept the reality that young people change and that assessments of them at one point may not be relevant later. The practical effect of this is the elimination of rigid tracking, the institutional form of stereotyping.

The parents' plea to me-the-principal that my school not pigeonhole their child, that I should see instead the complex and forming person before me, cuts deep. I myself had once been pigeonholed, as "not really college material." Only by the vociferous advocacy of my father did I get a fair shot. What of the youngster who has no such advocate, whom the school system, with all its well-intentioned "science," has written off?

3. How Much Should Schools Change to Help Students Succeed?

WHAT SCHOOLS MUST DO TO IMPROVE LATINO HIGH SCHOOL GRADUATION RATES

Harriet D. Romo and Toni Falbo

This article is excerpted from the book, Latino High School Graduation: Defying the Odds, *which was based on a four-year longitudinal study of 100 Hispanic "at risk" youth. The students were 15 years old when the authors first interviewed them and their families. Romo and Falbo then followed the students through the next four years in order to observe the series of choices that led either to high school graduation or to dropping out. The high number of students leaving school before graduation is regarded as a major national problem, but particularly in terms of the Hispanic population. Hispanic rates of graduation are on the* decline *while the rates for Anglos and African Americans are on the* increase. *The editor of the book from which this piece is excerpted claims that adopting Romo and Falbo's policy recommendations, only a few of which are made here, could make a major contribution to the future of our society by giving Latino students and their families new hopes and greater opportunities to succeed in their school and their lives.*

This chapter describes the changes schools must make in order to improve the graduation rates of Mexican-origin youth. Our recommendations for change are

From Harriet D. Romo and Toni Falbo, *Latino High School Graduation: Defying the Odds,* (Austin: U of Texas P, 1996), pp. 218–253.

derived from our observations of the disparity between what the students in our study needed and what schools provided them. For the most part, the schools blamed the parents for the low achievement, bad attitudes, and scholastic gaps of the students. We argue that the schools must accept the students and their families as they are, assess the academic skills of students, and meet their academic needs promptly and effectively.

Our recommendations for change are based on the premise that *schools* have the primary responsibility for educating students. Parents and communities have a part to play in the formal educational process, but schools must assume the leading role in assuring that our youth have the scholastic skills they will need to be productive adults and good citizens.

PREVENTING SCHOOL FAILURE

We believe that most of the students we studied could have graduated if the schools had been organized so that no students were allowed to fail. *We recommend that when a student is not making enough progress toward meeting academic standards, teachers and other school personnel should mobilize to change the way they have been delivering the student's education.* School personnel should identify the cause of the slow pace of progress quickly and take action immediately to increase the student's pace of learning. Students would not be passed on unprepared to the next grade level. Promotion would be based on performance, not on time served in class. Students would move up by mastering a task, skill, or topic, not by completing a course or passing a grade level. Each student would receive the appropriate instruction until the task or skill was mastered. Students should never be allowed to flunk a course or a whole grade level.

Good Teachers

The measure of a good teacher should be how many students they turn around, not how many students they flunk. It has been assumed that teachers who flunk students are good teachers because they have high standards. This will change when the absolute standards, described above, are used by all teachers. Then, an excellent teacher will be one who has brought students from making little or no progress to making average or above-average progress in meeting standards. All students should be in classrooms where instruction is at a high level. The school and the teacher should be responsible to make certain that support services and additional resources are made available so that no students fail.

This will require giving some students more time than we give others to learn the skills they need to meet the standards. In the case of learning to speak, read, and write the English language, students who speak other languages will generally need more time than native speakers of English to meet the standards. This means that such students will probably need longer school days, more school days per year, after-school tutoring and Saturday Morning School in order to meet the graduation standards by the time they are 18 years old.[1] This exten-

---

[1] National Education Commission on Time and Learning. (1994). *Prisoners of time.*

sion of their learning time should begin the moment that students get off the pace needed to lead to high school graduation at age 18.

MAKING SCHOOLS ACCESSIBLE

One of the most significant changes that schools need to make is to reach out to parents in order to get their help in educating their children. In general, the secondary schools we studied had not made enough effort to form partnerships with the parents of "at risk" youth. They expected parents to come to the school when the school summoned them, always during regular school hours, to work out the problems with school staff—at times convenient to the staff and in the language of the staff. . . .

Schools and Parents as Partners

Before schools can build partnerships with parents, they will have to learn how to communicate with parents in respectful and meaningful ways. The failure of teachers and other school personnel to treat parents with respect convinced many parents that the schools were prejudiced against people of Mexican origin. Parents interpreted the bad treatment that they and their children received as instances of discrimination. This perception of discrimination aroused anger in the parents and their children, and they decided to avoid school personnel altogether. . . .

We recommend that teachers, counselors, and all other school personnel learn how to behave in a respectful manner to all parents and learn how to give helpful advice to parents on how to solve their children's problems. Teachers and other school personnel ought to be able to suggest solutions for the child's problem, by referring the parents to counselors, social workers, or other parents who have solved similar problems in the past.

Speaking Spanish

A major problem for some parents in our sample was their inability to find someone at the school who spoke Spanish. . . .

In the school district we studied, there was only one major alternative language, Spanish, and yet most of the schools did not have staff members who could speak Spanish well enough to deal with sensitive issues such as school failure. Often parents were forced to rely on their own children to translate for them, resulting in poor communication between parent and school. Many of the children who were stuck in the role of translator simply were too immature to do the appropriate translation. Other children, when put in the role of translator, intentionally misled both their parents and school personnel in order to avoid blame, punishment, or embarrassment. *We recommend that schools have staff members trained to facilitate the communication between non-English-speaking parents and school personnel.*

CREATING PATHWAYS TO GOOD OUTCOMES

Partnerships between schools and families will facilitate communication so that students can do what they need to do in order to graduate. But before "at risk" students will stay in school long enough to graduate, they and their parents will need to be persuaded that spending more time in school will make a difference for their futures. This will be a hard sell to many students, particularly those who have had academic difficulties. For example, 76% of the students in our study told us, when they were 15, that they did not feel that school was "going to do anything" for them.

The Value of a High School Diploma

Among the students in our sample, even those who graduated, few believed that the high school diploma would really make a difference in the kinds of jobs they would get. . . .

If American students are to be motivated to meet high scholastic standards, then they will need incentives. This might be the most difficult aspect of the changes we recommend, because these changes require the cooperation of employers outside the school and strong linkages between high schools and post-secondary training schools. It requires that communities structure job and training opportunities so that the hard work of all students will pay off in jobs with bright futures.

CONCLUSION

Our analysis has convinced us that the chief cause of the high dropout rate of Hispanic youth lies not with Hispanics but within schools and communities. All the students and their families we studied embraced the ideology that education was essential for getting a good job and for having a better life. The students wanted to earn a high school diploma, but they saw no way to fulfill their aspirations within their own schools.

Many students in our study made a reasonable decision when they decided to drop out. They were correct when they realized that school was wasting their time. They recognized that they were gaining few marketable skills in school. They felt demeaned and demoralized by the way teachers and other school personnel treated them. Getting pregnant, working dead-end jobs, and even staying home and watching TV offered more satisfying alternatives than school.

As citizens, we must all take responsibility for the education of our youth. We must demand that the schools implement these reforms in partnership with parents and the community. Schools must take responsibility for educating all students to have the skills that will qualify them for success at post-secondary training or good jobs soon after graduation. To maintain the status quo will result in more dropouts, more juveniles incarcerated, more teen mothers, and the growth of an underclass of citizens who are alienated from the rest of society.

We have the opportunity to make a difference for the children of the students we studied. Their children began arriving in kindergarten in the fall of 1995.

WHERE HOMEBOYS FEEL AT HOME IN SCHOOL

Tina Juarez

Juarez is the principal of Walter Prescott Webb Middle School in Austin, Texas.

Four months after becoming principal of Webb Middle School in Austin, Texas, my worst nightmare came true. Shortly after dismissing students for the day, I learned that gang members were exchanging gunfire on a street outside the school.

After calling the police, I rushed outside, where students were hugging the ground to avoid flying bullets. Thankfully, police quickly apprehended the "shooters," and none of my students was hurt. Another consolation: the culprits turned out to be high school dropouts, not students at Webb.

The enormous relief that teachers and I felt was tempered, however, by some discomfiting facts. Some of my students, boys and girls alike, clearly stood in awe of the young men who were willing to put their lives on the line for their "homeboys." Whether formally in the gangs or not, a growing number of Webb students were beginning to wear gang colors and flash gang signs in the school hallways.

Though I quickly banned wearing colors and flashing signs at Webb, it was all too clear that some of the boys were joining gangs. Their bruised and cut faces were telltale signs of their membership: the result of "walking the line," an initiation ceremony in which a gang "wannabe" has to stand his ground against the flailing fists and kicking feet of the gang members he wants to join.

Again and again, I would bring these boys to my office. "Why do you let yourselves be beat to a pulp just to join a group of boys who are very likely going to wind up in prison or in an early grave?" I asked them. They would glance at me and then to the floor before answering. "We protect each other, Miss. We're family. Homeboys care what happens to each other. Nobody else does."

"Your teachers care what happens to you," I always insisted. Teachers at Webb work long hours and are very dedicated to our students. How could these boys not understand that we care for them, that we want them to succeed? One

---

Educational Leadership, 53, no. 5 (1996): 30–32.

day in my office, a boy explained. "Miss, in school we are 'nothings,'" he said in a courteous but matter-of-fact manner. "In a gang, we are somebodies."

AN ANTIDOTE TO WEAK SELF-IDENTITY

The boy who told me about "nothings" and "somebodies," a bright, handsome 12-year-old, spoke volumes. His words confirmed what we're learning about why some youngsters are drawn to gangs, even though they know that it's a path to almost certain destruction.

Many young people who turn to gangs have a weak sense of self-identity (Vigil 1988). The support and loyalty that gang members extend to one another is to many youngsters a powerful antidote to feelings of being a nothing in what they see as an uncaring world. The gang provides a sense of self-identity grounded in the security of a group-identity.

Educators may find it difficult to fathom why boys and girls would turn to a gang to surmount feelings of alienation, when schools exist to prepare them to function successfully in the world. Why do these youths not recognize the school as their ally in securing the tools to control their fate?

At least part of the reason is that many of these youngsters have repeatedly been labeled by schools as failures (Laska and Juarez 1992). To some young people, school transcripts laden with *F*'s are just one more confirmation that no one—in the school, the home, or the community—really thinks they have any value. No one, that is, except the gang.

Gangs appear to be effective at meeting the identity needs of many youngsters in difficult environments. And many of our students face extraordinary challenges. More than 85 percent of them qualify for the free or reduced-cost lunch program, and 65 percent of our students come from single-parent homes, where oftentimes the parent leaves the house at 5 A.M. to go to a low-paying job, not returning home until late at night.

Obviously, however, not all young people in such circumstances join gangs. How do they meet their identity needs in more productive and healthy ways?

Heath and McLaughlin (1993) studied the reasons for the success of youngsters "whose home and community lives should have foretold disaster." They found that many such youngsters drew support from neighborhood-based organizations that helped them to build a strong sense of self. The youngsters touched by these organizations felt no need to join gangs or engage in other forms of destructive behavior because they were too busy preparing for a better future.

The organizations studied by Heath and McLaughlin, such as YMCA/YWCA groups, Boy Scouts, Girl Scouts, Boys and Girls Clubs, and various civic and church-affiliated youth groups, were quite varied. But a common thread among the organizations was their focus on helping young people build a positive sense of identity. They created the conditions for the boys and girls to "*do* something and *be* someone in the eyes of others" (Heath and McLaughlin 1993). In these places of hope, there were no symbols of failure imposed by an official authority; there were instead many opportunities to keep trying until youngsters achieved success.

AN ALL-OUT EFFORT

After the incident of gang violence on the street outside Webb Middle School, we decided to make an all-out effort to deal with the problem of gangs in and around our school. We knew we had to take some immediate and positive action beyond simply banning colors and signing.

Our vision was to provide ways for each of our students to "do something and be something in the eyes of others." One key idea was to form clubs that would meet during the school day. School staff would serve as sponsors, providing their time and expertise. We were determined to find something of interest to every student.

With the help of students, we brainstormed a variety of different clubs, addressing virtually every interest a middle school child might have. Before long, the roster of clubs grew to almost 50 in number, including: Video, Yoga, Floral Design (yes, the boys liked it!), Sports, International Pen Pal, Astronaut, Ceramics, Science, Movie, We Make a Difference (visiting senior citizens homes), Drama, Rugby, Soccer, Reading, Math Counts, Singing, Macintosh, Poetry, Create Your Own Futures, Environmental, Ham Radio, Walking, Fishing, Ultimate Frisbee, Chess, Dominoes, Tejano Dance, Jazz Band, Publications, Scholarship, and so on.

We adjusted our class schedule to make time for club meetings to accommodate everyone, and students chose the clubs they wanted to join. The key idea was that there were no failures in these clubs, only opportunities to succeed. Some students who were making *F*'s in their academic courses demonstrated extraordinary abilities in the clubs, and we began to see success in the clubs carry over to success in the academic classroom.

To supplement the establishment of clubs, we actively sought community volunteers to help us at Webb. We encouraged employees of nearby businesses to tutor our students, act as mentors, or simply share their time. Some local professionals offered their help.

For example, the local Young Lawyers Association sponsored a series of sports tournaments for all students (not just those on the organized school teams). Everyone was a winner in these tournaments.

Such partnerships benefited both students and volunteers. For our students, some of whom had never met people from outside their immediate neighborhoods, new friendships began to open doors to exciting new career opportunities. For adults, the mentor program offered an outlet for many people who had wanted to help our students but were uncertain about how to become involved.

Other benefits became apparent as well. Soon after establishing the club program and inviting volunteer mentors, we began to see sharp reductions in our truancy and dropout rates. During my first year as principal, these rates were worse than the benchmarks designated by the state. Some student were spending their days in and around vacant buildings and lots, places where gang activity often breeds.

After our first year of clubs, the truancy and dropout rates dropped to almost zero. Instead of gang colors, our students were donning the colors of club uniforms donated by neighborhood businesses now eager to help our students. And the only signs flashed by students were smiles when they saw our volunteers enter the building. Clearly, our school clubs and volunteer mentors were beginning to meet the identity needs that compelled some youngsters to seek out gang membership in the first place.

ANOTHER LOOK AT ACADEMICS

Our success with the club and volunteer mentor programs led us to take another look at our academic program. We decided to make our instructional strategies more activities-based.

For example, instead of teaching math exclusively out of the book, which encourages passive learning, we began to develop activities that pushed students to participate more actively. We had math students build model bridges, and we linked the building of the bridges to lessons in science, social studies, and language arts. We tried many such strategies, with the common goal being that students would participate in classwork in a way that ensured their capacity to demonstrate what they'd learned and to "be something" in the eyes of others.

Additionally, we began to move away from the *F* grade in our academic program, and this year we abolished it entirely. Our students most susceptible to gang membership hate the *F* grade, and many stop putting forth effort after receiving one *F*.

We now give students who have not achieved sufficiently an *I* for incomplete. The transition in grading has raised difficult issues: What grade do you enter for students who never demonstrate they've learned the curriculum? How do you provide time for reteaching and retesting when students' work is incomplete? These problems are tough, but not insurmountable (Juarez 1994). In any case, some administrative disorder is still a better alternative than continuing to fail students, robbing them of the chance to build a positive self-identity.

One way to gain the flexibility needed to reteach and retest material is to use a year-round schedule. One reason the *F* grade has persisted is that education is wedded to the rigid nine-month school year and the six-weeks, back-to-back, grading scheme. This traditional format almost guarantees there will be no time or structure for reteaching and retesting.

This year, Webb became the first secondary school in our district to embark on year-round schooling. One advantage is that it affords us time during the intersessions (breaks) to work with students who need extra help to master learning objectives. During the intersessions, we also offer enrichment activities for all students, and we expand the activities of the clubs and the volunteer mentors program.

FROM NOBODY TO SOMEBODY

Our efforts at Webb Middle School are not driven exclusively by a belief that what we do will reduce gang violence or deter our potential gang wannabes from gang membership. Our clubs and volunteer mentors, and our changes in grading and the school calendar, are strategies we believe will benefit all students, the vast majority of whom will never consider joining a gang. Nevertheless, we believe these efforts will make a difference in the impact of gangs on our students' lives.

Whatever the causes for their poor sense of self-identity (and the reasons are multiple and complex), gang members and gang wannabes have special learning needs, styles, and problems. When such students receive positive opportunities to "be someone and do something in the eyes of others," they will be too busy (and too happy) to feel the need to join a gang.

References

Health, S. B., and M. W. McLaughlin. (1993). "Building Identities for Inner-City Youth." In *Identity & Inner-City Youth: Beyond Ethnicity and Gender*, edited by S. B. Heath and M. W. McLaughlin. New York: Teachers College Press.

Juarez, T. (1994). "Mastery Grading to Serve Student Learning in the Middle Grades." *Middle School Journal* 26, 1: 37–41.

Laska, J., and T. Juarez. (1992). *Grading and Marking in American Schools: Two Centuries of Debate*. Springfield, Ill.: Charles C Thomas.

Vigil, J. D. (1988). *Barrio Gangs: Street Life and Identity in Southern California*. Austin: University of Texas Press.

LOOK WHO'S AT SCHOOL: PARENTS RETURN TO HELP TEACHERS

Betsy Wagner and Monika Guttman

Wagner and Guttman wrote this article for U.S. News and World Report.

On a sweltering summer evening, Severo Escobar waits patiently for the doors of the Sun Valley Middle School to open. He's attending another session of the Parent Institute, an eight-week course designed to motivate students by educating their parents in the San Fernando Valley, Calif., school. Escobar says his 16-year-old daughter stays out until 11 each night and isn't "doing as well as I'd like." So to help her and four younger children, this father will spend the next two hours listening closely as a Spanish-speaking instructor explains everything from how

---

U.S. News and World Report, September 11, 1995, pp. 57–59.

to read a report card to how to detect signs of drug use. "You want your kids to go down a straight road," Escobar explains.

To keep kids out of life's hairpin turns and in school, parents across the country—from the poorest to the wealthiest districts—are taking a more active role in their children's education. The trend involves everything from elaborate fund-raising events to more involvement in the classroom. While this should not seem radical, for many public schools it is. "Parents thought they should send their kids to school and let the professionals handle them. And the professionals thought parents should butt out," says Anne Henderson of the Center for Law and Education in Washington, D.C. But the division of labor is fading, with parents demanding a bigger stake in the schools and teachers asking for more help.

In class, this means more and more places have a parent or two or more in school each day. Mothers kneel beside desks leading small children through math drills; shelves contain calculators and world atlases bought by the local parents' associations. As budgets get slashed in some places and courts order states to help poor districts in others, parents are scrambling to plug the financial gap. They raffle off mountain bikes, throw formal dinner dances, even solicit donations directly from other parents. "It raises the dilemma of whether this fund-raising will further the inequities between rich and poor districts," says Education Commission of the States spokesperson Chris Pipho.

Experts insist children do better when their parents get involved, whether attending school meetings, running for the school board or even cleaning erasers. A 1994 study found that parental involvement was a "significant predictor" of student achievement and behavior of kids of all races and incomes. While many parents cannot find the time to pitch in, a significant number do: A recent study says 42 percent of third through fifth graders have parents who have attended school functions and volunteered within the past year; a quarter of high school students have parents who have done so.

To get more parents involved, many schools are trying harder to make them feel welcome. Sun Valley Middle School just opened a small parent center. Katy Elementary School, 20 miles outside Houston, posts a cheery volunteer in the hallway to greet parents, and invites adults to stop by—even for lunch with their children. For parents pressed for time or intimidated by teachers, Katy officials hold meetings in community centers or church basements. "They make you feel like they want to see you and like they want you to know what they are doing," says Shirley Archie, whose 8-year-old daughter attends the school.

Homework help. Other programs try to help students by teaching their parents about how schools work. In a study released last week, almost a third of all parents said they have trouble helping their children with homework because they "teach things a lot differently" today. At Allenwood Elementary School in Temple Hills, Md., parents are invited to attend math workshops that show them how to assist their kids. Such programs often help. The Parent Institute, a California-based grass-roots organization that collaborates with school districts, has programs in San Diego and Los Angeles and is currently setting up shop in San Francisco. Since its founding eight years ago, it has graduated more than 50,000 parents, many of whom are immigrants with little formal education and almost no knowledge of how American schools work. "Before, I didn't know what kind of homework [my son] had or what I could do to help," says Joaquina Lobatos, who is attending sessions at Sun Valley School out of concern for her 13-year-old. "Now I want to come talk to [his] teacher."

Meanwhile, at the Excel School in Durango, Colo., parents are pitching in at a public school they helped dream up three years ago over coffee. Now in its second year, Excel teaches grades six through 10 and is one of 200 "charter" schools, a new breed of schools that are publicly funded by but run independent of school districts. Nestled in 16 rooms of a two-story 1950s brick building that it shares with another charter, Excel has small classes, few frills and an active bunch of parents. Each year, parents of all 160 students must sign a pledge promising that they will oversee their children's education and volunteer in the school. "There is something strong and clear about having it down on paper," says Olivia Reynolds, whose daughter is a seventh grader.

Every little bit helps schools' ever thinning bottom lines. Jim Ewing, Excel's only administrator, estimates that last year the school saved over $40,000, thanks to parents who volunteered during the day to supervise students and keep the school clean. On top of such savings, parents contributed $50,000 they raised through auctions, carnivals, fund drives and, yes, bake sales. To manage such sums, roughly 2,000 public high schools—or 13 percent of the nation's total—have created nonprofit fund-raising foundations that were once the hallmark of colleges or elite prep schools.

Many grown-ups think parents should be involved in schools from kindergarten through high school graduation. But what do their children think? During the day at Excel, Miles Green, a 14-year-old sophomore, occasionally bumps into his mother, who serves on several committees and sometimes supervises the lunch room. "I am a teenager. Of course I'm embarrassed," he says laughing. "But she doesn't come up to me and give me a hug or a kiss. She's there to do a job. I think it's great."

QUESTIONS TO HELP YOU THINK AND WRITE ABOUT EDUCATION ISSUES

1. Read the articles by Katz and Sollod. Draw a line down the middle of two sheets of paper, and make lists of the advantages and disadvantages of teaching self-esteem on the first, and the advantages and disadvantages of teaching spirituality on the second. What do you value? Why? What is consistent with your current educational experiences? Explain in detail.

2. Identify the claim, support, and warrants in the article by Katz. Do you share her opinions about teaching self-esteem in the public schools? Have you noticed any differences in the efforts of your primary and secondary school teachers and your college professors in their efforts to teach self-

esteem? Is a student's self-esteem a legitimate concern of college professors? Why or why not? Try to think in terms of human motivation and values as you work with this issue.

3. Sollod offers yet another possible subject for the schools to teach. What do you think the public schools should be responsible for teaching? What do you think the colleges and universities should be responsible for teaching? Think in terms of what constitutes a successful life and a successful society by your standards. Discuss how schools can contribute to success in some areas and how they should not be expected to contribute in others.

4. The articles by Borkat and Wiesenfeld deal with the problem of grade inflation in different ways. What is your response to these authors' ideas? Do you think this is a problem? What is its cause? Is it harmful? Why or how? What should be done about it?

5. What is Borkat's claim in her essay? Why do you think so? What technique is she using to state her claim?

6. Read Sizer's essay. Now draw a line down the middle of a piece of paper and list the reasons in favor of standard tests in one column and the reasons against them in the other. What conclusions does Sizer draw? What are your conclusions on this issue? Give reasons.

7. How much do you think schools should change to help students succeed? Think in terms of your own experience. From the three articles on this subject by Romo and Falbo, Juarez, and Wagner and Guttman, list the ideas you accept and those you cannot accept. Describe your idea of an ideal public school.

8. Compare Bacon's ideas about education with modern education as reflected by the other articles in this section and your own experience. What is the same? What is different? What elements of 17th century education do you wish were part of your education? Which elements are you glad are not a part of your education? Why? How would Bacon respond to the ideas in the essays by Katz and Sollod concerning what schools should teach?

9. Israeloff (see "Don't Know Much About History," page 83) reports that students are learning less about history than when she was in school. Do you think this is true? List all of the reasons you can think of why history is important to know and understand. Can you build a strong case that history is unimportant? How do you think history should be taught in schools?

SECTION III

Issues Concerning Crime and the Treatment of Criminals

WHAT ARE THE ISSUES?

1. How Tough Should Drug Sentencing Be?

An expert on addiction and substance abuse describes the problem and offers some solutions for dealing with drug offenders. A senator and an ex-convict provide perspectives on minimum sentences for drug cases.

2. How Should We Punish Crime?

Newman explains the psychology that drives the punishment of criminals. Clarence Darrow, a lawyer writing in 1932, and J. Edgar Hoover, the former FBI chief writing in 1959, provide historical perspectives on capital punishment. The arguments in this section question the effectiveness of the death penalty, give reasons for retaining it, provide a firsthand account of an execution, and suggest how some positive social good could come from it. For a very different view, see also "Giving People a Second Chance," page 55.

3. What Should Be Done with Young Offenders?

The focus of this section is on the escalating problem of children and teenagers who commit crimes and acts of violence. The arguments establish the nature of the problem, discuss its causes, evaluate how bad the problem is, and propose some ways for solving this problem. For another approach to this problem, see "Where Homeboys Feel at Home in School," page 486.

Extend Your Perspective with Film and Literature Related to Crime and the Treatment of Criminals

Films: Clockwork Orange, 1971; *Dead Man Walking,* 1996; *Boyz N the Hood,* 1991.
Literature: poem: "The Ballad of Reading Gaol" by Oscar Wilde; short story: "Billy Budd" by Herman Melville: novels: *Crime and Punishment* by Fyodor Dostoyevsky, *Of Mice and Men* by John Steinbeck, and *Clockwork Orange* by Anthony Burgess.

THE RHETORICAL SITUATION

Everyone seems to have opinions about the issues associated with crime and criminals. All of the recent presidents of the United States have made it a major issue in their campaigns and presidencies, yet the problems persist. According to the perceptions of many, the country is becoming increasingly lawless. Motivational warrants linked to the need for safety are implicit in many of the arguments about crime issues.

The issues related to crime that are included in this section deal with the degree of severity that should be required in sentencing drug cases, with the punishment of murderers and others who commit particularly horrible crimes, and with the growing problem of very young offenders. Drug sentencing causes severe overcrowding in jails and prisons, so some people question whether first offenders should receive mandatory jail sentences that keep them there for extended periods of time. Capital punishment is still controversial. Even though 87 percent of the people in a *Parade* magazine survey conducted in 1993 said they favored the death penalty, it is still debatable, as you will see. The death penalty has had an interesting history. It was banned in this country in 1972 and ruled constitutional again in 1976. Children and young teenagers breaking the law and committing particularly heinous crimes is a fairly new problem that concerns many people. This problem has become so serious that some people believe severe punishment is as justified for young offenders as it is for adult offenders. Others argue for various types of prevention, intervention, and rehabilitation for all criminals, whether they are young or old. There is a strong exigency in the United States to understand and solve the problems associated with crime in this country.

1. How Tough Should Drug Sentencing Be?

IT'S DRUGS, STUPID

Joseph A. Califano, Jr.

Califano is president of the Center on Addiction and Substance Abuse at Columbia University and a former Secretary of Health, Education, and Welfare.

For 30 years, America has tried to curb crime with more judges, tougher punishments and bigger prisons. We have tried to rein in health costs by manipulating payments to doctors and hospitals. We've fought poverty with welfare systems that offer little incentive to work. All the while, we have undermined these efforts with our personal and national denial about the sinister dimension drug abuse and addiction have added to our society. If [politicians] want to prove to us that they can make a difference in what really ails America, they should "get real" about how drugs have recast three of the nation's biggest challenges.

Law, Order and Justice. In 1960 there were fewer than 30,000 arrests for drug offenses; in 30 years, that number soared beyond one million. Since 1989, more individuals have been incarcerated for drug offenses than for *all violent crimes*—and most violent crimes are committed by drug (including alcohol) abusers.

New York Times Magazine, January 29, 1995, pp. 40–41.

Probation and parole are sick jokes in most cities. As essential first steps to rehabilitation, many parolees need drug treatment and after-care, which means far more monitoring than their drug-free predecessors of a generation ago required, not less. Yet in Los Angeles, for example, probation officers are expected to handle as many as 1,000 cases at a time. With most offenders committing drug- or alcohol-related crimes, it's no wonder so many parolees go right back to jail: 80 percent of prisoners have prior convictions and more than 60 percent have served time before.

Congress and state legislatures keep passing laws more relevant to the celluloid gangsters and inmates of classic 1930s movies than 1990s reality. Today's prisons are wall to wall with drug dealers, addicts, alcohol abusers and the mentally ill (often related to drug abuse). The prison population shot past a million in 1994 and is likely to double soon after the year 2000. Among industrialized nations, the United States is second only to Russia in the number of its citizens it imprisons: 519 per 100,000, compared with 368 for next-place South Africa, 116 for Canada and 36 for Japan.

Judges and prosecutors are demoralized as they juggle caseloads of more than twice the recommended maximum. In 1991 eight states had to close their civil jury trial systems for all or part of the year to comply with speedy trial requirements of criminal cases involving drug abusers. Even where civil courts remain open, the rush of drug-related cases has created intolerable delays—4 years in Newark, 5 in Philadelphia and up to 10 in Cook County, Ill. In our impersonal, bureaucratic world, if society keeps denying citizens timely, individual hearings for their grievances, they may blow off angry steam in destructive ways.

Health Care Cost Containment. Emergency rooms from Boston to Baton Rouge are piled high with the debris of drug use on city streets—victims of gunshot wounds, drug-prompted child and spouse abuse, and drug-related medical conditions like cardiac complications and sexually transmitted diseases. AIDS and tuberculosis have spread rapidly in large part because of drug use. Beyond dirty needles, studies show that teen-agers high on pot, alcohol or other drugs are far more likely to have sex, and to have it without a condom.

Each year drugs and alcohol trigger up to $75 billion in health care costs. The cruelest impact afflicts the half-million newborns exposed to drugs during pregnancy. Crack babies, a rarity a decade ago, crowd $2,000-a-day neonatal wards. Many die. It can cost $1 million to bring each survivor to adulthood.

Even where prenatal care is available—as it is for most Medicaid beneficiaries—women on drugs tend not to take advantage of it. And as for drug treatment, only a relatively small percentage of drug-abusing pregnant mothers seek it, and they must often wait in line for scarce slots. Pregnant mothers' failure to seek prenatal care and stop abusing drugs accounts for much of the almost $3 billion that Medicaid spent in 1994 on inpatient hospital care related to drug use.

The Fight Against Poverty. Drugs have changed the nature of poverty. Nowhere is this more glaring than in the welfare systems and the persistent problem of teen-age pregnancy.

[Current politicians] are hell-bent to put welfare mothers to work. But all the financial lures and prods and all the job training in the world will do precious little to make employable the hundreds of thousands of welfare recipients who are addicts and abusers.

For too long, reformers have had their heads in the sand about this unpleasant reality. Liberals fear that admitting the extent of alcohol and drug abuse among welfare recipients will incite even more punitive reactions than those now fashionable. Conservatives don't want to face up to the cost of drug treatment. This political denial assures failure of any effort to put these welfare recipients to work.

The future is not legalization. Legalizing drug use would write off millions of minority Americans, especially children and drug-exposed babies, whose communities are most under siege by drugs. It has not worked in any nation where it's been tried, and our own experience with alcohol and cigarettes shows how unlikely we are to keep legalized drugs away from children.

Drugs are the greatest threat to family stability, decent housing, public schools and even minimal social amenities in urban ghettos. Contrary to the claim of pot proponents, marijuana is dangerous. It devastates short-term memory and the ability to concentrate precisely when our children need them most—when they are in school. And a child 12 to 17 years old who smokes pot is 85 times as likely to use cocaine as a child who does not. Cocaine is much more addictive than alcohol, which has already hooked more than 18 million Americans. Dr. Herbert D. Kleber, a top drug expert, estimates that legalizing cocaine would give us at least 20 million addicts, more than 10 times the number today.

It's especially reckless to promote legalization when we have not committed research funds and energies to addiction prevention and treatment on a scale commensurate with the epidemic. The National Institutes of Health spend some $4 billion for research on cancer, cardiovascular disease and AIDS, but less than 15 percent of that amount for research on substance abuse and addiction, the largest single cause and exacerbator of those diseases.

Treatment varies widely, from inpatient to outpatient, from quick-fix acupuncture to residential programs ranging a few weeks to more than a year, from methadone dependence to drug-free therapeutic communities. Fewer than 25 percent of the individuals who need drug or alcohol treatment enter a program. On average, a quarter complete treatment; half of them are drug- or alcohol-free a year later. In other words, with wide variations depending on individual circumstances, those entering programs have a one-in-eight chance of being free of drugs or alcohol a year later. Those odds beat many for long-shot cancer chemotherapies, and research should significantly improve them. But a recent study in California found that even at current rates of success, $1 invested in treatment saves $7 in crime, health care and welfare costs.

Here are a few suggestions for immediate action to attack the dimension drugs have added to these three problems:

- Grant Federal funds to state and Federal prison systems only if they provide drug and alcohol treatment and after-care for all inmates who need it.
- Instead of across-the-board mandatory sentences, keep inmates with drug and alcohol problems in jails, boot camps or halfway houses until they experience a year of sobriety after treatment.

- Require drug and alcohol addicts to go regularly to treatment and after-care programs like Alcoholics Anonymous while on parole or probation.
- Provide Federal funds for police only to cities that enforce drug laws throughout their jurisdiction. End the acceptance of drug bazaars in Harlem and southeast Washington that would not be tolerated on Manhattan's Upper East Side or in Georgetown.
- Encourage judges with lots of drug cases to employ public health professionals, just as they hire economists to assist with antitrust cases.
- Cut off welfare payments to drug addicts and alcoholics who refuse to seek treatment and pursue after-care. As employers and health professionals know, addicts need lots of carrots and sticks, including the threat of loss of job and income, to get the monkey off their back.
- Put children of drug- or alcohol-addicted welfare mothers who refuse treatment into foster care or orphanages. [...] The compassionate and cost-effective middle ground is to identify those parents who abuse their children by their own drug and alcohol abuse and place those children in decent orphanages and foster care until the parents shape up.
- Subject inmates, parolees and welfare recipients with a history of substance abuse to random drug tests, and fund the treatment they need. Liberals must recognize that getting off drugs is the only chance these individuals (and their babies) have to enjoy their civil rights. Conservatives who preach an end to criminal recidivism and welfare dependency must recognize that reincarceration and removal from the welfare rolls for those who test positive is a cruel Catch-22 unless treatment is available.

Fortunately, [current politicians] are certain not to legalize drugs. Unfortunately, it is less clear whether they will recognize the nasty new strain of intractability that drugs have added to crime, health costs and welfare dependency, and go on to tap the potential of research, prevention and treatment to save billions of dollars and millions of lives.

If a mainstream disease like diabetes or cancer affected as many individuals and families as drug and alcohol abuse and addiction do, this nation would mount an effort on the scale of the Manhattan Project to deal with it.

DON'T LET JUDGES SET CROOKS FREE

Phil Gramm

Phil Gramm is a Republican U.S. Senator from Texas. He wrote this article for the New York Times *in 1993.*

Two Federal judges recently announced that they would refuse to take drug cases because they oppose mandatory minimum sentences. One judge, Jack Weinstein

New York Times, July 8, 1993, p. A1.

of Brooklyn, confessed to a "sense of depression about much of the cruelty I have been party to in connection with the war on drugs." The other, Whitman Knapp of Manhattan, heartened that President Clinton "has not committed himself to the war on drugs in such a way as the Republican Administration had," hoped his action would influence the President to abandon tough mandatory sentencing.

If the Clinton Administration listens to these voices, and their echoes, and tries to roll back minimum mandatory sentences, it will certainly win applause from some criminal defense lawyers, judges and the media—and no doubt many criminals—but it will betray millions of Americans who took the President at his word when he promised to be tough on crime.

Contrary to conventional wisdom, most criminals are perfectly rational men and women. They don't commit crimes because they're in the grip of some irresistible impulse. They commit crimes because they think it pays. Unfortunately, in most cases they are right: In America today, crime *does* pay.

Morgan Reynolds, an economist at Texas A&M University, has calculated the amount of time that a person committing a serious crime in 1990—the last year for which we have complete statistics—could reasonably expect to spend in prison. By analyzing the probability of arrest, prosecution, conviction, imprisonment and the average actual sentence served by convicts for particular crimes, Professor Reynolds has reached some shocking conclusions.

On average, a person committing murder in the United States today can expect to spend only 1.8 years in prison. For rape, the expected punishment is 60 days. Expected time in prison is 23 days for robbery, 6.7 days for arson and 6.4 days for aggravated assault. And for stealing a car, a person can reasonably expect to spend just a day and a half in prison.

Given this extremely low rate of expected punishment, is it any wonder that our nation is deluged by a tidal wave of crime? In trying to account for the six million violent crimes committed annually, analysts point to the breakdown of the family, the effects of television violence and the failure to teach moral values in our schools. While these factors have an impact, they overlook the main culprit: a criminal justice system in which the cost of committing crimes is so shamelessly cheap that it fails to deter potential criminals.

Mandatory minimum sentences deal with this problem directly. When a potential criminal knows that if he is convicted he is *certain* to be sentenced, and his sentence is *certain* to be stiff, his cost-benefit calculus changes dramatically and his willingness to engage in criminal activity takes a nose dive.

Again, Professor Reynold's statistics are revealing. He found that since 1950, the expected punishment for a serious criminal has declined by two-thirds, while the annual number of crimes has risen seven-fold. In 1950, each perpetrator of a serious crime risked, on average, 24 days in prison. By 1988, the amount of risked time was 8.5 days. Over 38 years, soft sentencing—treating criminals as victims of dysfunctional families, of predatory capitalism, of society at large—has brought a dramatic decline in the cost of committing a crime and a dramatic increase in crime.

Critics of mandatory minimum sentences point out, often with considerable indignation, that mandatory sentencing denies judges discretion in imposing sentences. And they are perfectly right. That's what we want.

Americans have lost faith in our criminal justice systems. Too many violent criminals have walked away with light or even no prison sentences. Mandatory minimum sentencing is a massive no-confidence vote by the American people in the discretionary powers of our judges. If judges and parole boards were legally liable for the actions of convicted felons who walk the streets due to their decisions, I would have more confidence in their judgment. But they are not.

"But what about fairness?" critics of mandatory minimum sentencing ask. "Is it fair that someone who has never committed a crime in his life should go to prison for 10 years because one day he sold drugs to some kid? Shouldn't we distinguish between a major drug dealer and a minor drug offense?"

Once again, the critics are right: There is a distinction between major and minor drug offenses. A minor drug offense takes place when a pusher sells drugs to somebody else's child; a major drug offense takes place when he pushes drugs on yours. Only when our nation's elites are as outraged about what happens to someone else's child as they would be were it happening to their own will we deal with crime effectively.

Of course, there is the cost issue to be considered. At a time when we are desperately trying to reduce the Federal deficit, we can really afford to sentence more criminals to jail for lengthier periods of time?

Of course we can. In 1990, the Department of Justice's bureau of statistics found that it costs from $15,000 to $30,000 to keep a felon in prison for a year. A Rand Corporation study calculated that the active street criminal imposes a financial cost of $430,000 a year on the general public—not to mention such immeasurable but very real costs as grief, fear and anger. By Washington standards (or anybody's, for that matter), spending $30,000 a year to save $430,000 a year is a brilliant allocation of resources.

In dealing with our nation's crime problem, cost is not the fundamental issue. Indifference is. I am appalled by the shoulder-shrugging approach some Americans take to the issue of crime in this country. Americans saw the pictures of starving children in Somalia and were outraged; we saw "ethnic cleansing" in Bosnia and were furious. But our outrage and fury evaporate when American children are the victims of criminals.

Like Judge Weinstein, all too many are ready to agonize over the "cruelty" that mandatory sentencing inflicts on drug pushers, and to overlook the cruelty that mandatory sentencing avoids by keeping these criminals off the streets and preventing them from brutalizing your children, mine or even Judge Weinstein's.

With the end of the cold war, domestic crime is now the greatest threat to the safety and well being of Americans. And just as the U.S. developed a military strategy—"containment"—to deter Soviet aggression by raising its costs, so today we need a legal strategy to contain, and reverse, the growth of violent crime.

That is why, along with many other Americans, I am a strong supporter of mandatory minimum sentences. In fact, I will go so far as to say that as long as I am in the Senate, we will be imposing more minimum sentences, not repealing them.

A CASE FOR DISCRETION

Michael Brennan

Brennan is an ex-convict who was released from custody in October of 1995. He lives in Portland, where he works as a writer.

I stood before federal district court judge Kimberly Frankel. The date was May 28, 1995; the place, Portland, Ore. I had just pleaded guilty to five shoplifting charges and one felony count of cocaine possession.

In a similar case in San Diego, Steven White, 32, faced a mandatory sentence of 25 years to life for shoplifting a $130 VCR. He decided instead that a bullet through the brain was the less painful way to go. The suicide note he left offered apologies to his parents for the heartbreak he caused them, but suggested that spending that much time in prison was too high a price to pay for a misdemeanor. The sentence White faced is a result of one of the many federal and state "mandatory minimum" sentencing acts that have been enacted by Congress and various state legislatures since 1986. White's case fell under California's so-called "three strikes you're out" law.

Like me, White had a sporadic history of heroin addiction and nonviolent criminal offenses. His first two strikes—burglary convictions—dated to 1983. His "third strike"—the shoplifting charge, which occurred in 1994—was elevated to a felony by being classed as "petty theft with a prior conviction of theft." Two judges pleaded with prosecutors not to seek the 25-to-life sentence that the recently enacted law called for. They refused.

Many groups oppose mandatory minimum sentences, including the National Association of Veteran Police Officers, the U.S. Sentencing Committee, the American Bar Association and Families Against Mandatory Minimums. Supreme Court Chief Justice William Rehnquist calls mandatory minimums "a good example of the law of unintended consequences."

There are currently 1.2 million people incarcerated in federal and state prisons in this country. The majority of them are up on drug-related crimes, and many are there as a result of mandatory minimum sentences. The average cost of housing a federal prisoner is $20,804 annually. It is ultimately the taxpayer who foots this enormous bill. Furthermore, the hodgepodge of state and federal mandatory drug sentences sometimes leads to violent offenders—Florida's rapists, robbers and murderers, for example—being released early to make room for nonviolent, first-time drug offenders serving lengthy, mandatory-minimum sentences.

Ironically, I came close to being classed as a violent offender. On one of my shoplifting sprees I struggled with a Fred Meyer's department-store security guard as I tried to escape her grasp. If she had described my desperate struggle as

---

Newsweek, November 13, 1995, p. 18.

resistance and my shoplifting partner's presence as a threat, I could have been charged with robbery 2, which now carries a mandatory five-year sentence under Oregon's Measure 11. But the issue is only partially whether the punishment fits the crime. There are a number of federal prisoners doing life without parole for marijuana sales, for example, while rapists are routinely paroled after only four years.

The more central question, however, is this: is it the American way to remove all discretion from judges and invest prosecutors with an extraordinary degree of power? Are there no circumstances—youth, a previously clean record or varying levels of culpability among codefendants—that might mitigate the degree of punishment that must be meted out? Not under any of the mandatory minimum sentences.

In my case, by the time I appeared before Judge Frankel I had behind me a 15-year on-again, off-again history of heroin addiction that resulted in numerous petty-theft convictions, three felony heroin-possession convictions and four stints in county jails.

Judge Frankel was free to weigh this unsavory history against what I had accomplished in the four drug-free years prior to my recent relapse. After my release from jail in 1989 I went from a homeless ex-offender to a working writer. I also initiated and managed a self-help work project in Boston that successfully employed 19 individuals who were dealing with homelessness, AIDS, addiction and mental illness.

The judge, using the discretionary powers that have been an integral part of the American judicial system for 200 years, sentenced me to 30 days in jail, 90 days of work-release, $700 in restitution fees and two years' probation. The work-release program allowed me to pay society back through community-work programs, maintain family connections, earn money at outside work to pay a substantial portion of my incarceration costs and to save funds for post-release living expenses.

Contrast my experience with that of Stephanie Lomax, a former Portland, Ore., resident whose family shared her story with me. Lomax and two codefendants were convicted in Nebraska on conspiracy charges involving crack cocaine. White House drug czar Lee Brown recently stated that crack-cocaine mandatory sentences primarily affect African-Americans, thus adding a racial bias to federal drug laws. He calls crack-cocaine mandatory sentences "bad law" based on "bad information."

Lomax, a 25-year-old pregnant black mother and first-time offender with no previous criminal history, continues to maintain her innocence. She was sentenced to life without parole. This means, literally, that she will die in the same prison system where she gave birth to the child she can no longer hold.

Americans are understandably frightened and frustrated by the impact of drugs and crime on society. One can only hope that our fears have not also destroyed our sense of compassion and justice, and that we can still respond to Stephanie Lomax (and untold thousands like her).

"Does anyone care about what is going on in the system today?" she writes from her cell at the Pleasanton federal prison in California. "I am poor. I have no assets and I'm very much in need of help. Can you help me and my family?"

2. How Should We Punish Crime?

ON CRIMES AND THEIR PUNISHMENTS: THE PSYCHOLOGY OF RETRIBUTION

Graeme Newman

These are excerpts from Newman's book Just and Painful: A Case for the Corporal Punishment of Criminals, *published in 1983. Compare the ideas in this selection with the ideas in "Turning Bad into Good" on page 515, which is a more recent article by Newman on the subject of how to treat criminals.*

From ancient myths to modern myths, retribution has played a central role in the resolution and definition of evil deeds. For example, Aeschylus borrowed the ideas for his Orestian tragedy from the dim beginnings of Greek history—an unending cycle of killings in which: King Agamemnon sacrifices his daughter Iphegenia for a propitious opening to his military campaign; his Queen Clytemnestra revenges their daughter by murdering the King; in turn, the Queen is murdered by their son Orestes. And the gods are hesitant to condemn any of the killings as totally unjustified.

Modern myths view retribution in a similar way. Take, for example, a modern play, the movie *Superman II*—not a tragedy, but a romance which is more typical of today's popular culture:

> Superman, having lost his super powers, accompanies Lois Lane as Clark Kent into that great belly of American culture, the diner. He leaves to make a telephone call, she sits up at the counter. A rough character takes Clark's seat and starts to bother Lois. Clark returns, asks the fellow to move, and a brawl ensues. The former Superman gets pummelled, and tastes his own blood for the first time.
>
> The audience sits on edge. Superman goes on to regain his super powers and perform the impossible: he defeats in mighty combat not one, but three evil persons who had equivalent super powers to his own.
>
> The audience lets out a sigh of relief. But the movie is not yet over.
>
> Clark Kent returns to the diner. The same ugly character is there insulting the diner's food. Clark picks a fight with him and—you guessed it—pummels the ruffian into the floor.
>
> The audience cheers loudly. Justice was done! And how the bully *deserved* what he got!

From Graeme Newman, *Just and Painful: A Case for the Corporal Punishment of Criminals* (New York: Macmillan, 1983), pp. 19–21, 22.

Why should a superman, one who had won a huge battle with three evil supermen, find it necessary to even up the score with a pathetic earthling? Surely a man so big and powerful could have shrugged it off?

The writers of this movie shrewdly saw that there would have been no end to this story had they not provided this last scene of redress. The need to settle a score, to even up old wrongs is deeply embedded into the meaning of justice in almost all cultures of the world.

This is the "psychological reality" of punishment—as Sigmund Freud called it—and it is well over two thousand years old. Philosophers and legal theorists call it "retribution" or "just deserts."

Here, justice is equated with the logic of the history and psychology of punishment.

Historically, punishment has always been linked to the crime: it has been made to fit the crime.

Psychologically we *feel* that the link between the crime and its punishment is right. We recognize that to reward crimes would make us feel extremely frustrated. (Indeed, this may be why so many people feel dissatisfied with our criminal justice system because it does seem to reward many criminals.) And at the very least, to sit by and do nothing about criminal behavior makes us jittery, even though we personally would rather not be those who actually meted out the punishment. Nevertheless, we insist that something be done to criminals who have committed offenses.

In the past, those who vociferously demanded retribution were considered to be conservatives. Today it has become a favorite banner of reformers such as Professor Von Hirsch in his book *Doing Justice.* In 1976 the Committee on Incarceration with Professor Von Hirsch as its Director, argued for a return to a just deserts model of punishment, claiming, among other things, that it would limit the overall length of time offenders spent in prison. It would replace the "treatment model" of criminal punishment which was blamed for the excesses of the "indeterminate sentence" (that is, the offender was incarcerated until such time that it was thought he was "cured"). The Committee argued that punishment according to just deserts would ensure that there were fixed limits to the punishment that could be applied to a particular crime, because the theory of just deserts requires that a person can only be punished:

1. For the particular crime, and only that crime, which he has committed and
2. By a punishment that fits the crime.

The oldest idea of making the punishment fit the crime was to reflect both the quality and gravity of the crime in the punishment. Thus, the hand of the thief was cut off—the old principle of an eye for an eye (often associated with the law of Moses, but the principle can be found to underlie the punishment systems of most cultures). There are many other variations of this theme. In colonial America, garrulous women who nagged at their husbands too much were, appropriately, gagged by the punishment of a metal bridle (called the "scold's bridle") that was placed over their heads and clamped on their mouths—a painful contraption which responded directly to the offense. Another reflection of the quality of the crime in the punishment was to punish a criminal on the very spot where he had committed the offense, a practice in English criminal law up until the 18th century. Or certain parts of the body were identified as the seat of the crime: to cut out the heart of a traitor, remove the kidneys of a thief.

The great Italian poet Dante Alighieri was a master at concocting reflecting punishments. In Dante's Hell, suicides, because they did not respect their own bodies, were turned into trees which were periodically snapped at and chewed by dogs. Thieves who had not respected the distinction between "mine" and "thine" were turned into reptiles, then transformed again into each other, destined never to retain their own true form. How apt, we say. There seems to be something inherently right about the choice of punishment. By "inherently" we mean that we have a "gut feeling" that it is right. This is why the audience cheers so loudly when Superman evens up the score.

MAKING THE PUNISHMENT FIT THE CRIME

This is a brief example of creative sentencing in an effort to make the punishment fit the crime. It was reported in The New Republic *in 1993. No author was listed.*

An Indiana judge recently sentenced fourteen abortion protesters to sit silently in an abortion clinic's waiting room for eight hours, without handing out anti-abortion literature. "I didn't want to send them to jail," said Judge Bernard Carter of the Lake County Superior Court, "but I did want them to do something that would make them uncomfortable, make them think about what they're doing." Carter's creative sentencing wins the prize for proportionate justice: a thought punishment for a thought crime.

WHY CAPITAL PUNISHMENT?

Clarence Darrow

These excerpts come from Clarence Darrow's autobiography, The Story of My Life, *published in 1932. Darrow was a criminal lawyer who opposed the death penalty and was able to avoid it even for some of his most horrendous criminal cases. It was legal in his time.*

So long as men discuss crime and penalties they will discuss capital punishment. It is not easy to select the valid reasons for and against any sort of punishment.

The New Republic, December 13, 1993, p. 10.
Clarence Darrow, *The Story of My Life* (New York: Scribner and Sons, 1932), pp. 359–365.

One who really seeks to know and understand goes over and over the question, and winds up at last by denying the validity of all punishment. Which means, of course, that society should not deliberately cause any one to suffer for any act that he commits. The difference between the one penalty and another depends entirely upon the reactions of the individual who fixes the penalties or discusses the subject.

It is almost universally believed that the death penalty is the most serious infliction that can be visited upon any individual. This is the reason people range on the opposite sides of the much-mooted topic. Those who are for it believe in this penalty because it is the worst fate that man can visit upon his fellow man. Those who are against are influenced by the same reason. No one is either for or against it on account of the effect on society, for it is out of the question to tell whether it increases the number of murders or lessens it. Even if this could be told, it would not settle the question. If so, more men would believe in some obvious form of physical torture like regular beatings or maimings, or starving or branding, or burning or boiling, or continuous torment of the victim up to the time of death.

There are various reasons why this cannot be settled. First, no one knows the effect of the different sorts of punishment toward preventing others from killing. Nor do they know which gives the most pain to the sufferer, or just how the pain administered upon one human being will affect others who know it, or whether men, women and children in general should be allowed to see the sufferings of the guilty or be compelled to see these victims while in agony, so that the spectacle of agony shall be expected to keep others from committing the same crime. Neither do they know whether visualizing and hearing of the effects of punishment of one deters others, or induces others. Or whether, even if it served to deter in this particular way, it might not render men, women and children callous to human distress.

A Chicago sheriff once had an unusual brainstorm: Instead of hiding the condemned, the execution, and the executioner, he took the other course. He had the scaffold erected in the jail corridor so that the prisoners would be obliged to see and hear all that occurred at the righteous killing. Of course, the brainstorm sheriff assumed that the jail contained the future murderers of Chicago, and assumed that if they saw and heard all the grim act, they would never kill, if, indeed, they ever got out. But this noble experiment does not seem to have produced the intended effect.

The hanging or electrocuting of a human sacrifice can be witnessed by only a few, although nothing else would draw such audiences as this everyday viciousness. Nor are the pictures allowed to be shown in the movies, although this would bring the matter most vividly before the people. And if capital punishment deters, nothing else than witnessing the hangings and other executions could produce the result. No one has yet settled whether the event of execution should be exploited or advertised. If not made public, how can it deter others? If made public, what effect will it have on the born and unborn? Before one starts on a journey, he should know where he wants to go, else he may take the wrong road. Only one thing is certain about capital punishment or its effect, that it is administered for no reason but deep and fixed hatred of the individual and an abiding thirst for revenge.

Whether one is for or against capital punishment depends, in the last analysis, on what sort of person he is; whether he is sensitive and imaginative and emotional, or whether he is cold and stolid and self-centred. And what he is depends on his inherited structure and his environment. So far as I can remember, I got my first impression of capital punishment from my father when I was very young, probably not over seven or eight years old. He told me about a murder that was committed when he was a young man, which happened in the town adjoining the one where he lived. In those days the murderer was hanged outdoors in broad daylight, and every one was invited to see the act and all the grewsome [sic] details that went with it. It was an eager, boisterous and anxious assembly, each pushing and crowding to be in at the moment of the death. My father managed to get well in front where he could watch the spectacle; but, he told me, when he saw the rope adjusted around the man's neck and the black cap pulled over his head, he could stand no more. My father turned away his head and felt humiliated and ashamed for the rest of his life to think that he could have had that much of a hand in killing a fellow man.

In most of the countries of the world the death penalty has been reserved for murder, on the theory, I suppose, that it is the most terrible crime ever committed. How is it so terrible? Is it because a human being has been put to death? If so, execution is just as bad, and much more deliberate. Is it, then, that it is more evil to take life than to commit any other act? If it is because to kill is evil, it means that he has what the law terms a wicked and malignant heart; although, as a matter of fact, the heart is not involved. Should the culprit be hanged because he has a wicked heart? Then all people merit death upon the same logic, for when one hates or despises another he usually wishes the other were dead, and has a feeling of pleasure if he learns of the death. Probably very few people have lived long in this world without wishing that some person or persons would die.

The killer's psychology is not different from that of any other man. Indeed, in a large proportion of the cases the murderer had no malice toward the dead. Is it, then, a worse crime if there is no malice? What then becomes of the wicked and malicious heart, said to be the reason for the crime and for the punishment? Something else must be found as a reason for putting the offender to death. Is he to suffer death because he has so grossly violated some other person's right? There are many other ways of destroying peoples' lives, and it is done day by day, by the slanderer, the libeller, and the one who takes away another's means of livelihood, whether in or out of the protection of the law.

But capital punishment is not administered for murder alone. Even in the State of Illinois there are two offenses punishable by death: murder and kidnapping. The latter is a recent statute passed, like all other new penal laws, when such reason as man has was lost through hatred and fear. Really, this law was passed so that in case a kidnapper takes a child and holds it for ransom, and for some reason the distracted parents cannot or do not pay the ransom, the kidnapper will kill the child to prevent its giving evidence in court. In some States rape is also subject to the death penalty; this, too, is a direct inducement for a ravisher to kill as well as rape; if caught, he must die anyhow, so he is persuaded by the law to kill the evidence of his guilt.

Up to a hundred and twenty-five years ago England punished some two hundred offenses by death. Amongst these were: picking pockets, gypsies remaining in the kingdom one month, the unlawful hunting or killing of deer, stealing fish out of a pond, injuring Westminster Bridge or any other bridge. The early American colonists made twelve offenses punishable by death, among which were blaspheming, the hitting or striking of a parent by a child over sixteen years old, and witchcraft, a favorite crime for which our Puritan fathers provided the death penalty; all the preachers and most of the judges abhorred this offense. To quote Warden Lewis Lawes, of Sing Sing prison, "When they stopped killing witches, witches ceased to exist."'

Why does a portion of the world still insist upon the death penalty for murder? Different people would give different reasons for this, but the real reason is that human beings enjoy the sufferings of others. The issue is always clouded by false statements, foolish inferences, and a wild appeal to the mob. Are there any facts to justify the belief that the death penalty lessens murder? Most of Europe has either abolished it by law or has practically ceased to use it. Italy abolished it for more than fifty years. When Mussolini came into power it was revived for political offenses. But Italy is in the hands of one man who no doubt thinks that his rule rests on arbitrary power. England has kept the death penalty on its books for many years but seldom uses it. England and Wales together, with some fifty million population, do not execute more than from fifteen to twenty people a year. Perhaps thirty or thirty-five are convicted and given the death penalty, but nearly half of these are reprieved in the Home Office; and in England a life term means not more than twenty years.

It has for years been the stock-in-trade of the haters to tell how much better the law is enforced in England than in the United States, and that this is the reason that there is less crime in Great Britain. But the statement is absurd and untrue. In proportion to the population, the United States executes four times as many as England and Wales, and this takes no account of the quasi-judicial killing by lynching of negroes in the South, and even in the North. So long as the hangers here could get by with the statements of the stern enforcement of the law in England they seemed to rest content; but when every one learned the truth they took up a new refrain: It was not that England punished individuals, but that their punishments were surer and quicker. The deterrent is not many punishments, but sure and quick ones, they now say.

No one knows much about why men violate the law, or why they do not. It is probable that the criminal statutes and the convictions have little to do with the conduct that we call crime. Human conduct is not controlled by statutes. It is true that of the people arrested a much larger proportion are convicted in England than here, but what does this prove? Scotland Yard seldom takes any one into custody except on thorough investigation and convincing proof. This is not brought about by the third degree. No officer could remain on the police force in that country if he resorted to the shameless beating and brutality that everywhere prevails in America. When the English police take one into custody he is pretty sure to be guilty. In America it is not uncommon to arrest five or ten, or even fifty, and subject them all to all sorts of indignities in order to find the one man. In the meantime, if the matter is at all sensational, the police are spurred on by continuous startling stories broadcast by the press, and the whole populace gleefully and righteously joins in the man hunt. I do not know how swift and sure is justice in the United States, or in any other land. In truth, I know little about the meaning of the word, and in this all men are alike. But I know this, that there is no country in the world, so far as I have investigated, where in any case that attracts attention a defendant is placed on trial so soon after the alleged offense as in our country. Professionals who criticise the courts in the interest of cruelty are given to pointing to cases that have been long waiting for trial. These delays sometimes happen before trial, sometimes after conviction and retrial. In almost every instance these delays are caused by the prosecution, when they do not dare dismiss the case for fear of criticism and know that they cannot convict.

Here in America it often happens that one is indicted one day and on the way to doom the next; and sometimes on the very same day. In the last few months we have been regaled with the quick responses of judges to public opinion. Really there is no reason for judges to intervene between the mob and the prisoner. They do not, in fact, intervene, but obey orders, and frequently are a part of the mob. These judges have been giving sentences running all the way from one year to one hundred and fifty years. It is only fair to note that in England the public press cannot comment on the facts, or alleged facts, of a criminal case until it is on trial, and then give only the barest report of the testimony. In this country, every detail, clue, surmise, and theory is given out every day until the public is as certain of the guilt of the defendant as the prohibitionist is of the sanctity of the Volstead Act.

When men recover from the obsession that it is only punishment and its dread that keep others from crime, they will be able to undertake the question of social order sanely and scientifically. They will accomplish real results without violating the safeguards of freedom, destroying liberty, and making a nightmare of life. There are more violations of law in America than in any European country; probably many more. What is the cause and what is the remedy? Is it bigger and better laws, or more and harder laws, or bigger and better prisons, or bigger and hotter frying-pans on which to sizzle the victims of luck and chance? Or, is it nothing of the sort?

STATEMENTS IN FAVOR OF THE DEATH PENALTY

J. Edgar Hoover

J. Edgar Hoover directed the Federal Bureau of Investigation from 1924 until his death in 1972. The statements reprinted here about his opinions on the death penalty were made in 1959, 1960, and 1961.

I

The question of capital punishment has sent a storm of controversy thundering across our Nation—millions of spoken and written words seek to examine the question so that decisions may be reached which befit our civilization.

The struggle for answers concerning the taking of men's lives is one to which every American should lend his voice, for the problem in a democracy such as ours is not one for a handful of men to solve alone.

As a representative of law enforcement, it is my belief that a great many of the most vociferous cries for abolition of capital punishment emanate from those areas of our society which have been insulated against the horrors man can and does perpetrate against his fellow beings. Certainly, penetrative and searching thought must be given before considering any blanket cessation of capital punishment in a time when unspeakable crimes are being committed. The savagely mutilated bodies and mentally ravaged victims of murderers, rapists and other criminal beasts beg consideration when the evidence is weighed on both sides of the scales of Justice.

At the same time, nothing is so precious in our country as the life of a human being, whether he is a criminal or not, and on the other side of the scales must be placed all of the legal safeguards which our society demands.

Experience has clearly demonstrated, however, that the time-proven deterrents to crime are sure detection, swift apprehension, and proper punishments. Each is a necessary ingredient. Law-abiding citizens have a right to expect that the efforts of law enforcement officers in detecting and apprehending criminals will be followed by realistic punishment.

It is my opinion that when no shadow of a doubt remains relative to the guilt of a defendant, the public interest demands capital punishment be invoked where the law so provides.

Who, in all good conscience, can say that Julius and Ethel Rosenberg, the spies who delivered the secret of the atomic bomb into the hands of the Soviets, should have been spared when their treachery caused the shadow of annihilation to fall upon all of the world's peoples? What place would there have been in civilization for these two who went to their deaths unrepentant, unwilling to the last to help their own country and their own fellow men? What would have been the

Reprinted from the *F.B.I. Law Enforcement Bulletin*, Vol. 29 (June 1960), Vol. 30 (June 1961), and *Uniform Crime Reports*, 1959, p. 14, respectively.

chances of rehabilitating Jack Gilbert Graham, who placed a bomb in his own mother's luggage and blasted her and forty-three other innocent victims into oblivion as they rode an airliner across a peaceful sky?

A judge once said, "The death penalty is a warning, just like a lighthouse throwing its beams out to sea. We hear about shipwrecks, but we do not hear about the ships the lighthouse guides safely on their way. We do not have proof of the number of ships it saves, but we do not tear the lighthouse down."

Despicable crimes must be dealt with realistically. To abolish the death penalty would absolve other Rosenbergs and Grahams from fear of the consequences for committing atrocious crimes. Where the death penalty is provided, a criminal's punishment may be meted out commensurate with his deeds. While a Power transcending man is the final Judge, this same Power gave man reason so that he might protect himself. Capital punishment is an instrument with which he may guard the righteous against the predators among men.

We must never allow misguided compassion to erase our concern for the hundreds of unfortunate, innocent victims of bestial criminals.

II

The capital punishment question, in which law enforcement officers have a basic interest, has been confused recently by self-styled agitators "against the evil of capital punishment." A brochure released not long ago, pleading for "rehabilitation" of murderers while passing lightly over the plight of the killers' innocent victims and families, charges that law enforcement officers "become so insensitized by their dealings with vicious criminals that they go to the extreme of feeling that the death penalty is absolutely necessary."

To add to the burden of conscience borne by peace officers, prosecutors, and jurists and to brand law enforcement officers as callous, unfeeling men "insensitized" to the sanctity of human life are gross acts of injustice to these servants of the public. This ridiculous allegation is mutely refuted by the compassion which wells up in quiet tears flowing down the cheeks of hardened, veteran officers who too often see the ravaged bodies of victims of child molesters.

There can be no doubt of the sincerity of many of those who deplore capital punishment. A realistic approach to the problem, however, demands that they weigh the right of innocent persons to live their lives free from fear of bestial killers against statistical arguments which boast of how few murderers kill again after "rehabilitation" and release. No one, unless he can probe the mind of every potential killer, can say with any authority whatsoever that capital punishment is not a deterrent. As one police officer has asked, how can these "authorities" possibly know how many people are not on death row because of the deterrent effect of executions?

Maudlin viewers of the death penalty call the most wanton slayer a "child of God" who should not be executed regardless of how heinous his crime may be because "God created man in his own image, in the image of God created he him." (Genesis 1:27) Was not this small, blonde six-year-old girl a child of God? She was choked, beaten, and raped by a sex fiend whose pregnant wife reportedly helped him lure the innocent child into his car and who sat and watched the assault on the screaming youngster. And when he completed his inhuman deed, the wife, herself bringing a life into the world, allegedly killed the child with several savage blows with a tire iron. The husband has been sentenced to death. Words and words and words may be written, but no plea in favor of the death penalty can be more horribly eloquent than the sight of the battered, sexually assaulted body of this child, truly a "child of God."

The proponents of "rehabilitation" for all murderers quote those portions of the Bible which they believe support their lavender-and-old-lace world where evil is neither recognized nor allowed. But the Bible clearly reveals that enforcement of moral justice is nothing new to our age. In fact, in referring to man as the "image of God," the Old Testament, so freely quoted by opponents of the death penalty, also states, "Whoso sheddeth man's blood, by man shall his blood be shed: for in the image of God made he man." (Genesis 9:6). There are many passages in the Old Testament which refer to capital punishment being necessary to enforce the laws of society. Since the Old Testament was written about and to a nation while the New Testament was written to individuals and to a nonpolitical body known as the Church, there is a difference in emphasis and approach. Certainly, however, the moral laws of the Old Testament remain with us today.

Misguided do-gooders frequently quote the Sixth Commandment, "Thou shalt not kill," to prove that capital punishment is wrong. This Commandment in the twentieth chapter, verse 13, of Exodus has also been interpreted to mean: "Thou shalt do no murder." Then the twenty-first chapter, verse 12, says, "He that smiteth a man, so that he die, shall be surely put to death." We can no more change the application to our society of this basic moral law in the Old Testament than we can change the meaning of Leviticus 19:18: "thou shalt love thy neighbor as thyself," which Jesus quoted in the New Testament.

To "love thy neighbor" is to protect him; capital punishment acts as at least one wall to afford "God's children" protection.

III

Most states have capital punishment; a few do not. For the most part, capital punishment is associated with the crime of murder. Some states have high murder rates; some do not. Of those states with low murder rates, some have capital punishment; some do not. The number of murders that occur within a state as indicated by rates is due to a wide range of social, human and material factors.

It would be convenient for a study of the effects of capital punishment as a deterrent if states fell neatly into two groups: (1) those with low murder rates and capital punishment; and (2) those with high murder rates and no capital punishment. Or, if the user of these statistics is making a case against capital punishment, he would prefer to demonstrate that the states with low murder rates are those that do not have capital punishment. But to expect such an oversimplification of a highly complex subject is to engage in wishful thinking or a futile groping for proof that is not there.

Some who propose the abolishment of capital punishment select statistics that "prove" their point and ignore those that point the other way. Comparisons of murder rates between the nine states which abolished the death penalty or qualified its use and the forty-one states which have retained it either individually, before or after abolition, or by group are completely inconclusive.

The professional law enforcement officer is convinced from experience that the hardened criminal has been and is deterred from killing based on the prospect of the death penalty. It is possible that the deterrent effect of capital punishment is greater in states with a high murder rate if the conditions which contribute to the act of murder develop more frequently in those states. For the law enforcement officer the time-proven deterrents to crime are sure detection, swift apprehension, and proper punishment. Each is a necessary ingredient.

WITNESS TO AN EXECUTION

Terry FitzPatrick

Terry FitzPatrick wrote this firsthand account of an execution in Texas for the Texas Observer *in 1992. You will need to infer his claim.*

I must confess that I *wanted* to see the execution of Johnny Frank Garrett. It took a bit of journalistic hustle to secure a place on the five-member press pool. My friends told me that I should examine my motives before I went. I didn't. I marched toward the Death House at midnight to satisfy insatiable journalistic curiosity. I just wanted to get *inside*.

The Death House is a brick bunker tucked inside The Walls prison unit in downtown Huntsville. Inside it's painted milky blue. It must be the most brightly lighted place in the entire Texas prison system. The room is small; only a few feet and silver, metal prison bars separated Garrett from his family. I stood directly behind Garrett's mother. The executioner stood in a separate room behind a pane of mirrored glass. Thin intravenous tubes ran through a small opening in the wall, into both arms of the prisoner.

Garrett was strapped to a gurney, with white leather belts across his chest, belly, thighs, knees, and ankles. His hands were concealed by tape. His arms were strapped outward at right angles. From above, it must have looked like he was on a crucifix.

Garrett was in a defiant mood and was clearly agitated. He was already on the gurney when the press contingent entered a few minutes past midnight. I'd seen Garrett many times before, in courtrooms, in jails, in those undignified hallway shuffles past the packs of reporters and cameras. He had always seemed

Texas Observer, February 28, 1992, p. 10.

calm, a bit detached. Back then, his prison haircuts, long sideburns, and thick eyebrows made him look like a Neanderthal. But here in the Death House, Garrett was clean shaven with his hair neatly combed back. He was very thin, clothed in pressed prison blues and new, white canvas shoes. His last meal had been chocolate ice cream. He had the look of panic: wide eyes, short breaths, tense movements of the head. Despite the psychiatrist's assessment that Garrett didn't believe a lethal injection would kill him, it seemed to me that Johnny Frank Garrett knew he was about to die.

His family was tightly huddled when I entered. His mother, two sisters, stepfather, and brother-in-law clutched the prison bars as Garrett strained to turn his head to the right to speak his final words.

"I'd like to thank my friends who tried to pull me through all this. My guru for helping me go through this. I'd like to thank my family for loving me. And the rest of the world can kiss my ass."

Garrett looked at the warden as he spoke that last part. Then he jerked his head toward the white ceiling to show he was ready. Garrett began to recite some kind of prayer or mantra to himself and the warden made a barely perceptible signal to the anonymous executioner behind the mirrored glass.

It was over in an instant: Garrett's mouth caught open in mid-speech, his eyes open—frozen with a small squint of recognition that poison was racing through his veins.

His mother kept saying "I love you son, it's okay. Go to sleep," as if it were a lullaby. Garrett's sisters were angry. "They're gonna' pay," one sister said.

With that, Garrett's mother tried to console her daughters. "God forgives those who forgive his brothers," she said. "He's at peace. He paid his debt. We all have to do that."

"He's in a better place than we are," the sister replied. "There aren't any assholes to tell him what to do."

The family sang Amazing Grace in broken tearful voices.

Texas uses three drugs in executions: sodium thiopental to relax the prisoner and induce sleep, pancuronium bromide to paralyze the muscles and prevent breathing, and potassium chloride to stop the heart. The dose is large enough to kill 10 people. The injection lasted four minutes, though life had slipped from Garrett's body just seconds after it began.

The executioner placed a roll of white adhesive tape in the small opening in the wall, beside the clear intravenous tubes, to indicate the injection was over. A prison doctor ambled in and searched perfunctorily for a pulse on Garrett's neck and arm, and then listened to Garrett's chest through a stethoscope for just an instant. He turned to the warden and compared the time on their watches. "I figure 12:18."

With that the heavy metal doors swung open with a startling thud. We filed out of the Death House behind the family. Nobody said a word. Officials looked at the floor as they walked. And Garrett lay there still. There were no gestures of respect for his corpse. Nobody covered him with a sheet, or closed his lifeless eyes. There was no dignity in this death.

We stepped outside the prison into the glare of television lights. A crowd of students from the nearby university broke out in cheers and applause, singing "na-na-na-na, hey-hey-hey, good bye." I felt ashamed as I walked with Garrett's family to the prison administration building across the street. The students weren't jeering at just the family, they were jeering at me. I felt my privileged press-pool access made me a participant in the execution as well as an observer. As a citizen of Texas, I realized that Johnny Frank Garrett had been executed in my name.

TURNING BAD INTO GOOD

Graeme Newman

Graeme Newman, a professor at the School of Criminal Justice of the State University of New York at Albany, writes arguments about the treatment of criminals that have original slants. These are excerpts from an article that first appeared in the magazine Chronicles *in 1992.*

In 1983 I noted in *Just and Painful: A Case for the Corporal Punishment of Criminals* that there were approximately 315,000 individuals incarcerated in federal and state prisons, plus some 158,000 persons in jails of various kinds. The annual cost of this incarceration was estimated then to be $20,000 per inmate, amounting to an annual expenditure of some $10 billion.

The solution I advocated at that time was to replace much of the punishment of prison with corporal punishment of a specific type: one that applied acute pain (that is, intense sharp pain of very brief duration). [. . .]

But I am humbled by the fact that hardly anyone takes my solution to the punishment problem seriously, especially since things have become much worse since 1983. Today there are over 600,000 persons in prison plus some 405,000 in jails. The annual cost is somewhere in the vicinity of $40,000 per inmate, and to build a new cell costs approximately $100,000. Why has the situation become so much worse? Why has no credible alternative to prison arisen? [. . .]

There have, of course, been alternatives to prison, but these attempts themselves demonstrate the very failure to understand the profound centrality of punishment to social life. The most well-known "alternative" was, of course, probation, introduced on a large scale in the United States early this century. It turned out to be largely an add-on "punishment" simply finding additional offenders. Worse, probation failed to convince the general public that it was in fact punitive enough. The great solution of the 1980's was supposed to be "community service," but unless its punitive element is sharpened, it will go the way of probation: people will see it, justifiably, as yet another attempt to subvert the punishment process. It turns "punishment" into "service" and "service" into "punish-

Chronicles, May 1992, pp. 19–22.

ment" by taking away the intrinsic merit of service from those who would normally volunteer for it.

Yet the idea embedded in community service is morally attractive: it tries to draw out of the punishment process something "good"—service to the community. This is an important idea that, unfortunately in the way it is currently implemented, will go the way of other "alternatives" to punishment, because it does not address the fact that punishment must be punishment. The public, in my view, understands and demands this. Legislators understand this to a point, by enacting severe prison terms, but they ignore the fiscal implications of their legislation. These alternatives to prison have simply subverted the central idea of punishment: the intentional and deliberate infliction of pain and suffering on the offender. [. . .]

I propose, therefore, to turn to the other end of the criminal justice system, and ask what we might do to those few who have been condemned to death for the most hideous of crimes. Theirs is behavior that is not so difficult to pronounce as evil, and whose behavior we might try to avoid in our punishment. At the same time, though, in an effort to raise ourselves above the level of the murderer, we must try to extract something good out of the evil that we do to the murderer (such as the application of the death penalty) even though he may well deserve to suffer terribly for his crimes.

What "good" did the execution of the serial killer Ted Bundy do? We know that such penalties do not deter, so this was not the "good." Did it "satisfy" justice? But what kind of justice is it that feeds on the killing of individuals? Is it good to feel satisfied after killing someone, even though the person deserved it? I do not argue that the motives for killing are identical, but I do insist that there are psychological elements of both acts that are similar. The most obvious similarity is that both killings are intentional. I contend that there is no positive aspect in the infliction of pain or suffering on an individual, even when it is justified. We need to work hard, therefore, to turn this act of violence into something that *is* positive. The mere taking away of the murderer's life does not fulfill this need.

The answer lies in the very common complaint of murderers on death row. They announce that they are "sorry" for what they did (though it's often hard to believe them), but add, what can they do? Their victims are dead, they say, and they can't bring them back to life. True enough. But if we pause for a moment, we see the answer: while they cannot bring their victims back to life, they can save the life (and perhaps lives) of others. They could donate their body parts. In this way, one executed criminal's body could possibly save several lives. I would go so far as to say that the condemned murderer should be *made* to give up his body organs. The social and moral good could be enhanced tremendously by this practice.

There is a critical shortage of donor organs. As of 1987, for example, there were over 13,000 individuals waiting for organs of one kind or another, and the number is closer to 20,000 today. The U.S. government spent $300,000 in 1990 on Medicare assistance for each of the 60,000 Americans who require kidney dialysis. Thus, each executed murderer is "worth" at least $600,000 just for the two kidneys alone. In 1987 there were more than 12,000 individuals waiting for kidney transplants, and only some 2,500 donors. A liver transplant costs about $150,000. The need, therefore, is critical.

The fantastic service that executed murderers could provide by saving lives is tremendous. While their suffering may not make up for the specific suffering and loss of the particular victim, the victim's family and society as well can at least take comfort in the fact that two terrible deeds—the murder and the execution—have been turned at least to a truly positive outcome: saving lives and improving the quality of life of many others. This is true community service, while at the same time preserving the punitive element of the punishment.

There are, of course, many obvious objections to this idea. I anticipate, for example, complaints that the government will execute more murderers in order to obtain more body parts. This is indeed a cynical view of government. It should be possible to introduce legislative safeguards to fend off this pitfall, if it is a pitfall. There may also be some concern about an individual living with a serial murderer's heart or other body part. Patients receiving such organs would need to be counseled carefully. Whether it should even be known from whom the organs came is a question that would need to be addressed. Others might complain of a slippery slope, since some organs, such as kidneys, could be extracted from prisoners without killing them. Why not trade off years in prison for donating a kidney? And could an inmate "freely volunteer" parts of his body in order to get out of prison? For the moment, we should begin only with executed prisoners, and if this works, then look to its extension in other settings.

When I advocated corporal punishment for most offenders some nine years ago, I thought that the enormous cost of using prisons for punishment would sooner or later bring the system down. The massive increase in the use of prisons since that time has so far proven me wrong. The problem of punishment is not motivated or limited by fiscal concerns. Rather, it is a problem of moral psychology, as I have argued in this essay. We must try hard to solve this distinctly late-20th-century problem of punishment by beginning to acknowledge the deep-seated shame we have about punishing. We should not be ashamed to use punishment in order to save lives. In doing so, we may turn not only the bad of the offender into good, but also the bad of the punishment process itself into something good.

3. What Should Be Done with Young Offenders?

PUNISHMENT

Patricia Cohen

Cohen wrote this article for the magazine George.

It's Friday, the equivalent of open-mike night in Judge Michael Corriero's Manhattan courtroom. There's the ninth-grader who went on a robbery spree, the two girls who wielded a butcher's knife to steal a 12-year-old's knapsack, the 15-year-

George, June/July 1996, p. 99.

old accused of fatally shooting a man. Judge Corriero, who could pass for Al Pacino's younger brother, listens intently before deciding who gets jail and who gets probation, who gets youthful-offender status and who gets thrown into the much harsher adult system.

Rehabilitation or punishment? This vexing question, which Corriero weighs dozens of times each day, lies at the heart of a major political and philosophical battle over juvenile crime, which could have the emotional explosiveness of last year's welfare reform debate.

This crackdown on young lawbreakers has been fueled by the rising number of juveniles arrested for violent crimes. After remaining virtually constant between 1972 and the late '80s, the juvenile crime rate nation-wide began to spike in 1990 and by 1992 had reached a 20-year high. From 1988 to 1991, the youth murder-arrest rate climbed 80 percent. A handful of stomach-churning incidents also made teenage offenders seem more impulsive and vicious. Now, Hawaii is the only state that treats all kids under age 16 as juveniles. In Illinois and North Carolina, 13-year-old offenders can be treated as adults; in Vermont, 10 is the cut-off. In New York, only murder suspects under age seven are automatically treated as juveniles, and Governor George Pataki recently vowed to further toughen the state's law.

Both Democrats and Republicans have recognized the political rewards of outraged fist-pounding: 700 legislative proposals to prosecute minors as adults were introduced last year, a trend that President Clinton promised, in his State of the Union address, to pursue.

Meanwhile, 24 states allow kids under the age of 18 to get the death penalty. Although no criminal has been executed while a minor, some sentenced while minors have been put to death. Currently, 42 juveniles sit on death row.

CRACKDOWN ON KIDS: GIVING UP ON THE YOUNG

Mike Males and Faye Docuyanan

Males and Docuyanan are social ecology doctoral students at the University of California, Irvine.

Madness is the word Stephen Bruner uses to describe the summer of 1992. "The things I did, things I had done to me. . . . Madness." It was the summer after eighth grade. He and his gang Panic Zone hung out where the rural black community of Spencer intersects the southeast Oklahoma City suburb of Midwest City. He rattles off the names of a dozen gangs—Hoover Street, Westside, Candlewood, 6–0—that inhabit the district.

The Progressive, February 1996, pp. 24–26.

For his contribution to the madness, Bruner spent his ninth grade in an Oklahoma juvenile lockup. Now Bruner works as an intern for Wayne Thompson at the Oklahoma Health Care Project in Founder's Tower overlooking the city's opulent northwest side. Thompson himself spent three years in prison in the 1970s at Terminal Island and Lompoc for armed bank robbery on behalf of the San Francisco Black Panther chapter.

Madness, Thompson suggests, is "the natural, predictable reaction" of youths to the "larger, hostile adult culture that is anti-youth, particularly anti-African-American youth."

Twenty thousand more Oklahoma City children and teenagers live in poverty than a quarter of a century ago. "These kids are at risk of extinction if they depend upon adults to protect them," Thompson says. It is not just parents who fail them, but an adult society increasingly angry and punishing toward its youth. "That is the perception of the young people who are being ground up in this culture and the grinder of the juvenile-justice system. Their perception of their situation is very correct."

Today, state after state is imposing harsher penalties on juveniles who run afoul of the law. "The nationwide trend is to get tough on juvenile crime," says Gary Taylor of Legal Aid of Western Oklahoma. Rehabilitation and reintegration into the community are concepts that have already fallen out of fashion for adult criminals. Now they are fast becoming passé for juveniles, as well. Instead of prevention and rehabilitation programs, more prisons are being built to warehouse juveniles along with adults. The trend began in California; it is now sweeping the nation.

Juveniles are being waived into adult court at lower and lower ages. In Wisconsin, ten-year-olds can now be tried as adults for murder. Juveniles convicted of drug offenses in adult court receive lengthy mandatory sentences. In California, studies by the state corrections department show that youths serve sentences 60 percent longer than adults for the same crimes. Oklahoma wants to try thirteen-year-olds as adults and petitioned the Supreme Court to allow executions of fourteen- and fifteen-year-olds.

And it's not just the states. It's the [Federal] Administration, too. *The New York Times* reported in December [1995] that "proposals by the Administration would allow more access to juvenile records and give federal prosecutors discretion to charge serious juvenile offenders as adults."

In short, we are giving up on human beings at a younger and younger age.

Juvenile crime is on the rise. But the reason is not media violence, rap music, or gun availability—easy scapegoats that have little to do with the patterns of violence in real life. Rather, the reason is rising youth poverty.

Sensational press accounts make it seem as though juvenile crime is patternless. It is hardly that. Juvenile crime is closely tied to youth poverty and the growing opportunity gap between wealthier, older people and destitute, younger people. Of California's fifty-eight counties, thirty-one with a total of 2.5 million people recorded zero teenage murders in 1993. Central Los Angeles, which has roughly the same number of people, reported more than 200 teen murders.

In the thirty-one counties free of teenage killers, the same blood-soaked media and rock and rap music are readily available (more, since white suburban families over-subscribe to cable TV), and guns are easy to obtain. Nor can some "innate" teenage qualities be the cause, since by definition those qualities are as present in youths in areas where violent teenage crime is rare as in areas where it is common.

"We see kids from *all* walks of life," says Harry Hartmann, counselor with the L.A. Office of Education. But "the races are skewed to blacks and Hispanics," he acknowledges. Very skewed—six out of seven of those who are arrested for violent juvenile crimes are black or Hispanic. By strange coincidence, that is just about the proportion of the county's youths in poverty who are black or Hispanic.

"Poverty in a society of affluence, in which your self-esteem is tied to failure to achieve that affluence," is a more accurate explanation for our uniquely high level of violence, says Gilbert Geiss, a criminologist formerly with the University of California, Irvine. It's not just "poverty, per se."

L.A. County is a clear illustration. Its per-capita income is much higher, and its general poverty rate lower, than the United States as a whole. But its youth poverty rate is staggering: 200,000 impoverished adolescents live in the county.

L.A. County is home to one in fifteen teenage murderers in the United States. Its vast basin harbors such a bewildering array of gangs and posses that estimates of the number of youths allied with them at any one time are almost impossible to pin down.

Jennifer, seventeen, at the Search to Involve Pilipino Americans (SIPA), a local community center, rattles off the names of twenty youth gangs, takes a breath, admits she has left some out. Los Angeles County (population 9 million) has more teen murders than the dozen largest industrial nations outside the United States combined. Of L.A.'s 459 teen murder arrestees in 1994, just twenty-four were white. Blacks and Hispanics predominated, but Asian Americans comprise the fastest-rising group of violent juveniles.

"I tried to ask them, 'Why are you in it?'" Jennifer says. "They don't know. A lot of people regret it after. 'Yeah, that was some stupid shit.' They thought it was so cool." But if stupid, confused kids were the whole problem, why are black kids in Los Angeles a dozen times stupider than white kids? Why are Asians getting stupider faster than anyone else?

As youth poverty rises and becomes more concentrated in destitute urban neighborhoods, violence becomes more concentrated in younger age groups.

But today's reigning criminal-justice experts—UCLA's James Q. Wilson, Northwestern's James Allen Fox, Princeton's John D'Iulio, former Robert Kennedy aide Adam Walinsky—dismiss poverty as a cause of youth violence. Instead, they talk about an insidious culture of poverty, and they argue relentlessly that only more cops and more prisons will bring down juvenile crime. Instead of proposing more money for alleviating poverty or for crime prevention, they want more law enforcement—at a cost of tens of billions of dollars.

Writing in the September 1994 *Commentary*, Wilson calls the growing adolescent population "a cloud" that "lurks . . . just beyond the horizon." It will bring "30,000 more muggers, killers, and thieves than we have now." Wilson downplays poverty, racism, poor schools, and unemployment as "not . . . major causes of crime at all." The real problem, he writes, is "wrong behavior" by a fraction of the population (he pegs it at 6 percent) with bad temperament, concentrated in chaotic families and "disorderly neighborhoods."

If more prisons and surer sentences were the solutions to crime and delinquency, California should be a haven where citizens leave doors unlocked and stroll midnight streets unmenaced. California inaugurated the new era of imprisoning juvenile offenders in Ronald Reagan's second term as governor in 1971, and since then the state has incarcerated a higher percentage of its youths than any other state. By 1993, a state corrections study found teenagers served terms nearly a year longer than adults for equivalent offenses.

"I tell parents who want to release their kid to the [juvenile-justice] system: he might come out worse than when he went in," says Gilbert Aruyao of SIPA.

Eleven hundred new state laws passed during the 1980s set longer, more certain prison terms, especially for juveniles. California's forty-one-prison, 140,000-inmate system is the third-largest in the world; only the United States as a whole and China have larger inmate systems.

The Golden State's biggest growth industry is corrections. Seven new prisons opened in California from 1989 to 1994, at a cost of $1.3 billion, to accommodate 16,000 more prisoners; today, they confine 28,000 prisoners. From 1995 through 1996, four new prisons, costing $839 million, will open their doors. There's a new prison built every eight months. Each one is full upon opening.

"For that incorrigible 25 percent (of youth offenders), prisons may be the only way to go," says Harry Hartmann of the L.A. Office of Education. "It's really hard for them to change." In California in 1994, 140,000 persons under the age of twenty were arrested for felonies—including one out of five black males, and one in ten Hispanic males ages sixteen through nineteen. If even one-tenth of that number must be imprisoned more or less permanently, the state's minority teenage male population will require four new prisons every year to contain them.

As youth poverty mushrooms and the attitudes of the larger society become harsher, the traditional markers of race and class are sliding toward new realignments. "There's still a racial element, sure," says Thompson. "But this has gone beyond race now. There's a larger madness."

Says Bruner: "There are white kids in black gangs, blacks in Mexican gangs, Mexicans in white gangs, blacks in white gangs, Asians in black gangs. We don't fight each other that way. It isn't a race thing. It's who's in the 'hood.'"

The *1995 Kids Count Factbook* lists 47,000 impoverished children and adolescents in the Oklahoma City metropolitan area—21,000 whites, 13,500 blacks, 4,500 Native Americans, 3,000 Asian Americans, 5,000 Latinos.

A November 1995 *Daily Oklahoman* series on the metropolis's exploding poverty reported that these adolescents are increasingly isolated, jammed together in a chain of destitute neighborhoods ringing downtown and extending eastward past the suburbs.

"You go to school with them, people ask of this guy you know, 'Is he OK with you, 'cause if he's OK with you, he's OK with me,'" says Bruner. "If you're in a subcultural group, it's no different in society's eyes whether you're in a gang or not. Kids had no choice but to hang with us. Racism is here. You can't run away from it. [But] racism is not just black or white." Nonwhite youths, white youths on the wrong side, "we are all targets."

Bruner is training in office management and in television production and editing through Thompson's program. Enough of his friends remain trapped in the justice system. Bruner sees that as surrender. "They didn't get out like I did; now they're up for murder one."

Bruner says the system is rigged: "I believe they want to keep me and every other black male and minority male and poor kid in the system permanently, send us all to the penitentiary."

In 1988, Oklahoma petitioned the U.S. Supreme Court to execute fourteen- and fifteen-year-olds (and lost only on a 5–4 vote).

"Society wants to kill these kids," says Thompson. "The death penalty. Shooting them in the street. If it can't do that, then killing their spirit."

Gary Taylor, deputy director of Legal Aid of Western Oklahoma, recounts his agency's efforts to reform a juvenile prison system whose brutality and puni- tive excesses had been exposed nationally. "Beatings, sexual assaults, hog tying, extreme medical punishments, extreme isolation," said Taylor. "It was kid-kid; it was staff-kid."

There was no notion of rehabilitation. San Francisco lawyers for convicted murderer Freddy Lee Taylor investigated his incarceration in the Oklahoma juve- nile prison system and found "a concentration-camp environment," attorney Robert Rionda said.

Many of these youths were wrongly imprisoned: they had been removed from their homes because their parents were abusive or neglectful, or the youths had committed minor offenses like curfew violations or truancy. Rionda's firm did not have to look hard to find Freddy Taylor's co-inmates: most were now in state prison serving terms for major felonies.

"There were many, many kids who were in the system because they were poor and in need of supervision, and they turned them into monsters," Rionda said.

In recent years, twice as many Oklahoma youths have been placed in the adult prison system as in the juvenile system. Oklahoma imprisons more of its citizens than any other state except Texas. If forcing youths into the adult prisons and administering harsh punishment is the remedy, Oklahoma, like California, should be a paradise of peace.

Yet arrest figures over the last decade show Oklahoma's juvenile violence growing at twice the already alarming national pace.

Los Angeles County and Oklahoma City officials stress prevention but note that it is underfunded. The most effective prevention effort by far is to raise fewer children in poverty. However, "reducing child poverty, much less eliminating it, is no longer a paramount priority for either political party," *U.S. News & World Report* pointed out in November 1995.

Wayne Thompson in Oklahoma City takes prevention seriously. "We ap- proach juvenile crime as a public-health problem, not a law-enforcement problem," says Thompson. "Intervene, then trace the pathology back to its source." The source inevitably turns out to be "the low social, educational, and economic status of the families and communities" violent youths come from.

Thompson's program uses employment training and a variety of family services to reintegrate youths who have already been convicted back into their communities. "We want to empower these young people to change the social and economic circumstances of their lives," he says.

An initial evaluation showed that Thompson's program was more effective than law-enforcement approaches in preventing recidivism among delinquent youths as well as preventing younger members of their families from following in their older siblings' footsteps. The clientele served by the program is small— fewer than 100 youths per year.

The adults most responsive to Thompson's approach are in the business community, Republicans more than Democrats, he notes. "That's frightening," he says. "The social services, academia, are bound like serfs to the status quo."

When he talks to Oklahoma City's business groups, Thompson finds growing concern over the costs of more prisons and "alarm in the white community because the gangs are becoming more integrated." He doesn't push charity or altruism.

"I tell them, 'You're going to die in fifteen or twenty years, and you have grandchildren. They're going to have to live with the environment we've created. And we've created a hellacious environment.' This is not just some teenage rite-of-passage problem. The alienation of young people from the traditional institutions is profound. This is the legacy we're leaving: armed camps. If we don't learn how to share with the people who are now powerless, this culture is ultimately going to acquire the means to bring our society to an end."

WHO SHOT JOHNNY?

Debra Dickerson

Dickerson is a lawyer in Washington, D.C.

Given my level of political awareness, it was inevitable that I would come to view the everyday events of my life through the prism of politics and the national discourse. I read *The Washington Post, The New Republic, The New Yorker, Harper's, The Atlantic Monthly, The Nation, National Review, Black Enterprise* and *Essence* and wrote a weekly column for the Harvard Law School Record during my three years just ended there. I do this because I know that those of us who are not well-fed white guys in suits must not yield the debate to them, however well-

The New Republic, January 1, 1996, pp. 17–18.

intentioned or well-informed they may be. Accordingly, I am unrepentant and vocal about having gained admittance to Harvard through affirmative action; I am a feminist, stoic about my marriage chances as a well-educated, 36-year-old black woman who won't pretend to need help taking care of herself. My strength flags, though, in the face of the latest role assigned to my family in the national drama. On July 27, 1995, my 16-year-old nephew was shot and paralyzed.

Talking with friends in front of his home, Johnny saw a car he thought he recognized. He waved boisterously—his trademark—throwing both arms in the air in a full-bodied, hip-hop Y. When he got no response, he and his friends sauntered down the walk to join a group loitering in front of an apartment building. The car followed. The driver got out, brandished a revolver and fired into the air. Everyone scattered. Then he took aim and shot my running nephew in the back.

Johnny never lost consciousness. He lay in the road, trying to understand what had happened to him, why he couldn't get up. Emotionlessly, he told the story again and again on demand, remaining apologetically firm against all demands to divulge the missing details that would make sense of the shooting but obviously cast him in a bad light. Being black, male and shot, he must, apparently, be gang- or drug-involved. Probably both. Witnesses corroborate his version of events.

Nearly six months have passed since that phone call in the night and my nightmarish, headlong drive from Boston to Charlotte. After twenty hours behind the wheel, I arrived haggard enough to reduce my mother to fresh tears and to find my nephew reassuring well-wishers with an eerie sangfroid.

I take the day shift in his hospital room; his mother and grandmother, a clerk and cafeteria worker, respectively, alternate nights there on a cot. They don their uniforms the next day, gaunt after hours spent listening to Johnny moan in his sleep. How often must his subconscious replay those events and curse its hosts for saying hello without permission, for being carefree and young while a would-be murderer hefted the weight of his uselessness and failure like Jacob Marley's chains? How often must he watch himself lying stubbornly immobile on the pavement of his nightmares while the sound of running feet syncopate his attacker's taunts?

I spend these days beating him at gin rummy and Scrabble, holding a basin while he coughs up phlegm and crying in the corridor while he catheterizes himself. There are children here much worse off then he. I should be grateful. The doctors can't, or won't, say whether he'll walk again.

I am at once repulsed and fascinated by the bullet, which remains lodged in his spine (having done all the damage it can do, the doctors say). The wound is undramatic—small, neat and perfectly centered—an impossibly pink pit surrounded by an otherwise undisturbed expanse of mahogany. Johnny has asked me several times to describe it but politely declines to look in the mirror I hold for him.

Here on the pediatric rehab ward, Johnny speaks little, never cries, never complains, works diligently to become independent. He does whatever he is told; if two hours remain until the next pain pill, he waits quietly. Eyes bloodshot, hands gripping the bed rails. During the week of his intravenous feeding when he was tormented by the primal need to masticate, he never asked for food. He just listened while we counted down the days for him and planned his favorite meals. Now required to dress himself unassisted, he does so without demur, rolling himself back and forth valiantly on the bed and shivering afterwards, exhausted. He "ma'am"s and "sir"s everyone politely. Before his "accident," a simple request to take out the trash could provoke a firestorm of teenage attitude. We, the women who have raised him, have changed as well; we've finally come to appreciate those boxer-baring, oversized pants we used to hate—it would be much more difficult to fit properly sized pants over his diaper.

He spends a lot of time tethered to rap music still loud enough to break my concentration as I read my many magazines. I hear him try to soundlessly mouth the obligatory "mothafuckers" overlaying the funereal dirge of the music tracks. I do not normally tolerate disrespectful music in my or my mother's presence, but if it distracts him now . . .

"Johnny," I ask later, "do you still like gangster rap?" During the long pause I hear him think loudly, *I'm paralyzed Auntie, not stupid.* "I mostly just listen to hip hop," he says evasively into his *Sports Illustrated.*

Miserable though it is, time passes quickly here. We always seem to be jerking awake in our chairs just in time for the next pill, his every-other-night bowel program, the doctor's rounds. Harvard feels a galaxy away—the world revolves around Family Members Living With Spinal Cord Injury class, Johnny's urine output and strategizing with my sister to find affordable, accessible housing. There is always another long-distance uncle in need of an update, another church member wanting to pray with us or Johnny's little brother in need of some attention.

We Dickerson women are so constant a presence the ward nurses and cleaning staff call us by name and join us for cafeteria meals and cigarette breaks. At Johnny's birthday pizza party, they crack jokes and make fun of each other's husbands (there are no men here). I pass slices around and try not to think, "17 with a bullet."

Oddly, we feel little curiosity or specific anger toward the man who shot him. We have to remind ourselves to check in with the police. Even so, it feels pro forma, like sending in those $2 rebate forms that come with new pantyhose: you know your request will fall into a deep, dark hole somewhere but, still, it's your duty to try. We push for an arrest because we owe it to Johnny and to ourselves as citizens. We don't think about it otherwise—our low expectations are too ingrained. A Harvard aunt notwithstanding, for people like Johnny, Marvin Gaye was right that only three things are sure: taxes, death and trouble. At least it wasn't the second.

We rarely wonder about or discuss the brother who shot him because we already know everything about him. When the call came, my first thought was the same one I'd had when I'd heard about Rosa Parks's beating: a brother did it. A non-job-having, middle-of-the-day malt-liquor-drinking, crotch-clutching, loud-talking brother with many neglected children born of many forgotten women. He lives in his mother's basement with furniture rented at an astronomical interest rate, the exact amount of which he does not know. He has a car phone, an $80 monthly cable bill and every possible phone feature but no savings. He steals Social Security numbers from unsuspecting relatives and assumes their identities to acquire large TV sets for which he will never pay. On the slim chance that he is brought to justice, he will have a colorful criminal history and no coherent explanation to offer for this act. His family will raucously defend him and cry cover-up. Some liberal lawyer just like me will help him plea bargain his way to yet another short stay in a prison pesthouse that will serve only to add another layer to the brother's sociopathology and formless, mindless nihilism. We know him. We've known and feared him all our lives.

As a teenager, he called, "Hey, baby, gimme somma that boodie!" at us from car windows. Indignant at our lack of response, he followed up with, "Fuck you, then, 'ho!" He called me a "white-boy lovin' nigger bitch oreo" for being in the gifted program and loving it. At 27, he got my 17-year-old sister pregnant with Johnny and lost interest without ever informing her that he was married. He snatched my widowed mother's purse as she waited in pre-dawn darkness for the bus to work and then broke into our house while she soldered on an assembly line. He chased all the small entrepreneurs from our neighborhood with his violent thievery, and put bars on our windows. He kept us from sitting on our own front porch after dark and laid the foundation for our periodic bouts of self-hating anger and racial embarrassment. He made our neighborhood a ghetto. He is the poster fool behind the maddening community knowledge that there are still some black mothers who raise their daughters but merely love their sons. He and his cancerous carbon copies eclipse the vast majority of us who are not sociopaths and render us invisible. He is the Siamese twin who has died but cannot be separated from his living, vibrant sibling; which of us must attract more notice? We despise and disown this anomalous loser but, for many, he *is* black America. We know him, we know that he is outside the fold, and we know that he will only get worse. What we didn't know is that, because of him, my little sister would one day be the latest hysterical black mother wailing over a fallen child on TV.

Alone, lying in the road bleeding and paralyzed but hideously conscious, Johnny had lain helpless as he watched his would-be murderer come to stand over him and offer this prophecy: "Betch'ou won't be doin' nomo' wavin', motha' fucker."

Fuck you, asshole. He's fine from the waist up. You just can't do anything right, can you?

PEACE IN THE STREETS

Geoffrey Canada

Canada is president and CEO of Harlem's Rheedlen Center for Children and Families, which serves at-risk inner-city children. Canada is also largely responsible for the Beacon Schools and the Peacemakers program in Harlem and is the East Coast coordinator for the Children's Defense Fund's Black Community Crusade for Children. This is an excerpt from his book, Fist Stick Knife Gun *as printed in the* Utne Reader *magazine.*

It's a Wednesday night in October and I'm early for my martial arts class in Harlem. I walk into the brightly lit gym and all eyes turn toward me. I'm walking with purpose, quickly and silently. A little boy begins to run over to me and an older student grabs his arm. I see him whispering in the younger boy's ear. I'm sure he's telling him, "You can't talk to him before class." And he's right. I stand in front of my class, looking unhappy and displeased. Everyone wonders who is out of place or not standing up straight. This is part of my act. Finally I begin the class and then I'm lost in the teaching. I'm trying to bring magic into the lives of these kids. To bring a sense of wonder and amazement. I can feel the students losing themselves and focusing on me. They are finally mine. I have them all to myself. I have crowded all the bad things out of their minds: The test they failed, the father who won't come by to see them, the dinner that won't be on the stove when they get home. I've pushed it all away by force of will and magic.

This is my time and I know all the tricks. I yell, I scream, I fly through the air with the greatest of ease. And by the time the class is ending my students' eyes are wide with amazement and respect, and they look at me differently. I line them up and I talk to them. I talk to them about values, violence, and hope. I try to build within each one a reservoir of strength that they can draw from as they face the countless tribulations small and large that poor children face every day. And I try to convince each one that I know their true value, their worth as human beings, their special gift that God gave to them. And I hope they will make it to the next class with something left in that reservoir for me to add to week by week. It is from that reservoir that they will draw the strength to resist the drugs, the guns, the violence.

My two best students usually walk with me after class and stay with me until I catch a cab. I tell them it's not necessary, but they are there to make sure I get home all right. What a world. So dangerous that children feel that a second-degree black belt needs an escort to get home safely.

This community, like many across this country, is not safe for children, and they usually walk home at night filled with fear and apprehension. But when I walk with them after class they are carefree, as children ought to be. They have no fear. They believe that if anything happens they'll be safe because I'm there. I'll fly through the air and with my magic karate I'll dispatch whatever evil threatens them. When these children see me standing on the corner watching them walk into their buildings they believe what children used to believe, that there are adults who can protect them. And I let them believe this even if my older students and I know different. Because in a world that is so cold and so harsh, children need heroes. Heroes give hope, and if these children have no hope they will have no future. And so I play the role of hero for them even if I have to resort to cheap tricks and theatrics.

If I could get the mayors, the governors, and the president to look into the eyes of the 5-year-olds of this nation, dressed in old raggedy clothes, whose jacket zippers are broken but whose dreams are still alive, they would know what I know—that children need people to fight for them. To stand with them on the most dangerous streets, in the dirtiest hallways, in their darkest hours. We as a country have been too willing to take from our weakest when times get hard. People who allow this to happen must be educated, must be challenged, must be turned around.

If we are to save our children we must become people they will look up to. We must stand up and be visible heroes. I want people to understand the crisis and I want people to act: Either we address the murder and mayhem in our country or we simply won't be able to continue to have the kind of democratic society that we as Americans cherish. Violence is not just a problem of the inner cities or of the minorities in this country. This is a national crisis and the nation must mobilize differently if we are to solve it.

Part of what we must do is change the way we think about violence. Trying to catch and punish people after they have committed a violent act won't deter violence in the least. In life on the street, it's better to go to jail than be killed, better to act quickly and decisively even if you risk being caught.

There are, however, things that governments could and should do right away to begin to end the violence on our streets. They include the following:

CREATE A PEACE OFFICER CORPS

Peace officers would not be police; they would not carry guns and would not be charged with making arrests. Instead they would be local men and women hired to work with children in their own neighborhoods. They would try to settle "beefs" and mediate disputes. They would not be the eyes and ears of the regular police force. Their job would be to try to get these young people jobs, to get them back into school, and, most importantly, to be at the emergency rooms and funerals where young people come together to grieve and plot revenge, in order to keep them from killing one another.

REDUCE THE DEMAND FOR DRUGS

Any real effort at diverting the next generation of kids from selling drugs *must* include plans to find employment for these children when they become teenagers. While that will require a significant expenditure of public funds, the savings from reduced hospitalization and reduced incarceration will more than offset the costs of employment.

And don't be fooled by those who say that these teenagers will never work for five dollars an hour when they can make thousands of dollars a week. I have found little evidence of this in my years of working with young people. Most of them, given the opportunity to make even the minimum wage, will do so gladly. The problem for many young people has been that they have looked for work year after year without ever finding a job. In some cities more than 40 percent of minority youth who want to work can't find employment.

REDUCE THE PREVALENCE OF DOMESTIC VIOLENCE AND CHILD ABUSE AND NEGLECT

Too many children learn to act violently by experiencing violence in their homes. Our society has turned a blind eye to domestic violence for so long that the smacking, punching, and beating of women has become almost routine. And in many of the same homes where women are being beaten, the children are being beaten also. Our response as a society has been to wait until the violence has gotten so bad that the woman has to go to a battered-women's shelter (often losing the only place she has to live), or we have to take the abused child from the family. In both cases we break up a family, and common sense tells us this ends up costing us more money than it would have if we had intervened early and kept the family together.

The best mode of early intervention for really troubled families is family preservation services—intensive, short-term interventions designed to teach families new coping skills. The family preservation worker spends as much time as needed with a family to ensure that it gets the type of support and skills that it needs to function as a supportive unit rather than a destructive one.

REDUCE THE AMOUNT OF VIOLENCE ON TELEVISION AND IN THE MOVIES

Violence in the media is ever more graphic, and the justification for acting violently is deeply implanted in young people's minds. The movie industry promotes the message that power is determined not merely by carrying a gun, but by carrying a big gun that is an automatic and has a big clip containing many bullets.

What about rap music, and especially "gangsta rap"? It is my opinion that people have concentrated too much attention on this one source of media violence. Many rap songs are positive, and some are neither positive nor negative—just kids telling their stories. But there are some rap singers who have decided that their niche in the music industry will be the most violent and vile. I would love to see the record industry show some restraint in limiting these rappers' access to fame and fortune.

But by singling out one part of the entertainment industry as violent and ignoring others that are equally if not more violent (how many people have been killed in movies starring Arnold Schwarzenegger, Sylvester Stallone, and Clint Eastwood?) we will have no impact on reducing violence in this country. The television, movie, and record industries must all reduce the amount of violence they sell to Americans.

REDUCE AND REGULATE THE POSSESSION OF HANDGUNS

I believe all handgun sales should be banned in this country. Recognizing, however, that other Americans may not be ready to accept a ban on handguns, I believe there are still some things we must do.

Licensing

Every person who wants to buy a handgun should have to pass both a written test and a field test. The cost for these new procedures should be paid by those who make, sell, and buy handguns.

Insurance

Gun manufacturers and dealers should be required to register every handgun they manufacture and sell. This registration would be used to trace guns that wind up being used for crimes, and the manufacturers and dealers should be held liable for damages caused by any gun they manufacture and sell. Individual citizens would be required to carry insurance policies for liability and theft on their handguns, which would increase the pressure on citizens to make sure that their guns were safely locked away.

Ammunition Identification

While we are beginning to bring some sane regulations to the handgun industry, we must also begin to make the killing of Americans with handguns less anonymous than it is today. One way to do this is to make all handgun ammunition identifiable. Gun owners should have to sign for specially coded ammunition, the purchase of which would then be logged into a computer. The codes should be etched into the shell casing as well as the bullet itself, and the codes should be designed so that even when a bullet breaks into fragments it can still be identified.

Gun Buy-Backs

The federal government, which recently passed a $32 billion crime bill, needs to invest billions of dollars over the next ten years buying guns back from citizens. We now have more than 200 million guns in circulation in our country. A properly cared-for gun can last for decades. There is no way we can deal with handgun violence until we reduce the number of guns currently in circulation. We know that young people won't give up their guns readily, but we have to keep in mind that this is a long-term problem. We have to begin to plan now to get the guns currently in the hands of children out of circulation permanently.

The truth of the matter is that reducing the escalating violence will be complicated and costly. If we were fighting an outside enemy that was killing our children at a rate of more than 5,000 a year, we would spare no expense. What happens when the enemy is us? What happens when those Americans' children are mostly black and brown? Do we still have the will to invest the time and resources in saving their lives? The answer must be yes, because the impact and fear of violence has overrun the boundaries of our ghettos and has both its hands firmly around the neck of our whole country. And while you may not yet have been visited by the spectre of death and fear of this new national cancer, just give it time. Sooner or later, unless we act, you will. We all will.

QUESTIONS TO HELP YOU THINK AND WRITE ABOUT THE ISSUES CONCERNING CRIME AND THE TREATMENT OF CRIMINALS

1. Read the two selections about drug sentencing by Gramm and Brennan. What is at issue in these selections? What is the position of each author? Which author provides the best logical appeal? Emotional appeal? Ethical appeal? Which author provides the most convincing argument for you? Why? (Consider the warrants that you share or do not share with each of them.)

2. Read Brennan's and Califano's articles together and form some opinions about prison as a form of punishment. Is prison a good or bad form of punishment? In what ways could it be improved? What are some alternatives to prison?

3. The articles by Califano, Brennan and Gramm propose different solutions to the issue of how to deal with drug criminals. Which solutions, in your opinion, are the best? Can you think of others?

4. Read Newman's essay about the psychology of retribution. Explain what he means by retribution. What are your opinions about Newman's claims concerning the "psychological reality" of punishment?

5. Compare the articles about capital punishment written by lawyer Clarence Darrow, FBI director J. Edgar Hoover, and journalist Terry FitzPatrick. Do they rely on logical, emotional, or ethical proof? What are the strengths of each argument? What are the weaknesses? How would you refute each of these arguments? What is your own opinion on the issue of capital punishment? Were you influenced in your thinking by any of these authors?

6. Read Newman's essay, "Turning Bad into Good" and the short piece "Making Punishment Fit the Crime." Give some specific examples of the concept of making the punishment fit the crime. Give some examples that violate this concept. Evaluate this concept. Is it good or bad? Can you think of some other creative ways for making the punishment fit the crime?

7. Make two columns on the chalkboard or on a piece of paper and list all of the problems associated with young offenders (poverty, gangs, etc.) in the first column and possible solutions for each problem in the second column. Refer to the articles in part four to help you. Circle the two best solutions and say why you think they might contribute to a solution for the general problem.

8. Suppose that Males and Docuyanan, Dickerson, and Canada have been appointed to a national committee to make recommendations on how to deal with young offenders. What warrants would each of these individuals bring to this committee? What are two suggestions that each of these authors might make for dealing with juvenile offenders? How would you reconcile their positions? What final recommendations would you like to see made?

SECTION IV
Freedom of Speech Issues

WHAT ARE THE ISSUES?

1. Should Reading Material Be Censored or Screened to Protect Readers?

A seventeenth century author, a nineteenth century author, and three modern authors provide different perspectives on the enduring issue of censoring books. Modern perspectives focus on the books that students should either be allowed or forbidden to read in school. Value warrants are important in these arguments. See if you can discover the values involved and how they come into conflict with each other. See also "What's Happened to Disney Films?" page 146 and "Rap's Embrace of 'Nigger' Fires Bitter Debate," page 184.

2. Should the Internet Be Censored or Screened to Protect Users?

Four authors provide perspectives on the issues that are related to censoring or failing to censor objectionable materials on the Internet. This is a complex issue that has legal, ethical, and technical aspects. It is also a global issue since people all over the world communicate on the Internet.

Extend Your Perspective with Film and Literature Related to Freedom of Speech

Film: The Front, 1976; *Absence of Malice,* 1981; *Inherit the Wind,* 1960; *The People vs. Larry Flynt,* 1996.
Literature: novels: *Fahrenheit 451* by Ray Bradbury, *1984* by George Orwell, *Animal Farm: A Fairy Story* by George Orwell; play: *An Enemy of the People* by Henrik Ibsen.

THE RHETORICAL SITUATION

No argument textbook would be complete without a section on freedom of speech. This is a right provided by the First Amendment to the U.S. Constitution, and one purpose of this book is to teach responsible and productive ways to exercise that right. Since freedom of speech is a constitutional issue, many legal controversies are referred to the U.S. Supreme Court and lower courts for debate and final resolution. Consequently, much of what is written about free speech includes references to court decisions as one type of evidence. You will find examples in this collection of articles.

One way to develop a perspective on free-speech issues is to place the essays you read somewhere on a continuum that begins with genuinely objective writing like almanacs or weather reports at one end and proceeds to extremist writing that may use emotionally loaded language in a hateful or discriminatory manner at the other end. Think also of movies, television, and material on the Internet in the same way. Objective writing and objective, unemotional visual materials do not usually spark controversy. Writing and visuals at the other end of this continuum do, however, because people fear they may arouse strong emotions in readers and viewers that may result in antisocial behavior and even harm to others. Language and pictures that challenge people's value systems are also controversial, particularly for those who hold opposing values. Socrates was put to death because people thought he was distorting the values of Athens' youth. The modern writer Salman Rushdie has had to protect his life from those who have threatened to assassinate him because of the views and values expressed in his writings.

A self-regulatory film industry committee to determine what could and could not be shown in moving pictures was formed in the 1920s. It was headed by Will H. Hays. The Hays Code, formatted by this committee, influenced what was shown on the screen from that time until 1966, when the film industry started its rating system. Both the Hays Code and film ratings have been industry attempts to respond to the public's views about the relative appropriateness of different types of visual materials for mass audiences. The Communications Decency Act which was signed into law in 1996 and declared unconstitutional about four months later sought to control the images and texts that could appear on the Internet. You may be able to think of other examples of conflict resulting from books, essays, or visual media that are inflammatory to certain audiences.

In the nineteenth century, John Stuart Mill, in his famous essay "On Liberty," made the statement, "If all mankind minus one were of one opinion, and only one person were of the contrary opinion, mankind would be no more justified in silencing that one person, than he, if he had the power, would be justified in silencing mankind." (Excerpts from Mill's essay appear on p. 536.) The U.S. Constitution was written in this spirit. The First Amendment states,

> Congress shall make no law respecting an establishment of religion, or prohibiting the free exercise thereof; or abridging the freedom of speech, or of the press; or the right of the people peaceably to assemble, and to petition the Government for a redress of grievances.

In spite of the free-speech guarantee, however, the suspicions and fear of powerful language and images persist; every age debates what should be permitted, and what should be suppressed. The issue surfaces when something happens: A parent discovers her child can easily access "bikini babes" or worse on the home computer; someone says he shot a policeman because of a song he heard on the radio; someone leaves a note at a murder scene that contains hate language; a professor gives a biased, racially discriminatory lecture and claims he is exercising freedom of speech; an employer discovers his employees are using company time to look at pornography on their work computers; or a report circulates that quantifies the number of murders and shootings children see on television each year. Fear, the desire to protect the innocent, the values associated with free speech, and the perceived responsibility to report and interpret free-speech infractions provide both exigence and contraints for authors who write about freedom of speech issues.

1. Should Reading Material Be Censored or Screened to Protect Readers?

AREOPAGITICA

John Milton

Milton wrote Areopagitica *in 1644 at a time when prepublication censorship of books in England was being threatened. Some of the most famous passages from this well-known essay that argues against censorship are excerpted here.*

[. . .] For books are not absolutely dead things, but do contain a potency of life in them to be as active as that soul was whose progeny they are; nay, they do preserve as in a vial the purest efficacy and extraction of that living intellect that bred them. I know they are as lively, and as vigorously productive, as those fabulous dragon's teeth; and being sown up and down, may chance to spring up armed men. And yet, on the other hand, unless wariness be used, as good almost kill a man as kill a good book: who kills a man kills a reasonable creature, God's image; but he who destroys a good book, kills reason itself, kills the image of God, as it were, in the eye. Many a man lives a burden to the earth; but a good book is the precious life-blood of a master spirit, embalmed and treasured up on purpose to a life beyond life. 'Tis true, no age can restore a life, whereof, perhaps, there is no great loss; and revolutions of ages do not oft recover the loss of a rejected truth, for the want of which whole nations fare the worse. We should be wary, therefore, what persecution we raise against the living labors of public men, how we spill that seasoned life of man preserved and stored up in books; since we see a kind of homicide may be thus committed, sometimes a martyrdom; and if it extend to the whole impression, a kind of massacre, whereof the execution ends not in the slaying of an elemental life, but strikes at that ethereal and fifth essence, the breath of reason itself, slays an immortality rather than a life. [. . .]

Good and evil we know in the field of this world grow up together almost inseparably; and the knowledge of good is so involved and interwoven with the knowledge of evil, and in so many cunning resemblances hardly to be discerned, that those confused seeds which were imposed on Psyche as an incessant labor to cull out and sort asunder, were not more intermixed. It was from out of

---

From John Milton, *The Portable Milton*, ed. Douglas Bush, ed., (New York: Penguin Books, 1949), pp. 155–156, 166–167, 193–194.

the rind of one apple tasted that the knowledge of good and evil, as two twins cleaving together, leaped forth into the world. And perhaps this is that doom which Adam fell into of knowing good and evil, that is to say, of knowing good by evil. As therefore the state of man now is, what wisdom can there be to choose, what continence to forbear, without the knowledge of evil? He that can apprehend and consider vice with all her baits and seeming pleasures, and yet abstain, and yet distinguish, and yet prefer that which is truly better, he is the true warfaring Christian. I cannot praise a fugitive and cloistered virtue, unexercised and unbreathed, that never sallies out and sees her adversary, but slinks out of the race where that immortal garland is to be run for, not without dust and heat. Assuredly we bring not innocence into the world, we bring impurity much rather; that which purifies us is trial, and trial is by what is contrary. That virtue therefore which is but a youngling in the contemplation of evil, and knows not the utmost that vice promises to her followers, and rejects it, is but a blank virtue, not a pure; her whiteness is but an excremental whiteness; which was the reason why our sage and serious poet Spenser, whom I dare be known to think a better teacher than Scotus or Aquinas, describing true temperance under the person of Guyon, brings him in with his palmer through the cave of Mammon and the bower of earthly bliss, that he might see and know, and yet abstain. Since therefore the knowledge and survey of vice is in this world so necessary to the constituting of human virtue, and the scanning of error to the confirmation of truth, how can we more safely, and with less danger, scout into the regions of sin and falsity than by reading all manner of tractates and hearing all manner of reason? And this is the benefit which may be had of books promiscuously read. [. . .]

Where there is much desire to learn, there of necessity will be much arguing, much writing, many opinions; for opinion in good men is but knowledge in the making.

ON LIBERTY

John Stuart Mill

John Stuart Mill was a nineteenth-century philosopher and economist. In his autobiography he says that he wanted "to be a reformer of the world." He wrote On Liberty *in 1859. The passages presented here express his well-known commitment to freedom of speech.*

[. . .] If all mankind minus one, were of one opinion, and only one person were of the contrary opinion, mankind would be no more justified in silencing that one person, than he, if he had the power, would be justified in silencing mankind. Were an opinion a personal possession of no value except to the owner; if to be

From Charles Frederick Harold and William D. Templeman (ed.), *English Prose of the Victorian Era* (New York: Oxford UP, 1938), pp. 677–680.

obstructed in the enjoyment of it were simply a private injury, it would make some difference whether the injury was inflicted only on a few persons or on many. But the peculiar evil of silencing the expression of an opinion is, that it is robbing the human race; posterity as well as the existing generation; those who dissent from the opinion, still more than those who hold it. If the opinion is right, they are deprived of the opportunity of exchanging error for truth: if wrong, they lose, what is almost as great a benefit, the clearer perception and livelier impression of truth, produced by its collision with error.[. . .]

When we consider either the history of opinion, or the ordinary conduct of human life, to what is it to be ascribed that the one and the other are no worse than they are? Not certainly to the inherent force of the human understanding; for, on any matter not self-evident, there are ninety-nine persons totally incapable of judging of it, for one who is capable; and the capacity of the hundredth person is only comparative; for the majority of the eminent men of every past generation held many opinions now known to be erroneous, and did or approved numerous things which no one will now justify. Why is it, then, that there is on the whole a preponderance among mankind of rational opinions and rational conduct? If there really is this preponderance—which there must be unless human affairs are, and have always been, in an almost desperate state—it is owing to a quality of the human mind, the source of everything respectable in man either as an intellectual or as a moral being, namely, that his errors are corrigible. He is capable of rectifying his mistakes, by discussion and experience. Not by experience alone. There must be discussion, to show how experience is to be interpreted. Wrong opinions and practices gradually yield to fact and argument: but facts and arguments, to produce any effect on the mind, must be brought before it. Very few facts are able to tell their own story, without comments to bring out their meaning. The whole strength and value, then, of human judgement, depending on the one property, that it can be set right when it is wrong, reliance can be placed on it only when the means of setting it right are kept constantly at hand. In the case of any person whose judgement is really deserving of confidence, how has it become so? Because he has kept his mind open to criticism of his opinions and conduct. Because it has been his practice to listen to all that could be said against him; to profit by as much of it as was just, and expound to himself, and upon occasion to others, the fallacy of what was fallacious. Because he has felt, that the only way in which a human being can make some approach to knowing the whole of a subject, is by hearing what can be said about it by persons of every variety of opinion, and studying all modes in which it can be looked at by every character of mind. No wise man ever acquired his wisdom in any mode but this; nor is it in the nature of human intellect to become wise in any other manner. The steady habit of correcting and completing his own opinion by collating it with those of others, so far from causing doubt and hesitation in carrying it into practice, is the only stable foundation for a just reliance on it: for, being cognisant of all that can, at least obviously, be said against him, and having taken up his position against all gainsayers—knowing that he has sought for objections and difficulties, instead of avoiding them, and has shut out no light which can be thrown upon the subject from any quarter—he has a right to think his judgement better than that of any person, or any miltitude, who have not gone through a similar process.[. . .]

Strange it is, that men should admit the validity of the arguments for free discussion, but object to their being 'pushed to an extreme'; not seeing that unless the reasons are good for an extreme case, they are not good for any case. Strange that they should imagine that they are not assuming infallibility, when they acknowledge that there should be free discussion on all subjects which can possibly be *doubtful*, but think that some particular principle or doctrine should be forbidden to be questioned because it is so *certain*, that is, because *they are certain* that it is certain. To call any proposition certain, while there is any one who would deny its certainty if permitted, but who is not permitted, is to assume that we ourselves, and those who agree with us, are the judges of certainty, and judges without hearing the other side. [. . .]

WHAT SHOULD BE DONE ABOUT BIAS IN OUR CHILDREN'S TEXTBOOKS?

Paul C. Vitz

This excerpt is from the book Censorship: Evidence of Bias in Our Children's Textbooks, *published in 1986. Identify the value warrants in this selection.*

[. . .] Studies make it abundantly clear that public school textbooks commonly exclude the history, heritage, beliefs, and values of millions of Americans. Those who believe in the traditional family are not represented. Those who believe in free enterprise are not represented. Those whose politics are conservative are almost unrepresented. Above all, those who are committed to their religious tradition—at the very least as an important part of the historical record—are not represented.

Even those who uphold the classic or republican virtues of discipline, public duty, hard work, patriotism, and concern for others are scarcely represented. Indeed, the world of these virtues long advocated by believers, as well as by deists and skeptics such as Thomas Paine, Benjamin Franklin, and Thomas Jefferson, is not found here. Even what one might call the "noble pagan" has ample reason to reject these inadequate and sentimentalized books which seem to be about an equal mixture of pap and propaganda.

Over and over, we have seen that liberal and secular bias is primarily accomplished by exclusion, by leaving out the opposing position. Such a bias is much harder to observe than a positive vilification or direct criticism, but it is the

From Paul C. Vitz, *Censorship: Evidence of Bias in Our Children's Textbooks* (Ann Arbor, MI: Servant Books, 1986), pp. 77–81.

essence of censorship. It is effective not only because it is hard to observe—it isn't *there*—and therefore hard to counteract, but also because it makes only the liberal, secular positions familiar and plausible. As a result, the millions of Americans who hold conservative, traditional, and religious positions are made to appear irrelevant, strange, on the fringe, old-fashioned, reactionary. For these countless Americans it is now surely clear that the textbooks used in the public schools threaten the continued existence of their positions.

A natural question to raise is: how could this textbook bias have happened? What brought it about? Some have suggested that religion is downplayed because of concern over maintaining the separation of church and state. This concern seems either unlikely or a rationalization of an underlying distaste for religion. After all, to identify the historical or contemporary importance of religion is to respect the facts; it is not to advocate religion. To teach *about* religion is not to teach religion.

Furthermore, the rejection of religion in these books is part of a very general rejection of the entire conservative spectrum of American life. Recall that these books omit marriage and the traditional family, along with traditional sex roles, patriotism, and free enterprise. In short, the bias in these books is not accidental; much of it is certainly not the result of some misunderstanding about separating church and state.

Another possible answer is that the publishers of these books have attempted to avoid controversial subjects. According to this theory, the books have been written in a style which will avoid offending anyone. In fact, some publishers do give guidelines to authors on what kinds of people and issues to avoid. But the evidence of this study makes clear that a desire to avoid offense and controversy *cannot* explain much of the bias observed here. [. . .] Consider the profeminist position found in several social studies texts and throughout the basal readers for grades 3 and 6. That feminism is controversial cannot be seriously denied, even by feminists. And consider that positive representations of traditional feminine role models are obviously absent from these books. The regular procoverage of environmental issues also makes clear that the only people and topics which are avoided in these books are those on the political right, those that are "controversial" to a liberal frame of mind.

One explanation of the antireligious bias in these books is that religion is so especially controversial that publishers want to avoid the subject. Curiously, the religions that do get some mention, e.g., Catholicism, Judaism, and Islam, are hardly uncontroversial. (In any case, why religion is supposedly more controversial than race, ethnic identity, feminism, or politics remains to be explained.)

The real issue is how a book handles religion. For example, magazines like the *Reader's Digest* and others often have articles about the positive accomplishments of people of different religious denominations. Such articles celebrating the different religions and their contributions to this country are uncontroversial, well received, and appear to help sales. Yet, such a positive treatment of America's religious life is without any example in the ninety books evaluated in this entire study.

Religious concepts and vocabulary are certainly censored in these text-books. A most revealing example of this censorship was recently published in the article "Censoring the Sources" by Barbara Cohen.[1] The issue centered on a children's story of hers called "Molly's Pilgrim." The story has an important Jewish religious theme; it focuses on the Jewish harvest holiday of Sukkos, a holiday that influenced the Pilgrims in initiating Thanksgiving. A major textbook publisher (Harcourt Brace Jovanovich) wanted to reprint part of the story for their third grade reader. But like most such stories, the publishers wanted to shorten it greatly and to rewrite parts to make it more acceptable. They phoned Ms. Cohen and asked her for permission to reprint their modified version. But her story wasn't just modified, it was maimed. "All mention of Jews, Sukkos, God, and the Bible"[2] had been removed. So Barbara Cohen refused to give them permission. They called back dismayed and tried to convince her to let them go ahead with the heavily censored version. They argued, "Try to understand. We have a lot of problems. If we mention God, some atheist will object. If we mention the Bible, someone will want to know why we don't give equal time to the Koran. Every time that happens, we lose sales."[3] "But the Pilgrims did read the Bible," Barbara Cohen answered.[4] Yes, you know that and we know that, but we can't have anything in it that people object to, was the reply!

After more debate and give and take, a compromise was reached. The publisher allowed a reference to worship and the Jewish harvest holiday of Sukkos to stay in. But God and the Bible were "eternally unacceptable"[5] and they had to go. The publisher claimed, "We'd get into terrible trouble if we mentioned the Bible."[6]

This true but incredible story ends with Barbara Cohen stating: "Censorship in this country is widespread, subtle, and surprising. It is not inflicted on us by the government. It doesn't need to be. We inflict it on ourselves."[7] At the very least, the publishers should hear from the millions of Christians and Jews that if God and the Bible are left out, the publishers will also lose sales. And, God willing, lots more sales will be lost than when publishers leave God and the Bible in. The schools and the publishers must learn that what is left out of a textbook can be just as offensive as what is let in.

Of course, the central issue hinges on the *facts* of America's past and present. And the facts are clear: religion, especially Christianity, has played and continues to play a central role in American life. To neglect to report this is simply to fail to carry out the major duty of any textbook writer—the duty to tell the truth.

To explain the liberal and secular prejudice of the texts, some have proposed that a deliberate, large-scale conspiracy is involved. I doubt very much, however, that this is the case. The number of people writing, editing, publishing, selecting, and using these books is far too large and varied for this explanation to be plausible. Instead, the bias is, I believe, the consequence of the widespread, dominant, secular worldview found throughout the upper levels of the field of education,[8] especially among those who control the schools of education, the publishers, the federal and state education bureaucracies, and the National Education Association. But, whatever the source of the bias, it certainly exists. Thus, the question is "What should be done?" Let us consider the major possibilities.

One possibility that I will call *Scenario One* is as follows. In this possible future the public school leadership acknowledges that the majority of America's parents are religious in their sympathies and generally conservative in their moral and social life. Recognizing this, educators move clearly and positively back into the mainstream of American life. Religion is given a positive and realistic portrayal in textbooks and other curriculum. The traditional family and moral values are recognized and integrated into the school programs. Finally, the new emphasis on character education continues to grow and become widely influential.

The result of making these changes is a revival of confidence in the public schools and increased community support. As a result, many religious Americans return their children to the public schools. Meanwhile more secular Yuppy parents note the increased morale of teachers and students and they also return to active public school support. After all, the private schools favored by many of the young upwardly mobile professionals are quite expensive. Revitalized public schools would be welcomed by many of them. In short, in this scenario the public schools are positively transformed and gain a new long lease on life.

NOTES

1. Barbara Cohen, "Censoring the Sources," *School Library Journal,* March 1986.
2. Cohen, 97.
3. Cohen, 98.
4. Cohen.
5. Cohen, 99.
6. Cohen.
7. Cohen.
8. This is also the opinion of Mel and Norma Gabler in *What Are They Teaching Our Children?* (Wheaton, IL: SP Publications, 1985).

WHY TEACH US TO READ AND THEN SAY WE CAN'T?

Nat Hentoff

Nat Hentoff has written many books about freedom of speech. This is an excerpt from
Free Speech for Me—But Not for Thee: How the American Left and Right Relentlessly Censor Each Other, *published in 1992.*

Children in many American schools are instructed early in thought control. This is not the term used by their school boards and principals. They call it the removal of "inappropriate" books.

From Nat Hentoff, *Free Speech for Me—But Not for Thee: How the American Left and Right Relentlessly Censor Each Other* (New York: HarperCollins, 1992), pp. 374–379.

For a long time, a book near the top of the hit list has been J. D. Salinger's *Catcher in the Rye.* In Boron, California, in 1990, a parent noted in alarm that the book "uses the Lord's name in vain two hundred times. That's enough reason to ban it right there," she explained. "They said it describes reality. I say let's back up from reality. Let's go backwards. Let's go back to when we didn't have an immoral society."

That parent is more candid than most of those on the political and religious right who object to certain books on their children's required or optional reading lists. They genuinely fear that forces—some say satanic forces—beyond their control have taken over the majority culture. And their responsibility, as parents and as Christians, is to protect their children—and all other children—from the infectious permissiveness of the larger society.

Strategically, it is a mistake to underestimate the seriousness of purpose and strength of will of these book police. I've spoken to many of them. They are not "kooks."

The resolution of the *Catcher in the Rye* furor in Boron, North Carolina, was the removal of the book from the high school language arts supplemental reading list.

In Clay County, in north Florida, school officials banished *My Friend Flicka* from the optional reading lists of fifth- and sixth-grade kids. The book has become an outlaw because in it, a female dog is described as a "bitch."

The harm that can be found in writing that has previously been considered free of malignities has also been exposed by school officials in Citrus County, Florida. As reported by Howard Kleinberg in the Los Angeles legal newspaper, the *Daily Journal,* a school cultural contest in Citrus County was canceled in 1990 "on the grounds that Joyce Kilmer, whose poem was part of the project, used the words 'breast and bosom' in it."

Attempts to control what children read, and thereby think, have been increasing across the country, according to annual accounts by the American Library Association and People for the American Way. There is a great deal of underreporting, however, as I've discovered in interviews with teachers and librarians through the years.

Many principals, for instance, yield immediately to complaints rather than have to deal with the controversy that comes with review committees and public hearings. And once there has been trouble in a school, some librarians do their own self-censoring of books they decide not to order.

Judy Blume's books, for example, are widely popular, especially among girls, but because they deal with real problems familiar to real youngsters, they are often attacked. At a meeting of librarians a few years ago, two of them from Minnesota told me how much they admired Judy Blume's ability to understand what's troubling kids. Then one of them added: "But we're not going to buy another book of hers. Too much damn trouble."

An increasing preoccupation of many fundamentalist Christians—to whom the Devil is no abstraction—has to do with satanism in books for children. Since the Devil can take on many forms, one has to sniff very carefully for the scent of brimstone. In Yorba Linda, California, parents insisting that satanism be removed root and branch filed objections to the presence of Old Nick in, among other books in the school, *Romeo and Juliet,* Maurice Sendak's *Where the Wild Things Are,* and a story by Nathaniel Hawthorne.

In response to the complaints, most of the children of the Satan-detectors were moved to safe classrooms in which those works were not taught.

Not all the putative censors win. By and large, those schools with a clearly worded and structured review procedure can often withstand these attacks. The parent or other complainer has to fill out a form specifying his or her objections. Faced with the form, some parents let the issue drop. But others go on. The review committee—consisting of librarians, teachers, and sometimes members of the community—usually provide some due-process protections for both the objecting parents and the accused books. And then there is the school board for final review. That being a political body, it can be more concerned with the next election than the First Amendment. But not always.

Here's how this review procedure worked in Watanga County, North Carolina. A philosophy professor and father of a child in kindergarten challenged a 1901 edition of Rudyard Kipling's *Just So Stories.* In one of the stories, "How the Leopard Got His Spots," the word "nigger" appears. A five-member review committee decided to remove the book.

Two librarians, however, appealed to the school board to reverse the sentence. The chairman of the school board—as reported in the American Library Association's *Newsletter on Intellectual Freedom*—said: "Freedom of speech is the vehicle through which can come the defense against those who would use words to harm human beings."

But the philosophy professor disagreed: "There are two things I very much want my daughter not to become. I don't want her to be a drug addict, and I don't want her to be a racist."

One of the librarians, however carried the day: "In the end the only way we learn there are such issues as racism is by discussing them with our children. We ask that you vote to leave this book on the shelf."

The vote was unanimous. Rudyard Kipling's stories still have a home in the Watanga County elementary school library.

Another victory for free expression took place in Colonie, New York. At issue was the future in the Shaker High School Library of *The Progressive* magazine, a national liberal political journal. A sophomore—complaints do come from students as well as from all manner of school employees—wanted the magazine banned because it has contained ads for *The Anarchist Cookbook, Women Loving Women,* and *Prove Christ Fictional.* Also offensive to the student was a full-page ad by the Jewish Committee on the Middle East.

The student saw no reason that his family's tax dollars should be spent to enrich this offensive magazine. And 123 of his fellow students signed a petition agreeing with him. On the other hand, the library director brandished a petition signed by 395(!) students supporting the magazine: "Libraries should provide information on all points of view."

A review committee of school employees noted that *The Progressive* "would have to be of little value as a library source or be incendiary in nature to warrant a recommendation for its removal. There is no support for either conclusion."

The review committee also pointed out that the magazine had been part of the media center collection for ten years, and it would stay there. "We do students a disservice," said the committee, "if we feel they will succumb to every enticement they encounter. They are fully capable of ignoring the advertisements [the student] cites as objectionable."

Sooner or later, however, a very careful reader may come across the numbers 666 in an issue of *The Progressive* or in some book. That is the Devil's number, and in some other town, another review committee may be formed to banish the devil from the school library. In Wilton Manors, Florida, an elementary school play—with the number 666 in it—was denounced by parents and a local minister. The play was then revised, but by then, it was too late in the school year for it to be produced.

There once was a school—the Mowat Middle School in Florida—where everybody was an exultant reader. The school had become so lively a center of learning—where kids actually read books they didn't have to—that in 1985 it was one of 150 American and Canadian secondary schools designated a Center of Excellence by the National Council of Teachers of English.

In each classroom, there were libraries from which students could choose what they wanted—though no one had to read anything, including in class, that he or his parents objected to. By 1986, the ninth-graders at Mowat were scoring on the high-twelfth-grade reading level. As a parent said, "I've caught my son reading sometimes on weekends. I also caught him writing a letter to his grandmother without my telling him to do it."

Then came the affair of *I Am the Cheese,* by Robert Cormier, one of the most honored of all young adult novels (and a 1977 Library of Congress Children's Book of the Year). A parent didn't like some of the language, and the district superintendent, Leonard Hall, didn't like its negative attitude toward government. (The boy in the book is part of a family in the not-always-caring Witness Protection Program.)

I Am the Cheese was immediately removed from the curriculum, the superintendent having ignored the usual review procedure when there is a complaint about a book. Other books began to be cast into darkness.

Superintendent Hall commanded teachers to examine classroom books closely and separate them into three categories. In the first would be books without "vulgar, obscene or sexually explicit material." In the second category would be those with "very limited vulgarity and no sexually explicit or obscene material." In the dread third category would be books with "quite a bit of vulgarity or obscene and/or sexually explicit material."

"Quite a bit" was not made more specific—nor were any of the other terms in the formula. Teachers in the district's two high schools poured over the books and presented Hall with sixty-four titles that were flagrantly impure by his standards and so belonged in category three. Hall removed them all from the reading lists. Among the titles:

The Red Badge of Courage, Intruders in the Dust, Oedipus Rex, Animal Farm, Twelfth Night, The Autobiography of Benjamin Franklin, The Canterbury Tales, John Ciardi's translation of *The Inferno, Hamlet,* and, of course, *Fahrenheit 451,* Ray Bradbury's novel about a future time when the only way to keep certain books alive is to go into hiding and memorize them, for otherwise they would be burned by the state.

At a crowded school board meeting to consider this remarkable new way of grading Western literature, students and teachers wore black armbands. Outside the room, a number of kids held up posters: "Why Teach Us to Read and Then Say We Can't?"

The school board put most of the books back on the classroom lists (*I Am the Cheese* excepted). But the superintendent and the principals under him retained the power to remove "unclean" books.

Subsequently, a number of books were banished from the Mowat School by its principal, including a young-adult novel of mine, *The Day They Came to Arrest the Book.* It's about attempts in a high school by black parents, fundamentalist Christian parents, and feminists to ban *Huckleberry Finn.* My novel was exiled because it has a "goddamn" in it.

Gloria Pipkin, a brave teacher at the Mowat Middle School, told me, as the censorship went on, that "ten of the eleven women in the English department at its peak have bailed out." Why does she keep on? That's what she was asked by a school board member who could not understand why she kept appearing before the board to convince it to bring back *I Am the Cheese,* among other books.

"Because it's worth it," Pipkin said.

She was the school's teacher of the year in 1983. Before the place was cleaned up.

During the unsuccessful resistance of teachers and students to the purges of the school library and curriculum, the superintendent said publicly that he was very disturbed at the effect of this battle over censorship on the children.

"All this talk of their rights," he said, "has distracted them from their studies. It has confused them."

CENSORSHIP FOLLIES, TOWN BY TOWN

Peggy Orenstein

Orenstein is the author of Schoolgirls: Young Women. Self-Esteem and the Confidence Gap, *a book that was banned in a town in Ohio and that raised censorship issues, as you will see.*

I had to go to the library to find a map detailed enough to show Cortland, Ohio, which, it turned out, is a small town in the northeastern corner of the state. There's not much there by big-city standards: 6,000 people and no movie theaters. But there is one courageous high school teacher who went to battle to keep his school board from banning my book.

New York Times, December 7, 1996, Sec. A, p. 17.

At the beginning of the school year, with the approval of his principal, Robert Walls assigned his 11th and 12th grade students my book, "Schoolgirls," which discusses the self-image of young women.

Then the parents of one student asked Mr. Walls to pull the book. They said they objected to its "rotten, filthy language" (this consists of a few quotations that include profanity) and a section on sexual harassment. The real concern, I suspect, was the book advocates teaching girls about their sexuality.

Mr. Walls refused to drop the book (although he did offer the parents a black marker with which to delete any offending passages from their daughter's copy). Suddenly, he found himself the object of a campaign by the student's parents as well as their church and a couple of school board members. They wanted the book banned.

As a first-year untenured teacher, Mr. Walls had absolutely no job security. Nevertheless, he insisted on arguing his case before the board. He was confident that, whatever the decision, his job would be safe, but he says his colleagues weren't so sure.

"People have told me to wait until I have tenure, then assign the book," he said when the controversy first broke. "But I can't put aside something I believe in for another two years."

I'd like to say this was an isolated confrontation, but it wasn't. According to People for the American Way, a First Amendment watchdog group, there were 300 attempts to censor school materials in the 1995–1996 school year, 120 of which were successful. The books challenged included "Canterbury Tales," "A Wrinkle in Time," a science-fiction classic, and "Ordinary People."

"I Know Why the Caged Bird Sings" by Maya Angelou is No. 1 on the censors' hit parade, because it depicts the rape of an 8-year-old girl. In one Louisiana town, a high school principal banned any book that mentioned sex from the school library; more than 200 such books were removed.

Even in communities where such attempts at censorship were defeated, teachers might think twice before assigning their students anything controversial or even material that depicts real-life events.

The obvious lesson is that one can never be too complacent about the right to the freedom of ideas. But there is another message here as well. While the big (and certainly important) cultural wars, like the fight against financing cutbacks in the arts, get national attention, there are countless small, local battles that depend on people who fight alone, unnoticed and often unsupported.

Because of Mr. Walls, my story had a happy ending. After his two-hour presentation in mid-November, the school board relented and voted to let him retain the book.

"A lot of people said this was a crazy thing to do," he said afterward.

I only hope that the rest of us could be brave enough to be that crazy.

2. Should the Internet Be Censored or Screened to Protect Users?

THE NEXT FRONT IN THE BOOK WARS

Stephen Bates

> *This article was written in 1994. The problem of children accessing the Internet was gaining national attention. Bates calls attention to the problem and predicts that there will be censorship battles down the line.*

In two suburban Chicago high schools this year, students are analyzing satellite photos of current weather, tracking wildfires in California, questioning atmospheric scientists about their research and collaborating on writing projects with students thousands of miles away. "The Internet is making the school a more integral part of the world," said Barry Fishman, manager of the federally funded CoVis Network which provides the schools' Internet hookup.

But the Internet is also bringing seamier elements of the world into the schoolhouse. Sooner or later, Mr. Fishman and other educators realize, people will complain about what the Internet is making available to schoolchildren and the ceaseless battles over schoolbooks will soar into cyberspace.

The cyberspace battles may prove especially contentious, because the Internet contains a great many works not found on the shelves of most schools. "The School Stopper's Textbook," for instance, tells how to short-circuit electrical wiring, set off explosives in school plumbing and "break into your school at night and burn it down."

"The Big Book of Mischief" features detailed bomb-making instructions.

"Suicide Methods," based in part on Derek Humphry's book "Final Exit," comprehensively analyzes various ways of killing oneself.

A drug archive offers recipes for marijuana brownies and a guide to constructing "bongs, pipes and other wonderful contraptions."

On several archives and Usenet discussion groups, hackers provide tips on breaking into computer networks, telephone systems and cash machines.

Some Usenet groups contain pornographic stories; others have photos of naked men, women and, occasionally, children.

"I don't think parents have ever had quite this challenge before," said Steve Bennett, an author who has developed computer activities for children. "You think your kid is mastering the Internet so he'll be ready for a technically sophisticated job—then you find he's got 'Popular Gynecology' up on the screen."

Schools can keep a pornographic book off the library shelf by not buying it, but they can't keep it from entering the building through cyberspace. The Internet is a headless web of computer networks, designed by Defense Department

New York Times, November 6, 1994, Sec. 4A, pp. 22–23.

contractors in the 1960's to withstand nuclear war. Limiting a user's access to material on it is nearly impossible. "The Net interprets censorship as damage and routes around it," said John Gilmore, a leading activist for freedom of speech in cyberspace.

So when educators contemplate bringing the Internet into public schools, "the situation is essentially all or nothing," said Libby Black, director of the Boulder Valley School District's Internet Project in Colorado, which provides Internet accounts to more than 1,600 public school students. Like the fledgling CoVis and other publicly and privately funded networks that provide information services to schools, Boulder Valley excludes the "alt.sex" discussion groups from Usenet's "alternative" hierarchy, but an enterprising user can venture out on the Internet and find a network that does receive them. Even from the confines of an E-mail-only account, a student can instruct several automated systems to send Usenet posts, including those from the alt.sex groups, by return mail. It is the electronic equivalent of interlibrary loan, only beyond the librarian's control.

"You can't prevent it," said Peg Szady, who teaches a course on the Internet at Monta Vista High School in Cupertino, Calif. "There's just no way."

Consequently, schools must rely on discipline and supervision. Early on in the CoVis project, Mr. Fishman sat down with teachers at the two pilot schools. "We attempted to get a sense of how we could educate people to use these tools for good, and minimize people using them for resources not directly related to improving education," he said.

The result is a network-use policy that the student and a parent must sign. The form stipulates that "network use is primarily intended for the support of project work conducted in participating CoVis classes, and far less significantly for other purposes that students and teachers determine to be of educational value."

Other schools send permission forms home with students. The Poudre School District in Fort Collins, Colo., alerts parents to the possibility of "defamatory, inaccurate, abusive, obscene, profane, sexually oriented, threatening, racially offensive, or illegal material" on-line. At Monta Vista, the policy instructs students not to access "areas of cyberspace that would be offensive to any students, teachers, or parents." Many schools limit students' electronic speech, prohibiting profanity, sexually oriented remarks, advertising, political lobbying and "flames" (vituperative verbal attacks). Violators can lose their accounts.

Some systems monitor students' use of the Internet. At Long Island's Oceanside High School, students must fill out a form summarizing each on-line session. Students at several schools in Chicago will soon log onto their Internet accounts using "smartcards," which will record their online movements for subsequent review by teachers. At the Poudre District in Fort Collins, administrators reserve the right to examine users' E-mail and other files. "You really have to do that with kids," said Larry Buchanan, a Poudre educational technologies specialist. "When they know somebody's watching them, they behave differently."

Schools impose such restrictions "to cover their butts," in the view of Russell Smith, a technology consultant for the state of Texas who has reviewed several schools' written policies. "Nobody wants to get sued."

The fear of litigation has a basis. "Some jurisdictions have laws that place a duty on everyone, not just schools, to prevent minors from being exposed to sexually related materials," said Mike Goodwin, online counsel of the Electronic Frontier Foundation. "Even if the material is not legally obscene—for instance, Playboy magazine—it may be that a party can be liable for giving that kind of sexually oriented material to a minor." Some states also prohibit "exposing minors to dangerous material or information," he added, but the courts have not definitively ruled on the constitutionality of such laws.

The seamy material on the Internet has not yet generated litigation, or in fact much controversy. At the relatively few schools now offering Internet accounts, students have had their accounts suspended for hacking, abusive E-mail and similar misbehavior more frequently than for accessing objectionable photos and texts.

Even so, educators know that cyberspace has the potential to ignite a sizable controversy. "The nightmare [public school educators] have," Steve Cisler, a senior scientist in the Apple Computer library, wrote in a newsletter last year, "is of some legislator waving around a raunchy [digitized] image 'paid for with tax dollars and found on the State Educational Network,' or reading some choice posting from alt.sex.necrophilia." The furor becomes increasingly likely as more and more schools put students on-line frequently with accounts they can access from home, beyond the scrutiny of school officialdom—and as the public schools' traditional critics begin paying attention to the Internet.

"There's a lot of fundamentalist groups out there," said Mr. Smith, the Texas consultant. "I don't think they know what's up with the Internet yet."

Representatives of three conservative organizations—Concerned Women for America, Focus on the Family and the American Family Association—said they had not yet studied Internet access in public schools.

Conservative Christians won't be the only ones to take offense. Indeed, most protests so far in universities rather than public schools have come from other groups, according to a list prepared by Carl Kadie, co-editor of the electronic periodical Computers and Academic Freedom News.

Women have complained about the newsgroups devoted to pornographic photos and sex chatter, and several universities have banned them. In 1989 Stanford banned a Usenet discussion group over a joke that some users deemed anti-Semitic; accused of censorship, the university later backed down. In September of this year, the Education Department's Office for Civil Rights contended that a males-only on-line discussion group at a California junior college violated Federal anti-discrimination law.

Whether the complaints come from the right or the left, the Internet's on-line community generally supports absolute freedom of inquiry. The phrase "information wants to be free" is a commonplace of Usenet discussions.

Mirroring that viewpoint, some civil libertarians have decried efforts to restrict how students use the Internet. In a statement issued in August, the Minnesota Coalition Against Censorship called for all public school students to enjoy unfettered Internet privileges, including access to "information that some have identified as controversial or of potential harm."

Most anti-censorship organizations are still studying the issue. "It's incredibly complex," said Candace Morgan, chairwoman of the American Library Association's Intellectual Freedom Committee. "The most difficult situations are those faced by school libraries."

People for the American Way, a liberal public-interest group, generally takes the position that no library materials should be kept from children, according to Leslie Harris, the organization's director of public policy. But, she added, pornographic images and some other materials on the Internet "may require a different answer."

"We are generally not for restrictions," said Roz Udow of the National Coalition Against Censorship. "But the Internet changes everything—it makes it all so accessible."

Meanwhile, computer engineers are looking for technical fixes. One approach is a "reverse firewall." Whereas a firewall keeps outsiders from entering a computer system, a reverse firewall would keep users from going beyond a few uncontroversial zones on the Internet, according to Denis Newman, director of education network systems at BBN Systems and Technologies. BBN, he said, is at work on a prototype. Other companies are also pursuing technical solutions, according to Nelson Heller, publisher of a newsletter on educational technology.

Mr. Fishman of CoVis thinks that network architecture won't provide the answer. "Roadblocks end up taking away what's valuable—the ability of students to perform tasks that their teachers couldn't even conceive of," he said. In his view, the better approach is for educators to "spend time up front thinking about what objections people might raise, then try to defuse those concerns through education."

He hopes that educators succeed in pre-empting the protests. "Losing the Internet in schools just because of some information on it—and we're really talking about a small percentage of the total information—it's a pretty bad investment," he said. "If a student was smuggling dirty pictures in their science textbook, would we take away all the science textbooks?"

INDECENCY ON THE INTERNET: CENSORSHIP OF STUDENT AND COLLEGE WEB PAGES

Jeffrey R. Young

The Communications Decency Act was passed overwhelmingly by Congress early in 1996 and signed into law by the President. The intent of the law was to banish pornography from the Internet. The law made it a felony, punishable by fines and imprisonment, to put objectionable material on the Internet where children might see it. The law was immediately controversial because many thought it threatened the First Amendment. This article explains how the law affected college campuses and college students at the time.

The Chronicle of Higher Education, April 26, 1996, p. A21+.

A Federal court's examination of new law regulating the Internet has left many academics more worried than ever that the statute will infringe on academic freedom.

At the judicial hearings here, the U.S. Justice Department presented evidence that the law is needed to protect children from "indecent" material on the Internet. In the material cited by the government were four World-Wide Web pages that college students had created on their campus computer systems.

Although most of what the government submitted came from commercial providers of pornography, the mention of the student Web pages worried a number of educators. Some observers also were troubled when a government witness agreed that, under the act, the statue of a nude figure in a university's art collection might need to be labeled as inappropriate for minors.

Lawyers for the American Civil Liberties Union said the examples were telling. If the government reviews student and scholarly activities on line, they said, the law will inevitably limit freedom of expression on the nation's campuses.

Trotter Hardy, a law professor at the College of William and Mary and editor of *The Journal of Online Law,* said that if the law is upheld, "universities have to worry about it. There's just no way around it."

But supporters of the law said educators were exaggerating its probable impact.

ENACTED IN FEBRUARY

The measure being challenged here was signed into law by President Clinton in February as part of a major telecommunications bill. It prohibits Internet users from sending "indecent" or "patently offensive" material to minors or from making such material available in a way that could be accessible to children.

Civil-liberties groups sued to block the law, which they say violates the freedom of speech guaranteed by the Constitution. Defenders of the act say it is no different from current restrictions on the distribution of printed pornography, some of which courts have approved.

Under provisions of the law, a three-judge panel is considering the legal challenges. Either side may appeal the case directly to the Supreme Court. The Justice Department has agreed not to enforce the law's provisions on indecency, pending the outcome of the legal proceedings.

The four student Web sites—all of which contained images of naked women—were produced at Duke University, Michigan State University, the University of Texas at Austin, and Whitman College.

Marjorie Heins, a lawyer for the A.C.L.U., called the mention of these sites significant. To include them in a list of commercial pornography providers indicates that students' computer activities will not be overlooked by law-enforcement officials should the law prevail, she said.

Some college administrators and legal scholars following the case wondered if academic institutions would be held liable for such materials, for which they provide Web space. "With the Internet you have so many intermediary people.

Who's responsible?" asked Mr. Hardy of William and Mary. "If that act stands and you're a prudent university, you're going to have to screen everything students post."

That prospect worries campus administrators. Joanne Hugi, director of university computing at the University of Oregon, said her institution does not regulate what students post on their home pages. Government supervision of students' home pages "increases my workload and potentially decreases the amount of information we can offer," she added.

'BEHIND BARS'

Other administrators noted that colleges couldn't monitor such Web pages even if they wanted to. "The volume of materials makes it impractical," said Philip Long, director of Academic Computing Services at Yale University. On the Internet, he said, "every student or faculty member is potentially a personal publisher. Who would do this screening?"

The only practical solution would be to restrict the Yale network to adults who were affiliated with the university, he said—and in that event, "the essence of discourse at Yale would be behind bars."

Supporters of the bill call such characterizations an overreaction. Russ Rader, press secretary for Sen. James Exon, the Nebraska Democrat who proposed the Internet restrictions, said the law provides a defense that "protects access providers from liability." Unless colleges were aware of "indecent" Web pages, he said, they would not be responsible for them.

But critics say this response points out how the law will turn colleges into censors of their students—which some fear is already the case on some campuses.

At Whitman College, the Web page cited by the government was forced off the system by administrators last month, before the hearings here. Paul J. Setze, Whitman's chief technology officer, said he had become aware of the page of nude photographs when it began attracting an enormous amount of traffic—up to 250 requests at a time.

The volume was slowing the entire campus network, he said. "We cannot allow this because it severely impacts every student who uses e-mail and many faculty as well," Mr. Setze wrote to the student. He said the content of the page had had no effect on the decision.

William T. Burkoth, the freshman who created the page, suspects that content did play a role. "I definitely feel censored," he said in an interview. The page showing centerfolds "doesn't offer anything you can't find on HBO or Cinemax after 10 at night."

At Duke, the student who created the Web page removed it after seeing it mentioned in *The New York Times*. "I'm not taking any risks," said Charles S. Hamilton.

Mr. Hamilton said that he had reviewed Duke's policy on Web pages before posting the material, and that he thought his page was not in violation. The policy's only restriction is that the pages not attract more than 10,000 requests per day.

Betty Le Compagnon, vice-president for information technology at Duke, said the university was not in the business of monitoring what's on its network. "We do not in any way control the content of the home pages," she said. The university's approach to the issue is based on "academic freedom, as opposed to censorship," she said.

Mr. Hamilton's Web page features an image of three nude cartoon characters fondling each other. During the hearing, the Justice Department pointed out that a child searching on the Web for "Jasmine," a character in the movie *Aladdin,* could reach Mr. Hamilton's page, which featured that character, unclothed, in an image.

WIDE RANGE OF MATERIALS

The final day of testimony last week focused on how the law might affect organizations that provide information in cyberspace. Judges and observers here showed surprise at the range of materials that might fall under the law.

Dan R. Olsen, Jr., the Justice Department's final witness and a computer scientist at Brigham Young University, described a rating system that would ostensibly give Internet users and content providers "safe harbor" from prosecution under the law.

Under his plan, Internet users would "tag" any material that they thought might be considered "indecent." The tag would consist of a four-character string, "-L18," placed in the computer file, which could block access to minors.

The judges sharply questioned Mr. Olsen on the viability of this system. Chief Judge Dolores K. Sloviter posed a hypothetical question: What if the University of Pennsylvania's Museum of Archaeology and Anthropology were to post the image of a nude statue in its on-line collection? "You might have to prescreen or block to be safe? Is that part of your scheme?"

"Yes," Mr. Olsen said.

The idea that one of their artifacts could be restricted on line surprised Pam Kosty, a museum spokeswoman. "I hadn't thought that it was a problem," she said.

The museum later issued a statement noting that it had on display a statue that might meet Judge Sloviter's description. The 2,000-year-old marble statue of a nude Greek goddess is currently seen by about 40,000 schoolchildren a year, according to the statement.

"It would be silly to be forbidden to put her photograph on the Net. We consider such material art and we consider it history. We would be amazed if anybody considered it indecent," the statement said.

The law's supporters replied that classic art would be safe on line. But Ms. Heins of the A.C.L.U. said there was "too much danger that a museum director would restrict access to a nude statue," fearing prosecution under the law.

EXCERPT FROM JUDGE DALZELL'S OPINION
AGAINST INTERNET DECENCY LAW

Stewart Dalzell

In June of 1996 a panel of three Federal judges declared unconstitutional the parts of the new Communications Decency Act, signed into law only four months earlier, that sought to regulate indecent materials on the Internet. Judge Dalzell's opinion was published in the New York Times *on that occasion, and it was widely quoted because of the way Judge Dalzell characterized the Internet.*

The Internet is a far more speech-enhancing medium than print, the village green, or the mails. Because it would necessarily affect the Internet itself, the C.D.A. would necessarily reduce the speech available for adults on the medium. This is a constitutionally intolerable result.

Some of the dialogue on the Internet surely tests the limits of conventional discourse. Speech on the Internet can be unfiltered, unpolished, and unconventional, even emotionally charged, sexually explicit, and vulgar—in a word, "indecent" in many communities. But we should expect such speech to occur in a medium in which citizens from all walks of life have a voice. We should also protect the autonomy that such a medium confers to ordinary people as well as media magnates.

Moreover, the C.D.A. will almost certainly fail to accomplish the Government's interest in shielding children from pornography on the Internet. Nearly half of Internet communications originate outside the United States, and some percentage of that figure represents pornography. Pornography from, say, Amsterdam will be no less appealing to a child on the Internet than pornography from New York City, and residents of Amsterdam have little incentive to comply with the C.D.A.

My analysis does not deprive the Government of all means of protecting children from the dangers of Internet communication. The Government can continue to protect children from pornography on the Internet through vigorous enforcement of existing laws criminalizing obscenity and child pornography.... As we learned at the hearing, there is also a compelling need for public education about the benefits and dangers of this new medium, and the Government can fill that role as well. In my view, our action today should only mean that the Government's permissible supervision of Internet content stops at the traditional line of unprotected speech.

Parents, too, have options available to them. As we learned at the hearing, parents can install blocking software on their home computers or they can subscribe to commercial online services that provide parental controls. It is quite clear that powerful market forces are at work to expand parental options to deal

---

New York Times, June 13, 1996, p. A18.

with these legitimate concerns. More fundamentally, parents can supervise their children's use of the Internet or deny their children the opportunity to participate in the medium until they reach an appropriate age. . . .

Cutting through the acronyms and argot that littered the hearing testimony, the Internet may fairly be regarded as a never-ending worldwide conversation. The Government may not, through the C.D.A., interrupt that conversation. As the most participatory form of mass speech yet developed, the Internet deserves the highest protection from governmental intrusion. . . .

The absence of governmental regulation of Internet content has unquestionably produced a kind of chaos, but as one of the plaintiffs' experts put it with such resonance at the hearing: "What achieved success was the very chaos that the Internet is. The strength of the Internet is that chaos." Just as the strength of the Internet is chaos, so the strength of our liberty depends upon the chaos and cacophony of the unfettered speech the First Amendment protects.

For these reasons, I without hesitation hold that the C.D.A. is unconstitutional on its face.

NEW ISSUE AT WORK: ON-LINE SEX SITES

Trip Gabriel

After the repeal of the Communications Decency Act (CDA) articles like this one began appearing again in the public press, signaling that indecency on the Internet is, indeed, a problem that will not go away. Trip Gabriel wrote this article for the New York Times *a couple of weeks after the three judges declared the CDA unconstitutional.*

Hunkered over computer screens, the six founders of an on-line magazine, five men and a woman, worked in a cramped Manhattan office late into the night to make their start-up business take flight.

Occasionally, one of the men, a graphic designer, would call his male colleagues over to gawk and laugh at images he downloaded from the World Wide Web. One night he beckoned the company's 30-year-old business manager, the sole woman, and told her, "I want to show you a marketing program." It turned out to be a partially nude woman in a sex act with an animal.

That such raunchy images can be found by rummaging through cyberspace is no secret. The right to disseminate them electronically was upheld earlier this month by a panel of three Federal judges in Philadelphia. But such viewing would seem to be so furtive an act that it would be confined to the privacy of the home, in the hours around midnight.

New York Times, June 27, 1996, p. B1+.

And yet, with Web access the latest fixture in many offices, sexually explicit images are popping up on computer screens in even the nicest workplaces. A survey released in April by Nielsen Media Research showed that the on-line edition of Penthouse magazine is called up thousands of times a month by employees at International Business Machines, Apple Computer, AT&T, NASA and Hewlett-Packard.

Compaq Computer recently dismissed about 20 employees, mostly in Houston, each of whom logged more than 1,000 hits on sexually explicit Web sites. (A hit is a click of the mouse to request a file from a site.)

Men who surf into such sites, say women and experts on sexual harassment, can create an uncomfortable and humiliating atmosphere for their female colleagues. The climate exists whether the images are glimpsed while passing a co-worker's cubicle, imagined from the guffaws of others gathered around a screen or explicitly pointed out.

"I was disgusted and angered by the fact he felt so little of me to ask me over," said the business manager of her co-worker. She asked that she and her company not be identified for fear that she would be ostracized.

"This is pornography, which he assumed I would find enjoyable or funny," she added. "It showed a complete lack of respect."

A growing number of companies and government agencies are restricting employees' access to sexually explicit sites, concerned about being held liable should they be sued for sexual harassment by women who find the images demeaning.

No suits have been filed yet, experts say, probably because widespread Internet access in offices is so new. (About 16 million to 20 million people in North America are estimated to use the Internet, with about half gaining access primarily at work.) In the meantime, employers and employees—men as well as women—are grappling with what is appropriate on-line behavior.

"In every training program I've done in the last year, the issue of surfing the Net and sexually explicit visuals has come up," said Trisha Brinkman of San Francisco, a consultant to corporations about sexual harassment. About 40 of Ms. Brinkman's clients, including law firms and brokerage houses, have taken her advice to update their harassment policies to prohibit viewing sexually explicit sites at the office.

Pornography by no means dominates the Internet, an ocean of information on cancer research, car reviews, Botticelli reproductions and "Star Trek" synopses. But it is a perennial favorite. Yahoo, the popular Internet search service, has reported that a significant percentage of requests are for sex-related sites.

When it comes to defining sexual harassment, surfing into sex sites falls into the same gray zone as hanging pinups over a desk—the closest pre-digital equivalent.

For some companies, there is no debate. "That behavior is definitely prohibited," said Marlene Somsak, a spokeswoman for Hewlett-Packard, one company that gained a bit of unwanted publicity from the Penthouse survey.

For workers, the offensiveness of sex sites can be in the eye of the beholder: there are many variations of how a woman might be exposed to them, and reactions seem to depend on the context.

A 28-year-old woman, who is now a computer systems consultant, recalled that when she worked as an analyst at a Wall Street investment bank, male colleagues continuously downloaded sexually graphic material.

I knew it was going on—there were always a lot of references to it—but whenever I'd walk by they'd say, 'No, no, we can't show you *that* one," she said. "It was never directed at me, and I didn't feel victimized at all."

A few women's rights advocates dismiss the behavior as trivial compared to more threatening situations.

"I don't really consider that sexual harassment," said Cheryl Kondratow, a founder of Women Against Sexual Harassment, a support group with chapters in New Jersey and elsewhere. "What a person does in their cubicle is their business. If I don't like it, I can walk by him. If everybody's sitting around laughing, I don't have to join in."

But Esther Nevarez, a sex-harassment educator for the New Jersey Division on Civil Rights, said such behavior "affects the esprit de corps in an office because it eliminates certain groups of people from participating."

Carter Hodgkin, an artist and Web designer, said that when she worked for a design company in New York last year, a colleague's frequent jokes about sexual material that he downloaded became a basis for male bonding that left her out.

"I wasn't included on such important social events as taking breaks, going to lunch, going out after work," she said. A subtle office divide was created that led to her exclusion from important projects, she asserted.

Although she was offended by the crudeness of the material, Ms. Hodgkin said, she was reluctant to complain for fear of being labeled a spoilsport. She also feared that as a freelancer she might not continue to get work from the company, which she declined to name for the same reason.

"The guy managing the graphics area loved all this bad-boy stuff," Ms. Hodgkin, 44, said. Only when the male designer responsible for the surfing left the company did the problem fade, she said.

Most experts say that openly viewing sexually explicit Web sites, along with variations like using Playboy screen savers and posting lewd jokes on on-line company bulletin boards, falls within the realm of intimidation that can create "a hostile working environment," which the Supreme Court ruled a form of sexual discrimination in 1986.

One instance of such activity would not be grounds for a legal case, experts say, but if it is part of a broad pattern of intimidation or ridicule, that is a graver matter.

Yael Foa, director of the Boston office of 9 to 5, the National Association of Working Women, said that in recent weeks two callers to the organization's hot line complained that unwelcome exposure to Internet sex sites had been part of a pattern of harassment where they work.

In one case, male colleagues of a female laboratory technician at a cancer research institute grabbed pornography off the Net and left it for her to see on a shared computer. The men also brought in sex toys to show her.

An increasing number of companies are taking a strong step to keep employees away from sex sites: blocking the sites from company computers with software like Surf Watch, which was originally designed for parents who want to restrict children's access to adult material.

Jay Friedland, sales manager of Surf Watch, said 15 to 20 percent of the company's sales are now to businesses. "In many cases, the calls that come in are driven by human resource departments," he said.

He said that corporate clients typically have two worries: their liability in the event of a harassment claim, and the loss of productivity when employees surf the Web, which can include looking for sites offering sports scores or movie gossip.

Compaq, which provides Internet access to most of its 17,000 employees, dismissed the workers singled out for heavy use of sex sites after a company-wide monitoring effort. Computer system administrators, using logs that are automatically recorded, can trace every individual's use of Web sites, news groups and E-mail.

The employees were let go for "misuse of company resources," said Nora Hahn, a Compaq spokeswoman.

On-line monitoring has added new fuel to an old debate over workplace privacy. Legally, employers have a right to regulate use of their computer systems, experts say. Many employees know that E-mail messages can be read by bosses, but not all realize that their Net surfing, which leaves a digital trail, can also be checked.

"An employee shouldn't have to give up his or her First Amendment rights when they enter the work-place," said David Banisar, a lawyer and policy analyst at the Electronic Privacy Information Center, a public interest group in Washington.

Some companies have policies that allow employees to surf the Net for personal use on lunch breaks or after business hours. But employees should not infer, experts say, that the road is open to the Web's red-light district.

Freada Klein, president of Klein Associates, a sexual harassment consultant group in Boston, said, "If there is a possibility that there will be intended or unintended observation of what you're doing—and if what you're doing could reasonably be construed as unwelcome sexual attention or creating a hostile environment—then you need to be advised you do so at your own risk."

QUESTIONS TO HELP YOU THINK AND WRITE ABOUT FREEDOM OF SPEECH ISSUES

1. Read the five articles about whether reading material should or should not be screened to protect readers. What positions do the authors of these articles take on this issue? What are the underlying warrants for each position? Which of these warrants are most acceptable to you?

2. Compare Milton's and Mill's positions with those of Vitz, Hentoff, and Orenstein. How has the question of censorship of print material changed over time, and how has it remained the same?

3. Read the essays in "The Rhetoric," "Rap's Embrace of 'Nigger' Fires Bitter Debate," (p. 184) and "What's Happened to Disney Films?" (p. 146) What are your views on the censorship of popular music (like rap music), television programs, and modern films? Do you think Milton's and Mill's positions on censorship would change or remain the same if they were to apply them to modern music, television, film, and pornographic materials on the Internet? Why do you think so?

4. Consider the contexts for the use of the word "nigger" described by Marriott in his essay "Rap's Embrace of 'Nigger' Fires Bitter Debate," (p. 184). How do contexts change the usual meaning of language? Can you think of other examples of words that might be acceptable in one context but not in another, or words that might be acceptable to one culture but not to another? Should controversial language of this nature be used or suppressed by the media? Consider that the media includes material with global circulation, like music, television, film, and the Internet, as well as printed materials.

5. Should there be any limits on what schoolchildren and older students are allowed to read? What criteria would you use to decide what they should read and what they should not read? Frame your answer in terms of grade-school children, high-school students, and college students.

6. Compare the situation created by censorship of the Internet just after the Communications Decency Act was passed, as described by Young, with the situation just after the Act was repealed, as described by Gabriel. What are the conflicts described in these articles? How do you think they can be resolved?

7. How does Dalzell characterize the Internet in his opinion against the Communications Decency Act? What might you add? Why is the Internet difficult to censor? What is the current status of the Internet censorship issue as you discuss it today? How do you think it will finally be resolved?

8. What might be done to control what people can access on the Internet without censoring it? Read the essay by Gabriel for some ideas. Are these ideas acceptable to you or not? Why? What would you propose?

SECTION V
Issues Concerning Racism in America

WHAT ARE THE ISSUES?

1. Are Racial Minorities in Crisis?

Cornel West says that African-Americans are the victims of nihilism, or a hope-lessness and a sense of meaninglessness in life, Andrew Hacker claims white Americans are intensely aware of racial discrimination, and Wang and Wu de-bunk the "model minority myth" that claims Asians have "made it" and no longer need affirmative action.

See also Haizlip, "We Knew What Glory Was," page 49, and D'Sousa, "Black America's Moment of Truth," page 163.

2. What Should Be Done to Solve Racial Problems?

The authors of the articles in this section explore some of the possible solutions for racial problems. Leadership is the subject of articles by Gates and DuBois. DuBois, writing in 1903, provides historical perspective for this issue. He urges the development of a talented black leadership to help solve racial problems. Gates provides a modern perspective on DuBois. Matthews explores the effects that interracial families and multiracial children may have on the problem. Isasi-Diaz makes a case for racial understanding.

See also "A View from Berkeley," page 52; "A Camp Sows the Seeds of Peace," page 253; "A Call for Unity," page 271; "Letter from Birmingham Jail," page 272; "A Simple 'Hai' Won't Do It," page 58; and Jobs Illuminate What Riots Hid: Young Ideals," page 80.

Extend Your Perspective with Film and Literature Related to Racism in America

Film: *Mississippi Burning,* 1988; *Lone Star,* 1996; *Ghosts of Mississippi,* 1996.
Literature: poems: "Incident" by Countee Cullen; "Poem for the Young White Man" by Lorna Dee Cervantes; autobiography: *Borderlands* by Gloria Anzaldua; "How It Feels to be Colored Me" by Zora Neale Hurston; play: "A Raisin in the Sun" by Lorraine Hansberry; novels: *Beloved* by Toni Morrison; *To Kill a Mocking-bird* by Harper Lee; *I Know Why the Caged Bird Sings* by Maya Angelou; and *The Joy Luck Club* by Amy Tan.

THE RHETORICAL SITUATION

Issues associated with race are difficult for many people because of the strong emotions associated with them. You will discover striking examples of emotional proof in this collection of articles about race. But you will also discover effective ethical and logical proof. The warrants associated with this issue are related to what is regarded as an acceptable quality of life, equal opportunities for self-development, and the ways and means necessary for achieving these goals.

The issues related to race in this section include the fact issue, Are racial minorities in crisis? and the policy issue, What should be done? Most authors agree that racial minorities are in crisis and cite as their evidence the current status of the urban poor, the disproportionate number of minorities in prison, the general dissatisfaction of middle-class minority members, and the various types of exclusion endured by minorities.

Possible solutions for racial problems examine the relative advantages of complete assimilation and equality between the races, so that racial differences would eventually cease to exist, versus valuing and preserving the uniqueness of one's own race and culture and maintaining a close identification, association, and appreciation for it. "Interracial" marriages and "multiracial" children may help blur racial distinctions, or, by creating a whole new racial category, may intensify them. Another exigency for issues involving race is provided by those minority members who have not made it into the middle class and who, instead, live in poverty and create horrendous social problems for the rest of society. Affirmative action and other preference programs that provide minority members with a "leg up" in life are also controversial. Some argue that such programs are no longer needed and may even be harmful, and others think they should be expanded. Minority participation and leadership is still an issue. We have not yet elected a president of the United States who represents a minority group. The number of mayors, governors, and Congressmen who represent these groups has certainly increased in recent years, however. There is disagreement among the authors in this section about the quality of minority leadership.

For some individuals, the racial issue is the most important issue in their lives, and for others, it barely exists. How do you regard this issue, and what provides the exigency for your interest or lack of interest?

1. Are Racial Minorities in Crisis?

NIHILISM IN BLACK AMERICA

Cornel West

These are excerpts from West's book Race Matters, *published in 1993. West is a philosopher, theologian, and activist who is professor of religion and director of Afro-American studies at Princeton University.*

The proper starting point for the crucial debate about the prospects for black America is an examination of the nihilism that increasingly pervades black communities. *Nihilism is to be understood here not as a philosophic doctrine that there are no*

From Cornel West, *Race Matters* (Boston: Beacon Press, 1993), pp. 14–20.

rational grounds for legitimate standards or authority; it is, far more, the lived experience of coping with a life of horrifying meaninglessness, hopelessness, and (most important), lovelessness. The frightening result is a numbing detachment from others and a self-destructive disposition toward the world. Life without meaning, hope, and love breeds a coldhearted, mean-spirited outlook that destroys both the individual and others.

Nihilism is not new in black America. The first African encounter with the New World was an encounter with a distinctive form of the Absurd. The initial black struggle against degradation and devaluation in the enslaved circumstances of the New World was, in part, a struggle against nihilism. In fact, the major enemy of black survival in America has been and is neither oppression nor exploitation but rather the nihilistic threat—that is, loss of hope and absence of meaning. For as long as hope remains and meaning is preserved, the possibility of overcoming oppression stays alive. The self-fulfilling prophecy of the nihilistic threat is that without hope there can be no future, that without meaning there can be no struggle.

The genius of our black foremothers and forefathers was to create powerful buffers to ward off the nihilistic threat, to equip black folk with cultural armor to beat back the demons of hopelessness, meaninglessness, and lovelessness. These buffers consisted of cultural structures of meaning and feeling that created and sustained communities; this armor constituted ways of life and struggle that embodied values of service and sacrifice, love and care, discipline and excellence. In other words, traditions for black surviving and thriving under usually adverse New World conditions were major barriers against the nihilistic threat. These traditions consist primarily of black religious and civic institutions that sustained familial and communal networks of support. If cultures are, in part, what human beings create (out of antecedent fragments of other cultures) in order to convince themselves not to commit suicide, then black foremothers and forefathers are to be applauded. In fact, until the early seventies black Americans had the lowest suicide rate in the United States. But now young black people lead the nation in suicides.

What has changed? What went wrong? The bitter irony of integration? The cumulative effects of a genocidal conspiracy? The virtual collapse of rising expectations after the optimistic sixties? None of us fully understands why the cultural structures that once sustained black life in America are no longer able to fend off the nihilistic threat. I believe that two significant reasons why the threat is more powerful now than ever before are the saturation of market forces and market moralities in black life and the present crisis in black leadership. The recent market-driven shattering of black civil society—black families, neighborhoods, schools, churches, mosques—leaves more and more black people vulnerable to daily lives endured with little sense of self and fragile existential moorings.

Black people have always been in America's wilderness in search of a promised land. Yet many black folk now reside in a jungle ruled by a cutthroat market morality devoid of any faith in deliverance or hope for freedom. Contrary to the superficial claims of conservative behaviorists, these jungles are not primarily the result of pathological behavior. Rather, this behavior is the tragic response of a people bereft of resources in confronting the workings of U.S. capitalist society. Saying this is not the same as asserting that individual black people are not responsible for their actions—black murderers and rapists should go to jail. But it must be recognized that the nihilistic threat contributes to criminal behavior. It is a threat that feeds on poverty and shattered cultural institutions and grows more powerful as the armors to ward against it are weakened.

But why is this shattering of black civil society occurring? What has led to the weakening of black cultural institutions in asphalt jungles? Corporate market institutions have contributed greatly to their collapse. By corporate market institutions I mean that complex set of interlocking enterprises that have a disproportionate amount of capital, power, and exercise a disproportionate influence on how our society is run and how our culture is shaped. Needless to say, the primary motivation of these institutions is to make profits, and their basic strategy is to convince the public to consume. These institutions have helped create a seductive way of life, a culture of consumption that capitalizes on every opportunity to make money. Market calculations and cost-benefit analyses hold sway in almost every sphere of U.S. society.

The common denominator of these calculations and analyses is usually the provision, expansion, and intensification of *pleasure*. Pleasure is a multivalent term; it means different things to many people. In the American way of life pleasure involves comfort, convenience, and sexual stimulation. Pleasure, so defined, has little to do with the past and views the future as no more than a repetition of a hedonistically driven present. This market morality stigmatizes others as objects for personal pleasure or bodily stimulation. Conservative behaviorists have alleged that traditional morality has been undermined by radical feminists and the cultural radicals of the sixties. But it is clear that corporate market institutions have greatly contributed to undermining traditional morality in order to stay in business and make a profit. The reduction of individuals to objects of pleasure is especially evident in the culture industries—television, radio, video, music—in which gestures of sexual foreplay and orgiastic pleasure flood the marketplace.

Like all Americans, African Americans are influenced greatly by the images of comfort, convenience, machismo, femininity, violence, and sexual stimulation that bombard consumers. These seductive images contribute to the predominance of the market-inspired way of life over all others and thereby edge out nonmarket values—love, care, service to others—handed down by preceding generations. The predominance of this way of life among those living in poverty-ridden conditions, with a limited capacity to ward off self-contempt and self-hatred, results in the possible triumph of the nihilistic threat in black America.

A major contemporary strategy for holding the nihilistic threat at bay is a direct attack on the sense of worthlessness and self-loathing in black America. This *angst* resembles a kind of collective clinical depression in significant pockets of black America. The eclipse of hope and collapse of meaning in much of black America is linked to the structural dynamics of corporate market institutions that affect all Americans. Under these circumstances black existential *angst* derives from the lived experience of ontological wounds and emotional scars inflicted by white supremacist beliefs and images permeating U.S. society and culture. These beliefs and images attack black intelligence, black ability, black beauty, and black character daily in subtle and not-so-subtle ways. Toni Morrison's novel, *The Bluest Eye,* for example, reveals the devastating effect of pervasive European ideals of beauty on the self-image of young black women. Morrison's exposure of the harmful extent to which these white ideals affect the black self-image is a first step toward rejecting these ideals and overcoming the nihilistic self-loathing they engender in blacks.

The accumulated effect of the black wounds and scars suffered in a white-dominated society is a deep-seated anger, a boiling sense of rage, and a passionate pessimism regarding America's will to justice. Under conditions of slavery and Jim Crow segregation, this anger, rage, and pessimism remained relatively muted because of a well-justified fear of brutal white retaliation. The major breakthroughs of the sixties—more psychically than politically—swept this fear away. Sadly, the combination of the market way of life, poverty-ridden conditions, black existential *angst,* and the lessening of fear of white authorities has directed most of the anger, rage, and despair toward fellow black citizens, especially toward black women who are the most vulnerable in our society and in black communities. Only recently has this nihilistic threat—and its ugly inhumane outlook and actions—surfaced in the larger American society. And its appearance surely reveals one of the many instances of cultural decay in a declining empire.

What is to be done about this nihilistic threat? Is there really any hope, given our shattered civil society, market-driven corporate enterprises, and white supremacism? If one begins with the threat of concrete nihilism, then one must talk about some kind of *politics of conversion.* New models of collective black leadership must promote a version of this politics. Like alcoholism and drug addiction, nihilism is a disease of the soul. It can never be completely cured, and there is always the possibility of relapse. But there is always a chance for conversion—a chance for people to believe that there is hope for the future and a meaning to struggle. This chance rests neither on an agreement about what justice consists of nor on an analysis of how racism, sexism, or class subordination operate. Such arguments and analyses are indispensable. But a politics of conversion requires more. Nihilism is not overcome by arguments or analyses; it is tamed by love and care. Any disease of the soul must be conquered by a turning of one's soul. This turning is done through one's own affirmation of one's worth—an affirmation fueled by the concern of others. A love ethic must be at the center of a politics of conversion.

A love ethic has nothing to do with sentimental feelings or tribal connections. Rather it is a last attempt at generating a sense of agency among a downtrodden people. The best exemplar of this love ethic is depicted on a number of levels in Toni Morrison's great novel *Beloved*. Self-love and love of others are both modes toward increasing self-valuation and encouraging political resistance in one's community. These modes of valuation and resistance are rooted in a subversive memory—the best of one's past without romantic nostalgia—and guided by a universal love ethic. For my purposes here, *Beloved* can be construed as bringing together the loving yet critical affirmation of black humanity found in the best of black nationalist movements, the perennial hope against hope for trans-racial coalition in progressive movements, and the painful struggle for self-affirming sanity in a history in which the nihilistic threat *seems* insurmountable.

The politics of conversion proceeds principally on the local level—in those institutions in civil society still vital enough to promote self-worth and self-affirmation. It surfaces on the state and national levels only when grassroots democratic organizations put forward a collective leadership that has earned the love and respect of and, most important, has proved itself *accountable* to these organizations. This collective leadership must exemplify moral integrity, character, and democratic statesmanship within itself and within its organizations.

Like liberal structuralists, the advocates of a politics of conversion never lose sight of the structural conditions that shape the sufferings and lives of people. Yet, unlike liberal structuralism, the politics of conversion meets the nihilistic threat head-on. Like conservative behaviorism, the politics of conversion openly confronts the self-destructive and inhumane actions of black people. Unlike conservative behaviorists, the politics of conversion situates these actions within inhumane circumstances (but does not thereby exonerate them). The politics of conversion shuns the limelight—a limelight that solicits status seekers and ingratiates egomaniacs. Instead, it stays on the ground among the toiling everyday people, ushering forth humble freedom fighters—both followers and leaders—who have the audacity to take the nihilistic threat by the neck and turn back its deadly assaults.

WHITE RESPONSES TO RACE AND RACISM

Andrew Hacker

This excerpt from Hacker's book Two Nations: Black and White, Separate, Hostile, Unequal, *published in 1992, was quoted or referred to by most of the reviewers who wrote about the book. It particularly caught their attention. Hacker is a political science professor who has written extensively about racial issues.*

Most white Americans will say that, all things considered, things aren't so bad for black people in the United States. Of course, they will grant that many problems remain. Still, whites feel there has been steady improvement, bringing blacks closer to parity, especially when compared with conditions in the past. Some have even been heard to muse that it's better to be black, since affirmative action policies make it a disadvantage to be white.

What white people seldom stop to ask is how they may benefit from belonging to their race. Nor is this surprising. People who can see do not regard their vision as a gift for which they should offer thanks. It may also be replied that having a white skin does not immunize a person from misfortune or failure. Yet even for those who fall to the bottom, being white has a worth. What could that value be?

From Andrew Hacker, *Two Nations: Black and White, Separate, Hostile, Unequal* (New York: Macmillan, 1992), pp. 31–32.

Let us try to find out by means of a parable: suspend disbelief for a moment, and assume that what follows might actually happen:

THE VISIT

You will be visited tonight by an official you have never met. He begins by telling you that he is extremely embarrassed. The organization he represents has made a mistake, something that hardly ever happens.

According to their records, he goes on, you were to have been born black: to another set of parents, far from where you were raised.

However, the rules being what they are, this error must be rectified, and as soon as possible. So at midnight tonight, you will become black. And this will mean not simply a darker skin, but the bodily and facial features associated with African ancestry. However, inside you will be the person you always were. Your knowledge and ideas will remain intact. But outwardly you will not be recognizable to anyone you now know.

Your visitor emphasizes that being born to the wrong parents was in no way your fault. Consequently, his organization is prepared to offer you some reasonable recompense. Would you, he asks, care to name a sum of money you might consider appropriate? He adds that his group is by no means poor. It can be quite generous when the circumstances warrant, as they seem to in your case. He finishes by saying that their records show you are scheduled to live another fifty years—as a black man or woman in America.

How much financial recompense would you request?

When this parable has been put to white students, most seemed to feel that it would not be out of place to ask for $50 million, or $1 million for each coming black year. And this calculation conveys, as well as anything, the value that white people place on their own skins. Indeed, to be white is to possess a gift whose value can be appreciated only after it has been taken away. And why ask so large a sum? Surely this needs no detailing. The money would be used, as best it could, to buy protections from the discriminations and dangers white people know they would face once they were perceived to be black.

BEYOND THE MODEL MINORITY MYTH

Theodore Hsien Wang and Frank H. Wu

Wang is a staff attorney with the Lawyers' Committee for Civil Rights of the San Francisco Bay Area, where he works on affirmative action and voting rights issues. His voting rights work resulted in the placement of voting booths in public housing developments, procedures to allow prisoners to vote in county jails, and procedures to implement the federal motor voter law in California. Wu is an assistant professor of law at Howard University in Washington, D.C. He has written widely on affirmative action.

From George E. Curry (ed.), *The Affirmative Action Debate* (Reading, Mass: Addison-Wesley, 1996), pp. 191–197, 204–206.

Race is no longer literally a black-or-white matter. It is increasingly clear that the word "minority" means more than black and "American" means more than white. Asian-Americans are finally being introduced into the discussion about race. Unfortunately, we are being used as pawns in the debate over affirmative action.[1]

One of the increasingly prominent fallacies in the attacks on affirmative action is that Asian-Americans are somehow the example that defeats the rationale for race-conscious remedial programs. House Speaker Newt Gingrich and California governor Pete Wilson are two of the many political leaders who point to Asian-Americans and their supposed success in American society to assert that affirmative action is not needed. Their views present the latest incarnation of the model minority myth.

No matter how frequently and thoroughly the model minority image is debunked, it returns as a troublesome stereotype in race relations. According to this popular portrayal of an entire race, Asian-Americans have achieved their notable economic success through a combination of talent, hard work, and conservative values, not through government entitlements, racial preferences, or complaints about discrimination. In this image, which can be seen everywhere from magazine articles to popular movies, Asian-Americans are depicted as champion entrepreneurs and college whiz kids, the immigrant parents working as urban greengrocers as their American children win the annual Westinghouse Science Talent Search.

Contrary to popular perceptions, however, only *some* Asian-Americans have made significant strides in socioeconomic status. Overall, Asian-Americans remain underrepresented in many areas and continue to experience discrimination. Most often, Asian-Americans are treated as if they are all foreigners who are getting ahead by unfair competition, and they face the "glass ceiling" that allows them to progress only up to a point. Furthermore, opponents of affirmative action—including some Asian-Americans—forget that Asian-Americans have benefited greatly from the civil rights movement.

As people who continue to experience racism, Asian-Americans should play a role in fighting for affirmative action. The many experiences of Asian-Americans show that our society remains highly color-conscious and has not become a color-blind meritocracy, that in racial reality black and white are not simple mirror images, and that straightforward racial discrimination and the efforts to remedy it are not the same. We should avoid allowing ourselves and our communities to be used as a wedge by politicians whose own ideologies and ambitions explain their sudden concern for Asian-Americans.[2]

THE ORIGINS OF THE MODEL MINORITY MYTH

Complimentary on its face, the model minority myth is disingenuous at heart. The myth has a long lineage, dating back to the arrival of Asians in this country during the nineteenth century. In the past as well as today, the praise lavished on

Asian-Americans has been used to denigrate other racial minority groups, primarily African-Americans.[3]

After the Civil War, southern plantation owners developed grand schemes to import Chinese laborers to compete against recently freed black slaves. As the Reconstruction governor of Arkansas explained, "Undoubtedly the underlying motive for this effort . . . was to punish the Negro for having abandoned the control of his old master, and to regulate the conditions of his employment and the scale of wages to be paid him."

This peculiar plan failed, but there were similar efforts throughout the country in the nineteenth century. More than twelve thousand Chinese men worked on the construction crews responsible for laying the transcontinental railroad, and in isolated cases Chinese men were used as strikebreakers in northeastern factories.

Almost a century later, during the civil rights era, the sociologist who introduced the model minority image was explicit in marveling at Asian-Americans in contrast to blacks.[4] The author of the 1966 *New York Times Magazine* article "Success Story, Japanese-American Style" opened his account with a lengthy history of official discrimination against Japanese-Americans. The point of his remarks was that, "this kind of treatment, as we all know these days, creates what might be termed, 'problem minorities.'" A nod and wink weren't necessary to identify those "problem minorities." The author went on to explain that Japanese-Americans, except for a few juvenile delinquents who had joined black or Mexican gangs, were a model minority.

Like historical accounts of Asian-Americans, the contemporary casting of Asian-Americans as the model minority all but explicitly says to African-Americans and other racial minorities, They made it—why can't you? But like other Americans, Asian-Americans by and large remain ignorant of their own history. Efforts to include a more multicultural perspective on past events are dismissed as politically correct, eliminating any context for understanding contemporary race relations.

Within that context, the model minority myth can be used against Asian-Americans as well. The exaggerated success of Asian-Americans can be held against them, leading to hatred and violence. In the nineteenth century, backlash against Chinese immigrants made a negative out of the formerly positive trait of industriousness. The result was the Chinese Exclusion Act, which marked the end of an era of open immigration by simply prohibiting Chinese from becoming citizens. In the early twentieth century, reaction against Japanese-Americans again was based on the trait of their being hardworking. The result was the Alien Land Laws, which prevented Japanese-Americans from owning the very farms that had formed the basis of their modest prosperity.

Repeatedly, during difficult economic circumstances accompanied by trade tensions with Asian nations, Asian-Americans have been seen as part of an economic juggernaut: Japan Inc., the Pacific century, the rise of the East and decline of the West are all concepts that update the "yellow peril" of the past. The blaming of Asian-Americans can become violent, as during the recession of the 1980s in Detroit, when two unemployed white autoworkers murdered a Chinese-American, Vincent Chin, mistaking him for a Japanese national.

On college campuses across the country, the model minority myth has developed into a powerful expression of anxiety about the assumed accomplishments of Asian-Americans. White Americans sarcastically suggest that UCLA stands for "United Caucasians Lost among Asians" and MIT, "Made In Taiwan." At the peak of the controversy over Asian-Americans and quotas in college admissions, a white Yale student stated, "If you are weak in math or science and find yourself assigned to a class with a majority of Asian kids, the only thing to do is transfer to a different section." The white president of the University of California at Berkeley explained, "Some students say if they see too many Asians in a class, they are not going to take it because the curve will be too high." The white president of Stanford repeated an apocryphal story about a professor who asked a student about a poor exam result in an engineering course, to be asked in return, "What do you think I am, Chinese?"[5]

THE TRUTH BEHIND THE STEREOTYPE

The model minority myth is based on poor social science. It reveals the risk of relying on racial generalizations. It is inappropriate to compare Asian-Americans and African-Americans because no matter how much racial discrimination Asian-Americans have faced in this country—and Asian-Americans have faced racial discrimination—they have never been enslaved. Even during periods of official discrimination, they were sometimes treated as "honorary" whites. By any socioeconomic measure, from housing segregation to employment discrimination, Asian-Americans enjoy advantages over African-Americans. Even the selective nature of immigration ensures that Asian immigrants arrive with significant educational and professional advantages; interestingly, contemporary African immigrants also display exceptional credentials.

Nevertheless, Asian-Americans are at a significant disadvantage compared to Caucasian Americans. The frequently cited statistic that average Asian-Americans family income is equal to or higher than average white family income obscures many facts: Asian-Americans are better educated than whites, again on the average; more Asian-American individuals contribute to family income; and Asian-Americans are concentrated in the high-income, high-cost states of California, New York, and Hawaii. Comparing equally qualified individuals, and controlling for immigrant status, Asian-Americans consistently earn less than whites.[6]

That Asian-Americans suffer the glass ceiling effect has been documented repeatedly, including most recently in the report of the bipartisan Glass Ceiling Commission. That studies show that though there are many Asian-Americans in engineering, science, and technical professions, they are significantly underrepresented in higher administrative, sales, and managerial positions as well as in the fields of law, education, social services, and media. Asian-American men earn between 10 and 17% less than their white counterparts. Asian-American women earn as much as 40% less than white men with the same credentials.

Even in higher education, Asian-American students' achievements have been exaggerated. When the University of California Regents were debating whether to eliminate affirmative action, reports circulated indicating that Asian-Americans would greatly benefit because they had the best credentials. A recent study by the university itself, however, revealed that Asian-American applicants had slightly lower high school grades and test scores than white applicants.[7] In other words, whites, not Asian-Americans, would be the primary beneficiaries of an admissions policy without affirmative action.

At best, labeling Asian-Americans a model minority is inaccurate. The Census Bureau's definition of "Asian-American" is problematic. Within this category, individuals from sixteen countries of origin and more than twenty Pacific Island cultures have been lumped together, even though there are tremendous differences among these groups. The fastest growing Asian-American ethnic group is Vietnamese-Americans. More than a quarter of Vietnamese-Americans live in poverty, compared to 13% of the general population. The percentages are even higher for other groups, including Laotians (35% below the poverty line) and Cambodians (43% below the poverty line). Southeast Asian groups are not unique; a higher portion of Chinese-, Pakistani-, Korean-, Thai-, and Indonesian-Americans also live in poverty. For most Asian-American ethnic groups, ironically, the average income of native-born individuals is lower than the average income of immigrants. This suggests that Asian-Americans are proof of selective immigration policies rather than modern-day Horatio Alger heroes.

Indeed, the model minority myth ensures that poor Asian-Americans will be ignored, sometimes by their own communities. For example, more than 44% of Chinese-Americans who live in California are not fluent in English. Lacking education and the language and cultural skills necessary to obtain work, these Asian-Americans have needs that are overlooked, even by policy makers who are trying to help the disadvantaged.

The model minority myth also shows the continuing significance of race in shaping our society. A recent survey asked white Americans to compare themselves with racial minorities on a number of traits. While whites regarded Asian-Americans more highly than they did African-Americans and Latinos, they thought of them as worse than themselves. On the whole, whites considered Asian-Americans to be more lazy, more violence-prone, less intelligent, and more likely to prefer being on welfare than are whites. Asian-Americans, then, may be regarded as a "model," but only for other minorities. [. . .]

Race may well become less important over time. Reasonable and sincere people can have different views on whether race should become less important. But individuals who wish to envision and achieve a color-blind society do their cause a disservice by being acutely conscious of Asian-Americans for the purpose of attacking affirmative action.

The time has come to move beyond black and white, and to do so constructively and cooperatively—regardless of the ultimate decisions that are made on affirmative action. There are many real issues that must be addressed in a society that is not only multiracial but also multicultural. The dilemma of Asian-Americans and affirmative action, however, should be recognized as a problem manufactured for political purposes. And opponents of affirmative action, including Asian-Americans, should be prepared to answer the inquiry, real rather than rhetorical, of what alternatives to affirmative action they might propose to achieve racial justice.

NOTES

1. There are only a few articles and books discussing Asian-Americans and affirmative action. Some sources are Frank H. Wu, "Neither Black Nor White: Asian-Americans and Affirmative Action," *Boston College Third World Law Journal*, 15, no. 2 (1995): 225; Pat K. Chew, "Asian-Americans: The 'Reticent' Minority and Their Paradoxes," *William and Mary Law Review*, 36, no. 1 (1994): 1; Dana Y. Takagi, *The Retreat from Race: Asian-American Admissions and Racial Politics* (New Brunswick, N.J.: Rutgers, 1992); and Grace W. Tsuang, "Assuring Equal Access of Asian-Americans to Highly Selective Universities," *Yale Law Journal*, 98, no. 2 (1989): 659.

2. The role of Asian-Americans in race relations is described in Gary Y. Okihiro, *Margins and Mainstreams: Asians in American History and Culture* (Seattle: Univ. of Washington Press, 1994); Mari Matsuda, "We Will Not Be Used," *UCLA Asian Pacific Islands Law Journal*, 1 (1993): 79.

3. The best sources of historical information about Asian-Americans are Ronald Takaki, *Strangers from a Different Shore: A History of Asian-Americans* (New York: Viking, 1989); Sucheng Chan, *The Asian-Americans: An Interpretive History* (New York: Macmillan 1991); and Roger Daniels, *Asian America: Chinese and Japanese in the United States Since 1850* (Seattle: Univ. of Washington Press, 1988).

4. William Petersen, "Success Story, Japanese-American Style," *New York Times Magazine*, Jan. 9, 1966, 20.

5. The examples are from Takaki, *Strangers from a Different Shore*, 479; Bret Easton Ellis, *Less Than Zero* (New York: Viking, 1985), 13; David Brand, "The New Whiz Kids: Why Asian-Americans Are Doing So Well, and What It Costs Them," *Time*, Aug. 31, 1987, 42; Jay Mathews, "Asian Students Help Create a New Mainstream," *Washington Post*, Nov. 14, 1985; Fox Butterfield, "Why Asians Are Going to the Head of the Class," *New York Times*, Education Supplement, Aug. 3, 1986.

6. The best sources for social science data concerning Asian-Americans are Jayjia Hsia, *Asian-Americans in Higher Education and at Work* (Mahwah, N.J.: Lawrence Erlbaum Assoc., 1988); Susan B. Gall and Timothy Gall, eds., *Statistical Record of Asian-Americans* (Detroit: Gale Research, 1993); Herbert R. Barringer et al., eds., *Asians and Pacific Islanders in the United States* (New York: Russell Sage Foundation, 1993); U.S. Department of Commerce, Bureau of the Census, *We the American Asians* (Washington, D.C.: GPO, 1993). Unless otherwise indicated, all statistics are drawn from these sources.

7. University of California, Office of the President, "The Use of Socio-Economic Status in Place of Ethnicity in Undergraduate Admissions: A Report on the Results of an Exploratory Computer Simulation" (May 1995): 14–15.

2. What Should Be Done to Solve Racial Problems?

THE TALENTED TENTH

W.E.B. Du Bois

This essay was originally published in 1903 in a book entitled The Negro Problem. *It was held up as a model in the social, political, and ethical roles of the new so-called "crossover" generation. Du Bois believed that education was the answer for positive change, as clearly shown in the essay.*

The Negro race, like all races, is going to be saved by its exceptional men. The problem of education, then, among Negroes must first of all deal with the Talented Tenth; it is the problem of developing the Best of this race that they may guide the Mass away from the contamination and death of the Worst, in their own and other races. Now the training of men is a difficult and intricate task. Its technique is a matter for educational experts, but its object is for the vision of seers. If we make money the object of man-training, we shall develop money-makers but not necessarily men; if we make technical skill the object of education, we may possess artisans but not, in nature, men. Men we shall have only as we make manhood the object of the work of the schools—intelligence, broad sympathy, knowledge of the world that was and is, and of the relation of men to it—this is the curriculum of that Higher Education which must underlie true life. On this foundation we may build bread winning, skill of hand and quickness of brain, with never a fear lest the child and man mistake the means of living for the object of life.

If this be true—and who can deny it—three tasks lay before me; first to show from the past that the Talented Tenth as they have risen among American Negroes have been worthy of leadership; secondly, to show how these men may be educated and developed; and thirdly, to show their relation to the Negro problem.

You misjudge us because you do not know us. From the very first it has been the educated and intelligent of the Negro people that have led and elevated the mass, and the sole obstacles that nullified and retarded their efforts were slavery and race prejudice; for what is slavery but the legalized survival of the unfit and the nullification of the work of natural internal leadership? Negro leadership, therefore, sought from the first to rid the race of this awful incubus that it might make way for natural selection and the survival of the fittest. In colonial days came Phillis Wheatley and Paul Cuffe striving against the bars of prejudice; and Benjamin Banneker, the almanac maker, voiced their longings when he said to

From Henry Louis Gates, Jr. and Cornel West, *The Future of the Race* (New York: Alfred A. Knopf, 1996), pp. 133–140, 156–157.

Thomas Jefferson, "I freely and cheerfully acknowledge that I am of the African Race, and in colour which is natural to them, of the deepest dye; and it is under a sense of the most profound gratitude to the Supreme Ruler of the Universe, that I now confess to you that I am not under that state of tyrannical thraldom and inhuman captivity to which too many of my brethren are doomed, but that I have abundantly tasted of the fruition of those blessings which proceed from that free and unequalled liberty with which you are favored, and which I hope you will willingly allow, you have mercifully received from the immediate hand of that Being from whom proceedeth every good and perfect gift.

"Suffer me to recall to your mind that time, in which the arms of the British crown were exerted with every powerful effort, in order to reduce you to a state of servitude; look back, I entreat you, on the variety of dangers to which you were exposed; reflect on that period in which every human aid appeared unavailable, and in which even hope and fortitude wore the aspect of inability to the conflict, and you cannot but be led to a serious and grateful sense of your miraculous and providential preservation, you cannot but acknowledge, that the present freedom and tranquility which you enjoy, you have mercifully received, and that a peculiar blessing of heaven.

"This, sir, was a time when you clearly saw into the injustice of a state of Slavery, and in which you had just apprehensions of the horrors of its condition. It was then that your abhorrence thereof was so excited, that you publicly held forth this true and invaluable doctrine, which is worthy to be recorded and remembered in all succeeding ages: 'We hold these truths to be self evident, that all men are created equal; that they are endowed with certain inalienable rights, and that among these are life, liberty and the pursuit of happiness.'"

Then came Dr. James Derham, who could tell even the learned Dr. Rush something of medicine, and Lemuel Haynes, to whom Middlebury gave an honorary A.M. in 1804. These and others we may call the Revolutionary group of distinguished Negroes—they were persons of marked ability, leaders of a Talented Tenth, standing conspicuously among the best of their time. They strove by word and deed to save the color line from becoming the line between the bond and free, but all that they could do was nullified by Eli Whitney and the Curse of Gold. So they passed into forgetfulness.

But their spirit did not wholly die; here and there in the early part of the century came other exceptional men. Some were natural sons of unnatural fathers and were given often a liberal training and thus a race of educated mulattoes sprang up to plead for the black men's rights. There was Ira Aldridge, whom all Europe loved to honor; there was that voice crying in the Wilderness, David Walker, and saying:

"I declare it does appear to me as though some nations think God is asleep, or that he made the Africans for nothing else but to dig their mines and work their farms, or they cannot believe history, sacred or profane. I ask every man who has a heart, and is blessed with the privilege of believing—Is not God a God of justice to all his creatures? Do you say he is? Then if he gives peace and tranquility to tyrants and permits them to keep our fathers, our mothers, ourselves and our children in eternal ignorance and wretchedness to support them and their families, would he be to us a God of Justice? I ask, O, ye Christians, who hold us and our children in the most abject ignorance and degradation that ever a people were afflicted with since the world began—I say if God gives you peace and tranquility, and suffers you thus to go on afflicting us, and our children, who have never given you the least provocation—would he be to us a God of Justice? If you will allow that we are men, who feel for each other, does not the blood of our fathers and of us, their children, cry aloud to the Lord of Sabaoth against you for the cruelties and murders with which you have and do continue to afflict us?"

This was the wild voice that first aroused Southern legislators in 1829 to the terrors of abolitionism.

In 1831 there met that first Negro convention in Philadelphia, at which the world gaped curiously but which bravely attacked the problems of race and slavery, crying out against persecution and declaring that "Laws as cruel in themselves as they were unconstitutional and unjust, have in many places been enacted against our poor, unfriended and unoffending brethren (without a shadow of provocation on our part), at whose bare recital the very savage draws himself up for fear of contagion—looks noble and prides himself because he bears not the name of Christian." Side by side this free Negro movement, and the movement for abolition, strove until they merged into one strong stream. Too little notice has been taken of the work which the Talented Tenth among Negroes took in the great abolition crusade. From the very day that a Philadelphia colored man became the first subscriber to Garrison's "Liberator," to the day when Negro soldiers made the Emancipation Proclamation possible, black leaders worked shoulder to shoulder with white men in a movement, the success of which would have been impossible without them. There was Purvis and Remond, Pennington and Highland Garnet, Sojourner Truth and Alexander Crummell, and above all, Frederick Douglass—what would the abolition movement have been without them? They stood as living examples of the possibilities of the Negro race, their own hard experiences and well-wrought culture said silently more than all the drawn periods of orators—they were the men who made American slavery impossible. As Maria Weston Chapman once said, from the school of anti-slavery agitation "a throng of authors, editors, lawyers, orators and accomplished gentlemen of color have taken their degree! It has equally implanted hopes and aspirations, noble thoughts, and sublime purposes, in the hearts of both races. It has prepared the white man for the freedom of the black man, and it has made the black man scorn the thought of enslavement, as does a white man, as far as its influence has extended. Strengthen that noble influence! Before its organization, the country only saw here and there in slavery some faithful Cudjoe or Dinah, whose strong natures blossomed even in bondage, like a fine plant beneath a heavy stone. Now, under the elevating and cherishing influence of the American Anti-slavery Society, the colored race, like the white, furnishes Corinthian capitals for the noblest temples."

Where were these black abolitionists trained? Some, like Frederick Douglass, were self-trained, but yet trained liberally; others like Alexander Crummell and McCune Smith, graduated from famous foreign universities. Most of them rose up through the colored schools of New York and Philadelphia and Boston, taught by college-bred men like Russworm, of Dartmouth, and college-bred white men like Neau and Benezet.

After emancipation came a new group of educated and gifted leaders: Langston, Bruce and Elliot, Greener, Williams and Payne. Through political organization, historical and polemic writing and moral regeneration, these men strove to uplift their people. It is now the fashion of to-day to sneer at them and to say that with freedom Negro leadership should have begun at the plow and not in the Senate—a foolish and mischievous lie; two hundred and fifty years that black serf toiled at the plow and yet that toiling was in vain till the Senate passed the war amendments; and two hundred and fifty years more the half-free serf of to-day may toil at his plow, but unless he have political rights and righteously guarded civic status, he will still remain the poverty-stricken and ignorant plaything of rascals, that he now is. This all sane men know even if they dare not say it.

And so now we come to the present—a day of cowardice and vacillation, of strident wide-voiced wrong and faint hearted compromise; of double-faced dallying with Truth and Right. Who are to-day guiding the work of the Negro people? The "exceptions" of course. And yet so sure as this Talented Tenth is pointed out, the blind worshippers of the Average cry out in alarm: "These are the exceptions, look here at death, disease and crime—these are the happy rule." Of course they are the rule, because a silly nation made them the rule: Because for three long centuries this people lynched Negroes who dared to be brave, raped black women who dared to be virtuous, crushed dark-hued youth who dared to be ambitious, and encouraged and made to flourish servility and lewdness and apathy. But not even this was able to crush all manhood and chastity and aspiration from black folk. A saving remnant continually survives and persists, continually aspires, continually shows itself in thrift and ability and character. Exceptional it is to be sure, but this is its chiefest promise; it shows the capability of Negro blood, the promise of black men. Do Americans ever stop to reflect that there are in this land a million men of Negro blood, well-educated, owners of homes, against the honor of whose womanhood no breath was ever raised, whose men occupy positions of trust and usefulness, and who, judged by any standard, have reached the full measure of the best type of modern European culture? Is it fair, is it decent, is it Christian to ignore these facts of the Negro problem, to belittle such aspiration, to nullify such leadership and seek to crush these people back into the mass out of which by toil and travail, they and their fathers have raised themselves?

Can the masses of the Negro people be in any possible way more quickly raised than by the effort and example of this aristocracy of talent and character? Was there ever a nation on God's fair earth civilized from the bottom upward? Never; it is, ever was and ever will be from the top downward that culture filters. The Talented Tenth rises and pulls all that are worth the saving up to their vantage ground. This is the history of human progress; and two historic mistakes which have hindered that progress were the thinking first that no more could ever rise save the few already risen; or second, that it would better the unrisen to pull the risen down.

How then shall the leaders of a struggling people be trained and the hands of the risen few be strengthened? There can be but one answer: The best and most capable of their youth must be schooled in the colleges and universities of the land. We will not quarrel as to just what the university of the Negro should teach or how it should teach it—I willingly admit that each soul and each race-soul needs its own peculiar curriculum. But this is true: A university is a human invention for the transmission of knowledge and culture from generation to generation, through the training of quick minds and pure hearts, and for this work no other human invention will suffice, not even trade and industrial schools. . . . Men of America, the problem is plain before you. Here is a race transplanted through the criminal foolishness of your fathers. Whether you like it or not the millions are here, and here they will remain. If you do not lift them up, they will pull you down. Education and work are the levers to uplift a people. Work will not do it unless inspired by the right ideals and guided by intelligence. Education must not simply teach work—it must teach life. The Talented Tenth of the Negro race must be made leaders of thought and missionaries of culture among their people. No others can do this work and the Negro colleges must train men for it. The Negro race, like all other races, is going to be saved by its exceptional men.

PARABLE OF THE TALENTS

Henry Louis Gates, Jr.

Henry Louis Gates, Jr. graduated summa cum laude *from Yale University with a degree in history and he received his Ph.D. in English from Cambridge University. He has written many books, including* The Future of the Race, *co-authored by Cornel West, from which this following excerpt is taken. In the Preface, the authors, who now both teach at Harvard, say, "Had it not been for affirmative action, we, like so many of our ancestors, familial and fraternal, would have met at one of the superb historically black colleges or universities, such as Spelman or Talledega, Howard or Morehouse, Fisk or Lincoln, and not in the Ivy League" (xi).*

HOW TO JOIN THE BLACK OVERCLASS

Twenty-five years ago, I left West Virginia for Yale University, to join the blackest class in the history of that ivy-draped institution. I drove up on my own, without my parents. They were never comfortable in that island of leaded glass and

From Henry Louis Gates, Jr. and Cornel West, *The Future of the Race* (New York: Alfred A. Knopf, 1996), pp. 3–6, 9, 19–21, 24–25, 33, 38.

Gothic spires, although you might say they spent much of their lives making sure I arrived there. My father worked two jobs—loading trucks at a paper mill, plus a night shift as a janitor for the phone company—to keep us well fed and well clothed, and to pay the premiums on "college insurance policies," a thousand dollars when we reached eighteen. It never occurred to me that we might be poor until much later a sociologist told me so, pinpointing "the Gateses" in a mass of metallic-tasting demographics that left me numb with the neatness of it all.

I suppose that Yale represented both a betrayal and a fulfillment of their dreams. Blacks are wedded to narratives of ascent, to borrow a phrase from literary critic Robert Stepto, and we have made the compounded preposition "up from" our own: up from slavery, up from Piedmont, up from the Bronx, always up. But narratives of ascent, whether or not we like to admit it, are also narratives of alienation, of loss. Usually the ascent is experienced not as a gradual progression but as a leap, and for so many of my generation that leap as the one that took us from our black homes and neighborhoods into the white universities that had adopted newly vigorous programs of minority recruitment. It should be said that the adjustment was a two-way street: we were as strange to the institutions in which we found ourselves as those institutions were to us. In short, we were part of a grand social experiment—a blind date, of sorts. We weren't a tenth, of course; and whatever talent we had wasn't necessarily greater than our compeers who were passed over, or who opted out; but we were here. You might call us the crossover generation.

To speak in strictly chronological terms, we are among the late-bloomers who now occupy the White House and the Congress—an age grade that includes Bill Clinton and Robert Reich and William Kristol. But the sense of generational affinity is intensified within the race: ours was the first generation to attend integrated schools in the wake of *Brown v. Board*; to have watched, as children, the dismantling of Jim Crow and to wonder where the process might end; to be given the chance, through affirmative action, to compete against white boys and girls; to enter and integrate the elite institutions just as the most expansive notions of radical democracy made an entrance.

I picked Yale almost out of a hat. After a year at a junior college near my home, a place where "nigger" was hung on me so many times that I thought it was my name, I decided to head north, armed with a scholarship and a first edition of Strunk and White's *The Elements of Style*.

By day—and it was still light when I first arrived in New Haven—the university is a tangible, mortar-and-stone manifestation of an Oxonian ideal of Gothic perfection. By night, the sense of enchantment increased: the mammoth structures, strangely out of keeping with the surrounding town, guarded their streets with bearded shadows made by the half-light of the lampposts. At Yale, battle hymns were Congregational, with delicate changes of key. The building that just *had* to be the college cathedral turned out to be Sterling Library. Every feature of the place was alarming and exhilarating. Welcome to Never-Never Land, I told myself. This is your world, the world you've longed for and dreamed of. This was where the goods and entitlements of the American century were stored and distributed. It was the grown-up version of the world of Captain Midnight Decoders; the repository of all those box tops I used to ship off to Kellogg's in fair exchange for laser guns. If college was a warehouse for what we've modishly learned to call "cultural capital," the question wasn't how to get it but what to do with it.

Many of the black kids at Yale were the first in their families to attend college, and they congregated in the pre-med and pre-law tracks, searching for a secure place in the newly integrated arenas of the nation's elite. Others were scions of old "colored money." Most of us took at least one course in the new program in Afro-American Studies, probably in part out of a sense of team spirit, partly out of a yearning to tap our cultural unconscious. I took several such courses, and at least three times found myself assigned to read Du Bois's essay "The Talented Tenth." (Only Harold Cruse's *The Crisis of the Negro Intellectual* was assigned more often.) Du Bois's essay was read and critiqued, almost defensively, for its vanguardism; but its vision of the educated bourgeoisie as the truly revolutionary class—Marx stood on its head, you might say—exerted an unmistakable sway on us.

LIFTED AS WE CLIMBED

In the year I was born, 1950, 5 percent of employed blacks held professional or managerial jobs; another 5 percent held clerical or sales jobs. So, depending on the elasticity of your definition, maybe a tenth would have qualified as "middle-class." To spell out the obverse: Among even those blacks who held jobs, 90 percent failed, by conventional standards, to qualify as middle-class. If educational attainment was your measure, the situation looked bleaker; even ten years later, only 3 percent of blacks had a college degree. And more than half of blacks fell below the poverty line. In the year I graduated from high school, almost half of black households took in less than fifteen thousand dollars a year, in today's dollars; less than 6 percent took in more than fifty thousand. [. . .]

THE TIMOROUS TENTH

The year I graduated from college, 1973, marked the beginning of a growing divergence between poor blacks and prosperous ones, such that the well-off became better-off while the poor became poorer; and in the years since, poverty has, in lockstep, kept pace with privilege. First, though, the good news. Today, roughly a third of black families can be counted as middle-class. I've mentioned that in 1950, only 5 percent of black workers were professionals or managers; today, the figure is greater than 20 percent. The number of black families earning more than fifty thousand dollars a year has quadrupled since 1967, and doubled in the eighties alone. In 1973, the top one hundred black-owned businesses had sales of $473 million; today, the figure is $11.7 billion. In 1970, only one in ten blacks had attended college; today, one in three has.

The black middle class has never been in better shape—and it has never felt worse about things. Du Bois had conjured up a Talented Tenth that would be a beacon of hope; it is ninety years later, and they are, instead, a sump of gloom. Middle-class messianism has given way to middle-class malaise. Jennifer Hochschild, the political scientist, calls this paradox "succeeding more and enjoying it less."

Certainly the data she has assembled are striking. Over the past generation, poor and affluent black Americans have switched places with respect to their attitudes toward America and their expectations of economic progress and of the future of race relations; the result is a kind of ideological chiasmus. Professor Hochschild writes:

> When asked what is important for getting ahead in life, poor blacks are almost as likely to choose being of the right sex and more likely to choose religious conviction and political connections than to choose being of the right race. Well-off blacks, however, think race matters more than any of those characteristics. Affluent blacks are almost more likely to see blacks are economically worse off than whites, and to see discrimination as blacks' most important problem. . . . As the African American middle class has become larger, more powerful, and more stable, its members have grown disillusioned with and even embittered about the American dream.[1]

This represents a dramatic reversal of the situation during the years of my childhood, in the fifties and sixties. In 1964, 70 percent of middle-class blacks surveyed said they thought most whites want to see blacks get a better break; by 1992, only 20 percent thought so. The Talented Tenth has a surprising susceptibility to racial paranoia, too: blacks with a college education are especially likely to seriously entertain claims that AIDS was concocted to infect blacks, or that the government conspired to make drugs available in poor neighborhoods in an effort to harm blacks. Material success has led to the death of trust. In short, even as the numbers of the affluent have swollen, the hopefulness of the affluent has plunged. Antonio Gramsci, famously, recommended pessimism of the intellect and optimism of the will; for much of the black elite, pessimism has prevailed on both fronts.

Why should this be? We're certainly free to speculate. Some critics would probably implicate the oppositional culture of the sixties, as incubated in the very elite institutions that secured us a place among the educated bourgeoisie. It isn't unknown for an oppositional creed to decay into a kind of routinized cynicism. Then there's the fact that economic advancement entails greater intimacy with whites, and so greater opportunities for friction. You might even wonder about the effects of stigmatizing black upward mobility; certainly the figure of the inauthentic buppy has passed from the sociological study into popular black films and novels. Culturally speaking, the "street" has been deemed the repository of all that is real, that is "black," and alternative models of ethnic solidarity have

---

[1] Jennifer L. Hochschild, *Facing Up to the American Dream: Race, Class, and the Soul of the Nation*. Princeton: Princeton University Press, 1995, p. 79.

been late in coming. But probably more significant is the matter of dashed hopes: of great expectations, and the mourning after.

THE POVERTY PERPLEX

What makes all this of particular concern is the swelling ranks of the black poor, a category that (like the black middle class) now encompasses about a third of black families. More than half of all black males between twenty-five and thirty-four are jobless or "underemployed." Other social indices are equally discouraging: In 1993, 2.3 million black men were sent to jail or prison while 23,000 received a college diploma—a ratio of a hundred to one. (The ratio for whites was six to one.) And the plight of the black poor is even more alarming if you look not just at household earnings but at assets. The poorest fifth of whites have a median net worth of ten thousand dollars; the median net worth of their black counterparts is . . . zero.

On a rational level, of course, we know that black prosperity doesn't derive from black poverty; on a symbolic level, however, the chronic hardship of a third of black America is a standing reproach to those of us who once dreamed of collective uplift. It makes it hard to invoke the salvific conception of the "Talented Tenth" without bitterness. If your name is Auchincloss, say, you do not worry overmuch about those impoverished Appalachians who share your Scottish descent; few blacks have the luxury of such detachment.

Du Bois once believed that educated Negroes would uplift the race; give or take a few revolutionary flourishes, most of my black classmates at college would have concurred. It *sounded* different, our creed, but it came to the same thing. So it's easy to take our collective misfortunes personally. Forty years after *Brown v. Board,* most black students attend majority black schools; a third attend schools that are 90 to 100 percent black. Everything was supposed to have been different from the way it turned out. [. . .]

And so the hand-wringing and the talk about the crisis of leadership. If only we could get *that* part right—some blacks have started to think—we could start to get a handle on the grassroots problems. The trouble is, no one can agree on what that leadership should look like; no one ever could.

Pollsters have long known of the remarkable gap between the leaders and the led in black America. A 1985 survey found that most blacks favored the death penalty and prayer in public schools while most black leaders opposed these things. Most blacks opposed school busing, while most black leaders favored it. Three times as many blacks opposed abortion rights as their leaders did. Indeed, on many key social issues, blacks are more conservative than whites. If the numbers of black Republicans are on the rise, as these opinion surveys suggest, it would be unwise to dismiss the phenomenon. Given the breach between the black leadership and its putative constituency, we shouldn't be surprised at the motley company who seek to fill it. [. . .]

The real crisis in black leadership, then, is that the very idea of black leadership is in crisis. On this score, we can't turn for help to our vested elites—not even to our Grand Polemarches and Supreme Basileuses. For black America needs a politics whose first mission isn't the reinforcement of the idea of black America; and a discourse of race that isn't centrally concerned with preserving the idea of race and racial unanimity. We need something we don't yet have: a way of speaking about black poverty that doesn't falsify the reality of black advancement; a way of speaking about black advancement that doesn't distort the enduring realities of black poverty. I'd venture that a lot depends on whether we get it.

MORE THAN IDENTITY RIDES ON A NEW RACIAL CATEGORY

Linda Mathews

Linda Mathews wrote this article for the New York Times.

Edward Cooper, a Portland, Ore., businessman, is black. His wife and business partner, Barbara McIntyre, is white. Their 12-year-old son, Ethan McCooper, is, like his name, a blend of his parents, and harder to classify.

On Ethan's school forms and other official papers, his parents sometimes check both the "white" and the "black" boxes. If "other" is available, they check that and write in "interracial." When ordered to choose between "black" and "white," they resolutely leave the form blank.

What they would like to call the light-skinned, dark-eyed boy with the reddish-brown hair is "multiracial." They may yet get their way, if the Federal Government yields to growing pressure and adds a "multiracial" category to the census in the year 2000.

"This is an issue that isn't going away," said Mary Waters, a Harvard professor of sociology who teaches a course on race. "We're riding such a big wave of interracial marriages that inevitably there are going to be many more people who can claim a multiracial identity if it's permitted."

Creating another category for people who do not fit the existing racial categories—or whose children do not fit—is not a simple matter. Indeed, a proposal to do so, which has been pending before the Federal Office of Management and Budget for three years, has been denounced by some of the nation's leading civil rights organizations as an unnecessary, expensive move that would deplete the ranks of blacks and other racial minorities and curtail their political power. A decision is expected from O.M.B. by mid-1997.

New York Times, July 6, 1996, pp. 1, 7.

At least five million people will be affected by the Government's decision—the three million Americans who told the Census Bureau in 1990 that they were married to or living with someone of a different race, and their two million children.

In percentage terms, of course, the numbers are still small. A 1995 telephone test survey by the Federal Government found that Americans who identify themselves as "multiracial" account for only 1.6 percent of the population.

But interracial marriages doubled from 1960 to 1970 and tripled from 1970 to 1980, spurred in part by a Supreme Court decision that struck down state laws prohibiting mixed marriages. While the pace slowed during the 1980's, by 1990 there were 1.5 million such marriages.

Unions between blacks and whites are still relatively rare, accounting for only about one-seventh of all interracial marriages, though a study released this week reported that the number of these marriages is accelerating. Only 6 percent of black men and 2 percent of black women marry outside their race, compared to 12 percent of Asian men, 25 percent of Asian women, and 59 percent of American Indian men and 60 percent of American Indian women. For whites, 1.6 percent of the men and 1.4 percent of the women marry non-whites.

While a new Census category may not deter society from seeing a multiracial person as black or Asian, some children of mixed marriages are planning a demonstration on July 20 in Washington in support of the addition. Styled on the Million Man March for black men last fall, the Multiracial Solidarity March, planners say, is to let participants "publicly and proudly affirm their multiraciality."

THE MOVEMENT: EMERGING GROUPS WITH AN AGENDA

In the past decade, interracial couples have emerged as a political force. They have organized political groups, both at the local and the national level, founded magazines and businesses that cater to the needs of families like theirs and established web pages and chat groups on the Internet.

Specifically, the goal for many of these groups is official recognition for multiracial Americans as separate from the four racial categories the Census Bureau has used since 1977: white; black; American Indian and Alaska native, and Asian and Pacific islander. The 1990 census also listed another category, called "other," and separately asked Americans whether they were of "Hispanic" or "Spanish" origin.

One of the largest and most vocal multiracial organizations, Project RACE, for Reclassify All Children Equally, has already succeeded in persuading seven state legislatures to enact laws requiring a "multiracial" classification on government documents.

"We have members who are black, white, Hispanic, Asian and Native American, or combinations thereof," says Susan Graham, the executive director of Project RACE, which is based in Rosewell, Ga., "and what they have in common is a simple wish to call themselves or their children what they are—multiracial."

Ms. Graham, who is white and married to a black, said that her son, now 11, had been classified as "white by the census, black at school and biracial at home."

She particularly resented being told by a census official in 1990 that "a mixed child should take the race of the mother" regardless of the family's preferences. Her son's kindergarten teacher decided he was black because his father dropped him off at school. "Calling him and his sister multiracial is really the most accurate way to go," Ms. Graham said.

"This is not just a feel-good issue for us," Ms. Graham said. She noted that census-takers no longer decided a person's race after a brief interview, as was the case before 1980. The modern census, conducted largely by mail, is based on self-identification—respondents get to declare their own race and the race of everyone else in their households, as a matter of right. In Ms. Graham's view, multiracial Americans should be extended the same right.

THE DISSENT: STRESSING COMFORT WITH SELF

The multiracial world is hardly a monolith when it comes to finding the right label. Candy Mills, the publisher and founding editor of three magazines, Interrace, Black Child and Child of Colors, once favored the multiracial category but has changed her mind.

"I think we should all resist categorization," said Ms. Mills, who is African-American and Native American and the mother of two biracial children, Gabriela 12, and Laszlo, 3. "A multiracial category would give more credence to other categories, when in fact we all know that there's no such thing as race. There are colors, but there's only one race, the human race."

Ms. Mills, who lives in Atlanta, said she and her husband, Gabe Grosz, who is white, had resisted labeling their children multiracial because they feared it would "separate them from all the things they have in common with both the black and white aspects of their lives."

"I tell my daughter I want her to grow up to be just Gabriela," Ms. Mills said, "and if she wants to call herself black or white or even Asian, I couldn't care less."

Ms. Mills is impatient with those who contend that a multiracial category is necessary to build the self-esteem and establish the identity of children like hers.

"It's the parents of many multiracial children who have the identity problem, not the children themselves," she declared. "Many of these multiracial activists, both black and white, want to minimize their child's African heritage.

"I think they see a multiracial category as a way to elevate their children, to say, 'You're not black. You're better than that.'" Now, I ask you, what's so bad about being called black?"

Kenya M. Mayfield, a senior at Cornell University who has written for Interrace magazine, also doubts the need for a multiracial category.

"I'm skeptical that the category will have any impact on anyone's self-esteem," Ms. Mayfield said. "A multiracial box may affect politics or the allocation of Federal funds but not anyone's identity."

Ms. Mayfield, 22, who grew up in Oklahoma City with a mother who is African-American and Cherokee and a father who is white, said her parents taught her that "I had the best of all worlds."

Some parents say they have complex motives for supporting a multiracial category. Ms. McIntyre, who owns a Portland mail-order company with her husband, says: "There may be some parents who like the multiracial idea because they want their children to be better than black, but there are also plenty like me who just want to be acknowledged. I'm part of this kid, too, no matter who he looks like.

"I favor what I call the three-in-one approach. My child is black, he's white and he's mixed. I want him to be comfortable in this world. If someone calls him African-American, I want him to accept that. If someone calls him whitey or honky, well, that's cool. Or mixed—that's O.K., too."

THE PROBLEMS: FEARING A LOSS OF POWER

The multiracial campaign has drawn the support of some people who are actively involved in civil rights issues. In Georgia, the bill that mandated a multiracial category on state documents was introduced by State Senator Ralph David Abernathy 3d, the son of the Rev. Ralph David Abernathy, who was president of the Southern Christian Leadership Conference.

But the proposal to do the same thing nationwide has drawn fire from other civil rights groups, including the National Urban League, the National Association for the Advancement of Colored People, the National Council of La Raza and the Lawyers Committee for Civil Rights Under Law.

Their objection, spelled out in letters, public testimony and journal articles, is that the availability of a multiracial category would reduce the number of Americans claiming to belong to long-recognized racial minority groups, dilute the electoral power of those groups and make it more difficult to enforce the nation's civil rights laws.

Dozens of Federal programs—to assist minority businesses, to insure that banks award mortgages fairly in black neighborhoods, to protect minority communities from environmental hazards—depend on racial data from the census. Those same figures had been used for reapportioning Congressional districts, state legislatures, county boards and city councils, though recent Supreme Court decisions have called into question how big a factor race should play in drawing voting lines.

Gary L. Flowers, a spokesman for the Lawyers Committee for Civil Rights Under Law, said the multiracial debate was "a very big deal for us," adding: "This multiracial hocus-pocus pleases only a relatively few individuals, and for everyone else, it's dangerous. It contributes to the pigmentocracy that already exists in America, that says it's better to be light-skinned than dark-skinned. Will it be better to be multiracial than to be black?"

Mr. Flowers, who calls himself African-American, said he also worries that "behind this is an attempt to say America is a melting pot and a color-blind society."

"We appreciate diversity," he said, "but anyone who says we've achieved a color-blind society is deluded."

Despite such fears, the 1995 telephone survey, conducted by the Bureau of Labor Statistics on nearly 60,000 households, found that when the multiracial category was available there was no statistically significant decline in the number of Americans identifying themselves as blacks, whites, or Asians. The only group whose numbers declined when the multiracial category was available were Native Americans.

The results surprised even the professional demographers.

"Some researchers had suggested that the multiracial question might affect the count of blacks, since such a high percentage have mixed racial heritage," said Nampeo R. McKenney, director of the program for special population statistics at the Census Bureau. Some surveys done by the Census Bureau have suggested that at least 75 percent of all black Americans have at least one white or American Indian ancestor.

Ms. McKenney speculated that an individual's decision to be identified as multiracial might depend on whether the ancestor of a different race was close or remote.

The telephone survey turned up other problems with the multiracial question, chiefly that many Americans apparently confuse race and ethnicity. Dr. Ruth B. McKay, an anthropologist at the Bureau of Labor Statistics, noticed, for example, that some people claiming to be multiracial said, in answer to a follow-up question, that they were both Irish-American and Italian-American. Others claimed to be both black and African-American, or white and Armenian.

"This is a problem at all educational levels, even the college-educated," Dr. McKay said. "Obviously, before we can get good data on multiracial Americans, we need to have good definitions that people can understand and use."

The apparent decline in the number of people calling themselves American Indians has caused alarm among some of the nation's 500 tribes as well as interracial organizations. Joann K. Case, executive director of the National Congress of American Indians and a member of the Mandan and Hidatsa tribes of North Dakota, says that a drop in the Government's official count of Native Americans "would have a devastating impact on our communities."

"So many programs—not just at the Bureau of Indian Affairs but at Agriculture, Commerce, Education, Health and Human Services—are tied directly to population," Ms. Case said.

She said she was also concerned that "native people are undercounted anyway, because of the remoteness of their homes and the fact that the census isn't especially user-friendly."

"We don't want to see the numbers diluted any further," she said.

Others distrust the Bureau of Labor Statistics survey.

"My take is that the bureau's sample of American Indians was so small that it could not be nationally representative," said Norm DeWeaver, Washington representative of the Indian and Native American Employment and Training Coalition. "The survey was very urban-oriented, by necessity, so that it would be nationally representative of other minority groups. But the Indian population is not well-represented in the cities—it's mostly rural—and the bureau didn't over-sample native people."

To test the multiracial proposal further, the Census Bureau this year is conducting two more surveys, these by mail, following the usual census practice. In March, a general mailing, not focused on race but including a multiracial question, went to 90,000 households. The Census Bureau is surveying another 120,000 households from all minorities as well as families, asking questions specifically designed to test racial identity. Once the results of both studies are tabulated and analyzed, the Office of Management and Budget will make its decision.

THE OUTLOOK: EVOLVING FEELINGS ON DEFINITIONS

The wish, often expressed among multiracial families, that racial distinctions would disappear seems unrealistic to professional demographers.

"The notion of race is extremely entrenched in our society," said Professor Waters, the Harvard sociologist who has been a consultant to the Federal Government on multiracial issues.

She said she went "back and forth" over whether a multiracial category would make for sound policy.

"As a technocrat, I understand the reasons for putting people in mutually exclusive categories," Professor Waters said. "And, realistically, that will happen whether a particular person calls himself multiracial or not. A school official will decide he's one or the other, or a funeral director.

"Of course, when I talk to people who are multiracial, I realize that telling the census who they are isn't a technocratic problem but an affirmation of their identity, a civic event that's important. The way we count people reinforces the feeling that that's who you are."

Whether the 2000 census includes the multiracial category or not, Professor Waters said, "the color line is definitely shifting."

"Some Asians and Hispanics are already stepping over the line," she said. "By the time they've been here a few generations and have intermarried, they consider themselves white."

Change comes more slowly for blacks, she said, though she noted that one-third of the children with one black parent and one white parent were identified as whites on the 1990 census.

"That's pretty amazing when you consider how long the one-drop rule has been around," she added, referring to the past Census Bureau practice of classify-

Interracial Families
Cumulative totals; for the Census years shown

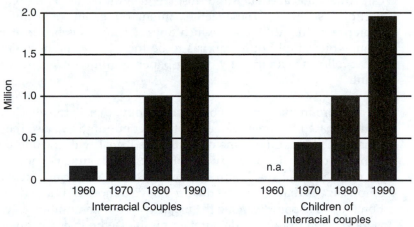

Source: Bureau of the Census

ing people black if they had any black ancestry at all. "My pet theory is that the definition of white is going to change, to become far more encompassing. That may be the only thing standing in the way of whites becoming a minority by the year 2040."

HISPANICS IN AMERICA: STARTING POINTS

Ada María Isasi-Diaz

Isasi-Diaz is the author (with Yolanda Tarango) of the 1988 book, Hispanic Women: Prophetic Voice in the Church. *She is the 1982 recipient of the Chicago Catholic Women's Woman of the Year award. Isasi-Diaz lives and writes in New York.*

The twenty-first century is rapidly approaching and with it comes a definitive increase in the Hispanic population of the United States. We will soon be the most numerous ethnic "minority"—a minority that seems greatly problematic because a significant number of us, some of us would say the majority, behave differently from other immigrant groups in the United States.

Our unwillingness to jump into the melting pot; our insistence on maintaining our own language; our ongoing links with our countries of origin—due mostly to their geographic proximity and to the continuous flow of more Hispan-

From Sonia Maasik and Jack Solomon (eds.), *Signs of Life in the U.S.A.* (Boston: Bedford Books, 1994), pp. 503–507.

ics into the United States; and the fact that the largest groups of Hispanics, Mexican Americans and Puerto Ricans, are geographically and politically an integral part of this country: These factors, among others, make us different. And the acceptance of that difference, which does not make us better or worse than other groups but simply different, has to be the starting point for understanding us. What follows is a kind of working paper, a guide toward reaching that starting point.

A preliminary note about terminology. What to call ourselves is an issue hotly debated in some segments of our communities. I use the term "Hispanic" because the majority of the communities I deal with include themselves in that term, though each and every one of us refers to ourselves according to our country of origin: Cubans, Puerto Ricans, Mexican Americans, etc. What I do wish to emphasize is that *"Latina/o"* does *not* have a more politicized or radical connotation than "Hispanic" among the majority of our communities. In my experience it is most often those outside our communities who insist on giving *Latina/o* such a connotation. The contrary, however, is true of the appellation, *"Chicana/o,"* which does indicate a certain consciousness and political stance different from but not necessarily contrary to the one of those who call themselves Mexican Americans.

The way Hispanics participate in this society has to do not only with us, but also with U.S. history, economics, politics, and society. Hispanics are in this country to begin with mostly because of U.S. policies and interests. Great numbers of Mexican Americans never moved to the United States. Instead, the border crossed *them* in 1846 when Mexico had to give up today's Southwest in the Treaty of Guadalupe-Hidalgo. The spoils of the Spanish American War at the end of the nineteenth century included Puerto Rico, where the United States had both military and economic interests. Without having any say, that nation was annexed by the United States.

Cuba suffered a somewhat similar fate. The United States sent troops to Cuba in the midst of its War of Independence against Spain. When Spain surrendered, the United States occupied Cuba as a military protectorate. And though Cuba became a free republic in 1902, the United States continued to maintain economic control and repeatedly intervened in Cuba's political affairs. It was, therefore, only reasonable that when Cubans had to leave their country, they felt they could and should find refuge here. The United States government accepted the Cuban refugees of the Castro regime, giving them economic aid and passing a special law making it easy for them to become residents and citizens.

As for more recent Hispanic immigrants, what can be said in a few lines about the constant manipulation by the United States of the economies and political processes of the different countries of Central America? The United States, therefore, has the moral responsibility to accept Salvadorans, Guatemalans, Hondurans, and other Central Americans who have to leave their countries because of political persecution or hunger. In short, the reasons Hispanics are in the United States are different from those of the earlier European immigrants, and the responsibility the United States has for our being here is vastly greater.

In spite of this difference, many people believe we Hispanics could have become as successful as the European immigrants. So why haven't we? For one thing, by the time Hispanics grew in numbers in the United States, the economy was no longer labor-intensive. Hispanics have lacked not "a strong back and a willingness to work," but the opportunity to capitalize on them. Then, unlike the European immigrants who went west and were able to buy land, Hispanics arrived here after homesteading had passed. But a more fundamental reason exists: racism. Hispanics are considered a nonwhite race, regardless of the fact that many of us are of the white race. Our ethnic difference has been officially construed as a racial difference: In government, businesses, and school forms "Hispanic" is one of the choices under the category *race*.

No possibility exists of understanding Hispanics and being in dialogue with us unless the short exposition just presented is studied and analyzed. The starting point for all dialogue is a profound respect for the other, and respect cannot flourish if the other is not known. A commitment to study the history of Hispanics in the United States—from the perspective of Hispanics and not only from the perspective presented in the standard textbooks of American history—must be the starting point in any attempt to understand Hispanics.

A second obstacle to dialogue is the prevalent insistence in this country that one American Way of Life exists, and it is the best way of life for everybody in the world. The melting pot concept has provided a framework in which assimilation is a must, and plurality of cultures an impossibility. Hispanic culture is not seen as an enrichment but as a threat. Few understand that Hispanic culture provides for us, as other cultures do for other peoples, guidelines for conduct and relationships, a system of values, and institutions and power structures that allow us to function at our best. Our culture has been formed and will continue to be shaped by the historical happenings and the constant actions of our communities—communities in the United States that are influenced by what happens here as well as in our countries of origin.

It is only within our own culture that Hispanics can acquire a sense of belonging, of security, of dignity, and of participation. The ongoing attempts to minimize or to make our culture disappear will only create problems for the United States. They engender a low sense of identity that can lead us to nonhealthy extremes in our search for some self-esteem. For us, language is the main means of identification here in the United States. To speak Spanish, in public as well as in private, is a political act, a means of asserting who we are, an important way of struggling against assimilation. The different state laws that forbid speaking Spanish in official situations, or militate against bilingual education, function as an oppressive internal colonialism that ends up hurting U.S. society.

The majority of Hispanics are U.S. citizens who have lived here all of our lives. To engage with us, Americans belonging to the dominant group, as well as to different marginalized racial and ethnic groups, must be open to new possibilities, to new elements becoming part of the American Way. Above all, they must reach beyond the liberal insistence on individualism, now bordering on recalcitrant self-centeredness. This is all the more urgent given the importance of community and family in Hispanic culture. Community for us is so central that we understand personhood as necessarily including relationship with some form of community. Family has to do not only with those to whom we are immediately related or related only by blood; it is a multilayered structure constituted by all those who care, all those to whom we feel close, who share our interests, commitments, understandings, and to whom we will always remain faithful. This sense of family is closer to the model that is becoming prevalent in the United States instead of the now almost mythical nuclear family. Indeed, Hispanics have much to contribute to the changing concept of family in this society.

The importance of community also finds expression in the way we relate to others at our work places. Our business contacts and dealings have at their center personal relationships much more than institutionalized procedures and structures. It is often better to know someone, even someone who knows someone, than to present the best plan, have the highest bid, or be the first one there. And the very prosperous Hispanic businesses that do exist here, though limited in number when one considers that more than 18 million Hispanics live in this country, clearly show that the way we do business can also be successful.

Hispanics know that we wear our emotions pinned on our sleeves, that we express what we believe and feel quite readily. Not to feel deeply seems to us to diminish our sense of humanity. We do not find it valuable to hide our subjectivity behind a so-called objectivity and uniform ways of dealing with everyone. We proudly and quickly express our opinions. For us time is to be used to further and enjoy our sense of community. It is more important to wait for everyone to be present than to start a meeting exactly on time. It is more important to listen to everybody and to take time to dwell on the personal than to end a meeting on time.

And those who want to deal with Hispanics need to know that conscience plays a very prominent role in our lives because we live life intensely. We do not take anything lightly, whether it is play, work, love, or, unfortunately, hate. We often think in ethical terms even in inconsequential matters. This intensity and insistence in giving serious consideration to almost all aspects of life are a constitutive element of our high sense of honor, our way of talking about our standard of morality and personhood, which we are willing to defend no matter the cost.

Finally, those who wish to understand Hispanics need to know that our religious practices—what is often referred to as *religiosidad popular*—express our close relationship with the divine. A personal relationship with God and the living-out of that relationship in day-to-day life is much more important to us than establishing and maintaining relationships with church structures and going to church on Sundays. Christianity, and specifically Roman Catholicism, are an intrinsic part of Hispanic culture—something not always understood and taken into consideration in this secular culture. Many of the cultural traditions and customs still prevalent today in Hispanic communities are closely entwined with religious rituals. Processions, lighting candles, relating to the saints, arguing and bartering with God through *promesas*—all of these are not only a matter of religion but a matter of culture.

The dominant groups in U.S. society must acknowledge that Hispanics have much to contribute to the United States and that in order to do so we must be allowed to be who we are. Meanwhile, the dominant groups in society, especially, need to be open to cultural, religious, social, and even organizational pluralism. The nations that have failed and disappeared from the map of our world are not those that have been open to change but rather those that insist on rigidity, uniformity, and believing they are better than others. That is what should be adamantly opposed in the United States—not a multiplicity of language, cultures, and customs.

QUESTIONS TO HELP YOU THINK AND WRITE ABOUT RACISM IN AMERICA

1. What does West mean by nihilism? What are the causes for nihilism in contemporary black culture? Is this a problem in other cultures? How great and pervasive a problem do you think it is? What can be done to solve the problems it creates?

2. Hacker's parable received a lot of attention when it was first published in 1992. What do you think of it? Imagine the terms of the parable are different. Would you be willing to make *any* change in your sex or your race? If so, what change would you be willing to make, and put a price on it. Justify your terms. You may want to conduct this discussion in small groups and then report back to the class. What conclusions do you draw?

3. Compare the views about affirmative action in the articles by Wang and Wu, and Chancellor Chang-Lin Tien, (see "A View from Berkeley," p. 52). List the reasons in favor of affirmative action and the reasons against. Do you favor continuing or discontinuing affirmative action programs? Give some reasons for your opinion.

4. Imagine Du Bois, Gates ("The Parable of the Talents"), and West in a conversation on a modern television talk show. The subject is modern black leadership. What positions would you expect each of these individuals to take on this subject? If you were the fourth participant in this conversation, what perspective would you offer?

5. Read the articles by Matthews and Isasi-Diaz, and think about the value of strong group identification. What are some of the advantages and some of the disadvantages of group identification?

6. Read the essay by Isasi-Diaz. What special characteristics of the Hispanic culture does this author identify? How are these characteristics similar to or different from the ways you would characterize your own culture?

7. Do you believe that it might be possible for racial distinctions to eventually disappear, as suggested in the article by Matthews? Provide reasons for your answer.

SECTION VI
Issues in Modern Electronic Media

WHAT ARE THE ISSUES?

1. What Effect Does Television Have on Its Viewers?

Several authors take positions on the benefits and harms of television. How it changes or influences the ideas and behavior of its viewers is a major facet of the issue.

2. What Effect Do Computers Have on Their Users?

Some of the leading theorists and major players in the current computer revolution speculate about the changes that computers will create and the effect of these changes on computer users both in the workplace and in their personal lives. See also "Computers in Class," page 172; "The Road to Unreality," page 86; "We're Too Busy for Ideas," page 179, and the articles about censoring the Internet, pages 547 to 558.

3. Extend Your Perspective with Films and Literature Related to Modern Electronic Media

Films: Alphaville, 1965; *The Net,* 1996; *War Games,* 1983; *Johnny Mnemonic,* 1995; *Hackers,* 1996; *Strange Days,* 1996.
Literature: poem: "Back from the Word Processing Course, I Say to My Old Typewriter" by Michael Blumenthal; play: *R. U. R.* by Karel Capek; novel: *Neuromancer* by William Gibson; and *Player Piano* by Kurt Vonnegut.

THE RHETORICAL SITUATION

As you will learn from reading these essays, anxieties and concerns about modern electronic media generate issues and argument. Changes in the way people communicate and transmit information have always generated issues. Socrates cautioned that writing would destroy people's memories, and Plato worried about the dangers of storytellers. In our own time, many people wonder about the changes in society that television and computers may eventually cause.

The authors in this section who write about the issues associated with modern television and computers organize most of their arguments around four of the five types of claims identified in Chapter 7: definition, cause (including effects), value, and policy. Definition articles help the layman understand modern media in new ways. Postman, for example, writes about the nature of television and Negroponte defines the special qualities of computers. Hamill, Gates, and the authors of the personal essays about television describe some of the effects that television and computers have on society. Other authors evaluate modern electronic media and argue how it may be either good or bad for society. Postman evaluates the effects of television and Kadi evaluates the effects of computers. Ann Landers suggests possible policy for one problem generated by modern computer technology.

As you read these articles, notice the ways in which these authors think modern life has already been changed and may still be changed even more in the future by modern television and computers. Science and science fiction may seem closely related. In fact William Gibson's science fiction novel *Neuromancer*, published in 1984, has become an inspiration to computer buffs and has also provided them with vocabulary. "Cyberspace" was first coined by Gibson. It is now used to describe the place where people are when they communicate on the Internet and the World Wide Web. As you read, separate fact from fiction, but also notice the fiction that has now become fact.

1. What Effect Does Television Have on Its Viewers?

THE AGE OF SHOW BUSINESS

Neil Postman

> *The following is an excerpt from Postman's well-known book* Amusing Ourselves to Death *which is about the effect that television has had on our lives. Postman is a professor at New York University. See if you agree with the claim Postman makes about television.*

A dedicated graduate student I know returned to his small apartment the night before a major examination only to discover that his solitary lamp was broken beyond repair. After a whiff of panic, he was able to restore both his equanimity and his chances for a satisfactory grade by turning on the television set, turning off the sound, and with his back to the set, using its light to read important passages on which he was to be tested. This is one use of television—as a source of illuminating the printed page.

But the television screen is more than a light source. It is also a smooth, nearly flat surface on which the printed word may be displayed. We have all stayed at hotels in which the TV set has had a special channel for describing the day's events in letters rolled endlessly across the screen. This is another use of television—as an electronic bulletin board.

Neil Postman. *Amusing Ourselves to Death.* (New York: Penguin Books, 1985), pp. 83–88, 90, 91–94, 97–98.

Many television sets are also large and sturdy enough to bear the weight of a small library. The top of an old-fashioned RCA console can handle as many as thirty books, and I know one woman who has securely placed her entire collection of Dickens, Flaubert, and Turgenev on the top of a 21-inch Westinghouse. Here is still another use of television—as bookcase.

I bring forward these quixotic uses of television to ridicule the hope harbored by some that television can be used to support the literate tradition. Such a hope represents exactly what Marshall McLuhan used to call "rear-view mirror" thinking: the assumption that a new medium is merely an extension or amplification of an older one; that an automobile, for example, is only a fast horse, or an electric light a powerful candle. To make such a mistake in the matter at hand is to misconstrue entirely how television redefines the meaning of public discourse. Television does not extend or amplify literate culture. It attacks it. If television is a continuation of anything, it is of a tradition begun by the telegraph and photograph in the mid-nineteenth century, not by the printing press in the fifteenth.

What is television? What kinds of conversations does it permit? What are the intellectual tendencies it encourages? What sort of culture does it produce?

These are the questions to be addressed, . . . and to approach them with a minimum of confusion, I must begin by making a distinction between a technology and a medium. We might say that a technology is to a medium as the brain is to the mind. Like the brain, a technology is a physical apparatus. Like the mind, a medium is a use to which a physical apparatus is put. A technology becomes a medium as it employs a particular symbolic code, as it finds its place in a particular social setting, as it insinuates itself into economic and political contexts. A technology, in other words, is merely a machine. A medium is the social and intellectual environment a machine creates.

Of course, like the brain itself, every technology has an inherent bias. It has within its physical form a predisposition toward being used in certain ways and not others. Only those who know nothing of the history of technology believe that a technology is entirely neutral. There is an old joke that mocks that naive belief. Thomas Edison, it goes, would have revealed his discovery of the electric light much sooner than he did except for the fact that every time he turned it on, he held it to his mouth and said, "Hello? Hello?"

Not very likely. Each technology has an agenda of its own. It is, as I have suggested, a metaphor waiting to unfold. The printing press, for example, had a clear bias toward being used as a linguistic medium. It is *conceivable* to use it exclusively for the reproduction of pictures. And, one imagines, the Roman Catholic Church would not have objected to its being so used in the sixteenth century. Had that been the case, the Protestant Reformation might not have occurred, for as Luther contended, with the word of God on every family's kitchen table, Christians do not require the Papacy to interpret it for them. But in fact there never was much chance that the press would be used solely, or even very much, for the duplication of icons. From its beginning in the fifteenth century, the press was perceived as an extraordinary opportunity for the display and mass distribution of written language. Everything about its technical possibilities led in that direction. One might even say it was invented for that purpose.

The technology of television has a bias, as well. It is conceivable to use television as a lamp, a surface for texts, a bookcase, even as radio. But it has not been so used and will not be so used, at least in America. Thus, in answering the question, What is television?, we must understand as a first point that we are not talking about television as a technology but television as a medium. There are many places in the world where television, though the same technology as it is in America, is an entirely different medium from that which we know. I refer to places where the majority of people do not have television sets, and those who do have only one; where only one station is available; where television does not operate around the clock; where most programs have as their purpose the direct furtherance of government ideology and policy; where commercials are unknown, and "talking heads" are the principal image; where television is mostly used as if it were radio. For these reasons and more television will not have the same meaning or power as it does in America, which is to say, it is possible for a technology to be so used that its potentialities are prevented from developing and its social consequences kept to a minimum.

But in America, this has not been the case. Television has found in liberal democracy and a relatively free market economy a nurturing climate in which its full potentialities as a technology of images could be exploited. One result of this has been that American television programs are in demand all over the world. The total estimate of U.S. television program exports is approximately 100,000 to 200,000 hours, equally divided among Latin America, Asia and Europe.[1] Over the years, programs like "Gunsmoke," "Bonanza," "Mission: Impossible," "Star Trek," "Kojak," and more recently, "Dallas" and "Dynasty" have been as popular in England, Japan, Israel and Norway as in Omaha, Nebraska. I have heard (but not verified) that some years ago the Lapps postponed for several days their annual and, one supposes, essential migratory journey so that they could find out who shot J.R. All of this has occurred simultaneously with the decline of America's moral and political prestige, worldwide. American television programs are in demand not because America is loved but because American television is loved.

We need not be detained too long in figuring out why. In watching American television, one is reminded of George Bernard Shaw's remark on his first seeing the glittering neon signs of Broadway and 42nd Street at night. It must be beautiful, he said, if you cannot read. American television is, indeed, a beautiful spectacle, a visual delight, pouring forth thousands of images on any given day. The average length of a shot on network television is only 3.5 seconds, so that the eye never rests, always has something new to see. Moreover, television offers viewers a variety of subject matter, requires minimal skills to comprehend it, and is largely aimed at emotional gratification. Even commercials, which some regard as an annoyance, are exquisitely crafted, always pleasing to the eye and accompanied by exciting music. There is no question but that the best photography in the world is presently seen on television commercials. American television, in other words, is devoted entirely to supplying its audience with entertainment.

Of course, to say that television is entertaining is merely banal. Such a fact is hardly threatening to a culture, not even worth writing a book about. It may even be a reason for rejoicing. Life, as we like to say, is not a highway strewn with flowers. The sight of a few blossoms here and there may make our journey a trifle more endurable. The Lapps undoubtedly thought so. We may surmise that the ninety million Americans who watch television every night also think so. But what I am claiming here is not that television is entertaining but that it has made entertainment itself the natural format for the representation of all experience. Our television set keeps us in constant communion with the world, but it does so with a face whose smiling countenance is unalterable. The problem is not that television presents us with entertaining subject matter but that all subject matter is presented as entertaining, which is another issue altogether.

To say it still another way: Entertainment is the supraideology of all discourse on television. No matter what is depicted or from what point of view, the overarching presumption is that it is there for our amusement and pleasure. That is why even on news shows which provide us daily with fragments of tragedy and barbarism, we are urged by the newscasters to "join them tomorrow." What for? One would think that several minutes of murder and mayhem would suffice as material for a month of sleepless nights. We accept the newscasters' invitation because we know that the "news" is not to be taken seriously, that it is all in fun, so to say. Everything about a news show tells us this—the good looks and amiability of the cast, their pleasant banter, the exciting music that opens and closes the show, the vivid film footage, the attractive commercials—all these and more suggest that what we have just seen is no cause for weeping. A news show, to put it plainly, is a format for entertainment, not for education, reflection or catharsis. And we must not judge too harshly those who have framed it in this way. They are not assembling the news to be read, or broadcasting it to be heard. They are televising the news to be seen. They must follow where their medium leads. There is no conspiracy here, no lack of intelligence, only a straightforward recognition that "good television" has little to do with what is "good" about exposition or other forms of verbal communication but everything to do with what the pictorial images look like. [. . .]

When a television show is in process, it is very nearly impermissible to say, "Let me think about that" or "I don't know" or "What do you mean when you say . . . ?" or "From what sources does your information come?" This type of discourse not only slows down the tempo of the show but creates the impression of uncertainty or lack of finish. It tends to reveal people in the *act of thinking,* which is as disconcerting and boring on television as it is on a Las Vegas stage. Thinking does not play well on television, a fact that television directors discovered long ago. There is not much to *see* in it. It is, in a phrase, not a performing art. [. . .]

I do not say categorically that it is impossible to use television as a carrier of coherent language or thought in process. William Buckley's own program, "Firing Line," occasionally shows people in the act of thinking but who also happen to have television cameras pointed at them. There are other programs, such as "Meet the Press" or "The Open Mind," which clearly strive to maintain a sense of intellectual decorum and typographic tradition, but they are scheduled so that they do not compete with programs of great visual interest, since otherwise, they will not be watched. After all, it is not unheard of that a format will occasionally go against the bias of its medium. For example, the most popular radio program of the early 1940's featured a ventriloquist, and in those days, I heard more than once the feet of a tap dancer on the "Major Bowes' Amateur Hour." (Indeed, if I am not mistaken, he even once featured a pantomimist.) But ventriloquism, dancing and mime do not play well on radio, just as sustained, complex talk does not play well on television. It can be made to play tolerably well if only one camera is used and the visual image is kept constant—as when the President gives a speech. But this is not television at its best, and it is not television that most people will choose to watch. The single most important fact about television is that people *watch* it, which is why it is called "tele*vision*." And what they watch, and like to watch, are moving pictures—millions of them, of short duration and dynamic variety. It is in the nature of the medium that it must suppress the content of ideas in order to accommodate the requirements of visual interest; that is to say, to accommodate the values of show business.

Film, records and radio (now that it is an adjunct of the music industry) are, of course, equally devoted to entertaining the culture, and their effects in altering the style of American discourse are not insignificant. But television is different because it encompasses all forms of discourse. No one goes to a movie to find out about government policy or the latest scientific advances. No one buys a record to find out the baseball scores or the weather or the latest murder. No one turns on radio anymore for soap operas or a presidential address (if a television set is at hand). But everyone goes to television for all these things and more, which is why television resonates so powerfully throughout the culture. Television is our culture's principal mode of knowing about itself. Therefore—and this is the critical point—how television stages the world becomes the model for how the world is properly to be staged. It is not merely that on the television screen entertainment is the metaphor for all discourse. It is that off the screen the same metaphor prevails. As typography once dictated the style of conducting politics, religion, business, education, law and other important social matters, television now takes command. In courtrooms, classrooms, operating rooms, board rooms, churches and even airplanes, Americans no longer talk to each other, they entertain each other. They do not exchange ideas; they exchange images. They do not argue with propositions; they argue with good looks, celebrities and commercials. For the message of television as metaphor is not only that all the world is a stage but that the stage is located in Las Vegas, Nevada.

In Chicago, for example, the Reverend Greg Sakowicz, a Roman Catholic priest, mixes his religious teaching with rock 'n' roll music. According to the Associated Press, the Reverend Sakowicz is both an associate pastor at the Church of the Holy Spirit in Schaumberg (a suburb of Chicago) and a disc jockey at WKQX. On his show, "The Journey Inward," Father Sakowicz chats in soft tones about such topics as family relationships or commitment, and interposes his sermons with "the sound of *Billboard*'s Top 10." He says that his preaching is not done "in a churchy way," and adds, "You don't have to be boring in order to be holy."

Meanwhile in New York City at St. Patrick's Cathedral, Father John J. O'Connor put on a New York Yankee baseball cap as he mugged his way through his installation as Archbishop of the New York Archdiocese. He got off some excellent gags, at least one of which was specifically directed at Mayor Edward Koch, who was a member of his audience; that is to say, he was a congregant. At his next public performance, the new archbishop donned a New York Mets baseball cap. These events were, of course, televised, and were vastly entertaining, largely because Archbishop (now Cardinal) O'Connor has gone Father Sakowicz one better: Whereas the latter believes that you don't have to be boring to be holy, the former apparently believes you don't have to be holy at all.

In Phoenix, Arizona, Dr. Edward Dietrich performed triple bypass surgery on Bernard Schuler. The operation was successful, which was nice for Mr. Schuler. It was also on television, which was nice for America. The operation was carried by at least fifty television stations in the United States, and also by the British Broadcasting Corporation. A two-man panel of narrators (a play-by-play and color man, so to speak) kept viewers informed about what they were seeing. It was not clear as to why this event was televised, but it resulted in transforming both Dr. Dietrich and Mr. Schuler's chest into celebrities. Perhaps because he has seen too many doctor shows on television, Mr. Schuler was uncommonly confident about the outcome of his surgery. "There is no way in hell they are going to lose me on live TV," he said.[2]

As reported with great enthusiasm by both WCBS-TV and WNBC-TV in 1984, the Philadelphia public schools have embarked on an experiment in which children will have their curriculum sung to them. Wearing Walkman equipment, students were shown listening to rock music whose lyrics were about the eight parts of speech. Mr. Jocko Henderson, who thought of this idea, is planning to delight students further by subjecting mathematics and history, as well as English, to the rigors of a rock music format. In fact, this is not Mr. Henderson's idea at all. It was pioneered by the Children's Television Workshop, whose television show "Sesame Street" is an expensive illustration of the idea that education is indistinguishable from entertainment. Nonetheless, Mr. Henderson has a point in his favor. Whereas "Sesame Street" merely attempts to make learning to read a form of light entertainment, the Philadelphia experiment aims to make the classroom itself into a rock concert.

In New Bedford, Massachusetts, a rape trial was televised, to the delight of audiences who could barely tell the difference between the trial and their favorite mid-day soap opera. In Florida, trials of varying degrees of seriousness, including murder, are regularly televised and are considered to be more entertaining than most fictional courtroom dramas. All of this is done in the interests of "public education." For the same high purpose, plans are afoot, it is rumored, to televise confessionals. To be called "Secrets of the Confessional Box," the program will, of course, carry the warning that some of its material may be offensive to children and therefore parental guidance is suggested. [...]

What all of this means is that our culture has moved toward a new way of conducting its business, especially its important business. The nature of its discourse is changing as the demarcation line between what is show business and what is not becomes harder to see with each passing day. Our priests and presidents, our surgeons, and lawyers, our educators and newscasters need worry less about satisfying the demands of their discipline than the demands of good showmanship. Had Irving Berlin changed one word in the title of his celebrated song, he would have been as prophetic, albeit more terse, as Aldous Huxley. He need only have written, There's No Business But Show Business.

NOTES

1. On July 20, 1984, *The New York Times* reported that the Chinese National Television network had contracted with CBS to broadcast sixty-four hours of CBS programming in China. Contracts with NBC and ABC are sure to follow. One hopes that the Chinese understand that such transactions are of great political consequence. The Gang of Four is as nothing compared with the Gang of Three.
2. This story was carried by several newspapers, including the *Wisconsin State Journal*, February 24, 1983, Section 4, p. 2.

CRACK AND THE BOX

Pete Hamill

Pete Hamill wrote this essay for Esquire *magazine in 1990. It was reprinted in the* Networker *later that year.*

One sad, rainy morning last winter I talked to a woman who was addicted to crack cocaine. She was 22, stiletto-thin, with eyes as old as tombs. She was living in two rooms in a welfare hotel with her children, who were two, three, and five years of age. Her story was the usual tangle of human woe: early pregnancy, dropping out of school, vanished men, smack and then crack, tricks with johns in parked cars to pay for the dope. I asked her why she did drugs. She shrugged in an empty way and couldn't really answer beyond "makes me feel good." While we talked and she told her tale of squalor, the children ignored us. They were watching television.

Walking back to my office in the rain, I brooded about the woman, her zombie-like children, and my own callous indifference. I'd heard so many versions of the same story that I almost never wrote them anymore; the sons of similar women, glimpsed a dozen years ago, are now in Dannemora or Soledad or Joliet; in a hundred cities, their daughters are moving into the same loveless

Networker, November/December 1990, pp. 28, 29.

rooms. As I walked, a series of homeless men approached me for change, most of them junkies. Others sat in doorways, staring at nothing. They were additional casualties of our time of plague, demoralized reminders that although this country holds only two percent of the world's population, it consumes 65 percent of the world's supply of hard drugs.

Why, for God's sake? Why do so many millions of Americans of all ages, races, and classes choose to spend all or part of their lives stupefied? I've talked to hundreds of addicts over the years; some were my friends. But none could give sensible answers. They stutter about the pain of the world, about despair or boredom, the urgent need for magic or pleasure in a society empty of both. But then they just shrug. Americans have the money to buy drugs; the supply is plentiful. But almost nobody in power asks, *Why?* Least of all, George Bush and his drug warriors.

William Bennett talks vaguely about the heritage of '60s permissiveness, the collapse of Traditional Values, and all that. But he and Bush offer the traditional American excuse: It Is Somebody Else's Fault. This posture sets the stage for the self-righteous invasion of Panama, the bloodiest drug arrest in world history. Bush even accused Manuel Noriega of "poisoning our children." But he never asked *why* so many Americans demand the poison.

And then, on that rainy morning in New York, I saw another one of those ragged men staring out at the rain from a doorway. I suddenly remembered the inert postures of the children in that welfare hotel, and I thought: *television*.

Ah, no, I muttered to myself: too simple. Something as complicated as drug addiction can't be blamed on television. Come on . . . But I remembered all those desperate places I'd visited as a reporter, where there were no books and a TV set was always playing and the older kids had gone off somewhere to shoot smack, except for the kid who was at the mortuary in a coffin. I also remembered when I was a boy in the '40s and early '50s, and drugs were a minor sideshow, a kind of dark little rumor. And there was one major difference between that time and this: television.

We had unemployment then; illiteracy, poor living conditions, racism, governmental stupidity, a gap between rich and poor. We didn't have the all-consuming presence of television in our lives. Now two generations of Americans have grown up with television from their earliest moments of consciousness. Those same American generations are afflicted by the pox of drug addiction.

Only 35 years ago, drug addiction was not a major problem in this country. There were drug addicts. We had some at the end of the 19th century, hooked on the cocaine in patent medicines. During the placid '50s, Commissioner Harry Anslinger pumped up the budget of the old Bureau of Narcotics with fantasies of reefer madness. Heroin was sold and used in most major American cities, while the bebop generation of jazz musicians got jammed up with horse.

But until the early '60s, narcotics were still marginal to American life, they weren't the $120 billion market they make up today. If anything, those years have an eerie innocence. In 1955, there were 31,700,000 TV sets in use in the country (the number is now past 184 million). But the majority of the audience had grown up without the dazzling new medium. They embraced it, were diverted by it, perhaps even loved it, but they weren't *formed* by it. That year, the New York police made a mere 1,234 felony drug arrests; in 1988, it was 43,901. They confiscated 97 *ounces* of cocaine for the entire year, last year it was hundreds of pounds. During each year of the '50s in New York, there were only about a hundred narcotics-related deaths. But by the end of the '60s, when the first generation of children *formed* by television had come to maturity (and thus to the marketplace), the number of such deaths had risen to 1,200. The same phenomenon was true in every major American city.

In the last Nielsen survey of American viewers, the average family was watching television seven hours a day. This has never happened before in history. No people has ever been entertained for seven hours a *day*. The Elizabethans didn't go to the theater seven hours a day. The pre-TV generation did not go to the movies seven hours a day. Common sense tells us that this all-pervasive diet of instant imagery, sustained now for 40 years, must have changed us in profound ways.

Television, like drugs, dominates the lives of its addicts. And though some lonely Americans leave their sets on without watching them, using them as electronic companions, television usually absorbs its viewers the way drugs absorb their users. Viewers can't work or play while watching television; they can't read; they can't be out on the streets, falling in love with the wrong people, learning how to quarrel and compromise with other human beings. In short, they are asocial. So are drug addicts.

One Michigan State University study in the early '80s offered a group of four- and five-year-olds the choice of giving up television or giving up their fathers. Fully one third said they would give up Daddy. Given a similar choice (between cocaine or heroin and father, mother, brother, sister, wife, husband, children, job), almost every stone junkie would do the same.

There are other disturbing similarities. Television itself is a consciousness-altering instrument. With the touch of a button, it takes you out of the "real" world in which you reside and can place you at a basketball game, the back alleys of Miami, the streets of Bucharest, or the cartoony living rooms of Sitcom Land. Each move from channel to channel alters mood, usually with music or a laugh track. On any given evening, you can laugh, be frightened, feel tension, thump with excitement. You can even tune in "MacNeil/Lehrer" and feel sober.

But none of these abrupt shifts in mood is *earned*. They are attained as easily as popping a pill. Getting news from television, for example, is simply not the same experience as reading it in a newspaper. Reading is *active*. The reader must decode little symbols called words, then create images or ideas and make them connect; at its most basic level, reading is an act of the imagination. But the television viewer doesn't go through that process. The words are spoken to him or her by Dan Rather or Tom Brokaw or Peter Jennings. There isn't much decoding to do when watching television, no time to think or ponder before the next set of images and spoken words appears to displace the present one. The reader, being active, works at his or her own pace; the viewer, being passive, proceeds at a pace determined by the show. Except at the highest levels, television never demands that its audience take part in an act of imagination. Reading always does.

In short, television works on the same imaginative and intellectual level as psychoactive drugs. If prolonged television viewing makes the young passive (dozens of studies indicate that it does), then moving to drugs has a certain coherence. Drugs provide an unearned high (in contrast to the earned rush that comes from a feat accomplished, a human breakthrough earned by sweat or thought or love).

And because the television addict and the drug addict are alienated from the hard and scary world, they also feel they make no difference in its complicated events. For the junkie, the world is reduced to him or her and the needle, pipe, or vial; the self is absolutely isolated, with no desire for choice. The television addict lives the same way. Many Americans who fail to vote in presidential elections must believe they have no more control over such a choice than they do over the casting of "L.A. Law."

The drug plague also coincides with the unspoken assumption of most television shows: Life should be *easy*. The most complicated events are summarized on TV news in a minute or less. Cops confront murder, chase the criminals, and bring them to justice (usually violently) within an hour. In commercials, you drink the right beer and you get the girl. *Easy!* So why should real life be a grind? Why should any American have to spend years mastering a skill or craft, or work eight hours a day at an unpleasant job, or endure the compromises and crises of a marriage?

The doper always whines about how he or she *feels*; drugs are used to enhance feelings or obliterate them, and in this the doper is very American. No other people on earth spend so much time talking about their feelings; hundreds of thousands go to shrinks, they buy self-help books by the millions, they pour out intimate confessions to virtual strangers in bars or discos. Our political campaigns are about emotional issues now, stated in the simplicities of adolescence. Even alleged statesmen can start a sentence, "I feel that the Sandinistas should . . ." when they once might have said, "I *think* . . ." I'm convinced that this exaltation of cheap emotions over logic and reason is one by-product of hundreds of thousands of hours of television.

Most Americans under the age of 50 have now spent their lives absorbing television; that is, they've had the structures of drama pounded into them. Drama is always about conflict. So news shows, politics, and advertising are now all shaped by those structures. Nobody will pay attention to anything as complicated as the part played by Third World debt in the expanding production of cocaine; it's much easier to focus on Manuel Noriega, a character right out of "Miami Vice," and believe that even in real life there's a Mister Big.

What is to be done? Television is certainly not going away, but its addictive qualities can be controlled. It's a lot easier to "just say no" to television than to heroin or crack. As a beginning, parents must take immediate control of the sets, teaching children to watch specific television *programs*, not "television," to get out of the house and play with other kids. Elementary and high schools must begin teaching television as a subject, the way literature is taught, showing children how shows are made, how to distinguish between the true and the false, how to recognize cheap emotional manipulation. All Americans should spend more time reading. And thinking.

For years, the defenders of television have argued that the networks are only giving the people what they want. That might be true. But so is the Medellin Cartel.

WATCHING TV

The Sun magazine invites its readers to write short essays each month on topics that it designates. One of those topics was "Watching TV." Here are three of a variety of responses that were sent in by readers. As you read through them, you might think about what your response would be if you were to write on this topic.

I often meet people who say that television is evil, that children should not be allowed to watch it, that it is a waste of time. I never feel quite at ease around these individuals. They talk about "real" relationships with living, breathing human beings as opposed to TV characters. I can't help but wonder, Are their relationships so different from mine? Most of my encounters with people are either superficial or emotionally exhausting. Only a small number are truly enjoyable or intimate.

I could never explain to anti-television types the sense of camaraderie I find with the characters of *Seinfeld* or *Dream On*, whom I consider my beloved friends. They expose all their weaknesses and allow me to partake of their experiences without demand or expectation. Most importantly, their lives provide a sense of conclusiveness and completeness always lacking in my own. Even though I can't call these characters up for a chat, can't share my stories with them or ask them for advice, their example helps me survive the grind of daily life.

R. Lurie
Santa Fe, New Mexico

My mother once dreamed that I had married Peter Jennings; I could tell that she was pleased by the thought. She likes to fill me in on television gossip: Tim Allen's drug problem, Vanna White's baby, Oprah's handsome boyfriend.

My parents got their first TV back in the fifties. They felt very sophisticated inviting friends over to watch boxing. Both were from poor, rural families, and now here they were in their smart ranch house, eating meat that came from the butcher, driving a car with chrome bumpers, and watching television.

The Sun, July 1996, pp. 27–29.

I am just old enough to remember the first moon landing. We went down the street to watch it on the color set at the Montgomerys' house. "Watch this," my father said. "You'll remember it the rest of your life."

My mother often reminded me how lucky I was to have TV: "People were so dumb back in my day," she said. "They weren't exposed to all the things kids are today." I imagined her and her seven brothers and sisters in their dark house, bored and sullen, fighting over a one-armed doll, or maybe a soiled checkerboard. Our family's evenings, by contrast, were neatly scheduled by our television viewing. Everyone respected my Friday-night passion for *The Brady Bunch* and *The Partridge Family.* Monday nights my father hid away in the basement to watch *Gunsmoke.* We ate TV dinners on TV trays and called Saturday night a "good TV night."

Now I'm an adult, and I consider myself more sophisticated than my parents. For one thing, I don't like TV. I own one and occasionally spend an evening in front of it, but afterward I feel miserable and guilty.

TV, however, has remained my mother's constant friend. All her children have moved away, her husband has died, and her neighborhood has deteriorated, but every day she sits on her overstuffed couch, a blanket over her lap, her face twitching with the palsy of old age, and wields her remote. She does not hug people, she has no friends, and she bickers constantly with her sisters. "TV is good company," she tells me. My mother's favorite shows usually depict two people raising irascible but ultimately endearing children; she chooses to remember her own life as having been the same. Didn't she once have a house full of children? Didn't they say cute things like these children?

This is not the ending I would have wanted for her.

Theresa H.
Lenexa, Kansas

My family was the last on our block to get a television. I was sixteen when my father finally broke down and bought a small black-and-white set. Before this, I'd been in the habit of going to the movies every weekend for a double feature—both Saturday and Sunday if I could—to escape my misery and loneliness. While television never had the magic and glamour of the movies, I quickly became addicted to the small screen, as well.

When I began living on my own, in a small New York apartment, with no one around to tell me what to watch or when to turn it off, the television became my best friend. I felt less lonely in the company of the flickering screen. I often felt ashamed for enjoying what some people thought was stupid and banal.

Now that I'm married, I have much less need to escape into the tube, and am more selective in my viewing. There is so much more I want to do with my life. Still, TV is a respite from family problems, unpleasant chores, the exhausting trials of daily living. When I need some time alone and there's a good movie on, or a sitcom I like, or a one-hour murder mystery, I'll turn on the television and watch. And I always will.

Allegreta Behar-Blau
Woodland Hills, California

2. What Effect Do Computers Have on Their Users?

AN AGE OF OPTIMISM

Nicholas Negroponte

> *Negroponte is Professor of Media Technology at MIT. The following article is the epilogue to his book,* Being Digital. *In it, Negroponte claims that the computer has four powerful qualities that will "result in its ultimate triumph." Identify these qualities and see if you agree with them.*

I am optimistic by nature. However, every technology or gift of science has a dark side. Being digital is no exception.

The next decade will see cases of intellectual-property abuse and invasion of our privacy. We will experience digital vandalism, software piracy, and data thievery. Worst of all, we will witness the loss of many jobs to wholly automated systems, which will soon change the white-collar workplace to the same degree that it has already transformed the factory floor. The notion of lifetime employment at one job has already started to disappear.

The radical transformation of the nature of our job markets, as we work less with atoms and more with bits, will happen at just about the same time the 2 billion–strong labor force of India and China starts to come on-line (literally). A self-employed software designer in Peoria will be competing with his or her counterpart in Pohang. A digital typographer in Madrid will do the same with one in Madras. American companies are already outsourcing hardware development and software production to Russia and India, not to find cheap manual labor but to secure a highly skilled intellectual force seemingly prepared to work harder, faster, and in a more disciplined fashion than those in our own country.

As the business world globalizes and the Internet grows, we will start to see a seamless digital workplace. Long before political harmony and long before the GATT talks can reach agreement on the tariff and trade of atoms (the right to sell Evian water in California), bits will be borderless, stored and manipulated with absolutely no respect to geopolitical boundaries. In fact, time zones will probably play a bigger role in our digital future than trade zones. I can imagine some software projects that literally move around the world from east to west on a twenty-four-hour cycle, from person to person or from group to group, one working as the other sleeps. Microsoft will need to add London and Tokyo offices for software development in order to produce on three shifts.

As we move more toward such a digital world, an entire sector of the population will be or feel disenfranchised. When a fifty-year-old steelworker loses his job, unlike his twenty-five-year-old son, he may have no digital resilience at all. When a modern-day secretary loses his job, at least he may be conversant with the digital world and have transferable skills.

From Nicholas Negroponte, *Being Digital* (New York: Alfred A, Knopf, 1995), pp. 227–231.

Bits are not edible; in that sense they cannot stop hunger. Computers are not moral; they cannot resolve complex issues like the rights to life and to death. But being digital, nevertheless, does give much cause for optimism. Like a force of nature, the digital age cannot be denied or stopped. It has four very powerful qualities that will result in its ultimate triumph: decentralizing, globalizing, harmonizing, and empowering.

The decentralizing effect of being digital can be felt no more strongly than in commerce and in the computer industry itself. The so-called management information systems (MIS) czar, who used to reign over a glass-enclosed and air-conditioned mausoleum, is an emperor with no clothes, almost extinct. Those who survive are usually doing so because they outrank anybody able to fire them, and the company's board of directors is out of touch or asleep or both.

Thinking Machines Corporation, a great and imaginative supercomputer company started by electrical engineering genius Danny Hillis, disappeared after ten years. In that short space of time it introduced the world to massively parallel computer architectures. Its demise did not occur because of mismanagement or sloppy engineering of their so-called Connection Machine. It vanished because parallelism could be decentralized; the very same kind of massively parallel architectures have suddenly become possible by threading together low-cost, mass-produced personal computers.

While this was not good news for Thinking Machines, it is an important message to all of us, both literally and metaphorically. It means the enterprise of the future can meet its computer needs in a new and scalable way by populating its organization with personal computers that, when needed, can work in unison to crunch on computationally intensive problems. Computers will literally work both for individuals and for groups. I see the same decentralized mind-set growing in our society, driven by young citizenry in the digital world. The traditional centralist view of life will become a thing of the past.

The nation-state itself is subject to tremendous change and globalization. Governments fifty years from now will be both larger and smaller. Europe finds itself dividing itself into smaller ethnic entities while trying to unite economically. The forces of nationalism make it too easy to be cynical and dismiss any broad-stroke attempt at world unification. But in the digital world, previously impossible solutions become viable.

Today, when 20 percent of the world consumes 80 percent of its resources, when a quarter of us have an acceptable standard of living and three-quarters don't, how can this divide possibly come together? While the politicians struggle with the baggage of history, a new generation is emerging from the digital landscape free of many of the old prejudices. These kids are released from the limitation of geographic proximity as the sole basis of friendship, collaboration, play, and neighborhood. Digital technology can be a natural force drawing people into greater world harmony.

The harmonizing effect of being digital is already apparent as previously partitioned disciplines and enterprises find themselves collaborating, not competing. A previously missing common language emerges, allowing people to understand across boundaries. Kids at school today experience the opportunity to look at the same thing from many perspectives. A computer program, for example, can be seen simultaneously as a set of computer instructions or as concrete poetry formed by the indentations in the text of the program. What kids learn very quickly is that to know a program is to know it from many perspectives, not just one.

But more than anything, my optimism comes from the empowering nature of being digital. The access, the mobility, and the ability to effect change are what will make the future so different from the present. The information superhighway may be mostly hype today, but it is an understatement about tomorrow. It will exist beyond people's wildest predictions. As children appropriate a global information resource, and as they discover that only adults need learner's permits, we are bound to find new hope and dignity in places where very little existed before.

My optimism is not fueled by an anticipated invention or discovery. Finding a cure for cancer and AIDS, finding an acceptable way to control population, or inventing a machine that can breathe our air and drink our oceans and excrete unpolluted forms of each are dreams that may or may not come about. Being digital is different. We are not waiting on any invention. It is here. It is now. It is almost genetic in its nature, in that each generation will become more digital than the preceding one.

The control bits of that digital future are more than ever before in the hands of the young. Nothing could make me happier.

PLUGGED IN AT HOME

Bill Gates

Bill Gates is Chairman and Chief Executive Officer of Microsoft Corporation, a company he co-founded in 1975. He has consistently believed that computers and software should be easy to use, and this vision has ensured the success of Microsoft, the arguable leader in the software industry. This excerpt from Gates' book, The Road Ahead, *claims that computers will increase the time people spend socializing. Notice the examples of socializing that Gates uses. Is this the same as your idea of socializing?*

One of the many fears expressed about the information highway is that it will reduce the time people spend socializing. Some worry that homes will become such cozy entertainment providers that we'll never leave them, and that, safe in our private sanctuaries, we'll become isolated. I don't think that's going to happen. [. . .]

From Bill Gates, *The Road Ahead* (New York: Viking, 1995), pp. 205–209, 211–214.

In the 1950s, there were those who said movie theaters would disappear and everyone would stay home watching the new invention, television. Pay TV and, later, movie video rentals provoked similar fears. Why would anyone spend money for parking and baby-sitters, buy the most expensive soft drinks and candy bars in the world, to sit in a dark room with strangers? But popular movies continue to fill theaters. Personally, I love movies and enjoy the experience of going out to see them. I do it almost every week, and I don't think the information highway will change that.

The new communications capabilities will make it far easier than it is today to stay in touch with friends and relatives who are geographically distant. Many of us have struggled to keep alive a friendship with someone far away. I used to date a woman who lived in a different city. We spent a lot of time together on e-mail. And we figured out a way we could sort of go to the movies together. We'd find a film that was playing at about the same time in both our cities. We'd drive to our respective theaters, chatting on our cellular phones. We'd watch the movie, and on the way home we'd use our cellular phones again to discuss the show. In the future this sort of "virtual dating" will be better because the movie watching could be combined with a videoconference.

I already play bridge on an on-line system that allows the players to see who else is interested in joining a game because it has a waiting room. Players have a primitive ability to choose the way they want to appear to the other players: their sex, hairstyle, body build, etc. The first time I connected to the system, I was in a rush to a keep a bridge appointment, and I didn't spend any time setting up my electronic appearance. After my friends and I had started playing, they all began to send me messages about how I was bald and naked (from the waist up, the only part of the body it showed). Even though this system didn't allow video or voice communication the way future systems will, the ability to send text messages to each other while we were playing made it a real blast.

The highway will not only make it easier to keep up with distant friends, it will also enable us to find new companions. Friendships formed across the network will lead naturally to getting together in person. Right now our methods for linking up with people we might like are pretty limited, but the network will change that. We will be meeting some of our new friends in different ways from the ones we use today. This alone will make life more interesting. Suppose you want to reach someone to play bridge with. The information highway will let you find cardplayers with the right skill level and availability in your neighborhood, or in other cities or nations. The idea of interactive games played by far-flung participants is hardly new. Chess players have been carrying on games by mail, one move at a time, for generations. The difference will be that applications running on the network will make it easy to find others who share similar interests and also to play together at the same pace you would face-to-face.

Another difference will be that while you are playing a game—say, bridge or *Starfighter*—you will be able to chat with the other players. The new DSVD modems I discussed earlier will let you use a normal phone line to carry on a voice conversation with the other players while watching the play unfold on your computer screen.

The experience of playing a friendly group game, as you do at the traditional card table, is pleasurable as much for the fellowship as for the competition. The game is more fun when you are enjoying the conversation. A number of companies are taking this multiplayer-game concept to a new level. You'll be able to play alone, with a few friends, or with thousands of people, and it will eventually be possible to see the people you are playing with—if they choose to permit you to. It will be easy to locate an expert and watch him play or take lessons from him. On the highway, you and your friends will not only be able to gather around a game table, you'll also be able to "meet" at a real place, such as Kensington Gardens, or in an imaginary setting. You'll be able to play a conventional game in a remarkable location, or play a new kind of game in which exploring the virtual setting is part of the action.

Warren Buffett, who is famous for his investment savvy, is a good friend of mine. For years I kept trying to think of how to entice him to use a personal computer. I even offered to fly out and get him started. He wasn't interested until he found out he could play bridge with friends all over the country through an on-line service. For the first six months he would come home and play for hours on end. Despite the fact that he had studiously stayed away from technology and technology investing, once he tried the computer, he was hooked. Now, many weeks Warren uses on-line services more than I do. The present system doesn't require you to enter your true appearance, or name, age, or sex. However, it seems that most of the users are either kids or retirees—neither of which describes Warren. One feature that had to be added into the system was a limit that permits parents to restrict the amount of time (and money) their kids spend on-line.

I think on-line computer-game playing will catch on in a big way. We'll be able to choose from a rich set of games, including the classic board and card games as well as action adventure and role-playing games. New styles of games will be invented specifically for this medium. There will be contests with prizes awarded. From time to time, celebrities and experts will come onto the system and everyone else will be able to watch as the celebrities play, or sign up to play against them. [. . .]

We can be sure we'll use the highway's unique capabilities to help us find communities of others with common interests. Today you may belong to the local ski club so you can meet other people who like to ski. You may also subscribe to *Recreational Skier* so you can get information about new ski products. Tomorrow you will be able to join such a community on the information highway. It will not only provide you with up-to-date information about weather conditions instantly, but will also be a way for you to stay in touch with other enthusiasts. [. . .]

Already, thousands of newsgroups on the Internet and countless forums on commercial on-line services have been set up as locations for small communities to share information. For example, on the Internet there are lively text-based discussion groups with such names as alt.agriculture.fruit, alt.animals.raccoons, alt.asian-movies, alt.coffee, bionet.biology.cardiovascular, soc.religion.islam, and talk.philosophy.misc. But these topics aren't nearly so specialized as some of the subjects I expect electronic communities will address in the future. Some communities will be very local, and some will be global. You won't be overwhelmed by the number of choices of communities any more than you are now by the telephone system. You'll look for a group that interests you in general, and then you'll search through it for the small segment you want to join. [. . .]

As on-line communities grow in importance, they will increasingly be where people will turn to find out what the public is really thinking. People like to know what's popular, which movies friends are watching, and what news others think is interesting. I want to read the same "newspaper front page" as those I'm going to meet with later today, so we can have something in common to talk about. You will be able to see what places on the network are being looked at often. There will be all sorts of "hot lists" of the coolest places.

Electronic communities, with all the information they reveal, will also create problems. Some institutions will have to make big changes as on-line communities gain power. Doctors and medical researchers are already having to contend with patients who explore medical literature electronically and compare notes with other patients who have the same serious disease. Word of unorthodox or unapproved treatments spreads fast in these communities. Some patients in drug trials have been able to figure out, by communicating with other patients in the trial, that they are receiving a placebo rather than the real medication. The discovery has prompted some of them to drop out of the trials or to seek alternate, simultaneous remedies. This undermines the research, but it is hard to fault patients who are trying to save their lives.

It's not just medical researchers who will be affected by so much access to information. One of the biggest concerns is parents having to contend with children who can find out about almost anything they want to, right from a home information appliance. Already, rating systems are being designed to allow parental control over what kids have access to. This could become a major political issue if the information publishers don't handle it properly.

On balance, the advantages will greatly outweigh the problems. The more information there is available, the more choices we will have. Today, devoted fans plan their evenings around the broadcast times of their favorite television shows, but once video-on-demand gives us the opportunity to watch whatever we like whenever we like, family or social activities, rather than a broadcaster's time slots, will control our entertaining schedules. Before the telephone, people thought of their neighbors as their only community. Almost everything was done with others who lived nearby. The telephone and the automobile allowed us to stretch out. We may visit face-to-face less often than we did a century ago because we can pick up the telephone, but this doesn't mean we have become isolated. It has made it easier for us to talk to each other and stay in touch. Sometimes it may seem too easy for people to reach you.

A decade from now, you may shake your head that there was ever a time when any stranger or a wrong number could interrupt you at home with a phone call. Cellular phones, pagers, and fax machines have already made it necessary for businesspeople to make explicit decisions that used to be implicit. A decade ago we didn't have to decide whether we wanted to receive documents at home or take calls on the road. It was easy to withdraw to your house, or certainly to your car. With modern technology you have to decide when and where you want to be available. In the future, when you will be able to work anywhere, reach anyone from anywhere, and be reached anywhere, you will be able to determine easily who and what can intrude. By explicitly indicating allowable interruptions, you will be able to reestablish your home—or anywhere you choose—as your sanctuary.

The information highway will help by prescreening all incoming communications, whether live phone calls, multimedia documents, e-mail, advertisements, or even news flashes. Anyone who has been approved by you will be able to get through to your electronic in-box or ring your phone. You might allow some people to send you mail but not to telephone. You might let others call when you have indicated you're not busy and let still others get through anytime. You won't want to receive thousands of unsolicited advertisements every day, but if you are looking for tickets to a sold-out concert, you'll want to get responses to your solicitations right away. Incoming communications will be tagged by source and type— for instance, ads, greetings, inquiries, publications, work-related documents, or bills. You'll set explicit delivery policies. You'll decide who can make your phone ring during dinner, who can reach you in your car, or when you're on vacation, and which kinds of calls or messages are worth waking you in the middle of the night. You'll be able to make as many distinctions as you need and to change the criteria whenever you want. Instead of giving out your telephone number, which can be passed around and used indefinitely, you will add a welcome caller's name to a constantly updated list indicating your level of interest in receiving his messages. If someone not on any of your lists wants to get to you, he'll have to have someone who is listed forward the message. You'll always be able to demote someone to a lower level or delete a name altogether from all level lists.

CYBER SWEETIE LEAVES SOUR TASTE

Ann Landers

Cyber romance is becoming a fairly common occurrence with the growing popularity of "chat" rooms and e-mail. Some of the social issues are even being dealt with by Ann Landers in her daily column. What are some of the issues that are evoked by the following letter?

Dear Ann Landers: I would like to respond to "Shocked in Texas," who lost her husband to a cyber lover. I feel eminently qualified because I left my marriage of 20-plus years under the same circumstances.

Now, after time to reflect and much counseling (that I refused in the beginning), I realize that my marriage had other problems or I would not have been such an easy target. But I may have worked it out if the computer hadn't been so handy.

Fort Worth *Star-Telegram,* July 18, 1996, p. E4.

Keep telling your readers, Ann, that this new "cyber" world is creating social issues that are brand-new and catching a multitude of basically good people completely off-guard. The ability to communicate intimately without seeing one another makes even those who would have thought themselves unlikely candidates for infidelities extremely vulnerable.

Everyone has problems, and to be able to communicate and empathize with a perfect stranger makes it incredibly easy to believe that person is your "soul mate." Why waste any more time with a flawed, real-life mate, who has not met all your needs, when you have this perfect lover who wants you right now?

It's sad that so many of us, in the midst of a raging midlife crisis, have thrown caution to the wind and gone head over heels for a "flawless" cyber soul mate. My only recommendation to "Shocked" is: Get therapy. Your husband might come to his senses, and whether he does or not, a competent therapist will help you learn from the past and deal with the future.

—Been there in California

Dear Calif.: I warned my readers several months ago that the cyber sweetie contagion is destined to be a major plague in the next millennium. It appears to have arrived earlier than expected.

There is no way to inoculate oneself against romantic fantasies. I can say, however, when you find yourself checking airline schedules and buying new underwear, make an appointment with your minister, friend, rabbi or guru and talk things over. Your cyberspace dreamboat could wind up being nothing more than a leaky canoe.

WELCOME TO CYBERBIA

M. Kadi

Kadi claims that there are some problems with the Internet. Can you identify them as Kadi describes them? Think about whether or not you agree with the ideas in this article and articulate your reasons why. If you accept these ideas, what ramifications do they have on the so-called global community that is simulated on the Internet? If you do not accept these ideas, offer support for your claims.

"Computer networking offers the soundest basis for world peace that has yet been presented. Peace must be created on the bulwark of understanding. International computer networks will knit together the peoples of the world in bonds of mutual respect; its possibilities are vast, indeed."—*Scientific American*, June 1994

Computer bulletin board services offer up the glories of e-mail, the thought provocation of newsgroups, the sharing of ideas implicit in public posting, and

Utne Reader, March–April 1995, pp. 57–59.

the interaction of real-time chats. The fabulous, wonderful, limitless world of communication is just waiting for you to log on. Sure. Yeah. Right. What this whole delirious, interconnected, global community of a world needs is a little reality check.

Let's face facts. The U.S. government by and large foots the bill for the Internet, through maintaining the structural (hardware) backbone, including, among other things, funding to major universities. As surely as the Department of Defense started this whole thing, AT&T or Ted Turner is going to end up running it, so I don't think it's too unrealistic to take a look at the Net as it exists in its commercial form in order to expose some of the realities lurking behind the regurgitated media rhetoric and the religious fanaticism of net junkies.

The average person, J. Individual, has an income. How much of J. Individual's income is going to be spent on computer connectivity? Does $120 a month sound reasonable? Well, you may find that a bit too steep for your pocketbook, but the brutal fact is that $120 is a "reasonable" monthly amount. The major online services have a monthly service charge of approximately $15. Fifteen dollars to join the global community, communicate with a diverse group of people, and access the world's largest repository of knowledge since the Alexandrian library doesn't seem unreasonable, does it? But don't overlook the average per-hour connection rate of $3 (which can skyrocket upwards of $10, depending on your modem speed and service). You might think that you are a crack whiz with your communications software—that you are rigorous and stringent and never, ever respond to e-mail or a forum while you're on-line—but let me tell you that no one is capable of logging on efficiently every time. Thirty hours per month is a realistic estimate for on-line time spent by a single user engaging in activities beyond primitive e-mail. Now consider that the average, one-step-above-complete-neophyte user has at least two distinct BBS [bulletin board system] accounts, and do the math. Total monthly cost: $120. Most likely, that's already more than the combined cost of your utility bills. How many people are prepared to double their monthly bills for the sole purpose of connectivity?

In case you think 30 hours a month is an outrageous estimate, think of it in terms of television. Thirty hours a month in front of a television is simply the evening news plus a weekly *Seinfeld/Frasier* hour. Thirty hours a month is less time than the average car-phone owner spends on the phone while commuting. Even a conscientious geek, logging on for e-mail and the up-to-the-minute news that only the net services can provide, is probably going to spend 30 hours a month on-line. And, let's be truthful here, 30 hours a month ignores shareware downloads, computer illiteracy, real-time chatting, interactive game playing, and any serious forum following, which by nature entail a significant amount of scrolling and/or downloading time.

If you are really and truly going to use the net services to connect with the global community, the hourly charges are going to add up pretty quickly. Take out a piece of paper, pretend you're writing a check, and print out "One hundred and twenty dollars—" and tell me again, how diverse is the on-line community?

That scenario aside, let's pretend that you have as much time and as much money to spend on-line as you damn well want. What do you actually do on-line?

Well, you download some cool shareware, you post technical questions in the computer user group forums, you check your stocks, you read the news and maybe some reviews—hey, you've already passed that 30-hour limit! But, of course, since computer networks are supposed to make it easy to reach out and touch strangers who share a particular obsession or concern, you are participating in the on-line forums, discussion groups, and conferences.

Let's review the structure of forums. For the purposes of this essay, we will examine the smallest of the major user-friendly commercial services—America Online (AOL). There is no precise statistic available (at least none that the company will reveal—you have to do the research by HAND!!!) on exactly how many subject-specific discussion areas (folders) exist on America Online. Any on-line service is going to have zillions of posts—contributions from users—pertaining to computer usage (the computer games area of America Online, for example, breaks into 500 separate topics with over 100,000 individual posts), so let's look at a less popular area: the "Lifestyles and Interests" department.

For starters, as I write this, there are 57 initial categories within the Lifestyles and Interests area. One of these categories is Ham Radio. Ham Radio? How can there possibly be 5,909 separate, individual posts about Ham Radio? There are 5,865 postings in the Biking (and that's just bicycles, not motorcycles) category. Genealogy—22,525 posts. The Gay and Lesbian category is slightly more substantial—36,333 posts. There are five separate categories for political and issue discussion. The big catchall topic area, the Exchange, has over 100,000 posts. Servicewide (on the smallest service, remember) there are over a million posts.

You may want to join the on-line revolution, but obviously you can't wade through everything that's being discussed—you need to decide which topics interest you, which folders to browse. Within the Exchange alone (one of 57 subdivisions within one of another 50 higher divisions) there are 1,492 separate topic-specific folders—each containing a rough average of 50 posts, but many containing closer to 400. (Note: America Online automatically empties folders when their post totals reach 400, so total post numbers do not reflect the overall historical totals for a given topic. Sometimes the posting is so frequent that the "shelf life" of a given post is no more than four weeks.)

So, there you are, J. Individual, ready to start interacting with folks, sharing stories and communicating. You have narrowed yourself into a single folder, three tiers down in the America Online hierarchy, and now you must choose between nearly 1,500 folders. Of course, once you choose a few of these folders, you will then have to read all the posts in order to catch up, be current, and not merely repeat a previous post.

A polite post is no more than two paragraphs long (a screenful of text, which obviously has a number of intellectually negative implications). Let's say you choose 10 folders (out of 1,500). Each folder contains an average of 50 posts.

Five hundred posts, at, say, one paragraph each, and you're now looking at the equivalent of a 200-page book.

Enough with the stats. Let me back up a minute and present you with some very disturbing, but rational, assumptions. J. Individual wants to join the on-line revolution, to connect and communicate. But J. is not going to read all one million posts on AOL. (After all, J. has a second on-line service.) Exercising choice is J. Individual's God-given right as an American, and, by gosh, J. Individual is going to make some decisions. So J. is going to ignore all the support groups—after all, J. is a normal, well-adjusted person, and all of J.'s friends are normal, well-adjusted people; what does J. need to know about alcoholism or incest victims? J. Individual is white. So J. Individual is going to ignore all the multicultural folders. J. couldn't give a hoot about gender issues and does not want to discuss religion or philosophy. Ultimately, J. Individual does not engage in topics that do not interest J. Individual. So who is J. meeting? Why, people who are *just like* J.

J. Individual has now joined the electronic community. Surfed the Net. Found some friends. *Tuned in, turned on, and geeked out.* Traveled the Information Highway and, just a few miles down that great democratic expressway, J. Individual has settled into an electronic suburb.

Are any of us so very different? It's my time and my money and I am not going to waste any of it reading posts by disgruntled Robert-Bly drum-beating men's-movement boys who think that they should have some say over, for instance, whether or not I choose to carry a child to term simply because a condom broke. I know where I stand. I'm an adult. I know what's up and I am not going to waste my money arguing with a bunch of neanderthals.

Oh yeah; I am so connected, so enlightened, so open to the opposing viewpoint. I'm out there, meeting all kinds of people from different economic backgrounds (who have $120 a month to burn), from all religions (yeah, right, like anyone actually discusses religion anymore from a user standpoint), from all kinds of different ethnic backgrounds and with all kinds of sexual orientations (as if any of this ever comes up outside of the appropriate topic folder).

People are drawn to topics and folders that interest them and therefore people will only meet people who are interested in the same topics in the same folders. Rarely does anyone venture into a random folder just to see what others (the Other?) are talking about.

Basically, between the monetary constraints and the sheer number of topics and individual posts, the great Information Highway is not a place where you will enter an "amazing web of new people, places, and ideas." One does not encounter people from "all walks of life" because there are too many people and too many folders. Diversity might be out there (and personally I don't think it is), but the simple fact is that the average person will not encounter it because with one brain, one job, one partner, one family, and one life, no one has the time!

Just in case these arguments based on time and money aren't completely convincing, let me bring up a historical reference. Please take another look at the opening quote of this essay, from *Scientific American*. It was featured in their 50

Years Ago Today column. Where you read "computer networking," the quote originally contained the word *television*. Amusing, isn't it?

QUESTIONS TO HELP YOU THINK AND WRITE ABOUT ISSUES IN MODERN ELECTRONIC MEDIA

1. What claim does Postman make about the effect of television on its viewers? Think of some recent examples from your experience that either support or refute his view.

2. What types of proof does Hamill use to develop his argument about the main effect of television? Are they effective? Why?

3. Compare the views of Hamill and Postman on the effect of television on its viewers. Which of their ideas do you agree with? Frame a rebuttal for the ideas you disagree with.

4. Read the three short essays about how television has impacted the lives of the readers of *The Sun* magazine. You and your classmates should now write similar short accounts of the effect television has had on each of you. Read these essays aloud and make some judgments about the good or bad effects that television has had on your class as a whole.

5. Read the four articles in part 2 about computers. Speculate about the good effects of computers. Also consider some of the dangerous effects, according to your system of values. What are your reasons for considering them valuable or dangerous or both for the future development of the human race?

6. Bill Gates describes a number of ways that computers can be used in the future. Which of these appeal to you? Which do not? Why? If you had Bill Gates's money, how would you employ modern computer technology in your life?

7. Repeat the assignment in question 5, only this time make computers the subject of the class' essays. Class members should write short accounts of the effects of computers on each of them. These essays should be read aloud so that the class can make some judgments about the good or bad effects that computers have had on the class as a whole.

SECTION VII

Issues Concerning Responsibility

WHAT ARE THE ISSUES?

I. Who Should Share Responsibility for the Children?

Most people would immediately agree that parents should be responsible for their children. But what happens when one or both parents work? Or, when parents do not take responsibility? Swift's "Modest Proposal" provides historical perspective for this issue. Three modern authors provide perspectives on day care and the idea of seeking permission to have children in the first place.

2. Who Should Take Responsibility for the Poor?

Is there still sufficient opportunity for poor people to "pull themselves up by their bootstraps" and get back on their feet, or is this an area where government needs to intervene with various types of welfare and self-development programs? This issue cuts across many of the other issues in this book, including crime and education. In this section you will read accounts of two people who have been involved with public assistance programs and a plan by Newt Gingrich to reform the present welfare system in this country.

3. Who Should Be Responsible for the Life or Death Decisions That Affect the Terminally Ill?

Some people believe that the issue of doctor-assisted suicide will become as emotionally charged and intensely debated as the abortion issue as more and more cases of doctor-assisted suicides are reported and as the courts become involved. The question is: should any person take the responsibility to end a human life? Several perspectives are provided on this issue in this section. See also "Doctor-Assisted Suicide: Is It Ever an Option?" page 258 and the Annotated Bibliography on Euthanasia, page 369.

4. Extend Your Perspective with Films and Literature Related to Issues Concerning Responsibility

Films: Kramer vs. Kramer, 1979; *Schindler's List,* 1995; *Rain Man,* 1988.
Literature: poem: "Ethics" by Linda Pastan; short story: "Bartleby the Scrivener" by Herman Melville and "The Ones Who Walked Away from Omelas" by Ursula LeGuin; novel: *The Lord of the Flies* by William Golding.

THE RHETORICAL SITUATION

What constitutes individual responsibility and what constitutes social responsibility has been an issue since humans first organized themselves in society. John Stuart Mill, in his essay "On Liberty" (1849), offers a historical perspective that is much in line with what many people would be willing to accept today. Mill provides the individual with considerable freedom of responsibility as long as the individual does not hurt others and is willing to be responsible for the consequences of his or her actions.

In our own day responsibility issues focus in general on whether or not we can expect every individual to be responsible for his or her actions or whether, in certain cases, social institutions need to take responsibility for them. Some people also wonder whether or not individuals, given freedom, can always be trusted to do what is best both for themselves and for society. When they do not, society needs to be able to intervene. Some examples of specific responsibility issues in our time focus on whether the government, private business, or individuals should be responsible for health care, day care, homeless shelters and food for the homeless, drug addicts and their care, the rehabilitation of criminals, employees who have been "laid off," single mothers with no source of income, the disabled, and the otherwise disadvantaged.

No one escapes the responsibility issue and its ramifications in modern life. Responsibility issues permeate politics, determine how we spend much of the national treasury, and have profound personal effects on the daily well-being of many of us.

The articles in this section focus on responsibility issues concerning children, the poor, and the terminally ill. They will get you started thinking about responsibility, but they clearly do not exhaust all aspects of the issue. Which responsibility issues will affect your life?

1. Who Should Share Responsibility for the Children?

A MODEST PROPOSAL FOR PREVENTING THE CHILDREN OF IRELAND FROM BEING A BURDEN TO THEIR PARENTS OR COUNTRY

Jonathan Swift

Swift wrote this piece in 1729 when England was exploiting Ireland to the point of debilitation. Swift's proposal is satirical, to be sure, but what claim is implicit in the piece? Does Swift ever finally offer an answer to the question of who is responsible for the children of Ireland?

From Jonathan Swift, *Satires and Personal Writings*, ed. William Alfred Eddy, (London: Oxford University Press, 1932), pp. 21–31.

It is a melancholly Object to those, who walk through this great Town or travel in the Country, when they see the Streets, the Roads and Cabbin-doors crowded with Beggers of the Female Sex, followed by three, four, or six Children, all in Rags, and importuning every Passenger for an Alms. These Mothers instead of being able to work for their honest livelyhood, are forced to employ all their time in Stroling to beg Sustenance for their helpless Infants, who, as they grow up, either turn Thieves for want of Work, or leave their dear Native Country, to fight for the Pretender in Spain, or sell themselves to the Barbadoes.

I think it is agreed by all Parties, that this prodigious number of Children in the Arms, or on the Backs, or at the Heels of their Mothers, and frequently of their Fathers, is in the present deplorable state of the Kingdom, a very great additional grievance; and therefore whoever could find out a fair, cheap and easy method of making these Children sound and useful Members of the Common-wealth, would deserve so well of the publick, as to have his Statue set up for a Preserver of the Nation.

But my Intention is very far from being confined to provide only for the Children of professed Beggers, it is of a much greater Extent, and shall take in the whole Number of Infants at a certain Age, who are born of Parents in effect as little able to support them, as those who demand our Charity in the Streets.

As to my own part, having turned my Thoughts, for many Years, upon this important Subject, and maturely weighed the several Schemes of other Projectors, I have always found them grossly mistaken in their computation. It is true, a Child just dropt from its Dam, may be supported by her Milk, for a Solar Year with little other Nourishment, at most not above the Value of two Shillings, which the Mother may certainly get, or the Value in Scraps, by her lawful Occupation of Begging; and it is exactly at one Year Old that I propose to provide for them in such a manner, as, instead of being a Charge upon their Parents, or the Parish, or wanting Food and Raiment for the rest of their Lives, they shall, on the Contrary, contribute to the Feeding and partly to the Cloathing of many Thousands.

There is likewise another great Advantage in my Scheme, that it will prevent those voluntary Abortions, and that horrid practice of Women murdering their Bastard Children, alas! too frequent among us, Sacrificing the poor innocent Babes, I doubt, more to avoid the Expence than the Shame, which would move Tears and Pity in the most Savage and inhuman breast.

The number of Souls in this Kingdom being usually reckoned one Million and a half, Of these I calculate there may be about two hundred thousand Couple whose Wives are Breeders; from which number I substract thirty Thousand Couples, who are able to maintain their own Children, although I apprehend there cannot be so many, under the present Distresses of the Kingdom; but this being granted, there will remain an hundred and seventy thousand Breeders. I again Substract fifty Thousand, for those Women who miscarry, or whose Children die by accident, or disease within the Year. There only remain an hundred and twenty thousand Children of poor Parents annually born: The question therefore is, How this number shall be reared, and provided for? which, as I have already said, under the present Situation of Affairs, is utterly impossible by all the Methods hitherto proposed; for we can neither employ them in Handicraft or Agriculture; we neither build Houses, (I mean in the Country) nor cultivate Land: They can very seldom pick up a Livelihood by Stealing till they arrive at six years Old; except where they are of towardly parts; although, I confess, they learn the Rudiments much earlier; during which time they can however be properly looked upon only as Probationers; as I have been informed by a principal Gentleman in the County of Cavan, who protested to me, that he never knew above one or two Instances under the Age of six, even in a part of the Kingdom so renowned for the quickest proficiency in that Art.

I am assured by our Merchants, that a Boy or a Girl before twelve years Old, is no saleable Commodity, and even when they come to this Age, they will not yield above three Pounds, or three Pounds and half a Crown at most, on the Exchange; which cannot turn to Account either to the Parents or Kingdom, the Charge of Nutriment and Rags having been at least four times that Value.

I shall now therefore humbly propose my own Thoughts, which I hope will not be liable to the least Objection.

I have been assured by a very knowing American of my acquaintance in London, that a young healthy Child well Nursed is at a year Old a most delicious nourishing and wholesome Food, whether Stewed, Roasted, Baked, or Boiled; and I make no doubt that it will equally serve in a Fricasie, or a Ragoust.

I do therefore humbly offer it to publick consideration, that of the Hundred and twenty thousand Children, already computed, twenty thousand may be reserved for Breed, whereof only one fourth part to be Males; which is more than we allow to Sheep, black Cattle, or Swine, and my Reason is, that these Children are seldom the Fruits of Marriage, a Circumstance not much regarded by our Savages, therefore, one Male will be sufficient to serve four Females. That the remaining Hundred thousand may at a year Old be offered in Sale to the Persons of Quality and Fortune, through the Kingdom, always advising the Mother to let them Suck plentifully in the last Month, so as to render them Plump, and Fat for a good Table. A Child will make two Dishes at an Entertainment for Friends, and when the Family dines alone, the fore or hind Quarter will make a reasonable Dish, and seasoned with a little Pepper or Salt will be very good Boiled on the fourth Day, especially in Winter.

I have reckoned upon a Medium, that a Child just born will weigh 12 pounds, and in a solar Year, if tolerably nursed, encreaseth to 28 Pounds.

I grant this food will be somewhat dear, and therefore very proper for Landlords, who, as they have already devoured most of the Parents seem to have the best Title to the Children.

Infant's flesh will be in Season throughout the Year, but more plentiful in March, and a little before and after; for we are told by a grave Author an eminent French Physician, that Fish being a prolifick Dyet, there are more Children born in Roman Catholick Countries about nine Months after Lent, than at any other Season; therefore reckoning a Year after Lent, the Markets will be more glutted than usual, because the Number of Popish Infants, is at least three to one in this Kingdom, and therefore it will have one other Collateral advantage, by lessening the Number of Papists among us.

I have already computed the Charge of nursing a Begger's Child (in which List I reckon all Cottagers, Labourers, and four fifths of the Farmers) to be about two Shillings per Annum, Rags included; and I believe no Gentleman would repine to give Ten Shillings for the Carcass of a good fat Child, which, as I have said will make four Dishes of excellent Nutritive Meat, when he hath only some particular Friend, or his own Family to dine with him. Thus the Squire will learn to be a good Landlord, and grow popular among his Tenants, the Mother will have Eight Shillings neat Profit, and be fit for Work till she produces another Child.

Those who are more thrifty (as I must confess the Times require) may flay the Carcass; the Skin of which, Artificially dressed, will make admirable Gloves for Ladies, and Summer Boots for fine Gentlemen.

As to our City of Dublin, Shambles may be appointed for this purpose, in the most convenient parts of it, and Butchers we may be assured will not be wanting; although I rather recommend buying the Children alive, and dressing them hot from the Knife, as we do roasting Pigs.

A very worthy Person, a true Lover of his Country, and whose Virtues I highly esteem, was lately pleased, in discoursing on this matter, to offer a refinement upon my Scheme. He said, that many Gentlemen of this Kingdom, having of late destroyed their Deer, he conceived that the Want of Venison might be well supply'd by the Bodies of young Lads and Maidens, not exceeding fourteen Years of Age, nor under twelve; so great a Number of both Sexes in every Country being now ready to Starve, for want of Work and Service: And these to be disposed of by their Parents if alive, or otherwise by their nearest Relations. But with due deference to so excellent a Friend, and so deserving a Patriot, I cannot be altogether in his Sentiments; for as to the Males, my American acquaintance assured me from frequent Experience, that their Flesh was generally Tough and Lean, like that of our Schoolboys, by continual exercise, and their Taste disagreeable, and to fatten them would not answer the Charge. Then as to the Females, it would, I think with humble Submission, be a Loss to the Publick, because they soon would become Breeders themselves: And besides it is not improbable that some scrupulous People might be apt to Censure such a Practice, (although indeed very unjustly) as a little bordering upon Cruelty, which, I confess, hath always been with me the strongest Objection against any Project, how well soever intended.

But in order to justify my Friend, he confessed, that this expedient was put into his Head by the famous Sallmanaazor, a Native of the Island Formosa, who came from thence to London, above twenty Years ago, and in Conversation told my Friend, that in his Country when any young Person happened to be put to Death, the Executioner sold the Carcass to Persons of Quality, as a prime Dainty, and that, in his Time, the Body of a plump Girl of fifteen, who was crucified for an attempt to poison the Emperor, was sold to his Imperial Majesty's prime Minister of State, and other great Mandarins of the Court, in Joints from the Gibbet, at four hundred Crowns. Neither indeed can I deny, that if the same Use were made of several plump young Girls in this Town, who, without one single Groat to their Fortunes, cannot stir abroad without a Chair, and appear at a Play-house, and Assemblies in Foreign fineries, which they never will pay for; the Kingdom would not be the worse.

Some Persons of a desponding Spirit are in great concern about that vast Number of poor People, who are Aged, Diseased, or Maimed, and I have been desired to imploy my Thoughts what Course may be taken, to ease the Nation of so grievous an Incumbrance. But I am not in the least Pain upon that matter, because it is very well known, that they are every Day dying, and rotting, by cold and famine, and filth, and vermin, as fast as can be reasonably expected. And as to the younger Labourers, they are now in almost as hopeful a Condition. They cannot get Work, and consequently pine away for want of Nourishment, to a degree, that if at any Time they are accidentally hired to common Labour, they have not Strength to perform it, and thus the Country and themselves are happily delivered from the Evils to come.

I have too long digressed, and therefore shall return to my Subject. I think the Advantages by the Proposal which I have made are obvious and many, as well as of the highest Importance.

For *First*, as I have already observed, it would greatly lessen the Number of Papists, with whom we are Yearly over-run, being the principal Breeders of the Nation, as well as our most dangerous Enemies, and who stay at home on purpose with a Design to deliver the Kingdom to the Pretender, hoping to take their Advantage by the Absence of so many good Protestants, who have chosen rather to leave their Country, than stay at home, and pay Tithes against their Conscience, to an Episcopal Curate.

Secondly, The poorer Tenants will have something valuable of their own which by Law may be made lyable to Distress, and help to pay their Landlord's Rent, their Corn and Cattle being already seized, and Money a Thing unknown.

Thirdly, Whereas the Maintenance of an hundred thousand Children, from two Years old, and upwards, cannot be computed at less than Ten Shillings a Piece per Annum, the Nation's Stock will be thereby increased fifty thousand Pounds per Annum, besides the Profit of a new Dish, introduced to the Tables of all Gentlemen of Fortune in the Kingdom, who have any Refinement in Taste, and the Money will circulate among our Selves, the Goods being entirely of our own Growth and Manufacture.

Fourthly, The constant Breeders, besides the gain of eight Shillings Sterling per Annum, by the Sale of their Children, will be rid of the Charge of maintaining them after the first Year.

Fifthly, This Food would likewise bring great Custom to Taverns, where the Vintners will certainly be so prudent as to procure the best Receipts for dressing it to Perfection; and consequently have their Houses frequented by all the fine Gentlemen, who justly value themselves upon their Knowledge in good Eating; and a skilful Cook, who understands how to oblige his Guests, will contrive to make it as expensive as they please.

Sixthly, This would be a great Inducement to Marriage, which all wise Nations have either encouraged by Rewards, or enforced by Laws and Penalties. It would encrease the Care and Tenderness of Mothers towards their Children, when they were sure of a Settlement for Life, to the poor Babes, provided in some Sort by the Publick, to their annual Profit instead of Expence; we should soon see an honest Emulation among the married Women, which of them could bring the fattest Child to the Market. Men would become as fond of their Wives, during the Time of their Pregnancy, as they are now of their Mares in Foal, their Cows in Calf, or Sows when they are ready to farrow, nor offer to beat or kick them (as is too frequent a Practice) for fear of a Miscarriage.

Many other Advantages might be enumerated. For Instance, the Addition of some thousand Carcasses in our Exportation of Barrel'd Beef: The Propagation of Swine's Flesh, and Improvement in the Art of making good Bacon, so much wanted among us by the great Destruction of Pigs, too frequent at our Tables, which are no way comparable in Taste, or Magnificence to a well grown, fat yearling Child, which roasted whole will make a considerable Figure at a Lord Mayor's Feast, or any other Publick Entertainment. But this, and many others, I omit, being studious of Brevity.

Supposing that one thousand Families in this City, would be constant Customers for Infant's Flesh, besides others who might have it at merry Meetings, particularly at Weddings and Christenings, I compute that Dublin would take off Annually about twenty thousand Carcasses, and the rest of the Kingdom (where probably they will be sold somewhat cheaper) the remaining eighty Thousand.

I can think of no one Objection, that will possibly be raised against this Proposal, unless it should be urged, that the Number of People will be thereby much lessened in the Kingdom. This I freely own, and 'twas indeed one principal Design in offering it to the World. I desire the Reader will observe, that I calculate my Remedy for this one individual Kingdom of Ireland, and for no Other that ever was, is, or, I think, ever can be upon Earth. Therefore let no man talk to me of other Expedients: Of taxing our Absentees at five Shillings a Pound: Of using neither Cloaths, nor Household Furniture, except what is of our own Growth and Manufacture: Of utterly rejecting the Materials and Instruments that promote Foreign Luxury: Of curing the Expensiveness of Pride, Vanity, Idleness, and Gaming in our Women: Of introducing a Vein of Parcimony, Prudence and Temperance: Of learning to love our Country, wherein we differ even from Laplanders, and the Inhabitants of Topinamboo: Of quitting our Animosities, and Factions, nor act any longer like the Jews, who were murdering one another at the very Moment their City was taken: Of being a little cautious not to sell our Country and Consciences for nothing: Of teaching Landlords to have at least one Degree of Mercy towards their Tenants. Lastly, Of putting a Spirit of Honesty, Industry, and Skill into our Shop-keepers, who, if a Resolution could now be taken to buy only our Native Goods, would immediately unite to cheat and exact upon us in the Price, the Measure, and the Goodness, nor could ever yet be brought to make one fair Proposal of just Dealing, though often and earnestly invited to it.

Therefore I repeat, let no Man talk to me of these and the like Expedients, till he hath at least some Glimpse of Hope, that there will ever be some hearty and sincere Attempt to put them in Practice.

But as to my self, having been wearied out for many Years with offering vain, idle, visionary Thoughts, and at length utterly despairing of Success, I fortunately fell upon this Proposal, which as it is wholly new, so it hath something Solid and Real, of no Expence and little Trouble, full in our own Power, and whereby we can incur no Danger in disobliging England. For this kind of Commodity will not bear Exportation, the Flesh being of too tender a Consistence, to admit a long Continuance in Salt, although perhaps I cou'd name a Country, which wou'd be glad to eat up our whole Nation without it.

After all, I am not violently bent upon my own Opinion, as to reject any Offer, proposed by wise Men, which shall be found equally Innocent, Cheap, Easy, and Effectual. But before something of that Kind shall be advanced in Contradiction to my Scheme, and offering a better, I desire the Author or Authors, will be pleased maturely to consider two Points. *First*, As Things now stand, how they will be able to find Food and Raiment for a hundred Thousand useless Mouths and Backs. And *Secondly*, There being a round Million of Creatures in Human Figure, throughout this Kingdom, whose whole Subsistence put into a common Stock, would leave them in Debt two Millions of Pounds Sterling, adding those, who are Beggers by Profession, to the Bulk of Farmers, Cottagers and Labourers, with their Wives and Children, who are Beggers in Effect; I desire those Politicians, who dislike my Overture, and may perhaps be so bold to attempt an Answer, that they will first ask the Parents of these Mortals, Whether they would not at this Day think it a great Happiness to have been sold for Food at a Year Old, in the manner I prescribe, and thereby have avoided such a perpetual Scene of Misfortunes, as they have since gone through, by the Oppression of Landlords, the Impossibility of paying Rent without Money or Trade, the Want of common Sustenance, with neither House nor Cloaths to cover them from the Inclemencies of the Weather, and the most inevitable Prospect of intailing the like, or greater Miseries, upon their Breed for ever.

I profess in the Sincerity of my Heart, that I have not the least Personal Interest in endeavouring to promote this necessary Work, having no other Motive than the Publick Good of my Country, by advancing our Trade, providing for Infants, relieving the Poor, and giving some Pleasure to the Rich. I have no Children, by which I can propose to get a single Penny; the youngest being nine Years Old, and my Wife past Child-bearing.

GIVING CHILDREN A CHANCE IN LIFE

David T. Lykken

Lykken is a professor of psychology at the University of Minnesota.

Natural selection has produced a human species designed to live relatively amicably in extended families. Just as we evolved an innate readiness to learn language, so we evolved a proclivity to learn and obey basic social rules—to nurture

The Chronicle of Higher Education, XLII, no. 22, February 9, 1996, pp. B1–B2.

our children, help our neighbors, and pull our weight in the group effort for survival. But, like the ability to acquire language, our innate readiness to become socialized does not appear automatically: Unless other humans help us develop and practice the necessary skills during childhood, we remain undisciplined and unprepared to play a productive role in society.

Traditional societies in which children are socialized communally—the way our species evolved—have little crime. Any persistent offender is likely to be a psychopath—that is, someone whose innate temperament makes him unusually resistant to socialization.

In our society, where extended families are seldom available to train children in social skills, we now entrust this basic responsibility to the biological parents alone—which means increasingly to single mothers. Nearly two of every five American children today are being reared by single mothers. About half of these youngsters are children of divorce, whose fathers have essentially abandoned paternal responsibility. The other half were born out of wedlock; many of them never knew their fathers. In 1994, one in five American women of childbearing age who had never married had at least one child. Many of these mothers are immature or unsocialized themselves, hardly well qualified to teach social rules to their children. I call the unsocialized offspring of indifferent, incompetent, or overburdened parents *sociopaths.*

The *Star Tribune,* of Minneapolis, recently printed the story of a single mother who has 10 children under the age of 16. Just arrived from Chicago, she and her family have been repeatedly ejected from our local homeless shelters because of the children's undisciplined behavior. Until her welfare check can be rerouted from Chicago to Minneapolis, my county is putting the family up in a motel, whose owner is charging a steep price because of the children's noise and destructiveness.

I admit to feeling a certain resentment that I and other taxpayers have to underwrite the costs of this woman's career of illegitimate parenthood. But, more important, what about those 10 hapless children? Some will never learn to read or do their sums. Most of the boys will soon be known to our juvenile-corrections system. Most of the girls are likely to follow their mother's example, beginning not long after puberty. This case made the newspaper because the family is unusually large, but, in fact, this mother and children represent the tiny tip of an enormous iceberg.

In the United States, among boys aged 12 to 17, the percentage who are arrested for violent crime has doubled in the past 15 years. Not coincidentally, the percentage of children under 18 who are being reared without fathers also has doubled during this period. Nationally, about 70 per cent of school dropouts, 70 per cent of teenage girls who are pregnant and unmarried, and 70 per cent of incarcerated juvenile delinquents were raised without fathers.

The social historian David Blankenhorn, president of the Institute for American Values, argues persuasively in *Fatherless America: Confronting Our Most Urgent Social Problem* (BasicBooks, 1995) that being reared without a father is the primary cause of these social pathologies. Indeed, one can show that a boy raised without a father is nearly seven times more likely to end up in prison than a boy reared by both biological parents.

Gerald Patterson, a developmental psychologist at the Oregon Social Learning Center, has demonstrated that some parents of problem children can be taught to handle more effectively the daily challenges of parenting. But the process is usually slow and requires many supervised sessions of parent-child interaction. And not all immature, inept, or indifferent parents are willing or able to enroll in parental-training programs such as the one created by Mr. Patterson. How can we give their children a brighter future and also prevent them from becoming burdens on society?

Bad parenting is not a new phenomenon, of course; lurid examples can be found in the novels of Charles Dickens and Thomas Hardy. What is new is the size of the problem, and the rapid increase in the number of children who become sociopaths or are abused or even murdered by the adults who should be caring for them. Last year, thousands of American children were abused or killed by their harried mothers or their mothers' current boyfriends.

This problem is compounded by the counterproductive "family preservation" philosophy of many social workers, who believe that children should be kept with their biological mother unless she is hopelessly addicted to drugs or alcohol or is in prison. In the latter cases, social workers often favor placing the child with the maternal grandmother, who failed so badly in rearing the mother. Unless we can come to grips with the fact that, by any rational, moral bookkeeping, the rights of the children outweigh the rights of the biological parents, we will never solve the problem of children whose parents cannot socialize them.

We need to invest in parental training for those parents who can benefit from it, and in an adequate system of professionalized foster care for the children of those parents for whom training will not work. If parenting is as difficult—yet as important—as we know it to be, and if thousands of children like those 10 in my example desperately require a new and better chance in life, then surely we shall need a vastly expanded system of foster care, with foster parents adequately trained, supervised, and compensated. Many married women who now work outside the home, for example, might well prefer to work as foster parents, if the pay were better. Government action now assuredly will save us money later.

Group homes with five to 10 children seem to work better than foster parents for youngsters who have spent their first 10 years or so with inept parents. With several staff members of both sexes, such homes provide a broader choice of parent substitutes. Group homes essentially provide foster care on a communal scale, in some ways more like the extended-family system of socialization to which our species is evolutionarily adapted.

James Q. Wilson, a professor of management and public policy at the University of California at Los Angeles, has suggested that it would be cost-effective to establish boarding schools for children whose parents are not able or willing to socialize them. This seems like another logical option. In my county, for instance, it costs $150 a day to keep a youngster in the juvenile-corrections center, which works out to $37,800 per school year, nearly $55,000 per calendar year—far more than tuition at any boarding school would be.

It is clear that an investment now would pay huge dividends in the future. Sociopaths breed high-risk children, because sociopaths are bad parents. Therefore, reducing the number of children in the present generation who become sociopaths will also reduce the proportion of high-risk children in the next generation.

But if we really want to tackle the problem, it is time that we begin a serious discussion of the feasibility (and ethics) of limiting the reproductive "rights" of our citizens. I see several important reasons for making this suggestion: If parents cannot or will not take responsibility for supporting and rearing their children, society will have to take on that responsibility. If parents keep but fail to socialize their children, taxpayers will have to bear the costs, which Jack Westman, a child psychiatrist at the University of Wisconsin at Madison, estimates in *Licensing Parents: Can We Prevent Child Abuse and Neglect?* (Plenum, 1994) are roughly $50,000 per sociopath per year. These costs include the added burden on the criminal-justice system (more expensive per capita than Ivy League colleges) and lost productivity and taxes—not to mention injury and losses to the sociopaths' victims.

But more important than the cost is the welfare of the vulnerable children themselves. Most members of the anti-abortion movement express what I am sure is a genuine emotional concern for the welfare of the fetus. But I hope these kind-hearted people are equally concerned about what may become of an unwanted or abused child, a socially maladjusted adolescent, or a criminal or drug-dependent adult.

In our nation, it is taboo to suggest any infringement by society upon the procreative rights of individuals. Yet one must obtain a license to get married. Courts and social-service agencies require prospective adoptive parents to meet reasonable standards before, in effect, licensing them to adopt a child. I believe that it is not wildy unreasonable, therefore, at least to consider and discuss the imposition of a similar requirement upon prospective biological parents. Many practical problems would have to be solved to implement such a plan, but we will never know whether they could be solved if we shrink from even discussing them, if we permit the taboo that surrounds the issue of procreative rights to silence rational debate.

As a first step, I would recommend that child-welfare agencies be directed to keep careful track of children whose parents are statistically more likely to produce unsocialized children: parents who would not normally be permitted to adopt a child because they are unmarried, under 21, unable to support themselves, or because they have serious criminal records or incapacitating mental illness. Such children would be visited at least annually by child-protection workers, who would evaluate each child's health, educational progress, and social development.

I believe that after several years of carefully collecting data on these children—the rates of neglect and abuse, truancy and school dropout, delinquency and teen pregnancy—we would see rates for this high-risk group so many times higher than those for other children that the need for further action would be obvious to everyone.

By that time, we might be willing to require people who want to become parents to get a license, perhaps from the same authorities who now issue marriage licenses. Most people would easily qualify for such a license (by showing that they do not fall into any of the categories of high-risk parents listed above). Others, such as gay couples or individuals with sufficient resources to provide the equivalent of two-parent nurturing, could appeal to family court for an exemption.

Our present social policies actually make it easy for immature, incompetent, or unsocialized people to produce children at will, and then to maintain those children under conditions that are almost guaranteed to leave them unfit for happy or successful lives. We have been so concerned about parental rights that we have ignored what is more important by any means of moral reckoning—namely, the rights of those innocent children. I believe it is time we changed our social priorities.

DAY CARE: A GRAND AND TROUBLING SOCIAL EXPERIMENT

Dorothy Conniff

Dorothy Conniff is director of community services in Madison, Wisconsin. She has worked in the field of day care for over twenty years. Contrast Conniff's views with the views of Susan Faludi, whose article follows this one.

We won't find real solutions to the need for good child care until we solve a fundamental problem: We value children only sentimentally. Children's real needs and concerns do not register as essential.

We have abundant research about the lasting negative effects of early deprivation and the strikingly positive effects of high-quality early education. Yet today we shuffle millions of middle-class children off to day-care settings duplicating the sort of deprivation that used to be suffered only by the poorest and most disadvantaged.

Take infant care, for example.

In many states, there are no regulations governing the number of infants a staff member may care for. In those where there are, many states allow five or six. In Wisconsin, where I live, the maximum is four infants per worker. [According to the National Association for the Education of Young Children, 29 states require this four-to-one ratio, while only three—Kansas, Maryland, and Massachusetts—

Utne Reader, May/June 1993, pp. 66–67.

require a three-to-one ratio. Most of the remaining states have five-to-one or six-to-one ratios.]

Consider the amount of physical care and attention a baby needs—say 20 minutes for feeding every three hours or so, and 10 minutes for diapering every two hours or so, and time for the care giver to wash her hands thoroughly and sanitize the area after changing each baby. In an eight-and-a-half-hour-day, then, a care giver working under the typical four-to-one ratio will have 16 diapers to change and 12 feedings to give. Four diaper changes and three feedings apiece is not an inordinate amount of care over a long day from the babies' point of view.

But think about the care giver's day: Four hours to feed the babies, two hours and 40 minutes to change them. If you allow an extra two and a half minutes at each changing to put them down, clean up the area, and thoroughly wash your hands, you can get by with 40 minutes for sanitizing. (And if you think about thoroughly washing your hands 16 times a day, you may begin to understand why epidemics of diarrhea and related diseases regularly sweep through infant-care centers.)

That makes seven hours and 20 minutes of the day spent just on physical care—if you're lucky and the infants stay conveniently on schedule.

Since feeding and diaper changing are necessarily one-on-one activities, each infant is bound to be largely unattended during the five-plus hours that the other three babies are being attended to. So, if there's to be any stimulation at all for the child, the care giver had better chat and play up a storm while she's feeding and changing.

Obviously, such a schedule is not realistic. In group infant care based on even this four-to-one ratio, babies will not be changed every two hours and they will probably not be held while they're fed.

They also will not get the kind of attention and talk that is the foundation of language development. If a child is deprived of language stimulation for eight to ten hours a day, how much compensation—how much "quality time"—can concerned parents provide in the baby's few other waking hours at home?

Unfortunately, the situation is not much better for toddlers. Group care is almost as new a service for toddlers as for infants. In many centers, even in the better ones, young, unskilled staff struggle with large groups of very young children. Staff turnover rates exceed 30 percent a year, so most don't stay long enough to be trained.

One common sign of staff inexperience is the Big Toddler Lineup. Inexperienced staff tend to fall back on their only model for dealing with groups of children: the elementary school. What do you do in school each time an activity changes? Line up. Not realizing that forming a line is developmentally beyond the capacity of such young children, staff struggle for long periods to get their toddlers to line up for routine events. The results are comical and predictable—babies wander off, sit down and stare into space, cry—and staff lose patience. What's not so comical is that this kind of distressingly inappropriate expectation and the impatience, disapproval, and unhappiness that result are the chronic daily experience of the children.

Toddlers learn through all their senses. They cannot make sense of words alone; they need to touch and heft objects, move through space, put two things side by side. Without this opportunity, children become apathetic or uncontrollable—and sometimes both by turns.

When children under 3 are put into impoverished or chaotic environments with inexperienced, discouraged staff who expend most of their energy just trying to maintain order, the children suffer. Some of their pain is physical, because toddlers need to move around a lot. Some is mental, because of the continual frustration of basic developmental impulses. And some is emotional, because of the constant disapproval, which the child is powerless to correct.

Preschoolers ages 3 and up are the group that most day-care centers have been accustomed to serve. These kids are more amenable to groups, but without skilled staff they also suffer. To serve 3-year-olds well, teachers somehow have to make time to answer their questions even though they have 20 or more active little ones to organize, feed, nap, and otherwise get through the day.

Learning to pose questions and receive information that is satisfying is a key social as well as intellectual experience in a child's development. Children who don't have a successful experience at this stage, or whose experience is frustrated or perverted, stop participating in the learning process. They stop expressing their questions, and eventually may stop thinking them up.

If their world is structured so that formulating and getting answers to questions is difficult or impossible, the developmental process is seriously damaged. And this is the most consistent drawback of day-care centers where staff are overloaded and inexperienced. Staff resort to forcing children into the same boring activity all at the same time to maintain control. The kind of repressive control that keeps them sitting down to meaningless tasks day after day hurts their self-esteem and impairs their relationship with learning.

We have no idea how destructive a situation we have created. It is a social experiment on a grand scale with virtually no controls.

THE KIDS ARE ALL RIGHT

Susan Faludi

Faludi originally wrote this article for Mother Jones *magazine.*

What should be most curious to anyone reviewing the voluminous research literature on day care is the chasm between what the studies find and what people choose to believe. Despite a pervasive sense that day care is at best risky for children and at worst permanently damaging, much of the research indicates that

Utne Reader, May/June 1993, pp. 68–70.

if day care has any long-term effect on children at all, it has made them somewhat more social, experimental, self-assured, cooperative, creative. At the University of California at Irvine, Alison Clarke-Stewart, professor of social ecology, found that the social and intellectual development of children in day care was six to nine months ahead of that of children who stayed home.

The research on day care points to other bonuses, too. Day-care kids tend to have a more progressive view of sex roles. Canadian researchers Delores Gold and David Andres found that the girls they interviewed in day care believed that housework and child care should be evenly divided; the girls raised at home still believed these tasks are women's work. We are reminded constantly by the press that children in day care turn out to be too "aggressive." But researchers point out that what is being billed as aggression could as easily be labeled assertiveness, not at all a bad quality in a child.

As for the supposed and much-publicized daycare child abuse "epidemic," a three-year, $200,000 study by the University of New Hampshire's Family Research Laboratory found in 1988 that if there is an "epidemic" of child abuse, it's in the home—where children are almost twice as likely to be molested as in day care. And, ironically, the researchers found that children were *least* likely to be sexually abused in day-care centers located in high-crime, low-income neighborhoods (there tends to be more supervision in these centers). Despite frightening stories in the media, the researchers concluded that there is no indication of some special high risk to children in day care.

Although many of the celebrated tales of day-care workers molesting children have turned out to be tall tales, we continue to believe their message. "The consequences of all the negative play in the press about the McMartin case were really quite dramatic," says Abby Cohen, managing attorney of the Child Care Law Center, referring to the 1984 sex-abuse scandal at the McMartin Pre-School in Manhattan Beach, California. "Because, unfortunately, up until then there hadn't been very much play about child care, period. So it was terribly detrimental that the first real wide attention to it was in such a negative light."

For children of poverty, day care may be their ticket out of the ghetto. The studies find that the futures of low-income kids brighten immeasurably after a couple of years in day care. The Perry Pre-School Project of Ypsilanti, Michigan, followed 123 poor black children for 20 years. The children who spent one to two years in preschool day care, the researchers found, stayed in school longer, were not as prone to teenage pregnancy and crime, and improved their earning prospects significantly. A New York University study of 750 Harlem children came up with similar results: The children enrolled in preschool were far more likely to get jobs and pursue education beyond high school.

Presented with the evidence, some day-care critics will concede that preschool may have a negligible negative effect on toddlers, but then they move quickly to the matter of infants. So 3-year-olds may survive day care, they say, but newborns will suffer permanent damage. Their evidence comes from two sources. The first is a collection of studies conducted in the 1940s, '50s, and '60s in France, England, and West Germany. These studies concluded that infants who were taken from their mothers had tendencies later toward juvenile delinquency and mental illness. But there's a slight problem in relying on these findings: The studies were all looking at infants in orphanages and hospital institutions, not day-care centers.

The other source frequently quoted is the much-celebrated turnabout by Pennsylvania State University psychologist Jay Belsky, once a leading supporter of day care. In 1982 Belsky had reviewed the child-development literature and concluded that there were few if any significant differences between children raised at home and those in day care. Then in September 1986 he announced that he had changed his mind: Children whose mothers work more than 20 hours a week in their first year, he said, are at "risk" for developing an "insecure" attachment to their mothers. Belsky's pronouncement provided grist for the anti-day-care mill—and was widely reported. What did not receive as wide an airing, however, is the evidence Belsky cited to support his change of heart. Two of the studies he used flatly contradict each other: In one of them, the study's panel of judges found the infants in day care to be more insecure; in the other, the panel found just the opposite. The difference in results was traced to the judges' own bias against day care. In the study where the judges were not told ahead of time which babies were in day care and which were raised at home, the judges said the children's behavior was indistinguishable. In the study where they did know ahead of time which babies were in day care, they concluded that the day-care children were more insecure.

It is this bias that makes our day-care terrors so intractable. If the feeling comes from the gut, if it is an internalized, strictly personal belief, then its truth must be of a higher order, unassailable by any number of studies. But what many people fail to see is how our seemingly personal perceptions of day care are not so personal after all; how they have been shaped by forces that have little to do with gut instinct. Our opinions have been hammered by years of relentless anti-day-care and anti-working-mother rhetoric from the Reagan and Bush administrations and from the media, where bashing day care seems to be a sanctioned sport. (A few headlines from well-read magazines: "'Mommy, Don't Leave Me Here!': The Day Care Parents Don't See." "When Child Care Becomes Child Molesting: It Happens More Often Than Parents Like to Think." "Creeping Child Care…Creepy.")

Other cultural forces are at work here, too. We suffer a compulsion to replicate our childhoods, no matter how unpleasant those early years might have been. If our mothers stayed home, that must be the "healthy" way. What we forget is that it's only been since the 1940s that public opinion has so insistently endorsed the 24-hour-mom concept. The Victorians may have kept their women at home, but not for the sake of the children. "An educated woman," writer Emily Davies advised mothers in the 1870s, "blessed with good servants, as good mistresses generally are, finds an hour a day amply sufficient for her domestic duties." An early version of quality time.

The paranoia may ease once the younger generation reaches adulthood; they are not freighted with the same cultural assumptions about child care as those weaned in the 1950s. When I brought up the matter of child rearing to teenagers at Lowell High School in San Francisco, they all seemed to favor day care more than their parents do. How come? "Well," one 17-year-old girl reasoned, in what turned out to be a typical response, "I went to day care when I was little and I had a really good time."

2. Who Should Take Responsiblity for the Poor?

UNSUPPORTED SUPPORT

Datina M. Herd

Herd lives in Kentucky. She wrote this article for Newsweek *magazine.*

My heart pounded against my chest as my husband slowly walked into the bedroom. "How'd it go?" I asked, resisting the sudden urge to cross my fingers. Keeping his eyes downcast, he said, "They doubled it. They doubled my child support." Talk about exhaling; all of the air left my body. How could they double it? Didn't they take our four children and me into account when they made the decision? We already cannot pay all of our bills. How can they justify giving so much to one child when we have five to support?

I almost felt sorry for him, as he looked around as if wishing he could disappear. "They said that under the law, it is based on each parent's income. Since she is on welfare, I have to pay 70 percent and she pays 30, regardless of who else is affected. I told them that since the state is actually contributing her 30 percent through her welfare allotment, she is not paying anything, but they said that is how it works." He left to go to work and I sat there trying to swallow this new setback.

My husband and I have been together for almost 13 years. His oldest child was born after her mother ended their brief relationship. During those 13 years, I have always worked and his child's mother is dependent on welfare. She is my age—35—and has held certification as a nursing assistant since the '80s, when I first met her. She is not unskilled or unemployable. She completed her schooling and certification while I was still in college. She was on welfare then, too—there was already a child by another man. I worked full time to pay my way through college. This mother now has at least three children by three different fathers—that's the only reason I can figure she isn't required to work. She has never married.

Being on welfare means that there's always an agency working on her behalf to make sure my husband supports their child. Many of us working moms contribute fully to their kids' upkeep. Will there ever be a time when this person will be required to give monetary support to her child? Isn't welfare meant to be short term?

Newsweek, April 22, 1996, p.16.

The court even requested our past tax returns so that any income from me could be taken into account to reward a mother more child support while she stays home. At that time, the returns showed only my husband was working. I called my close girlfriends sobbing from the unfairness and helplessness I felt. We work and pay taxes, part of which support welfare. My husband pays child support, which goes to the welfare system. The system works backward. A woman being rewarded for being irresponsible, and I'm being punished for taking responsibility!

I can remember a comment made by an attorney during a TV show dealing with child support. The audience was told that welfare mothers can get child support by going to court and that money can be obtained from the new wife's income by attaching her tax refund. Why should welfare recipients profit from former partners wives' willingness to work and provide a certain standard of living for their families?

Don't get me wrong. I know my husband has to support his child. But the system is unfair. My husband has been laid off and unemployed several times. At times, the financial strain on us both has almost caused a divorce, but we have held on knowing it has to get better. No agency stepped in to make my husband support our children "by any means necessary" on my behalf. I've had to work to support my family. I started at minimum wage after college, worked two jobs (one part time and one full time) while nine months pregnant and reached the professional level as a federal employee. The stress has affected my health, and I was forced to resign from my job last summer. At home I had thought I might try writing articles for extra money. Family finances have slapped me back to reality and I realize that it's now necessary for me to return to work at once. I'd hoped it wouldn't be so soon. As the law seems to work against me, maybe I should have divorced my husband and applied for welfare.

Because of the additional child support, I have accepted a position for which I am overqualified. I hope once again to work my way up to a better job. After being laid off from a four-year temporary position as a mail carrier, my husband has become a fast-food restaurant manager. The job pays better than you might think, but it is a substantial reduction in income when compared to his previous job. He is also attending school, hoping to gain additional skills that will enable him to make better wages.

It is obvious that we are not wealthy. When only my husband worked because I'd become ill, I found out that we would qualify for food stamps. Unless we face going hungry, we don't want them, because we worry about the example it would set for our children since we're able to work. We live in a fixer-upper house and have one vehicle. Even when we both work, we just manage to keep our heads above water, make do with what we have and set goals to do better. More children are out of the question even if we wanted them. When I get back to work, there will be the additional costs of paying child care again. For the short time that I have been home, I have been able to attend school programs and PTA meetings and spend a lot more time with the children. The increased support to my husband's first child has left me no choice but to return to work immediately. We'll have even less time and money for the children we have together.

I have accepted that my husband's paychecks will be smaller after this new deduction. I'm resigned to the fact that I'll probably work until my children are adults. I had hoped that I would be a stay-at-home mom for a while, spending more time with my kids. My plan had been to return to work when my 4-year-old started school this fall. I don't begrudge children the support they are entitled to from an absent parent. What I refuse to accept is that it is my responsibility to be forced to leave my own children and go to work while someone else can stay at home and profit from it.

DOWN-SIZING AND WELFARE

Ann Landers

Ann Landers writes a daily nationally syndicated advice column.

Dear Ann Landers: The letter from "Oakland, Calif." about welfare recipients prompted me to write and confirm what she said. "Oakland" needed assistance because she was mentally ill and unable to work. I, too, needed welfare to make it. Never in my wildest dreams did I imagine I would be in such a spot.

As an executive in a major company, I was "sized down" when the company was swallowed by a bigger fish. Even though I was 55 at the time, I assumed that my education and professional background would make me attractive to other companies.

The weeks went by, then months and then a couple of years. Not only had I gone through all my financial resources, but I had to sell off antiques, oil paintings and my wife's jewelry—much of which she had inherited from her grandmother. When the sheriff delivered a foreclosure notice on our beautiful home, only then did I force myself to apply for public assistance—a euphemism I prefer to "welfare."

It was the most humiliating experience of my life, especially when a social worker came to check out our home and expressed amazement that we were asking for government help. Swallowing my pride made me gag, but I survived and finally got back on my feet, thanks to welfare. No, we are not all lazy freeloaders. Many of us are respectable people who were victims of the times. If it could happen to us, it could happen to anybody. We learn from life.

—**Washington, D.C.**

Dear D.C.: Thank you for a letter that will open some eyes and some hearts as well.

Fort Worth *Star-Telegram*, July 22, 1996, p. C4.

REPLACING THE WELFARE STATE WITH AN OPPORTUNITY SOCIETY

Newt Gringrich

Gingrich has served in the U.S. Congress since 1979. The following is excerpted from his book, To Renew America.

The greatest moral imperative we face is replacing the welfare state with an opportunity society. For every day that we allow the current conditions to continue, we are condemning the poor—and particularly poor children—to being deprived of their basic rights as Americans. The welfare state reduces the poor from citizens to clients. It breaks up families, minimizes work incentives, blocks people from saving and acquiring property, and overshadows dreams of a promised future with a present despair born of poverty, violence, and hopelessness.

When a welfare mother in Wisconsin can be punished for sewing her daughter's clothing and saving on food stamps so she can set aside three thousand dollars for her daughter's education, you know there is something wrong.

When a woman who sells candy out of her apartment in a public housing project cannot open a store because she would lose her subsidized rent and health care and end up paying in taxes and lost benefits all she earned in profit, you know there is something wrong.

Gary Franks, congressman from Connecticut, tells of going into grade schools and asking young children what they hope to be when they grow up. Basketball players, football players, and baseball players are the three answers, in that order. What if you can't be an athlete? he then asks. They have no answer. It is beyond the experience of these children to consider becoming a lawyer or an accountant or a businessman. The public housing children, no matter what their ethnic backgrounds, have simply no conception of the world of everyday work. Clearly something is wrong.

Charlie Rangel, the senior congressman from Harlem, asked me to imagine what it would be like to visit a first- or second-grade classroom and realize that every fourth boy would be dead or in jail before he was twenty-five years old. As I think of my three nephews, Charlie's comment drives home to me the despair and rage at the heart of any black leader as he looks at the lost future of a generation of poor children. Clearly something is wrong.

The defenders of the status quo should be ashamed of themselves. The current system has trapped and ruined a whole generation while claiming to be compassionate. The burden of proof is not on the people who want to change welfare. It is on those who would defend a system that has clearly failed at incalculable human cost.

Consider the facts. Welfare spending is now $305 billion a year. Since 1965 we have spent $5 trillion on welfare—more than the cost of winning World War II. Yet despite this massive effort, conditions in most poor communities have

---

From Newt Gingrich, *To Renew America* (Harper Collins Publishers, 1995), pp. 71–85.

grown measurably worse. Since 1970 the number of children living in poverty has increased by 40 percent. Since 1965 the juvenile arrest rate for violent crimes has tripled. Since 1960 the number of unmarried pregnant teenage girls has nearly doubled and teen suicide has more than tripled. As welfare spending increased since 1960, it has exactly paralleled the rise in births outside of marriage. On a graph, the two lines move together like a pair of railroad tracks. The more we spend to alleviate poverty, the more we assure that the next generation will almost certainly grow up in poverty. Clearly something is profoundly wrong.

We owe it to all young Americans in every neighborhood to save them from a system that is depriving them of their God-given rights to life, liberty, and the pursuit of happiness. There can't be true liberty while they are trapped in a welfare bureaucracy. There can't be any pursuit of happiness when they are not allowed to buy property or accumulate savings. And there can't be any reasonable right to a long life in an environment that is saturated with pimps, prostitutes, drug dealers, and violence.

Make no mistake: replacing the welfare state will not be an easy job. It will not work simply to replace one or two elements while leaving everything else intact. It will be necessary to think through the entire process before we begin.

Replacing the welfare state with an opportunity society will require eight major changes, which need to be undertaken simultaneously. Trying to change only one or two at a time will leave people trapped in the old order. We have an obligation to begin improving the lives of the poor from day one.

When people tell me I am intense on this issue, I ask them to imagine that their children were the ones dying on the evening news and then tell me how intense they would be to save their own children's lives. That is how intense we should all be.

One of the encouraging developments of the last few years has been that a lot of truly caring, intelligent people have spent a lot of time thinking about the tragedy of modern welfare systems. As a result, we now have a fairly good idea of what works and what doesn't. The eight steps we need for improving opportunities for the poor are:

1. Shifting from caretaking to caring
2. Volunteerism and spiritual renewal
3. Reasserting the values of American civilization
4. Emphasizing family and work
5. Creating tax incentives for work, investment, and entrepreneurship
6. Reestablishing savings and property ownership
7. Learning as the focus of education
8. Protection against violence and drugs

Let us consider each one of these in turn.

1. Shifting from Caretaking to Caring

In *Working Without a Net*, Morris Schechtman emphasizes the distinction between (1) caretaking—a more casual attitude, in which the important concern is to make the provider feel good, no matter what the outcome and (2) caring—a more selfless but positive approach, in which the outcome for the person being helped is the first concern. Caretaking has established the Supplemental Security Income (SSI) system, which has allowed, for example, forty disabled alcoholics to have their government checks registered directly at a Denver liquor store. Caring, on the other hand, would require any poor or disabled person to be partners in their own self-improvement.

The distinction between the deserving and the undeserving poor is at the heart of Marvin Olasky's great book, *The Tragedy of American Compassion*. Olasky emphasizes that indiscriminate aid actually destroys people. In addition, the sight of undeserving people getting resources while refusing to be responsible for themselves sends a devastating message to those working poor who are trying to make the effort to improve their lot. Besides undermining individual morality, indiscriminate aid undermines society as a whole.

From Colonial times until the 1960s, Olasky argues, American reformers made a clear distinction between poverty, a condition in which an individual or family did not have much money but their morality had not been undermined, and pauperism, a condition of passive dependency in which the work ethic has been completely lost. Social reformers emphasized that nothing could be more destructive than giving people help they didn't deserve. These experienced, traditional reformers saw as the most dangerous persons the wealthy caretaker who passed out money to make himself feel good even as it ruined people in the process.

Olasky's model for true caring requires a level of detailed knowledge that is not possible for government bureaucracies. Because of the very magnitude of the task they attempt to undertake, government caretakers can do nothing more than provide indiscriminate handouts for income maintenance.

2. *Volunteerism and Spiritual Renewal*

In the nineteenth century, Olasky notes, there was an average of one volunteer for every two poor people. Under these circumstances, volunteers could actually get to know individuals and their families and could trace whether they were making progress. It takes detailed knowledge to assess what people and their families need. The resulting system emphasized both volunteerism and spiritual salvation.

Olasky cites again and again the difference between trying to maintain people in poverty, alcoholism, and addiction and helping them rise above their circumstances. Maintenance programs will eventually attract more people into the kind of pauperism we are tying to avoid than it will help escape from poverty. This was the consistent concern of nineteenth-century reformers, and we now have more than enough evidence to prove they were right.

Olasky also cites the role of spiritual transformation in saving people from poverty. Unless people get some kind of religious bearings, it is unlikely they will make the effort needed to change their circumstances. It is no accident that Alcoholics Anonymous gives God a central place in any effort to recover from addiction. For two generations we have tried to replace spiritual transformation with secular counseling. The experiment has failed miserably. Since no secular bureaucracy can (or should) engage in spiritual renewal, it is clear this effort must be undertaken by churches, synagogues, mosques, or other charitable and nonprofit institutions.

Congressmen Jim Kolbe and Joe Knollenberg have come up with a stunning suggestion for transforming welfare. Instead of the government taking billions of dollars from reluctant taxpayers and scattering it among the poor, individual tax-payers would be allowed to check off contributions of up to one hundred dollars for donation to their favorite charity—just as you are now allowed to check off three dollars for the Presidential Election Campaign Fund. This would shift $9 billion a year into private organizations offering spiritual help. It would also give taxpayers some control over how their money is being spent. Taxpayers would be able to vote with their checkbooks if a charitable effort were having counter-productive results.

I am proud to work with Habitat for Humanity, which helps poor people build their own homes. Millard and Linda Fuller founded Habitat after becoming convinced that a spiritually based approach was necessary to help the poor. Habitat screens families to find people who they believe deserve help (something the government cannot do). Those who are chosen are required to take a twenty-four-hour course on how to be a homeowner (something that HUD's lawyers say cannot be required). Habitat first asks the family to invest one hundred hours of sweat equity in helping build someone else's house and then three hundred hours in building their own home. Finally, Habitat sells them a $70,000 house for $36,000 with the understanding that if they try to sell it before the mortgage is paid off, they will have to pay off a second mortgage that covers the whole price of the home.

Volunteers like myself also come on Saturdays to work on the projects. It is a rewarding experience to see the future homeowning family there alongside public-spirited citizens. Habitat for Humanity is a program that combines prayer with practical help, a model for volunteerism and spiritual renewal of the kind Olasky writes about. That is why I wear a Habitat pin on my lapel.

3. Reasserting the Values of American Civilization

Every day on television and radio poor people see and hear things that reinforce the message that income transfer is what matters and spiritual transformation is unimportant. In her great book *The Demoralization of Society*, Gertrude Himmel-farb argues that the values and attitudes people have about themselves depend on the messages the culture sends them. She also notes that these attitudes can change in a very short period of time.

I believe we are at the end of the era of tolerating alcoholism, addiction, spouse and child abuse, parental indifference, and adult irresponsibility. We have all seen society change for the better in recent years in its views on smoking, drunk driving, and racism. There is no reason that views on acceptable standards of behavior for the poor cannot change as well.

When I spoke in March 1995 to the National League of Cities, I cited Him-melfarb's book and asserted that the time had come to reestablish shame as a means of enforcing proper behavior. It is shameful, I said, to be a public drunk at three in the afternoon and we ought to say so. People began applauding. It is shameful, I said, for males to have children they refuse to support and we ought to say so. The applause grew louder. And on it went.

It is shameful for radio stations to play songs that advocate mutilating and raping women. Government can't and shouldn't censor it, but decent advertisers could announce they will boycott any radio station that plays that kind of music. Within weeks these brutal, barbaric songs would be off the air.

Cultural signals are a powerful and legitimate means of enforcing proper behavior. One of the responsibilities of public leaders is to encourage the kind of public environment we want. Our culture should be sending over and over the message that young people should abstain from sexual intercourse until marriage, that work is a part of life, and that any male who does not take care of his children is a bum and deserves no respect. If you want a sense of the personal values we should be communicating to children, get the Boy Scout or Girl Scout handbook. Or go and look at *Reader's Digest* and *The Saturday Evening Post* from around 1955. Healthy societies send healthy signals to their children and to those who have become temporarily confused at any age. Look at the sick signals we are now sending through the entertainment industry and popular culture. Is it any wonder that society is so confused if not downright degenerate?

4. Emphasizing Family and Work

Charles Murray's *Losing Ground* was one of the first books to point out that the current welfare state is actually discouraging family formation, breaking up intact families, and trapping people in poverty for generations. Leon Dash's *When Children Want Children* then built a devastating case that the culture of poverty and violence was actually offering positive incentives for teenage girls to have children outside of marriage. Dash noted that over half the boys offered to marry the girl and were turned down. The tragedy is that the welfare state now offers young girls an alternative to marriage.

Yet while being pregnant outside of marriage may be appealing at first sight, it turns out to be a terrible trap. Three-fourths of all unmarried teen mothers end up on welfare within five years. More than 40 percent remain on the rolls for more than ten years. The daughters of teenage mothers are two and a half times more likely to become teen mothers themselves, and when they do, they are three times as likely to live in poverty.

Murray argues that the tax code, the welfare laws, and the rules of the bureaucracy all add up to a system that is antiwork, antifamily, and antiopportunity. We have to rewrite these laws so they do not punish people for taking responsibility. If a couple with children earns $11,000 apiece, they will pay $2,700 less in taxes if they remain unmarried. That's a 12 percent marriage tax. Then we wonder why births outside marriage have skyrocketed.

We have to reemphasize identifying the father and requiring the father to accept at least financial responsibility for the child (ideally he should also accept psychological and emotional responsibility, but let's start with the sense that if you have a child you have an obligation to help pay for that child's upbringing).

We need to revise welfare so that going to work never lowers your standard of living. When you add up housing, health care, food stamps, aid to family and dependent children, and other programs, there is actually a substantial disadvantage in joining the labor force. We need to redesign the system so people have a sense of reward at each step up the ladder of opportunity.

5. Tax Incentives for Work, Investment, and Entrepreneurship

People can work only when jobs are available; job creation requires investment. Today America's poorest neighborhoods offer such poor returns on investment that people simply won't go there to create jobs. The result is that few jobs are likely to be available, even if welfare rules are changed to encourage work. In addition, big cities often have the most red tape, the highest local taxes, and the most difficult bureaucracies. As a result, the poor are cheated out of jobs.

Hernando De Soto, a Peruvian economist, has written a brilliant book entitled *The Other Path*, in which he describes how lawyer-dominated big-city bureaucracies kill jobs in Latin America. Although he uses Lima, Peru, as his main example, every lesson applies to the United States.

In a brief introduction, Mario Vargas Llosa, a Peruvian novelist, describes the illegal activities of entrepreneurial Peruvians who refuse to let their government stop them from earning a living. At the time the book was written, 93 percent of the buses in Lima were illegal. The entire city had learned to operate outside the city's regulated transportation system.

Almost every public housing project in the United States has the same underground economy of people working for cash or barter without securing government licenses or paying taxes. Jack Kemp has been the leading advocate of "enterprise zones" that would encourage job creation within the legal system. Kemp has long proposed massive tax and regulatory breaks for anyone who would invest in poor neighborhoods. Since these neighborhoods pay almost no taxes anyway and since they drain the public treasury through welfare payments, the cost of giving them tax breaks would be relatively small. If new investment helped poor people make the long-term transition from welfare to productive work, these enterprise zones would more than pay for themselves. With Kemp's leadership, we are now working to apply this model in Washington, D.C. We hope to have a full-blown experiment by 1996.

People can create jobs as well as find jobs. Amway, Mary Kay, BeautiControl, Tupperware, and a host of other companies are examples of job creation. Anyone with a little money, some free time, and a willingness to learn marketing can make money. It is just as important to convince the poor that they can create their own jobs as it is to help them find jobs. We want to arouse an entrepreneurial spirit. A generation of small-business creation among African and Hispanic Americans would transform everything. If there were five Steve Jobses or one Bill Gates in Harlem, the entire nature of the community would change.

If city governments truly want to help the poor, they will make life dramatically easier for small businesses. What most poor neighborhoods need more than anything is a small-business renaissance. Cities should be cutting taxes and eliminating regulations to make it easy for poor people to start their own enterprises.

Bill Marriott, founder of the famous hotel chain, started with a single pushcart. Today license regulations would probably make that pushcart illegal, and fees and taxes would make it unprofitable.

6. Reestablishing Savings and Property Ownership

If you are going to go to work or start your own small business, you have to believe you are going to keep the fruits of your labor. The history of immigrants in America has been a history of people working two and three jobs and scrimping and saving to put their children through school or open a first business. Immigrants dreamed of a better future and then worked to make those dreams come true. The greatest human damage done by the welfare state has been to kill people's dreams and destroy their ability to imagine themselves improving their lot.

The first step toward financial independence is to accumulate savings and acquire a little property. The current welfare system prohibits both. We want to ensure that, from day one, people who work hard can see their work pay off.

Part of this process involves giving people control over their own housing. Poor people ought to be given a chance to buy the property they live in. Public housing run as a cooperative or as a condominium would be vastly different from public housing run by middle-class bureaucrats who see the poor as clients rather than customers.

Jack Kemp has encouraged an experiment in the Kennilworth Apartments in Washington, D.C., in which residents took control of their own housing project. The first change they made was to require that maintenance people live in the project. Overnight the quality of maintenance improved. Custodians did a better job since, if they didn't, residents showed up at their door and complained. Trying to minimize their own work, maintenance workers quickly discovered who was breaking windows and engaging in vandalism. The guilty children were taken to their parents. The entire project began to look nicer within two months. When people are consumers instead of clients, their habits change drastically.

7. Learning as the Focus of Education

The greatest single misallocation of taxpayers' money has been the unionized monopolies of inner-city education. It is astonishing how much is spent per child on these cumbersome, red-tape-ridden bureaucracies—and how little ever gets to the individual child.

I was radicalized on this subject by former governor Tom Kean of New Jersey. He showed me a thousand-page study of the Jersey City schools, which were spending over $7,000 per child and hardly educating anyone. Governor Kean's study group discovered the schools had been looted by the local political machine for patronage purposes. There was a $54,000-a-year fire extinguisher inspector who failed to show up for three years. Not only was he freeloading, but the schools were left with faulty fire extinguishers. A fire would have been a disaster. The study led to a state takeover of the city school system.

My radicalization was completed by a *Chicago Tribune* series on one particularly bad school in the Windy City. After spending a year in the schools, a team of reporters wrote a devastating series of articles. The most telling was an interview with a teacher who was so destructive that every principal she had ever worked for had tried to fire her. The tenure system always saved her. She still had eleven years of teaching time left. When asked her professional goal, she said she wanted to retire with a full pension. This teacher regularly failed to educate thirty students a year, yet the system was designed to protect her incompetence. Remember, when young people fail to get educated in the Information Age, they lose all sense of purpose and dignity. When we tolerate a school that is failing to educate children, we put not just their education but their lives at risk.

The first breath of hope for me came in Milwaukee, where Polly Williams, a former welfare mother, has led a remarkable effort to reform the system. A Wisconsin state legislator and former state co-chair for Jesse Jackson's presidential campaign, Williams eventually concluded that inner-city children were being cheated by the education monopoly. She persuaded the legislature to adopt a voucher system that allows inner-city children to attend private schools at state expense. The Wisconsin teachers' union and the traditional liberals fought her bitterly, but Governor Tommy Thompson and the Republicans gave her the backing she needed. Even though the Republicans now control the state legislature, they have installed Williams as chair of the Inner City Education Reform Committee. She leads a broad bipartisan coalition that seeks to break the public-school monopoly and find new ways to educate poor children.

From home schooling to vouchers, from a drastic overhaul of the present system to allowing private companies to take over whole school districts—we simply have to take whatever steps are necessary to ensure that poor children can participate in the Information Age. There is no other strategy that will give them a full opportunity to pursue happiness.

8. Protection Against Violence and Drugs

Safety is simply the most fundamental concern of government. After all, none of our God-given rights matter much if we can be raped, mugged, robbed, or killed. And the poorest neighborhood is as entitled to be safe as the richest. No economic incentives a government can devise will entice businesses to open factories in a neighborhood where employees are likely to be in constant physical danger. Nor will any amount of education make up for your child being preyed upon by drug dealers and pimps. Addiction and prostitution will quickly wipe out the fruits of any educational reform.

In Part Four, I will outline proposals for ending the drug trade and saving children from violent crime. Here I will simply say that both measures are essential and should be applied first to the poorest neighborhoods. The United States Constitution was written to protect us from enemies both foreign and domestic. We are doing a good job on foreign enemies, but a pathetic job of protecting ourselves and our children from those who behave like domestic enemies.

Everything else will fail if we cannot suppress drugs and violent crime. Establishing safety is the first foundation of creating opportunity for the poor.

SUMMARY

If we are truly serious about helping the poor, we must undertake all eight reforms simultaneously. The poor today are trapped both in a bureaucratic maze and in a culture of poverty and violence. No simple steps will suffice. It will take an immense effort and a lot of volunteers to replace the current welfare state with an opportunity society.

Imagine a poor child who is failing to learn in a public monopoly, whose life is at risk when she walks to the store, who knows no one who goes to work regularly, and who is likely to be pregnant at age twelve or thirteen. Now imagine that this child is your daughter. How hard would you work to save her life? How much effort would you put into forcing change? How intensely would you work to eliminate the bureaucracies that are exploiting her instead of serving her?

All I ask is that you look at your fellow Americans and decide that they deserve the same passion, the same commitment, the same courage you would show for your children. Together we can replace the culture of poverty and violence. Together we can replace the welfare bureaucracy. Together we can create a generation of hope and opportunity for all Americans.

3. Who Should Be Responsible for the Life and Death Decisions That Affect the Terminally Ill?

TERMINAL CARE: TOO PAINFUL, TOO PROLONGED

Geoffrey Cowley and Mary Hager

Cowley and Hager wrote this article for Newsweek *magazine.*

Hazel Welch was 92, severely disabled and living in a Connecticut nursing home when a perforated stomach ulcer landed her in the emergency room at Yale-New Haven Hospital. The physician on call, Dr. Sherwin Nuland, proposed emergency surgery to repair her exploded digestive tract. To his surprise, she refused, explaining that she had already outlived her friends and relatives, and that 92 years on this planet was quite long enough anyway. Her odds of surviving the operation were just one in three, but as Nuland recounts in his 1993 book, "How We Die," the need to intervene seemed obvious. So he pressured her, she gave in and he operated. She survived for a few pain-filled weeks, then died of a massive stroke. "Although my intentions were only to serve … her welfare, I was guilty of the worst sort of paternalism," Nuland reflects. "I had won out over [the ulcer] but lost the greater battle of humane care."

Newsweek, December 4, 1995, pp. 74–75.

Hazel Welch died in 1978, but as a disturbing new study makes clear, American medicine has yet to grasp the meaning of her story. Under a $28 million grant from the Robert Wood Johnson Foundation, researchers recently monitored the care given some 9,000 critically ill patients at five major medical centers. Their findings, published in last week's Journal of the American Medical Association, suggest that despite two decades of right-to-die activism, vast numbers of Americans continue to die in intensive-care units, alone and in pain, after days or weeks of futile treatment—even if they have living wills. Moreover, the researchers discovered that a huge, well-organized effort to prevent needless care made no difference. "We thought we knew how to solve the problem," says Dr. William Knaus of the University of Virginia Health Sciences Center, who headed the study, "but the system doesn't know when to stop."

Needless pain: The study, known as SUPPORT, was carried out in two phases. In the first, chronicling the care given 4,300 critically ill patients, the researchers found a dearth of doctor-patient communication, an excess of aggressive treatment and a lot of needlessly prolonged pain. Only 49 percent of the patients who requested do-not-resuscitate orders actually got them, and 70 percent were never asked their preferences. Nearly 40 percent of the patients who died spent at least 10 days in an intensive-care unit, kept alive by machines. And half of those who were conscious spent at least half of their final hospital stay in pain.

For the second phase, Knaus and his colleagues assembled 4,800 critically ill patients and placed half in a program to foster more humane end-of-life care. Specially trained nurses were assigned to help patients and families translate their preferences into advance directives. The hospital doctors got daily reports detailing patients' wishes and assessing their chances for recovery. Yet, to the researchers' dismay, patients from the two groups were equally likely to have their advance directives ignored, to spend their last days in intensive care and to die in pain.

Why did such an ambitious experiment fail so miserably? For one thing, SUPPORT assumed that patients know in advance what they want, and that anyone given good information will make rational choices about dying. But a crisis can change everything. "When I discuss [intensive care] with patients in advance," says Dr. Russell Phillips of Boston's Beth Israel Hospital, "they say they don't want it if the quality of life is bad. But what we think of as poor quality of life doesn't seem so bad if that's all you have left."

Sometimes patients don't change their minds, but the press of circumstance leads to advance directives being ignored. When someone stops breathing, for example, there isn't always time for consultation between specialist and primary-care physician. Even when there's time for contemplation, doctors can disagree. Jane Becker of Arlington, Mass., recalls dealing with a small army of surgeons and residents, an internist and an intensive-care physician when trying to decide whether to withdraw her dying mother's life support. "I wanted everyone in the same room, having one conversation," she says. Instead she got specialists pulling her aside to offer their own views. "I had an overwhelming sense of trying to get around a big machine," she says. "There was no place to jump in and say, 'Wait, I don't want that.'."

The larger problem, most analysts agree, is that American medicine lacks any conception of death as a part of life. Insurance policies rarely cover hospice or home care, so dying patients end up in hospitals, surrounded by nurses who talk of miracles and doctors who are hellbent on performing them. In his reflection on Hazel Welch, Nuland notes that even if he'd been wise enough to honor her death wish, peer pressure would have forced him to intervene. "I would have had to defend the result at the weekly surgical conference (where it would certainly be seen as *my* decision, not hers)."

To help wean physicians from their warrior mentality, the American Medical Association has established a Task Force on Quality Care at the End of Life. Somehow, says Dr. Thomas Reardon, who chairs the AMA task force, doctors must learn to "sit down and say, 'There's nothing more I can do, but I'll be here to see you through'." But Knaus, the study director, doubts that's enough. Patients' preferences should be recorded as routinely as their blood types, he says—and checked just as carefully by anyone contemplating a heroic procedure. "Blood matching isn't voluntary," he says. "This shouldn't be either." That may sound blunt, but as the new findings make clear, every one of us is currently at risk of dying on someone else's terms.

DEATH AND THE MAIDEN

Stephanie Gutmann

Gutmann is a writer living in New York. She wrote this piece for The New Republic.

Who would use the services of the right-to-die movement's death assisters? If suicide were "medicalized," if there were a death dispenser in every neighborhood staffed with a knowledgeable, certified facilitator, what kind of person would partake? What, in psychologists' jargon, would be his "presenting problem?" And just what kind of assistance would the physician in the physician-assisted suicide really supply?

For a preview of that brave new landscape, there is no better place to look than at the record being so industriously compiled by Dr. Jack Kevorkian, Royal Oak, Michigan's notorious "Dr. Death." The enterprising pathologist has been at it for six years and has, at this writing, assisted twenty-eight suicides—though only his ever-present lawyer knows when and where he will surface next, schlepping the bottles and tubes of the Rube Goldbergian death equipment he calls the "Thanatron" or, more recently, the "Mercitron."

The New Republic, June 24, 1996, pp. 20–21, 24, 28.

In the absence of competitors, Kevorkian has attracted a broad spectrum of people seeking a physician-assisted way out. They have come from the proverbial all walks of life, from the trailer park and the manicured suburb. In many respects, the doctor's clients represent a pretty good sample of the general population. Except for the fact that most of them are women.

Like the men, they are younger than you might expect—ranging from age 40 to early 80s—with a surprising number (or perhaps not so surprising, given mid-life crises, menopause, empty nests) in their 50s. The most striking fact about the field, though, is how much what one might call the "objective despair index" differs by sex. Most of Kevorkian's men were declared terminally ill by their own doctors; they were in constant, severe pain from medically diagnosed causes and were often physically incapacitated. Whatever you think about suicide or physician-assisted suicide, these were easier calls.

Many of the women, on the other hand, had more ambiguous complaints: in a chart like the one compiled by Kalman Kaplan, director of the Suicide Research Center at Columbia-Michael Reese Hospital in Chicago, we see that most of the Kevorkian women were not diagnosed terminal and had not been complaining of severe or constant pain. We see conditions like breast cancer (for which there is now great hope), emphysema, rheumatoid arthritis and Alzheimer's (a condition that usually burdens relatives more than the people who have it). Reading the case histories it is clear that many of these women's lives were messy and unattractive. But in all-too-typical female fashion, the patient often seems to have been most worried about the disease's impact on others. Is it possible that a certain type of woman—depressive, self-effacing, near the end of a life largely spent serving others—is particularly vulnerable to the "rational," "heroic" solution so forcefully proposed by Dr. Death?

Kevorkian is far too media-savvy to have been sanguine for long about his disproportionate number of female patients. As the deaths of his first eight women clients were registered and charges of misogyny started ringing from the editorial pages, he began, in his fashion, to make his oeuvre look more like America. The number of men grew as the work progressed, finally bringing the total to eleven. But even with the added effort to diversify, one problem remains: Kevorkian seems to like to feint and bobble, to flirt and play coy with his clients. Some of this tendency stems from his problems finding appropriate venues for medicides and from his responsible attempts to make sure patients have explored the range of treatments. But much of it seems to have come out of Dr. K's pleasure in the process, in playing God.

The upshot is that many of Kevorkian's male prospective clients had already killed themselves by the time Kevorkian got around to "setting the date."

Kevorkian's experience with men is mirrored in suicide records from the National Center for Health Statistics. Women attempt suicide three times more often than men, according to the center. The reason we end up with far more completed male suicides—24,000 men to 6,000 women in 1992—is that men generally seem determined to succeed. They blow their heads off and throw themselves off buildings. Women tend to take overdoses of pills. Sexist as it may sound, women's suicide attempts are more like the classic "cry for help"—a perverse way of reaching out, of bringing people to the bedside and hands to the body.

Some social scientists have even noticed an erotic component to aging women's fantasies and unconscious feelings about death. Administering TAT (Thematic Apperception Test) card tests to terminally ill women in their 60s, Harvard University's David McClelland found a recurring figure in the stories the women told to explain the ambiguous situations pictured in the cards. McClelland called this figure "the harlequin"—enigmatic, seductive but dangerous—and he concluded from other contextual comments that the harlequin represented death. In men's imagery, death is more often represented by big, all-encompassing things like the ocean. What this suggests is that for women death is a more social affair; if it is given a human face by a soothing physician/assister there is all the more reason why the super-altruistic woman with a life spent serving others would want to put down her burdens, and succumb.

Hence the basis of the Kevorkian charm. Affable, worldly, Dr. Jack made death into a prize—frequently he toyed with his clients, telling them they "were not ready," then finally relented, all the while lacing the interaction with rousing messianic language. (Why did he assist his first client in a rusty van in a parking lot? asked prosecutors. "One reason for that," snarled Dr. K. "No Room At The Inn." So what if the van he used was dilapidated, Kevorkian would say, "The savior of a major fraction of mankind was born in the most abject conditions possible. . . . It's all I could do. I'm alone . . . a formidable mind in the Dark Ages.")

Janet Adkins, Kevorkian's first client, certainly got many such pep talks from Dr. K, and the ringing language, the formality, the jargon, the bureaucracy (even the concept of death-by-machine), must have been very attractive to a woman who seems to have spent her life attempting to be perfect. Adkins—who lived with her stockbroker husband in an affluent Oregon suburb—is one of Kevorkian's most curious and disturbing cases, a key example of the ambiguous female case. (Initially Kevorkian was charged with Adkin's murder, but the prosecution ran out of steam, in part, I am convinced, because of quasi-feminist arguments that it was patronizing to question whether Adkins "knew her own mind.")

Adkins—whose case is well documented in *Appointment With Dr. Death*, a fascinating book by former Detroit *Free Press* reporter Michael Betzold—certainly looked the part of a strong, willful woman. Though she didn't have a full-time career, she raised three successful sons, climbed Mount Hood, went hang gliding and generally behaved like a cyclone of energy, according to neighbors. At 54 she found herself forgetting things. Her husband complained to Dr. K that he had to remind her of the times of her tennis lessons and that she "kept leaving her purse in the house."

"These are things that keep slipping away," said Ron Adkins, who made the first contact with Kevorkian after reading about him in *Newsweek,* who then played liaison throughout the logistical discussions, and who appears to have answered for Janet throughout the pre-death conference with Kevorkian. Doctors at a Portland hospital told her that eventually—Alzheimer's can take around fifteen years to fully develop—she would be dependent on her husband for feeding and bathing. Setting the date for November 30, 1989—so she "wouldn't spoil Christmas for the kids"—she made plans to go. Though she was still able to carry on clear conversations and demolish her son at tennis, her husband explained that "if she was going to err she'd rather err on the side of going too soon rather than too late."

The week before she died (with the date now pushed forward to June), "Janet selected the music and the readings for the memorial service," writes Betzold. She "arranged for a therapist to mediate final 'closure' sessions with her family." The night before her death she stayed up past midnight in a restaurant with friends, and rhapsodized about Bach with Dr. K.

So many things are worrisome about Adkins's death: Alzheimer's is notoriously hard to diagnose, for one. Only an autopsy finally confirms it, and its early symptoms—confusion, clumsiness, memory problems—are identical to those of moderate to severe depression. It's chilling to think that perhaps Dr. Kevorkian merely colluded with a suburban Super Mom's Stepfordism. Most chilling of all, though, is the barrenness, the loneliness of the whole affair. One ponders if, in the midst of the meticulous death planning—while she was listening to her husband's oh-so-rational, oh-so progressive, oh-so-unpatronizing wish that she just "do what's right for her"—Janet Adkins might have longed for someone to show a tiny wisp of passion about whether or not she stuck around.

If we can trust Dr. K's perceptions, there was a tiny wisp of passion, a calling card from the harlequin, while Janet Adkins lay, hooked to the Thanatron, on a cot in the back of Kevorkian's VW van. As the EKG flattened: "Her eyelids flickered a little," Kevorkian told Ron Rosenbaum, who covered the story for *Vanity Fair*, "and she looked like she was rising up to almost kiss me. I leaned over and the first thing that came to mind is to say, 'Have a nice trip.' That's all. 'Have a nice trip.' Those were the last words said."

For his next medicide Kevorkian promised Sherry Miller and Marjorie Wantz "a beautiful setting on a little lake in a little woods." When the group—Kevorkian's entourage, Wantz's husband, Miller's best friend—convened at a state park near Detroit, they found production values worthy of a Hemlock Society self-deliverance brochure. The only false note in the bucolic scene (complete with rustic cabin, candles and last-minute exchanges of endearments) are the confused motives of the two middle-aged women involved. Both cases are as troubling in their own way as Adkins's: one woman seems to have been suffering from depression rather than organic disease, and the other from a particularly self-abnegating sense of the trouble her disease caused others.

Wantz, 58, had suffered from pelvic pain ever since a 1988 operation to remove non-cancerous growths from inside her vagina. Though she had many vivid explanations for her torments—third-degree burns, a needle left behind after the surgery—doctor after doctor could find no organic cause for them. At various times, she was diagnosed with "major depression" and "somatization syndrome," for which doctors prescribed anti-depressants and even psychiatric hospitalization. Wantz turned these down, requesting a spinal cord severment (to end the pain), and, failing that, medicide with Dr. K, followed by an "extremely, extremely thorough autopsy" in which, she stipulated, she would have to "be cut, like, ten ways." An autopsy cited by the Oakland County prosecutor's office found nothing wrong.

Sherry Miller, who died the same day on the cot next to Wantz, was also roiled by powerful emotions—above all, one would assume, rage at the husband who had divorced her and taken her children just as her multiple sclerosis had worsened. But at 43, confined to a wheelchair and living with her elderly parents, Miller hardly discussed the recent divorce, Betzold writes, and "never spoke a word of blame." Instead she focused her formidable energies on persuading Dr. Kevorkian to help her die.

At one of Kevorkian's trials, in a cross-examination conducted by assistant prosecutor Michael Modelski, Miller said she was worried about her elderly parents and beginning to realize she would have to move to Texas to be cared for by relatives there. "In that context I asked her if it wasn't that she thought she was going to be a burden on others whether she would want to die. There was a long pause," Modelski recalls, "and she said, 'Well, I can't really deal with ifs.'"

"Not being a bother" seemed to preoccupy Miller: During the detailed, pre-death conferences with Kevorkian, she became "very quiet," Betzold wrote. Her best friend "knelt down by her and said: 'It will be OK.' [Miller] started crying. 'I just don't want all this fuss,' she said."

RUSH TO A LETHAL JUDGMENT

Stephen L. Carter

Carter is the William Nelson Cromwell Professor of Law at Yale University. He wrote the following for the New York Times.

Many years ago, a psychiatrist who was treating someone I loved asked me to remember that she had the right to kill herself if she wanted to. Sometimes, he said softly, the decision to commit suicide is the decision of a rational mind, a reasonable if tragic answer to the question of whether life is worth continuing.

When he said "right," he did not, of course, mean constitutional right; he meant moral right, a part of human dignity. As long as her mind was sound, she had the right as an autonomous individual to decide whether to continue living.

New York Times Magazine, July 21, 1996, pp. 28–29.

Her responsibilities to her loved ones and her community might have carried weight in the moral calculus, but the final decision had to be hers alone.

Although I saw the logic of his position then and see it now, the law has traditionally offered a rather different understanding. Suicide was a felony under England's common-law regime, and was illegal everywhere in the United States into this century. Some cynics have identified the age-old prohibition on suicide as a matter of royal selfishness—at common law, if you committed a felony, your worldly goods went to the crown—but the better answer is that the laws reflected a strong belief that the lives of individuals belonged not to themselves alone but to the communities in which they lived and to the God who gave them breath.

Nowadays, we have a broader notion of individual autonomy. Our laws increasingly reflect the belief that our lives do belong to us alone. Some anti-suicide statutes are still on the books, but today the societal distaste for suicide is registered through the civil, not the criminal, law: people who try suicide but do not succeed may be involuntarily hospitalized to determine whether they are continuing threats to themselves. So although we certainly try to prevent suicide, we no longer punish it.

There is one exception: most jurisdictions continue to treat the person who directly assists someone else's suicide as a felon. That is the basis, for example, of Michigan's prosecutions of the notorious "suicide doctor," Jack Kevorkian, who, as of this writing, has been involved in more than 30 suicides. Many a family harbors its secret story of indirect assistance—leaving the bottle of sleeping pills within reach of the dying relative, for example—but the reason for the secrecy in part has been the traditional view that assistance of any kind is at least immoral and often illegal.

In recent months, however, two Federal appellate courts have held that terminally ill patients have a constitutional right to seek the assistance of physicians in ending their lives. With the entire dispute plainly on its way to the Supreme Court anyway, opponents and supporters of what has come to be called the "right to die" are even now battling their way through the implications. The moral questions raised by assisted suicide are weighty, but our ability as a society to deal with them has been seriously weakened by the judicial rush to enshrine one side's moral answer in the framework of constitutional rights.

The two cases presented the same basic question, but the courts dealt with it in very different ways. In March, the Court of Appeals for the Ninth Circuit, based in San Francisco, decided the case of Compassion in Dying v. State of Washington, resting the right to assisted suicide for the terminally ill on the due process clause of the 14th Amendment, the same provision in which the courts have located the abortion right. The right to choose how to end one's own life, the court explained, was a direct descendant of the right to choose whether to bear a child, and, as with abortion, the state must have a very strong reason before it may interfere.

Then, less than a month later, the Second Circuit struck down New York's assisted-suicide ban in the case of Quill v. Vacco. The Second Circuit rejected the due process argument, pointing out that the United States Supreme Court has limited that approach to cases in which the state is interfering with a fundamental liberty "deeply rooted in this Nation's history and tradition," like the freedom to marry or procreate. The right to obtain assistance in suicide, the court sensibly concluded, does not fit this definition. But the Quill court found a rationale of its own: the right to assisted suicide is supported, said the judges, by another part of the 14th Amendment—the equal protection clause. Why? Because New York allows mentally competent terminally ill patients on life support to direct the removal of the supporting apparatus, even when the removal will hasten or directly cause their deaths, but prohibits those who do not need life support from obtaining drugs to hasten or directly cause their deaths. So the state is discriminating, in the court's terms, by allowing some of the terminally ill, but not others, to die quickly.

The logic of Quill, although more attractive than that of Compassion in Dying, seems terribly forced, not least because the state allows many other distinctions among the terminally ill—for example, wealthier patients often have access to experimental drugs and therapies that others do not. These distinctions may not always seem sensible or fair but they hardly rise to the level of constitutional concern.

And there is a larger analytical problem with both decisions. If the right to choose suicide with the help of a physician is of constitutional dimension, it is difficult to discern how it can be limited to those who are terminally ill. Terminal illness is not a legal category—it is a medical category, and one that even doctors sometimes have trouble defining. Some of us who teach constitutional law—the old-fashioned types, I suppose—still tell our students that constitutional rights arise by virtue of citizenship, not circumstance. This implies that each of us (each who is a competent adult, at least) possesses an identical set of rights. So if there is indeed a constitutional right to suicide, assisted or not, it must attach to all citizens.

If the right to pursue assistance in suicide attaches to all citizens, then the Constitution is at present being violated by all the state laws permitting the involuntary hospitalization of individuals who try suicide. Instead of locking them up, we should be asking them if they would like assistance in their task. In fact, the Second Circuit has matters precisely backward: if everybody except the terminally ill were allowed to seek the assistance of physicians in suicide, the equal protection claim might have merit. If, on the other hand, the terminally ill are allowed to seek suicide, the court's concern for equality might suggest that everybody should be allowed to do it, lest the state discriminate between two groups who want do die, those who desire to commit suicide because they are terminally ill and those who desire to commit suicide because they are dreadfully unhappy.

Except in emergencies, a court decision is the worst way to resolve a moral dilemma. Constitutional rights, as they mature, have a nagging habit of bursting from the analytical confinements in which they are spawned. When the Supreme Court struck down organized classroom prayer in 1962, nobody other than a few opponents of the rulings, dismissed as cranks, envisioned a future in which courts would order traditional religious language and symbols stripped from official buildings and state seals. And did the justices who voted to legalize abortion in 1973 really imagine that two decades later, the United States would be home to 1.5 million abortions a year?

In the case of the right to assisted suicide, the risks are many. For example, it is far from obvious that the right can be limited to adults. The abortion right isn't. The Supreme Court has ruled that pregnant minors must be allowed to demonstrate to a judge that they are mature enough to make up their own minds about abortion. It does not take much of a stretch to imagine a judge concluding that a young person mature enough to decide that a child should not come into the world is also mature enough to decide that her (or his) own life is not worth living.

And there are other, more ominous difficulties. Some worried medical ethicists have predicted that a right to assisted suicide might lead exhausted families to encourage terminally ill relatives to kill themselves. Moreover, women are more likely than men to try suicide, but men succeed much more often than women. With the help of health care workers, women, too, might begin to succeed at a high rate. Is this form of gender equality what we are looking for?

But the biggest problem with the idea of a constitutional right to assisted suicide is that the courts (if the decisions stand) are preempting a moral debate that is, for most Americans, just beginning. To criticize the constitutional foundation for the recent decisions is not at all to suggest that the policy questions are easy ones. There are strong, thoughtful voices—and plausible moral arguments—on both sides of the assisted-suicide debate, as there are in the larger euthanasia debate. The questions are vital ones: Do our mortal lives belong to us alone or do they belong to the communities or families in which we are embedded? Will this new right give the dying a greater sense of control over their circumstances, or will it weaken our respect for life?

These are, as I said, weighty questions, and the policy arguments on either side are the stuff of which public political and moral debates are made. And a thoughtful, well-reasoned debate over assisted suicide is precisely what we as a nation need; we do not need judicial intervention to put a decisive end to a conversation that we as a people have scarcely begun. Because the arguments on both sides carry such strong moral plausibility—and because the claim of constitutional right is anything but compelling—the questions should be answered through popular debate and perhaps legislation, not through legal briefs and litigation. In an ideal world, the Supreme Court would swiftly overturn Quill and Compassion in Dying, allowing the rest of us the space and time for the moral reflection that the issue demands.

QUESTIONS TO HELP YOU THINK AND WRITE ABOUT ISSUES CONCERNING RESPONSIBILITY

1. What does Swift propose, literally, in his "Modest Proposal?" What does he really mean? In your opinion, who do you think Swift believes should be responsible for the children of Ireland? Compare Swift's views with Lykken's views.

2. Lykken proposes that parents seek a license to have children just as they seek a license to get married. What are some advantages and some disadvantages of this idea? Would you support it? Why, or why not?

3. Conniff and Faludi present opposing views on day care. What are their positions? Who is more convincing? Why? Consider their use of *ethos, pathos,* and *logos* to help you decide.

4. React and respond to Conniff's claim, "We value children only sentimentally. Children's real needs and concerns do not register as essential." Do you agree? Disagree? Why? Give reasons.

5. In your opinion, would Gingrich's plan to replace the welfare state with an opportunity society address the needs of the individual problems described in the articles by Herd and Ann Landers? Go into detail as you frame your answer, showing how his plan might help and how it might not.

6. Critique Gingrich's eight steps for improving opportunities for the poor, one by one. In your opinion, which will work? Which will not work? State why you think so.

7. Make four columns on a sheet of paper or on the chalkboard with the headings: the patient, the caregiver, the physician, and society as a whole. Consider the issue of assisted suicide from these four points of view. List the concerns of each party involved. Which of these parties, in your view, should have the greatest power of decision making? Which the least? Or, would a combination be better? Propose how decisions for assisted suicide ought to be made.

8. Cowley and Hager claim, "American medicine lacks any conception of death as a part of life." What does that mean to you? What changes in current health care are implied by that statement?

9. Carter points out that women are more prone to try suicide than men. Consider this generalization in regard to the specific cases detailed in Gutmann's article. Should the information in Gutmann's article help form public policy in assisted suicides for women?

10. Carter concludes his essay with two "vital" questions: Do our mortal lives belong to us alone or do they belong to the communities or families in which we are embedded? Will this new right [to assisted suicide] give the dying a greater sense of control over their circumstances, or will it weaken our respect for life? How would you respond?

Credits (*continued from page ii*)

655

Topic Index

Author–Title Index

PRENTICE HALL
Upper Saddle River, NJ 07458

http://www.prenhall.com

ISBN 0-13-096448-4

9 780130 964489

90000>